Economic Report
of the President

Transmitted to the Congress
February 2004

together with

THE ANNUAL REPORT
of the
COUNCIL OF ECONOMIC ADVISERS

UNITED STATES GOVERNMENT PRINTING OFFICE

WASHINGTON : 2004

For sale by the Superintendent of Documents, U.S. Government Printing Office
Internet: bookstore.gpo.gov   Phone: toll free (866) 512-1800;   DC area (202) 512-1800
Fax: (202) 512-2250 Mail: Stop SSOP, Washington, DC 20402-0001

ISBN 0-16-051539-4

CONTENTS

* For a detailed table of contents of the Council's Report, see page 9

ECONOMIC REPORT
OF THE PRESIDENT

ECONOMIC REPORT OF THE PRESIDENT

To the Congress of the United States:

As 2004 begins, America's economy is strong and getting stronger. Over the past several years, this Nation has faced major economic challenges resulting from the decline of the stock market beginning in early 2000, a recession that began shortly after, revelations about corporate governance scandals, slow growth among many of our major trading partners, terrorist attacks, and the war against terror, including in Afghanistan and Iraq. These challenges affected business and consumer confidence and resulted in hardship for people in many industries and regions of our Nation. Americans have responded to each challenge, and now we have the results: renewed confidence, strong growth, new jobs, and a mounting prosperity that will reach every corner of America.

This *Report*, prepared by my Council of Economic Advisers, describes the economic challenges we faced, the actions we took, and the results we are seeing. It also discusses our plan to continue growing the economy and creating jobs.

In May 2003, I signed a Jobs and Growth bill that focused on three key goals. First, we accelerated previously passed tax relief and let American households keep more of their own money to save, invest, and spend. Second, we increased incentives for small businesses to invest in new equipment and plant expansions. Third, we enacted important tax relief on dividend income and capital gains to help investors and businesses. These actions were designed to promote investment, job creation, and income growth. By all three measures of performance, we are seeing signs of success.

Since May 2003, we have seen the economy grow at its fastest pace in nearly 20 years. Consumers and businesses have gained confidence. Retail sales are strong, and Americans are buying, building, and renovating houses at a record pace. Investment has strengthened, with spending on business equipment the best in 5 years. The unemployment rate has fallen from its peak of 6.3 percent last June to 5.7 percent in December, and employment is beginning to rise as new jobs are created, especially in small business. Productivity growth has been strong, leading to higher incomes for workers, while the tax relief we passed means that American families keep more of their money instead of sending it to Washington.

We are moving in the right direction, but have more to do. I will not be satisfied until every American who wants a job can find one. I have outlined a six-point plan to promote job creation and strong economic growth. This plan includes initiatives to help manage rising health care costs to make health care more affordable and accessible for American workers and families; reduce the burden of junk lawsuits on the economy; ensure a reliable and affordable energy supply; simplify and streamline government regulations; open foreign markets for American goods and services; and allow businesses and families to keep more of their hard-earned money and plan with confidence by making our tax relief permanent. This year, I will work with the Congress to achieve these goals.

I will also continue to work with the Congress on another important shared goal: controlling federal spending and reducing the deficit. The federal budget is in deficit, foremost because of the economic slowdown and then recession that began in 2000 and the additional costs of fighting the war on terror and protecting the homeland. We are continuing to take action to restrain spending and bring the deficit down. By carefully evaluating priorities and being good stewards of the taxpayer's money, we will cut the budget deficit in half over the next five years.

The task of reducing the deficit will become easier because America's economy is growing. We have taken the actions needed to restore growth, and we are pursuing additional policies to help create jobs for American workers and families. I'm optimistic about the future of our economy because I know the values of America and the decency and entrepreneurial spirit of our people.

THE WHITE HOUSE
FEBRUARY 2004

THE ANNUAL REPORT
OF THE
COUNCIL OF ECONOMIC ADVISERS

LETTER OF TRANSMITTAL

COUNCIL OF ECONOMIC ADVISERS,
Washington, D.C., January 30, 2004

MR. PRESIDENT:

The Council of Economic Advisers herewith submits its 2004 Annual Report in accordance with the provisions of the Employment Act of 1946 as amended by the Full Employment and Balanced Growth Act of 1978.

Sincerely,

N. Gregory Mankiw
Chairman

Kristin J. Forbes
Member

Harvey S. Rosen
Member

CONTENTS

9

LIST OF BOXES

Overview

The U.S. economy made notable progress in 2003, propelled forward by pro-growth policies that led to a marked strengthening of activity in the second half of the year and put the United States on a path for higher sustained output growth in the years to come.

The recovery was still tenuous coming into 2003, as continued fallout from powerful contractionary forces—the capital overhang, corporate scandals, and uncertainty about future economic and geopolitical conditions—was offset by stimulus from expansionary monetary policy and the Administration's 2001 tax cut and 2002 fiscal package. The contractionary forces dissipated over the course of 2003, and the expansionary forces were augmented by the Jobs and Growth Tax Relief Reconciliation Act (JGTRRA) that was signed into law at the end of May.

The economy appears to have moved into a full-fledged recovery, with real gross domestic product (GDP), the most comprehensive measure of the output of the U.S. economy, expanding at an annual rate of more than 8 percent in the third quarter of the year. Based on data available through the middle of January, a further solid gain appears likely in the fourth quarter (the GDP estimate for the fourth quarter was released after this *Report* went to press). Job growth, however, began to pick up only late in 2003.

This *Report* discusses this turning of the macroeconomic tide, along with a number of other economic policy issues of continuing importance. The 14 chapters of this *Report* cover five broad topics: macroeconomic policy, fiscal policy, regulation, reforms of the health care and tort systems, and issues in international trade and finance. In all of these areas, the *Report* highlights how economics can inform the design of public policy and discusses Administration policies.

The Administration's pro-growth tax policy, in concert with the dynamism of the U.S. free-market economy, has laid the groundwork for sustainable rapid growth in the years ahead. Well-timed fiscal stimulus combined with expansionary monetary policy to offset and eventually reverse the contractionary forces impacting the economy. But there is still much to be done. The tax cuts must be made permanent to have their full beneficial impact on the economy. A stronger economy will also result from progress on the other aspects of the Administration's economic agenda, including making health care more affordable; reducing the burden of lawsuits on the economy; ensuring an affordable and reliable energy supply; streamlining regulations; and opening markets to international trade. These initiatives are discussed in this *Economic Report of the President*.

Macroeconomic Policy

Chapter 1, *Lessons from the Recent Business Cycle*, discusses the distinctive features of the recent recession and subsequent recovery, and draws five key lessons for the future. The recent business cycle was unusual in that it was characterized by especially weak business investment but robust consumption and housing investment. This makes clear the first lesson, that structural imbalances such as the "capital overhang" that developed in the late 1990s can take some time to resolve. A number of events contributed to a climate of uncertainty in 2003, including the terrorist attacks of September 11, 2001, corporate governance and accounting scandals, and geopolitical tensions surrounding the war with Iraq. The second lesson from the recent business cycle is that the effects of the uncertainty from these events on household and business confidence can have important effects on asset prices, household spending, and investment. Resolution of some of the uncertainties appears to have contributed to the resurgence of growth.

Monetary and fiscal policies played a critical role in moving the economy back toward potential. The third lesson is that aggressive monetary policy can help make a recession shorter and milder. The fourth lesson is that tax cuts can likewise boost economic activity. Tax cuts raise after-tax income, while at the same time promoting long-term growth by enhancing incentives to work, save, and invest. Tax relief enacted in 2001 and 2002 helped lessen the severity of the recession, while the 2003 tax cut appears to have propelled the economy forward into a strong recovery. Job creation has lagged behind, even as demand has surged. Thus, the fifth lesson of the recent recession is that strong productivity growth, as was experienced in 2003, means that much faster economic growth is needed to raise employment. This productivity growth, however, is not to be lamented, since it ultimately leads to higher standards of living for both workers and business owners.

Chapter 2, *The Manufacturing Sector*, examines recent developments and long-term trends in manufacturing and considers policy responses. Manufacturing was affected by the economic slowdown earlier, longer, and harder than other sectors of the economy and manufacturing employment losses have only recently begun to abate. The severity of the recent slowdown in manufacturing was largely due to prolonged weakness in business investment and exports, both of which are heavily tied to manufacturing.

Over the past several decades, the manufacturing sector has experienced substantial output growth, even while manufacturing employment has declined as a share of total employment. The manufacturing employment decline over the past half-century primarily reflects striking gains in productivity and increasing consumer demand for services compared to manufactured goods. International trade has played a relatively small role by comparison. Consumers and businesses generally benefit from the lower prices made possible by increased manufacturing productivity, and strong productivity growth has led to real compensation growth for workers. While the shift of jobs from manufacturing to services has caused dislocation, it has not resulted, on balance, in a shift from "good jobs" to "bad jobs." The best policy response to recent developments in manufacturing is to focus on stimulating the overall economy and easing restrictions that impede manufacturing growth. This Administration has actively pursued such measures.

Chapter 3, *The Year in Review and the Years Ahead*, reviews macroeconomic developments in 2003 and discusses the Administration forecast for 2004 through 2009. Real GDP growth picked up appreciably in 2003, with growth in consumer spending, residential investment, and, particularly, business equipment and software investment increasing noticeably in the second half of the year. The labor market began to rebound in the final five months of 2003. Inflation remained well in check, with core consumer inflation declining by the end of the year to its lowest level in decades. The improvement in the economy over the course of the year stemmed largely from faster growth in household consumption, extraordinary gains in residential investment, and a sharp acceleration of investment in equipment and software by businesses. Payroll employment bottomed out in July and increased by 278,000 over the remainder of the year. Financial markets responded favorably to the strengthening of the economy, with the total value of the stock market rising more than $3 trillion, or 31 percent, over the course of 2003.

The Administration expects the economic recovery to strengthen further in 2004, with real GDP growth running well above its historical average and the unemployment rate falling. Boosted by pro-growth policies and expansionary monetary policy, and on the foundation of the underlying strength of the free-market society in the United States, the economy is expected to continue on a path of strong, sustainable growth.

Fiscal Policy

Chapter 4, *Tax Incidence: Who Bears the Tax Burden?*, discusses the analysis of how the burden of a tax is distributed among taxpayers. This question is important to policy makers, who want to know whether the distribution of the tax burden (between rich and poor, capital and labor, consumers and producers, and so on) meets their criteria for fairness. The key result is that the economic incidence of a tax may have little to do with the legal specification of its incidence. Rather, it depends on the actions of market participants in response to the imposition of the tax.

Distributional tables showing the tax burdens borne by different income groups are an important application of incidence analysis. When used properly, distributional tables can contribute to informed decision making on the part of citizens and policy makers. Unfortunately, mainstream economic analysis suggests that these tables do not always accurately describe who bears the burden of certain taxes. This problem does not arise from bias or lack of economic knowledge on the part of the economists who prepare these tables. Instead, it reflects resource and data limitations, uncertainty about some of the economic effects of taxes, and variations in the time frame considered by the analyses. Nevertheless, the shortcomings of distributional tables can lead to misperceptions of the impact of tax changes.

An important implication of the economic analysis of incidence is that, in the long run, a large part of the burden of capital taxes is likely to be shifted to workers through a reduction in wages. Analyses that fail to recognize this shift can be misleading, suggesting that lower income groups bear an unrealistically small share of the burden of such taxes and an unrealistically small share of the gain when capital income taxes are lowered.

Chapter 5, *Dynamic Revenue and Budget Estimation*, examines how taxes affect the behavior of firms, workers, and investors and discusses the implications for the estimated effects of a tax change on revenue. Changes in taxes and spending generally alter incentives for work, investment, and other productive activity—a higher tax on an activity tends to discourage that activity. Revenue estimation is called *dynamic* if it incorporates the behavioral responses to tax changes and *static* if it does not incorporate these behavioral responses.

To make informed decisions about a policy change, policy makers should be aware of all aspects of its budgetary implications. Currently, official revenue estimates of proposed tax changes incorporate the revenue effects of many microeconomic behavioral responses. However, these estimates are not fully dynamic because they exclude the effects of macroeconomic behavioral responses. Several obstacles have prevented macroeconomic behavioral responses from being incorporated in such estimates. This chapter discusses the ongoing efforts to provide a greater role for fully dynamic revenue and budget estimation in the analysis of major tax and spending proposals. At least in the near term, it may not be practical for macroeconomic effects to be incorporated in official estimates. But estimates of these effects should be provided as supplementary information for major tax and spending proposals. Dynamic estimation of policy changes should distinguish aggregate demand effects from aggregate supply effects, include long-run effects, apply to spending as well as tax changes, reflect the differing effects of various policy changes, account for the need to finance policy changes, and use a variety of models.

Reform of entitlement programs remains the most pressing fiscal policy issue confronting the Nation. Chapter 6, *Restoring Solvency to Social Security*, examines the largest entitlement program. Social Security is a *pay-as-you-go* system in which payroll taxes on the wages of current workers finance the benefits being paid to current retirees. While the program is running a small surplus at present, deficits are projected to appear in 15 years; by 2080, the Social Security deficit is projected to exceed 2.3 percent of GDP. These deficits are driven by two demographic shifts that have been underway for several decades: people are having fewer children and are living longer. The President has called for new initiatives to modernize Social Security to contain costs, expand choice, and make the program secure and financially viable for future generations of Americans.

This chapter assesses the need to strengthen Social Security in light of its long-term financial outlook. The most straightforward way to characterize the financial imbalance in entitlement programs such as Social Security is by considering their long-term annual deficits. Even after the baby-boom generation's effect is no longer felt, Social Security is projected to incur annual deficits greater than 50 percent of payroll tax revenues. These deficits are so large that they require a meaningful change to Social Security in future years. Reform should include moderation of the growth of benefits that are unfunded and would otherwise require higher taxes in the future. However, the benefits promised to those in or near retirement should be maintained in full. A new system of personal retirement accounts should be established to help pay future benefits. The economic rationale for undertaking this reform in an era of budget deficits is as compelling as it was in an era of budget surpluses.

Regulation

Chapter 7, *Government Regulation in a Free-Market Society*, discusses the role of the free market in providing for prosperity in the United States and considers situations in which government interventions such as regulations would be beneficial. An important reason for Americans' high standard of living is that they rely primarily on markets to allocate resources. The government enables the system to work by enforcing property rights and contracts. Typically, free markets allocate resources to their highest-valued uses, avoid waste, prevent shortages, and foster innovation. By providing a legal foundation for transactions, the government makes the market system reliable: it gives people certainty about what they can trade and keep, and it allows people to establish terms of trade that will be honored by both sellers and buyers. The absence of any one of these elements—competition, enforceable property rights, or an ability to form mutually advantageous contracts—can result in inefficiency and lower living standards. In some cases, government intervention in a market, for example through regulation, can create gains for society by remedying shortcomings in the market's operation. Poorly designed or unnecessary regulations, however, can actually create new problems or make society worse off by damaging the elements of the market system that do work.

Chapter 8, *Regulating Energy Markets*, discusses economic issues relevant to several energy markets, including natural gas, gasoline, electricity, and crude oil. While energy markets generally function well, some parts of the energy industry have characteristics associated with market failures. These could stem from the large fixed costs required to construct distribution networks for electricity and natural gas that give rise to *market power* in the form of a natural monopoly. Alternatively, the market may not function well in the presence of *negative externalities*, such as when energy producers and consumers do not fully take into account the fact that burning fossil fuels may cause acid rain or smog.

Minimizing disruptions is an important consideration in the design of regulations to address shortcomings in energy markets. Federal, state, and local regulations can have conflicting goals. If the conflicting goals are not balanced, competing regulations could lead to worse problems than the market failures the regulations attempt to address. Moreover, regulations need to be updated as markets evolve over time to ensure that their original goals still apply and that these regulations are still the lowest-cost means of meeting those goals.

The chapter also examines global trade in energy products. The United States benefits from international trade in energy products because meeting all U.S. energy needs from domestic sources would require significant and costly changes to the U.S. economy, including changes in the types of transportation fuels used by Americans. But this leads to the possibility of occasional supply disruptions. An important consideration is that the price of oil is set in global markets, so that disruptions to the supply of oil from areas that do not supply the United States affect domestic prices of oil even if U.S. imports are not directly affected. Fortunately, changes in the U.S. economy over the past three decades and the increasing sophistication of financial markets have diminished the impact of supply disruptions and temporary price changes on the United States.

Finally, the chapter considers the role for government in subsidizing research and development into new energy sources. In general, policy makers should avoid forcing commercialization of new energy sources before market signals indicate that a shift is required. One potential problem with forcing this process is that technological breakthroughs may lead to alternatives in the future that are hard to imagine today. Premature adoption of new technologies would raise energy costs before the need arises, causing society as a whole to spend more on energy than needed.

Chapter 9, *Protecting the Environment*, discusses market-oriented approaches to safeguarding and improving the environment. While the free-market system typically promotes efficiency and economic growth, the absence of property rights for environmental "goods" such as clean air and water can lead to negative externalities that reduce societal well-being. This problem can be addressed by establishing and enforcing property rights that will lead the interested parties to negotiate mutually beneficial outcomes in a market setting. If such negotiations are expensive, however, the government can design regulations that consider both the benefits of reducing the environmental externality as well as the costs of the regulations.

Regulations should be designed to achieve environmental goals at the lowest possible cost, promoting both environmental protection and continued economic growth. Indeed, economic growth can lead to increased demand for environmental improvements and provide the resources that make it possible to address environmental problems. Some policies aimed at improving the environment can entail substantial economic costs. Misguided policies might actually achieve less environmental progress than alternative policies for the same cost. Environmental risks should be evaluated using sound scientific methods to avoid possible distortions of regulatory priorities. Market-based regulations, such as the cap-and-trade programs promoted by the Administration to reduce common air pollutants, can achieve environmental goals at lower cost than inflexible command-and-control regulations.

Reforms of Health Care and the Legal System

Chapter 10, *Health Care and Insurance*, discusses the roles of innovation, insurance, and reform in the health care market. U.S. markets provide incentives to develop innovative health care products and services that benefit both Americans and the global community. The breadth and pace of innovation in the provision of health care in the United States over the past few decades have been astounding. New treatment options, however, have also been associated with higher costs and concerns about affordability. Research suggests that between 50 and 75 percent of the growth in health expenditures in the United States is attributable to technological progress in health care goods and services. A strong reliance on market mechanisms will ensure that incentives for innovation are maintained while providing high-quality care in the most cost-efficient manner.

Health insurance plays a central role in the workings of the U.S. health care market. An understanding of the strengths and weaknesses of health insurance as a payment mechanism for health care is essential to the design of reforms that retain incentives for innovation while reining in unnecessary expenditures. Over-reliance on health insurance as a payment mechanism leads to an inefficient use of resources in providing and utilizing health care. Reforms should provide consumers and health care providers with more flexibility, more choices, more information, and more control over their health care decisions.

Chapter 11, *The Tort System*, discusses the role of the U.S. tort system and the considerable burden it imposes on the U.S. economy. The tort system is intended to compensate accident victims and to deter potential defendants from putting others at risk. Empirical evidence, however, is mixed on whether the tort system effectively deters negligent behavior. Moreover, the tort system is a costly method of providing insurance against a limited number of injuries. Research suggests that tort liability also leads to lower spending on research and development, higher health care costs, and job losses.

Ways to reduce the burden of the tort system include limits on noneconomic damages, class action reforms, trust funds for payments to victims such as in asbestos, and allowing parties to avoid the tort system contractually. The Administration has proposed a number of reforms to reduce the burden of the tort system while ensuring that people with legitimate claims can recover damages.

International Trade and Finance

Chapter 12, *International Trade and Cooperation*, discusses how growing trade helps to spur U.S. and global growth. Since the end of the Second World War, international trade has grown steadily relative to overall economic activity. Over time, countries that have been more open to international flows of goods, services, and capital have grown faster than countries that were less open to the global economy. The United States has been a driving force in constructing an open global trading system. The Administration has pursued, and will continue to pursue, an ambitious agenda of trade liberalization through negotiations at the global, regional, and bilateral levels.

New types of trade deliver new benefits to consumers and firms in open economies. Growing international demand for goods such as movies, pharmaceuticals, and recordings offers new opportunities for U.S. exporters. A burgeoning trade in services provides an important outlet for U.S. expertise in sectors such as banking, engineering, and higher education. The ability to buy less expensive goods and services from new producers has made household budgets go further, while the ability of firms to distribute their production around the world has cut costs and thus prices to consumers. The benefits from new forms of trade, such as in services, are no different from the benefits from traditional trade in goods. Outsourcing of professional services is a prominent example of a new type of trade. The gains from trade that take place over the Internet or telephone lines are no different than the gains from trade in physical goods transported by ship or plane. When a good or service is produced at lower cost in another country, it makes sense to import it rather than to produce it domestically. This allows the United States to devote its resources to more productive purposes.

Although openness to trade provides substantial benefits to nations as a whole, foreign competition can require adjustment on the part of some individuals, businesses, and industries. To help workers adversely affected by trade develop the skills needed for new jobs, the Administration has worked hard to build upon and develop programs to assist workers and communities that are negatively affected by trade.

The Administration has also worked to strengthen and extend the global trading system. International cooperation is essential to realizing the potential gains from trade. International trade agreements have reduced barriers to international commerce, and contributed to the gains from trade. A system through which countries can resolve disputes can play an important role in realizing these gains.

Chapter 13, *International Capital Flows*, discusses the economic benefits and risks associated with the transfer of financial assets, such as cash, stocks, and bonds, across international borders. Capital flows have become an increasingly significant part of the world economy over the past decade, and an important source of funds to support investment in the United States. Around $2 trillion of capital flowed into all countries in the world in 2002, with around $700 billion flowing into just the United States. Different types of capital flows—such as foreign direct investment, portfolio investment, and bank lending—are driven by different investor motivations and country characteristics. Countries that permit free capital flows must choose between the stability provided by fixed exchange rates and the flexibility afforded by an independent monetary policy.

Capital flows can have a number of benefits for economies around the world. For example, foreign direct investment can facilitate the transfer of technology, allow for the development of markets and products, and improve a country's infrastructure. Portfolio flows can reduce the cost of capital, improve competitiveness, and increase investment opportunities. Bank flows can strengthen domestic financial institutions, improve financial intermediation, and reduce vulnerability to crises.

A series of financial crises in emerging market economies, however, has raised some concerns that financial liberalization can also involve risks. In countries with weak institutions, poorly regulated banking systems, or high levels of corruption, capital inflows may not be channeled to their most productive uses. One approach to limiting the risks from capital flows when legal and financial institutions are poorly developed is to restrict foreign capital inflows. Experience suggests, however, that capital controls impose substantial, and often unexpected, costs. Instead, countries are more likely to benefit from free capital flows and minimize any related risks, if they adopt prudent fiscal and monetary policies, strengthen financial and corporate institutions, and develop sound regulations and supervisory agencies. The Administration has promoted policies to help countries reap the benefits from the free flow of international capital.

Chapter 14, *The Link Between Trade and Capital Flows*, shows that trade flows and capital flows are inherently intertwined. Changes in a country's net international trade in goods and services, captured by the current account, must be reflected in equal and opposite changes in its net capital flows with the rest of the world. The large net inflow of foreign capital experienced by the United States in recent years has funded more investment than could be supported by U.S. national saving. Corresponding to these inflows is the large U.S. current account deficit. These patterns reflect fundamental economic forces, notably strong growth in the United States that has made investment in this country attractive compared to opportunities in other countries.

An adjustment of the U.S. current account deficit could come about in several ways. Faster growth in other countries relative to the United States could increase demand for U.S. net exports. Trade flows could also adjust through changes in the relative prices of U.S. goods and services compared to the prices of foreign goods and services. Any narrowing of the U.S. current account deficit would also require reduced net capital inflows into the United States. This might occur if U.S. national saving increased, reducing the need for foreign funds to finance U.S. domestic investment, or if U.S. investment declined, so that the United States required less capital inflows. Lower investment is the least desirable form of balance of payments adjustment, however, as it could slow the expansion of U.S. productive capacity and reduce economic growth.

It is impossible to predict the exact timing or magnitude of any adjustment in the U.S. current account balance. After a large increase in the U.S. current account deficit in the 1980s, the ensuing adjustments were gradual and benign. Public policies can facilitate smooth changes in the U.S. current account and net capital flows by creating a stable macroeconomic and financial environment, promoting growth abroad, and encouraging greater saving in the United States.

Conclusion

The future of the U.S. economy is bright. This is a testament to the institutions and policies that have unleashed the creativity of the American people and their spirit of entrepreneurship. History teaches that the forces of free markets are the bedrock of economic prosperity.

In 1776, as the Founding Fathers signed the Declaration of Independence, the great economist Adam Smith wrote: "Little else is requisite to carry a state to the highest degree of opulence from the lowest barbarism but peace, easy taxes, and a tolerable administration of justice: all the rest being brought about by the natural course of things." The economic analysis presented in this *Report* builds on the ideas of Smith and his intellectual descendants by discussing the role of the government in creating an environment that promotes and sustains economic growth.

CHAPTER 1

Lessons from the Recent Business Cycle

Economic conditions in the United States improved substantially during 2003, with real gross domestic product (GDP), the most comprehensive measure of the output of the U.S. economy, expanding at an annual rate of more than 8 percent in the third quarter of the year. Based on data available through the middle of January, a further solid gain appears likely in the fourth quarter (the GDP estimate for the fourth quarter was released after this *Report* went to press). The improvement in the economy over the course of the year stemmed largely from faster growth in household consumption, extraordinary gains in residential investment, and a sharp acceleration of investment in equipment and software by businesses. Payroll employment bottomed out in July and increased 278,000 over the remainder of the year. Financial markets responded favorably to the strengthening of the economy, with the total value of the stock market rising more than $3 trillion, or 31 percent, over the course of 2003.

Despite this improvement, the U.S. economy has further to go to make up for the weakness that began showing even before the economy slipped into recession roughly three years ago. Until recently, the recovery has been slow and uneven. Employment has lagged behind gains in other areas. Strong fiscal policy actions by this Administration and the Congress, together with the Federal Reserve's stimulative monetary policy, have softened the impact of the recession and have also put the economy on an upward trajectory. The Administration's pro-growth tax policy, in particular, has laid the groundwork for sustainable rapid growth in the years ahead.

This chapter discusses the distinctive features of the recent recession and recovery, and it draws lessons for the future. The key points in this chapter are:

- Structural imbalances, such as the "capital overhang" that developed in the late 1990s, can take some time to resolve.
- Uncertainty matters for economic decisions, and was likely a factor weighing on investment in recent years.
- Aggressive monetary policy can reduce the depth of a recession.
- Tax cuts can boost economic activity by raising after-tax income and enhancing incentives to work, save, and invest.
- Strong productivity growth raises standards of living but means that much faster economic growth is needed to raise employment.

Overview of the Recent Business Cycle

The recent recession and recovery mark the seventh business cycle in the U.S. economy since 1960. This cycle shares some common features with previous business cycles. According to the National Bureau of Economic Research (NBER), the unofficial arbiter of U.S. business cycles, a *recession* is "a period of falling economic activity spread across the economy, lasting more than a few months, normally visible in real GDP, real income, employment, industrial production, and wholesale-retail sales." The recent recession, like others, has involved a downturn in economic activity of sufficient depth, duration, and breadth to be judged a recession by the NBER.

The NBER also identifies the *peaks* and *troughs* of economic activity that mark when recessions begin and end. In November 2001, the NBER determined that the economy had peaked in March 2001. However, revisions to economic data since the NBER's initial decision suggest that the peak in activity was actually months earlier (Box 1-1). In July 2003, the NBER determined that the economy had reached a trough in November 2001.

Despite the similarities between the recent business cycle and previous ones, this most recent cycle was distinctive in important and instructive ways. One noteworthy difference is that real GDP fell much less in this recession than has been typical. Chart 1-1 shows the path of real GDP over the past several years compared with the average path of the six prior recessions, with the level of real GDP at the economy's peak set equal to 100 in each case. (All of the charts in this *Report* assume that the peak for the recent recession was in the fourth quarter of 2000.) The chart shows that the decline in real GDP in the recent recession was smaller than the historical average; indeed, it was the second smallest in any recession since 1960.

Box 1-1: When Did the Recent Recession Begin?

The National Bureau of Economic Research (NBER) uses a variety of economic data to determine the dates of business-cycle peaks and troughs. This task is made more difficult because many of these data series are subject to revision. For example, on November 26, 2001, the NBER announced that a recession had begun in March 2001. Since then, the four data series that the NBER used to determine the timing of the recession have been revised. The revisions to these series suggest that the recent recession began earlier than March 2001.

The four series cited by the NBER in their decision about the recent business-cycle peak were revised as follows:

Box 1-1 — *continued*

- *Real personal income less transfers:* When the NBER dated the recession, this series showed a generally steady rise throughout 2000 and early 2001. Subsequent revisions reveal that income peaked in October 2000.
- *Nonfarm payroll employment:* The data at the time of the recession announcement showed employment growing at a substantial pace in early 2001, with 287,000 jobs added from December 2000 to its peak in March 2001. Revised data show that employment grew less than one-third of this amount in early 2001 and peaked in February 2001.
- *Industrial production:* The original data used by the NBER showed that this series peaked in September 2000. Revised data show that this peak came even earlier, in June 2000.
- *Manufacturing and trade sales:* Original data showed a peak in August 2000; the most recent data show a peak in June 2000.

Thus, the revised data show that the *latest* peak among the four series was February 2001, with some series peaking considerably earlier. Moreover, another data series, which the NBER has recently announced it will incorporate into its business-cycle dating process, also shows a peak before March 2001: *monthly GDP* reached a high point in February 2001, according to the most recently available estimates computed by a private economic consulting firm.

While some arbitrariness in determining the date on which a recession began is inevitable, revisions since the NBER made its decision for the most recent recession strongly suggest that the business-cycle peak was before March 2001. The median date of the peak for the five series discussed here is October 2000. Other data support the notion that economic activity had slowed sharply or even begun to decline by this point, including the stock market, business investment, and initial unemployment claims. For these reasons, the analyses throughout this chapter (including the charts that compare this recession to past recessions) use the fourth quarter of 2000 as the peak of economic activity and the start of the recession.

In October 2003, the NBER announced that it would defer consideration of whether the latest business-cycle peak should be revised until the results of the coming comprehensive revision of the National Income and Product Accounts were released. The major results of this revision were announced in December 2003, but the monthly manufacturing and trade sales data and some of the detail needed to estimate monthly GDP had not been released at the time this *Report* went to press.

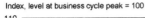

Chart 1-1 **Real GDP**
Real GDP fell less in the recent recession than it typically has.

Index, level at business cycle peak = 100

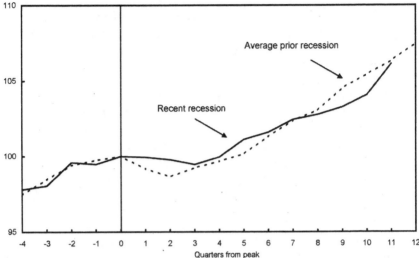

Note: Recent peak set by Council of Economic Advisers at 2000:Q4. Average based on prior recessions since 1960.
Source: Department of Commerce (Bureau of Economic Analysis).

This relatively mild decline in output can be attributed to unusually resilient household spending. Consumer spending on goods and services held up well throughout the slowdown, and investment in housing increased at a fairly steady pace rather than declining as has been typical in past recessions. In contrast, business investment in capital equipment and structures has been quite soft in this cycle. As discussed below, business spending during the past few years has likely been held down by overinvestment in the late 1990s, as well as by heightened business caution owing to terrorism and corporate scandals. As a result of these forces, investment weakened sooner and has recovered more slowly than in the typical cycle.

Another distinguishing feature of this cycle has been the weakness in labor markets relative to output. In particular, the recovery in employment—although now under way—lagged the upturn in output by a much longer period than in prior recessions. This difference was associated with unusually large productivity gains.

The balance of this chapter draws five distinctive lessons from the recent business cycle in the United States. Chapter 3, *The Year in Review and the Years Ahead,* presents details about developments over the past year and discusses the Administration's forecast.

Lesson 1: Structural Imbalances Can Take Some Time to Resolve

Business investment in equipment and software surged in the late 1990s. Real investment increased at an average annual rate of roughly 13 percent between the fourth quarter of 1994 and the fourth quarter of 1999, compared with an average annual rate of less than 7 percent over the preceding three decades. The surge in investment was led by purchases of high-tech capital goods—computers, software, and communications equipment—which increased at an average annual rate of 20 percent over the period.

Economic theory implies that businesses invest when they believe that there are profits to be made from that investment. In the late 1990s, several developments fed a perception that the expected future return from newly installed capital would be considerably greater than the cost of this capital. Rapid advances in technology had lowered the price of high-tech capital goods dramatically throughout the 1990s and especially in the second half of the decade. For example, the quality-adjusted price index for business computers and peripheral equipment fell at an average annual rate of 22 percent between late 1994 and late 1999. In addition, rapidly growing demand for business output led firms to believe that newly installed capital would be used productively, boosting the expected return to investment.

Moreover, technological progress and legislation provided incentives for strong investment in high-tech equipment. The development of the World Wide Web enabled new and established firms to enter e-commerce, and rapidly increasing household and business access to the Internet provided a large base of potential customers for these firms. The Telecommunications Act of 1996 provided for substantial deregulation of the telecommunications industry and may have spurred investment in that sector. In addition, concern that some computer systems might be inoperable after December 1999 caused a wave of so-called Y2K-related investment. Some analysis indicates that Y2K spending alone boosted the growth rate of real equipment and software investment by more than 3½ percentage points per year in the latter part of the 1990s.

Optimism about the potential gains from new capital, and from high-tech capital in particular, was reflected not only in investment decisions but also in a sharp rise in stock prices. From late 1994 to late 1999, the Wilshire 5000—a broad index of U.S. stock prices—nearly tripled. The Nasdaq stock price index, which is heavily weighted toward high-tech industries, registered an even more dramatic ascent, increasing more than fourfold over this period. The increase in stock prices stimulated investment by reducing the cost of equity capital. In addition, the rise in stock prices fueled a consumption boom by boosting the wealth of a growing number of Americans and more generally signaling better future economic conditions. This consumption boom encouraged further business investment.

In mid-2000, business equipment investment abruptly slowed. After rising at an annual rate of 15 percent in the first half of the year, real spending on business equipment and software inched up at about a ¼ percent annual rate in the second half. The slowdown in high-tech equipment investment was especially dramatic. For example, real outlays for computers had skyrocketed at an annual rate of 40 percent in the first half of the year, but grew at less than one-quarter of that pace in the second half. This stalling of investment preceded the downturn in the overall economy; by contrast, in the typical business cycle, investment has turned down at the same time as overall economic activity (Chart 1-2). The unusual timing of the investment slow-down in this recession is the reason that the recent business cycle has been widely viewed as an "investment-led" recession.

The sharp break in investment occurred in parallel with an apparent reevaluation of future corporate profitability among financial market partic-ipants. By the end of 2000, the Wilshire 5000 index of stock prices was down 13 percent from its peak, and analysts had substantially marked down their forecasts for S&P 500 earnings over the coming year. The movements were even more dramatic in the high-tech sector. The Nasdaq index of stock

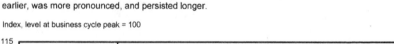

Chart 1-2 **Real Investment in Equipment and Software**
Relative to the average prior recession, the weakness in investment in the recent recession occurred earlier, was more pronounced, and persisted longer.

Index, level at business cycle peak = 100

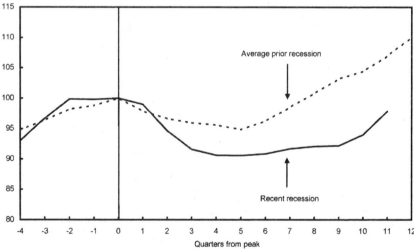

Note: Recent peak set by Council of Economic Advisers at 2000:Q4. Average based on prior recessions since 1960.
Source: Department of Commerce (Bureau of Economic Analysis).

prices dropped nearly 50 percent from its peak in March 2000 to the end of the year. The prices of technology, telecommunications, and Internet shares fell particularly sharply, along with near-term earnings estimates. The elevated valuations of many such companies also declined markedly. Indeed, the price-earnings ratio (where "earnings" are those expected over the next year) for the technology component of the S&P 500 fell from a peak of more than 50 in early 2000 to less than 35 by the end of the year.

These facts and considerable anecdotal evidence suggest that business managers and investors sharply revised downward the expected gains from new capital investment during this period. One factor that may have contributed to the downward revision is a possible slowing of the pace of technological advance—the rate at which computer prices were declining eased (from more than 20 percent in the late 1990s to about half that in 2000), and the software industry reportedly developed no new so-called "killer applications" that required or spurred purchases of new hardware. In addition, firms may have been disappointed by the response of households to e-commerce opportunities and to new communications technologies such as broadband. Finally, previous investments had not uniformly translated into higher profitability, perhaps because the true potential of new forms of capital could be realized only by changing other aspects of production processes. For example, new computer systems designed to lower inventory management costs might have required an expensive reconfiguration of warehouses.

This reassessment of the gains from capital investment also implied that existing stocks of some types of equipment exceeded the amount of equipment that firms could put to profitable use. Such an excess of the existing capital stock relative to the desired stock (often called a *capital overhang*) is one type of *structural imbalance* that can slow or reverse economic expansion. In the case of an excess supply of capital, investment would be expected to slow until the capital overhang dissipates through a combination of depreciation in the existing stock and an increase in the desired stock due to lower costs of capital or stronger final demand.

Resolving the structural imbalance that developed in the late 1990s took considerable time. Real business spending on equipment and software dropped more than 9 percent during the four quarters of 2001 and posted less than a 2 percent gain during the four quarters of 2002. The high-tech categories showed especially sharp breaks in their upward trends. In these categories, the effects of the capital overhang were likely exacerbated by a reduction in normal replacement demand following the Y2K-related investment spurt. The prolonged period of sluggishness in business investment is another distinctive feature of this business cycle. Real investment in equipment and software typically has fallen less and has recovered more quickly than it did in the current recession and recovery (Chart 1-2).

A similar structural adjustment appears to have taken place overseas, where investment demand was also weak. The global slowdown in investment hampered U.S. export growth, since capital goods traditionally account for about one-third of the value of U.S. exports. Real exports fell sharply in this recession and have recovered only a little of their lost ground. In past recessions, exports have typically leveled off but not declined (Chart 1-3). Soft investment and weak export demand led to a long period of weakness in manufacturing output, a topic discussed in the next chapter.

Several forces have more recently moved existing capital stocks into better alignment with desired stocks and thereby set the stage for a renewal of robust investment demand. Previously installed capital has depreciated, a process that occurs especially quickly for many types of high-tech equipment. Rising demand for business output and falling costs for high-tech capital (caused by ongoing technological progress) have increased firms' desired capital stocks. The elimination of capital overhangs, together with improved business confidence and reductions in tax rates on capital income discussed later in this chapter, are consistent with the marked upturn in business investment spending in the second half of 2003.

Chart 1-3 **Real Exports**
Real exports have also been unusually weak in recent years relative to the average prior recession.

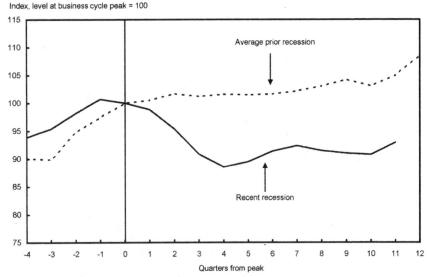

Note: Recent peak set by Council of Economic Advisers at 2000:Q4. Average based on prior recessions since 1960.
Source: Department of Commerce (Bureau of Economic Analysis).

Lesson 2: Uncertainty Matters for Economic Decisions

The U.S. economy has been hit hard in the past few years by a number of unexpected developments, including the tragic terrorist attacks of September 11, 2001, the corporate governance and accounting scandals of 2002, and the geopolitical tensions surrounding the war with Iraq in 2003. In addition to having direct effects on the economy, each of these events contributed to a climate of uncertainty that weighed on household and business confidence and thereby affected spending decisions.

The terrorist attacks have had substantial consequences for many aspects of the U.S. economy. The heightened focus on security at home, together with the determined efforts against terrorism around the world, have required increases in some types of government spending. The attacks hurt some industries directly: for example, fear of new attacks and the inconveniences associated with heightened airport security reduced air travel and tourism. Beyond these direct economic effects, the unprecedented attacks on the United States also generated uncertainty about future economic conditions.

Another setback for the economy was the series of revelations during 2002 regarding incomplete or misleading corporate financial reporting and, in some cases, wrongful conduct by corporate management. The number of financial restatements—that is, corrections to previous statements of earnings—by U.S. public corporations reached a record high in 2002. Although most of the restatements were not linked to misconduct, they raised questions about the reliability of accounting practices and the credibility of corporate financial disclosures. The combination of these concerns and allegations of misconduct by high-profile executives heightened investors' uncertainty about the quality of corporate governance and the reliability of earnings reports and projections.

In early 2003, uncertainty about the economic outlook increased during the period leading up to the war with Iraq. One source of this uncertainty was the potential effect of the conflict on the capacity for producing and transporting oil in the Persian Gulf, and thus on the future supply and price of oil. Observers were also concerned about the amount of additional government spending that would be needed to finance military operations and subsequent reconstruction, as well as the danger of retaliatory terrorist attacks on the United States. Finally, consumer confidence fell sharply in early 2003, raising concerns that the consumer demand that had supported the economy over the previous couple of years might falter. Such concerns were plausible, given that the 1990 Gulf War roughly coincided with a marked drop in consumer confidence and the start of the 1990-1991 recession.

Chart 1-4 **The Wilshire 5000 Index of Stock Prices**
A broad measure of stock prices moved down after the terrorist attacks of September 2001, during the period of revelations of corporate misreporting, and before the war with Iraq.

Index, January 1980 = 1,078.29

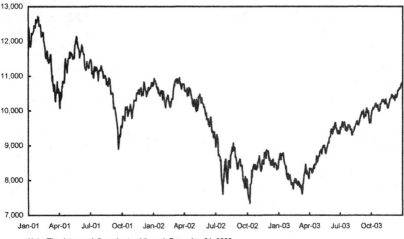

Note: The data are daily and extend through December 31, 2003.
Source: Wilshire Associates.

The uncertainties created by the three developments described above had significant effects on financial markets. Stock prices dipped noticeably in September 2001, recovered subsequently, but moved down during the summer of 2002 and fell again in early 2003 (Chart 1-4). *Risk spreads* (the difference between interest rates on corporate bonds and on comparable Treasury bonds) jumped temporarily after the terrorist attacks and rose again in late 2002 during the peak of concerns about corporate governance. Because risk spreads generally reflect the extra return investors require to hold riskier corporate assets, the rise in spreads in 2002 indicated investors' greater perceived probability of default, lesser willingness to take on risk, or both. Investor uncertainty also was reflected in measures of the expected volatility of stock prices based on option prices, which were elevated during each of the episodes noted above (Chart 1-5).

Reductions in share prices and increases in bond yields raised the cost of funding capital expenditures and thus directly discouraged business investment. Increased uncertainty likely also had *direct* effects on business decisions about investment and hiring: uncertainty may cause firms to wait until they have more information before committing to an investment. In this case, firm managers hesitate to respond to a change in demand. Anecdotal evidence from the past few years as well as some statistical analyses

Chart 1-5 **Expected Near-Term S&P 500 Volatility**

Expected stock price volatility was elevated after the terrorist attacks of September 2001, during the period of revelations of corporate misreporting, and before the war with Iraq.

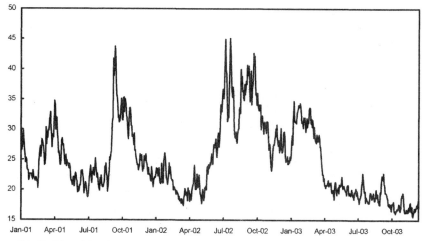

Note: The data are daily and extend through December 31, 2003.
Source: Chicago Board Options Exchange.

suggest that uncertainty has a noticeable damping effect on investment. Anecdotal evidence also suggests that uncertainty has held back hiring in the past few years.

Household spending may also have been affected by uncertainty. Economic theory and empirical evidence suggest that greater uncertainty about future economic conditions may lead households to raise saving and reduce spending. However, such effects are not immediately apparent in the recent cyclical downturn—as will be explained shortly, household spending has shown remarkable resiliency over the past few years. A possible explanation for the seeming discrepancy between this pattern and empirical work based on earlier data is that the negative effects of greater uncertainty were offset by lower taxes and the effects of lower interest rates.

While the uncertainty created by these unexpected developments has hampered the economic recovery, household and business confidence strengthened considerably during the second half of 2003. This Administration and the Congress moved swiftly to address problems with corporate governance. In March 2002, the President proposed a set of reforms aimed at a wide range of corporate governance issues, and in July 2002, Congress passed the landmark Sarbanes-Oxley Act. As concerns about corporate governance have abated, and the durability of the recovery has become more apparent, firms have begun to invest and hire.

Lesson 3: Aggressive Monetary Policy Can Reduce the Depth of a Recession

When the economy showed signs of weakening three years ago, the Federal Reserve moved decisively to reduce interest rates to stimulate the economy. During 2001, the Federal Reserve cut the Federal funds rate eleven times for a total reduction of 4¾ percentage points. When the economy failed to gain much forward momentum, the Federal Reserve reduced the funds rate another ½ percentage point in November 2002 and a further ¼ percentage point last June, to 1 percent. The decline in the Federal funds rate in this economic downturn was larger and occurred more rapidly than in previous downturns (Chart 1-6). One factor that likely contributed to the Federal Reserve's willingness to cut the funds rate so sharply was the low level of inflation. Core consumer price inflation, as measured by the 12-month change in the consumer price index excluding food and energy, was around 2¾ percent in early 2001 and fell to just over 1 percent by late last year. Thus, the Federal Reserve was able to lower the Federal funds rate and keep it low with little apparent risk of triggering an undesirably high inflation rate.

Chart 1-6 **The Effective Federal Funds Rate**
The decline in the Federal funds rate in the recent recession was larger and occurred earlier than in the average prior recession.

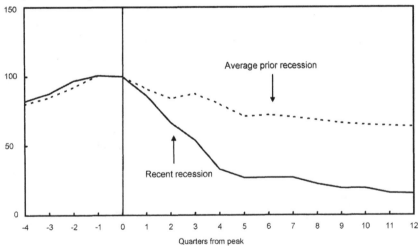

Index, level at business cycle peak = 100

Quarters from peak

Note: Recent peak set by Council of Economic Advisers at 2000:Q4. Average based on prior recessions since 1960.
Source: Board of Governors of the Federal Reserve System.

Long-term interest rates on government securities and high-grade corporate securities began falling in late 2000, likely in part reflecting an anticipated decline in the Federal funds rate in response to a weaker economic outlook. Throughout 2001, short-term and medium-term interest rates declined along with the Federal funds rate. However, long-term rates changed little, on net, because market participants apparently expected the downturn to be short-lived and believed that the Federal Reserve would soon begin raising the funds rate. Then, in 2002, persistently weak economic conditions, combined with the Federal Reserve's decisions to hold the funds rate steady for much of the year and cut it further in November, persuaded market participants that short-term rates were likely to stay low for some time. As a result, long-term rates fell substantially, on balance, in 2002. Long-term rates fluctuated in 2003, but finished the year a little above where they started.

Interest rates on fixed-rate mortgages tracked long-term government yields over this period, as they typically have. In 2003, the interest rate on 30-year fixed-rate mortgages averaged more than 2 percentage points below the average in 2000. Low and falling mortgage rates have provided strong support for housing demand over the past few years. Indeed, residential investment has increased at a fairly steady pace throughout the period of overall economic weakness—a stark contrast to the pattern in past recessions, when residential investment tended to fall sharply (Chart 1-7).

Chart 1-7 **Real Residential Investment**
Real residential investment has steadily increased over the past few years, in stark contrast to the considerable decline seen in the average prior recession.

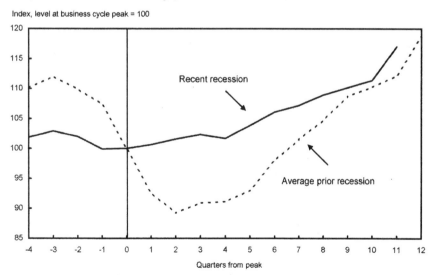

Index, level at business cycle peak = 100

Note: Recent peak set by Council of Economic Advisers at 2000:Q4. Average based on prior recessions since 1960.
Source: Department of Commerce (Bureau of Economic Analysis).

Declining mortgage interest rates have also fueled an enormous wave of mortgage refinancing. (The response has been particularly strong because technological and institutional advances in mortgage markets have reduced the costs of such transactions.) In many refinancing transactions, homeowners have "cashed out" some of their accumulated home equity by taking out new mortgages that are larger than the remaining balance on their previous mortgages. According to a survey of households, more than half of the liquefied equity funded either home renovations or household consumption and thus may have helped to sustain aggregate demand. Another substantial portion reportedly was used to pay down credit card debt, which generally carries a higher interest rate than mortgage debt and, unlike mortgage debt, is not tax-deductible. By moving from a high-cost form of debt to a lower-cost one, households have been better able to cope with their debt burdens. In particular, the transition has held down the fraction of their income committed to regular debt service payments, and thus has increased the amount of income available for spending on discretionary items.

Low long-term interest rates have also reduced the cost of funds to businesses. In some cases, this lower cost has been passed directly to households. For example, motor vehicle manufacturers made low-interest-rate loans available to car buyers in late 2001 and have generally maintained a high level of financing incentives since then. These incentives have bolstered consumer outlays for motor vehicles.

More generally, lower interest rates make it cheaper for firms to finance new investment projects. The aggressive easing of monetary policy since early 2001 has likely helped to support business investment, even though the forces discussed earlier have, on balance, caused investment to be weak.

Firms have also taken advantage of low long-term interest rates to restructure their balance sheets. Net issuance of commercial paper and net borrowing from banks were both negative in each of the past three years, while net bond issuance was strong. By issuing longer-term bonds and paying down short-term debt, businesses have substantially lengthened the overall maturity of their debt. This restructuring reduced firms' near-term repayment obligations and locked in low rates for longer periods. The strengthening of businesses' financial positions means that financial constraints are less likely to restrain a further pickup in hiring and investment.

Lesson 4: Tax Cuts Can Boost Economic Activity by Raising After-Tax Income and Enhancing Incentives to Work, Save, and Invest

The use of *discretionary fiscal policy*—explicit changes in taxes and government spending, as opposed to those that occur automatically as economic activity changes—to reduce cyclical fluctuations in the economy has fallen out of favor with many economists over the past several decades. Some have pointed to the difficulties of crafting and implementing discretionary policy quickly enough to provide stimulus while the economy is still weak rather than accentuating an upturn that is already under way. It has also been noted that a temporary reduction in taxes might be mostly saved by households and thus encourage relatively little additional spending. Moreover, some have argued that expansionary fiscal policy can push up interest rates and thereby "crowd out" interest-sensitive spending. All told, before the recent business cycle, many economists believed that monetary policy made the use of discretionary fiscal policy unnecessary to stabilize the economy.

The experience of the past three years, however, shows that well-designed and well-timed tax cuts are a useful complement to expansionary monetary policy. Over this period, three bills have made significant changes to the personal and corporate tax systems. The President came into office with proposals for permanently reducing taxes on work and saving. With the budget surplus having reached its highest level relative to GDP in half a century, the proposals were aimed predominantly at reducing tax-based impediments to long-term growth. The proposals resulted in the Economic Growth and Tax Relief Reconciliation Act (EGTRRA), which the President signed into law in June 2001. In the wake of the terrorist attacks of September 2001 and continuing softness in the economy, the Congress passed the Job Creation and Worker Assistance Act (JCWAA), which the President signed into law in March 2002. And, in early 2003, with the pace of economic growth still falling below its potential and the labor market lagging behind, the President proposed and the Congress enacted the Jobs and Growth Tax Relief Reconciliation Act (JGTRRA), which the President signed into law in May.

These three bills provided substantial short-term stimulus to economic activity and helped put the economy on the road to recovery. One source of stimulus has been the large boost to after-tax personal income stemming from lower marginal tax rates, a larger child tax credit, reduced tax rates on dividends and capital gains, and other changes in the tax law. Real after-tax income has increased much more than before-tax income over the past three

Chart 1-8 **Growth in Personal Income, Before and After Taxes**
Real after-tax income has increased much more than before-tax income in recent years.

Percent change in annual average

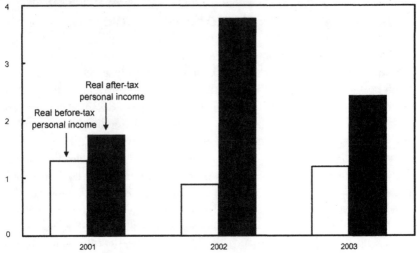

Note: Average for 2003 based on data through November. Before-tax personal income deflated by the price index for personal consumption expenditures.
Sources: Department of Commerce (Bureau of Economic Analysis) and Council of Economic Advisers.

years (Chart 1-8). Over the preceding five years, average annual growth in real after-tax income was more than ½ percentage point below the growth rate of real before-tax income. Numerous studies have shown that long-term tax cuts foster higher consumer spending. Thus, the additional income provided by the tax cuts is likely to have substantially boosted aggregate demand since 2000.

The tax cuts provided further stimulus by increasing incentives for business investment. Some of these incentives came in the form of *bonus depreciation* for business investment, an expansion in the amount of expensing of investment available for small businesses. The bonus depreciation was introduced in the 2002 tax cut (JCWAA), which specified that 30 percent of the price of investments made by September 10, 2004 could be treated as an immediate expense under the corporate profits tax and the remaining 70 percent depreciated over time according to the regular depreciation schedules. Moving the depreciation closer to the time of new investment increased the present value of depreciation allowances and the net after-tax return on investment. The 2003 tax cut (JGTRRA) raised the bonus depreciation to

50 percent of the price of new equipment and extended the period of eligibility so that investments made by the end of 2004 would be covered. It also increased the cap on small-business expensing from $25,000 to $100,000 per year through 2005, effectively lowering the cost of investment for small businesses. These tax changes lowered firms' cost of capital and likely provided support for investment at a crucial time.

The tax cuts also reduced the cost of capital and increased incentives for business investment by lowering tax rates on personal capital income. The 2001 tax cut (EGTRRA) phased out the estate tax and reduced marginal tax rates on all forms of income. These steps lowered the tax burden on capital income received from corporations and also on income received through sole proprietorships, partnerships, and S corporations (corporations for which income is taxed through individual tax returns). In addition, the 2003 tax cut (JGTRRA) reduced taxes on corporate dividends and capital gains.

Altogether, these three tax bills provided $68 billion in tax stimulus in fiscal year 2001, $89 billion in fiscal year 2002, $159 billion in fiscal year 2003, and $272 billion in fiscal year 2004. However, the bills were designed not only to provide short-term stimulus, but also to encourage stronger economic growth over the long run. Lower tax rates on labor income provide an incentive to increase work effort. Lower tax rates on capital income—the reward for saving and investment—provide an incentive to do more of these activities. Investment increases the amount of capital for each worker and also increases the rate at which new technology embodied in capital can be put to use. According to one study, the cut in taxes on capital income in the 2003 tax package (JGTRRA) reduced the marginal effective total tax rate on income from corporate investment by 2 to 4 percentage points. Lower taxes on dividends and capital gains also move the tax system toward a more equal treatment of debt and equity, of dividends and capital gains, and of corporate and noncorporate capital. This move increases economic efficiency because it promotes the allocation of capital based on business fundamentals rather than a desire for tax avoidance.

In sum, the tax cuts supported by this Administration provided a substantial short-term stimulus to consumption and investment and promoted strong and sustainable long-term growth. In weighing the merits of countercyclical monetary and fiscal policy, the stimulus provided by discretionary fiscal policy may be especially important in the low-inflation, low-interest-rate environment the country now enjoys. Under these circumstances, the Federal Reserve may have less room to cut interest rates, and direct stimulus to demand from fiscal policy may be needed to ensure that the Nation's resources are fully utilized in the face of cyclical weakness.

Lesson 5: Strong Productivity Growth Raises Standards of Living but Means that Much Faster Economic Growth is Needed to Raise Employment

One distinctive feature of this recession and recovery has been the remarkably fast growth of *labor productivity*—the amount of goods and services that a worker with given skills produces from each hour of work. The late 1990s had already witnessed an acceleration of productivity growth from an average annual rate of around 1½ percent between the fourth quarters of 1972 and 1995 to a roughly 2½ percent rate between the fourth quarters of 1995 and 2000. Productivity growth then picked up further, contrary to the usual experience in which productivity growth has typically softened in the quarters surrounding business-cycle peaks. In the latest recession, productivity growth leveled off for just one quarter before beginning to rise rapidly (Chart 1-9). Since the fourth quarter of 2000, productivity has increased at an exceptional annual rate of more than 4 percent per year.

Labor productivity growth can be decomposed into the skills of the workforce *(labor quality)*, increases in the amount of capital services per worker-hour *(capital deepening)*, and increases in *total factor productivity*—a

Chart 1-9 **Productivity in the Nonfarm Business Sector**
Productivity has risen unusually rapidly relative to the average prior recession/recovery period.

Index, level at business cycle peak = 100

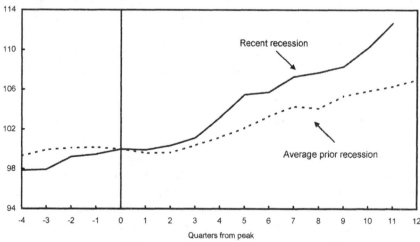

Quarters from peak

Note: Recent peak set by Council of Economic Advisers at 2000:Q4. Average based on prior recessions since 1960. Data based on productivity available as of December 3, 2003 (that is, prior to the benchmark revision of the National Income and Product Accounts).
Source: Department of Labor (Bureau of Labor Statistics).

residual category that captures the change in aggregate output not explained by changes in capital and labor inputs. According to this framework (as detailed in last year's *Report*), productivity growth stepped up in the mid-1990s partly because the rapid pace of business investment generated large increases in the amount of capital available to each worker. Yet a larger part of this acceleration owes to faster growth in the unexplained residual category of total factor productivity.

The explanation for faster productivity growth in the past couple of years is not clear (especially since the information needed to decompose productivity growth over this period is quite limited). One possibility is that weaker profits and skepticism about the return to new physical investment have encouraged firms to make better use of the resources they already had rather than investing in new technology and capacity. This effort to increase what is sometimes called *organizational capital* might involve, for example, restructuring production processes and retraining workers to take maximum advantage of new information-technology equipment installed in the late 1990s. Another possibility is that firms somehow induced extra work effort for a time because they were hesitant to hire new workers until they were more confident that increases in final demand would persist. A third possibility is that the slower recent pace of gross investment may have been accompanied by slower depreciation of the existing capital stock so that firms lengthened replacement cycles and held on to their existing equipment for longer periods. If this were the case, net investment and the growth rate of the capital stock would have been stronger than indicated by measures based on historical depreciation rates.

In the long run, productivity growth is the key determinant of growth in living standards. Without labor productivity growth, our nation's output and income would grow only at the rate at which the labor force expands; if the labor force grows proportionally with population, this would mean that income per person would be unchanged. With productivity growth, income per person increases. Indeed, U.S. average income is close to eight times as high as it was one hundred years ago, similar to the increase in productivity over this period. The recent robust gains in productivity have boosted both corporate profits and employees' compensation. Corporate profits declined sharply during the recession, but turned around and rose briskly in 2003 (based on data through the first three quarters). Average hourly earnings of production workers in private industry have risen at an average annual rate of close to 3 percent over the past three years. Moreover, productivity growth has reduced inflationary pressures by holding down growth in unit labor costs. As a result, wage gains after adjusting for inflation have been even more impressive by historical standards. In this recession, real average hourly earnings, published in the Bureau of Labor Statistics employment release, never fell below their pre-recession levels, and increased nearly 3 percent in the eleven quarters after the recession began. The experiences in past recessions have been diverse, but many show a net decline in real hourly earnings or much weaker growth even eleven quarters after the start of the recession.

By definition, labor productivity multiplied by hours worked equals output. Thus, in an arithmetic sense, faster productivity growth generally implies that output must expand more rapidly to generate employment gains. The same principle explains why the rapid pace of productivity growth over the past couple of years has meant that gains in output occurred without gains in employment, until recently.

Indeed, the performance of employment over the past couple of years has been appreciably weaker than in past business cycles (Chart 1-10). Employment was slow to pick up in the average previous recovery, perhaps because employers delayed hiring until they became confident that the increases in demand were sustainable. However, such sluggishness typically has been short-lived (a quarter or two) and followed by vigorous expansion. In contrast, in the current business cycle, employment did not begin its recovery until nearly two years after the upturn in real GDP. The performance of employment in this cycle has lagged even that of the so-called "jobless recovery" from the 1990-1991 recession. (Chart 1-10 shows data from the *establishment survey* done by the Bureau of Labor Statistics (BLS). The BLS *household survey* can show a different pattern—as it has done over the past couple of years. As discussed in Box 1-2, however, the BLS views the establishment survey as a more accurate indicator of labor market conditions.)

Chart 1-10 **Total Nonfarm Employment**
The performance of employment in this recovery has lagged that in the typical recovery and even that in the "jobless recovery" of 1990-1991.

Index, level at business cycle peak = 100

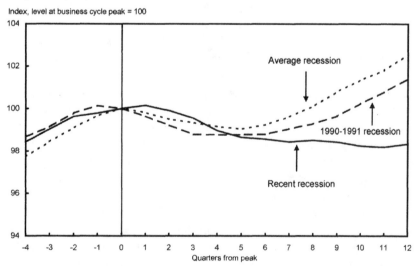

Note: Recent peak set by Council of Economic Advisers at 2000:Q4. Average based on prior recessions since 1960.
Source: Department of Labor (Bureau of Labor Statistics).

Nonetheless, one should not conclude that rapid productivity growth *causes* low employment growth. Rapid productivity growth means that output must increase faster for employment to expand, but it also means that the economy is capable of growing faster. In the long run, the faster rate of *potential output growth* is undoubtedly a good thing for living standards.

Box 1-2: Two Surveys of Employment

Everyone who works is either employed by a firm or is self-employed. Therefore, to count the total number of workers, one could ask each person whether he or she is employed, or one could ask each firm how many workers it employs. The Bureau of Labor Statistics, the agency responsible for tracking employment, uses both approaches. When the BLS asks individuals about their employment status, the results are summarized in the *household survey* of employment. When the BLS asks firms, it produces the *establishment survey* of employment.

Though both surveys ask about employment, they have some important differences that can cause their results to diverge. For example, the establishment survey obtains data from about 160,000 businesses and government agencies that represent about 400,000 worksites and employ over 40 million workers. The sample covers about one-third of all nonfarm payroll jobs in America. The household survey, in contrast, collects data from about 60,000 households, thereby directly covering fewer than 100,000 workers. The establishment survey's larger base of respondents means the calculated margin of error of its estimates is significantly smaller than that associated with the household survey estimates. In addition, the establishment survey is revised annually to match complete payroll records from the universe of establishments participating in state unemployment insurance programs, while the household survey is not.

Furthermore, definitional differences affect the scope of employment measured by the surveys. The establishment survey estimate represents the number of *payroll jobs*, or the number of jobs for which firms pay compensation, while the household survey estimate represents the number of employed persons. Because some people hold more than one job, the total number of payroll jobs can exceed the total number of employed persons. On the other hand, the household survey includes employees working in the agricultural sector, the unincorporated self-employed, unpaid family workers, workers in private households, and workers on unpaid leave from their jobs. The establishment survey excludes all of these categories because they are not reported on the nonfarm business payrolls that provide the source data for the survey.

Box 1-2 — *continued*

These differences and other factors create a gap between the household and establishment surveys' employment estimates, though they tend to display similar long-term trends. The average gap since 1990 has been about 6 percent, or 8 million workers.

While long-term trends in the two surveys are similar, over shorter periods of time their trends have sometimes diverged. This has been the case since late 2001, when employment from the two surveys has trended in opposite directions. For the first time in the two series' histories, one showed a large and sustained *decrease* in employment while the other showed a large and sustained *increase*. In particular, the establishment survey reported a decline in employment of over 1.0 million from the end of the recession in November 2001 to August 2003, while the household survey reported an increase of over 1.4 million. In every month of 2003, the establishment survey showed employment below the November 2001 level, while the household survey showed it above this level. Such a sustained string of divergence is unprecedented.

One possible explanation is that the establishment survey misses some new firms and therefore may underestimate employment at the start of an economic expansion. Past revisions to the establishment survey offer some support for this theory. For the recent data, however, this theory can explain at most the divergence since March 2003, because establishment survey data up to that point appear consistent with unemployment insurance records that cover all establishments. Another possible explanation is that the household survey results are overstated because of the way in which the survey results are extrapolated to represent the entire population. Specifically, information from the 2000 Census, together with estimates of how the population is changing over time, are used to determine how many actual U.S. households correspond to each household in the sample. If, for example, immigration has been unexpectedly low because of tighter border controls and the weaker labor market over the past few years, the estimated number of U.S. households corresponding to each household in the sample may be overstated. As a result, the estimates of total employment (and other aggregates based on the population estimates) from the household survey could be too high.

Both surveys contain valuable information about current economic developments, but, as with all economic statistics, the data from both surveys are imperfect. The Bureau of Labor Statistics has stated that the establishment survey is generally the more reliable indicator of current trends in employment. Still, the explanation for why these two surveys' results have diverged so markedly over the last few years, and what this might indicate about the economic recovery, remains a puzzle.

Conclusion

The U.S. economy is much stronger now than it was a year ago and, as will be discussed in Chapter 3, prospects for the coming year look solid. Nonetheless, the experiences of the past several years remain relevant for the future. Understanding the negative forces that weighed against the economy, as well as the policies that contributed to the recovery, can help policy makers ensure that economic activity maintains a strong upward trend in the years ahead.

The Manufacturing Sector

The manufacturing sector was affected by the latest economic slowdown earlier, longer, and harder than other sectors of the economy and only recently have manufacturing employment losses begun to abate. Over the past several decades, the manufacturing sector has experienced substantial output growth, even while manufacturing employment has declined as a share of total employment. This chapter examines recent developments and long-term trends in manufacturing and considers policy responses.

The key points in this chapter are:

- The severity of the recent slowdown in manufacturing was largely due to prolonged weakness in business investment and exports, both of which are heavily tied to manufacturing.
- The manufacturing employment decline over the past half-century primarily reflects striking gains in productivity and increasing consumer demand for services compared to manufactured goods. International trade plays a relatively small role.
- Consumers and businesses generally benefit from the lower prices made possible by increased manufacturing productivity, and strong productivity growth has led to real compensation growth for workers. The shift of jobs from manufacturing to services has caused dislocation but has not resulted, on balance, in a shift from "good jobs" to "bad jobs."
- The best response to recent developments in manufacturing is to focus on stimulating the overall economy and easing restrictions that impede manufacturing growth. This Administration has actively pursued such measures.

Manufacturing and the Recent Business Cycle

This section looks at the characteristics and causes of the recent economic downturn with particular focus on the manufacturing sector. Output in manufacturing held up relatively well in the recent recession, but employment declined sharply. Data released over the past few months are encouraging regarding the prospects for recovery in the manufacturing sector.

The Recent Downturn in Manufacturing Output

Manufacturing output dropped 6.8 percent from its peak in June 2000 to its trough in December 2001. This was a larger decline than that for real GDP, which fell only 0.5 percent from its peak in the fourth quarter of 2000 to its trough in the third quarter of 2001. This gap is not out of line with historical experience: manufacturing output has dropped much more than real GDP during past business cycles (Chart 2-1). What is more unusual is that the recovery in manufacturing output has been far weaker than the recovery in real GDP.

As discussed in Chapter 1, *Lessons from the Recent Business Cycle*, investment demand was especially weak during the recent recession. A slowing of demand for equipment investment disproportionately hurts the manufacturing sector because nearly all business equipment involves manufactured products. The rest of final demand, in contrast, involves a mix of manufactured goods, agricultural products, services, and structures. The industries within manufacturing contributing most to the downturn in manufacturing output were those primarily associated with the production of business equipment. In particular, slower growth in production of computers and other electronics, machinery, and metals accounts for nearly two-thirds of the swing in manufacturing output from its rapid growth in the late 1990s (an annual rate of 6.9 percent) to its decline in the 18 months after

Chart 2-1 **Real GDP and Manufacturing Industrial Production**
Manufacturing industrial production is more volatile than real GDP.

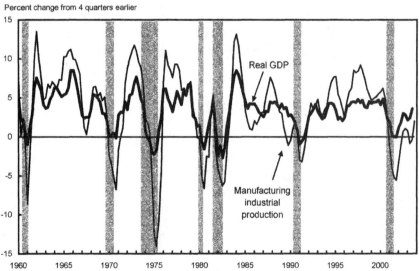

Note: Shaded areas indicate recessions. Recent peak set by Council of Economic Advisers at 2000:Q4.
Sources: Department of Commerce (Bureau of Economic Analysis) and Board of Governors of the Federal Reserve System.

mid-2000 (an annual rate of -4.6 percent). Some parts of manufacturing saw especially difficult times. The metalworking machinery industry, of which the hard-hit tool and die industry makes up 40 percent of employment, has seen its payrolls decline by almost 25 percent from mid-2000 to the end of 2003. Real production in the metalworking machinery industry fell by more than 35 percent over this period.

The timing of the manufacturing slowdown also strongly suggests a link to the decline in business investment (Chart 2-2). Manufacturing output declined substantially in the middle of 2000, months before real GDP turned downward around the fourth quarter of 2000. This pattern mirrors that of business investment in equipment and software, which also peaked in mid-2000—well before the overall economy. The prolonged period of weakness in manufacturing output also bears a notable similarity to the sluggish recovery in investment in equipment and software.

Lackluster demand for U.S. exports has been another source of weakness in the manufacturing sector over the past three years. Exports have been depressed, in part due to slow growth in other major economies. Since the fourth quarter of 2000, the average annual rates of real GDP growth in the euro area and Japan have been less than half that of the United States. Industrial supplies and capital goods make up the bulk of U.S. goods exports. Lower exports of manufactured goods can account for all of the decline in exports since 2000.

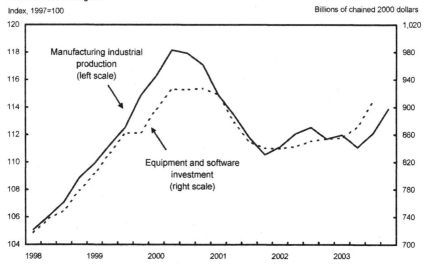

Chart 2-2 **Manufacturing Industrial Production and Real Investment**
Manufacturing industrial production has been low, in part reflecting low investment, since the recent recession began.

Sources: Department of Commerce (Bureau of Economic Analysis) and Board of Governors of the Federal Reserve System.

Manufacturing Employment in Recent Years

Manufacturing employment declined more than manufacturing output during the recent downturn, just as overall employment declined more than overall output. Manufacturing employment declined 16 percent from June 2000, the peak of manufacturing production, to December 2003—a steeper decline than in recessions on average (Chart 2-3). In fact, the recent drop in manufacturing employment was the largest cyclical decline since 1960.

As with the overall economy, the weakness of manufacturing employment relative to output during and after the recent recession has been reflected in rapid productivity growth (Chart 2-4). From the fourth quarter of 2000 through the third quarter of 2003, productivity in the nonfarm business sector and in the manufacturing sector rose more than 4 percent at an annual rate—appreciably faster than in recessions on average since 1960. This rise has allowed businesses to increase output without a corresponding increase in labor input.

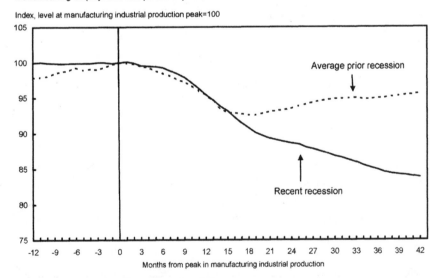

Chart 2-3 **Manufacturing Employment**
Manufacturing employment was particularly hard-hit in the recent recession.

Index, level at manufacturing industrial production peak=100

Note: Average based on prior recessions since 1960.
Sources: Department of Labor (Bureau of Labor Statistics) and Board of Governors of the Federal Reserve System.

Chart 2-4 **Productivity in Manufacturing**
Manufacturing productivity grew more quickly during the recent recession and recovery than in
the average prior recession.

Index, level at business cycle peak=100

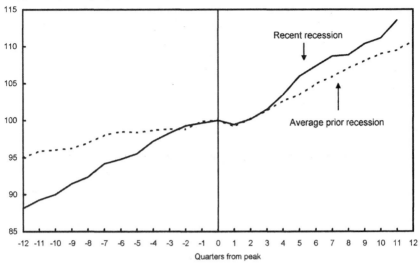

Quarters from peak

Note: Recent peak set by Council of Economic Advisers at 2000:Q4. Average based on prior recessions since 1960.
Source: Department of Labor (Bureau of Labor Statistics).

Signs of Recovery in the Manufacturing Sector

Data for the second half of 2003 suggest a noticeable firming in the manufacturing sector. Orders and shipments of capital goods began to increase around the middle of 2003. Industrial production rose at an average annual rate of 5.9 percent during the second half of the year, the largest six-month gain since the first half of 2000. In addition, the new orders index from the Institute of Supply Management's monthly survey of purchasing managers rose to its highest level in two decades, indicating widespread optimism that activity is picking up. Moreover, some of the factors that have historically affected firms' production decisions support a further strengthening—the cost of capital is low by the standards of the last decade and manufacturers' profits are well above their levels of two years ago.

Although manufacturing employment fell throughout 2003, recent developments hint at improving employment conditions for the sector as a whole. To be sure, some industries continue to lag—for example, textiles, apparel, printing, and petroleum and coal industries have seen employment fall substantially more than overall manufacturing employment since mid-2003. More broadly, however, the rate of decline in overall manufacturing employment eased noticeably in the fourth quarter of 2003, with the smallest quarterly loss in three years. In addition, the rise in temporary-help services since the spring of 2003 is consistent with a future rebound in permanent employment. The temporary-help sector supplies a substantial share of its workers to the manufacturing sector, and over the past decade has tended to lead movements in the permanent payrolls of manufacturing firms (Chart 2-5).

Chart 2-5 **Employment in Manufacturing and Temporary-Help Services**
Changes in temporary-help services employment tend to lead changes in manufacturing employment.

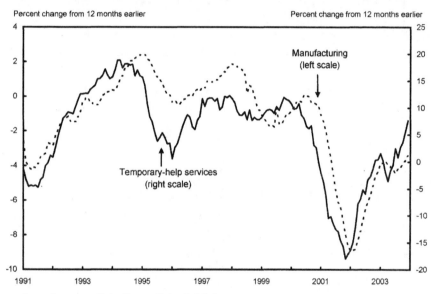

Source: Department of Labor (Bureau of Labor Statistics).

Long-Term Trends

To place the recent experience of the American manufacturing sector in perspective, this section examines the evolution of the manufacturing sector as a whole over the 50 years from 1950 to 2000 along three key dimensions: output, productivity and demand, and employment.

Manufacturing Output over the Long Term

Manufacturing output increased dramatically from 1950 to 2000, with particularly strong growth in the 1990s (Chart 2-6). *Manufacturing industrial production*, a measure of real manufacturing output, increased more than sixfold from 1950 to 2000 before declining in the recent recession. Over the same period, annual growth in manufacturing industrial production averaged 3.8 percent, faster than real GDP growth of 3.4 percent. From 1990 to 2000, manufacturing industrial production expanded at an annual rate of 4.6 percent, outpacing real GDP growth by more than a percentage point. Per capita consumption of manufactured goods has also risen: consumption of goods excluding food and fuel more than quadrupled in real 2000 dollar terms from $1,400 per person in 1950 to $6,000 per person in 2000.

Chart 2-6 **Real GDP and Manufacturing Industrial Production**
Manufacturing industrial production increased at a faster rate than real GDP over the period 1950 to 2000.

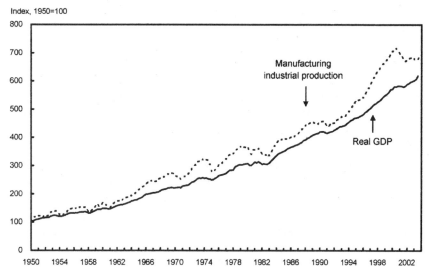

Index, 1950=100

Sources: Department of Commerce (Bureau of Economic Analysis) and Board of Governors of the Federal Reserve System.

In contrast to real manufacturing output, *nominal manufacturing output* (the dollar value of manufacturing output) has grown more slowly than *nominal* GDP (the dollar value of GDP). As a result, the share of nominal GDP accounted for by manufacturing roughly halved, from 29 percent in 1950 to 15 percent in 2000 (based on GDP by industry data available when this *Report* went to press; that is, prior to the 2003 benchmark revision of the National Income and Product Accounts).

Manufacturing Productivity and Demand over the Long Term

Two factors are driving the declining share of manufacturing in U.S. nominal output. First, and most significant, productivity growth in manufacturing lowered the relative price of manufactured goods, but demand did not respond proportionately. Second, imported manufactured goods increased their market share.

Productivity, as measured by output per hour worked, has grown more rapidly in manufacturing than in the overall nonfarm business sector over the last three decades. From 1950 to 1973, manufacturing productivity grew at about the same pace as productivity overall. Over the period from 1973 to 1995, manufacturing productivity growth exceeded productivity growth overall by about 1 percentage point per year. The disparity is even wider over the period from 1995 to 2000, when manufacturing productivity grew at an annual rate nearly 2 percentage points higher than nonfarm business productivity (Chart 2-7). An hour of work in manufacturing produced about four times as much in 2000 as it did in 1950, whereas an hour of work in the nonfarm business sector produced less than three times as much in 2000 as it did in 1950.

This dramatic productivity differential has contributed to a decline in the price of manufactured goods relative to services, which in turn helps to explain the difference between the behavior of nominal and real manufacturing output. Increased labor productivity in a sector means that fewer hours are required to make a given amount of output. This reduces the cost of production and, typically, the relative price of that output. In the same way, relative prices tend to increase in sectors that have experienced less productivity growth, such as services. For example, the falling prices of computers and other electronics have contrasted sharply with the rising costs of services. This example is confirmed by the aggregate data: the average price of consumption goods relative to services fell more than 50 percent between 1950 and 2000. In contrast to the nearly ninefold increase in the prices for

Chart 2-7 **Productivity Growth**
Growth in manufacturing productivity outpaced that in nonfarm business productivity over
the periods 1973 to 1995 and 1995 to 2000.

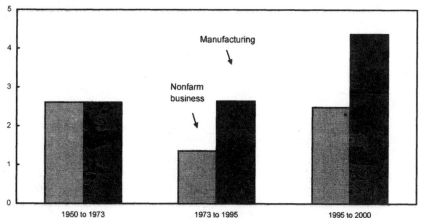

Percent, at an annual rate

Note: Nonfarm productivity based on data available as of December 3, 2003 (that is, prior to the benchmark
revision of the National Income and Product Accounts). Manufacturing productivity based on revised estimates
beginning 1987 (released on January 7, 2004); as revised data for earlier years are not yet available, growth
rates are assumed to be the same as the previously-published SIC-based estimates.
Sources: Department of Labor (Bureau of Labor Statistics) and Council of Economic Advisers.

services, prices for *durable goods* (goods such as cars and refrigerators that are
expected to last, on average, three years or more) rose by a factor of only
2½ and prices for *nondurable goods* rose by a factor of about 5 from 1950 to
2000 (Chart 2-8). Expressed another way, to equal the buying power of
$100 worth of durable goods in 1950, a consumer would have spent $250 in
2000, while for $100 worth of services in 1950, a consumer would have
spent $890 in 2000.

The slower growth of manufactured goods prices has increased the
purchasing power of incomes relative to what it otherwise would have been,
but the portion of this increase that Americans have allocated to manufactured goods has not been large enough to maintain manufacturing's share of
nominal output. The boost to real income from the relative price decline of
manufactured goods has supported demand not only for these goods but
also for services such as health care and financial advice. That is, Americans
have used the resources made available from the relatively slow growth in
manufacturing prices to buy many things, not just manufactured goods.
Increased demand for services, combined with rising relative prices for services, is reflected in the fact that health services and business services each

Index, 1950=100

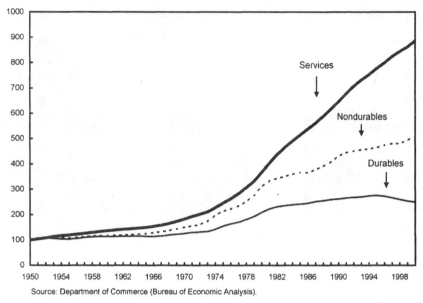

Source: Department of Commerce (Bureau of Economic Analysis).

have increased their share of total nominal output about 4 percentage points since 1950. The finance, insurance, and real estate industry has increased its share a dramatic 9½ percentage points. The opposite trend has held for manufacturing, in which relative price declines have not been fully offset by increases in demand. This explains why the share of manufacturing in total nominal output has roughly halved since 1950. (All calculations of industry share of nominal GDP are based on the pre-benchmark data available when this *Report* went to press.)

In other words, U.S. demand for manufacturing products has been relatively *price inelastic*. That is, demand has not been very responsive to price declines. For example, a family that purchased a car may have reacted to lower relative car prices (and the increased real income they create) by paying for college or hiring a home health care aide, rather than by putting those gains toward the purchase of another car. As a numerical example of inelastic demand, suppose that people buy 10 compact discs at $20 each (for a total expenditure of $200). Now suppose the price falls from $20 to $10. If people buy twice as many compact discs at $10, the value of overall sales will still be $200 (20 compact discs at $10 each). But if people increase their purchases to 15 compact discs, the value of overall sales will be only $150, a decline of 25 percent. This is similar to what has happened in manufacturing.

Productivity gains have tempered price increases, and demand has not responded strongly enough to keep nominal revenues constant as a share of nominal GDP.

A second factor that has led to a decline in manufacturing's share of GDP is that Americans are purchasing more goods from abroad. Goods purchases as a share of total domestic purchases have been declining for about 30 years. The share of domestically produced goods has fallen somewhat faster, particularly in the 1970s and 1990s. Domestically produced goods were 91 percent of overall domestic goods purchases in 1970; by 2000, they had fallen to 68 percent. In other words, imports have made up an increased share of goods bought in the United States (Chart 2-9).

Growth in exports of manufactured goods from the United States over the past several decades has offset only some of the growth in imports (Chart 2-10). As a result, net imports of nonagricultural goods (imports minus exports) have risen materially, reaching about 30 percent of manufacturing production in 2000 (based on the pre-benchmark data available when this *Report* went to press) (Chart 2-11). In relation to the overall economy, net nonagricultural goods imports have also risen, but remained below 5 percent of GDP in 2000. China has been a growing source of manufacturing imports, although this growth has not been a major factor in the increase of the U.S. trade deficit (Box 2-1).

Chart 2-9 **U.S. Imports and Domestic Production of Goods**
Goods produced in the United States have made up a declining share of all goods purchases in the United States since the 1960s.

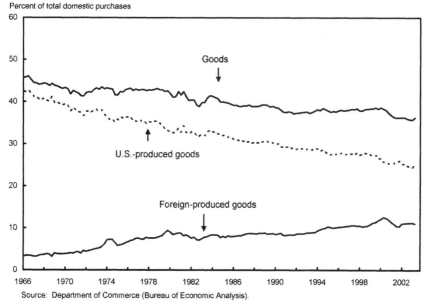

Percent of total domestic purchases

Source: Department of Commerce (Bureau of Economic Analysis).

Chart 2-10 Nonagricultural Goods Trade as a Percent of Manufacturing Output
Imports and exports have increased relative to manufacturing output.

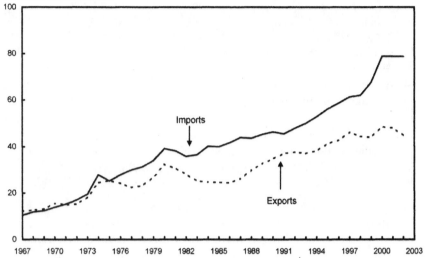

Percent of manufacturing output

Note. Manufacturing output based on data released prior to the 2003 benchmark revision of the National Income
and Product Accounts.
Source: Department of Commerce (Bureau of Economic Analysis).

Chart 2-11 Nonagricultural Goods Net Imports as a Percent of Output
Net imports of goods have risen as a percent of manufacturing GDP over the last 30 years but
remain small as a share of overall GDP.

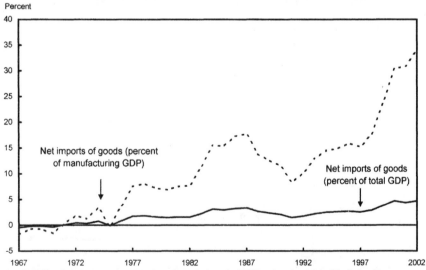

Percent

Note: Manufacturing output based on data released prior to the 2003 benchmark revision of the National Income
and Product Accounts.
Source: Department of Commerce (Bureau of Economic Analysis).

Box 2-1: China and the U.S. Manufacturing Sector

The recent decline in employment in U.S. manufacturing has coincided with a sizable increase in the overall U.S. trade deficit and a sharp increase in the U.S. bilateral trade deficit with China. In part because of the high visibility of Chinese imports, which are primarily everyday consumer goods, these events have raised concerns that imports of Chinese goods come at the expense of American manufacturing workers.

China's Trade with the World
While China's exports and imports grew quickly starting in the early 1990s, China's trade with the rest of the world has been modest until very recently (Chart 2-12). The growth in China's trade has been well balanced in that increased exports to the world have been matched by rising imports from the world. According to data from China's official statistical agency, China has had a trade deficit with the world excluding the United States for several years. China recently ran trade deficits with a number of other countries, including industrial countries such as Germany and Japan.

China's Trade with the United States
China has a significant trade surplus with the United States, its most important export market and the destination of one-quarter of all Chinese goods exports. The U.S. trade deficit with China—about $124 billion through November 2003 at an annual rate—is the single largest bilateral goods and services trade deficit for the United States. The next-largest bilateral deficit is with Japan, at $66 billion through November 2003 at an annual rate.

The U.S. trade deficit excluding China has also risen dramatically since the mid-1990s and is about 3½ times larger than the bilateral deficit with China (Chart 2-13). China's share of the overall U.S. trade deficit in goods has actually fallen since 1997—exactly the period over which trade with China grew rapidly.

Greater trade with China does not appear to have contributed to an increased overall U.S. trade imbalance, as the higher share of U.S. imports from China has been more than offset by a declining share of imports from other Asian countries. The share of U.S. imports from the Pacific Rim as a whole has fallen since the mid-1990s (Chart 2-14). Restrictions on imports from China would be expected to increase imports from other low-cost foreign producers, rather than to increase production and employment for American manufacturers. That is, any job gains from reduced Chinese imports are more likely to occur in other developing countries rather than the United States.

Box 2-1 — *continued*

U.S. exports to China have grown strongly in the last several years, with exports to China up more than 60 percent since 2000. As of the third quarter of 2003, China was the sixth-largest U.S. export market. Exports to China have grown even while exports to the rest of the world have stagnated (Chart 2-15).

The Impact of Trade with China on U.S. Manufacturing Employment
Imports from China affect the prospects for domestic firms with which they compete, and this impact often extends to workers and communities associated with these firms. This is especially the case for firms that make items that are relatively intensive in the use of less-skilled labor, as these are goods in which China has a comparative advantage in production. This may raise the question of whether imports from China are a primary factor in the displacement of American manufacturing workers.

A closer look at the data indicates this is not the case. The low level of U.S. imports from China before the mid-1990s suggests that declines in employment prior to that period were not due to U.S. trade with China. The data on more-recent job losses in manufacturing indicate that China is not a primary factor in these declines, either. With the exception of apparel, the largest job losses have occurred in export-intensive industries for the United States, and job losses in U.S. manufacturing have been mainly in industries in which imports from China are small. For example, the computer and electronic equipment industry accounts for 15 percent of all manufacturing job losses since January 2000, but imports from China were only 8 percent of U.S. output in 2002. Other export-intensive industries that have suffered large job losses include fabricated metal products (9 percent of manufacturing job losses and 2 percent of U.S. output), machinery (10 percent and 2 percent), and transportation equipment (12 percent and 0.4 percent).

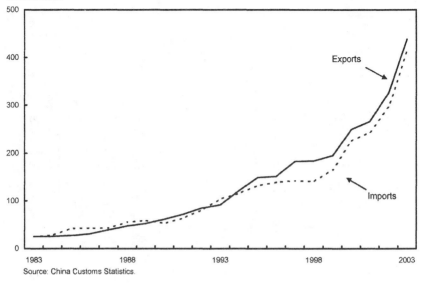

Chart 2-12 **China's Trade in Goods**
The recent growth in China's trade has been divided fairly evenly between growth in imports and growth in exports.

Billions of dollars

Source: China Customs Statistics.

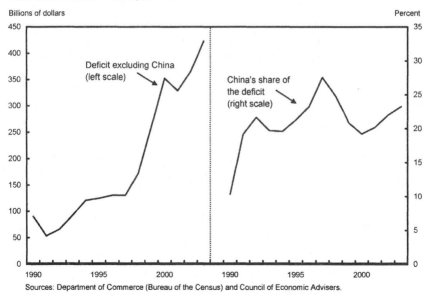

Chart 2-13 **U.S. Trade Deficit in Goods**
The U.S. trade deficit with countries other than China has risen dramatically, while China's share of the overall deficit has fallen since its peak in 1997.

Billions of dollars   Percent

Sources: Department of Commerce (Bureau of the Census) and Council of Economic Advisers.

Chapter 2 | 67

Chart 2-14 **U.S. Imports of Goods**
While the share of U.S. imports of goods from China has been increasing, the share of imports from all Pacific Rim countries combined has been falling.

Percent of U.S. imports

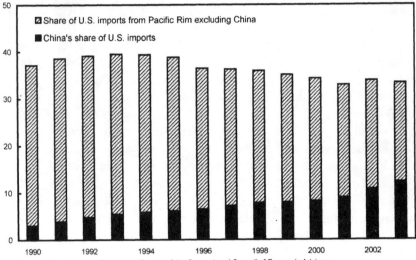

Sources: Department of Commerce (Bureau of the Census) and Council of Economic Advisers.

Chart 2-15 **U.S. Exports of Goods**
Exports to China have increased dramatically over the past several years compared with lackluster growth in exports to the rest of the world.

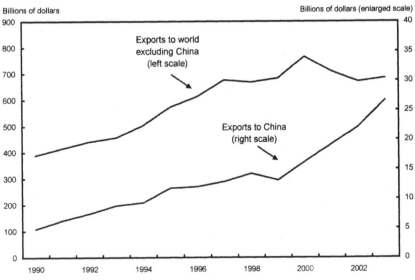

Sources: Department of Commerce (Bureau of the Census) and Council of Economic Advisers.

Manufacturing Employment over the Long Term

Employment in manufacturing as a share of total employment peaked in the early 1940s at about one-third of all farm and nonfarm workers. By 2000, it had declined to just below 13 percent (17 million out of 135 million employees). Employment in service-providing sectors (including transportation, wholesale and retail trade, finance, insurance, and real estate, and services) increased from 35 percent of payroll employment in the early 1940s to 65 percent (86 million workers) of all employees in 2000 (Chart 2-16).

The two main reasons for this shift from the manufacturing sector to service-providing sectors in the labor market are related to the explanations for the declining nominal share of manufacturing output. First, increased demand for services and relatively slow productivity growth in service-providing sectors have led to rising demand for workers in these sectors. In manufacturing, inelastic demand for manufactured goods and faster productivity growth have lowered the relative demand for manufacturing workers.

Second, manufacturing employment likely has fallen in response to the transfer of manufacturing jobs abroad. The jobs affected have generally been those involved in the production of goods requiring relatively low skills.

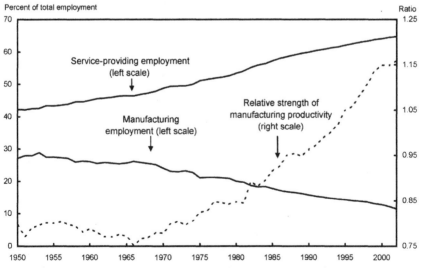

Chart 2-16 **Employment and Relative Productivity**
The decline in manufacturing's share of employment is largely due to rapid productivity gains.

Note: Ratio of manufacturing productivity to nonfarm business productivity available as of December 3, 2003 (that is, prior to the benchmark revision of the National Income and Product Accounts); both indexed to 1992=100.
Sources: Department of Labor (Bureau of Labor Statistics) and Council of Economic Advisers.

Indeed, this is part of the explanation for the rapid growth in manufacturing productivity over the last 50 years (Chart 2-16). The relatively highly-skilled American manufacturing workforce has been increasingly focused on higher-productivity activities. This shift can be seen by looking at compensation for the industries in which employment decreased or increased the most from 1950 to 2000 (Table 2-1). With a few exceptions, employment fell dramatically in industries with relatively low-skilled jobs and rose dramatically in industries with relatively highly-skilled jobs.

This specialization is a natural outcome of the opening of economies all over the world to trade. As a result of such specialization, world efficiency increases and world output goes up as countries focus on the activities in which they are relatively more productive. All countries that participate in trade benefit from this increased output.

The effect of long-term productivity improvements on the shift to service-providing jobs is far more important than increased manufacturing imports. Two simple hypothetical exercises can help to illustrate this. In the first exercise, imagine that manufacturing productivity was fixed at its value in 1970. To match the actual amount of manufacturing output in 2000, one-third of total U.S. nonfarm employment would have been required by manufacturing, compared with the 13 percent required at 2000 productivity levels. That is, without the increase in manufacturing productivity, manufacturing's share of nonfarm employment would have *increased* 8 percentage

TABLE 2-1.— *Employment in Selected Manufacturing Industries*

Industry	Change in employment, 1950 to 2000 (percent)	Compensation per employee as percent of average for all sectors, 2000
Panel A		
Manufacturing industries with employment that grew the fastest		
Rubber and miscellaneous plastics products	213	95
Instruments and related products	207	155
Printing and publishing	102	113
Transportation equipment other than motor vehicles and equipment	83	140
Electronic equipment	77	152
Panel B		
Manufacturing industries with employment that declined the fastest		
Leather and leather products	-82	78
Tobacco products	-65	195
Textile mill products	-58	77
Apparel and other textile products	-50	67
Petroleum and coal products	-42	177

Note.—Data relate to full-time equivalent employees and include some definitional changes. Not yet available are data based on the December 2003 benchmark revision of the National Income and Product Accounts.

Source: Department of Commerce (Bureau of Economic Analysis).

points rather than *decreased* 12 percentage points from 1970 to 2000. As a second exercise, imagine that trade in manufactured goods was balanced in 2000, so that net exports were zero, but assume that the share of manufacturing employment in 1970 and productivity growth from 1970 to 2000 were their actual values. This would raise the amount of manufactured goods produced in the United States. Manufacturing employment as a share of total nonfarm employment, however, would have been only 1 percentage point higher—14 percent, compared with the actual figure of 13 percent—if there had been balanced trade in manufactured goods in 2000.

The Effects of Domestic Outsourcing and Temporary Workers on Measurement of Manufacturing Employment

The decline in manufacturing employment in the official statistics may somewhat overstate the number of actual manufacturing production jobs that have been lost. Changing business practices in the manufacturing sector have led to both the outsourcing of nonproduction work that used to be done "in house" and the increased use of temporary workers. Manufacturing firms that once employed lawyers or accountants in their legal or finance departments might now hire outside consultants to perform these services. Counting this outsourcing as a decline in manufacturing jobs is somewhat misleading, because these workers provide services whether they are working for a manufacturing firm or an outside firm.

Similarly, manufacturing firms are increasingly using temporary workers, especially during periods of uncertain demand. Such workers, previously counted as manufacturing employees, are now counted as service-sector employees in the payroll employment data, although many of them still produce manufactured goods. The way in which employment statistics capture the increased use of outsourcing and temporary workers thus over-states the shift from manufacturing to service-providing jobs.

Much of the outsourced work is taken on by industries that make up the employment category "Professional and Business Services," which includes the temporary-help services industry. The professional and business services category covers a rapidly growing sector of the labor market, so it is likely that the understatement of manufacturing employment has increased over time. Professional and business services grew from just under 3 million employees in 1950 to over 16 million employees in 2000 (Chart 2-17). Employment in subgroups of this category increased substantially in the 1990s (Chart 2-18).

Chart 2-17 **Manufacturing and Professional and Business Services Employment**
Employment in professional and business services has risen dramatically since 1950.

Millions of employees

Manufacturing

Professional and
business services

Source: Department of Labor (Bureau of Labor Statistics).

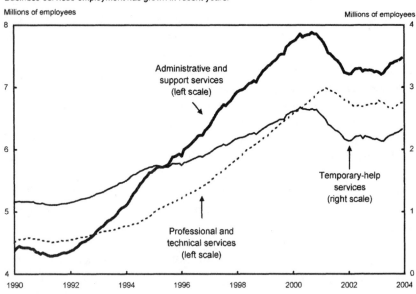

Chart 2-18 **Outsourcing and Temporary-Help Services Employment**
Business services employment has grown in recent years.

Millions of employees

Millions of employees

Administrative and
support services
(left scale)

Temporary-help
services
(right scale)

Professional and
technical services
(left scale)

Source: Department of Labor (Bureau of Labor Statistics).

Results from academic studies can be used to estimate the understatement of employment in the manufacturing sector, bearing in mind that outsourced jobs are not necessarily comparable to permanent ones (for example, a temporary worker may receive fewer benefits than a permanent employee). One widely-cited study estimates that about one-third of all temporary-help services employees work in the manufacturing sector. If the official manufacturing employment statistics are adjusted by this amount, the decline in the level of manufacturing employment in the 1990s is eliminated.

In terms of shares of overall nonfarm employment, adjusted manufacturing shows a decline of 2.8 percentage points over the 1990s, compared with a drop of 3.1 percentage points in the reported data. If outsourcing were also included, the decline in the actual share of employment in the manufacturing sector would probably be even smaller. In other words, at least one-tenth (and perhaps as much as one-fourth) of the decline in manufacturing's share of employment over the 1990s does not reflect a loss of manufactured goods-producing jobs. Rather, it reflects how measurement conventions used to calculate employment statistics account for manufacturers' increased use of outsourced workers for tasks previously performed internally. Another example of how measurement conventions can affect, and confuse, the evaluation of the manufacturing sector is in the definition of manufacturing (Box 2-2).

Box 2-2: What Is Manufacturing?

The value of the output of the U.S. manufacturing sector as defined in official U.S. statistics is larger than the economies of all but a handful of other countries. The definition of a manufactured product, however, is not straightforward. When a fast-food restaurant sells a hamburger, for example, is it providing a "service" or is it combining inputs to "manufacture" a product?

The official definition of manufacturing comes from the Census Bureau's North American Industry Classification System, or NAICS. NAICS classifies all business establishments in the United States into categories based on how their output is produced. One such category is "manufacturing." NAICS classifies an establishment as in the manufacturing sector if it is "engaged in the mechanical, physical, or chemical transformation of materials, substances, or components into new products."

This definition is somewhat unspecific, as the Census Bureau has recognized: "The boundaries of manufacturing and other sectors... can be somewhat blurry." Some (perhaps surprising) examples of manufacturers listed by the Bureau of Labor Statistics are: bakeries, candy stores,

Box 2-2 — *continued*

custom tailors, milk bottling and pasteurizing, fresh fish packaging (oyster shucking, fish filleting), and tire retreading. Sometimes, seemingly subtle differences can determine whether an industry is classified as manufacturing. For example, mixing water and concentrate to produce soft drinks is classified as manufacturing. However, if that activity is performed at a snack bar, it is considered a service.

The distinction between non-manufacturing and manufacturing industries may seem somewhat arbitrary but it can play an important role in developing policy and assessing its effects. Suppose it was decided to offer tax relief to manufacturing firms. Because the manufacturing category is not well defined, firms would have an incentive to characterize themselves as in manufacturing. Administering the tax relief could be difficult, and the tax relief may not extend to the firms for which it was enacted.

For policy makers, the blurriness of the definition of manufacturing means that policy aimed at manufacturing may inadvertently distort production and have unintended and harmful results. Whenever possible, policy making should not be based upon this type of arbitrary statistical delineation.

Effects of the Shift to Services on Workers' Compensation

Many workers affected by the structural developments in manufacturing have experienced difficult transitions. Studies indicate that displaced workers have a significant chance of being unemployed or employed in a part-time job for some time following their job loss. Many of those who are able to find new jobs suffer earnings declines compared to previous earnings. Furthermore, workers also experience losses in earnings growth relative to what they would have had if they had remained continuously employed. Because of these effects, an often-voiced concern is that the shift toward employment in services has meant that more Americans are working in low-paying jobs.

While the shift from the manufacturing sector to service-providing sectors has been painful for many displaced from the manufacturing sector, the average effect on compensation—and in particular on new entrants into the labor force who have chosen to work in services rather than manufacturing—has been less worrisome. Some service-providing industries pay less than some manufacturing industries, but much of the employment growth in service-providing sectors has occurred in industries with higher than average compensation. The third column of Panel A in Table 2-2 shows the total compensation per full-time equivalent employee in five service-providing industries relative to the average across industries: for example, compensation in wholesale trade in 2000 was 27 percent higher than the average (which equals 100 percent). The second column gives the change in employment from 1950 to 2000 for each industry: wholesale trade employment increased more than 4 million over this period. As Panel A reveals, four of the five service-providing industries with the largest employment increases paid compensation roughly at or above the average. Together, these five service-providing industries can explain nearly two-thirds of overall private employment growth from 1950 to 2000. Panel B of Table 2-2 shows that three of the five manufacturing industries with the highest job-loss rates paid less than the average private-sector job in 2000. For example, apparel employment fell nearly 600,000 from 1950 to 2000, and compensation of workers in the apparel industry in 2000 was only 67 percent of the average. As a result of the large increases in employment in some of these high-paying service-providing industries, the gap between compensation in service-providing sectors and manufacturing has been closing over the last couple of decades.

TABLE 2-2.— *Compensation in Selected Industries*

Industry	Change in employment, 1950 to 2000 (thousands)	Compensation per employee as percent of average for all sectors, 2000
Panel A: Service-providing		
Service-providing industries with the largest employment increases		
Retail trade	14,248	57
Business services	9,079	99
Health services	8,482	103
Finance, insurance, and real estate	5,406	158
Wholesale trade	4,259	127
Panel B: Manufacturing		
Manufacturing industries with the largest employment decreases		
Textile mill products	-715	77
Apparel and other textile products	-586	67
Primary metal industries	-491	124
Leather and leather products	-321	78
Petroleum and coal products	-91	177

Note.—Data relate to full-time equivalent employees and include some definitional changes. Not yet available are data based on the December 2003 benchmark revision of the National Income and Product Accounts.

Source: Department of Commerce (Bureau of Economic Analysis).

The Transition in Context

Individuals and communities tied to declining industries experience dislocation and distress. While many workers have made the transition from manufacturing to the service sector, the transition can be difficult. To ease it, the President has supported policies for worker retraining accounts and has extended unemployment insurance benefits when needed. The appropriate policy responses to this transition will be discussed in more detail later in this chapter. Before that, however, it is useful to place the evolution of the U.S. manufacturing sector in a broader context.

First, the shift to a relatively more service-oriented economy has involved substantial benefits for American consumers and producers. Real incomes have risen, allowing consumers to purchase more goods and services such as food, health care, transportation, and education, while measures of the quality of life and life expectancy have also increased. In addition, the growth of the service-providing sector has generated new opportunities for employment in industries such as information technology services, financial services, and entertainment.

Second, the shift of employment away from lower-productivity manufacturing toward higher-productivity manufacturing and service-providing sectors reflects economic growth and development, just as the shift away from agriculture toward manufacturing did in the last century (Box 2-3). The relative shift from manufacturing toward service-providing sectors has been shared by other advanced economies over the last few decades (Chart 2-19). Manufacturing employment declined from the mid-1990s to 2002 in a number of countries whose economies are rapidly developing, including China, Brazil, and South Korea. In fact, China, Brazil, South Korea, and Japan had steeper percentage declines in manufacturing employment over that period than the United States.

Chart 2-19 **Employment in Industry as a Percent of Total Employment**
A declining share of employment in manufacturing is common across developed economies.

Percent of total employment

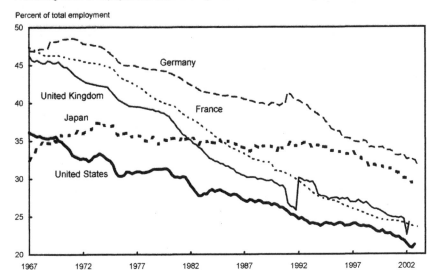

Note: Industry comprises manufacturing, mining, and construction. In 2001, manufacturing made up about two-thirds of industry in each country.
Source: Organization for Economic Cooperation and Development.

Box 2-3: The Evolution of the U.S. Agricultural Sector

The evolution of U.S. manufacturing from 1970 to 2000 mirrors, in important respects, that of U.S. agriculture from 1940 to 1970. Total real farm output increased more than 60 percent from 1940 to 1970. Over the same period, employment in farming declined nearly 6 million, or almost two-thirds of the level in 1940 (Chart 2-20). This translated into a decline in agriculture's share of total employment of 15 percentage points, from 19.4 percent in 1940 to 4.4 percent in 1970.

While the histories of agriculture and manufacturing in the United States differ in some ways, such as the prominent role of subsidies in the agricultural sector, their similarities help put the long-term story of the manufacturing sector in context.

In both sectors, a 30-year period of rapid productivity growth substantially reduced the share of the American workforce needed to meet demand for food and manufactured goods. Labor productivity in agriculture nearly quadrupled from 1940 to 1970 (Chart 2-21), a period that has been called the "second American agricultural revolution."

Box 2-3 — *continued*

This productivity boom has been attributed to the invention of new technologies, such as hybrid crop varieties, as well as the widespread application of existing technologies, such as machinery and conservation practices.

Agricultural productivity growth led to low growth in the price of food, bringing substantial benefits to American consumers and the U.S. economy as a whole and significantly improving U.S. competitiveness in world markets. Despite the mid-century expansion in the demand for agriculture's output, prices remained essentially flat. After the run-up in demand and prices during World War II and its immediate aftermath, agricultural prices increased only 4 percent from 1950 to 1970. The average price of all commodities, in comparison, increased 35 percent from 1950 to 1970 (Chart 2-22). The lack of food price inflation is mimicked by the low inflation in manufacturing in the last few decades, with a sizable benefit for American consumers in both cases.

The evolution of the agricultural sector has been good for the economy on the whole, but it meant dislocation for millions of agricultural workers—a process that continues today. Displaced farm workers faced uncertainty regarding their next job and the applicability of their skills in different sectors, just as manufacturing workers do today. The 1940s and 1950s saw the rapid growth of new industries that hired workers no longer needed on farms. Manufacturing itself likely absorbed a substantial percentage of former agricultural workers: nearly 8 million new manufacturing jobs were created between 1940 and 1970, 2 million more than the total decline in agricultural employment.

In the 1970s and 1980s, service-providing sectors likely absorbed workers not needed in manufacturing. This continued in the 1990s, as high-tech and financial services accounted for new employment growth. Looking forward, it is difficult to predict which industries will grow and require more workers. The past experience of the adjustment in agriculture suggests that market forces will continue to reshape the American workforce.

Chart 2-20 **Employment and Real Output in Agriculture**
Agricultural employment declined dramatically from 1940 to 1970, while real agricultural output increased substantially.

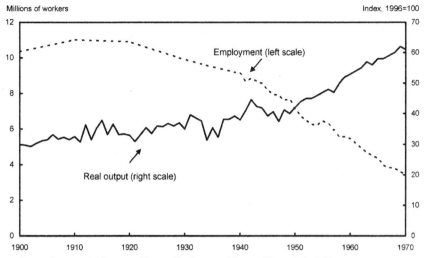

Sources: Department of Commerce (Bureau of the Census and Bureau of Economic Analysis) and Council of Economic Advisers.

Chart 2-21 **Agricultural Productivity**
Agricultural productivity on farms surged in the mid-20th century

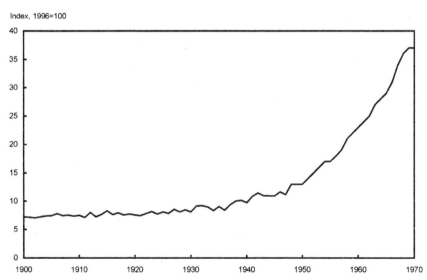

Sources: Department of Commerce (Bureau of the Census) and Council of Economic Advisers.

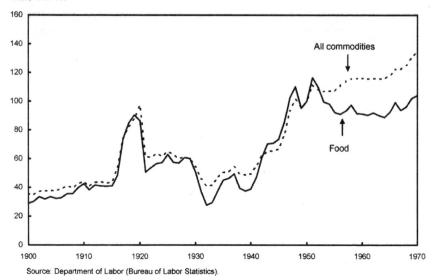

Chart 2-22 **Wholesale Prices**
The price of food relative to all commodities declined substantially in the mid-20th century.

Index, 1950=100

Source: Department of Labor (Bureau of Labor Statistics).

The Role of Policy

Markets operating free from government intervention will, in most cases, best allocate the Nation's resources across sectors. It is generally a mistake to target government assistance to a particular sector at the expense of other sectors, and manufacturing is no exception. That said, government policy can play a positive role. Policies targeted toward general education and training, such as the President's landmark education reforms and proposed funding to help displaced workers train for new opportunities, will help people adapt to ongoing structural changes. The President's Jobs for the 21st Century plan will support students and workers by improving high school education and strengthening post-secondary education and job training.

The short-run performance of the manufacturing sector is closely tied to fluctuations in overall economic activity. Policies that increase aggregate output and economic growth will help to improve the near-term outlook for the manufacturing sector. This Administration put forward a six-point plan for the U.S. economy in September 2003. The plan would help the manufacturing sector along with the overall economy, and it includes the following components:

Making Tax Relief Permanent

The Administration has undertaken several important fiscal measures to strengthen growth, including the 2001 tax relief program, the March 2002 stimulus package, and the May 2003 Jobs and Growth Act. These policies have already contributed to the current recovery in manufacturing. The President has proposed making provisions of the 2001 and 2003 tax cuts permanent. These include measures that lower the cost of capital and thereby encourage business investment. Capital investment makes up a relatively large share of manufacturers' costs, so a lower cost of capital provides a particularly important benefit to manufacturers. Moreover, manufacturers produce capital goods, so increased investment demand particularly benefits manufacturing firms.

Making Health Care Costs More Affordable and Predictable

The President's proposals aim to reduce frivolous litigation, help individuals save for future health expenses, and allow small businesses to pool together to purchase health coverage. Health care costs as a share of total compensation are one-third higher in manufacturing than in service-providing industries. The President's proposals will help manufacturers reduce the burden of increasing health care costs.

Reducing the Burden of Lawsuits on the Economy

The President seeks to address the burden that lawsuits impose on American businesses. For example, estimates suggest that roughly 60 companies entangled in asbestos litigation have gone bankrupt primarily because of asbestos liabilities, displacing between 52,000 and 60,000 workers.

Ensuring an Affordable, Reliable Energy Supply

Initiatives include modernizing the electricity grid and streamlining the process of acquiring permits for natural gas exploration. This is vital for manufacturing, which makes up about 15 percent of nominal GDP but accounts for around one-quarter of energy use in the United States.

Streamlining Regulations to Ensure that they are Reasonable and Affordable

Research has shown that manufacturing bore about 30 percent of the costs of regulation in the United States in 2000—nearly double its share of nominal output.

Opening International Markets to American Goods and Services

This has become particularly important for the manufacturing sector. While exports accounted for about one-sixth of American manufacturing production in 1970, they made up nearly half by 2002.

Conclusion

The manufacturing sector in the United States has undergone significant change in the last half-century. Productivity and real output in manufacturing have risen dramatically, and faster than in the economy as a whole. Productivity improvements have boosted real income in the United States. However, because Americans have spent much of their real income gains on services rather than manufactured goods, manufacturing's share of employment has declined. In the recent recession, manufacturing output and employment were hit particularly hard. The President's policies, aimed at stimulating the overall economy, easing restrictions that impede manufacturing growth, and ensuring that workers have the skills they need to be competitive, address the short-term difficulties of the sector and ensure its long-term health.

CHAPTER 3

The Year in Review and the Years Ahead

The U.S. economy made notable progress in 2003. The recovery was still tenuous coming into the year, as continued fallout from powerful contractionary forces—the capital overhang, corporate scandals, and uncertainty about future economic and geopolitical conditions discussed in Chapter 1, *Lessons from the Recent Business Cycle*—still weighed against the stimulus from expansionary monetary policy and the Administration's 2001 tax cut and 2002 fiscal package. However, the contractionary forces dissipated over the course of 2003, and the expansionary forces were augmented by the Jobs and Growth Tax Relief Reconciliation Act (JGTRRA) that was signed into law at the end of May. The economy now appears to have moved into a full-fledged recovery.

This chapter reviews the economic developments of 2003 and discusses the Administration's forecast for the years ahead. The key points in this chapter are:

- Real GDP growth picked up appreciably in 2003. Growth in consumer spending, residential investment, and, particularly, business equipment and software investment appear to have increased noticeably in the second half of the year.
- The labor market began to rebound in the final five months of 2003.
- Core consumer inflation declined to its lowest level in decades.
- The Administration's forecast calls for the economic recovery to strengthen further this year, with real GDP growth running well above its historical average and the unemployment rate falling. Looking further ahead, the economy is expected to continue on a path of strong, sustainable growth.

Developments in 2003 and the Near-Term Outlook

After rising 2.8 percent during the four quarters of 2002, real GDP expanded at an average annual rate of 4.4 percent during the first three quarters of 2003. The economy appears to have gained momentum as the year went on, with annualized real GDP growth averaging close to 2½ percent during the first half of the year and more than 8 percent in the third quarter. The available data suggest solid further growth in the fourth quarter, though not as spectacular as in the third quarter. (The *Report* went to print before GDP data for the fourth quarter were available.)

The Administration expects real GDP to grow at an annual rate of 4.0 percent during the four quarters of 2004, a figure that is close to the latest Blue Chip consensus economic forecast (as of January 10, 2004). The unemployment rate, which peaked at 6.3 percent in June 2003, is projected to fall to 5.5 percent by the fourth quarter of 2004.

The pace of real GDP growth during the first three quarters of 2003 was supported by robust gains in consumption, residential investment, and defense spending. Inventory investment, in contrast, declined over the first three quarters of last year. In 2004, the composition of GDP growth is expected to shift away from government spending and toward business fixed investment and net exports. Evidence of emerging momentum in investment accumulated over the course of 2003: businesses began to hire, build inventories, and increase shipments of nondefense capital goods. In addition, expected faster growth among our trading partners and the recent decline in the exchange value of the dollar make U.S. exporters well positioned for expansion.

Much of the growth of private demand during 2003 was attributable to the effects of expansionary fiscal and monetary policy designed to counteract the lingering effects of the stock market decline, the capital overhang, worries about geopolitical developments, and concern about accounting scandals. Much stimulus remains in the pipeline in the form of refunds on 2003 tax liabilities this spring and the ongoing effects of the current low interest rates. The fiscal stimulus will not disappear suddenly. The reduction in the tax withholding schedule included in the 2003 fiscal package (JGTRRA) only began in July 2003, and households are still adjusting to these lower tax rates. Moreover, tax refunds in the first half of 2004 are expected to be higher than usual: the tax cuts were retroactive to January 2003, but last year's withholding changes generally did not capture tax savings on income earned in the first half of the year. In addition, because of the 2002 and 2003 tax cuts, businesses will be able to cut their tax liabilities by expensing 50 percent of their equipment investment (rather than depreciating the new capital) through the end of 2004. The lower tax rates, higher tax refunds, and investment expensing included in the Jobs and Growth Tax Relief Reconciliation Act are expected to reduce tax collections by about $146 billion in 2004, up from about $49 billion (or about $98 billion at an annual rate) in the second half of 2003.

Consumer Spending

Consumer spending increased briskly in 2003. Real personal consumption expenditures increased at an average annual pace of 3 percent during the first half of the year, and then surged at an annual rate of 6.9 percent in the third quarter. Data on retail sales and motor vehicle purchases through December and services outlays through November are consistent with consumer spending remaining at a high level in the fourth quarter. As a result, real consumption growth in the second half of the year likely ran noticeably above that in the first half.

The pickup in spending growth in the second half of the year corresponded to an increase in the rate of growth of household income. After rising at an annual rate of 3.6 percent in the first half, real disposable personal income (that is, inflation-adjusted household income after taxes) jumped at an annual rate of 6.3 percent in the third quarter, boosted by tax relief, and appears to have held steady in the fourth quarter.

Wages and salaries increased moderately in the second half of the year, bolstered by the emerging recovery in the labor market. Moreover, the personal tax cuts included in the 2003 fiscal package (JGTRRA) meant that U.S. households were able to keep substantially more of their earnings. The reduction in withholding and the advance rebates of the child tax credit added $37 billion to disposable income (not at an annual rate) in the second half of the year.

Other factors also likely contributed to the strengthening of consumer spending over the course of 2003. The robust performance of equity markets and solid gains in home prices bolstered wealth. Household wealth (net financial resources plus the value of nonfinancial assets such as cars and homes) increased $2¼ trillion during the first three quarters of 2003, and it probably rose substantially further in the fourth quarter given the solid increase in broad indexes of stock prices in the last few months of the year. Consumer sentiment was depressed early in the year by the prospect of war with Iraq. Sentiment jumped in April and May following the successful resolution of major combat operations and then was little changed until November, when it picked up noticeably. By the end of the year, household sentiment was somewhat higher than it had been at the end of 2002 and much higher than it was just prior to the war with Iraq.

All told, consumption grew in line with household after-tax income during 2003. Personal saving as a fraction of disposable personal income averaged 2.3 percent in 2002 and remained at this level, on average, in the first three quarters of 2003. Swings in personal saving have contributed to movements in national saving in recent years (Box 3-1).

Growth of real consumption is expected to be lower than that of real GDP in coming years. As explained in Box 3-1, the relative flatness of the personal saving rate over the past couple of years is likely the result of offsetting forces. On the one hand, capital losses associated with the decline in the stock market from March 2000 to March 2003 probably tempered consumption (with some lag) and, in turn, caused the personal saving rate to increase. On the other hand, personal saving was likely depressed by the

Box 3-1: Personal Saving and National Saving

One important influence on the personal saving rate (the saving of the household sector divided by its after-tax income) over the past 10 years has been changes in households' wealth, although the past couple of years appear to have been an exception.

Driven by movements in stock prices, the ratio of household wealth to personal income climbed dramatically in the second half of the 1990s, peaked in early 2000, and then retreated substantially over the next two years. Economic theory suggests that increases in wealth tend to raise household spending, and decreases in wealth tend to lower household spending. This "wealth effect" often produces a negative correlation between household wealth and the personal saving rate because personal saving is defined in the national accounts as the difference between income excluding capital gains and spending (Chart 3-1).

Empirical studies suggest that an additional dollar of wealth leads to a permanent rise in the level of household consumption of about two to five cents, with the adjustment occurring gradually over a period of one to three years (the range depends on the exact specification—for example, one study found that including the components of wealth separately produces lower estimates). Such estimates of the wealth effect can explain the behavior of personal saving in the second half of the 1990s fairly well. For example, assuming that a dollar of wealth leads to an increase in consumption of three cents and that adjustment lags are typical, one would predict that the rise in wealth in the late 1990s would have caused the saving rate to decline by 4 percentage points between the end of 1994 and the end of 2000—close to the actual decline in the saving rate (ignoring the quarter-to-quarter volatility in the series).

The wealth effect also suggests that the (net) fall in wealth after 2000 would have caused a rebound in the personal saving rate of more than 2 percentage points. In fact, however, the personal saving rate has not risen materially. One potential explanation for the divergence is that households have raised consumption in anticipation that the labor market recovery will continue and, in turn, bolster income. Some of the additional consumption may have been funded through the wave of cash-out home mortgage refinancing enabled by the combination of low interest rates and technological advances that have made such transactions easier. Another possibility is that the availability of low-interest-rate loans on cars and other items has spurred households to replace cars and other durable goods earlier than they otherwise would have.

Box 3-1 — *continued*

Direct saving by households represents only part of the total saving done in the United States. Corporations also save in the form of retained earnings—the difference between after-tax profits and dividends. Most of the year-to-year variation in retained earnings stems from profits because dividend payments tend to have a fairly smooth upward trend over time. Profits rose in the early and mid-1990s, boosted by brisk productivity growth. After peaking as a share of GDP in 1997, profits fell over the next few years, owing to the 1998 global financial crisis, a catch-up of wages to productivity gains, and the economic slowdown. Retained earnings as a share of GDP also trended lower over this period. During the first three quarters of 2003, both profits and retained earnings picked up.

National saving is the sum of private saving (that is, the saving of households and corporations) and government saving (equal to the Federal budget surplus plus the state and local government budget surpluses). The saving of state and local governments tends to make a small positive contribution to government saving, but in the past few years, deteriorating fiscal conditions in states and localities have pushed their overall saving into slightly negative territory. Saving of the Federal government has declined sharply since 2000, as the recession and tax cuts have pulled down revenue, and homeland security and national defense expenditures have increased.

National saving rose (as a fraction of GDP) during the 1990s, but has fallen sharply since 2000 (Chart 3-2). As a fraction of GDP, it now stands at the low end of its range since World War II. Although both government saving and private saving are above their historic lows, the fact that they are both fairly low at the same time has led to the low level of national saving.

National saving is important because it represents the portion of our country's current income that is being set aside for investment in new capital. In particular, national saving plus the net capital inflow from abroad equals domestic investment. Greater saving and investment today boost future national income. To increase national saving, the President supports raising Federal saving by restraining Federal spending. He has also proposed Lifetime Savings Accounts and Retirement Savings Accounts, which are designed to increase incentives for households to save.

Chart 3-1 **Wealth-to-Income Ratio and Personal Saving Rate**
The "wealth effect" produces a negative correlation between household wealth and personal saving.

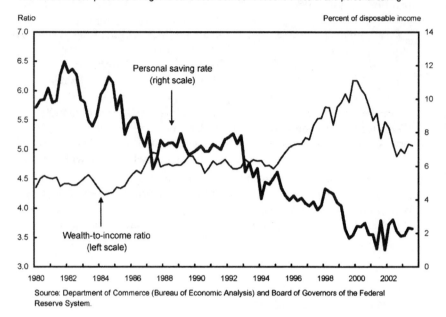

Source: Department of Commerce (Bureau of Economic Analysis) and Board of Governors of the Federal Reserve System.

Chart 3-2 **National Saving Rate**
Net national saving is at an extremely low level by historical standards, reflecting both low private saving and low government saving.

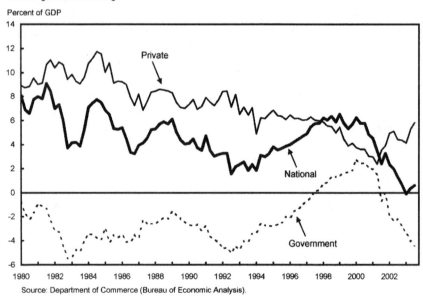

Source: Department of Commerce (Bureau of Economic Analysis).

boost to consumption from low interest rates (both directly through the availability of low-interest-rate loans on durable goods and indirectly through the funds made available by cash-out mortgage refinancings). As interest rates and incomes rise over the course of the next several years, the transitory forces boosting consumption growth should dissipate, and as a result, real consumption is expected to grow more slowly than real GDP over the forecast period.

An increase in corporate contributions for defined-benefit pension plans is likely to boost the saving rate in the near term from what it might be otherwise. The Pension Benefit Guarantee Corporation (PBGC) has estimated that corporate contributions to defined-benefit plans will increase sharply above 2003 levels. Indeed, rapid increases have already begun, according to separate data included in the Employment Cost Index. The contributions raise personal income, but because these funds are not placed in the hands of employees until retirement, they seem unlikely to affect current-year consumption. As a result, they should increase the personal saving rate.

Residential Investment

The housing sector continued to show remarkable vigor in 2003, with real residential investment climbing at an average annual rate of more than 10 percent in the first three quarters of the year. Housing starts moved above the already high 2002 level to 1.8 million units in 2003, the largest number of starts since 1978. In addition, sales of both new and existing single-family homes rose to record levels.

Some of the strength in housing demand reflected the same gains in after-tax income and wealth that bolstered real consumer spending. The low levels of mortgage interest rates were another important driving force. The interest rate on new fixed-rate 30-year mortgages slipped from an average of 6½ percent in 2002 to an average of 5¾ percent in 2003. This level is the lowest in the 32 years for which comparable data are available. Indeed, according to data from the Michigan Survey Research Center, consumers' assessments of home-buying conditions remained very positive in 2003, largely because of low mortgage interest rates. As a result of the very favorable conditions in the housing sector, the U.S. home-ownership rate climbed to 68.2 percent in the third quarter of 2003—equal to its highest level on record.

During 2004, real residential investment is expected to slip lower as housing starts edge down to levels determined by long-run demographics.

Business Fixed Investment

Real business fixed investment (firms' outlays on equipment, software, and structures) turned around in 2003, posting an annualized gain of 6.2 percent during the first three quarters of the year after declines of 10.2 percent during the four quarters of 2001 and 2.8 percent during the four quarters of 2002. The acceleration during the year was noteworthy, with real investment rising at an annual rate of 12.8 percent in the third quarter and indications of further growth in the fourth quarter, compared with an average annual pace of 3.1 percent in the first half of the year. The improvement from 2002 to 2003, as well as the pickup over the course of 2003, largely reflected a strengthening in real purchases of equipment and software.

Within the equipment and software category, the largest increases occurred for certain high-tech items. Real outlays for computers increased at an annual rate of 43 percent in the first three quarters of 2003, and real spending on communications equipment, which had performed particularly poorly during the recession, rose almost 15 percent. Shipments data suggest that spending in these categories remained strong in the fourth quarter. Meanwhile, real investment in software continued its solid upward trend, rising 12 percent during the first three quarters of the year. Outlays for transportation equipment were held down by further large declines in purchases of aircraft in the first three quarters of the year. Finally, the available data suggest that real spending on equipment outside of the high-tech and transportation categories posted a solid gain over the course of 2003.

The increased momentum in business purchases of capital goods in 2003 likely reflects the factors mentioned in Chapter 1. First, with capital overhangs probably behind them, firms were poised to take advantage of further declines in prices of high-tech goods stemming from continued technological advances. Second, striking gains in productivity and falling unit labor costs bolstered corporate profits. Third, the cost of capital was held down by a number of factors, including falling prices for high-tech capital goods, but also by low interest rates, rising stock prices, and the investment incentives introduced in the Job Creation and Worker Assistance Act of 2002 (JCWAA) and expanded in the 2003 fiscal package (JGTRRA).

The Administration expects the recovery in real business investment in equipment to strengthen further this year, reflecting the acceleration in output, continued low interest rates, and the investment incentives provided by the 2002 and 2003 tax cuts. Fixed investment in equipment and structures tends to be related to the pace of growth in output (along with the cost of capital), and so the pickup in real GDP growth from 2.8 percent during the four quarters of 2002 to 4.4 percent during the first three quarters of 2003 is projected to lead to an increase in investment during 2004.

One reason for the development of a capital overhang was the lowered business expectations of the future level of output that developed just prior to the past recession. As these projections fell, the demand for investment also fell. In contrast to that period, current projections of 2004 output have been rising since mid-2003 and are expected to lead to increased demand for capital goods in the initial quarters of the forecast.

Growth in equipment investment in 2004 should be further boosted as firms pull forward spending in anticipation of the expiration of the period when businesses are able to expense (rather than depreciate) 50 percent of the value of their equipment investment. The flip side of some investment being advanced into 2004 is that investment may grow more slowly in 2005. Even so, the growth of equipment investment in 2005 is projected to be solid.

Despite the emerging recovery in spending on equipment and software, business demand for structures remained soft in 2003. High overcapacity seems to have offset the impetus imparted by low interest rates and higher cash flow. In the office sector, vacancy rates rose substantially for the third consecutive year. Vacancy rates moved still higher in the industrial sector and now stand at extremely elevated levels. The good news is that the substantial declines in total spending on structures seem to have abated. Indeed, real investment in nonresidential structures was approximately flat over the first three quarters of 2003, in contrast with a plunge of more than 25 percent during the preceding two years. Strength in oil and gas drilling and an increase in construction of general merchandise stores during the year have offset continued softness in some other sectors.

The forces that shape the outlook for business structures—the growth of output and the cost of capital—are much the same as for business equipment. However, they operate with a longer lag because of the time it takes to plan and build these structures. Investment in business structures is projected to post a small gain during 2004.

Business Inventories

Businesses began 2003 with lean inventories following a massive liquidation in 2001 and little restocking during 2002. Inventory investment was substantially negative over the first three quarters of 2003, as increases in production lagged those in final demand. The reasons for this slow response of production are unclear. Firms may have been surprised by the strength of final demand, or they may simply have been waiting for compelling evidence that a sustainable recovery was under way.

The net decline in inventories during the first three quarters of 2003 left stocks in their leanest position relative to final sales of goods and structures in at least 50 years. (This lean position results, at least in part, from efficiencies generated by just-in-time inventory-management techniques.) Stockbuilding seems to have begun in September, however. Inventory investment appears likely to have made a positive contribution to GDP growth in the fourth quarter of 2003, and the contribution is projected to remain noticeably positive through the first half of 2004. Inventory investment is expected to plateau thereafter at a level that keeps stocks in line with rising sales throughout 2004 and 2005.

Government Purchases

Real Federal spending (consumption expenditures and gross investment) climbed at an annual rate of 8 percent during the first three quarters of 2003. The available data suggest that 2003 as a whole likely saw the largest increase in more than 30 years. The gain during the first three quarters was led by an annualized rise of 10 percent in real defense spending largely related to military operations in Iraq. Real nondefense spending rose at an average annual pace about 4 percent. This gain was less than half as large as the gain during the four quarters of 2002, when outlays were stepped up considerably for homeland security.

The defense supplemental appropriations for FY 2004, signed in November, allows for some further near-term growth in government purchases. Defense spending is projected to fall during FY 2005, and as a result, overall Federal spending is projected to edge down.

Like the Federal government, the governments of states and localities saw their tax receipts decelerate during the economic slowdown. Budgets have also deteriorated because of rising health care costs and increased demand for security-related spending. With many of these governments subject to balanced-budget rules, they have taken a variety of measures to address their fiscal imbalances, including drawing on accumulated reserves (so-called "rainy day funds"), raising taxes, and restraining spending. Real expenditures of state and local governments were little changed during the first three quarters of 2003, in contrast with an average annual gain of around 3 percent over the preceding five years. With state and local governments still under pressure, their real expenditures are projected to increase slowly during the coming year. Eventually, their fiscal situations should be improved by increases in tax revenue resulting from the strengthening of the economy.

Exports and Imports

The U.S. current account deficit as a share of GDP was little changed, on net, during the first three quarters of 2003, averaging about 5 percent. The deficit on trade in goods and services as a share of GDP also moved in a narrow range during the first three quarters. U.S. net investment income (the income paid to U.S. investors in foreign endeavors less that paid to foreign investors in U.S. projects) was roughly flat, as both receipts from abroad and payments to foreign investors rose somewhat during the first three quarters of 2003. Real imports of goods and services have likely been restrained in recent quarters by the decline in the value of the dollar. Real imports rose at an annual rate of 1 percent during the first three quarters of 2003, a substantially slower pace than during the four quarters of 2002. Real imports of capital goods (other than autos) rose solidly, as would be expected given the recovery in U.S. investment. Real oil imports increased at a faster pace (on an annual basis) than during the four quarters of 2002. Real services imports fell markedly in the first half of 2003 but turned up in the third quarter.

America's major trading partners have recovered from the global slowdown somewhat more slowly than has the United States. For example, an index of real GDP for our G-7 trading partners increased at an average annual pace of less than 2 percent during the first three quarters of 2003. As a result, foreign demand for U.S. exports was lackluster in the first half of 2003. Real exports picked up sharply around the middle of 2003, increasing at an annual pace of 10 percent in the third quarter. The increase was led by a gain in real exports of capital goods. Even so, the level of exports remained well below its peak in 2000.

Prospects for exports over the next two years look better. Growth among the non-U.S. OECD countries is projected by the OECD Secretariat to rise 2.6 percent during the four quarters of 2004, up from a pace of 1.6 percent during 2003. Growth is expected to rise further to 2.8 percent in 2005. The expected growth in foreign markets should support growth in U.S. exports. In addition, the effect will likely be augmented by a rise in the U.S. market share of world exports owing to the effects of the 23 percent decline in the value of the dollar against major currencies from its peak in early 2002 through the end of 2003. The effect of the recent dollar decline on exports will likely take a couple of years to be fully felt.

Real imports are projected to increase along with domestic output, but the growth of real imports is likely to be slowed by the recent decline in the dollar's value relative to other currencies. On balance, real imports are projected to grow at about the same pace as GDP, on average, during the next two years. Nominal imports will increase faster than real imports because import prices will rise in reaction to the recent dollar decline. Even so, the current account deficit, which rose to about 5 percent of GDP in the first three quarters of 2003, is projected to edge up in 2004 and decline thereafter.

Overall, real net exports are expected to be approximately flat during the next year and are likely to make a positive contribution to real GDP growth thereafter. Over the next six years, the returns to foreign owners of U.S. capital are likely to grow faster than the returns to U.S. owners of foreign capital, a legacy of a long period of strong foreign investment in the United

States during the past decade. As a result, real gross national product (GNP), which includes these net foreign returns to capital, is expected to grow slower than real gross domestic product (GDP).

The Labor Market

Nonfarm payroll employment fell an average of 50,000 workers per month in the first seven months of 2003, before increasing 35,000 in August, 99,000 in September, and an average of 48,000 per month in the fourth quarter. The strengthening was experienced in most sectors. Job gains in professional and business services stepped up appreciably from the modest upward pace seen earlier in the year. Construction employment began to expand in the second quarter after two years of modest job losses, and the quarterly averages of employment in the wholesale trade, transportation, and utilities industries turned up at the end of the year. The manufacturing sector continued to shed jobs through year-end, though the pace of decline slowed, and the factory workweek climbed more than 0.5 hour, on balance, in the final five months of 2003.

The unemployment rate increased in the first half of 2003, reaching a peak of 6.3 percent in June, before falling during the second half of the year. In the fourth quarter, the unemployment rate averaged 5.9 percent, the same as it had been a year earlier. Because the labor force is constantly expanding, employment must be growing moderately just to keep the unemployment rate steady. For example, if the labor force is growing at the same rate as the population (about 1 percent per year), employment would have to rise 110,000 a month just to keep the unemployment rate stable, and larger job gains would be necessary (and are expected) to induce a downward trend in the unemployment rate.

Looking ahead, temporary-help services employment—a leading indicator for the labor market—suggests substantial further employment growth. Average growth in temporary-help services employment over a six-month period has a striking positive correlation with growth in overall employment over the subsequent six months (Chart 3-3). Statistical analysis suggests that an increase of one job in temporary-help services corresponds to a subsequent rise of seven jobs in overall employment. Employment in temporary-help services has expanded 194,000 since last April, suggesting robust growth in overall employment this year. The unemployment rate is projected to fall to 5.5 percent by the fourth quarter of 2004.

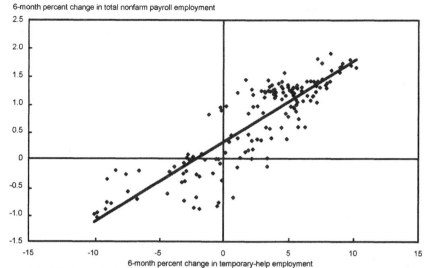

Chart 3-3 **Growth in Temporary-Help Services and Overall Employment, 1990-2003**
Growth in temporary-help services employment tends to lead growth in overall nonfarm employment.

6-month percent change in total nonfarm payroll employment

Note: The change in total employment covers the 6-month period following the 6-month period during which the
change in temporary-help employment is measured.
Source: Department of Labor (Bureau of Labor Statistics).

Productivity, Prices, and Wages

The consumer price index (CPI) increased 1.9 percent over the 12 months ended in December 2003, a little below the 2.4 percent rise experienced during the same period the previous year. Consumer energy prices fluctuated markedly over the course of 2003, but ended the year 6.9 percent above their level at the end of 2002. The core CPI (which excludes food and energy) rose only 1.1 percent during 2003, considerably below the 1.9 percent increase of the previous year. This deceleration likely stems from the slack in labor and product markets last year. In addition, unit labor costs were held down by an impressive performance for labor productivity, with output per hour in the nonfarm business sector rising at an annual pace of about 6 percent during the first three quarters of the year following an increase of roughly 4½ percent during the four quarters of 2002. This pace of productivity growth is well above the annual average of just over 2 percent experienced since 1960.

Hourly compensation of workers appears to have picked up a little last year. During the 12 months of 2003, the employment cost index (ECI) for private nonfarm businesses moved up 4 percent following a 3.2 percent gain during the previous year. The wages and salaries component of the index rose 3.0 percent during 2003, slightly below the 2.7 percent increase recorded for 2002. The benefits component of the ECI, however, surged 6.4 percent over the 12 months of 2003, much faster than the 4.7 percent pace during 2002. The increase in benefits was especially large in the first quarter of 2003, led by a jump in contributions to defined-benefit pension plans as employers began making up for losses in the value of pension fund assets. Employer-paid health premiums rose 10.5 percent during 2003, roughly the same pace as in 2002.

Core CPI inflation is expected to continue at a low level in 2004, and overall inflation is expected to be even lower as energy prices retreat further. Overall CPI inflation is projected to fall to 1.4 percent during the four quarters of 2004—close to the past year's pace of core inflation. With the unemployment rate expected to average 5.6 percent for the year as a whole (above our estimated 5.1 percent midpoint of the range of rates consistent with stable inflation) the level of slack—although less than in 2003—is still projected to hold down inflation during 2004. Also keeping inflation in check is the recent rapid pace of—and solid near-term prospects for—productivity growth. Offsetting this effect is the somewhat higher pace of import-price inflation (resulting from the recent dollar decline) and the quicker pace of GDP growth. Over the next five years, CPI inflation is expected to edge up, eventually flattening out at 2.5 percent, a level that is identical to the consensus forecast.

The path of inflation as measured by the GDP price index is similar, but a bit lower throughout the projection period. Inflation as measured by the GDP price index is projected fall to 1.2 percent during the four quarters of 2004, the same as the 1.2 percent pace of the core GDP price index during the first three quarters of 2003. GDP price inflation is projected to increase slowly thereafter—roughly parallel to the rise in CPI inflation.

The wedge between the CPI and the GDP measures of inflation has important implications for the Federal budget and budget projections. A larger wedge reduces the Federal budget surplus because cost-of-living adjustments for Social Security and other indexed programs rise with the CPI, whereas Federal revenue tends to increase with the GDP price index. For a given level of nominal income, increases in the CPI also cut Federal revenue because they raise income tax brackets and affect other inflation-indexed features of the tax code. Of the two indexes, the CPI tends to increase faster in part because it measures the price of a fixed market basket. In contrast, the GDP price index increases less rapidly than the CPI because it reflects the choices of households and businesses to shift their purchases away from items with increasing relative prices and toward items with decreasing relative prices. In addition, the GDP price index includes investment goods, such as computers, whose relative prices have been falling rapidly. Computers, in particular, receive a much larger weight in the GDP price index (0.8 percent) than in the CPI (0.2 percent).

During the eight years ended in 2002, the wedge between inflation in the CPI-U-RS (a version of the CPI designed to be consistent with current methods) and the rate of change in the GDP price index averaged 0.5 percentage point per year. With the core CPI and the core GDP price index both increasing at about a 1¼ percent pace during the past year, inertia suggests that the near-term wedge will be only about 0.2 percentage point in 2004. The wedge is expected to widen eventually to its recent mean of 0.5 percent by 2009.

Financial Markets

Stock prices skidded early in the year, but rallied in March and have been on a solid uptrend since then. During the 12 months of 2003, the Wilshire 5000 index—a broad measure of stock prices—rose 29 percent. An increase of this magnitude has not been seen since 1997. High-tech stocks did even better; for example, the Nasdaq index, which is heavily weighted toward high-tech industry, rose 50 percent during 2003. Nearly two-thirds of the rise in broad measures of stock prices occurred after the President signed the 2003 tax cut (JGTRRA) in late May; the Act reduced marginal tax rates on dividends and capital gains and thus likely contributed to the robust performance of stock prices.

Following a large decline in 2001, and a smaller one in 2002, the interest rate on 91-day Treasury bills fell an additional 29 basis points in 2003 and ended the year at 0.9 percent. These reductions reflected the Federal Reserve's efforts to stimulate the economy, leaving real short-term rates (that is, nominal rates less expected inflation) slightly negative. Following market-based expectations of interest rates (derived from rates on Eurodollar futures), the Administration does not expect real rates this low to persist once the recovery becomes firmly established, and nominal Treasury bill rates are projected to increase gradually. Long-term interest rates fell sharply last spring and then rebounded in the summer. For the year as a whole, long-term Treasury rates were about unchanged, but corporate interest rates dropped a bit as the spread over Treasury rates narrowed. The Administration projects that the yield on 10-year Treasury notes, which averaged 4.3 percent in December 2003, will edge up gradually next year, consistent with the path of short-term Treasury rates.

The Long-Term Outlook

The economy could well grow faster than in the projection presented here, as the long-run benefits from the full reductions in marginal tax rates are felt. These should lead to higher labor force participation than would occur otherwise, more entrepreneurial activity, and greater work effort by highly productive individuals. The Administration, however, chooses to adopt conservative economic assumptions that are close to the consensus of professional forecasters. As such, the assumptions provide a prudent and cautious basis for the budget projections.

Growth in Real GDP and Productivity over the Long Term

The economy continues to display supply-side characteristics favorable to long-term growth. Productivity growth has been remarkable, and inflation remains low and stable. As a result of stimulative fiscal and monetary policies, real GDP is expected to grow faster than its 3.1 percent potential rate during the next four years. The Administration forecasts that real GDP growth will average 3.7 percent at an annual rate during the four years from 2003 to 2007—in line with the consensus projection. Because this pace is somewhat above the assumed rate of increase in productive capacity, the unemployment rate is projected to decline over this period. In 2008 and 2009, real GDP growth is projected to continue at its long-run potential rate of 3.1 percent, and the unemployment rate is projected to be flat at 5.1 percent (Table 3-1).

The growth rate of the economy over the long run is determined by its supply-side components, which include population, labor force participation, productivity, and the workweek. The Administration's forecast for the contribution of different supply-side factors to real GDP growth is shown in Table 3-2.

TABLE 3-1.—*Administration Forecast*[1]

Year	Nominal GDP	Real GDP (chain-type)	GDP price index (chain-type)	Consumer price index (CPI-U)	Unemploy-ment rate (percent)	Interest rate, 91-day Treasury bills (percent)	Interest rate, 10-year Treasury notes (percent)	Nonfarm payroll employ-ment (millions)
	Percent change, fourth quarter to fourth quarter				Level, calendar year			
2002 (actual)	4.3	2.9	1.3	2.2	5.8	1.6	4.6	130.4
2003	5.8	4.2	1.5	2.0	6.0	1.0	4.0	130.1
2004	5.2	4.0	1.2	1.4	5.6	1.3	4.6	132.7
2005	4.9	3.4	1.4	1.6	5.4	2.4	5.0	136.3
2006	5.0	3.3	1.6	1.9	5.2	3.3	5.4	138.6
2007	5.2	3.3	1.8	2.2	5.1	4.0	5.6	140.6
2008	5.2	3.1	2.0	2.5	5.1	4.3	5.8	142.5
2009	5.2	3.1	2.0	2.5	5.1	4.4	5.8	144.4

[1] Based on data available as of December 2, 2003.

Sources: Council of Economic Advisers, Department of Commerce (Bureau of Economic Analysis), Department of Labor (Bureau of Labor Statistics), Department of the Treasury, and Office of Management and Budget.

TABLE 3-2.—*Accounting for Growth in Real GDP, 1960-2009*[1]

[Average annual percent change]

Item	1960 Q2 to 1973 Q4	1973 Q4 to 1990 Q3	1990 Q3 to 2003 Q3	2003 Q3 to 2009 Q4
1) Civilian noninstitutional population aged 16 or over	1.8	1.5	1.2	1.1
2) Plus: Civilian labor force participation rate	.2	.5	-.1	-.1
3) Equals: Civilian labor force [2]	2.0	2.0	1.1	1.0
4) Plus: Civilian employment rate [2]	.0	-.1	.0	.2
5) Equals: Civilian employment [2]	2.0	1.9	1.1	1.2
6) Plus: Nonfarm business employment as a share of civilian employment [2] [3]	.1	.1	-.1	.6
7) Equals: Nonfarm business employment	2.1	2.0	1.0	1.8
8) Plus:. Average weekly hours (nonfarm business)	-.4	-.4	-.1	.0
9) Equals: Hourall persons (nonfarm business)	1.7	1.7	.9	1.8
10) Plus: Output per hour (prods of uctivity, nonfarm business) ...	2.8	1.4	2.5	2.1
11) Equals: Nonfarm business output	4.6	3.1	3.4	3.9
12) Plus: Ratio of real GDP to nonfarm business output [4]	-.3	-.2	-.4	-.5
13) Equals: Real GDP	4.2	2.9	3.0	3.4

[1] Based on data available as of December 2, 2003.
[2] Adjusted for 1994 revision of the Current Population Survey.
[3] Line 6 translates the civilian employment growth rate into the nonfarm business employment growth rate.
[4] Line 12 translates nonfarm business output back into output for all sectors (GDP), which includes the output of farms and general government.

Note.—The periods 1960 Q2, 1973 Q4, and 1990 Q3 are business cycle peaks.
Detail may not add to totals because of rounding.

Sources: Council of Economic Advisers, Department of Commerce (Bureau of Economic Analysis), and Department of Labor (Bureau of Labor Statistics).

The Administration expects nonfarm labor productivity to grow at a 2.1 percent average annual pace over the forecast period, virtually the same as that recorded during the 43 years since the business-cycle peak in 1960. The projection is notably more conservative than the roughly 4½ percent average annual rate of productivity growth since the output peak in the fourth quarter of 2000. After such an extraordinary surge, a period of slower productivity growth is likely as firms shed their hesitancy to hire. In addition, the slower pace of productivity assumed in the forecast reflects the Administration's view that in the absence of a good explanation for the recent acceleration, it is wiser to base the productivity forecast on longer-term averages.

In addition to productivity, growth of the labor force (also shown in Table 3-2) is projected to contribute 1.0 percentage point per year to growth of potential output on average through 2009. Labor force growth results from growth in the working-age population and changes in the labor force partic-ipation rate. The Bureau of the Census projects that the working-age population will grow at an average annual rate of 1.1 percent through 2009—roughly the same pace as during the years between 1990 and 2003. The last year in which the labor force participation rate increased was 1997, so the long-term trend of rising participation appears to have come to an end. Since then, the participation rate has fallen at an average 0.2 percent annual pace—although some of the decline in 2001 and 2002 probably resulted from the recession-induced decline in job prospects. In 2003, the baby-boom cohort was 39 to 57 years old, and over the next several years the boomers will be moving into older age brackets with lower participation rates. As a result, the labor force participation rate is projected to edge down an average of 0.1 percent per year through 2009. The decline may be greater, however, after 2008, which is the year that the first baby boomers (those born in 1946) reach the early-retirement age of 62.

In sum, potential real GDP is projected to grow at a 3.1 percent annual pace, slightly above the average actual pace since 1973 of 3.0 percent. Actual real GDP growth during the six-year forecast period is projected to be slightly higher, at 3.4 percent, because the civilian employment rate (line 4 of Table 3-2) makes a small (0.2 percentage point) and transitory contribution to growth through 2007 as the unemployment rate falls. This contribution then ends as the unemployment rate stabilizes at 5.1 percent.

Interest Rates over the Long Term

The gradual increase in the interest rate on 91-day Treasury bills is projected to continue through 2009. The rate is expected to reach 4.4 percent by 2009, at which date the real interest rate on 91-day Treasury bills will be close to its historical average. The projected path of the interest rate on 10-year Treasury notes is consistent with that on short-term Treasury rates. By 2008, this yield is projected to be 5.8 percent, 3.3 percentage points above expected CPI inflation—a typical real rate by historical standards. By 2009, the projected term premium (the difference between the 10-year interest rate and the 91-day rate) of 1.4 percentage points is in line with its historical average.

The Composition of Income over the Long Term

A primary purpose of the Administration's economic forecast is to estimate future government revenue, which requires a projection of the components of taxable income. The Administration's income-side projection is based on the historical stability of the long-run labor and capital shares of gross domestic income (GDI). During the first three quarters of 2003, the labor share of GDI was on the low side of its historical average. From this jump-off point, it is projected to rise to its long-run average and then remain at this level over the forecast period. (The income share projections are consistent with data available through December 2, 2003. They exclude any effects of the later comprehensive revision to the National Income and Product Accounts.) The labor share consists of wages and salaries, which are taxable, employer contributions for employee pension and insurance funds (that is, fringe benefits), which are not taxable, and employer contributions for government social insurance. The Administration forecasts that the wage and salary share of compensation will decline while employer contributions for employee pension and insurance funds grow faster than wages. This pattern has generally been in evidence since 1960 except for a few years in the late 1990s. During the next five years, the fastest growing components of employer contributions for employee pension and insurance funds are expected to be employer-paid health insurance and contributions for defined-benefit pension plans.

The capital share (the complement of the labor share) of GDI is expected to fall before leveling off at its historical average. Within the capital share, a near-term decline in depreciation (an echo of the decline in short-lived investment during 2001 and 2002) helps boost corporate economic profits, which in the third quarter 2003 were noticeably above their post-1973 average of about 8 percent of GDI. The share of corporate economic profits in GDI is projected to be bolstered in 2004 by the strong recent productivity growth together with stable gains in hourly compensation, and an expected decline in depreciation. From 2005 forward, the profit share is expected to slowly decline back to its historical average of about 8 percent. The projected pattern of book profits (known in the national income accounts as "profits before tax") reflects the 30 percent expensing provisions of the Job Creation and Worker Assistance Act of 2002 and the 50 percent expensing provisions of the Jobs and Growth Tax Relief Reconciliation Act of 2003. These expensing provisions reduce taxable profits from the third quarter of 2001 through the fourth quarter of 2004. The expiration of the expensing provisions increases book profits thereafter, however, because those investment goods expensed during the three-year expensing window will have less remaining value to depreciate thereafter. The share of other taxable income (the sum of rent, dividends, proprietors' income, and personal interest income) is projected to fall, mainly because of the delayed effects of past declines in long-term interest rates, which reduce personal interest income during the projection period.

Conclusion

The Administration's policies have been a key force shaping recent economic developments and the prospects for economic growth in coming years. The policies are designed to enhance U.S. economic growth, not just maintain it. The remaining chapters of this *Report* illustrate the ways in which pro-growth economic policies can improve economic performance by striking a balance between encouragement and regulation of firms, by reducing barriers to trade, and by reducing tax-based disincentives to economic activity.

CHAPTER 4

Tax Incidence:
Who Bears the Tax Burden?

The study of *tax incidence* is the economic study of which taxpayers bear the burden of a tax. This question is of considerable importance to policy makers, who want to know whether the distribution of the tax burden (between rich and poor, capital and labor, consumers and producers, and so on) meets their criteria for fairness.

Distributional tables showing the tax burdens borne by different income groups are an important application of incidence analysis. The Joint Committee on Taxation (JCT) and the Department of the Treasury prepare distributional tables for the existing tax system and for some proposed and adopted tax changes. The Congressional Budget Office (CBO) prepares such tables for the existing tax system. In addition to these official analyses, some private groups also publish distributional tables.

When used properly, distributional tables can contribute to informed decision making on the part of citizens and policy makers. Unfortunately, mainstream economic analysis suggests that these tables do not always accurately describe who bears the long-run burden of certain taxes. This problem does not arise from bias or lack of economic knowledge on the part of the economists who prepare these tables. Instead, it reflects resource and data limitations, uncertainty about some of the economic effects of taxes, and variations in the time frame considered by the analyses. Nevertheless, the shortcomings of distributional tables can lead to misperceptions of the impact of tax changes.

This chapter discusses some of the ways in which distributional tables can be improved. The key points in this chapter are:

• The actual incidence of a tax may have little to do with the legal specification of its incidence. Official distributional tables recognize this fact in many contexts, but not in all of them.

• In the long run, a large part of the burden of capital taxes is likely to be shifted to workers through a reduction in wages. Analyses that fail to recognize this shift can be misleading, suggesting that higher income groups bear an unrealistically large share of the long-run burden of such taxes.

To begin, it is useful to review the basic economic principles of tax incidence and apply them to different types of taxes.

Theory of Tax Incidence

One crucial finding in the study of tax incidence is that the *economic incidence* of a tax (the identity of the person who bears the burden of the tax) can be completely different from its *statutory* or *legal incidence* (the identity of the person upon whom the law officially imposes the tax). In other words, the person who is legally responsible for paying the tax may not be the one who actually bears the burden of the tax. As explained below, the incidence of a tax depends upon the law of supply and demand, not the laws of Congress.

Another crucial principle is that only people can pay taxes. Businesses and other artificial entities cannot pay taxes. Although the corporate income tax is legally imposed on firms that are organized as corporations, the actual burden of the tax can fall only on people—perhaps the firm's owners, or its employees, or its customers—but certainly not on a legal artifact such as a corporation. Similarly, although the estate tax is legally imposed on the estate, the burden of the tax can fall only on people—perhaps the decedent who left the estate, perhaps the heirs, perhaps other people—but not the estate, which is merely a legal construct established to sort through the ownership of the decedent's assets.

It is simplest to first discuss the incidence of a simple *excise tax*, a tax levied on a specific good or service. As explained below, the key insights from this analysis can be extended to apply to other types of taxes.

Incidence of an Excise Tax

Consider a tax on apples. Suppose that when there is no tax, the price of apples is $1. Now, suppose that the government imposes a 10-cent excise tax on apples and that the producers are legally responsible for paying this tax. Do producers actually bear the economic burden of the tax?

The answer depends on what happens to the price of apples. If the price remains unchanged, producers bear the economic burden (the economic incidence of the tax is the same as the legal incidence). Consumers pay $1, the same as before, and suffer no burden. Producers, after collecting $1 from the consumers, must pay 10 cents to the government, so they clear only 90 cents. Alternatively, if the price rises by the amount of the tax, from $1 to $1.10, consumers bear the burden. Although they do not send any money to the government, they pay 10 cents more per apple than they did without the tax. The producers bear no economic burden, even though they are legally responsible for paying the tax. After collecting $1.10 from consumers and sending 10 cents to the government, they still clear $1, as they did without the tax. In this case, economists say that the producers *shift* the burden of the tax to consumers. To consider another possibility, if the price of apples rises by 5 cents, to $1.05, consumers and producers share the burden equally. Consumers bear a 5-cent burden because they pay $1.05 for each apple, compared to the $1 that they paid without the tax. Producers bear a 5-cent burden because they clear only 95 cents per apple, compared to the $1 they cleared without the tax: they collect $1.05 from consumers, but send 10 cents to the government.

As these examples show, the division of the tax burden between consumers and producers depends on what happens to the price of apples. When prices are free to adjust, they are likely to be determined by the law of supply and demand. If the price of apples was $1 with no tax, then the number of apples consumers wanted to buy at that price must have equaled the number of apples that producers wanted to sell at that price.

What happens when the 10-cent excise tax is imposed? It depends on how responsive consumers and producers are to changes in the prices they pay or receive. The relevant questions are: How many fewer apples do producers sell if the amount they clear per apple declines? How many fewer apples do consumers buy if the amount they pay per apple rises?

For example, suppose that producers are four times more responsive to price changes than consumers. Then, producers face a price change that is one-fourth as large as that faced by consumers. The 10-cent tax causes the price to rise from $1 to $1.08, putting an 8-cent burden on consumers and a 2-cent burden on producers. At that price, the number of apples consumers want to buy falls by the same amount as the number that producers want to sell. Alternatively, if consumers were four times more responsive than producers, then producers would bear 8 cents of the burden and consumers would bear only 2 cents.

The group that is less responsive bears more of the burden of the tax. The group that is more responsive escapes much of the burden because it responds to the tax, abandoning the taxed activity when threatened with a tax burden. The price-responsiveness of each group depends upon its flexibility. Do producers have good alternatives (in the form of other industries in which they can produce)? Do consumers have good alternatives (in the form of other products they can buy)?

The answers vary across products, types of producers (such as workers and owners of capital), and time frames. If the excise tax applied only to Granny Smith apples, consumers could switch to other, untaxed, kinds of apples. If it applied to all apples, consumers would have somewhat less flexibility. Some workers may have skills specific to the apple industry. Other workers may be more flexible because their skills are more general; they could avoid bearing the tax burden by finding a job in another industry. The owners of capital employed in a taxed industry may bear a significant short-run burden because the buildings and equipment in the industry may be designed specifically for its use and the owners may have little ability to move those resources elsewhere. In the long run, though, capital can leave the taxed industry: as buildings and equipment depreciate in the taxed industry, *new* buildings and equipment are constructed in other industries.

A similar logic applies if the product is subsidized rather than taxed. The group that is more responsive receives the smaller benefit because the subsidy prompts new members of that group to enter the market and compete away the benefits of the subsidy. Conversely, the group that is less responsive receives the greater benefit from the subsidy because little entry occurs.

Because the incidence of an excise tax depends upon the relative flexibility of consumers and producers, the burden may not always fall where the Congress intends. When the Congress imposed a "luxury" tax on yachts in 1991, for example, it intended the wealthy purchasers of yachts to bear the burden. Such purchasers, however, may be quite responsive to price because there are many alternative goods that they can purchase (expensive cars and jewelry, for example). If this is so, then a significant part of the burden of a yacht tax may fall on workers in the industry, who may be less well-off than owners of yachts. Indeed, after the tax was introduced, production and employment in the boat industry fell, leading some observers to claim that workers were bearing much of the burden of the tax. Although the validity of this claim cannot be conclusively determined (the industry's decline may have been caused by the 1990-1991 recession rather than the tax), the Congress responded to these concerns by repealing the tax in 1993.

Legal Incidence Is Unimportant

As long as prices can freely adjust, the economic incidence of a tax does not depend on the legal incidence. Suppose that, in the above example, the government imposes the 10-cent excise tax on apple consumers rather than apple producers. Consumers then must make the tax payment to the government, in addition to the price they pay to producers.

Because producers are four times more price-responsive than consumers, the price received by producers must still fall by 2 cents and the price paid by consumers must still rise by 8 cents. Despite the legislative change, that is still the only outcome that keeps the number of apples producers want to sell equal to the number that consumers want to buy. If the tax is legally imposed on producers, they shift 8 cents of the burden to consumers. If it is legally imposed on consumers, they shift 2 cents of the burden to producers.

Given that the price can freely adjust, it should not be surprising that the final outcome is unchanged. It is irrelevant whether the tax collector stands next to consumers and takes 10 cents from them when they buy an apple or stands next to producers and takes 10 cents from them when they sell an apple. It does not matter whether the consumer puts a dime in a bowl marked "taxes" or hands the dime to the producer who puts it in the same bowl.

Applied Distributional Analysis of Excise Taxes and Subsidies

The legal incidence of Federal excise taxes is sometimes placed on consumers, sometimes on manufacturers, and sometimes on other producers or importers. In most cases, this legal incidence rightly receives little attention. In accordance with the economic theory of tax incidence, the JCT and Treasury economists preparing distributional tables uniformly ignore the legal incidence of conventional excise taxes. The JCT generally allocates excise tax burdens to consumers. Treasury follows a similar, but more elaborate, approach.

These approaches are reasonable, since consumers are likely to bear much of the long-run burden of most excise taxes. In the long run, most producers are flexible, or price-responsive, because they can switch to other industries. Consumers are likely to have less flexibility, except in special cases where there are good substitutes for the product being taxed.

The theory of incidence also applies to more-subtle excise subsidies, such as those included within the individual income tax. The income tax law grants tax reductions for purchasers of various products—for example, an itemized deduction for medical expenses, a credit for electric cars, and the Hope and Lifetime Learning credits for the costs of higher education. The economic benefits of these provisions are likely to be divided between consumers and producers, with the greater benefit going to the group that is less price-responsive. The long-run benefits are likely to go largely to consumers, because they are likely to be less price-responsive than producers. Official distributional analyses generally allocate these income tax reductions to the consumers.

The basic insight that tax burdens fall more heavily on groups that are less flexible can be applied to a wide range of taxes. The remainder of this chapter applies this framework to payroll taxes, taxes on capital, and estate and gift taxes.

Payroll Taxes

The largest Federal payroll tax, earmarked to finance Social Security and Medicare Part A, is imposed at a 15.3 percent rate on the first $87,900 of earnings and at a 2.9 percent rate on earnings above that amount. A much smaller Federal payroll tax, earmarked to finance unemployment compensation, is imposed at a 0.8 percent rate on the first $7,000 of earnings. The legal incidence of the Social Security-Medicare tax is divided equally between employers and employees. The legal incidence of the Federal unemployment compensation tax is placed entirely on employers.

With a payroll tax, the product being taxed is labor and its price is the wage rate. Applying the insights obtained from the analysis of excise taxes, the relevant question is whether firms' demand for labor or workers' supply of labor is more responsive to changes in the wage rate. In the long run, it is likely that firms are more responsive, or flexible, particularly in a global economy in which they can relocate abroad. This conclusion implies that employees bear most of the payroll tax burden, a result supported by empirical studies. In other words, wages paid to employees are lower by an amount roughly equal to the employers' part of the payroll tax. In accord with this conclusion, official distributional analyses generally assign the full burden of payroll taxes to employees. The primary controversy in this area concerns whether the distributional analysis should also include the Social Security benefits that are financed by the payroll tax (Box 4-1).

Much of the individual income tax is also imposed on labor income. Based on the above discussion, the burden of the individual income tax on labor, like that of payroll taxes, should also fall on workers. Official distributional analyses generally allocate the individual income tax on labor income to workers.

Some taxes on and subsidies to labor income are more subtle. The income tax laws deny firms their normal business-expense deductions for some payments of labor income. For example, under certain circumstances, firms cannot deduct salaries greater than $1,000,000 per year paid to senior executives or some "golden-parachute" payments made to executives in connection with corporate takeovers. Because of this denial of deductibility, the firm pays a tax on these labor income payments, in addition to the regular tax on its owners' net income. This tax operates as an additional payroll tax legally imposed on employers, although of a much narrower scope than the payroll taxes discussed above. On the other hand, the income tax laws allow firms to claim tax credits for some other payments of labor income. Examples include the work opportunity tax credit, the welfare-to-work credit, the empowerment zone employment credit, and the Indian employment credit. (The work opportunity and welfare-to-work credits expired on December 31, 2003, but may be reinstated by future legislation.) In economic terms, these credits are subsidies to labor.

The fact that these taxes and subsidies are implemented as changes in the employer's (rather than the employee's) income tax does not change their economic incidence. The fact that they apply only to employees in specific jobs or in specific locations or to those receiving specific forms of compensation, however, may change their incidence. Because employees can, to some extent, change their jobs, locations, and forms of compensation, the flexibility of the employee may be greater than was assumed in the discussion of general taxes on labor income. As a consequence, the division of the burdens

Box 4-1: Social Security and Transfer Payments in Distributional Tables

In addition to collecting taxes, the government makes transfer payments to households. The net burden that the fiscal system imposes on households is better measured by looking at tax payments minus transfer payments received rather than by looking at tax payments alone. Official distributional tables, however, usually show only tax payments. They do not tabulate the distribution of transfer payments, except sometimes the refundable tax credits that are administered through the individual income tax, such as the Earned Income Tax Credit. For example, if a household has $20,000 of wage income, pays $5,000 in taxes, and receives transfer payments of $2,000, the distributional table would report that the household bears a $5,000 tax burden, overlooking the fact that its net burden imposed by the fiscal system is only $3,000. In some tables, transfer payments are included in the income measure that is used to classify households into different income groups—in this example, the household might be classified as having income of $22,000 rather than $20,000. But, the transfer payments are not netted against the taxes in measuring the household's burden.

This practice induces a potential political bias because policy makers receive "distributional credit" for helping the poor only if they do so through the tax system rather than through transfer payments.

The omission of government benefits from distributional tables may provide a misleading picture of Social Security. Official distributional tables generally show that the Social Security payroll tax imposes a smaller burden, as a fraction of income, on high income groups than on lower and middle income groups. However, if the analysis were expanded to include the Social Security benefits financed by the payroll tax, it would likely reveal that high income groups bear a larger net burden, as a fraction of income, than some other groups. Thus, distributional tables might be more accurate if these benefits were included in some manner. One possibility would be to treat the present value of the future benefits accrued by a worker each year as an offset to his or her payroll tax liability.

or benefits between employees and firms is not clear. Official distributional analyses generally allocate the burdens and benefits of these provisions in the same manner as firms' other income tax payments. (As discussed below, these analyses differ in their treatment of the corporate income tax.)

Taxes On Capital Income

The Federal tax system imposes taxes on capital income. Capital income generated by corporations is generally subject to the corporate income tax. Capital income received by individuals is generally subject to the individual income tax.

Many observers view capital income taxes as highly progressive because capital income is highly concentrated. However, economic analysis suggests that capital income taxes are particularly likely to be shifted, especially in the long run. Taxes imposed on owners of capital in one sector of the economy may be shifted to the owners of capital in other sectors. More importantly, capital income taxes may be partly shifted to workers through a reduction in wages. The extent of shifting differs across time horizons because savers (who provide capital and earn capital income) are more flexible in the long run than in the short run.

Shifting Across Sectors

Even if a tax is imposed on capital income in one sector of the economy, it is likely that owners of capital in all sectors bear the same economic burden in the long run. To see why, note that if capital is mobile across sectors, after-tax rates of return must be equalized across sectors, after adjustment for risk. Suppose that an economy contains two sectors and that, when there are no taxes, capital earns a 6 percent rate of return in each sector. Now, suppose that a 50 percent tax is imposed on capital income in one sector, while no tax applies in the other sector. In the very short run, capital in the taxed sector earns an after-tax return of only 3 percent, while capital in the tax-exempt sector earns an after-tax return of 6 percent. At this point, only the owners of capital in the taxed sector bear the burden.

This state of affairs cannot continue. Owners of capital in the taxed sector will move their money out of that sector and begin investing in the tax-exempt sector. As they do so, two things happen. First, the before-tax rate of return rises in the taxed sector as capital becomes more scarce. Second, the before-tax rate of return falls in the tax-exempt sector as capital becomes more plentiful. This movement continues until investors are indifferent between the two sectors, which happens when after-tax rates of return are once again in balance. For example, after a certain amount of capital has relocated, the before-tax rate of return in the taxed sector may rise from 6 to 8 percent, while the before-tax rate of return in the tax-exempt sector may fall from 6 to 4 percent. At this point, investors in both sectors earn the same 4 percent after-tax rate of return. Because all investors initially earned 6 percent and now earn 4 percent, they all bear the same burden from the tax, even though the tax legally applies to only one sector.

For example, the corporate income tax is likely to be shifted across sectors. This tax applies only to the corporate sector, but the above analysis suggests that the burden is shared by owners of capital in both the corporate and noncorporate sectors. Similarly, tax provisions that apply to only a single industry are likely to ultimately affect owners of capital in all industries.

Shifting to Workers

Shifting across sectors may not be the most important way in which the burden of capital income taxes is shifted. In the long run, much of the burden of capital income taxes (whether imposed at the firm or individual level) is likely to be shifted to workers. The reason is that such taxes reduce investment, which diminishes the capital stock. With a smaller capital stock, the before-tax rate of return to capital is higher, offsetting part of the burden that the owners of capital would otherwise bear. Also, workers are less productive because they have a smaller capital stock to work with and earn lower real wages. Part of the tax burden is therefore shifted to workers.

In accordance with the insights obtained by studying the incidence of excise taxes, owners of capital bear less of the burden if the supply of capital is more responsive to changes in its after-tax rate of return. This responsiveness, and hence the extent to which capital income taxes are shifted, depends upon several factors, including the amount of time that has elapsed since the tax was imposed, the willingness of consumers to substitute between current and future consumption, and the extent to which capital can escape the tax by relocating abroad.

The time frame is very important. The shifting of the tax burden to workers is likely to occur slowly because it takes time for large changes in the capital stock to occur. In the short run, the tax causes little change in the capital stock, because most of the capital on hand was already in existence when the tax was adopted. With little change in the capital stock, very little of the burden is shifted from owners of capital to workers. Over time, however, the tax has a greater impact on the capital stock as it discourages the accumulation of new capital. As a result, more of the tax burden falls on workers and less falls on owners of capital.

Under certain assumptions, the entire burden of the capital income tax is shifted to workers in the long run, although owners of capital bear much of the burden in the short run. A textbook model of economic growth, called the Ramsey model, provides an illustration of this effect. (The Appendix to Chapter 5, *Dynamic Revenue and Budget Estimation*, explains the basic features of this model.) Using plausible values for the key inputs to the Ramsey model demonstrates that the economy adjusts only gradually to a capital tax increase. Initially, 100 percent of the burden of a capital tax increase is borne by the owners of capital, since they have already invested in the capital currently in place. Five years after the tax increase, about a quarter of the tax burden has shifted to workers. Ten years after the tax increase, workers have taken on over 40 percent of the burden. It takes 50 years for the burden to shift nearly completely—by that time, capital owners bear only 6 percent of the burden and workers bear 94 percent.

If consumers are more willing to substitute between present consumption and the future consumption made possible by their savings, saving is more responsive to the after-tax rate of return and more of the capital income tax is shifted. The responsiveness of saving to the after-tax rate of return also depends on consumers' planning horizons. The Ramsey model assumes that consumers consider the impact of their saving decisions on their descendants. If, instead, consumers plan only for their own lifetimes, saving is less responsive to changes in its after-tax rate of return and less of the capital income tax burden is shifted to workers.

International capital flows also play a role. If the tax applies only to capital located in the United States and capital is mobile across international boundaries, the tax is more likely to be shifted to workers. The above example assumes that there are no international capital flows; incorporating such flows would increase the speed at which the tax is shifted.

Empirical work provides some evidence that capital income taxes are shifted to some extent: studies find that the before-tax return to capital income is higher when the tax rate on capital income is higher. However, the picture is not entirely clear, because other factors may cause tax rates and before-tax rates of return to move together.

The belief that a large portion of the capital income tax burden is shifted in the long run is common in the economics profession. In a 1996 survey, public finance economists were asked to state "the percentage of the current corporate income tax in the United States that is ultimately borne by capital." The average response was 41 percent, and three-quarters of the respondents gave answers of 65 percent or less. This survey indicates that the average public finance economist believes that more than half of the tax is eventually shifted from the owners of capital to workers or other groups.

Because labor income is more evenly distributed across taxpayers than capital income is, recognizing that part of the burden of capital income taxes is shifted to workers reveals that high income taxpayers bear a smaller share of the burden than is often assumed. Chart 4-1 classifies households by their levels of total income and tabulates the share of national labor income and national capital income earned by different groups. The chart shows, for example, that the 10 percent of households with the highest total incomes receive 37 percent of labor income and 62 percent of capital income. If half of capital taxes are shifted to workers in the long run, the fraction of the burden falling on this high-income group is reduced from 62 percent to 49 percent; if all capital taxes are shifted to workers in the long run, the high-income share of the burden falls to 37 percent.

Chart 4-1 **Distribution of Capital Income Tax Burden in the Long Run**
High-income individuals bear less of the long-run burden if part or all of the tax is shifted to workers.

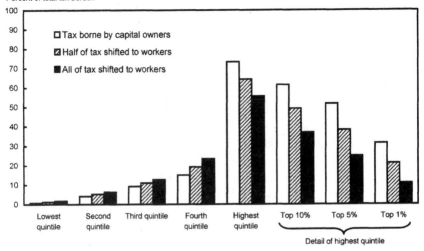

Note: Quintiles defined with respect to family economic income. Treasury model for 1989 extended to 2000.
Source: Julie-Anne Cronin, "U.S. Treasury Distributional Analysis Methodology," Department of the Treasury, Office of Tax Analysis, OTA Paper 85, September 1999.

Applied Distributional Analysis and the Choice of Time Frame

Official distributional analyses differ in their treatment of the corporate income tax. The JCT previously distributed the burden to owners of corporate capital, but now does not distribute it on the grounds that the incidence of the corporate income tax is uncertain. The CBO and Treasury now distribute the corporate tax burden to owners of all capital. None of these analyses currently recognizes the shifting of the tax to workers. The CBO previously presented analyses that allocated half of the burden to workers and Treasury did the same in its January 1992 corporate integration study. Official analyses generally allocate individual income taxes on capital income to the persons who bear the legal incidence of the taxes.

The time frame plays a key role in how tax incidence is treated. When the JCT adopted its former practice of allocating the corporate income tax to corporate capital, it stated that its analysis was intended to refer to the very short run, when little shifting of any kind would occur. Similarly, Treasury has justified allocating the burden to owners of all capital by stating that this is the most reasonable assumption for incidence over a 10-year horizon. These analyses serve the useful objective of informing policy makers of how the current tax burden is divided between current workers and current owners of capital.

Nevertheless, presenting estimates only for short time frames leaves an incomplete picture. If a tax change is intended to be permanent, it is important to also inform policy makers how its long-run burden will be divided between future workers and future owners of capital. Answering that question requires additional distributional tables that recognize the significant shifting to workers that is likely to occur in the long run.

Estate and Gift Taxes

Capital can also be subject to estate and gift taxes when its ownership changes hands due to an inheritance or gift. The lessons from the analysis of capital income taxes can therefore be applied to estate and gift taxes.

The estate and gift taxes apply on a cumulative basis to an individual's lifetime gifts and to the estate the individual bequeaths at his or her death. An individual may make up to $11,000 of gifts to any recipient per year, without counting them against the lifetime total. Bequests to surviving spouses are exempt, as are gifts and bequests to charitable organizations.

The taxes apply only when lifetime gifts plus the estate exceed an exemption amount, which was $675,000 in 2001. Under the laws in place at the beginning of 2001, the exemption amount was scheduled to increase to $1,000,000 starting in 2006. The taxes applied at rates of up to 55 percent.

The tax law adopted in June 2001 provides for further reductions in the estate and gift taxes for 2002 through 2009. This law increases the exemption amount to $1 million for 2002 and 2003 and gradually increases it to $3.5 million for 2009. The law reduces the top tax rate from 2002 to 2009, with top rates of 50 percent in 2002 and 45 percent in 2007 through 2009. For 2010, the law completely repeals the estate tax, but retains the gift tax with a top rate of 35 percent. It also increases, in some cases, the capital gains taxes paid by heirs who sell property that they inherit.

Because the 2001 tax law is scheduled to expire at the end of 2010, the estate and gift taxes are scheduled to return in 2011, at the levels specified by the previous laws. The President has proposed permanently extending the provisions of the 2001 tax law that are in effect in 2010, including the repeal of the estate tax.

The issue of who benefits from estate tax repeal has been a prominent one in the debate over repeal. Treasury allocates the burden of estate and gift taxes to the decedents (the individuals who have died) and donors. The JCT used to do the same, but has now stopped distributing them due to uncertainty about the taxes' incidence. The CBO's recent distributional analyses have not included estate and gift taxes. Allocating the estate tax burden to decedents supports the common view that the tax is highly progressive, since (at the current exemption amount) the tax applies to only the largest 2 percent of estates. It is virtually certain, however, that little of the economic burden of the estate tax is borne by the decedents. The burden of the estate tax is borne by them only if the tax prompts them to reduce their lifetime consumption and accumulate a larger estate, so that the tax can be paid without reducing the after-tax bequests left to their heirs. In other words, the estate tax must reduce lifetime consumption and promote estate accumulation for it to be borne by the decedents.

This condition is unlikely to hold. Because the estate tax makes estate building less attractive, it probably reduces the size of bequests. Empirical research confirms that the estate tax reduces the amount that decedents accumulate and pass on to their heirs. As a first step, it would make more sense to distribute the burden of the tax to heirs rather than to decedents.

Despite what one might expect, the heirs of wealthy decedents are not always wealthy. Economists have found that the correlation between the long-term labor earnings of successive generations is around 0.4 or 0.5. The correlation between long-term incomes (which includes the inheritances themselves) or between long-term consumption levels of successive generations has been estimated to be around 0.7. (Correlation is a number, ranging from -1 to 1, that measures the strength of the relationship between two variables. A correlation of 0.4 or 0.7 indicates that one variable tends to increase when the other increases, but that the relationship is not perfect.) Some bequests are left to grandchildren or nephews and nieces where the correlation between the incomes of decedents and the incomes of heirs may be even lower. Because heirs can be less wealthy than decedents, recognizing that the estate tax burden is more likely to fall on the former reveals that less of the burden is borne by the very wealthy.

A more important point, however, is that the reduction in estate building induced by the tax is likely to take the form of a reduction in capital accumulation. Because the estate and gift taxes are taxes on capital, part of their long-run burden is likely to be shifted to workers through a reduction in wage rates, as discussed above. Part of the burden is therefore likely borne by ordinary workers who never receive a bequest or taxable gift.

Conclusion

Distributional analysis can be a useful tool for policy makers. It is important, however, to recognize the limitations of existing analyses. Current analyses can be misleading, particularly with respect to the estate and gift taxes and other capital taxes. These taxes are likely to be shifted substantially to workers in the long run, reducing the extent to which their burden falls on high-income groups.

CHAPTER 5

Dynamic Revenue and Budget Estimation

A central conclusion of the study of taxation is that taxes affect behavior and distort the choices of firms, workers, and investors. In particular, a higher tax on an activity tends to discourage that activity relative to others. These behavioral responses to a tax change can, among other things, alter the revenue effect of the tax change, a topic that is the focus of this chapter. Revenue estimation is called *dynamic* if it incorporates the revenue implications of behavioral responses to tax changes and *static* if it does not incorporate these revenue implications. Like changes in taxes, changes in government spending can encourage or discourage certain behavior; budget estimates are dynamic if they incorporate the budgetary implications of these behavioral responses.

If policy makers are to make informed decisions about policy changes, all significant effects should ideally be included in estimates of the policy's budgetary implications. Several obstacles have prevented macroeconomic behavioral responses from being incorporated in such estimates. This chapter discusses the ongoing efforts to provide a greater role for fully dynamic revenue and budget estimation in the analysis of major tax and spending proposals.

The key points in this chapter are:

- Currently, official revenue estimates of proposed tax changes are not fully static because they incorporate the revenue effects of many microeconomic behavioral responses. These estimates are not fully dynamic, however, because they exclude the effects of macroeconomic behavioral responses.

- Changes in taxes and spending generally alter incentives for work, investment, and other productive activity. These macroeconomic behavioral responses have revenue and budgetary implications.

- Steps have recently been taken to provide more information about the revenue effects of macroeconomic behavioral responses. At least in the near term, it may not be practical for macroeconomic effects to be incorporated in official estimates. But estimates of these effects should be provided as supplementary information for major tax and spending proposals.

- Dynamic estimation of policy changes should distinguish aggregate demand effects from aggregate supply effects, include long-run effects, apply to spending as well as tax changes, reflect the differing effects of various policy changes, account for the need to finance policy changes, and use a variety of models.

Revenue Estimation and
Microeconomic Behavioral Responses

To frame the issues, it is useful to begin with a simple example of how a tax change can affect behavior and how the behavioral response then alters the revenue impact of the tax change.

An Example of Revenue Implications of Microeconomic Behavioral Responses

Consider an excise tax on apples (similar to that discussed in Chapter 4, *Tax Incidence: Who Bears the Tax Burden?*). If the current tax rate is 25 cents per apple and 1,000 apples are produced and consumed at this tax rate, tax revenue is $250. Now, suppose the tax rate is cut to 20 cents per apple. If apple output and consumption don't change, total tax revenue falls to $200, a decrease of $50. Therefore, a purely static estimate of the revenue loss would be $50.

The actual change in tax revenue is likely to be different, however, because consumers and producers respond to the tax rate change. The tax rate drives a wedge between the price paid by consumers (including the tax) and the price that producers receive (net of the tax). When the tax rate is reduced, this wedge is reduced, meaning that consumers are likely to pay a lower price and producers are likely to receive a higher price. For example, at the 25-cent tax rate, consumers might pay $1.13 per apple and producers might receive 88 cents per apple; at the 20-cent tax rate, consumers might pay $1.10 and producers might receive 90 cents. The lower price paid by consumers induces them to consume more apples and the higher price received by producers induces them to produce more apples. As explained in Chapter 4, the changes in the two prices must be such that consumers' desired increase in consumption equals producers' desired increase in production.

Suppose that 1,100 apples are produced and consumed at the lower tax rate. (The actual increase in the quantity of apples depends on how responsive consumers and producers are to their respective prices; the increase is larger when both groups are more responsive.) Tax revenue is then $220 (20 cents per apple times 1,100 apples), not $200. Thus, the tax cut lowers revenue by $30, not $50. Of the $50 static revenue loss, $20 is "paid for" by the increase in apple production and consumption caused by the tax cut. In other words, 40 percent of the tax cut "pays for itself" through this revenue feedback.

Conversely, increasing the tax from 25 cents to 30 cents yields $50 of additional revenue if the quantity of apples remains at 1,000. However, the quantity of apples is likely to fall as the tax rate increases. With the higher tax, consumers pay a higher price and producers receive a lower price, prompting a decline in the desired levels of apple production and consumption. If the quantity of apples falls from 1,000 to 900, revenue rises from $250 to $270, so that the revenue gain from the tax rate increase is $20 rather than the $50 that would occur with no behavioral response. The actual revenue effects of such a tax change may be more complex than this discussion suggests. As the quantity of apples changes, the quantities of other items produced and consumed also change. If those items are also subject to taxes, changes in those quantities also impact revenue. In any event, behavioral responses to a tax change can alter its revenue impact.

Incorporation of Microeconomic Behavioral Responses in Revenue Estimation

The insight that microeconomic behavioral responses to tax changes affect revenue has been incorporated into the official revenue-estimation process.

The staff of the Joint Committee on Taxation (JCT) prepares the official revenue estimates for thousands of proposed tax changes submitted by members of Congress each year. Similarly, the Department of the Treasury prepares official revenue estimates for tax changes proposed by the President and some changes considered by the Congress. Official estimation of the revenue effect of a tax change is commonly called *scoring*. Each revenue estimate presents the estimated change in revenues in the current fiscal year and up to 10 subsequent fiscal years, a period referred to as the "10-year window."

In preparing their estimates, JCT and Treasury economists routinely include the effects of microeconomic behavioral responses to tax changes. For example, when excise taxes change, JCT and Treasury estimates reflect how much sales of the taxed item are expected to change. So, official revenue estimates for the hypothetical apple tax change described above would reflect an estimate of the change in the quantity of apples. For changes in the tax treatment of a particular type of business investment, the revenue estimates reflect shifts between that type of investment and other types.

Changes in the capital gains tax rate provide another example of how behavioral changes play a prominent role in the scoring process. Economic theory and statistical studies have established that capital gains taxes deter *realization* of capital gains—the sale of assets that have risen in value. A cut in the capital gains tax rate, therefore, is likely to spur an increase in capital gains realizations. Put simply, investors are likely to sell their assets to take advantage of the lower tax rate on any gains they have already accrued. This increase in realizations will mean that the capital gains tax will be applied to a larger tax base, partially offsetting the cut in the tax rate itself. Indeed, depending on the timing and structure of the rate cut, it may actually raise revenue immediately after enactment. JCT and Treasury estimates recognize these effects.

Economists' understanding of—and data on—human behavior is incomplete. This makes it difficult to determine the exact magnitude of behavioral responses to tax changes and their exact impact on tax revenues. Nevertheless, a revenue estimate that ignores such behavioral responses will be inaccurate. By taking account of microeconomic behavioral responses, the JCT and Treasury produce estimates that are likely to be more accurate than strictly static estimates.

Macroeconomic Behavioral Responses to Policy Changes

Despite advances in making revenue estimates more dynamic, the incorporation of behavioral responses has been subject to one fundamental limitation. The official revenue estimates assume that macroeconomic aggregates, such as total investment, total labor supply, and GDP, are not affected by tax and spending changes. Because the estimates ignore these potentially important effects, they are not fully dynamic.

Lowering taxes on labor and capital income strengthens incentives to work and invest and is likely to spur increases in these activities. Additional work and investment boosts national income, which increases the tax base and thus partially offsets the revenue loss from lower tax rates.

As an example, suppose that the current income tax rate is 25 percent and that total national income is $1,000. Total tax revenue is $250. Now, suppose the tax rate is cut to 20 percent. If total income did not change, total tax revenue would be $200. The lower tax rate, however, is likely to encourage work and saving, boosting total income. If income rises to $1,100, total tax revenue will be $220, not $200. Thus, the tax cut lowers total tax revenue by $30, not $50. In other words, 40 percent of the tax cut ($20 of the $50 static revenue loss) "pays for itself."

Popular attention is often focused on the possibility that an income tax rate cut could stimulate so much additional income that it would *fully* pay for itself. Most economists believe that, starting from current U.S. tax rates, such an outcome is unlikely for a broad-based income tax change. It is important to realize, however, that any behavioral response alters the size of the revenue loss from a tax cut, even if it does not transform the loss into a revenue gain.

Official scoring of income tax rate changes already includes a number of microeconomic behavioral responses. The scoring takes into account a variety of ways in which the rate cut may raise taxable income, such as a shift from tax-exempt fringe benefits to taxable wages. However, the estimates do not recognize that lower income taxes can encourage greater labor supply and capital accumulation, and thereby raise total income in the economy. The exclusion of macroeconomic behavioral responses from official revenue estimation is not due to ignorance of these responses or disagreement about their existence. Instead, it reflects the judgment that accurately including these effects is impractical, due to the controversy about their magnitudes and the complexity of modeling them. Uncertainty about the correct model of the economy and the size of behavioral responses to tax changes, and disagreement about the appropriate time frame for revenue projections has made consensus difficult to achieve.

Ultimately, it may be possible for macroeconomic effects to become part of the official scoring process for those tax and spending proposals that are likely to have significant macroeconomic effects. However, given the time and resource constraints facing revenue estimators and the lack of consensus about these issues, that goal is not likely to be feasible in the near future. To promote informed policy making, though, it is essential that fully dynamic revenue estimates (incorporating macroeconomic as well as microeconomic effects) be presented as supplementary information for major tax and spending proposals.

Recently, estimators have taken major steps in precisely this direction. In November 1997, the JCT compiled and published estimates of the macroeconomic effects of fundamental tax reform prepared by nine sets of economists using nine different economic models. The JCT subsequently began developing its own macroeconomic models and formed a blue-ribbon panel of academic and private-sector economists to further explore dynamic revenue estimation. In January 2003, the House of Representatives adopted Rule XIII.3(h)(2), which requires the JCT to prepare analyses of the macroeconomic effects of major tax bills before such bills can be considered by the House. In May 2003, the JCT prepared such an analysis of the Ways and Means Committee's version of the Jobs and Growth tax bill. In December 2003, the JCT published a description of the methodology it used for this analysis. The Congressional Budget Office (CBO) provided a similar analysis of the President's 2004 Budget in March 2003 and provided a more detailed description of its analysis in a July 2003 technical document. Private organizations have also prepared dynamic analyses of proposed tax changes that reflect macroeconomic behavioral responses

User's Guide to Dynamic Revenue and Budget Estimation

Recent work suggests six guidelines for dynamic revenue and budget estimation.

Guideline 1: Dynamic Estimation Should Distinguish Aggregate Demand Effects and Aggregate Supply Effects

Tax cuts can affect output through two different channels, by changing aggregate demand and by changing aggregate supply. Any aggregate demand effects are likely to be concentrated in the first few years. Aggregate supply effects are likely to occur over a longer time period.

Changes in Aggregate Demand

In the short run, tax cuts may push an underperforming economy back toward its potential by raising consumers' disposable incomes and, thus, their demand for goods and services. Tax cuts may also increase firms' demand for investment goods. These effects increase the aggregate demand for goods and services.

The extent of the increase in aggregate demand depends upon how the tax cut is financed. If the tax cut is accompanied by reductions in government spending, little or no stimulus to aggregate demand is likely to occur. If the tax cut is financed by borrowing, then aggregate demand is more likely to be stimulated.

The net effect of a tax cut on aggregate demand also depends upon the reaction of the Federal Reserve. If taxes are cut in an under-performing economy, the Federal Reserve may perceive less need for interest-rate reductions. In such a case, the boost to aggregate demand from a tax cut would, at least in part, be offset by the reduced stimulus provided by the Federal Reserve.

The Federal Reserve is less likely to offset the aggregate demand stimulus from tax cuts, however, in a low-interest-rate economy, because interest rates cannot go below zero. Under these circumstances, the fiscal stimulus provided by a tax cut may reinforce, rather than replace, monetary stimulus. This case seems relevant for the 2003 tax cut; the Federal Reserve's target for the Federal funds interest rate was 1.25 percent from November 6, 2002, to June 25, 2003, and has since remained at 1 percent.

Aggregate demand effects are primarily relevant in the short run. These effects tend to fade over time as prices and wage rates adjust and the economy returns to its normal level of output. The bulk of the aggregate demand stimulus from a policy change is likely to be felt within a few years.

Changes in Aggregate Supply

Tax cuts can raise after-tax returns to work and investment, encouraging both activities. This effect increases aggregate supply because it increases the amount of goods and services that the economy is capable of producing. Tax changes can also improve the long-run allocation of resources, allowing greater output to be produced with a given set of resources. One way to do this is to make tax rates more uniform across different types of income, as exemplified by the reduction in dividend and capital gains tax rates adopted in the Jobs and Growth Tax Relief Reconciliation Act of 2003. This provision reduced the tax burden on investment in the corporate sector, which was more heavily taxed than investment in the noncorporate sector. Over time, this tax reduction is expected to make the allocation of resources more efficient, leading the economy to allocate more resources to the corporate sector.

Because some commercially available forecasting models tend to emphasize short-run aggregate demand effects, it may be necessary to develop models that place greater emphasis on long-run aggregate supply effects. In their recent dynamic analyses, the CBO and the JCT used a mix of models with varying emphases on short-run and long-run effects. The time frame over which tax revenues are estimated should be long enough to fully capture the longer-run, supply-side effects, which leads us to the second guideline.

Guideline 2: Dynamic Estimation Should Include Long-Run Effects

While official revenue scoring is confined to a 10-year "window," it is important that dynamic revenue estimation provide some information for a longer horizon. Presenting the dynamic revenue estimates as supplementary information, rather than as part of the official revenue estimate, facilitates the use of a longer horizon.

The longer horizon is necessary because exclusive use of the 10-year horizon skews the emphasis given to different macroeconomic effects. As discussed in guideline 1, aggregate demand effects are likely to be fully realized within the 10-year window but have little long-run importance. In contrast, aggregate supply effects may not fully materialize within the 10-year window: Although changes in labor supply may occur relatively quickly, changes in the capital stock occur more slowly.

Economic analysis indicates that, in a closed economy, such capital accumulation takes place over a period of decades. Consider an example in which the government cuts taxes slightly on capital income, starting from a 25 percent marginal tax rate. If standard parameter values are assumed for a leading model of economic growth (the Ramsey growth model used in Chapter 4 and described in the Appendix to this chapter), only 42 percent of the long-run increase in the capital stock is put in place within the first 10 years. That is, more than half of the increased capital stock accumulates outside the conventional 10-year window. In fact, only two-thirds of the increase takes place within 20 years. In an open economy, international capital flows may allow the capital stock to adjust somewhat more quickly. Still, this analysis indicates the importance of considering a long time horizon when estimating a tax cut's effect on aggregate supply.

A longer time horizon would give adequate emphasis to the tax cut's aggregate supply effects. It would also permit policy makers to accurately compare the fundamental consequences of different types of tax and spending changes. This leads to the third and fourth guidelines.

Guideline 3: Dynamic Estimation Should Be Applied to Spending Changes as well as Tax Changes

The logic behind dynamic estimation applies to spending as well as tax changes. As discussed more fully in guideline 4, spending programs can also affect aggregate demand and aggregate supply. To be sure, dynamic budget estimation for spending changes can be even more difficult, and has been less common, than dynamic revenue estimation for tax changes. Nevertheless, including macroeconomic effects only for tax changes would lead to an unbalanced and misleading comparison of policies.

Guideline 4: Dynamic Estimation Should Reflect the Differing Macroeconomic Effects of Various Tax and Spending Changes

Not all types of taxes or spending programs would be expected to have the same effects on the economy. Moreover, the policies that may have the most beneficial effects in the short run (because they provide a powerful boost to aggregate demand) can, in some cases, be the least beneficial, or even harmful, in the long run (because they fail to boost aggregate supply by increasing work and investment).

In the short run, the most immediate stimulus may be provided by an increase in government purchases of goods and services, an increase in transfer payments, or by tax cuts designed to boost consumer spending. These policies, however, are generally not the best ways to boost aggregate supply. Although some spending programs, such as infrastructure construction and education, may increase economic growth, others, particularly some transfer payments, would be expected to reduce aggregate supply by weakening incentives to work and invest.

In the long run, the strongest boost to aggregate supply is likely to come from tax cuts designed to boost investment. Tax cuts on capital income are most likely to have this effect. Their short-run revenue feedback may be small (because their aggregate demand effects may be limited), but their long-run revenue feedback may be large.

Consider again the example discussed above, in which the government cuts capital taxes slightly, starting from a 25 percent marginal tax rate. Using the same assumptions as before (as detailed in the Appendix to this chapter), increased growth resulting from the tax cut significantly moderates its revenue loss. This is particularly true in the very long run (after 50 years or so), as the economy settles back toward equilibrium. At that point, the reduction in tax revenues is about half of what conventional scoring would indicate. The estimated revenue feedback is so large for two reasons: the policy being considered is a reduction in the capital tax rate and the estimate refers to the very long run.

It is also possible for some tax cuts to reduce the incentive to work and save. In this case, the revenue loss from the tax cut is *larger* than it would have been without macroeconomic behavioral changes. A prime example is an increase in a tax credit or deduction that is phased out as income rises. Such a phase-out is another form of a higher marginal tax rate on income. For example, married couples filing jointly lose $5 of tax credits per child for each $100 of additional income above $110,000. For a couple with two children, this phase-out increases their effective marginal income tax rate by 10 percentage points. Given the existence of the phase-out, any increase in the size of the credit lengthens the interval of income to which this higher marginal tax rate applies. As with any increase in marginal income tax rates, parents in this income bracket have less incentive to work, save, or otherwise increase their income. This outcome does not mean that increasing the child credit is a bad idea. The President proposed such increases in 2001 and 2003 and advocates making the increases permanent. As long as the income phase-out remains in place, however, revenue estimates for increases in the credit should include the revenue lost because of the reduction in the parents' work and saving.

Dynamic estimation is not accurate unless it includes all of the policy changes that are required to support the tax change. This leads to our fifth guideline.

Guideline 5: Dynamic Estimation Should Account For the Need to Finance Policy Changes

Because the government is a going concern, it need never actually pay off its outstanding debt. Nevertheless, government debt cannot indefinitely grow faster than national income. One implication of this constraint is that, over the entire time frame of the economy's existence, the present value of tax revenue must equal the present value of noninterest government spending. (Present value takes into account the time value of money—the fact that monetary sums can earn interest over time.) In the long run, there can be no "unfunded tax cuts" or "unfunded spending increases." If current tax revenue is reduced while current spending is left unchanged or if current spending is increased while current revenue is left unchanged, government debt increases. Servicing this debt requires that future taxes be higher, future spending be lower, or both.

To be sure, it is infeasible for estimators to accurately predict which adjustments future Congresses and Presidents may adopt. Nevertheless, to avoid analyzing economically impossible policy specifications, dynamic revenue estimates should recognize that some such adjustments must occur. To ensure comparability across proposals, it may be best to adopt a few stylized assumptions about the nature of the financing. A few benchmark cases could then be considered; perhaps one in which the debt service is financed with reductions in government purchases, one in which it is financed with reductions in transfer payments, and one in which it is financed with higher income tax rates.

How a tax cut is financed can alter its effects in the short run and the long run. If current revenues are reduced through a tax cut while current spending is held fixed, the government's budget deficit will get larger. Such a deficit-financed tax cut has a strong positive effect on aggregate demand because consumers are likely to spend part of the tax cut and there is no offsetting reduction in government spending. It may do somewhat less to boost aggregate supply, however, if the deficit raises interest rates and, as a result, lowers investment. This effect is often called *crowding-out*, because a government's deficit spending reduces, or crowds-out, the amount of savings available for private firms to use for funding investment. On the other hand, if current spending is reduced along with current revenue, the aggregate demand effects of the tax cut are muted, because the spending cuts lower aggregate demand. The boost to aggregate supply is greater, however, because no crowding-out occurs.

To maximize the aggregate supply impact of the recent tax cuts, the President has stressed the need to restrain government spending.

Guideline 6: Dynamic Revenue Estimation Should Use a Variety of Models Until Greater Consensus Develops

One challenge facing estimators is that different models yield different results. Comparing the results from different models is the best way to resolve differences between possible approaches and to test the sensitivity of results to changes in assumptions. To improve our ability to distinguish among models, a set of models could be applied to clearly defined and relatively simple hypothetical policies. This would allow the different models' results to be compared and would make it easier to attribute any variation among their results to differences in their assumptions. As mentioned above, the JCT did such an exercise in 1997 when exploring the possible effects of fundamental tax reform. The CBO and the JCT also used a variety of models in their dynamic analyses in 2003. Presenting dynamic revenue estimates as supplementary information rather than as part of the official revenue estimates facilitates the use of a variety of models.

One reason that dynamic revenue estimation is subject to so much uncertainty is that fiscal changes may have important effects that are left out of standard models of economic growth. For example, standard growth models take the rate of technological progress as given. Some research, however, has suggested that technological progress may be a by-product of capital accumulation; if so, changes in capital income taxes can alter the rate of technological progress. As another example, standard models take the economy's equilibrium level of unemployment as given. Yet some research has indicated that the equilibrium unemployment rate depends on productivity growth, which can also be influenced by changes in capital taxation. Incorporating such nonstandard effects into dynamic revenue estimation is undoubtedly a formidable challenge, but if initial results on these effects are confirmed by future research, this challenge should not be avoided.

Conclusion

Fully dynamic revenue estimation that incorporates macroeconomic behavioral changes is an important step forward in applying economic insights to policy analysis. Significant progress has been made on this front; continued progress is essential to sound policy making.

Appendix: The Model Used in the Capital-Tax Example

The model underlying the capital-tax example is the growth model developed by Frank Ramsey in 1928. It is a leading textbook model, and most of its assumptions are standard among models of economic growth. For instance, output is produced by combining capital and labor, and productivity growth increases how much output a given amount of capital and labor can produce. Consumers maximize their welfare by deciding how much of their income to save. Businesses maximize profit and compete when hiring workers and selling products. Over the long term, the saving rate determines the capital stock and, thus, the level of output in the economy. The Ramsey model allows consumers to choose their saving rate, while simpler models impose a constant saving rate estimated from historical data.

Unlike some other models, the Ramsey model assumes that consumers are members of families comprised of an infinite number of generations and that they care about the well-being of their descendants. This means that consumers consider the effects of their choices on their children and subsequent generations. Some critics of the Ramsey model view this assumption as unreasonable. However, the results presented in the text do not change substantially if we assume that people care less about each successive generation and, for generations far enough into the future, hardly consider their welfare at all.

In the Ramsey model, the long-run equilibrium for the economy can be described by two relationships. Firms invest in capital equipment until the value of the output produced by the last unit of capital equipment just equals the interest rate—the cost borne by the firm to invest. The interest rate is, in turn, determined by consumers' choices about their consumption and savings. These choices depend on the growth rate of technology, the discount rate (a measure of how much consumers prefer having a dollar today compared to a dollar in one year), and consumers' flexibility with regard to spending in different time periods. To solve the model, we must make an assumption about how the government finances policy changes in the long run. In the capital-tax example, we assume that the government adjusts transfer payments accordingly.

Knowing this long-run equilibrium allows us to calculate the impact of a cut in tax rates on tax revenue taking into account the aggregate dynamic effects that this chapter has described. In particular, we can summarize the difference between a dynamic analysis and a static analysis with a few key parameters, or inputs, to the model. We assume that the tax rates on labor and capital income are each 25 percent, capital's share of total income is one-third, and the elasticity of substitution between capital and labor is one. Then, if dynamic effects are considered, a capital tax cut reduces tax revenue in long-run equilibrium by half as much as a static analysis would indicate.

CHAPTER 6

Restoring Solvency to Social Security

Much of the Federal government's budget is dedicated to *entitlement programs*, in which expenditures are determined not by discretionary budget allocations but by the number of people who qualify. Reform of entitlement programs remains the most pressing fiscal policy issue confronting the Nation. With projected expenditures of $478 billion in 2003, Social Security is the largest entitlement program and an appropriate place to begin. Social Security is designed as a *pay-as-you-go* system in which payroll taxes on the wages of current workers finance the benefits being paid to current retirees. While the program is running a small surplus at present, large deficits loom in the future. Deficits are first projected to appear in 15 years; by 2080, the Social Security deficit is projected to exceed 2.3 percent of GDP.

The coming deficits in Social Security are driven by two demographic shifts that have been in progress for several decades: people are having fewer children and are living longer. The President has called for new initiatives to modernize Social Security to contain costs, expand choice, and make the program secure and financially viable for future generations of Americans.

This chapter assesses the need to strengthen Social Security in light of its long-term financial outlook. The key points in this chapter are:

- The most straightforward way to characterize the financial imbalance in entitlement programs such as Social Security is by considering their long-term annual deficits. Even after the baby-boom generation's effect is no longer felt, Social Security is projected to incur annual deficits greater than 50 percent of payroll tax revenues.

- These deficits are so large that they require a meaningful change to Social Security in future years. Reform should include moderation of the growth of benefits that are unfunded and can therefore be paid only by assessing taxes in the future. A new system of personal retirement accounts should be established to help pay future benefits. The benefits promised to those in or near retirement should be maintained in full.

- The economic rationale for undertaking this reform in an era of budget deficits is as compelling as it was in an era of budget surpluses.

The Rationale for Social Security

All developed countries and most developing countries have publicly administered programs to provide benefits for the elderly, including programs to support surviving spouses and the disabled. Government involvement in markets for goods or services is typically predicated on a failure of private markets to achieve an efficient or equitable result. There are three main problems in the market for providing support to the elderly that justify a government role in old-age entitlement programs.

First, a strictly private market to support old age would require all individuals to choose the level of consumption that they would like in retirement and to save accordingly. Some individuals may not be capable of making the relevant calculations themselves and may not be able to enlist the service of a financial professional to advise them. For these people, Social Security provides a minimal level of financial planning. Social Security requires people who otherwise would not save for retirement to participate in a system that makes them pay for insurance against old-age poverty. It also provides a mechanism for everyone to share in the burden of taking care of those who are truly in need of assistance.

Second, well-being in retirement is subject to two types of risk that are not easily insured in private markets. The first risk is low income during working years, which can lead to poverty in old age. Low income may be caused by a specific event like disability, and Social Security provides workers with disability insurance. Private disability insurance plans exist but participation is quite low. Low income may also be caused by other events beyond an individual's control. However, these events do not lend themselves to private insurance contracts because income can also be low for a variety of reasons that are under an individual's control but that are difficult for an insurer to observe (such as low work effort). Social Security partially overcomes this problem through its progressive benefit formula—retirees with lower earnings during their working years get benefits that are higher as a share of preretirement earnings.

The other risk to well-being in old age is the possibility that retirees will live an unusually long time and thereby exhaust their personal savings. To protect against this risk, a portion of the retirement wealth that a worker has accumulated must be converted to an annuity, a contract that makes scheduled payments to the individual and his or her dependents for the remainder of their lifetimes. The annuity payments should be indexed to inflation, so that their purchasing power is not eroded over time. Inflation-indexed annuities are a fairly new financial product, and even today, relatively few people participate in the indexed annuity market. A public system of Social Security, in which the government pays benefits in the form of an annuity that keeps pace with the cost of living, can help protect retirees from outliving their means to support themselves.

Third, in other contexts, the government's fiscal policies are designed to redistribute resources from high- to low-income individuals. In most cases, such as the progressive income tax schedule, income is defined based on an annual measure. Social Security is unusual because it can redistribute income based on a lifetime average of earnings. By doing so, Social Security more accurately targets these transfers to the people who most need the assistance. Individuals with higher lifetime average earnings receive benefits from Social Security that are higher in dollar terms, but lower as a percentage of their earnings, than do those with lower lifetime average earnings.

All of these rationales are legitimate. Whether the U.S. system actually meets these goals, and whether it does so in an efficient and equitable manner, however, should be a subject of continued debate. An essential part of this debate is that none of these rationales require that Social Security be operated on a pay-as-you-go basis. Long-term solvency can be restored by advance funding of future obligations through personal retirement accounts. Personal retirement account proposals can be and often have been designed to allow for greater protection for surviving spouses and other vulnerable groups. The President has taken an important step in this debate by making the modernization and long-term solvency of Social Security a prominent feature of his Administration's domestic policy agenda.

Understanding the Financial Crisis

In a pay-as-you-go system like Social Security, the benefits paid to current beneficiaries are financed largely by the payroll taxes collected from current workers. In any given year, the system will be in balance when the *income rate* equals the *cost rate*. The income rate is the total amount of tax revenue collected (from both the payroll tax and the income taxation of Social Security benefits for moderate- and high-income beneficiaries) divided by the total amount of payroll on which taxes are levied. The cost rate is the total amount of scheduled benefits divided by the total payroll on which taxes are levied. The *annual balance* is the difference between the income rate and the cost rate in a given year.

The impending financial crisis in Social Security is due to the rapid growth in the cost rate relative to the income rate in the future. This growth is attributable to two demographic factors that have become critically important over the last half century: people are having fewer children and living longer in old age. As a result of these lower rates of both fertility and mortality, the size of the elderly cohort will expand relative to the younger cohort over time.

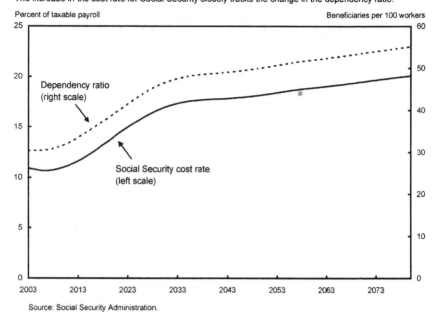

Chart 6-1 Demographic Change and the Cost of Social Security Through 2080
The increase in the cost rate for Social Security closely tracks the change in the dependency ratio.

Percent of taxable payroll

Beneficiaries per 100 workers

Dependency ratio
(right scale)

Social Security cost rate
(left scale)

Source: Social Security Administration.

Chart 6-1 compares the Social Security cost rate with the *dependency ratio*, which is the number of beneficiaries per hundred workers. The projections are based on the intermediate assumptions made by the Social Security Trustees in their 2003 report. The dependency ratio rises from 30.4 in 2003 to 55.2 in 2080, an increase of 82 percent. Stated another way, the number of workers paying payroll taxes to support the payments to each beneficiary will fall from 3.3 workers per beneficiary in 2003 to 1.8 in 2080. With fewer workers to support each retiree, it is not surprising that the cost rate is projected to increase, in this case from 10.89 percent of payroll in 2003 to 20.09 percent in 2080. This 84 percent increase is almost identical to the rise in the dependency ratio. While changes in productivity, immigration, interest rates, and other factors also affect the long-term solvency of the program, changes in population structure are at the center of the looming crisis.

Chart 6-2 graphs the single-year projections of Social Security's income and cost rates, along with its annual balances. The solid curve that rises over the period represents the cost rate (this is the same curve as in Chart 6-1). The dashed line is the projected income rate, which reflects revenue received by the Social Security trust funds from the payroll tax of 12.40 percent plus a portion of the income tax on current benefits. Income taxation on benefits currently being paid generates an amount equal to 0.30 percent of taxable payroll. Thus,

Percent of taxable payroll

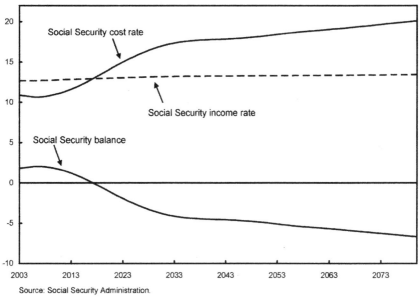

Source: Social Security Administration.

the income rate in 2003 was 12.70 percent. Because the income thresholds at which Social Security benefits become taxable are not indexed for inflation, a greater share of benefits become taxable over time as the price level rises. In 2080, income taxation of benefits is projected to generate 1.03 percent of taxable payroll, resulting in an income rate of 13.43 percent.

The annual balance, the difference between the income rate and the cost rate, is projected to deteriorate. For 2003, the annual balance is 1.81 percent of taxable payroll (12.70 − 10.89). The annual balance is graphed at the bottom of Chart 6-2 as a solid curve that declines over the period. The substantial increase in the cost rate relative to the income rate in the future causes this annual balance to change from surplus to deficit by 2018 and to widen considerably thereafter. In 2080, the annual balance will be -6.67 percent of taxable payroll (13.43 − 20.09, as reported in the Trustees Report, with the small discrepancy due to rounding).

Unless the Social Security system is reformed before that time, the payroll tax would have to rise from 12.40 percent to 19.07 percent to pay all benefits scheduled by current law, even with the assumption that benefit taxation continues under current law to provide a rising share of program revenues. Such an increase represents an expansion of the payroll taxes associated with the program of over 50 percent (Box 6-1).

The annual deficit of 6.67 percent of payroll is the most straightforward way to represent the long-term fiscal challenge confronting the Social Security program. To describe a proposed reform as having restored solvency to Social Security, the reform must greatly reduce or eliminate these annual deficits. The only desirable way to restore solvency is to do so without

---

Box 6-1: The Retirement of the Baby-Boom Generation

It is common in public discussions to associate the financial crisis in Social Security with the approaching retirement of the baby-boom generation, those born between the years 1946 and 1964. This explanation, however, is only partly correct. The problems confronting Social Security are more fundamental than the aging of an unusually large birth cohort. In 2080, for example, the youngest baby boomer will be 116 years old, and almost all benefits in that year will be paid to retirees who were born after the baby-boom generation. Even with virtually no baby boomers among the beneficiaries, Social Security in 2080 is projected to have an annual deficit equal to 6.67 percent of its payroll tax base.

The retirement of the baby-boom generation *does* have an important impact on the system's finances, as can be seen in Chart 6-1. The period of rapid increase in both the dependency ratio and the cost rate occurs during the two decades starting roughly in 2008 when the baby-boom generation becomes eligible for retirement benefits. Chart 6-2 shows that over this same period, the annual balance in Social Security will deteriorate by over 5 percentage points of payroll. If the retirement of the baby-boom generation were the only source of Social Security's financial crisis, then the cost rate would begin to decline as that generation passed away and the dependency ratio fell.

As shown in Chart 6-1, however, the cost rate continues to climb even as the baby boomers age and pass away. The dramatic increase in the cost rate associated with the retirement of the baby-boom generation is, in fact, a permanent transition to an economy in which a higher ratio of beneficiaries to workers makes pay-as-you-go entitlement programs more expensive to maintain. This transition would be more apparent already were it not for the presence of the baby-boom generation in the workforce today. The huge numbers of baby boomers in the workforce have held down the ratio of beneficiaries to workers over the past several decades. Judged from this point forward, the retirement of the baby-boom generation does not cause the financial crisis; it simply makes the long-term problem in the pay-as-you-go system appear sooner rather than later.

---

continued reliance on general revenues. While these numbers are only estimates and are revised over time, recent efforts by the actuaries at Social Security to consider the uncertainty in the projections show that there is essentially no chance that the system will be in balance in the long-term (Box 6-2).

Box 6-2: Long-Term Projections and Uncertainty

Recent experience with short-term forecasts has shown that there is considerable uncertainty about how the economy will evolve. That uncertainty is compounded over the 75-year period that the Social Security actuaries must consider. Traditionally, the Trustees Report has included projections based on three different sets of assumptions—low cost, intermediate cost, and high cost. The low-cost scenario has higher fertility rates, slower improvements in mortality, faster real wage growth, and lower unemployment. All of these changes work to reduce the projected deficits. The high-cost scenario changes the assumptions in the opposite direction and results in larger projected deficits.

Policy discussions seldom include any mention of the low- and high-cost scenarios. Part of the reason is that these alternatives are accompanied by no information on how likely they are to occur. In the 2003 Trustees Report, a new method of dealing with uncertainty was included in an appendix. The method, called *stochastic simulation*, is based on the idea that each of the main variables underlying the projection (like the interest rate or economic growth rate) will fluctuate around the value assumed in the intermediate scenario. These fluctuations are modeled by an equation that captures the relationship between current and prior years' values of the variable and introduces year-by-year random variation, as reflected in the historical period. A stochastic simulation consists of many different combinations of possible outcomes for the random variables. Each combination generates a unique path for the key financial measures, each one analogous to the single assumed path generated by the intermediate-cost scenario. Taken together, these paths represent a wide range of possible outcomes for Social Security.

Chart 6-3 shows the range of outcomes for the cost rate generated by the simulation model. These simulations are based on the assumptions and methods in the 2002 Trustees Report, when the deficits reported in the last year of the projection period (2076) were 1.11, 6.42, and 14.66 percent of taxable payroll in that year for the low-, intermediate-, and high-cost scenarios, respectively. Each curve, starting with the lowest, corresponds to a successively higher percentile of the distribution of outcomes each year. In the last year of the projection

---

Box 6-2 — *continued*

period, the median cost rate is 20.33 percent of taxable payroll, which is slightly higher than the value of 19.84 percent based on the interme-diate assumptions. Overall, 95 percent of the cost rates are between 14.53 and 28.98 percent of payroll. Thus, the low-cost estimate of 14.24 and the high-cost estimate of 28.51 correspond to very extreme outcomes in the overall distribution.

Modeling the uncertainty underlying the demographic and economic components of the projection is a large step forward in assessing the future obligations of Social Security. The simulation model used in the Trustees Report likely understates the variation that is possible for future costs of Social Security. Nonetheless, the simula-tions show that based on random year-to-year fluctuations, it is highly improbable that the system will have a cost rate below its income rate in the long-term. Uncertainty in the underlying projections only strengthens the case for reform.

Chart 6-3 **Probability Distribution of Projected Annual Cost Rates**
Simulations that incorporate economic and demographic uncertainty show a wide range of possible outcomes for Social Security's long-term costs.

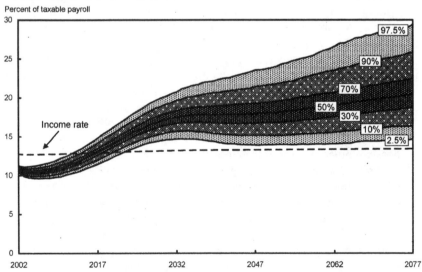

Note: Lines represent percentiles of the distribution, as labeled. Darker shaded areas are more likely outcomes.
Source: Social Security Administration.

Misunderstanding the Financial Crisis

Altough the Social Security program is operated on a largely pay-as-you-go basis, discussions of the financial condition of the program often focus on the trust funds out of which benefit payments are made. There are two trust funds—one for the old-age and survivors benefits and one for the disability benefits—that will be referred to collectively as the "Social Security trust fund." In a year when the government collects more in payroll taxes than it needs to pay out in Social Security benefits (net of the income taxes on benefits), surplus revenues are allocated to the Social Security trust fund. The trust fund is held in a portfolio that consists of special-issue Treasury bonds. The interest rate on the portfolio reflects the yields on long-term Treasury bonds. In a year when Social Security benefit payments exceed revenues, some of the bonds in the trust fund must be redeemed to cover the gap.

In the 2003 Trustees Report, the *trust fund ratio* for the Social Security program was reported as 288 percent for 2003. The trust fund ratio is the proportion of a year's benefit payments that could be paid with the funds available at the beginning of the year. Thus, a trust fund ratio of 288 percent means that in 2003, the amount of bonds held in the trust fund could have been redeemed to cover nearly three years of Social Security benefit payments. A positive trust fund ratio is the standard way of assessing the solvency of Social Security at a point in time. A trust fund ratio of 100 percent is considered to be an adequate reserve for unforeseen contingencies, such as an unexpected drop in payroll tax collections in a particular year.

When the Trustees Report is released, the reaction in the popular press almost always focuses on the date at which the trust fund is projected to go to zero as an indicator of Social Security's financial health. In the 2003 Trustees Report, this date was 2042, and this was widely reported as good news because the prior year's report had projected that date at 2041. The additional year before all of the bonds are redeemed reflects higher annual balances in Social Security through 2042 than were projected in the prior year's report.

Focusing on the date of trust fund exhaustion is inadequate as a measure of Social Security's financial health because this date by itself gives no indication of how dire the fiscal situation becomes *after* the trust fund hits zero. When the trust fund is projected to be exhausted in 2042, for example, the gap between the income and cost rates on the Social Security program is projected to be 4.54 percent of taxable payroll (or 37 percent of the revenues collected by the payroll tax). If such a gap existed in 2003, it would be nearly $200 billion. Reform proposals that are based on pushing back the date when the trust fund is exhausted by a few years will be insufficient to address Social Security's long-term financial imbalance.

As a means of providing a longer-range summary of the finances of the program, the Trustees Report also projects the 75-year *actuarial deficit* in Social Security. Long-range actuarial projections are made over 75 years because this is approximately the remaining lifetime of the youngest current Social Security participants. The 75-year actuarial deficit is equal to the percentage of taxable payroll that could be added to the income rate for each of the next 75 years, or subtracted from the cost rate for each year, to leave the trust fund ratio at 100 percent at the end of the 75-year period.

In the Trustees Report for 2003, this 75-year actuarial deficit was 1.92 percent of taxable payroll using the intermediate assumptions, up from 1.87 percent in the prior year's report. That is, in order to have one year's worth of benefits left in the trust fund in 2077 (the last year of the 75-year projection period starting in 2003), Social Security payroll taxes would have to be 14.32 percent each year for 75 years.

The 75-year actuarial deficit is a widely used measure of the system's financial condition. However, even this measure understates the long-term challenge facing Social Security's finances. Although an increase in the income rate of 1.92 percentage points in each of the next 75 years leaves the trust fund with a positive balance at the end of the 75-year period, the trust fund will rapidly decline to zero in the years after 2077. This occurs because the payroll tax increase of 1.92 percent does not cover the annual deficits of over 6.5 percent that are projected for those years.

Relying on the 75-year actuarial deficit as a guide to solvency is only marginally better than considering the date of trust fund exhaustion. A reform that purported to close the 75-year actuarial deficit would be sufficient only to push the date of trust fund exhaustion to a year just beyond the projection period.

The actuarial deficit over any finite period, even one as long as 75 years, can dramatically understate the financial imbalance in Social Security when the program's annual deficits are getting wider over that period. For example, the 2003 Trustees Report estimates that the present value of the unfunded obligations for the program over the next 75 years is $3.5 trillion. In other words, if this amount of money were available today and invested at the rate of return that is credited to trust fund assets, it would provide just enough to cover the program's deficits over the next 75 years. However, the Trustees Report also estimates that the present value of the program's unfunded obligations over the infinite horizon—the next 75 years and all years thereafter—is $10.5 trillion. The $7.0 trillion difference reflects the continued annual deficits that persist after the first 75 years. Thus, the first 75-year period represents only one-third of the present value of the total shortfall.

A projection period limited to 75 years also biases the discussion of potential reforms in favor of those that are based on pay-as-you-go, rather than advanced, funding. Some reform proposals would allow a portion of the payroll tax to be used to establish voluntary personal retirement accounts (PRAs). People who establish their own personal retirement accounts would be able to direct some of their payroll taxes into their PRAs in exchange for accepting lower benefits from the pay-as-you-go system in retirement. The additional funding requirements to maintain benefits for current retirees while allowing some of the payroll tax to be used for personal retirement accounts for current workers necessarily appear in the first 75 years. However, much of the benefit of advanced funding—in terms of reduced obligations of the pay-as-you-go system—occurs outside of the 75-year projection period.

Recognizing that even a 75-year actuarial deficit cannot fully reflect the long-term financial shortfalls in Social Security, the Trustees have increased their focus on the annual balance in the last year of the 75-year projection period as a guide to the financial shortfalls in the program. If the trust fund ratio is to continue to play a role in discussions of solvency, then, at the very least, the standard for restoring solvency to the program should be to have not only a positive trust fund in the terminal year of the projection period, but also a trust fund that is not declining toward zero in that year.

The Nature of a Prefunded Solution

To restore solvency to Social Security on an ongoing basis, the income and cost rates cannot be moving apart over time. If the income and cost rates are moving together at the same level, then there is no need for a large trust fund, because the program's annual balance will be roughly zero in each year. As noted above, the annual deficit is currently projected to grow to 6.67 percent of taxable payroll by 2080. Only by reducing annual benefits or increasing the payroll tax (or the income tax on benefits) by a total of 6.67 percent of taxable payroll can solvency be restored in the long term on a pay-as-you-go basis.

If these benefit cuts or tax increases are not desired, then an alternative is to allow the gap between the cost and income rates to persist (provided that it is not increasing over time) and rely on the investment income from a portfolio of assets to cover the gap. Such a portfolio would have to be accumulated in the intervening years, in order to prefund the difference between the program's scheduled obligations and revenues.

In 1983, the last time a major reform of Social Security was undertaken, the program was changed to begin accumulating annual surpluses in the Social Security trust fund. In 2003, the trust fund balance was $1.5 trillion. However, the intervening two decades provide little assurance that the Social Security surpluses during that time have increased the resources available to the government as a whole to pay future benefits.

The balance in the Social Security trust fund has a clear meaning as an accounting device. At any point in time, the trust fund balance shows the cumulative amount of additional revenue—plus interest—the Social Security program has made available to the Federal government to spend on other purchases. The special-issue Treasury bonds in the trust fund are IOUs from the rest of the government to the Social Security program to cover its deficits in future years. The trust fund balance shows the extent of the legal authority for the Social Security program to redeem those IOUs in the future. Administratively, the Social Security program is not authorized to pay benefits unless the trust fund ratio is positive; that is, it can only pay benefits to the extent that it has been a net creditor to the rest of the government.

The question of what the government has done with the revenues made available by past Social Security surpluses has important implications for what the trust fund represents in economic terms and for the design of Social Security reform. There are two competing conjectures about the government's actions. The first is that the surpluses in the Social Security program have had no effect on the surpluses or deficits in the rest of the government's budget. If this is true, every dollar that the government received from past Social Security surpluses and thus allocated to the trust fund served to reduce the amount of Treasury bonds held by the public by a dollar. In the future, drawing down the trust fund when Social Security is projected to run annual deficits simply involves selling the debt back to the public so that when the trust fund is exhausted, the amount of debt held by the public in the future will be the same as it would have been had there not been any Social Security surpluses. Under this conjecture about government budget policy, the Social Security surpluses have been a source of higher national saving and the trust fund represents real resources available to pay future benefits.

The second conjecture is that the surpluses in the Social Security program have encouraged the government to run smaller surpluses or larger deficits in the rest of its budget. If this conjecture is true, the Social Security surpluses have not been used to repurchase existing Treasury bonds held by the public but instead have been used to pay for government expenditures, such as defense, health care, or education. Drawing down the trust fund in future years will involve selling Treasury debt to the public, as in the first case. However, unless future government spending is reduced, the debt held by the public will be higher than it would have been in the absence of Social Security surpluses by the time the trust fund is exhausted. Under this conjecture about government budget policy, the Social Security surpluses have not resulted in higher national saving, and the balance in the trust fund does not represent additional real resources available to pay future benefits.

Analysts have argued in favor of both of these conjectures. Determining which one is correct requires making an assumption about what the government would have done in the counterfactual case that Social Security had not run annual surpluses. The unified budget deficit (including Social Security) has been the focus of budget discussions for almost all of the last two decades. This provides a strong *prima facie* case that government expenditures outside of Social Security were higher due to the presence of Social Security surpluses during this period.

Allocating Social Security surpluses to special-issue Treasury bonds in the trust fund provides no guarantee that future Social Security obligations are prefunded. It would therefore not be appropriate to simply accumulate government bonds in a trust fund as a way to restore solvency. One way to overcome the vagueness in trust fund accounting is to require that the prefunding occur by allocating a portion of Social Security's annual revenues to the purchase of private rather than government securities and to treat these purchases as annual expenditures of the Federal government. Doing so would break the link between Social Security surpluses and the issuance of debt by the Federal government. This would allow the Social Security program to accumulate a portfolio of financial claims on private sources to pay for future obligations.

Some simple arithmetic shows the size of the portfolio of private securities that would be required to close the entire long-term annual deficit in this manner. Suppose that investments in a portfolio of stocks and corporate bonds earn a 5.2 percent expected return, net of inflation and administrative costs. To obtain an income flow of 6.67 percent of taxable payroll (the annual deficit in 2080) would require a portfolio of assets equal to $6.67/5.2 = 128$ percent of taxable payroll. In 2080, taxable payroll is projected to be 34.7 percent of GDP, so that the required stock of assets would be equal to 44.5 percent of GDP. If such a fund existed in 2003, when GDP was estimated to be $10.9 trillion, the fund would have a value of $4.9 trillion. This calculation assumes that either taxpayers or beneficiaries will absorb the financial risk associated with investments in corporate stocks and bonds. Repeating the same arithmetic using a 3 percent real interest rate—the projected return on the Treasury bonds in the Social Security trust fund—shows that the fund would have to be $8.4 trillion.

For portfolios of this magnitude, prefunding by investing in private securities would require that individuals establish their own personal retirement accounts. To put these figures in some perspective, as of November 2003, the net assets of all mutual funds in the United States were estimated to be $7.24 trillion. Thus, in order to cover the annual deficit in 2080 through prefunding, a portfolio the size of at least two-thirds and possibly more than 100 percent of all mutual funds would have to be accumulated. A portfolio of this size is simply too large to be administered centrally without political interference and without disruption to the capital markets.

In light of these issues, a Social Security reform plan should have two components. First, it should restrain the growth of future pay-as-you-go benefits for those not currently in or near retirement to bring the cost rate of the program in line with the income rate in the long term. Second, it should establish personal retirement accounts for each worker. The personal retirement accounts serve a dual purpose. First, because the accounts can be located outside of the government's budget, the accumulation of assets in these accounts would not provide any impetus for higher government spending in the non-Social Security part of the budget. Second, the personal retirement accounts would provide a way for individual workers to accumulate assets to offset the reduction in their total retirement income that otherwise would occur due to the lower benefits in the pay-as-you-go part of the system.

Can We Afford to Reform Entitlements?

While Social Security's long-term solvency has been an ongoing concern for over 25 years, the report of the 1994-1996 Advisory Council on Social Security prompted a new round of policy discussions that included serious proposals to prefund future obligations with private securities. These discussions were bolstered by the appearance of surpluses in the Federal government's budget and budget forecasts during the late 1990s. Shortly after the President took office in 2001, a bipartisan commission on Social Security was established. The commission's final report discusses three reform options that would involve the use of personal retirement accounts to prefund a portion of future benefits.

Some critics of personal retirement accounts have suggested that Social Security reform requires surpluses in the unified budget (including Social Security) or even the non-Social Security portion of the budget to begin investing in the accounts while maintaining pay-as-you-go benefits to current retirees. Since the budget surpluses forecasted a few years ago have not materialized, critics argue that adding personal retirement accounts to Social Security is impossible or impractical. In reality, the need to add resources to the Social Security system is no less pressing now that the surpluses have disappeared; indeed, it may be even more so. The change in the budget outlook makes reform neither less necessary nor less economically feasible.

As an illustration, consider the recent President's Commission's Model 2, under the assumption that all eligible workers will voluntarily choose to establish a personal retirement account (thereby maximizing the transition costs to be discussed below). This plan has two main components. First, it slows the growth of benefits from the pay-as-you-go system by indexing future benefits to prices rather than to wages. Prices generally increase more slowly than wages. Second, the plan allows workers to receive a tax cut now, if they place the tax cut into a personal retirement account, in exchange for specific reductions in the pay-as-you-go benefits they would receive otherwise. When workers choose this option, private saving is increased. Under the conjecture that Social Security surpluses are saved rather than spent, government saving is reduced and national saving is essentially unchanged. However, the long-term solvency of the pay-as-you-go system is maintained, and government and national saving increase to the extent that having resources go into personal retirement accounts rather than the Social Security trust fund prevents the government from using Social Security revenues to pay for non-Social Security expenditures.

The economic rationale for undertaking this type of Social Security reform does not depend on the current budget situation. This is clearly true with respect to the first component of reform—restraining the growth of future pay-as-you-go benefits to a level that is commensurate with future payroll tax revenues. The value of pursuing this objective does not depend in any important way on whether, due to prior economic and budgetary events not related to the reform, future generations will be paying interest on a large or small stock of public debt. If anything, easing the payroll tax burden on future generations is *more* important if they face a greater interest burden. Relying on personal retirement accounts also remains necessary. Compared to government saving, saving in personal retirement accounts gives workers greater freedom to prepare for their own retirement. Saving in personal retirement accounts also ensures that the additional resources being accumulated for Social Security are not available to be tapped for additional government spending.

Even if both components of reform are still necessary, though, are they feasible? Chart 6-4 shows the plan's effect on the unified budget deficit and total government debt held by the public assuming that the first contributions to personal retirement accounts are made in 2004. Even under the favorable conjecture that Social Security surpluses do not facilitate higher government spending outside of Social Security, the deficit initially increases, but then falls as the reform is fully phased in. At its maximum, in 2022, the incremental deficit increase is less than 1.6 percent of GDP. The higher deficits in turn lead to a greater stock of debt in subsequent years, followed by repayment. The maximum increment to the debt is 23.6 percent of GDP, in 2036.

The hump-shaped pattern for the impact of reform on the deficit reflects the combined effects of the two parts of the reform. Personal retirement accounts widen the deficit by design—they refund payroll tax revenues to workers in the near term while lowering benefit payments from the pay-as-you-go system in later years. After 2048, an incremental surplus emerges as the benefit reductions phased in through price indexation begin to outweigh the net effect of the personal retirement accounts on the deficit.

Is this temporary increase in government borrowing a problem? Not from an economic perspective. The increased borrowing does not shift any burden to future generations. The tax cuts given to today's workers are paid for by reductions in the share of their future benefits that must be paid from future tax dollars. Nor are current workers harmed. They save this money in their own accounts, which can give them retirement income just as surely as if the government were promising it to them.

While the government's budget situation does not affect the *economic* necessity and feasibility of Social Security reform, under some assumptions about the political constraints on the budget process, the *political* feasibility and desirability of reform may be shaped by the overall budget picture.

Reforms will lead to larger unified budget deficits in the near term but smaller deficits in the long term. The presence of a deficit in the non-Social Security part of the budget may make it more difficult to persuade lawmakers to reform Social Security, if the transition costs of the reform cause the deficit to eclipse a previous record. However, avoiding Social Security reform will not keep deficits in check. If nothing is done to reform Social Security, under current projections, the growth of Social Security,

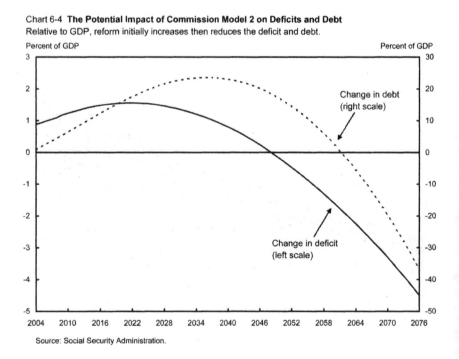

Chart 6-4 **The Potential Impact of Commission Model 2 on Deficits and Debt**
Relative to GDP, reform initially increases then reduces the deficit and debt.

Source: Social Security Administration.

Medicare, Medicaid, and the interest on the borrowing required to finance their growth will lead to unified budget deficits that surpass previous records as a share of GDP.

Chart 6-5 shows the projected costs and revenues in the unified budget under the assumption that no reforms are made to Social Security. The projections are based on the President's policies in the fiscal year 2004 budget, modified to include relief from the alternative minimum tax. The chart assumes that all scheduled Social Security benefit payments are made, financed through additional debt after the trust fund is exhausted. The stacked areas represent total scheduled Federal spending as a share of GDP. Even with nonentitlement spending fixed at 8.1 percent of GDP and excluding interest payments, Federal spending surpasses 20 percent of GDP in 2025, 25 percent in 2050, and 30 percent in 2080. The solid line shows total revenue. The budget deficit, which is the height of the areas above the black line, grows sharply in upcoming decades.

The impact of Social Security reform on the baseline deficit is shown in Chart 6-6, which graphs the evolution of the deficit under two scenarios: the baseline from Chart 6-5 in which no reform is implemented and a reform that includes all of Model 2, with 100 percent participation. Recall from Chart 6-4 that this reform causes the budget deficit to increase temporarily before falling to a lower share of GDP as the reform is fully phased in.

Chart 6-5 **The Long-Run Budget without Social Security Reform**
The unified budget deficit widens considerably over the coming decades.

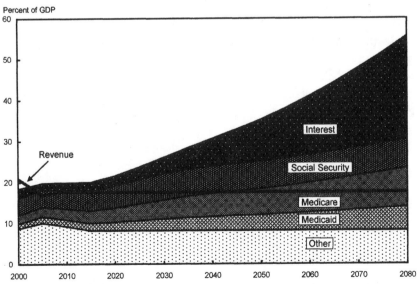

Sources: Social Security Administration, Centers for Medicare and Medicaid Services, Office of Management and Budget, and Council of Economic Advisers.

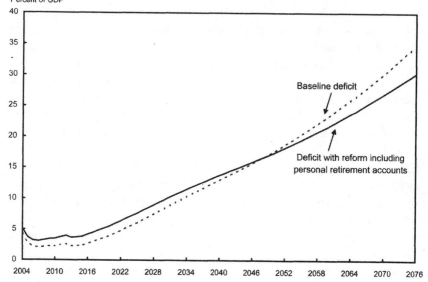

Chart 6-6 **The Long-Run Budget Deficit with Social Security Reform**
Enacting Social Security reform leads to lower unified deficits when fully phased in.

Percent of GDP

Baseline deficit

Deficit with reform including personal retirement accounts

Sources: Social Security Administration, Centers for Medicare and Medicaid Services, Office of Management and Budget, and Council of Economic Advisers.

With the reform, the unified budget deficit reaches 5 percent of GDP in 2019. Without reform, this deficit is reached instead in 2023. The benefits of the reform appear over time, making a positive impact on the Federal budget after 2048.

Policy makers concerned about the unified deficit will have to decide how they will restrain Federal spending over the upcoming decades—they will have to confront this question even if nothing is done to reform Social Security. The benefit of reforming Social Security is that it alleviates, to some extent, the financial burden that unreformed entitlement programs will place on future generations.

Conclusion

The Nation must act to avert a long-foreseen future crisis in the financing of its old-age entitlement programs. The crisis results mainly from the fundamental demographic shifts to lower birthrates and longer lives rather than the impending retirement of the baby-boom generation. However, the scope for enacting meaningful reform will disappear as the baby-boom generation begins to retire and an ever greater share of the population sees its current income arrive in the form of a government check. The design of the Social Security program has failed to keep pace with emerging demographic realities. The benefits promised to those currently in or near retirement must be honored, but a new course must be set to ensure that Social Security is viable and available to Americans in the future.

To do nothing at this point to restrain the growth of entitlement programs would bequeath to future generations an increasing tax on their income to support Social Security. The only way to avoid such an outcome without reducing the living standards of future retirees is to save more today. Greater saving will increase the capital stock and increase the productive capacity of the economy so that it can support those higher payments. The combination of reducing the projected cost of taxpayer-financed benefits and shifting the revenues into personal retirement accounts provides the best mechanism for achieving that result.

CHAPTER 7

Government Regulation in a Free-Market Society

An important reason for Americans' high standard of living is that they live in a free-market economy in which competition establishes prices and the government enforces property rights and contracts. Typically, free markets allocate resources to their highest-valued uses, avoid waste, prevent shortages, and foster innovation. By providing a legal foundation for transactions, the government makes the market system reliable: it gives people certainty about what they can trade and keep, and it allows people to establish terms of trade that will be honored by both sellers and buyers. The absence of any one of these elements—competition, enforceable property rights, or an ability to form mutually advantageous contracts—can result in inefficiency and lower living standards. In some cases, government intervention in a market, for example through regulation, can create gains for society by remedying any shortcomings in the market's operation. Poorly designed or unnecessary regulations, however, can actually create new problems or make society worse off by damaging the elements of the market system that do work.

The key points in this chapter are:

- Markets generally allocate resources to their most valuable uses.
- Well-designed regulations can address cases where markets fail to accomplish this goal.
- Not all regulations improve market outcomes.

How Markets Work

Free markets work through voluntary exchange. This voluntary nature ensures that only trades that benefit both parties take place: people give up their property only when someone agrees to exchange it for something that they value more highly. In most transactions, sellers receive money rather than goods in exchange for their property. Sellers then use that money to become buyers in other transactions.

What ensures that producers are providing the commodities that consumers want? Market prices play the critical role of coordinating the activities of buyers and sellers. Prices convey information about the strength of consumer demand for a good, as well as how costly it is to supply. By conveying information and providing an incentive to act on this information, prices induce society to shift its scarce resources to the production of goods that are valued by consumers. In this way, markets usually allocate resources in a manner that creates the greatest net benefits (benefits minus costs) to society. An *efficient* allocation is one that maximizes the net benefits to society.

In general, efficiency requires that the price of a good reflects the incremental cost of producing that good, including the cost of inputs and the value of the producer's time and effort. In this way, prices induce consumers to economize on goods that are relatively expensive to produce and to increase their purchases of goods that are relatively inexpensive to produce. A key advantage of free-market competition is that it generally leads to a situation in which price equals incremental production cost. This outcome occurs because in a competitive market environment, a seller who charges a price above the cost of production will be undercut by competitors, including new entrants. In contrast, if prices are artificially high because of limited competition, consumers will buy less of the good than they would if they faced the competitive price. Furthermore, some consumers who would benefit from buying the good at a competitive price may not buy it at all.

When market conditions change, prices usually change as well and signal buyers and sellers to modify their behavior. For example, if a disruption in the gasoline supply were to occur and prices and behavior remained unchanged, there would not be enough gasoline supplied to satisfy consumer demand at predisruption prices. The result would be a gas shortage. To eliminate this shortage, some form of rationing would be required to ensure that the quantity of gasoline demanded by consumers matched the quantity of gasoline provided by suppliers.

In a market economy, rationing is done by prices. As prices of gasoline increase, two changes in behavior typically occur. First, consumers as a whole reduce their consumption of gasoline, and second, producers as a whole increase the quantity of gasoline available for sale. These aggregate changes are the result of many individual decisions. For example, some consumers may carpool, others may cancel trips, and some may be willing to spend more on gasoline to continue on as before. On the supply side, producers may ship gasoline from areas not affected by the supply disruption, refineries may increase production, and firms may lower inventories of gasoline in storage. Eventually, prices increase to the point at which the reduced quantity of gasoline demanded equals the increased quantity of gasoline supplied. In a market economy, all of this happens without any centralized control mechanism.

Market Imperfections

Sometimes markets do not allocate resources efficiently. Under such circumstances, it may make sense for the government to intervene in markets beyond providing a legal foundation for market transactions. Chapters 8 and 9, which deal with energy and the environment, discuss some regulations designed to address two such market failures—externalities and market power. These chapters look at both the benefits and potential problems that can result from imposition of regulations.

Poorly designed or unnecessary government regulations can actually reduce society's overall well-being. The possible costs of government regulation include the costs imposed on consumers and producers, impeded innovation, and unintended negative consequences such as the creation of unforeseen barriers to competition. It is essential to consider whether the costs potential regulations impose on society are greater than the benefits society receives from fixing any market failures.

Regulation and Externalities

Externalities (also known as *spillover effects*) can lead to a situation in which the price of a commodity does not reflect its full incremental cost to society. A *negative externality* exists when the voluntary market transaction between two parties imposes involuntary costs on a third party. For example, a power plant might produce and sell electricity to consumers to both their advantage, but the production process might emit air pollution that negatively affects the population. The costs that this pollution imposes on the population might not be considered when the firm decides where to locate a plant, which technologies to use, or how much electricity to produce. It could be that if these costs were taken into account in the same way as all of the other costs of producing electricity, the plant might be relocated to a place where its pollution would affect fewer people, the firm might put greater emphasis on pollution-reducing technologies, or the plant may not produce as much electricity. The existence of a negative externality can lead to an outcome that is worse for society than one that takes the externality into account.

As discussed in Chapter 9, *Protecting the Environment*, in many cases the best remedy for externalities is to define property rights and allow the affected parties to transact privately to achieve a mutually beneficial outcome. Sometimes, however, establishing property rights can be expensive. Even with clearly defined property rights, it may be costly for affected parties to collectively agree on a mutually beneficial transaction. Under such circumstances, other forms of government intervention may be appropriate, including taxes, subsidies, and direct regulation.

Addressing Externalities Through Taxes

One approach to dealing with externalities would be to levy a tax (known to economists as a *Pigouvian tax*) on market participants such that the amount of tax collected equals the incremental cost of the externality. For example, if a power plant's emissions are easy to monitor and the costs of pollution are easy to assess, the tax on each unit of pollution could be set equal to the cost of the externality. Alternatively, if the amount of pollution is not easily monitored, the tax could apply to each unit of production (each kilowatt produced by the plant, for example) rather than the pollution itself, and could be set equal to the additional external cost of pollution from each unit of production.

In general, taxes distort economic activity (see the discussion of the income tax in Chapter 4, *Tax Incidence: Who Bears the Tax Burden?*). However, proponents of Pigouvian taxation argue that it can improve the allocation of resources by forcing producers and consumers to confront the full costs of production. Indeed, some advocates of the use of such taxes go further and argue that revenues from Pigouvian taxes could be used to finance a reduction in the rates on other taxes that do distort behavior, such as the income tax. This idea is sometimes called the *double-dividend hypothesis* because it increases efficiency in the market with the externality *and* in the markets that are distorted by the income tax.

This argument must be viewed with caution. To see why, recall that Pigouvian taxes drive up the prices of the goods that are produced using technologies that involve pollution. The increase in prices reduces the buying power of households' incomes. This is effectively a decrease in the real wage rate because a given dollar amount of wages buys fewer goods and services. Put another way, Pigouvian taxes are, to some extent, also taxes on earnings. If the labor market is already distorted because of an income tax (as is the case in the United States and other industrial economies), the Pigouvian tax makes the distortion worse. In some cases, the added distortions in the labor market can actually outweigh the gains from correcting the externality. The desirability of Pigouvian taxes as a policy instrument must be determined on a case-by-case basis.

Addressing Externalities Through Limits on Quantity

Another possible problem with Pigouvian taxes is that determining their magnitude can be challenging because it may be difficult to measure the amount of pollution, as well as the value of the damage it causes. Moreover, the appropriate tax may change with market conditions. If, for example, the cost of the externality increases with output, the optimal tax would need to go up if output increases.

It is also difficult to know beforehand the tax level that will reduce emissions by the desired amount. Moreover, as the economy changes, the tax will need to be adjusted to maintain the desired amount of emissions reduction. A system in which a firm must own a government-issued permit for each unit of pollution addresses these problems because the government determines the number of permits to create. A *cap-and-trade* system, which allows firms to trade these permits, accomplishes the environmental goal at least cost.

Addressing Externalities Through Subsidies

Another option for dealing with externalities is to subsidize alternative behaviors that do not produce the negative externality. For example, concern over externalities from fossil fuels has led to government subsidies of some alternative sources of electricity, such as wind and solar power. However, such subsidies have some limitations. First, using the example of electricity, subsidies encourage overconsumption by keeping the cost of electricity below the level that market forces would set if the costs of the externality were taken into account. Second, subsidies raise some difficult administrative issues. In particular, the government needs to identify all the behaviors that should qualify for a subsidy. In the case of the power plant that emitted pollution, a fully efficient policy would be to subsidize all other ways of generating electricity and all conservation activities. Such attempts quickly become unwieldy in practice.

Addressing Externalities Through Command-and-Control Regulation

The government can also attempt to limit negative externalities with *command-and-control* regulations that mandate certain behavior. For example, the government requires automobile producers to meet overall fuel-efficiency standards. There have also been proposals to mandate that a certain percentage of electricity be generated by renewable fuels such as wind and solar power.

Command-and-control regulations can sometimes be the only way to deal with an externality. In general, however, they should be avoided because they discourage flexible and innovative responses to externalities and can result in higher costs than alternative policies. For example, mandating use of a particular technology to lower emissions could lessen firms' incentives to develop more effective techniques to reduce pollution. Furthermore, people adapt to command-and-control regulations in unintended ways that can limit their effectiveness over time. For example, one unintended consequence of the automobile fuel-efficiency standards was to increase the demand for light trucks and sport utility vehicles (SUVs), which were not as stringently regulated.

Regulation and Market Power

Market power, which arises in the presence of impediments to competition, is another potential source of inefficiency in a free-market system. Firms that have *market power* typically have the ability to charge prices above the competitive price level and maintain those high prices profitably over a considerable period. In some cases, the impediment is a law that makes it difficult for competitors to enter a market, but market power can also arise from the nature of the industry itself. For example, the high cost of wiring residential neighborhoods for electricity makes it unlikely that multiple firms would be willing to compete to distribute retail electricity. In these cases, regulation can be useful to prevent firms with market power from charging consumers prices that substantially exceed the cost of providing the good.

Policy makers need to recognize, however, that regulations themselves affect firms' and consumers' behavior and incentives. Regulations that do not take these effects into account can result in excessive consumption, misaligned incentives, stunted innovation and investment, and needless waste. Even regulations that do account for these effects may be rendered obsolete or counterproductive by changes in the industry that occur over time. For this reason, it is important to periodically reevaluate regulatory policies. Chapter 8, *Regulating Energy Markets*, discusses opportunities for reevaluation in further detail.

Regulation in the Absence of a Market Failure

Some government regulations attempt to reverse what would otherwise be efficient market outcomes due to beliefs that a particular market-based allocation of resources is undesirable. For example, regulations to prevent "price gouging" might be seen as fair, but the economic consequences of these regulations must be recognized (Box 7-1). Attempts to circumvent the market in this way must confront a basic reality—resources are scarce, so that if market prices are not used to ration commodities, some other mechanism has to be used instead. For example, resources could be allocated to consumers using ration coupons, a lottery, or first-come, first-served. Resources could also be allocated based on cronyism or other discriminatory means. These nonprice methods cannot guarantee that the scarce resources go to the consumers who value them the most. Furthermore, they reduce suppliers' incentives to increase production. For example, if prices are capped, suppliers may not work overtime to increase supplies or pay extra transportation costs to bring in supplies from distant areas. As a result, resources are not put to their best uses.

Box 7-1: Market Responses to Unexpected Shortages

When there are large, unexpected increases in demand or decreases in supply for a good, a normal market response is for prices to increase by enough to restore balance between supply and demand. Consumers might accuse sellers of "price gouging" when such price increases occur in response to a natural disaster or a failure of supply infrastructure. A number of states have laws that make price gouging illegal. Even without such laws, some businesses might choose not to increase prices during an emergency for fear of a consumer backlash. If prices do not increase, however, consumers do not receive a signal to cut their consumption and suppliers might not have the proper incentives to increase supply adequately.

By not allowing market forces to restore the balance between supply and demand after the shock, nonprice rationing must be implemented instead. For example, after a pipeline break reduced the supply of gasoline into the Phoenix, Arizona, area in August 2003, press reports indicated that some stations ran out of gasoline, consumers waited in line for hours, and some drivers started following gasoline tankers as they made their deliveries.

Changes in demand can induce shortages as well. For example, in the days leading up to the arrival of Hurricane Isabel in the Mid-Atlantic states in September 2003, press reports indicated that many retailers sold out of flashlights and D batteries. The flashlights and batteries went to the first people to show up at the store, rather than to those who valued them the most. It also meant that people who were able to buy the goods might have bought more than they would have at the higher price, leaving fewer for others. Without price increases, there was no mechanism to allocate the available goods to their highest-valued uses. For example, if prices were higher, early customers may have decided not to buy new batteries for their fifth flashlight and later customers would not have been forced to sit in the dark.

While allowing prices to increase in the face of a natural disaster or a supply disruption may seem unfair, the alternative would be to restrict the allocation of scarce supplies and to possibly keep supplies from those who need them most. Artificially low prices remove incentives for consumers to conserve and for suppliers to meet unfilled demand, potentially prolonging the shortage. Society must decide whether the perceived fairness resulting from regulations to hold down prices is more important than allowing the market to provide incentives for resolving the shortage as quickly as possible, while making sure that scarce resources are available for those who value them the most.

Conclusion

In general, market systems allocate resources toward their most highly valued uses. Importantly, no one *directs* society to this result. Rather, it is the outcome of a process in which each consumer and each producer observe prices and privately make the decisions that maximize their well-being. The coordination of economic activity is done by prices, which provide signals of the costs to society of providing various goods. However, in the presence of market power, externalities, and other types of market failure, market-generated prices may not incorporate all of the relevant information about costs. Under these conditions, there are opportunities for government to intervene and improve the allocation of resources.

The fact that the market-generated allocation of resources is imperfect does not mean that the government necessarily can do better. For example, in certain cases the costs of setting up a government agency to deal with an externality could exceed the cost of the externality itself. Therefore, proposed remedies for market failure must be evaluated on a case-by-case basis.

Energy and the environment are two areas in which government intervention may play a role in correcting market failures. Such interventions are likely to be more successful when they harness market forces to the extent possible. The next two chapters illustrate the challenges in properly designing regulations in these areas. An important implication of the analysis of both chapters is that in order to make society better off, regulatory policy must be based on a solid economic foundation.

Regulating Energy Markets

Energy is essential to the U.S. economy, both as a final good and as an input into the production of most other goods. In 2000, energy expenditures equaled $703 billion, or 7.2 percent of GDP. The markets that provide this energy function well and are generally competitive. However, parts of the energy industry have characteristics that are associated with market failures. For example, the large fixed costs required to construct distribution networks for electricity and natural gas make it unlikely that more than one firm would be willing to invest in the infrastructure needed to serve residential customers in a particular area. The distribution company, therefore, may have *market power*, the ability to charge prices significantly above the competitive price level and profitably maintain those prices for a considerable period. Another type of market failure involves *negative externalities*, costs that economic transactions impose on third parties that the parties to the transaction do not face. For example, energy producers and consumers may not fully take into account the fact that burning fossil fuels may cause acid rain or smog.

This chapter discusses economic issues relevant to several different energy markets, including natural gas, gasoline, electricity, and crude oil. The use of these different types of energy involves different market structures and different potential market failures. An important focus of the chapter is on the design of regulations to address market failures in energy markets while minimizing disruptions to the market. The key points in this chapter are:

- Markets generally work well for energy products, which in most ways are like other products in the U.S. economy. While some aspects of energy markets may require regulation, most segments of these markets function well without regulation.
- Federal, state, and local regulations can have conflicting goals. If the conflicting goals are not balanced, competing regulations could lead to worse problems than the market failures the regulations attempt to address.
- Regulations need to be updated as markets evolve over time to ensure that the original goals still apply and that these regulations are still the lowest-cost means of meeting those goals.
- The United States benefits from international trade in energy products.

Market Forces and Regulation in the Market for Natural Gas

Some energy markets require regulation. For example, because of the high cost of natural gas distribution services, the market generally supports only one local distribution company. Thus, the delivery infrastructure, including pipelines and gas meters connected to individual residences, is regulated. However, certain segments of the natural gas industry are amenable to competition. They do not require regulation even though the distribution segment does. Indeed, in many areas of the country parts of the natural gas market have been deregulated. For example, producers of natural gas are no longer subject to price regulation. Furthermore, although prices for transporting natural gas to homeowners are regulated, in some states multiple firms now compete for the right to sell the gas to homeowners. This type of partial deregulation has also been applied to electricity markets; in many areas, local distribution lines are still regulated while generation and retail marketing are deregulated.

The last year has demonstrated how market forces have worked to allocate scarce resources in the natural gas market. Demand for natural gas is highly seasonal, with the greatest consumption by far during the winter heating season. During the summer, a portion of natural gas production is stored for use in the following winter. Natural gas inventories in spring 2003 were unusually low after a colder than normal winter in 2002-2003. This led to large increases in natural gas prices in the spot and futures markets. In turn, these high prices encouraged consumers to switch to other fuels or reduce consumption over the summer, encouraged producers to increase production, and encouraged importers to bring in additional natural gas from outside North America. In combination, these actions resulted in a near-record increase in natural gas inventories in time for the winter heating season. As a result, the United States entered the winter of 2003-2004 with slightly above-average natural gas inventories. High prices have also given firms an added incentive to invest in new projects, such as liquefied natural gas (LNG) facilities, to bring additional supplies of natural gas to the market in the future.

Market Forces and Regulation in Gasoline Markets

Recent and past events in the gasoline market have shown how unexpected shortages affect market prices and how government regulation can make the situation worse. Wage and price controls imposed in the early 1970s to combat inflation included government regulations that kept gasoline prices below the market level. As a result, when oil supplies were disrupted in 1973 and 1979 by geopolitical events in the Middle East, consumers wanted to buy more gasoline than suppliers were willing to supply at the artificially low prices.

Regulations that prevented suppliers from increasing prices meant that consumers had to wait in lines or face limits on the amount of gasoline they could purchase. As a result, some gasoline likely went to consumers who valued it less than other consumers because those who would have cut consumption as prices rose continued to buy gasoline at the artificially low price. Keeping gasoline prices artificially low also reduced the incentive for oil companies to refine new sources of crude oil into gasoline—a supply response that would have lessened the shortfall.

Gasoline markets also demonstrate how markets react to unexpected changes in supply when prices are not regulated. For example, several refinery problems on the West Coast in recent years have, on occasion, temporarily reduced the supply of California Air Resource Board (CARB) gasoline that meets strict California specifications for reducing air pollution. After these disruptions, prices typically increased quickly, and usually stayed high for only a matter of weeks. These increased prices led consumers to reduce their gasoline consumption.

During supply disruptions that were expected to last a relatively long time, the high prices also led distant refineries to produce and ship CARB gasoline to California. These refiners had to shift their operations to make CARB gasoline instead of their normal product, find an available tanker, and then ship the gasoline to California—a process that takes three weeks or more. High prices rewarded the refiners that were able to get CARB gasoline to California quickly, while refiners whose shipments arrived too late (that is, as prices started to come down again) would lose money. The price spike provided an incentive for distant refiners to risk making and shipping CARB gasoline to California, thus helping to alleviate California's gasoline shortage.

Local and Federal Regulations May Conflict

As illustrated in the example above, not all gasoline sold in the United States is the same. Differences in local specifications are often the result of how local and state governments have responded to the Clean Air Act of 1990. Chart 8-1 shows which areas of the United States have adopted different fuel specifications. Flexibility in how localities address air pollution abatement allows them to implement an approach that best meets their needs. However, different local or regional gasoline specifications add complexity to the national gasoline production and distribution infrastructure, reducing the reliability and availability of gasoline supplies.

The proliferation of fuel varieties produced for various locations (called *boutique fuels*) reduces the number of potential suppliers of each particular fuel and slows the industry response when there are local or regional disruptions to the gasoline supply. Boutique gasoline specifications likely contributed to the price spike in the Midwest in 2000, which occurred after several refineries experienced production problems around the same time that two major pipelines supplying the region went out of service. Chicago and Milwaukee were particularly hard-hit in part because of their local

Chart 8-1 **Required Specifications for Gasoline**
Different local environmental regulations have lead to a patchwork of gasoline specifications.

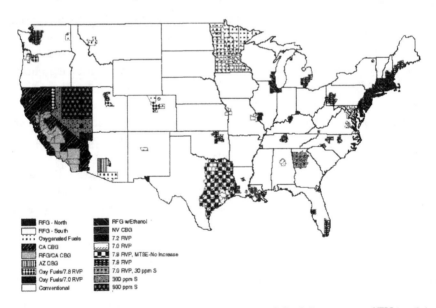

Note: RFG refers to reformulated gasoline, CBG to cleaner burning gasoline, RVP to Reid vapor pressure, MTBE to methyl tertiary butyl ether, and ppm S to parts per million sulfur.
Source: ExxonMobil, November 2003.

requirements for reformulated gasoline using ethanol. Nearby cities using reformulated gasoline had different specifications, so that existing reformulated gasoline stocks could not be shipped to the area.

The impact of boutique fuel regulations demonstrates that there may be benefits from standardizing regulations across geographic areas for goods that are sold regionally or nationally. Gasoline markets in the eastern half of the United States are interconnected by pipelines, barges, and tankers. Reducing the number of gasoline specifications could allow for increased flexibility of the gasoline supply system. For example, production lost because of a refinery problem in Chicago could be offset by shipments of gasoline from refiners in other areas. The President's National Energy Plan asked the Environmental Protection Agency (EPA) to study ways to increase the flexibility of the Nation's fuel supply.

While there may be benefits from standardizing regulations across geographic areas, standardization may require some areas to use gasoline that is more expensive than necessary to meet local air-quality standards. The benefits of standardization must be weighed against any increased costs.

Local and State Regulations Lead to Different Market Outcomes

State regulations can also increase the cost of marketing and distributing gasoline to consumers. For example, several states and the District of Columbia have divorcement laws that restrict refiners' ability to own and operate retail stations. These regulations have been found to increase prices at the pump; prices in states with divorcement laws are almost 3 percent higher than they would be without such laws. Similarly, regulations in Oregon and New Jersey ban self-service gasoline sales because of putative safety and environmental concerns. Economists have estimated that gasoline prices in these states are between 2 and 6 cents per gallon higher than they would be without the self-service ban (gasoline prices in New Jersey are lower than in surrounding states because of New Jersey's low gasoline taxes, but prices would be even lower if self-service were allowed).

Market Forces and Regulation in Electricity Markets

While a mix of market forces and well-designed regulation can lead a market with market failures to perform more effectively and efficiently, improper regulation can lead to worse outcomes than even an imperfect market without regulation. The market for electricity is a case in point.

Some existing regulations in the United States have the unintended effect of making the Nation's electricity supply less reliable and more expensive. The same attribute that makes competition in electricity difficult to achieve—provision of electricity over a single network on which the amount of electricity supplied must equal the amount of electricity consumed at every moment—makes the consequences of poorly designed regulation particularly costly. For example, California's rolling blackouts in January 2001 appear to have stemmed in part from regulations that fixed retail electric rates. As a result, there was an insufficient supply of electricity during the daily peak periods of demand. Fixed retail electric rates provided little incentive for consumers to reduce their consumption of electricity during these high-usage periods.

The Evolution of the Electric Industry from Local to Interstate Markets

As the electric industry has evolved from local, largely self-contained systems to a more national, integrated system, the appropriate combination of state and Federal regulations has changed as well. For many years, electricity was provided by integrated utilities—local monopolies that generated power and distributed it to residents and companies in a specific area—that were regulated by state public utility commissions.

Over time, a high-voltage transmission network linking the local monopolies developed. The network was originally designed to boost reliability, but it has also had the effect of reshaping the economics of the electricity market. The existence of this network (called the *transmission grid*) gave rise to a market for wholesale electricity through which utilities could buy electricity generated elsewhere for use by their own customers.

Regulatory changes complemented the technological and structural changes to make the electricity business more competitive. In 1978, new Federal regulations mandated by the Public Utilities Regulatory Policies Act (PURPA) required state-regulated utilities to buy power generated using renewable energy sources and cogeneration plants (plants that produce electricity while producing other products such as steam heating). These regulations led to an expansion of wholesale markets in which regulated utilities bought electricity generated by other firms and demonstrated that independent electricity generators could coexist with existing state-regulated utilities. In the late 1980s, Federal regulators began revising regulations to encourage the development of independent producers more generally. In 1996, Federal regulators began requiring the public utilities that owned transmission lines to make them available to independent electricity generators. Today, more than half of all the electricity generated is exchanged on the wholesale market before it is sold to consumers.

Electricity Regulation in an Evolving Market

Wholesale electricity generation will become more efficient over time as unregulated generating companies add new capacity based on competitive market signals. Market signals will influence both the timing of when new generation capacity is built and the type of fuel these plants will use. For fully regulated electric utilities, these decisions are made with the approval of local or state regulators. Without the discipline of competitive markets, regulated utilities are able to pass increased costs on to consumers regardless of whether the utilities have made the most efficient choices.

Effects of Regulation on Transmission Capacity

Regulations in the electricity market continue to impose barriers to competition and greater efficiency. Today's regulatory structure may not encourage regulators in one jurisdiction to take into account the full effects of their actions on the rest of the transmission grid because the regulatory system is based on an industry structure that no longer exists. For example, the transmission grid crosses state boundaries, so what happens in one state affects the residents of other states. However, state regulators might not consider the costs and benefits of their actions on citizens of other states. As a result, regulation of the transmission grid has not kept up with changes in the market.

Extensive blackouts in the Northeast and Midwest in August 2003 and in the West in August 1996 demonstrated the potential costs of not updating and coordinating Federal, state, and local regulations. Despite the growing demand for electricity and the growing demand for transmission capacity to satisfy the wholesale market, construction of new transmission facilities has declined by about 30 percent since 1990. The current mix of regulations has facilitated increased use of transmission capacity, but has not done enough to encourage companies to invest in building new capacity. For example, some state and local regulations have discouraged the construction of new local facilities, thus encouraging increased transmission from more distant locations.

State deregulation may also give local utilities the incentive to import lower cost electricity from generators in other states. The growth of interstate transmission of electricity has increased the need for Federal, state, and local governments to coordinate their regulations that affect the interstate transmission grid.

Another problem with existing regulation is that state and Federal regulators approve transmission rates to provide the owners of transmission lines a fixed rate of return, but the chosen rate may not be high enough to encourage firms to invest in sufficient new transmission capacity. One factor that is not fully considered in rate-of-return calculations is the lengthy and uncertain permitting process that requires companies to deal with multiple regulators. Because these costs are not fully accounted for, the effective rate of return often is too low to attract investment. Such regulatory uncertainties are just one of many factors that make investing in new transmission capacity risky. Higher rates of return may be needed to spur investment.

Insufficient investment in new transmission capacity is not the only problem stemming from improper regulation of rates of return. Such regulation may also prevent investment from being channeled to areas that most need new transmission capacity. Higher prices for use of the most congested parts of the grid would reduce transmission over these parts of the grid and send a signal to potential investors to expand capacity in those areas. Grid operators in some parts of the country now use locational marginal pricing to set prices in different locations based on both the cost of generation and the cost of congestion. Areas that are served by congested transmission lines pay higher prices reflecting the cost of such congestion.

Congestion in the transmission grid leads to both lower reliability and less competition. The lack of competition results from the low-cost generators' inability to send power to high-cost areas, forcing the high-cost areas to use less efficient, locally-produced electricity. Adding new transmission capacity between low-cost and high-cost areas could increase prices in low-cost areas in the short run. However, these price increases would likely lead to new generating capacity being built in low-cost areas, reducing prices back toward existing levels.

Regulations That Require Updating

As electricity markets have become more competitive, Federal regulations designed to prevent utilities from abusing their government-granted monopoly power may have ceased to serve the public interest. For example, the Public Utilities Holding Company Act (PUHCA) was originally passed in the 1930s to limit the size and type of operations in which a public utility may engage, including the types of companies that can own utilities. Today, these limits may actually increase prices to consumers by preventing utilities from engaging in activities that could make their businesses more efficient. These limits also may prevent public utilities from expanding their operations in ways that would increase competition in other parts of the country.

The evolution of the electric power industry from a natural monopoly to an increasingly competitive market calls for regulations that facilitate rather than hinder efficiency and innovation. The Federal Energy Regulatory Commission (FERC) is working on new regulations for wholesale electricity markets with the goal of having market forces encourage the lowest-cost generators to provide electricity.

Demand Response to Electricity Production Costs

Many residential electric rates today are fixed throughout the day at a level based on the average cost of generating and delivering electricity to the residential customer. The cost of producing electricity, however, is not fixed throughout the day. Instead, electricity generators constantly adjust production to meet demand hour by hour or even minute by minute. As a result, the marginal cost of electricity production—the cost to produce one extra unit of electricity—varies widely over the course of a day. Wholesale prices reflect this, with lower prices in the middle of the night (a period of low demand) and higher prices in late afternoon (a period of peak demand). Under the current regulatory structure, however, many consumers are charged the same rate regardless of the wholesale cost of electricity so that utilities cannot raise prices to reflect the true cost of generation. As a result, local regulated utilities must have access to enough generating capacity to meet peak demand, as well as enough transmission and distribution capacity to get the electricity to all customers. Chart 8-2 illustrates the fluctuations in electricity consumption and wholesale prices over a week in August 1999. During the week illustrated, the regulated utilities were at times forced to sell electricity at a loss because wholesale prices rose above the fixed retail rate.

It is not cost-effective to store large quantities of electricity. Therefore, the requirement that electric utilities meet all demand at fixed retail prices

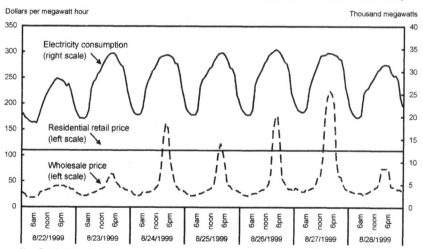

Chart 8-2 **Hourly Electricity Consumption, Wholesale Prices, and Retail Prices in California**
The volume and wholesale price of electricity consumed fluctuate throughout the day, while retail prices are fixed, so that residential consumers have no economic incentive to change their consumption as costs change.

Note: Residential retail price is the monthly average for August 1999.
Sources: California Energy Commission, California Power Exchange, and Department of Energy (Energy Information Admistration).

means that they must build enough capacity to meet the highest peak demand during the year. They also need to maintain reserve capacity to offset any supply lost due to generation or transmission problems. Some of this capacity is only required during the relatively few hours of the year when demand peaks, for example, on the hottest days in August.

Without the ability to increase retail prices during peak demand to encourage consumers to cut their energy consumption, insufficient generation capacity would lead to a rationing of supply, for example, rolling blackouts. While some electric utilities offer time-of-day pricing, a system in which retail rates are higher during periods of peak demand, these prices do not vary with the actual cost of generating electricity on a particular day. These programs reduce the average peak demand but do not provide the needed incentives to cut power usage on days with extreme peak demand.

Some consumers also receive lower rates in exchange for allowing the electric company to interrupt their service if wholesale costs increase above a certain level. There are some programs that allow the utility to cut off all of a consumer's power, while others simply allow the utility to turn off the consumer's air-conditioning. There are also typically limits on how long or how many times the utility can cut off power. These programs to reduce peak electricity usage thus represent only a partial implementation of variable pricing.

A reduction in peak demand achieved through variable pricing would allow regulated utilities to build less generation, transmission, and distribution infrastructure. Because they cannot increase retail prices, these utilities use other means to reduce peak demand, such as rebates to consumers who purchase energy-efficient appliances or incentives to improve weatherization of homes. While these programs reduce peak demand by increasing energy efficiency, they do not use the market to determine which ways of cutting electricity demand would have the lowest cost. Furthermore, as electricity markets evolve, there may no longer be one firm that can capture all of the benefits from reducing peak demand. As a result, these programs may not be able to continue because individual companies have less incentive to implement them.

Current programs that attempt to reduce peak demand still leave customers unaffected by changes in the cost of production until shortages and interruptions in service result. If retail prices were allowed to increase, consumers could decide to cut their consumption (possibly to zero). This approach could improve overall welfare by reducing the number of peaking plants needed; that is, it may be less costly to curtail demand than to add to supply by building expensive generation capacity that is rarely used. However, for variable pricing to be completely implemented, new meters and smart appliances may be needed so that consumers can acquire the information and technology needed to adjust their usage as electricity prices change.

Energy and Trade

The United States benefits greatly from global trade in energy markets. Gasoline and diesel fuels refined from crude oil are currently the most widely used transportation fuels. By importing petroleum, U.S. firms are able to continue to supply gasoline and diesel at real prices comparable to historical averages, even as environmental regulations have increased the costs of refining. Adjusted for inflation, gasoline prices are much lower than at their peak in 1981. However, this beneficial trade requires reliance on imports that could be subject to supply disruptions.

Because crude oil is traded throughout the world, its price is affected by global changes in supply and demand. Disruptions to the supply of oil from areas that do not supply the United States would affect domestic prices of oil even if U.S. imports are not directly affected. Indeed, domestic prices of oil would be affected even if the United States produced all of its oil domestically (unless petroleum exports were prohibited). The outcome is the same because the price of oil is set in global markets.

Meeting all U.S. energy needs from domestic sources would require significant changes to the U.S. economy, including changes in the types of transportation fuels used by Americans. The costs of these changes would probably exceed the costs resulting from periodic unexpected increases in the global price of oil. This is suggested by the fact that prior oil market disruptions did not lead to such structural changes in the U.S. economy. Moreover, oil markets have undergone tremendous changes since the 1970s that likely reduce the risks to the U.S. economy from a disruption in crude oil production and imports.

U.S. Energy Sources

Most energy consumed in the United States is produced in North America. In 2002, the main energy sources were petroleum (39 percent), natural gas (24 percent), coal (23 percent), and nuclear power (8 percent). In 2002, roughly 80 percent of U.S. energy needs were met by North American sources, including 59 percent of crude oil, 99 percent of natural gas, 100 percent of coal, and roughly 45 percent of uranium for nuclear power generation. Petroleum is the main energy source that the United States imports in significant amounts from outside North America. Hence, discussions of energy security focus on imports of crude oil. In the future, analysts expect the United States to import more natural gas, but there are many potential suppliers.

The United States also imports a large share of uranium from outside North America, but there are sufficient North American reserves of uranium that could be used if less-expensive foreign sources were not available. Furthermore, uranium fuel represents a relatively small portion of the cost of nuclear electricity generation. Also, most uranium is produced in stable parts of the world, with Canada and Australia producing about half of the world's total.

Changes in the Oil Market

A disruption in crude oil production in an area that does not supply the United States would still affect the United States by raising oil prices in the worldwide market. However, the power of the Organization of the Petroleum Exporting Countries (OPEC), or of any one country, to affect world oil prices is less today than it was in the past. OPEC's influence on the market has fallen with the decline of its market share from 55 percent in 1973 to 39 percent in 2002. Other evidence of the diversification of sources of crude oil is that in 1973, the top eight producing countries produced 75 percent of the world's oil, while in 2002 the top eight producing countries produced only 54 percent. Access to a greater number of sources of oil reduces the impact of a disruption in any one region on the world oil price. In addition, the increased sophistication of financial markets for oil and related products has made it easier to hedge oil price risks. With financial instruments such as futures contracts, firms are better able to avoid having potential disruptions in the crude oil market lead to substantial immediate cost increases from their energy inputs.

Another significant difference between today and the 1970s is that the United States no longer has price controls on gasoline and oil. During the oil shocks of the 1970s, Federal government mandates kept consumer prices artificially low and dampened the amount of gasoline conservation that otherwise would have occurred in response to increased prices. As a result, people wanted to consume more gasoline than suppliers were willing to supply at the artificially low price leading to shortages in the United States.

When prices are not regulated, large swings in oil prices do not disrupt the economy nearly as much. For example, between June 15, 1998, and November 27, 2000, the price of West Texas Intermediate (WTI) crude oil more than tripled from $11.69 to $36.24 per barrel without throwing the economy into disarray. These price increases did not cause major economic disruptions for two main reasons. First, energy consumption per 1996 dollar of real GDP has dropped 43 percent, from 18,360 British thermal units (BTU—a measure of the energy content in fuels) per dollar in 1973 to 10,450 BTU per dollar in 2001. Second, market signals have worked to increase the flexibility of U.S. energy markets, allowing them to adjust and adapt to market changes. This is why market forces work better to allocate goods than command-and-control measures such as price controls.

Another change from the 1970s has been the expansion of the strategic reserve of crude oil that can be used during severe disruptions to the oil market. Created in 1975, the Strategic Petroleum Reserve held 634.7 million barrels as of December 2003—enough oil to replace U.S. crude oil imports from the Persian Gulf for approximately 287 days. While maintaining the Strategic Petroleum Reserve entails storage and inventory costs, holding reserves to increase energy security is less likely to distort the market than other measures, such as attempting to replace U.S. oil imports with more expensive sources of energy.

Trade in Oil and Price Stability

In considering whether it is worth taking steps to decrease U.S. reliance on petroleum imports from outside North America, it is useful to compare the movement of oil prices with the prices of other commodities in which the United States is self-sufficient. It turns out that having a supply of a commodity in the United States or North America is not an assurance of stable prices. Numerous factors affect both the supply and the demand of goods so that commodities such as natural gas, wholesale electricity, and many agricultural goods also exhibit price volatility even when supplied wholly from North American sources.

Relying on imported oil reduces the United States' overall expenditures on energy. Without crude oil imports, the cost of gasoline and other petroleum products (or alternative transportation fuels) would be higher. Therefore, the United States would have to devote a greater portion of its resources to paying for the costs of energy, especially for transportation, than is the case today. Without petroleum imports, it would be necessary to use significantly less gasoline and more transportation fuels made from corn, soybeans, or other agricultural products, or liquid fuels from coal, natural gas, oil sands, or oil shale. Under current technologies, these substitutes all cost substantially more to produce than gasoline from crude oil.

The Evolution of Energy Markets

Energy sources have changed as society's needs have evolved over time. Wood was replaced by coal, which was replaced by petroleum. Eventually, the energy market may evolve to include substantial energy production from new sources, such as renewable energy, hydrogen, or nuclear fusion. Government policy can help move this evolutionary process forward by encouraging research in new energy technologies. However, forcing the transition to new technologies before the market signals that old technologies should begin to be phased out could involve tremendous costs to society.

Market signals have already altered U.S. energy consumption. In response to higher crude oil prices, U.S. crude consumption fell by 21 percent between 1978 and 1983 even as real GDP grew by 7.8 percent. Demand shifted towards coal, which experienced the smallest price increase of any major fuel, and away from oil and natural gas, which experienced the greatest increases. Even with the increased consumption of coal, total U.S. energy consumption declined 1.8 percent annually between 1978 and 1983. This decrease occurred despite the longer-term upward trend of energy consumption, which averaged 1.1 percent annually between 1971 and 2001. Energy conservation programs and other nonmarket forces may have been responsible for some of the reduced demand for energy. However, at least 80 percent (and probably more) of the demand reduction can be attributed to higher prices and overall changes in the economy.

Market signals have also triggered a great deal of innovation to lower the cost of finding and extracting oil. For example, three-dimensional seismic technologies have lowered the cost of finding oil, and directional drilling has lowered the cost of extracting oil so that reserves that were not viable in the past can be extracted profitably today. Similarly, technological advances have lowered the cost of extracting oil from oil sands so that production from oil sands is competitive at today's oil prices. As a result, at least one industry publication has classified a portion of Canada's large oil sand deposits as proved oil reserves; estimates of Canada's proved oil reserves are now second only to those of Saudi Arabia.

The technology exists to convert large North American reserves of oil sands, oil shale, natural gas, coal, wood, and agricultural products into liquid fuels such as gasoline, diesel, methanol, and ethanol. Some of these processes are now prohibitively expensive, but these fuels could compete with fuels produced from crude oil if oil prices increased or if research and development lowered their production costs. Chart 8-3 illustrates the range of estimated costs of producing synthetic fuels that could compete with oil in the market for liquid fuels. For example, at a price for oil of $20 a barrel, liquid fuels from oil sands and natural gas may be able to cover production costs, while oil shale, coal, ethanol, and biodiesel would not be viable sources. Higher prices could eventually make these alternatives commercially viable. Note that the extraction process for some of these fuels may have adverse environmental consequences that could limit their use and that some of these processes yield low-sulfur fuels that may burn more cleanly than fuels produced from crude oil. The chart does not consider either the costs of the externalities or the benefits of the cleaner fuels.

There is a role for government in subsidizing research and development into new energy sources. For example, hydrogen shows strong potential as a possible future fuel, though many technological hurdles must be overcome

Chart 8-3 **Production Costs and Reserves of Alternative Transportation Fuel Sources**
Synthetic fuels have the potential to become commercially viable if the price of oil increases sufficiently.
Energy reserves not traditionally used as a source of liquid fuels would become available at this point.

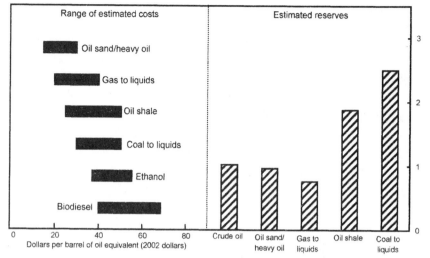

Note: Ethanol and biodiesel reserves are assumed to be infinite. Crude oil reserves are included for comparison.
Sources: Department of Agriculture, Department of Energy, and Council of Economic Advisers.

before it becomes practical for everyday use. Even if hydrogen became a feasible energy source, there would be still more problems to be resolved before the technology became economically competitive. Government subsidies for research and development may aid the private market in developing technology to produce, transport, and use hydrogen economically as a fuel. However, market forces should decide when commercial adoption of hydrogen as an energy source will be competitive.

Policy makers should avoid forcing commercialization of new energy sources before market signals indicate that a shift is required. One potential problem with forcing this process is that technological breakthroughs may lead to alternatives that are not seriously considered today. Premature adoption of new technologies would raise energy costs before the need arises, causing society as a whole to spend more on energy than needed, a misallocation of resources that would hurt the U.S. economy. For example, forcing adoption of energy sources other than oil to gain complete energy independence would be prohibitively expensive; it would require tremendous reductions in the use of energy derived from crude oil through the use of alternative energy sources that are far from competitive.

Conclusion

Regulations can improve the performance of energy markets by addressing market failures such as externalities and market power. However, it is essential to design regulations to address these potential market failures without reducing the benefits from markets. An added complication occurs when the goals of local and Federal regulators conflict. Regulators should adjust the rules as markets evolve and ensure that the regulations' goals are achieved. Finally, regulators should be careful not to adopt regulations that cause more harm than the potential market failure.

CHAPTER 9

Protecting the Environment

Economic growth and environmental improvements go hand-in-hand. Economic growth can lead to increased demand for environmental improvements and can provide the resources that make it possible to address environmental problems. Some policies aimed at promoting environmental improvements can entail substantial economic costs. Misguided policies might actually achieve less environmental progress than alternative policies for the same economic cost. It is therefore important to weigh the direct benefits of environmental regulations against their economic costs.

While the free-market system typically promotes efficiency and thus enhances economic growth, the absence of property rights for environmental "goods" such as clean air and water can lead to negative externalities that reduce societal well-being. This can be addressed by establishing and enforcing property rights that will lead the affected parties to negotiate mutually-beneficial outcomes in a market setting. If such negotiations are expensive, however, the government can design regulations that consider both the benefits of reducing the environmental externality as well as the costs the regulations impose on society. Regulations should be designed to achieve environmental goals at the lowest cost possible, thus helping to achieve environmental protection and continued economic growth.

The key points in this chapter are:

- Establishing and enforcing property rights for the environment can address environmentally-related market failures. Any needed regulations should consider both the benefits and the costs.
- Environmental risks should be evaluated using sound scientific methods to avoid possible distortions of regulatory priorities.
- Market-based regulations, such as the cap-and-trade programs promoted by the Administration to reduce common air pollutants, can achieve environmental goals at lower cost than inflexible command-and-control regulations.

The Free Market and the Environment

In a free-market system, only trades that benefit both parties will take place. Market prices coordinate the activities of buyers and sellers and convey information about the strength of consumer demand for a good, as well as how costly it is to supply. In the context of the environment, a market failure may occur if a voluntary transaction between parties imposes involuntary costs on a third party. These involuntary third-party costs are known as *negative externalities* (or *spillovers*), and their existence in a free market can lead to inefficient outcomes; that is, outcomes that fail to maximize the net benefits to society. For example, a plant might produce and sell a good to a consumer to both their advantage, but the production process may result in emissions of air pollutants that negatively affect others not involved in the transaction. The root of the market failure is that there are no clear property rights for the surrounding air. The interests of the third party—the people affected by the plant's emissions—are not represented in the market transaction.

If those affected by the plant's emissions had a right to demand compensation for the costs imposed on them by the pollution, then the firm would take these costs into account when making its production decisions. The plant would produce only up to the point where the benefit of another unit of production equals the additional cost of producing the good plus the cost to the people negatively affected by the pollution. Any additional emissions due to producing more goods would require compensation that is greater than the monetary gain the plant gets from selling the additional goods. Likewise, if the property right belonged to the plant, the people negatively affected by the emissions could compensate the plant for reduced emissions. Either way, all three parties (consumers, the firm, and those affected by the emissions) would transact voluntarily to everyone's benefit, resulting in an efficient outcome. If the government were to assign and enforce the property right, and if it were costless for parties to collectively agree on compensation, then an efficient use of resources would result from private bargaining, regardless of which party was assigned the property right. This insight is known as the *Coase theorem*.

The Role of Government in Regulating the Environment

The existence of property rights does not always guarantee an efficient outcome. If there are many sources of pollution or there are many parties affected by the emissions, then it might be difficult for the parties collectively to agree on the compensation, and an efficient outcome might therefore not be achieved. This presents an economic justification for government involvement and regulation. Government regulation might also be justified in order to address distributional concerns associated with environmental problems.

Regulations that address negative externalities can therefore improve societal welfare. To improve the environment while still promoting economic growth, sound policies must consider both the benefits and the costs of regulations. Economic growth itself can contribute to environmental improvements

(Box 9-1). As the economy grows, the demand for environmental improvements increases and the greater wealth provides more resources to better address environmental concerns. It is therefore important to weigh the direct environmental benefits of regulations against their economic costs.

Box 9-1: Economic Growth Can Improve the Environment

Much research has shown that economic growth contributes to environmental gains. In the early stages of economic development, environmental degradation may occur because nations place higher priority on basic needs such as food and shelter. As wealth increases, however, so does demand for a cleaner environment, and greater wealth provides more resources to better address these environmental concerns. After a certain level of national income is attained, the balance shifts and environmental degradation is arrested and then reversed. For several decades in the United States, many environmental indicators have been improving as the economy has also grown.

From 1975 to 2002, concentrations of five of the six common air pollutants (the pollutants for which there are reliable data) decreased by an average of 60 percent (Chart 9-1), as real gross domestic product (GDP) increased by about 130 percent, energy consumption increased by 35 percent, and the population increased by 34 percent. While the Nation's air quality has improved substantially since passage of the Clean Air Act of 1970, air quality was improving prior to 1970, perhaps due to market-induced technological advancements (such as improvements in energy efficiency) that accompany economic growth. The limited air-quality monitoring data available before 1970 indicate that average annual concentrations of particulate matter in urban air dropped 16 percent from 1957 to 1970 and these total suspended particulates (liquid or solid particles in the air) across the country fell by about six percent from 1958 to 1970 (Chart 9-2).

As the Nation's productive output has increased and environmental quality has improved, so too has the health and well-being of Americans. In the last century, life expectancy at birth increased from 48 to 80 years for women and from 46 to 74 years for men. Infant mortality dropped to the lowest level ever recorded in the United States. The death rates for heart disease, cancer, and stroke are also decreasing. This well-documented correlation between wealth and health extends across time and nations. More-developed countries have higher life expectancy, and globally, life expectancy has increased as per capita wealth has increased.

Chart 9-1 **National Concentrations of Air Pollutants**
Concentrations of five major air pollutants have been declining since 1975.

Index, 1975 = 100

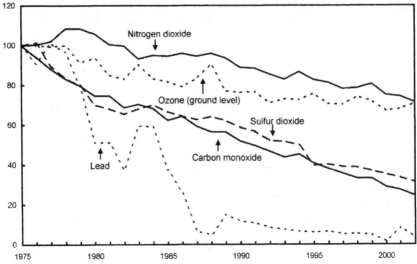

Note: The number of air monitors varies across pollutants and time.
Source: Environmental Protection Agency.

Chart 9-2 **Particulate Matter Concentrations**
While the data for monitoring airborne particulate matter have not been uniform, limited data indicate that particulate matter began declining steadily prior to passage of the Clean Air Act in 1970.

Micrograms per cubic meter

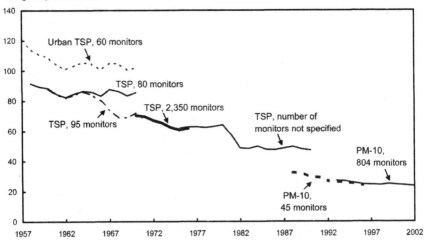

Note: TSP refers to total suspended particulates and PM-10 refers to particulates with diameter of 10 micrometers or less. The figures for monitors are the number that collected data for a particular series.
Sources: Environmental Protection Agency and Council on Environmental Quality.

Misplaced Reasons for Government Intervention

In making environmental policies, it must be recognized that government measures themselves might create further inefficiencies. When it is difficult to determine the extent of an environmental externality, an attempt to rectify it might end up making matters worse by imposing unintended costs on third parties without achieving an efficient outcome.

This inefficiency can arise even from well-intentioned environmental regulations. Two fallacious arguments are frequently used to justify inefficient regulations. One such misplaced rationale is that regulations improve the economy and spur job growth. The reasoning goes as follows: environmental regulations lead firms to install pollution-control technologies, which they must purchase from other firms. These technologies are built, delivered, installed, and operated by workers who otherwise would not be doing this work. Similarly, the regulations may promote environmentally-friendly industries that hire people who would not be hired otherwise. For these reasons, the regulations are said to "spur" the economy and job growth. By this reasoning, throwing a rock through a window also improves the economy, because it necessitates the hiring of someone to repair the window. What this ignores is that the resources spent to comply with an unnecessary or inefficient regulation are diverted from other uses. The money and people involved could have been used instead to produce more goods for consumers or to build new factories or machinery. The jobs associated with complying with environmental regulations are a cost of regulation, not a benefit.

Another misplaced view of environmental regulation is that the goal of regulations should be to eliminate or substantially reduce risks without considering costs. This approach is embodied in some well-intentioned laws. The 1970 Clean Air Act, for example, directs the Environmental Protection Agency (EPA) Administrator to set national ambient air quality standards (NAAQS) that achieve "an adequate margin of safety," and the Supreme Court has ruled that "the Clean Air Act…unambiguously bars cost considerations in the NAAQS setting process." Similarly, the stated goal of the Occupational Safety and Health Act of 1970 is "to assure so far as possible every working man and woman in the Nation safe and healthful working conditions," without considering the costs of doing so. While the goals of these laws are noble, they do not recognize the inevitable trade-offs involved. Not all environmental laws preclude cost considerations. For example, the Safe Drinking Water Act Amendments of 1996 explicitly acknowledge the importance of benefit-cost analysis when considering the appropriate level of regulation for contaminants in drinking water.

Regulations Impose Benefits and Costs

The failure to consider costs inhibits the goal of making regulations that maximize the difference between benefits and costs. Furthermore, the failure to consider costs can lead to a misallocation of resources, because a regulation that is made without considering costs might receive more resources than other regulations that warrant greater attention. While the benefits of many regulations include both health and non-health related benefits, many regulations primarily address fatality risks, and there is a wide range of cost per expected life saved across such regulations. For example, one survey of cost per life saved across regulations found that the regulation for childproof cigarette lighters costs approximately $100,000 per life saved (in 2003 dollars) whereas the formaldehyde regulation costs approximately $80 billion per life saved (in 2003 dollars). Shifting resources from regulations where the cost per expected life saved is high (for example, formaldehyde regulation) to regulations where it is low (for example, childproof lighter regulation) would result in more lives saved for the same cost to society. Many of the differences in cost per life saved occur because legislative mandates only sometimes allow agencies to consider costs when crafting regulations.

Stringent regulations may appear to be good for society because they save lives. However, because the Nation's ability to bear costs is limited, the wide range of costs per life saved across regulations implies that more lives could be saved at the same cost by shifting resources to the regulations with lower costs per expected life saved. One study found that society could save twice as many lives with the same budget if it designed regulations in a way that maximized lives saved. Some of the more costly health-based regulations might actually lead to a net increase in fatality risk because their high costs diminish the resources available for improving other health and environmental outcomes.

Using Science to Help Set Regulatory Priorities

Sound regulatory policy must be based on scientific assessments of environmental and health risks. Scientific assessments involve a careful examination of the risks involved and of the expected health outcomes for the people exposed to the risk at hand. This allows for an unbiased evaluation of environmental and health threats in which to target regulatory actions. Unfortunately, regulatory risk assessments at times overestimate some threats, or overemphasize risks to "hypothetical" (rather than real) people. These practices can lead to a distortion of regulatory priorities.

Overestimating the Risks: The Problem with "Cascading Conservatism"

In a well-intentioned attempt to be prudent, regulatory agencies sometimes rely on scientific assessments of environmental and health risks based on assumptions that overstate actual risks. When estimating chemical toxicity, for example, risk assessors have at times relied on high-end default assumptions that are likely to overestimate the actual risk of a chemical. Toxicity testing is evolving to use information that permits assessors to move away from assumptions that lead to overstated risks. When more data are available, regulatory risk assessors do not need to rely on high-end default assumptions and can instead attempt to estimate more accurately the expected level of risk. Because the EPA's primary goal is public health protection, however, it still relies on high-end default assumptions when there is uncertainty about scientific data.

Similarly, regulatory agencies sometimes use high-end estimates of the likelihood of people being exposed to a certain risk. These exposure estimates are then combined with toxicity estimates that are themselves likely to overstate risk. The multiplicative impact of combining several high-end component estimates is known as *cascading conservatism*. This practice can lead to risk estimates that greatly overstate the threat of environmental problems and thus overstate the benefits of regulating those risks. One study found that in a sample of hazardous waste sites, over 40 percent of the sites requiring cleanup under the Superfund program would shift into the discretionary cleanup range if not for the overestimation of risks resulting from cascading conservatism.

Such high-end risk estimates can lead to several types of problems. First, the practice overstates the risk of all environmental health problems relative to other types of hazards. This overstatement can cause too many resources to be allocated to addressing low-priority concerns. An example of such a distortion is the commonly-held view that synthetic chemical pollutants such as insecticides are a leading contributor to cancer. In reality, the evidence suggests that such chemicals account for a low percentage of human cancers. The main contributors to human cancer appear to be smoking and poor diet—each of which accounts for about one-third of cancers. The result is that regulatory efforts are directed at addressing the risks of synthetic chemicals that may well pose lower risks of causing cancer than many common natural chemicals.

A second problem with the high-end risk estimates caused by cascading conservatism is that they can distort the allocation of resources among different environmental health concerns. If each uncertain component that goes into a risk assessment overstates the risk, then the multiplicative impact of cascading conservatism will result in higher risk estimates for threats that have more uncertain components. For example, if there are two equally effective pesticides, with one posing a higher threat to the population than the other, the safer pesticide might be assessed as more of a threat if there are more uncertain components involved in its risk assessment. This assessment could result in the safer pesticide receiving stronger regulatory emphasis by the government. It is better to target regulatory dollars to the risks expected to be higher in a reasonable scenario or range of scenarios than to the risks that might be higher in a worst-case scenario.

Population-Weighted Risk Assessments

Regulatory efforts can also be distorted when risk assessments ignore the number of real people potentially exposed to an environmental risk. For example, an environmental hazard at one location might pose a greater risk to any person exposed to the hazard than an environmental hazard at a second location. However, if no one lives near the first location and many people live near the second location, the expected risk to society is higher at the second location.

The case of *United States* v. *Ottati & Goss* offers one example of such misplaced regulatory priorities. In this case, a company litigated for relief of an EPA-required cleanup that would have cost the company $9.3 million to remove small amounts of contaminants from a site that was already mostly decontaminated. The company had already spent $2.6 million to clean the site so that small children playing on the site could eat small amounts of dirt daily for 70 days each year for three and a half years without significant harm. The additional $9.3 million would be used to burn the soil, which would allow children to eat a small amount of dirt each day for 245 days per year without significant harm. However, there was little chance that children would ever be exposed to this site because it was located in a swamp. The courts ruled in favor of the private party and refused to enforce the proposed remediation goal.

Objective Versus Perceived Risk

Regulatory decisions should be based on scientific assessments of risks rather than perceived risks. This approach would help properly order priorities for regulatory decisions. Perceived risks often differ from expert assessments of risk because laypeople have difficulty assessing the frequency of low-probability events. Chart 9-3 compares survey respondents' perceived risks of dying from various hazards to the objectively measured risks of dying. In this chart, the dashed line represents where the perceived risk equals the actual risk; if all the points on the chart fell on this line, it would indicate that survey participants precisely estimated the risk of dying from various hazards. All points to the left of the dashed line represent hazards for which the

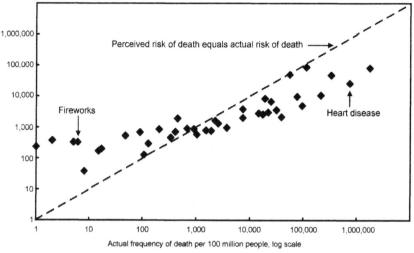

Chart 9-3 **Relationship Between Actual and Perceived Risk of Dying**
People tend to overestimate the risk of dying from low-fatality events and underestimate the risk of dying from high-fatality events.

Perceived frequency of death per 100 million people, log scale

Perceived risk of death equals actual risk of death ⟶

Fireworks

Heart disease

Actual frequency of death per 100 million people, log scale

Source: Sarah Lichtenstein, Paul Slovic, Baruch Fischhoff, Mark Layman, and Barbara Combs, "Judged Frequency of Lethal Events," *Journal of Experimental Psychology: Human Learning and Memory*, November 1978.

perceived risk of dying is higher than the actual risk, and all points to the right of the line indicate hazards for which people thought the risk of dying is lower than it actually is. The chart suggests that it is common to overestimate fatalities associated with low-probability events and to underestimate fatalities associated with high-probability events. These systematic misperceptions may lead to misplaced pressures to overregulate small environmental risks at the expense of addressing larger ones.

Achieving Goals Through Cost-Effective Regulations

As discussed in Chapter 7, *Government Regulation in a Free-Market Society*, when the assignment of property rights is insufficient to achieve an efficient outcome, government intervention may help achieve efficiency. Chapter 7 discusses government actions that can, in principle, achieve an efficient outcome by incorporating the costs of externalities into the market's price mechanism. It is important that any regulatory mechanism that addresses externalities do so in the least costly (that is, the most cost-effective) way so that society's scarce resources are not wasted. This section focuses on how to achieve air-quality goals cost effectively, but many of the lessons can be applied toward achieving other environmental goals, such as clean water protection and energy-efficiency standards.

Command-and-Control Regulations

Air-quality command-and-control regulations prescribe specific technologies that individual firms must use to control emissions, or they set specific emission rates for individual firms. The United States currently has many such environmental regulations. These regulations are inherently inflexible and are ill-suited to achieving emissions reductions in the least costly manner. While some command-and-control air-quality regulations may be just slightly more costly than cost-effective regulations, studies show that others are up to 22 times more expensive than the most cost-effective set of controls.

The reason command-and-control regulations are more expensive is straightforward: suppose the regulatory goal is to halve the emissions emanating from two firms. A command-and-control regulation might require each firm to cut its emissions by half. However, if it is less costly for one firm to reduce emissions, then—so long as the health effects of the emissions depend only on the total from the two emission sources—shifting the burden to the firm with lower abatement costs would result in the same environmental improvement at a lower cost. In general, the greater the differences across firms in their emissions before the regulation, and the greater the differences across firms in the rate at which each firm's costs rise with additional reductions, then the more costly a command-and-control approach is compared to more flexible approaches. Cost-effective emissions reduction is achieved when the cost of reducing an additional unit of emissions (the *marginal abatement cost*) is equal across all firms.

An example of an inflexible command-and-control regulation is the mechanism by which the Clean Air Act Amendments of 1990 address hazardous air pollutants (HAPs). The Act specifies that the emissions reduction standards for categories of existing HAP polluters must be set at "the average emission limitation achieved by the best performing 12 percent of the existing sources." While some flexibility is allowed in establishing the emission limitations, the command-and-control standard for regulating HAPs has frequently been interpreted in a way that ignores the differential costs of reducing emissions across existing sources within a category. This likely results in higher costs than would a more flexible regulation.

Command-and-control regulations also fail to provide market incentives for firms to explore less expensive means of reducing emissions. More flexible, incentive-based regulations would provide signals to the market of the increased demand for emissions reductions. With proper incentives in place, markets can respond to such an increase in demand with technological innovation and efficient reallocation of their scarce resources to achieve the goal.

Command-and-control regulations can also unintentionally lead to outcomes that are contrary to their environmental goals. An example of this is the New Source Review component of the 1977 Clean Air Act Amendments. This legislation required a strict control technology for most new industrial facilities and for facilities that undertook significant modifications, but it exempted existing facilities that did not make major modifications from the same standards. It was thought at the time to be more efficient to add new pollution control technology when plants were upgrading or when building new plants. This situation is known as *new source bias* because it provides an incentive for existing sources of emissions to continue their business operations for longer than would have been the case under normal market conditions without the regulation. It also provides an incentive for existing plants to forgo modifications.

New pollution-causing production sources tend to be cleaner than old ones even in the absence of regulations, so extending the business operations of older plants without making modifications could result in higher emissions. Applying different regulations for "routine" versus "major" modifications also leads to ambiguity, litigation delays, and uncertainty in business planning, all of which can harm the economy and may impede environmental improvements. The Administration recently addressed this problem by establishing clear rules that remove disincentives for facilities to modify and undertake routine maintenance, repair, and replacement activities that could improve the safety, reliability, and efficiency of the plants.

Market-Based Price Regulations: Emission Fees

Environmental regulations that provide firms with market-based incentives for emissions reduction avoid the complications of command-and-control regulations and achieve the same goals at lower costs. In particular, emission fees and cap-and-trade programs are usually less expensive than command-and-control approaches at achieving regulatory goals. An emission fee involves a charge to polluting sources for each unit of pollution emitted. Because each successive unit of emissions reduction typically involves increased costs, each source will reduce emissions until it would cost more to reduce the next unit of emissions than it would to pay the emissions fee. This results in equal marginal abatement costs across all affected firms.

With an emission fee, the total level of emissions reduction will depend on the per unit fee: a higher rate will achieve more emissions reduction. The emission fee also provides incentives to reduce emissions, because the better a firm is at reducing emissions, the lower the total fee the firm must pay. This sends a market signal that pollution has a price (equal to the emission fee), and any innovative means of reducing emissions will save firms from paying the fee. This market signal is likely more adept than the government at spurring technological innovation, adapting to changes in the economy, and shifting resources to reflect the increased demand for emissions reduction.

Market-Based Quantity Regulations: Cap-and-Trade

The main problem with an emission fee is that it is difficult to know beforehand what fee level will achieve the desired amount of pollution reduction. A cap-and-trade regulation addresses this issue and provides market incentives to reduce emissions in a cost-effective way. Such regulations "cap" the amount of allowable emissions and require that a firm own a permit for each unit of pollution emitted in a given period (for example, a year). This permit effectively establishes a legal property right for the air affected by the pollution, so that any emissions must be paid for by the firm. The government allocates the pollution permits to the emission sources and then allows the sources to buy and sell permits from each other.

Under a cap-and-trade system, a source with a high cost of reducing an additional unit of emissions would be willing to purchase a permit from a source with a lower marginal abatement cost. With a well-functioning market for the permits, sources will trade permits until the price for the permits equals the marginal abatement cost. As with the emission fee, the marginal abatement costs will be equal across sources, leading to a cost-effective result. The cap-and-trade system also provides an incentive to reduce emissions because each unit of emissions reduction saves the source the price of another permit. This regulation sends a market signal that there is a price for emissions and any innovative means of reducing emissions will save firms from paying the price. The cap-and-trade system therefore achieves the target level of pollution reduction at the lowest cost.

One consideration for a cap-and-trade system is how to allocate the permits initially. A cap-and-trade system that allocates the permits based on historic emissions or other firm characteristics, known as *grandfathering*, in essence gives away a valuable asset—the permits. A grandfathering system could establish a barrier to entry for new firms because any new entrant would have to purchase permits from existing firms.

One way to avoid these problems is to auction the permits at some regular interval to the highest bidders. Firms with higher marginal abatement costs would bid more for permits than those that can achieve less-costly emissions reductions. While auctioning the permits would result in lower profits for the regulated firms (compared to giving away the permits), it would not affect the firms' output decisions. Grandfathering versus auctioning the permits is primarily a question of distribution, not efficiency—it is a question of whether a public asset should be given to firms for free or sold as a means of generating public revenues.

A notable example of a cap-and-trade system is the sulfur dioxide (SO_2) trading program created under Title IV of the Clean Air Act Amendments of 1990. The program set a goal of reducing emissions by 10 million tons from the 1980 level by 2010. This was to be accomplished in two phases. The first phase, which began in 1995, initially capped the SO_2 emissions at 263 individual units which were owned by 110 electric utility power plants in 21 eastern and midwestern states. These plants, which were primarily coal-fired, emitted the greatest amounts of pollution among power plants in these regions. From 1995 to 2000, an additional 182 units were allowed into the program. The second phase, which began in 2000, further decreased the annual emissions of SO_2 and required all large fossil fuel-fired power plants in the contiguous 48 states and the District of Columbia to hold permits to cover their emissions.

In both phases, power plants could purchase permits from other power plants in order to meet their emissions coverage. The program also allowed plants to carry over (or *bank*) unused permits to use in later years, which gives firms even greater flexibility in achieving long-term pollution reduction. In contrast to a command-and-control system, this cap-and-trade system allows plants that find it costly to reduce their SO_2 emissions to purchase credits from plants that can reduce SO_2 at lower cost.

Evidence indicates that such cost-saving trades did indeed take place as firms took advantage of the system's inherent flexibility (Chart 9-4). Each bar in the following chart represents the emissions rate each plant achieved after trading permits in 1997. The superimposed line in the figure shows the level of emissions each plant would have had to achieve in the absence of trading. Bars below the line indicate plants that reduced their emissions by more than the required amount and sold their excess permits or banked them. Bars above the line indicate plants that purchased permits or used previously banked permits to avoid costly abatement. The figure shows that almost every plant took advantage of the flexibility of the system, suggesting that plant-level costs of reducing SO_2 emissions vary greatly.

The trading program has achieved its pollution-reduction goals at great cost savings. By the end of the first phase, emission reductions were almost 30 percent below the required level. The flexibility of this approach has been estimated to provide cost savings of approximately $0.9 billion to $1.8 billion a year compared to costs under a command-and-control regulatory alternative; other tradable-permit markets have had significant cost savings as well (Table 9-1).

Chart 9-4 **Unit-Level Sulfur Dioxide Emissions Trading in 1997**
Variation in actual plant-level emissions for units in the Acid Rain Program indicates that firms took advantage of the flexibility and cost-savings inherent in the cap-and-trade system.

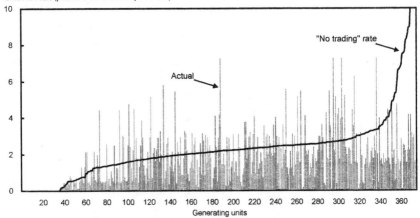

Note: Corresponding graphs for other years of the program show similar patterns.
Sources: Richard Schmalensee, Paul L. Joskow, A. Denny Ellerman, Juan Pablo Montero, and Elizabeth M. Bailey, "An Interim Evaluation of Sulfur Dioxide Emissions Trading," *Journal of Economic Perspectives*, Summer 1998. Update from personal communication between A. Denny Ellerman, Massachusetts Institute of Technology, and the Council of Economic Advisers.

TABLE 9-1.— *Cost Savings of Tradable-Permit Systems*

Program	Traded commodity	Years of operation	Cost savings (2003 dollars[1])
Emissions trading program	Criteria air pollutants	1974-present	Total, $1-$12 billion
Lead phasedown	Rights for lead in gasoline	1985-1987	Total, $400 million
Acid rain reduction	SO$_2$ emission reduction credits	1995-present	Annual, $0.9-$1.8 billion

[1] Base year for values for emissions trading program not specified.

Sources: Robert W. Hahn, "Economic Prescriptions for Environmental Problems: How the Patient Followed the Doctor's Orders," *Journal of Economic Perspectives*, Spring 2000; Curtis Carlson, Dallas Burtraw, Maureen Cropper, and Karen L. Palmer, "Sulfur Dioxide Control by Electric Utilities: What Are the Gains from Trade?" *Journal of Political Economy*, December 2000; and Environmental Protection Agency.

Emission Fees Versus Cap-and-Trade

As mentioned previously, one problem with emission fees is that it is difficult to know beforehand at what level to set the fee to achieve the desired pollution reduction. This might require periodic adjustments of the fee level, and such adjustments would introduce uncertainty that could interfere with firms' planning decisions. The emissions fee does, however, allow the government to set with certainty the marginal cost of emissions reduction. For each emission fee there is a corresponding allocation of permits that would achieve the same results; however, it is difficult to know beforehand what the market price for permits will be once trading actually takes place.

One way to reconcile these issues is to offer a cap-and-trade system with a *safety valve*. The safety valve sets a maximum price for a permit, which guarantees that the price of reducing emissions does not exceed the expected benefits. The regulatory agency issues and sells extra permits on request from any firm at this fixed safety valve price, thus guaranteeing that the market permit price does not exceed this level. A cap-and-trade program with a safety valve achieves the target level of emission reductions in a cost-effective manner, while protecting the regulated firms against unexpected short-term price increases in emissions reduction.

The President's Cap-and-Trade Program

An example of a well-designed incentive-based regulatory approach is the President's Clear Skies proposal for reducing emissions of sulfur dioxide, nitrogen oxides, and mercury from electric utility generators by approximately 70 percent by 2018. Clear Skies would cost-effectively reduce emissions by establishing a cap-and-trade system for each of the three pollutants. The EPA has estimated the benefits of the Clear Skies Act at $113 billion annually by 2020, compared with $6 billion in projected annual costs. These include $110 billion in annual health benefits (including the prevention of 14,100 premature deaths and 30,000 hospitalizations and emergency room visits) and $3 billion in annual benefits from increased visibility at national parks. Under the existing Clean Air Act, the EPA issues national air-quality standards for certain pollutants, including particulate matter and ozone. The EPA projects that compared with existing programs, the Clear Skies Act would lead 35 additional eastern U.S. counties to meet the particulate matter standard by 2020, leaving only eight counties not meeting the standard. The EPA expects that the remaining counties not meeting the standards would move closer to achieving them due to the Clear Skies Act.

To mitigate the effects of market shocks that potentially affect the costs of emissions reduction, Clear Skies would establish a safety valve price for permits of each pollutant. It would also provide regulatory certainty by achieving the reductions of all three pollutants in two phases. Firms would therefore plan their reductions of the three pollutants together and over the long term. Indeed, because the Clear Skies plan allows the banking of permits for future use, it provides an incentive for firms to achieve reductions quickly. Additionally, Clear Skies would provide revenue for the government because it phases in an auction system for the permits.

Clear Skies demonstrates the lessons learned from past regulatory experiences: instead of imposing an inflexible, command-and-control regulation to achieve emissions reduction, it offers a market-based, cost-effective, cap-and-trade program to achieve large reductions in emissions from electric utility generators.

Conclusion

Economic growth and environmental improvements are at times incorrectly seen as competing aims. Increased economic production can indeed lead to greater environmental degradation. However, an increase in economic resources provides more options (most notably, technological advancements) for addressing environmental problems. Moreover, a growing economy can also lead to increased demand for environmental improvements. It is therefore important to weigh the direct environmental benefits of a regulation against its economic costs. The goal should be to maximize the net benefits to society, while also giving due consideration to distributional issues. Maximizing net benefits is best achieved in a free-market setting unless there are spillover costs to third parties.

Spillover costs are best addressed by establishing property rights that will lead the affected parties to negotiate a mutually-beneficial outcome. If the costs of such negotiations are prohibitive, however, government should respond carefully and always keep in mind the possible government spillover costs. To make effective regulations, the government must first assess the environmental problems using sound, unbiased estimates of the hazards and then craft incentive-based regulations to address them. Such regulations can address the spillover costs of environmental problems at lower costs to society than the traditional command-and-control regulatory methods. These principles, and the lessons learned from our past regulatory experiences, as described throughout this chapter, should guide our future regulatory endeavors to achieve environmental improvements coupled with economic growth and efficiency.

CHAPTER 10

Health Care and Insurance

The breadth and pace of innovation and change in the provision of health care in the United States over the past few decades have been no less than astounding. Technological progress in the form of new medical knowledge, medicines, treatments, and medical devices has allowed Americans and people worldwide to live longer, healthier lives.

As new treatment options become available, it is not surprising that the United States and other major industrialized countries continue to shift more resources to health care. Research suggests that between 50 and 75 percent of the growth rate in health expenditures in the United States is attributable to technological progress in health care goods and services. However, the increase in resources devoted to health care has led to concern about its affordability, both for families worried about tight budgets and for the Nation as a whole. A strong reliance on market mechanisms will ensure that incentives for innovation are maintained while providing high-quality care in the most cost-efficient manner. Americans should have more choices, more information, and more control over their health care decisions.

Health insurance plays a central role in the workings of the U.S. health care market. An understanding of the strengths and weaknesses of health insurance as a payment mechanism for health care is essential to the design of reforms that retain incentives for innovation while reining in unnecessary expenditures.

This chapter discusses the roles of innovation, insurance, and reform in the health care market. The key points in this chapter are:

- U.S. markets provide incentives to develop innovative health care products and services that benefit both Americans and the global community.
- Over reliance on health insurance as a payment mechanism leads to an inefficient use of resources in providing and utilizing health care.
- Reforms should provide consumers and health care providers with more flexibility and information.

The U.S. Health Care System as an Engine of Innovation

Innovation and new technology have changed the practice of medicine over the past few decades. Diagnostic tools such as magnetic resonance imaging and computed tomography scanning have made it possible for doctors to see otherwise invisible problems. Innovations such as balloon angioplasty treat conditions that previously required extensive surgery. Minimally invasive surgical techniques such as arthroscopy provide treatment options that lead to shorter hospital stays and faster recoveries. Restorative surgeries such as hip and knee replacements are now commonplace and provide patients with improved mobility and thus improved quality of life. New pharmaceuticals treat conditions that were previously intractable or help to avoid more costly surgeries and lengthy hospital stays. The list of advances is long and impressive.

The Value of Health Care Innovation

Innovation in health care goods and services, including advances in scientific knowledge that have changed many people's day-to-day behavior, has markedly improved the lives of Americans. Life expectancy at birth in the United States increased from 68.2 years in 1950 to 77.2 years in 2001. Medical advances have also increased the quality of life through innovations that improve mobility, sight, and hearing.

Some might argue that these advances are not unique to the United States and that Americans spend too much for health care relative to other countries. The United States expends a higher fraction of GDP on health care than does any other industrialized country. According to an international comparison released in 2003, the United States spent 13.9 percent of GDP on health care in 2001, while the average among industrialized countries was 8.4 percent of GDP. Measures of health outcomes such as longevity and infant mortality, however, are not markedly different in the United States than in other advanced economies that spend substantially less on health care.

The argument that the U.S. health care system is overly costly relative to other countries implicitly assumes that if two countries spend different amounts for health care and get the same health outcomes, then the higher-spending country must be inefficient and wasteful. This argument is not correct in the case of health care for two reasons that are related to the leading role of the United States as a source of research and innovation.

First, in general terms, while all countries can benefit from research and development expenditures made by a single country, only the health expenditures in the innovating country will include the costs of research and development. Health expenditures in non-innovating countries will exclude the research and development costs.

Second, free markets incorporate incentives for innovation that generate products, services, and knowledge that potentially benefit all countries. Markets naturally encourage and reward innovation. Unfettered by government price controls or access restrictions, innovative products, talented health care practitioners, and skilled health care professionals are rewarded in the marketplace. This leads to technological advances by encouraging talented people to participate in the health care industry and by increasing investment in new products and research. The financial rewards for innovation will be reflected in U.S. health expenditures through a combination of higher prices and wages, and higher usage than in other countries. Once a product or service is developed through the combination of talent and capital, however, it becomes available for use outside the United States. Countries in which government regulation has supplanted market forces will still have the opportunity to take advantage of U.S. innovation without having to pay as much for it.

As an illustration of how U.S. health expenditures reflect the incentives for innovation, consider products such as medical devices and pharmaceuticals. The patent system exists to encourage innovation for these types of products. The innovator's incentive in a patent-based system is the opportunity to hold a monopoly on a product for a limited period of time. Therefore, the innovator can temporarily charge a higher price and earn more profits than he would without patent protection. The higher consumer expenditures that can result from monopoly pricing will be reflected in health care expenditures.

Once the patent system has led to the development of a product, it is available for use throughout the world, not just in the United States. This leads to an opportunity for other countries with centralized health agencies to negotiate a price close to production costs, thereby paying lower prices than they would in a free market that fully respected patent rights. What this implies is that other countries can reap the benefits of U.S. innovations in health care goods and services but pay only a fraction of the costs. It follows that if the United States attempted to reduce health expenditures by adopting cost-control policies found in other countries, innovation would slow and both Americans and citizens of other countries would be affected.

U.S. Leadership in Health Care Technology

Several pieces of evidence point toward the preeminence of the United States in providing health care technology. First, since 1975, the Nobel Prize in medicine or physiology has been awarded to more Americans than to researchers in all other countries combined. Second, according to data collected through 1993, 15 of the 19 marketed "biotech" drugs used for nondiagnostic purposes were the product of U.S. companies alone. U.S. companies shared credit with companies from other countries for two more of the 19 drugs. As of 2002, eight of the world's ten top-selling drugs were produced by companies headquartered in the United States.

A third example of U.S. leadership is that many important medical innovations in the past 30 years arguably originated in the United States. This evidence is based on a survey designed to determine the relative importance of a variety of medical innovations developed over approximately the last 30 years. Starting with a review of the medical literature, researchers compiled a list of 30 major medical innovations and then surveyed over 300 leading general internists in the United States concerning the relative importance to their patients of the innovations. Based on the survey, researchers ranked the innovations in order of importance. The first and second columns of Table 10-1 reflect the results for the top ten innovations.

The table also includes countries of origin, a category that was not included in the original research. Assignment of country was based on the

TABLE 10-1.— *Important Medical Innovations and Associated Country of Origin*

Rank	Technology	Description	Country of Origin
1	Magnetic resonance imaging (MRI); Computed tomography (CT)	Noninvasive methods to view internal workings of the body	United States, United Kingdom; United States, United Kingdom
2	Angiotensin converting enzyme (ACE) inhibitors	Drugs to treat hypertension and heart failure	United States
3.	Balloon angioplasty	Minimally invasive surgery to treat blocked arteries	Switzerland
4	Statins	Cholesterol-reducing drugs	United States, Japan
5	Mammography	Diagnostic tool to detect breast cancer	Indeterminate
6	Coronary artery bypass graft (CABG) surgery	Surgery for heart failure	United States
7	Proton pump inhibitors (PPIs); H2-receptor antagonists	Antiulcer drugs	Sweden; United States
8	Selective serotonin re-uptake inhibitors (SSRIs)	Antidepressant drugs	United States
9	Cataract extraction and lens implants	Eye surgery	United States
10	Hip replacement; Knee replacement	Joint replacement with mechanical prosthesis	United Kingdom; Japan, United Kingdom, United States

Sources: Victor R. Fuchs and Harold C. Sox Jr., "Physicians' Views of the Relative Importance of Thirty Medical Innovations," *Health Affairs*, September/October 2001. Descriptions and countries of origin from various sources.

location where the first clinically viable form of the innovation was developed or produced, or where research important to its creation occurred. The United States dominates this chart as the innovating country for these important medical developments. Of the ten, eight include the United States as a key country. The United Kingdom and Japan, the next closest sources, are associated with just two of the innovations each.

Table 10-1 should not be misinterpreted. Scientific advances by their nature are evolutionary, with recent advances building upon prior discoveries. The process of identifying a single person or team for progress that relies upon previous work is necessarily subjective. Nevertheless, such judgments are regularly made in selecting awards such as the Nobel Prize. But even taking into account the unavoidable limitations of such a list, it does suggest a dominant role for the United States in the development of new and useful medical technologies.

Box 10-1: Price Regulation and the Introduction of New Drugs

A recent study suggests that pharmaceutical firms tend to avoid or delay introducing new drugs in countries with price controls. In the study, which includes data from 25 countries on 85 new chemical entities introduced in the United States or the United Kingdom between 1994 and 1998, the three countries that did not require price approval before launch (the United States, Germany, and the United Kingdom) introduced the most new drugs. Analysis controlling for per capita income and other country and firm characteristics shows that countries with lower expected prices or smaller expected market size have fewer launches and longer launch delays. In the European Union, where drugs can be approved through a centralized procedure for use in the entire region, countries with price controls still experience significant launch delays.

According to the study, the connection between price controls and delayed access to drugs lies in the tendency for price controls to "spill over" from one country to another. Firms have an incentive to avoid or delay launching drugs in markets with price controls if they fear that the low prices will "spill over" to other markets. There are two main mechanisms by which price controls in one country can affect pharmaceutical profits in another: parallel trade and external referencing. With *parallel trade*, one country can take advantage of regulated low prices in another country through trade. With *external referencing*, countries can incorporate external price controls into domestic prices through price-setting formulas that depend on prices in other countries. Overall, the study suggests that there is a tradeoff between low prices and rapid access to new drugs.

Insurance Reform as a Means of Providing Health Care More Efficiently

While the U.S. health care market provides excellent incentives for innovation, there are legitimate concerns about cost. Rising health expenditures for families and firms can lead to difficult decisions over how best to allocate limited budgets. Pressure on government budgets continues to increase due to major health care programs such as Medicare (health insurance primarily for the elderly) and Medicaid (health insurance primarily for the poor). Physicians and hospitals struggle with government regulations, rising liability costs, and growing administrative burdens. To craft adequate responses to such challenges, it is important to understand the economic forces at work.

Technological progress in health care has been very beneficial, but it has led to growth in health care expenditures as the new technology has been applied to increase the length and to improve the quality of life. Research suggests that between 50 and 75 percent of the growth rate in health expenditures in the United States is attributable to technological progress in health care goods and services. Potential sources of the remaining 25 to 50 percent of the growth rate include: higher demand for health care due to increasing incomes and the aging of the U.S. population; the increased practice of "defensive medicine" (that is, medical procedures with limited therapeutic value that are performed by physicians to avoid lawsuits); and increased use of health insurance plans as a payment mechanism for health care.

There are various ways to reduce health care costs. Reducing the incentive to practice defensive medicine has the potential to lower the level of health care costs and is therefore an important objective. Modifying the health insurance system offers an especially attractive target for cost-saving reform because it would affect both the level and the growth rate of health expenditures. Reforms could be targeted to reduce administrative costs and the incentive to overuse health insurance as a payment mechanism. Understanding the strengths and the weaknesses of the health insurance system is central to developing policies that will lead to more cost-effective health care and to greater access to health care for those underserved by the current market.

The Appropriate Use of Insurance

Insurance is an indispensable tool in modern economies. Individuals insure automobiles against the possibility of an accident and homes against the possibility of a fire. Life insurance provides financial security to loved ones in case of an untimely demise. In each of these examples, the basic principle is the same: for a fee—the insurance premium—the insurer promises that some financial benefit will be forthcoming if a well-defined event takes place such as a car accident, a house fire, or a death.

Insurance is a valuable economic commodity. By giving up some income in the form of a premium, a consumer can avoid the large decline in wealth associated with an unfortunate event. Even if the event does not occur, a consumer benefits from the reduced uncertainty provided by insurance. Insurance is generally not needed when there is little uncertainty or when financial risks are small. For example, insurance policies usually do not pay for items such as groceries, clothing, or gasoline, although it would certainly be possible to create such policies. Suppose, for example, that an individual could purchase a clothing insurance policy with a "coinsurance" rate of 20 percent, meaning that after paying the insurance premium, the holder of the insurance policy would have to pay only 20 cents on the dollar for all clothing purchases. An individual with such a policy would be expected to spend substantially more on clothes—due to larger quantity and higher quality purchases—with the 80 percent discount than he would at the full price. However, the insurance company would need to charge a high premium to cover expenses. The premium would need to cover the 80 percent discount on the clothing that the individual would have bought had he or she been paying full price. Additionally, the premium would need to cover the insurer's expense for clothes purchased because the individual buys clothes as if they cost only 20 cents on the dollar. Few individuals would find such an expensive policy cost-effective.

Moral Hazard

The clothing insurance example suggests an inherent inefficiency in the use of insurance to pay for things that have little intrinsic risk or uncertainty. It also illustrates the broader problem in insurance markets known as moral hazard. *Moral hazard* refers to the idea that policy holders will make different choices when they are covered by an insurance policy than when they are not, but the insurer cannot fully monitor or restrict their actions. In the clothing example, moral hazard results in insured individuals spending more on clothing than they would without insurance.

Optimal insurance contracts must balance the value that consumers place on reducing their exposure to risk against the inefficiency arising from moral hazard. In the absence of uncertainty, insurance is wasteful because moral hazard will lead to excessive use and there is no benefit to the consumer from risk-reduction. Inefficient use of insurance will be reflected in an unnecessarily high cost for insurance. Standard features of insurance contracts such as coinsurance rates, copayments, and deductibles are attempts to mitigate the moral hazard problem. Even so, inefficiencies of this sort are pervasive in the U.S. health care system.

Adverse Selection

Another issue that arises in discussions of insurance markets is adverse selection. *Adverse selection* occurs when an insurance policy attracts certain types of people, and the insurer cannot identify these people before they enroll. If the premium is based on the average individual, but the policy disproportionately attracts those who spend more than the average person (in the clothing example, individuals with particularly expensive tastes in clothes), the policy will lose money for the insurer. The policy will then either increase in price or not last in the marketplace.

Adverse selection illustrates a problem that exists when the consumer knows more about his or her characteristics than the insurer. As a result there is a market inefficiency where, in the extreme, some consumers do not purchase insurance because the only policy available to them is priced for the most expensive consumers. If insurers could distinguish among different types of consumers, policies could be tailored to specific types and priced accordingly. With better information, an efficiently functioning insurance market would be able to provide insurance in a way that would maximize individual consumer welfare.

Health Insurance in the United States

Health insurance in the United States has several unique features. First, the employer portion of premiums for employer-provided health insurance is generally exempt from income and payroll taxes. The employee portion of premiums is similarly tax-exempt for the roughly one-half of workers covered by tax-advantaged health plans. This leads to the second, and unsurprising, feature, which is that most health insurance is provided through employers. Over 60 percent of all individuals in the United States have employer-provided health insurance. The central role of employer provision makes health insurance very different from other types of insurance, such as fire and car insurance.

Third, health insurance policies in the United States also tend to cover many events that have little uncertainty, such as routine dental care, annual medical exams, and vaccinations. For these types of predictable expenses, health insurance is more like prepaid preventative care than true insurance. If automobile insurance were structured like the typical health policy, it would cover annual maintenance, tire replacement, and possibly even car washes.

Fourth, health insurance tends to cover relatively low-expense items, such as an office visit to the doctor for a sore throat. Although often unforeseeable, this expense would not have a major financial impact on most people. To continue the analogy, it would be similar to car insurance covering relatively small expenses such as replacing worn brakes.

Box 10-2: Who are the Uninsured?

The U.S. Census Bureau estimates that in 2002, 242.4 million people in the United States had health insurance for the entire year, while the remaining 43.6 million people were uninsured. Uninsurance persists in the face of public programs such as Medicare, Medicaid, and the State Children's Health Insurance Program. In general, these programs provide health insurance to the elderly, the very poor, and the children of the moderately poor, respectively.

The uninsured are a diverse and perpetually changing group. The Congressional Budget Office claims that due to sampling techniques, the U.S. Census Bureau estimate of 43.6 million (15.2 percent of the population) more closely represents the number of people who are uninsured at a point in time than the number of people who are uninsured for an entire year. Just under half of all new spells of uninsurance end within four months. The number of people who were uninsured for all of 1998 (the most recent year for which comparative survey data are available) is estimated to have been 21 million to 31 million (7.6 to 11.2 percent of the population).

Some individuals included in survey-based counts of the uninsured may in fact have access to public coverage. For instance, the number of people who report having Medicaid is smaller than the number determined to be enrolled based on the program's administrative data. The reasons for this discrepancy are not well understood. People might fail to report this coverage because of a possible stigma associated with being on Medicaid or because the survey questions are confusing. In addition, some individuals who are uninsured are eligible for Medicaid but have not enrolled. These people are counted as uninsured in surveys, but they are effectively insured because they can enroll in Medicaid should they require medical treatment.

Others who lack insurance coverage possess economic or demographic characteristics that suggest many of them may remain uninsured as a matter of choice. For example, some have levels of household income that are above the median for the population. Over 32 percent of uninsured individuals report a household income of $50,000 or more. Others have access to employer-provided coverage but do not opt to participate. Researchers believe that as many as one-quarter of those without health insurance had coverage available through an employer but declined the coverage. Still others may remain uninsured because they are young and healthy and do not see the need for insurance. In fact, more than two-fifths of uninsured individuals are between the ages of 18 and 34.

A Brief History of Health Insurance in the United States

The historical background of health insurance coverage in the United States helps explain why health insurance is different from other types of insurance. In the early twentieth century, health insurance tended to cover wage loss rather than payment for medical services. This insurance is comparable to present-day disability insurance or workers' compensation. Limited health care coverage reflected the small number of options available to the medical profession for improving health—there were few costly treatments to insure against.

The first modern health insurance policy appears to have been started in 1929 when a group of teachers contracted with Baylor University Hospital. For an annual premium of $6, the policy guaranteed up to three weeks of hospital coverage. Providing insurance through employers, rather than to individuals, lowered administrative costs for insurers. It also mitigated the problems from adverse selection because the insured group was formed without regard to health status.

Employer-based coverage was encouraged by legal provisions during World War II that allowed employers to compete for employees by offering health benefits during a period of wage and price controls. Separately, a 1943 administrative tax court ruled that some employers' payments for group medical coverage on behalf of employees were not taxable as employee income.

A consequence of exempting premiums paid on employer-provided insurance is that tax receipts to the Federal government are lower than they otherwise would be. It has been estimated that Federal tax receipts in 2001 were about $120 billion lower as a result of the tax exemption. Research suggests that the tax preference for insurance induces people to buy more expansive health insurance—for example, people buy policies that cover a broad array of health services—and policies that have low deductibles and low coinsurance rates, which lead to the associated inefficiencies from moral hazard.

To summarize, health insurance markets can be improved in at least three ways. The first is to encourage contracts that focus on large expenditures that are truly the result of unforeseen circumstances. The second is to strengthen health insurance markets outside the traditional employer-based group markets. The third is to provide a more standardized tax treatment of all health care expenditures.

Proposals for Modernizing the Health Care Market

Health insurance reforms have the potential to increase the cost-effectiveness of health care markets without sacrificing the incentives that are essential to continued innovation. Reforms that lead to more direct interaction between consumers and health care providers, relying less on third-party payers such as insurance companies, have the potential to increase the efficiency and therefore the cost-effectiveness of health care markets. Coupled with changes that provide consumers with more flexibility and more information, such reforms would continue to provide the market signals important for developing new and useful health care innovations. The President has proposed several reforms that promise to move the Nation in the direction of achieving these goals. Taken together, these reforms will help preserve the innovative strengths that have proven so valuable to Americans and will improve the efficiency of the U.S. health care system.

Medicare Prescription Drug, Improvement, and Modernization Act of 2003

The Medicare Prescription Drug, Improvement, and Modernization Act of 2003, enacted in December, adds a prescription drug benefit to the Medicare program. The new drug benefit will give more Medicare beneficiaries access to prescription drug coverage and will provide benefits for individuals with limited means and low incomes. A prescription drug discount card will be available for beneficiaries until the full drug benefit is available nationwide.

The Act also establishes another key element of the President's health care agenda, Health Savings Accounts (HSAs). With an HSA, individuals and their employers may contribute pretax dollars to fund an account that can then be used to pay for medical expenses. Once established, this money belongs to the individual and can accumulate over time. The account remains with the individual if he or she changes employers. With such accounts, there is an increased incentive to purchase insurance that only covers events that are truly random and large, and to pay for other expenses using an HSA. Indeed, the law requires that such accounts be coupled with a high-deductible insurance plan.

With less reliance on insurance for routine health expenses, consumers would place a greater value on information about health care options and providers. More prudent use of insurance would also reduce "middle-man" costs of involving an insurance company in what could otherwise be a simple transaction between the patient and the caregiver.

Next Steps in Improving Health Care Markets

The passage of the Medicare bill was a major accomplishment, but much remains to be done. A number of proposals on the President's agenda for health care reform would lead to improvements in the health care market.

Association Health Plans (AHPs)

The AHP proposal enables small businesses and associations to purchase health insurance for employees and their families. These plans offer small businesses and self-employed individuals the potential for lower health insurance premiums resulting from decreased administrative costs and increased bargaining power with insurers and medical providers.

New Tax Deduction for Health Insurance Premiums

The President has proposed a new tax deduction for health insurance premiums. Individuals who purchase a high-deductible insurance policy coupled with an HSA would be able to deduct the value of the insurance premium from their income taxes even if they do not itemize their deductions. This would encourage the use of high-deductible insurance by providing a tax benefit similar to that given to employer-provided insurance.

Refundable Health Credit

Many workers do not have the option to obtain insurance through their employment. The President has proposed a refundable health credit that could be used to purchase insurance. This credit will help expand health care access for low- and middle-income workers who do not have good employer-based coverage options.

Reducing the Cost of Medical Care Through Liability Reform

Malpractice premiums are a significant cost for physicians and hospitals. The President has proposed the national adoption of standards to make the medical liability system more fair, predictable, and timely. Adoption of these proposals would lower the cost of providing health care (see the discussion of this subject in Chapter 11, *The Tort System*). Similarly, fear of litigation keeps health care providers from sharing vital information on quality problems and medical errors. The President has called for legislation to allay these fears and make it possible for health professionals to share information to reduce errors and complications.

Improving Efficiency Through the Use of Health Information Technology

The use of information technology in health care holds the promise of reducing medical errors, facilitating communication between care providers and patients, and reducing administrative costs. Computerized physician order entry, a type of technology that allows physicians to write medication orders electronically, has been shown to reduce significantly the rate of serious medication errors. Intensive care telemedicine, a type of technology that allows remote specialists to monitor patients continuously with video-conferencing and computer-based data transmission tools, has been found to decrease intensive care costs substantially in certain settings. The President is proposing to double the funding (for a total of $100 million) for the Department of Health and Human Services to increase the use of these new technologies through demonstration projects.

Conclusion

The U.S. health care system has provided tremendous benefits for both American citizens and the global community. New knowledge, innovative products, and life-saving medical procedures are the results of the U.S. market for health care. The proposed policies will help preserve the strengths of the U.S. market and will improve the efficiency and affordability of health care.

CHAPTER 11

The Tort System

Tort is the civil law through which injured individuals seek compensation from another party alleged to have caused or contributed to their injury. The tort system in the United States is intended to compensate accident victims and to deter potential defendants from putting others at risk. Expenditures in the U.S. tort system were $233.4 billion in 2002, equal to 2.2 percent of gross domestic product (GDP), more than twice the amount spent on new automobiles in 2002. The expansive tort system has a considerable impact on the U.S. economy. Tort liability leads to lower spending on research and development, higher health care costs, and job losses. This chapter examines the growth of the tort system, the benefits the United States receives from it, and how alternative injury-compensation systems compare with the present tort system in terms of costs.

The key points of the chapter are:

- The evidence is mixed on whether the tort system serves to deter negligent behavior.
- The tort system is a costly method of providing insurance against injuries, and has a number of adverse effects on the economy.
- Possible ways of reducing the burden of the tort system include limiting noneconomic damages, reforming class action procedures, setting up trust funds for payments to victims, and allowing parties to avoid the tort system contractually.

The Changing Role of Tort Law

Until the 1960s, tort law covered injuries involving strangers, such as those caused by automobile accidents. Injuries resulting from the interaction between individuals with a prior relationship, such as physicians and patients, were covered by contract law instead of torts, which enabled individuals to define the terms the court would use to resolve any injury disputes in advance. This division between the tort system and contracts limited the courts' role to hearing cases involving injuries in which one person had harmed another with no predetermined specification of damages by the parties—either because no contract existed or because the existing contract did not cover a particular set of circumstances. In essence, the courts' job was to decide if the defendant was *liable* (at fault) and to determine compensation for the plaintiff (the victim). An important feature of the legal environment was that courts assigned liability for an injury by applying the *negligence standard*, under which the court assessed whether the injury had occurred because the defendant had failed to exercise the caution of a reasonable person under the circumstances of the accident. Changes to tort law since the 1960s have altered the standard of care courts apply in considering claims for compensation. Although some tort cases, such as those alleging medical liability, still use the negligence standard, others, such as product liability, are now generally decided using *strict liability*. Under this standard, defendants are held responsible for any product-related injuries even if they were not negligent. More injuries have become eligible for compensation as a result of this change, thus increasing the number of injuries litigated in the tort system.

Another change since the 1960s is that the tort system now serves to provide insurance against harms relating to any goods or services consumers or businesses purchase. This function is in addition to the original purpose of punishing negligence in order to deter future injuries. The right to sue for damages means that the tort system today effectively obligates suppliers of goods and services to provide this insurance along with their products. As recently as the late 1950s, ladder manufacturers would not have been liable for falls from ladders, doctors would not have been liable for birth defects, and diving-board manufacturers would not have been liable for injuries resulting from diving; in today's tort system, they are. Courts used to presume that falls from ladders were caused by deviations from normal use and not, as is currently the case, that ladder manufacturers were potentially liable for not warning consumers about the dangers of their product.

The Expansion of Tort Costs

Expenditures associated with the tort system have risen along with its increased role in society. One estimate based on insurance industry data finds that aggregate expenditures in the tort system were $233.4 billion in 2002. This estimate includes the legal costs of defending policyholders, benefits paid to parties injured by policyholders, insurance companies' administrative costs, and estimates of medical liability and self-insurance costs. Tort costs as a percentage of GDP increased after 1974 and peaked in 1987 (Chart 11-1).

The number of injuries handled in the tort system has increased along with expenditures. The number of filings per capita started to rise in the early 1980s and peaked in the mid-1980s, at least in the 16 states for which data on lawsuit filings are available between 1975 and 2000 (Chart 11-2).

Chart 11-1 **Tort Costs as a Percent of GDP**
Tort costs as a percent of GDP have been rising since 1974 but, until recently, have fallen from
their peak in 1987.

Percent of GDP

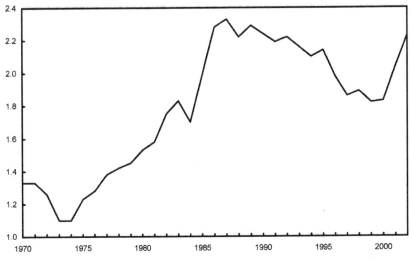

Source: Tillinghast-Towers Perrin, "U.S. Tort Costs: 2003 Update, Trends and Findings on the Costs of the
U.S. Tort System," 2003.

Much of the decline in filings since 1985 appears to have occurred in California, where medical liability reforms included a $250,000 limit for noneconomic damages that was found constitutional in 1985. Although there has been a decline in cases per capita since the 1980s, some types of tort awards have increased. For example, between 1990 and 2001, the median award in medical liability cases increased from about $100,000 to more than $300,000.

Expenditures in the tort system vary by the type of dispute (Table 11-1). In auto cases plaintiffs received a median award of $18,000 (in 57.5 percent of the cases). The most expensive cases tended to be those in which plaintiffs and defendants had preexisting relationships, such as product liability and medical liability. Plaintiffs won 23.4 percent of the time in medical liability cases and received a median award of $286,000. The median award in asbestos cases tried in state courts was $309,000, with 56 percent of plaintiffs receiving compensation. Large awards are relatively rare. In the 75 largest counties in the United States in 1992, 73 percent of the 377,421 tort cases disposed in state courts concerned auto accidents, which tend to result in relatively small awards at trial.

Chart 11-2 **Tort Filings in 16 States**
Tort filings rose through the 1980s but have returned to 1975 levels.

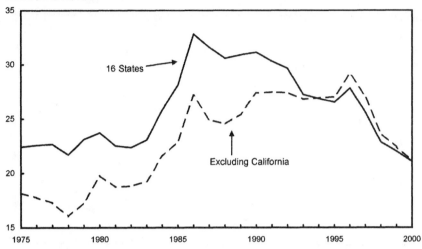

Note: The 16 States comprise: Alaska, California, Colorado, Florida, Hawaii, Idaho, Kansas, Maine, Maryland, Michigan, North Dakota, Ohio, Tennessee, Texas, Utah, and Washington.
Source: National Center for the Study of State Courts.

TABLE 11-1.— *Characteristics of State and Federal Tort Cases Decided by Trial, 1996*

Tort cases by type	Cases won by plaintiff (percent)	Median award	Percent of awards $250,000 or more	
			Total	$1 million or more
All tort cases				
State	48.2	$31,000	16.9	5.8
Federal	45.8	139,000	38.1	14.6
Automobile cases				
State	57.5	18,000	8.7	3.4
Federal	59.7	100,000	37.4	11.6
Medical liability				
State	23.4	286,000	51.0	20.2
Federal	39.8	252,000	54.3	22.9
Asbestos				
State	55.6	309,000	50.6	12.1
Federal	40.0	465,000	50.0	0.0
Product liability other than asbestos				
State	37.1	177,000	41.2	16.3
Federal	26.6	368,500	62.0	24.0

Source: Congressional Budget Office.

The Economic Effects of the Tort System

The economic effects of the tort system go beyond their direct impact in terms of expenditures. Resources that could be directed toward productive uses are diverted instead to the tort system or dissipated as firms and individuals take actions not needed for actual safety concerns but rather to avoid exposure to tort liability. Studies suggest that the gains to society from tort compensation and deterrence do not make up for these losses. A study of the impact of tort reform on productivity finds that limitations on the size of tort claims (for example, caps on punitive damages) enacted by states from 1972 to 1990 increased productivity by 1 to 2 percent a year, an amount equal to $955 per worker per year in 2002 dollars. Limitations on tort awards moved some injury payments out of the tort system so that the $955 figure represents an estimate of the cost of the tort system over alternative systems.

The gains from limits on the tort system come about because torts cause firms and individuals such as medical professionals to change the way they do business. Firms choose not to sell certain products so that they can avoid potential liability or they take costly extra precautions in the delivery of their products and services—precautions beyond the level that would reasonably balance costs and benefits to society. For example, torts cause doctors to practice defensive medicine, such as ordering extra tests that are a waste of time and resources. Some expenditures in the tort system, such as compensation for damages, are transfers of money from defendants to plaintiffs and do not consume resources. Other expenditures involve true economic costs in that the resources involved are not available for more productive uses; attorney's fees are an example. Additional costs include the profits and consumer benefits forgone by society when a potential defendant removes a product or service from the market or does not produce it in the first place in order to avoid frivolous lawsuits.

Torts as Injury Compensation

The tort system is not the only way in which society can deter injuries and compensate victims. There is an extensive system of regulations to improve the safety of products, medicines, and many other goods and services. Consumers have access to numerous publications and Internet Web sites that offer reviews and facilitate discussions of products. The availability of this information on product safety provides producers with a powerful financial incentive to make their products safer.

The question then becomes whether another system could provide the same benefits in terms of compensation and deterrence as the tort system but at lower cost. There is not enough evidence to determine the answer to this broad question. Nevertheless, some evidence indicates that in certain areas, such as product liability and medical liability, the tort system does not deliver enough deterrence benefits to justify the associated administrative costs (such as legal fees, overhead to process insurance claims, and the cost of running the tort system itself).

The Principal Injury-Compensation Methods

Injury-compensation systems can be broadly classified by the type of act that leads to the compensation being provided. A *fault-based* system compensates the injured party on the basis of negligent action, intentional harm, or strict liability. In contrast, a *cause-based* system is one in which the specific cause of the injury entitles an individual to compensation. The most widespread cause-based program in the United States is workers' compensation, which pays for many workplace injuries regardless of whether the employer was negligent with regard to the worker's injury. Finally, *loss-based* systems pay compensation based only on injury or illness. Loss-based systems include private systems like health insurance and public systems like Medicare.

The tort system is not the principal means by which injuries are compensated. Private health insurance, Medicaid, and Medicare are all substantially larger providers of compensation than the tort system (Table 11-2). The portion of tort expenditures that covers only economic damages such as current and future lost wages (that is, not including noneconomic damages such as for pain and suffering) is comparable in size to either the workers' compensation system or payments for life insurance.

Administrative Costs

The tort system is one of the most expensive compensation systems to run, with administrative costs equal to 54 percent of benefits. Sixty-one percent of these administrative costs (about a third of every dollar spent in the tort system) are the legal fees generated by attorneys for plaintiffs and defendants. In 2001, administrative costs of the health insurance industry were around 14 percent of benefits paid. The overhead for the Social Security disability system was around 3 percent of benefits in 2003; a study from the mid-1980s found that workers' compensation had overhead costs of around 20 percent of benefits. Some of the high cost of the tort system may arise because it deals with accidents that are more difficult to evaluate than those of other injury-compensation mechanisms.

Type of injury or illness compensation system	Compensation (billions of 2002 dollars)
Fault-based	
Tort economic payment[1]	51.3
Tort noneconomic payment[1]	55.9
Cause-based	
Workers' compensation[2]	48.0
Veterans' benefits[2]	26.0
Loss-based	
Health insurance (private first-party)[2]	408.2
Life insurance (private first-party)[2]	46.1
Social/public insurance	
Health:	
Medicaid[3] and Medicare[2]	362.1
Medicaid prescription drug[4]	13.1
Disability:	
Social Security Disability[1] and Supplemental Security Income[2]	94.1

[1]Data are for 2002.
[2]Data are for 2000.
[3]Data are for 1999.
[4]Data are for 1998

Sources: Department of Commerce (Bureau of Economic Analysis); Social Security Administration; Centers for Medicare and Medicaid Services; American Council of Life Insurers, "Life Insurers Fact Book," annual; and Tillinghast-Towers Perrin, "U.S. Tort Costs: 2000, Trends and Findings on the Costs of the U.S. Tort System," February 2002.

Compensation of Noneconomic Losses

Another way in which the tort system differs from other compensation methods is that it forces consumers to accept not only coverage for economic losses such as current and future lost wages and medical costs, but also nonpecuniary losses such as pain and suffering. Of the 46 cents of each dollar spent in the tort system that goes to plaintiffs, on average, 22 cents compensates them for economic losses and 24 cents compensates them for noneconomic damages.

Damages paid through the tort system are costs to firms—and higher costs ultimately translate into higher prices for goods and services. Tort awards can thus be seen as a form of insurance: consumers pay "premiums" in the form of higher prices for goods and services and receive compensation if injured. Torts cover only a limited set of possible injuries, however, so a consumer seeking comprehensive insurance against all possible economic and noneconomic losses would still have to purchase additional insurance. In reality, few people buy insurance against noneconomic losses such as pain and suffering; people do buy insurance against economic losses such as lost wages, medical expenses, or costs to rebuild a damaged house. This suggests that insurance policies against noneconomic losses are not worth their cost to potential buyers.

Extent of Coverage

Despite the expansion of the tort system, torts still provide compensation for a relatively limited number of injuries compared to other systems such as health insurance. For example, injuries that are the sole fault of the victim do not give rise to a legal claim for compensation and hence do not fall under the purview of the tort system. Many injuries are too small in economic terms to justify litigation. The long delays inherent before the tort system delivers monetary compensation likely also dissuade many potential lawsuits from being filed. In tort cases resolved in the 75 largest counties in the United States in 1992, the median time from filing to disposition was just over two years, with nearly one out of six cases taking more than four years. For medical liability, the median time to resolution was nearly three years with almost three out of ten cases taking longer than four years.

There is evidence that the eventual compensation does not match the injury well. In medical liability cases, the tort system appears to overcompensate minor injuries relative to the compensation that would have been provided by private insurance, while more serious injuries are undercompensated. This discrepancy may exist because factors other than the medical specifics of the injury could affect the compensation received by the plaintiff. For example, the location of the trial and the composition of the jury pool appear to affect the verdicts of some tort lawsuits and the size of the compensation. In addition, compensation may be tied more to the ability of the defendant to pay than to the actual injury suffered by the plaintiff. This is particularly a concern for punitive damages (Box 11-1).

Moreover, the tort system does a poor job of identifying which injuries are entitled to compensation and which are not. Many injuries that would meet the legal definition of negligence are never pursued, and the majority of those that are pursued appear not to merit compensation. A 1984 study of the outcomes of hospitalizations in New York City found that 3 to 4 percent of hospitalizations gave rise to adverse events such as drug reactions, with just over one-quarter of these due to negligent actions. However, more than half of the medical liability claims actually filed in the tort system arose from circumstances in which neither negligence nor any identifiable injury was present. One-third arose from instances in which the patient was injured but the doctor was not negligent (for example, for injuries resulting from a previously unknown drug allergy). Only one-sixth of the cases identified instances of true negligence and injury. Moreover, in this study, these claims represented a small fraction of injuries that actually arose due to negligence. Consequently, the majority of the compensation went to people who were not injured or were not injured by the doctor accused of malpractice, while the majority of those actually injured by doctor error were not compensated at all. Only in a minority of cases did those legally entitled to compensation receive it through the legal system.

Box 11-1: Punitive Damages

Compensatory damages are intended to "make the plaintiff whole" by offsetting an injured victim's losses. Punitive damages, on the other hand, are intended to punish the party whose negligent action caused the injury. Defendants may be liable for punitive damages if a jury finds that their actions were malicious, oppressive, gross, willful and wanton, or fraudulent. The Department of Justice studied civil trial cases in the country's 75 largest counties and found that punitive damages were awarded in 4.5 percent of cases that plaintiffs won (or 2.3 percent of all cases), but represented 21 percent of all damages awarded to plaintiffs. The median punitive award was $40,000 in those cases in which the plaintiff received an award. The threat posed by large punitive damages is that they may encourage more frequent and larger settlements.

Some are concerned that punitive damages are awarded against companies because they have deep pockets rather than because they have behaved egregiously. Indeed, the Supreme Court has expressed unease over the fact that the size of certain punitive awards has seemed out of proportion to the wrongfulness of the defendant's actions. This capriciousness also has implications for the deterrence effect of punitive damages, because a deterrence effect can be realized only if firms are able to take specific actions to avoid liability. If firms cannot tell which actions will likely incur liability, they cannot avoid them. Anecdotal evidence suggests that punitive-damage awards can indeed be unpredictable. Two identical allegations of fraud against BMW were heard in the same Alabama court and before the same judge. One purchaser was awarded $4 million in punitive damages; the second purchaser received no punitive damages.

Torts As Deterrence

The threat of a lawsuit can create and enforce appropriate standards of behavior. If the tort system made products and services in the United States safer, fewer accidents would occur and the higher administrative cost of torts would provide benefits to society in terms of reduced injury rates and associated health care costs. For example, the move by a number of states to no-fault automobile insurance in the 1970s appears to have led to as much as a 15 percent increase in the highway fatality rate. Such no-fault auto insurance laws eliminate or restrict liability for auto accidents so that each driver's own insurer typically pays for his or her own accident costs regardless of how the accident happened. Drivers who know that they will not be financially liable for other drivers' injuries in the event of an accident might be expected to take fewer safety precautions than if they were responsible for the financial consequences of their actions. In other areas of tort law such as medical liability and product liability, there is not consistent evidence that deterrence effects are large enough to justify the considerable administrative costs of the tort system. This suggests that alternatives to the tort system provide deterrence. For example, the possibility of losing a medical license could provide an adequate incentive for doctors to take steps to avoid negligence beyond the steps doctors take in the interests of their patients.

General Aviation and Deterrence

The experience of the general aviation industry over the past several decades provides an example of the role of tort liability in affecting product safety, firm profits, and the availability of goods to consumers. General aviation is the segment of the aviation industry composed of all civil aircraft not flown by commercial airlines or the military. General aviation manufacturers were the targets of a large volume of litigation in the 1970s and 1980s.

The general aviation accident rate has been declining for 50 years (Chart 11-3). In 1963, court rulings made lawsuits alleging manufacturing defects in the design of private and commercial aircraft subject to strict liability. In the most extreme cases, this meant that firms were responsible for accidents even if the accidents were caused by product defects that were not known or knowable at the time of manufacture. By the mid-1970s, this change in the law had led to a sharp rise in the number of product-liability cases and increased liability costs for the general aviation industry, with liability awards increasing nearly ninefold from 1977 to 1985.

The merits of these product-liability claims against airplane manufacturers were subject to question. A study of a sample of general aviation lawsuits filed between 1983 and 1986 showed that none of the accidents that led to lawsuits was caused by a design or manufacturing defect, as each suit had claimed. Thus, these lawsuits did not give manufacturers any additional incentives to produce safer aircraft, since the allegations of design defects appear to have been specious in the first place.

Indeed, the rise in tort claims had no discernible effect on the accident rate. An examination of the trends in the accident rate calculated over various periods shows that the steepest decline in general aviation accidents occurred between 1950 and 1969—before the dramatic rise in tort costs in the 1970s and 1980s (Chart 11-4). If liability exposure were driving the general aviation industry to build safer products, accident rates would have declined more rapidly as the increased likelihood of tort litigation pushed aircraft manufacturers to add safety features to their aircraft.

Chart 11-3 **General Aviation Liability Payouts and Accident Rates**
The increase in liability payouts between 1977 and 1985 did not cause a change in trends of the number of accidents or fatal accidents per 100,000 flight hours.

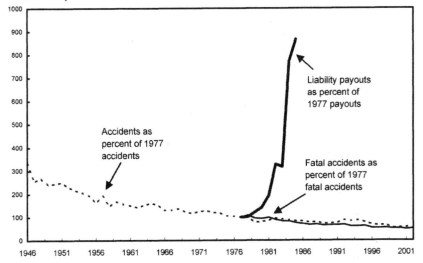

Sources: George L. Priest, "The Modern Expansion of Tort Liability: Its Sources, Its Effects, and Its Reform," *Journal of Economic Perspectives*, Summer 1991, and General Aviation Manufacturers Association.

Chart 11-4 **Accident Rate for Small Aircraft**
The rise in tort claims has had no discernible effect on the declining accident rate in general aviation. The steepest decline was between 1950 and 1969, which predated the rise in tort costs during the 1970s and 1980s.

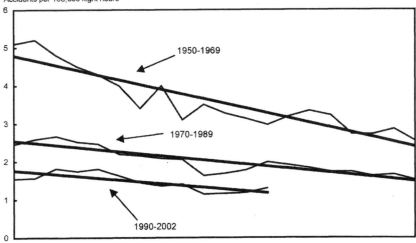

Source: General Aviation Manufacturers Association.

The rise in liability expenses did, however, cause great harm to the general aviation industry. During the period of expanding liability costs from 1977 to 1985, the financial health of the general aviation industry deteriorated markedly, with a number of firms shutting down production lines and one going bankrupt. As a result, small-aircraft production fell precipitously (Chart 11-5). By discouraging the production of new planes, tort law has created a situation in which the mix of planes in use actually presents a higher risk than would have been the case had older planes been retired and replaced by new ones. The General Aviation Revitalization Act of 1994, which exempted some general aviation aircraft older than 18 years from product-liability claims, appears to have led to a small resurgence in the industry.

Chart 11-5 **Small-Aircraft Production**
The increase in tort liability beginning in the 1970s caused a decrease in small-aircraft production. This effect was attenuated by the General Aviation Revitalization Act of 1994.

Percent of 1970 production

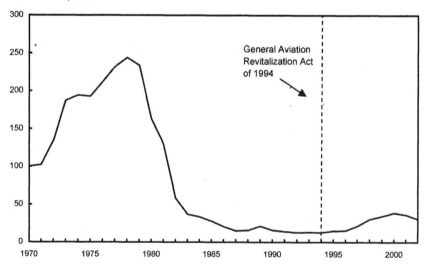

Source: General Aviation Manufacturers Association.

Other Evidence on Deterrence

It is difficult to find deterrence effects in other contexts. For example, studies examining injury rates for consumers and workers as well as death rates from workplace injuries show that such injuries did not decline more rapidly following a steep increase in litigation. Other research has examined the deterrence effect of medical liability by estimating the impact on treatment outcomes of state-imposed limits on damage awards at trial (such as California's $250,000 limit on noneconomic damages). Studies have found no appreciable impact on treatment outcomes—the lower threat of torts did not lead to more medical injuries. These findings suggest that there is at best limited deterrence from such cases.

The Limits of Tort Deterrence

Why does the tort system appear to be ineffective in improving product safety? One major reason is that market incentives already provide an important form of deterrence against unsafe products. Firms whose products cause injuries lose customers and suffer economic losses. In addition, many products and services face government regulation. The producers of such items are required to undertake investments in safety, and the tort system may have no incremental effect on safety. Similarly, medical services also face market incentives and regulation by governmental and professional bodies.

The current tort system makes it hard to predict which actions will be deemed negligent during litigation. Thus, the system does not provide much deterrence because people do not know what steps to take to avoid a lawsuit or an adverse judgment.

Potential Tort Reforms

One way to consider the effects of changes in the U.S. tort system is to compare the U.S. system with those in other advanced economies, such as Canada, Japan and the United Kingdom. Like the United States, many of these countries use a negligence standard for medical liability and strict liability for product-related injuries, yet they expend fewer resources in their tort systems than the United States (Chart 11-6). Possible explanations for this divergence are discussed in the following sections.

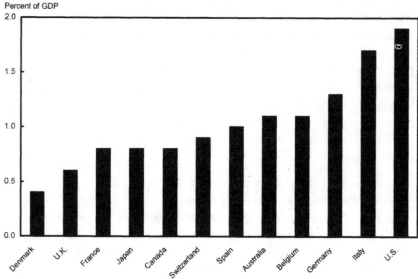

Chart 11-6 **International Comparison of Tort Costs, 1998**
Tort costs as a percent of GDP were higher in the United States than in other industrialized countries.

Percent of GDP

Source: Tillinghast-Towers Perrin, "U.S. Tort Costs: 2000, Trends and Findings on the Costs of the U.S. Tort System," February 2002.

Limiting Noneconomic Damages and Other Potential Reforms

One important reason for the divergence in tort costs between the United States and other countries is that awards for noneconomic damages, such as pain and suffering, appear to be much higher in the United States. Noneconomic damages account for half of all compensation awarded in the United States, but in other countries are either capped (as in Canada) or otherwise restricted (as in Germany). Reforms aimed at reducing or eliminating pain and suffering awards, such as the President's proposed $250,000 limitation on noneconomic damages in health-related cases, have the potential to reduce the cost of the U.S. tort system.

Several other differences appear to be less important in explaining the divergence than compensation for noneconomic damages. One difference is that in other countries, judges decide the vast majority of tort claims, while juries typically decide cases in the United States. Empirical evidence suggests that U.S. judges and juries decide cases in approximately the same way, suggesting this is not a major factor in explaining the divergence. Another difference is that in the United States each side pays its own legal costs, whereas in many other nations the losing side pays both sides' legal costs. A study of Florida's temporary use of a "loser-pays" method in medical liability cases found that when the losing side paid legal expenses, plaintiffs were more likely to receive compensation either at trial or in a settlement. Furthermore, the compensation was higher. This finding suggests that apportioning legal costs to the losers discourages plaintiffs from pursuing low-quality (nuisance) cases because they would have to pay all legal costs if the case went against them.

Procedural Reforms

Some of the costs of the tort system arise because there are incentives that encourage state judges and juries to extract financial compensation from out-of-town defendants. The vast majority of tort cases are litigated in state courts. Tort cases tried before elected state judges have been found to result in higher awards when the defendant is a corporation headquartered outside of the state than when the defendant is local. By removing national class action suits from state courts, the Federal government could reduce the ability of entrepreneurial lawyers to *forum shop*, that is, to file cases in a sympathetic state court. Some evidence on asbestos tort litigation suggests that forum shopping is indeed a problem. Research also suggests that certain small counties tend to be magnets for national class actions in the sense that they attract many more cases than would be expected on the basis of their populations.

The Class Action Fairness Act of 2003 would allow removal of some class actions to Federal court if any plaintiff is from a different state than any defendant (Box 11-2). Under current law, a plaintiff's attorney who does not like a particular judge's limitations in a class action can seek a less restrictive judge in a different jurisdiction. The proposed Act would make this more difficult by reducing the ability of plaintiffs' attorneys to file national class actions in state court.

Limiting the Scope of Tort Compensation

An alternative approach to the current system would be to resolve disputes and compensate victims outside the tort system. An example of this approach is the case of compensation for individuals exposed to asbestos. The proposed Fairness in Asbestos Injury Resolution Act of 2003 would create a trust fund to compensate those injured by asbestos exposure. Disbursements from the fund would be restricted to those who are actually suffering from asbestos-related illnesses. The use of asbestos has been all but abandoned in the United States, so the focus in resolving claims is now appropriately placed on compensating injured workers rather than deterring new instances of future liability (Box 11-3).

Box 11-2: The Role of Class Actions in the Tort System

A *class action* is a legal procedure in which individuals are joined together to litigate a single case (the class refers to the group of such individuals). Class actions are used in a variety of contexts, including cases involving securities fraud, consumer protection, employment, civil rights, and exposure to toxic chemicals or other pollutants. Class actions are intended to secure compensation in cases that involve substantial aggregate losses but relatively small individual losses. In practice, private attorneys often initiate these cases, each one in effect becoming a "Private Attorney General." In this role, lawyers identify both the legal violations and a number of individuals harmed by the violations and bring an action on these individuals' behalf. To induce attorneys to take on this role, they are compensated out of the settlement fund. In many cases, this compensation is based on a *contingent fee*, a percentage of the settlement or award.

An important concern about class action suits is that many of them are filed more for the benefit of the plaintiffs' attorneys than for the plaintiffs. In individual litigation, plaintiffs enter a contract with an attorney and have an incentive to monitor the attorney's effort to ensure a favorable outcome. In class action suits, most individual plaintiffs have only a small stake in the case's outcome and thus have little incentive to monitor the activities of their lawyers. In principle, judges are expected to monitor payments to plaintiffs' attorneys and the nature of settlements. With growing caseloads, however, many judges face pressure to clear their dockets as rapidly as possible. Accepting a settlement and associated attorneys' fees is one way to accomplish this.

Without the active scrutiny of clients or judges, plaintiffs' lawyers have an incentive to collude with defendants to set higher attorney's fees in exchange for lower overall payouts from defendants to plaintiffs. One study of a small number of class action cases found that in a substantial fraction of them, class counsel received more in fees and expenses than all of the plaintiffs combined.

Box 11-3: Asbestos and the Tort System

The tort system's treatment of asbestos cases demonstrates how the system can fall short of its purported objectives of deterring harmful behavior and funding compensation. Beginning in the 1970s, increased public awareness and concern about the health effects of asbestos led to regulations limiting exposure to asbestos. By 1989, all new uses were banned, and strict regulations have limited remaining asbestos use. Between 1973 and 2001, asbestos use in the United States fell by 98 percent. With extensive regulations in place and minimal use, the tort system's role in deterring harmful behavior has been substantially reduced simply because there is little activity to deter.

Yet even as the use of asbestos declined, the number of claims rose substantially. The total number of claimants is estimated to have grown from 21,000 in 1982 to over 600,000 by the end of 2000. To be sure, some additional claims are warranted because cancers caused by asbestos can take years to develop. An estimated 90 percent of the new claims, however, are by people who have no cancers and may never develop cancer. Claims by individuals without a diagnosed asbestos-related cancer account for almost all of the growth in asbestos case loads during the 1990s and most of the compensation received by claimants goes to those without malignant cancers. Only 43 percent of the money spent on asbestos litigation is recovered by claimants—the rest goes to lawyers and administrative costs. In short, the current system neither achieves deterrence in the use of this dangerous substance nor directs appropriate compensation to its victims.

Instead, asbestos litigation has imposed costs on workers, shareholders, and those who in the future will become ill from their previous exposure to asbestos. Estimates suggest that roughly 60 companies entangled in asbestos litigation have gone bankrupt primarily because of asbestos liabilities, with most of the bankruptcies occurring since 1990. One study estimated that between 52,000 and 60,000 workers were displaced because of these bankruptcies. Moreover, bankruptcy results in a shrinking pool of money to be divided up among future claimants. The growing number of bankruptcies raises concerns that those who become ill in the future will receive little or no compensation.

For other injuries, a possible approach to compensating accident victims would be a system akin to workers' compensation, in which compensation would be provided by an insurance system. New Zealand has replaced the personal injury and medical liability aspects of its tort system with a government-run compensation system. Such a system, however, can increase the prevalence of accidents because fully-insured individuals may not take sufficient care against a loss. This is not a concern in cases where accidents have already occurred, such as asbestos exposure. In other cases, such as product liability or medical liability, the effect of changes in the system on the behavior of potential victims is an important consideration. Moreover, like the tort system, workers' compensation systems tend to be costly to administer and may encourage frivolous claims. Replacing the tort system with a more general workers' compensation system could well mean replacing one costly and inefficient system with another.

Avoiding the Tort System

Recontractualization is an alternative approach to reform that has been the subject of considerable academic discussion. According to this idea, individuals and firms would be allowed to specify by contract the types of damages for which injurers would be liable. For example, consumers or their insurers could determine individual caps on damages in exchange for lower prices for goods and services. In principle, potential defendants would enter into such contracts if they reduced the expected costs of dealing with injuries. Such a system would be voluntary, so that individuals could refuse to participate if offered a contract by a potential defendant that was inferior to the insurance associated with the tort system.

A possible drawback to this approach is that the courts currently view contracts limiting damages or defining negligence with suspicion. Courts have held that warranties that limit liability are not enforceable because they are *contracts of adhesion*—agreements that the purchaser of a product or service has no choice but to accept. Hence, it is likely that any steps toward recontractualization would require substantial institutional and legal changes. This could explain why this approach has not received much attention from policy makers.

Conclusion

The tort system has expanded in the last 30 years. By expanding the number of accidents for which accident victims receive compensation, the current tort system in effect requires the suppliers of goods and services to provide insurance to their customers. This tort-based insurance against accidents appears to be more expensive than other methods of compensating victims. At least in the cases of product liability and medical liability, the expansion of the tort system does not appear to have had an appreciable effect in deterring negligent behavior.

The President has proposed several initiatives to reduce the burden of torts on the economy. These include placing limits on noneconomic damages, reforming class action procedures, and finding alternative methods to compensate injuries such as those that have been proposed for people suffering from asbestos-related ailments. These steps would focus the tort system on those cases it can deal with most effectively and lessen the costs to society of frivolous lawsuits and awards.

CHAPTER 12

International Trade and Cooperation

Since the end of the Second World War, international trade has grown steadily relative to overall economic activity. Countries that have been more open to international flows of goods, services, and capital grew faster than countries that were less open to the global economy. The United States has been a driving force in constructing an open global trading system. A series of international trade agreements has reduced barriers to trade in goods and services and has been an important element in U.S. and global growth.

During this period, new types of trade emerged and delivered new benefits to consumers and firms in trading countries. Growing international demand for goods such as movies, pharmaceuticals, and recordings offered new opportunities for U.S. exporters. A burgeoning trade in services provided an important outlet for U.S. expertise in sectors such as banking, engineering, and higher education. The ability to buy goods and services from new places has made household budgets go farther, while the ability of firms to distribute their production around the globe has cut costs and thus prices to consumers.

The key points in this chapter are:

- Trade has grown significantly since World War II. The benefits from new forms of trade, such as trade in services, are no different from the benefits of traditional trade in goods.
- The benefits of integration are substantial.
- International cooperation is an essential part of realizing the potential gains from international trade. A system through which countries can resolve disputes can play an important role in realizing these gains.

Increased Trade Flows: Facts and Trends

One way to measure the relative importance of international trade is to compare the value of trade flows to overall economic activity. In the latter half of the twentieth century and into the twenty-first, growth in world trade has outpaced growth in world output (Chart 12-1). As recently as 1950, the sum of merchandise exports of all countries equaled only 8 percent of world GDP. In 2002, the most recent year for which data are available, exports had increased to 19 percent of world output. For the United States, the sum of merchandise exports and imports rose from 7 percent to 18 percent of GDP over the same period.

Index, 1950=100

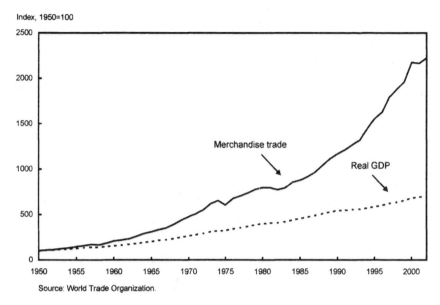

Source: World Trade Organization.

Increased trade has been accompanied by increased output growth, which can be attributed, at least in part, to the opening of markets and to the benefits derived from the international trading system. The growth in world trade also reflects lower transportation costs, which facilitate trade; new production processes, which allow companies to produce and assemble goods in different countries; and information technology, which facilitates communication between buyers and sellers. These allow trading countries to take advantage of variations in resource endowments and sectoral productivities across countries.

The United States is the largest importer and exporter of goods and services in the world, although its prowess at exporting is sometimes less apparent to the casual observer than the country's demand for imports. This is because many of the products that U.S. firms export are capital goods used in production and are not sold at the retail level to consumers (Table 12-1). The composition of U.S. exports reflects its abundance of skilled labor and high-technology expertise relative to other countries. This relative abundance explains why the United States is more likely to export aircraft and semiconductors and import footwear and clothing.

U.S. export levels depend partly on the vitality of export markets. When U.S. trading partners such as Europe and Japan experience slow growth, as has occurred in recent years, they import fewer goods from the United States. The developed countries of North America, Europe, and Japan still account for roughly two-thirds of world imports and exports of goods, and over 70 percent of world trade in services.

TABLE 12-1.— *Leading U.S. Net Exports of Goods, 2002*

Rank	Category	Millions of dollars
1	Aircraft	15,675
2	Semiconductors and related devices	15,233
3	Aircraft parts and auxiliary equipment	9,482
4	Plastics materials and resins	6,819
5	Soybeans	5,597
6	Oil and gas field machinery and equipment	5,296
7	Corn	4,988
8	Aircraft engines and engine parts	4,624
9	Motor vehicle parts	3,976

Source: Department of Commerce (International Trade Administration).

The Benefits of Free Trade

The benefits of free trade are often misunderstood. Discussions of the gains from trade often focus on the jobs created in industries that export goods and services rather than the benefits to consumers and producers from importing. The jobs created by exports are important—indeed, some research suggests that workers in export industries tend to have higher wages than those in other industries. The benefits of trade, however, are much greater. In fact, the claim that free trade is good mainly because it allows us to export misses much of the story. Free trade is good not just because it allows us to export, but also because it allows us to import. Providing goods and services to people in other countries is worthwhile because it allows Americans to consume the goods and services made in other countries. This is analogous to why most people work at their jobs—to earn the income with which to buy goods and services. That is, people "export" the product of their efforts and in return receive income with which to buy goods and services made by other people.

The benefits of exports are similar. The advantage of selling goods and services abroad is that U.S. exporters receive funds that can be spent on imports for Americans to consume. Imports allow Americans to purchase more varieties of goods and services at lower cost than if the same items were obtained from domestic producers. These cost savings free up resources to be used to produce other products. In this way, imports raise the standard of living in the United States.

Comparative Advantage

Free trade does not require that one country gains at another country's expense. Free trade is win-win. Just as the United States benefits from goods produced more cheaply abroad, other countries benefit from goods built more efficiently here. Each country gains from these exchanges because each has different capabilities. Free trade encourages countries to specialize in what they do best. Such a division of tasks raises economic well-being around the world, just as the specialization of individual workers into different jobs makes a company more productive.

Free trade also pushes American businesses to become as efficient as possible by exposing them to competition from foreign firms. For example, foreign competition over the past several decades has spurred improvements on the part of U.S. automakers. American firms and workers responded to the challenge of international competition by improving American cars and making them less expensive. American consumers are better off as a result of increased choice and better value.

Barriers to trade, in contrast, tend to help a relatively small number of firms and their workers at the expense of harming a much larger number of consumers who pay more for their goods as a result of protection. Each consumer might pay only modestly more while the beneficiaries of the protection gain substantially. The total financial costs of protection borne by consumers, however, are typically larger than the benefits that accrue to producers and workers.

The effects of trade policy on economic growth and the mechanisms by which trade affects growth have been controversial. In part, this is because it is difficult to disentangle the effects of trade liberalization on economic growth from the effects of the multitude of other policies that countries adopt. As late as the 1950s and 1960s, the idea that open markets spur economic growth was somewhat unconventional. The more common belief was that developing countries should close their borders to imports in order to support and encourage the growth of their own firms. This approach became known as "import substitution" because countries sought to develop home industries in place of imports. This was believed to be particularly important for the manu-facturing sector. Advocates of this view pointed to positive past experiences with protection among currently developed countries. Developing countries that followed this strategy and tried to substitute domestic production for imports often found initial success, but subsequently encountered serious economic difficulties.

Broad comparisons of countries' experiences support the assessment that openness to trade is significantly correlated with economic growth. One study examined the experience of 133 countries from 1950 to 1998. Countries' annual real incomes per capita grew about ½ percentage point faster after liberalizing trade policies than under their closed regimes. Further, the income gains from opening up to free trade have become increasingly significant; countries that removed trade barriers in the 1990s raised their growth rates 2½ percentage points, an additional 2 percentage points per year. While the results of these cross-country studies are not irrefutable, their findings are bolstered by studies of individual countries' problems with trade protection and successes with liberalization.

Assisting People and Communities Affected by Free Trade

Although openness to trade provides substantial benefits to the Nation as a whole, foreign competition can require adjustment on the part of some individuals, businesses, and industries. To help workers affected by trade develop the skills needed for new jobs, the Administration has built upon and developed programs to assist workers and communities that are negatively affected by trade. The Administration has reformed existing programs to make them more responsive and flexible. For example, the long-standing Trade Adjustment Assistance program offered training and income support to workers directly hurt by greater imports. This program was significantly enhanced by new legislation signed by the President in 2002 to extend eligibility to workers indirectly affected, such as upstream suppliers of the firms hurt by imports. The new legislation also expanded the benefits to include a health insurance tax credit and a wage supplement for older workers who found new jobs that did not pay as well as the jobs they had lost. This assistance, which will total $12 billion over 10 years, helps ease the adjustment for displaced workers and helps them move into jobs where they are most needed. In addition, the President has proposed a pilot program for Personal Reemployment Accounts, which would offer an innovative approach to worker adjustment. These accounts would provide unemployed individuals funds they can use for training, for job-search assistance, or as a cash reemployment bonus if they find new work quickly.

The creation and destruction of jobs is part of the way in which people and materials move from less-productive to more-productive functions in a free-market economy. Businesses fail and jobs are lost for many reasons; for example, changes in technology or new domestic competition can shake up industries and communities. In the 1980s, 70 percent of the changes in employment in U.S. manufacturing resulted from less demand for relatively low-skilled workers and greater demand for high-skilled workers within the same industry. This indicates that the job losses in the 1980s were not primarily due to foreign trade pushing workers out of a sector, but to the changing nature of manufacturing. Import competition, however, often receives a disproportionate share of the blame. This may be because there is less that can be done to prevent the dislocations associated with technological change.

New Facets of Trade

The nature of U.S. trade has changed dramatically over the last several decades. Whereas the United States once would have exported your father's Oldsmobile in exchange for foreign-made food or clothing, the United States is now as likely to export financial or educational services, Hollywood blockbusters, or life-saving medicines. The United States still imports food and apparel, but it also imports components that go into sophisticated products (such as computer hard drives). This section explores several ways in which modern trade has evolved from the classic exchange of manufactured and agricultural goods.

Intellectual Property

The kinds of goods that have been traded for centuries, such as wine or clothing, have two important attributes: the value of the good is linked to the physical object, and it costs roughly the same to produce the second unit of the good as the first. Many of the goods in which the United States now excels—movies, books, music, software, and pharmaceuticals—are dramatically different from traditional goods. The value of a book, movie, or computer software program lies in the ideas contained within, more than in the paper and binding or disk. The cost of producing the first book includes not just the paper and ink, but the intellectual contribution of the author. To produce the second copy of the book, however, only the raw materials are required, which makes it significantly less expensive. As discussed later in the chapter, trade in goods with valuable intellectual property raises different policy questions than does more-traditional trade.

Services

Services trade is growing in importance in the world economy (Chart 12-2). The services sector, for trade purposes, includes travel and transportation-related services, royalties and license fees, and other private services, such as finance, insurance and telecommunications. The service-providing sector is the largest component of the private economy in the United States, providing more than 86 million jobs in 2003 and accounting for over half of total GDP. In 2002, the United States exported services worth almost $300 billion, about 30 percent of total exports of goods and services.

Worldwide services trade totaled $1.5 trillion in 2002, compared to goods trade of over $6 trillion, but services trade has been growing faster. Unlike

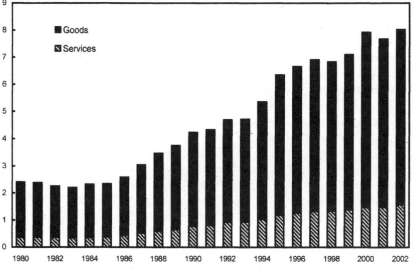

Trillions of U.S. dollars

Source: World Trade Organization.

goods trade, in which a product can be loaded on a ship at one port and off-loaded anywhere in the world with little need for the exporter and importer to interact, services trade generally requires extensive interaction. Some services can be provided at a distance, such as software services. For others, such as tourism, the customer must come to the location of the service provider. For others, such as some consulting work, the service provider must come to the customer. The liberalization of services trade involves the movement of individuals as well as the regulation of investment and other business activity. For American banks to sell many of their services abroad, they must open branches in their target markets (Box 12-1). As a result, negotiations to liberalize trade in services have moved beyond border measures such as *tariffs* (taxes on imports) to deal with subjects that have traditionally been the domain of domestic regulation.

One facet of increased services trade is the increased use of *offshore outsourcing* in which a company relocates labor-intensive service industry functions to another country. For example, a U.S. firm might use a call-center in India to handle customer service-related questions. The principal novelty of outsourcing services is the means by which foreign purchases are delivered. Whereas imported goods might arrive by ship, outsourced services are often delivered using telephone lines or the Internet. The basic economic forces behind the transactions are the same, however. When a good or service is produced more cheaply abroad, it makes more sense to import it than to make or provide it domestically.

Box 12-1: Trade in Financial Services

The United States is the world's top producer and exporter of financial services, with exports of roughly $16 billion in 2002. Foreign clients rely on U.S. firms for financial advice, fund management, credit-card services, credit-rating services, and housing finance. In developing countries that suffer from a shortage of capital or qualified human resources, foreign-provided services can offer vital support for economic development. Financial services can introduce new technologies, promote better business practices, and provide access to the global capital market.

The experience of foreign financial services firms in Mexico provides an example of the benefits of trade in financial services. In the aftermath of the peso devaluation in 1994, thousands of business went bankrupt. As a result, a number of Mexican banks failed and the government was forced to purchase $100 billion worth of nonperforming loans to prevent a systemic banking crisis. The Mexican government also encouraged foreign banks to invest in Mexican banks. The government hoped that foreign banks would inject much-needed liquidity into the financial system. U.S. and other foreign financial service companies are credited with helping to stabilize Mexico's financial sector. Together, foreign firms now manage a significant fraction of the assets of the Mexican banking system.

Intra-industry Trade and Intermediate Products

In classical descriptions of trade, a country with abundant land sends corn to a country with abundant capital in exchange for automobiles. In modern trade, it is common for two countries to send machine tools back and forth to each other. While the items traveling in both directions might all be machine tools, they are distinct products that draw on similar production capabilities. Even when a country is technologically capable of producing all varieties of a product, it is cost-effective to specialize in producing particular varieties and then trade with partner countries to obtain other types of the product. This type of trade is referred to as *intra-industry trade*.

Modern trade also differs from classical trade because the production of any given product may be spread across several countries. Final assembly might occur in the United States, for example, using parts (*intermediate inputs*) that were built in Canada and Brazil. In fact, a good deal of U.S. trade involves flows of intermediate inputs used for domestic production.

This kind of trade can have very different economic effects. In the conventional trade model, an increase in imports would drive out domestic production and jobs in the import-competing sectors. Evidence indicates, however, that increases in imports are correlated with increases in domestic employment in the same product category. One explanation for this result is that when production is integrated across countries, an increase in demand can stimulate both domestic and foreign production.

International Cooperation and Disputes

Countries can benefit from cooperation that increases trade. This has always been true for the shipment of goods across borders, but it is even more essential for the new types of trade described above. Trade in services and goods with high intellectual-property content often requires a deeper involvement on the part of the exporter in the importing country, as in the case of U.S. bank branches overseas.

Why Is There a Need for Cooperation?

Even if a nation understands and accepts the benefits of importing, there may still be an incentive to intervene in trade through policies such as tariffs. Countries that are large enough to affect world prices can potentially benefit by limiting their demand for imports and moving the *terms of trade* (the relative price of exports to imports) in their favor. If two large countries try to do this to each other, however, they can make their situations worse than under free trade.

One reminder of this lesson was the aftermath of the Smoot-Hawley Tariff Act of 1930. Though the United States had a trade surplus before 1930, the pressures of the nascent Great Depression led Congress to raise tariffs in an ill-conceived attempt to protect American jobs. Trading partners around the world responded by raising their own trade barriers. This was an important factor in the ensuing breakdown of international commerce, contributing to lower employment worldwide.

Many of the post-World War II international economic institutions established under U.S. leadership, such as the World Bank and the International Monetary Fund, were responses to perceived failures in international economic policy in the prewar period. The plan under which these two institutions were created also included a proposal for an organization, the International Trade Organization (ITO), to oversee cooperation in international trade. The ITO was never established due to political disputes.

For more than four decades the trading system was governed instead by a series of agreements known as the General Agreement on Tariffs and Trade

(GATT). GATT only became part of a formal organization, the World Trade Organization (WTO), in 1995. Despite the absence of a standing international body, substantial progress was made in global trade liberalization.

In the first GATT negotiations in the late 1940s, a relatively small group of countries, including the United States, looked for opportunities in which they could all benefit from reciprocally lowering barriers. This gathering to seek mutual gains from cooperation was known as a "round." The current multilateral trade talks were launched by well over 100 countries in Doha, Qatar, in 2001.

Early trade talks were primarily devoted to cutting tariffs. This era of import liberalization coincided with and contributed to an era of rapid worldwide economic growth. While tariff cuts could be painful for industries that faced new competition from imports, the United States gained better market access for exports, while consumers and firms benefited from lower prices of imports. At a practical level, tariff cutting was relatively easy. If the United States and France each had 40 percent tariffs in sensitive sectors, they could agree to cut those tariffs to 20 percent. Because of this simplicity, as well as the limited number of participating countries, the early GATT trade rounds were brief. Over time, however, GATT negotiations became more comprehensive and more complex. The negotiations were held less frequently and lasted much longer. Nonetheless, a good deal of progress was made in liberalizing world trade. Among developed countries, successive tariff cuts on manufactured goods lowered average tariff levels to below 5 percent. Barriers remained higher in developing countries.

Nontariff barriers to trade remain, but they are often more difficult to address. For example, countries' policies on protecting intellectual property can constitute a nontariff barrier with important trade consequences (Box 12-2). Other types of regulations could, if misused, also constitute a barrier to trade. For example, "sanitary and phytosanitary regulations" are rules designed to protect the health of people, plants, and animals. A foreign government seeking to block competition in a sensitive agricultural sector could seek to ban imports on the basis of a product-safety claim that is without a sound basis in science. The standard that was agreed upon in the Uruguay Round of trade talks in 1994 was that such claims must be based on sound scientific evidence. What constitutes such evidence has been the subject of dispute. This circumstance poses a challenge: trade restrictions based on sound science must be allowed and claims not founded on sound science must be avoided or dismissed, but determining the difference is frequently not an easy process.

Box 12-2: International Cooperation on Intellectual Property Rights

The protection of intellectual property is an important new trade issue. The United States has worked to ensure that copyrights, trademarks, and patents given to authors, companies, programmers, or other inventors are protected in other countries.

One implication of the high development and low production costs of goods with high intellectual property content is that they are relatively easy to steal. While it may cost $80 million to create a feature film, the blank videotape or DVD used to copy that film may cost just a few dollars. It is a fairly straightforward matter for the United States to prevent other countries from taking U.S. wheat without paying. It is more difficult to prevent an exported copy of a movie, recording, or drug from being reproduced, though the loss to the United States in forgone exports would be just as significant. These losses can occur not only through unauthorized duplication, but also through foreign government policies such as controls on drug prices. These price controls reduce the return that U.S. producers can earn from abroad and shift the burden of paying for development costs to the American consumer.

As trade in goods embodying valuable intellectual property has grown, the protection of intellectual property has emerged as an important policy concern. In the Uruguay Round of trade talks, which concluded in 1994, participating countries agreed to adopt high standards of intellectual property protection in the accord on Trade-Related Aspects of Intellectual Property Rights (TRIPS). Some have misconstrued it as preventing developing nations from addressing health emergencies such as the spread of AIDS in Africa. At Doha in 2001, WTO members agreed that the TRIPS Agreement does not and should not prevent members from taking measures to protect public health. Furthermore, in 2003, the United States and other WTO members agreed that developing countries that lack domestic manufacturing capacities in the pharmaceutical sectors should be able to override patent rights to import needed medicines from abroad in order to deal with domestic health problems.

The Administration has actively pursued measures in trade agreements to ensure the security of U.S. intellectual property rights. The inclusion of these measures in trade agreements illustrates a new way in which international cooperation benefits the United States. If countries are found to be in violation of their obligations under a trade agreement, the United States could retaliate against those countries across the entire range of transactions covered by the agreement.

The Benefits of Dispute Settlement

Another issue that arises with international cooperation in trade is the need for some way of solving disagreements among trading partners. Disputes might occur when one country disregards a commitment it made in negotiations, or when there is a disagreement over the interpretation of an agreement.

If one WTO member has a complaint about the behavior of another member, there is an established process for addressing the concern. First, the two countries are required to consult and determine whether the dispute can be resolved amicably. If this is not possible, a dispute settlement panel is established at the WTO. This panel consists of experts, generally selected from countries not involved in the dispute, who hear evidence from the complaining and responding countries and then issue findings. The panel determines whether a country has failed to follow through on commitments previously made in its trade agreements. Panel findings can be appealed to a standing body, which issues its own report and findings on the issues on appeal. Panel and Appellate Body reports are then submitted to the Dispute Settlement Body (DSB), also a standing body, for adoption. Once adopted, these findings become DSB recommendations and rulings.

After the conclusion of the dispute process, the difference between the WTO system and the domestic legal system becomes apparent. All WTO members have agreed that when a country loses a dispute settlement case at the WTO, the first preference is to bring the domestic law into compliance with the DSB recommendations and rulings. However, if the losing country chooses to maintain its initial policies, it must either negotiate compensation to the complaining country or else the complaining country can get authorization from the WTO to retaliate by withdrawing concessions of comparable value. If the latter happens, the net effect is the unwinding of the reciprocal liberalization that the countries had undertaken.

The virtue of an orderly dispute-settlement system that has the confidence of all participants is that the unraveling of cooperation is limited. Parties not involved in the dispute handle the facts and interpretation of the dispute, reducing the scope for disagreement over whether retaliation is legitimate.

The United States has had much success in complaints it has initiated against other countries' trade practices. As of September 2003, the United States had filed 63 complaints against other countries. Of the 39 that have been resolved through panel proceedings, the United States lost only 3 in litigation. In turn, the United States was a respondent in 77 cases over the same time period and successfully defended its practices in 4 of the resulting 38 panel proceedings. These statistics suggest that WTO complaints are not brought frivolously, in the sense that complaints, whether by or against the United States, have a high probability of success.

An effective dispute-settlement mechanism that has the confidence of all participants is an important part of the cooperative trading system. A dispute-settlement system can help to ensure that all parties to trade agreements receive the benefits on which they agreed.

Progress Toward Free Trade

The United States has pursued trade liberalization through negotiations at the global, regional, and bilateral levels. This multipronged approach allows for continuing progress even when one avenue for liberalization is blocked or stalled. Due to its global reach, the broadest and most important forum for liberalization is the World Trade Organization. This body now has 148 members. Among the central principles of the WTO is the requirement that the lowest tariff offered to one WTO member must be offered to all members. This principle, known as most-favored-nation (MFN) treatment, ensures that even if cooperative agreements are reached among a smaller group of countries, those countries will extend the benefits broadly to other WTO members. Although WTO rules permit important exceptions to the MFN principle, such as allowing countries to lower barriers with trade-agreement partners and as part of trade preference programs for poor countries, when the MFN principle is observed it creates a "level playing field" of equal tariffs on all trading partners so that countries will buy goods from the most-efficient producer.

The WTO encompasses agreements made under the GATT, as well as agreements on trade in services, intellectual property, and other issues. The WTO is driven by its members. It does not serve as a legislative body and passes no laws. What the WTO provides is a forum for countries to come together to negotiate. When there are decisions to be made, they are reached by consensus of the members rather than by majority vote. The principal task of the WTO Secretariat is to support the work of member countries as they pursue the goal of trade liberalization.

The Administration played a critical role in launching the Doha Development Agenda negotiations in 2001, following the failure of the 1999 Seattle ministerial meeting to initiate new multilateral trade negotiations. Participating nations agreed that the negotiations would focus on the needs of developing countries and their integration into the global trading system. The United States has put forward proposals for liberalization of trade in agriculture, consumer and industrial goods, and services—the three major areas for market access under negotiation. The Administration is committed to a successful completion of the Doha Development Agenda. This would substantially lower barriers to trade in all countries and provide expanded market access for American goods and services, while boosting economic prospects for developing countries. One study estimates that removal of tariff barriers, production subsidies, and export subsidies could raise annual world income by over $355 billion by 2015. According to another study, a successful round that lowered trade barriers around the world could raise the level of U.S. GDP by $144 billion each year, which translates into additional annual income of $2,000 or more for a family of four.

The WTO operates by consensus, so it takes little to halt progress. While the Administration seeks to continue work on global trade negotiations through the WTO, it has also independently pursued trade liberalization with developed and developing nations through far-reaching bilateral and regional agreements (Table 12-2). These free trade agreements (FTAs) remove substantially all barriers to trade between participants and allow for cooperation in other areas of concern, such as regulation of investments and the protection of intellectual property, the environment, and labor rights. Under WTO rules, countries may undertake preferential liberalization in a free trade agreement, as long as the accord is comprehensive and the liberalization is completed in a reasonable period of time.

TABLE 12-2.— *Status of Free Trade Agreements (FTAs) with the United States*

Country or Region	Status
Israel	In effect since April 22, 1985
Mexico and Canada (NAFTA)	In effect since January 1, 1994
Jordan	In effect since December 17, 2001
Singapore	In effect since January 1, 2004
Chile	In effect since January 1, 2004
Australia	In negotiation as of January 2004
Morocco	In negotiation as of January 2004
Central America (CAFTA)	
El Salvador, Guatemala, Honduras and Nicaragua	Negotiations concluded on December 17, 2003
Costa Rica	Negotiations concluded on January 25, 2004
Dominican Republic	In negotiation
Southern African Customs Union (Botswana, Lesotho, Namibia, South Africa, and Swaziland)	In negotiation
34 Western Hemisphere Countries (FTAA)	In negotiation
Bahrain	In negotiation
Thailand	Intentions to negotiate announced
Panama	Intentions to negotiate announced
Columbia, Peru, Bolivia, and Ecuador	Intentions to negotiate announced

Source: U.S. Trade Representative.

For each potential trading partner in a free trade agreement, the United States assesses the economic benefits such an agreement would bring to the United States, the extent to which the country is ready to undertake free trade obligations, and the role that the agreement would play in furthering the broader, worldwide trade-liberalization agenda. Throughout the process of selecting and negotiating with FTA partners, the Administration consults with members of Congress, public-interest groups, and industry representatives. The United States has demonstrated its willingness to liberalize trade with countries from around the world, both developing and developed. These agreements offer the benefits of trade and investment to the United States and our partner countries and help build a coalition of nations interested in achieving progress in multilateral talks.

The United States has worked to rapidly expand its set of FTA partners, while maintaining low trade barriers to goods and services from all countries through our global commitments.

Conclusion

The United States has benefited and continues to benefit enormously from the international exchange of goods and services. Trade allows countries to specialize in those activities that make the best use of their skills and resources, as well as to reap the benefits in terms of imported goods. These gains have increased as lower barriers, better transportation, and easier communication have expanded existing international markets and created new ones.

Another important but often overlooked benefit to the expansion of free trade is the expansion of freedom and democracy. Involvement in the global economy provides incentives for nations to ensure a degree of transparency and stability in order to attract investors and trading partners. It also encourages countries to embrace a more democratic and less corrupt system of government. Economic freedoms can lead to greater political freedoms.

As the complexity of international trade has increased, so too has the complexity of the agreements that govern it. The dispute-settlement mechanism in the WTO has been useful for resolving disagreements between WTO members. The United States has been challenged on certain trade practices, but in turn has used the dispute settlement system to assert its rights and challenge the practices of other countries.

The Administration is committed to an open and unfettered trading system to promote economic growth in the United States and around the world.

CHAPTER 13

International Capital Flows

International capital flows are the transfer of financial assets, such as cash, stocks, or bonds, across international borders. They have become an increasingly significant part of the world economy over the past decade and an important source of funds to support investment in the United States. In 2002, around $700 billion flowed into the United States. Inflows of international capital help to finance U.S. factories, support U.S. medical research, and fund U.S. companies. At the same time, U.S. investors provided nearly $200 billion in capital to other countries for a wide range of purposes.

Around $2 trillion flowed into countries around the world in 2002, equivalent to roughly 6 percent of global GDP (Chart 13-1). Although these world capital flows have dropped from a peak of over 13 percent of GDP in 2000, largely reflecting a global economic slowdown, they remain above the level of the early 1990s.

Chart 13-1 **Global Capital Flows as a Percent of World GDP**
The 1990s saw a surge in global capital inflows. Flows have since declined, but remain above their level in 1992.

Percent of world GDP

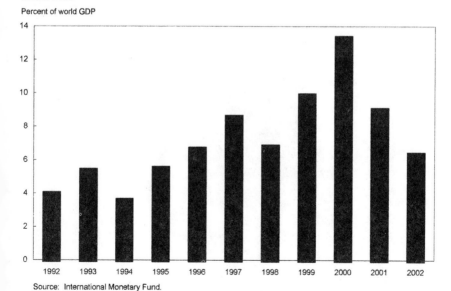

Source: International Monetary Fund.

This chapter describes the various types of international capital flows and discusses their benefits, as well as their risks. The key points in this chapter are:

- Capital flows have significant potential benefits for economies around the world.
- Countries with sound macroeconomic policies and well-functioning institutions are in the best position to reap the benefits of capital flows and minimize the risks.
- Countries that permit free capital flows must choose between the stability provided by fixed exchange rates and the flexibility afforded by an independent monetary policy.

Types of International Capital Flows

Not all capital flows are alike, and there is evidence that the motivation for capital flows and their impact vary by the type of investment. Capital flows can be grouped into three broad categories: foreign direct investment, portfolio investment, and bank and other investment (Chart 13-2).

Chart 13-2 **World Capital Inflows in 2002**
World capital inflows, which include direct investment, portfolio investment, and bank and other investment, totaled $2 trillion in 2002.

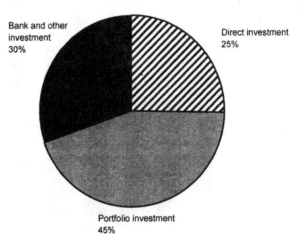

World capital inflows = $2,040 billion

Bank and other investment 30%

Direct investment 25%

Portfolio investment 45%

Source: International Monetary Fund.

Foreign Direct Investment

Foreign direct investment occurs when an investor, in many cases a firm rather than an individual, gains some control over the functioning of an enterprise in another country. This typically takes place through a direct purchase of a business enterprise or when the purchaser acquires more than 10 percent of the shares of the target asset.

A number of factors affect the flow of foreign direct investment. Trade links between investor and recipient countries tend to increase foreign direct investment, as demonstrated by the establishment of Japanese auto plants in the United States starting in the 1980s. Proximity to foreign markets also plays a role, as shown by the investment of U.S. companies in China to service Chinese consumers and firms. The political, economic, and legal stability of the recipient country also matters. Investors are reluctant to establish ownership of foreign companies or set up businesses abroad if corruption or political or social instability are likely to jeopardize operations.

In 2002, foreign direct investment made up roughly one quarter of world capital inflows. About 40 percent of these flows went to the major industrial countries—the United States, Canada, the United Kingdom, Japan, and countries in the euro zone. During much of the 1990s, the United States was the largest single recipient of foreign direct investment. Foreign direct investment flows to industrialized countries are driven largely by the desire for better distribution networks and market access. Another 30 percent of total foreign direct investment went to emerging markets. Relative to flows to industrial countries, these investments were driven more by the low production costs and growing markets of Asia, as well as the privatization of state-owned enterprises in many countries in Latin America and Eastern Europe.

Portfolio Investment

Portfolio investment occurs when investors purchase noncontrolling interests in foreign companies or buy foreign corporate or government bonds, short-term securities, or notes. This type of investment accounted for almost half of world capital inflows in 2002.

Economic and financial conditions in the recipient and investor countries are important influences on portfolio investment flows. The market for these assets is typically more liquid than that for direct investments; it is usually easier to sell a stock or bond than a factory. As a result, investors can quickly reshuffle portfolio investments if they lose confidence in their purchases. Not surprisingly, portfolio investment is far more volatile than foreign direct investment. Countries that receive large capital inflows in one year can see a quick reversal of these inflows if economic or political developments cause investors to reevaluate the expected return on their assets.

Sudden and destabilizing reversals of portfolio investment took place in countries such as Korea, Mexico, Russia, Brazil, and Argentina during the second half of the 1990s and early 2000s. These reversals partly reflected the concern that private-sector and government borrowers in emerging market economies might be unable to meet their financial obligations.

In the United States, portfolio investment in U.S. government securities has played an increasingly important role since 2001. Foreign purchases of U.S. government securities rose from 3 percent of total capital inflows in 2001 to 33 percent in the first three quarters of 2003. One of the most important factors explaining this change is a shift in the share of U.S. security purchases by foreign investors from equities into lower-risk assets, such as U.S. government obligations. Another important factor is increased purchases of U.S. government securities by foreign central banks. A decline in the number of mergers and acquisitions in the United States has also led to lower foreign purchases of private assets.

Bank Investment

Bank investment is the third major type of capital flow. Bank-related international investment includes deposit holdings by foreigners and loans to foreign individuals, businesses, and governments. These investments, grouped with a few other miscellaneous types of investments, accounted for over one quarter of total international capital inflows in 2002. For emerging markets, the importance of these bank-related and other investment flows has declined dramatically in the past decade. While these flows represented an average of 28 percent of capital inflows to emerging economies from 1992 to 1996, they represented an average of only 3 percent of inflows from 1997 to 2002. Economic crises in a number of Asian and Latin American countries since the mid-1990s have contributed to reduced bank lending to these regions since 1997, notably from banks in Japan and Europe.

Benefits of International Capital Flows

Capital flows can have a number of important benefits:
- International capital allows countries to finance more investment than can be supported by domestic saving, thereby increasing output and employment.
- Greater access to foreign markets can provide new opportunities for foreign and domestic investors to increase the return and reduce the risk of their portfolios.

- Foreign direct investment can facilitate the transfer of technology and managerial expertise to developing countries, thus improving productivity.
- Better risk management and other management techniques associated with foreign direct investment can help recipients modify their production processes to lower costs and raise productivity.
- Exposure to international capital markets and the resulting increased competition may induce governments and firms issuing assets to improve macroeconomic policy, management, and profitability. These improvements may, in turn, encourage additional foreign investment.
- Improved international access to investment opportunities in the country receiving capital inflows expands the number of potential investors in any domestic project. This will tend to reduce the cost of raising capital.
- Increased capital inflows can spur the development of domestic financial sectors. A well-developed financial sector can lead to greater investment and reduced financial-sector vulnerability.

Empirical evidence suggests that countries that are open to capital flows can enjoy many of these benefits. In the case of foreign direct investment, studies indicate that industries and some developing countries with more foreign direct investment grow faster than those with less foreign direct investment. In addition, extensive research has found that foreign-owned firms tend to have higher productivity and wages than do their domestic counterparts. Finally, for some developing countries, foreign direct investment can help catalyze the adoption of more-advanced technologies and management practices.

Foreign portfolio investment has played a key role in furthering the development of domestic equity and bond markets. In the case of equity markets, one report estimates that opening up to foreign shareholders leads to an almost 40 percent increase in the real dollar value of the stock market. This lowers the cost of equity capital for domestic firms, as a higher stock price means that a smaller portion of a company needs to be sold to raise a given amount of capital. Developing equity markets can help restrain the ability of corporate managers to pursue their own goals and can help align managerial incentives with earnings growth. In the case of debt markets, evidence indicates that foreign investment can widen the investor base and help businesses raise capital. Moreover, developing countries that lack debt markets may rely excessively on bank lending. Studies suggest that this may leave economies more vulnerable to financial crises because banks are less likely to hold well-diversified portfolios than are participants in developed bond markets.

For all of these reasons, financial market liberalization has been linked to greater investment and higher output growth. One study found that equity market liberalization raised annual economic growth by about 1 percentage point per year in the five years following liberalization. In a related study, the same researchers showed that 17 out of a set of 21 countries that opened their equity markets to foreign participation experienced faster average-growth rates than before liberalization.

A foreign banking presence can also have substantial benefits for the host economy. Foreign-owned financial institutions have been shown to improve the standards and efficiency of the domestic banking sector. This can raise the net yield on saving and enhance capital accumulation and growth. In Latin America, studies have shown that foreign banks in the latter half of the 1990s had higher and less-volatile loan growth than the average domestic bank. Foreign banks may also be a stabilizing force during periods of financial stress. This is partly because foreign banks are often better capitalized and have access to financing through their parent companies at times when domestic banks might be unable to raise capital. Because foreign banks are often better managed and less exposed to domestic downturns, they can also provide citizens some insurance against a collapse of the domestic banking sector. Drawing on the experiences of the Asian crises, academic work suggests that the greater the foreign bank presence in a developing country, the less likely the country was to experience a banking crisis. The ability to hold bank accounts in other countries and borrow from overseas financial institutions can also facilitate trade.

Risks of International Capital Flows

Many countries that reduced barriers to capital flows in the 1990s experienced large capital inflows, increased investment, and strong growth. Several of these countries, however, subsequently experienced economic crises. In the majority of these crises, capital outflows were associated with currency depreciations. The governments, firms, and citizens of many of these emerging markets had significant amounts of debt denominated in foreign currency but received income denominated in domestic currency. The currency depreciations therefore greatly impaired the capacity of these borrowers to service their debts. The resulting increase in bankruptcies and, in some cases, government defaults, weakened the banking sectors and other financial institutions in these countries. All of these factors contributed to sharp contractions in output and high unemployment rates. Such "currency crises" occurred in Mexico, Thailand, Korea, Russia, and Argentina from the mid-1990s through 2001. These experiences have led to a more guarded view of the advantages of capital flows.

One lesson learned from these crises is that a strong institutional framework is important if a country is to benefit fully from openness to capital flows. In other words, capital flows are more likely to yield substantial benefits and carry fewer risks in countries where the financial system is strong and well developed; laws and regulations are clear, reasonable, and enforced by the courts and public institutions; and the reporting of financial information is timely and accurate so that investors have a clear understanding of the conditions and strength of the assets in which they are investing. Corruption is also associated with lower foreign investment and weaker growth.

In countries with weak institutions or high levels of corruption, capital inflows may not be channeled to their most-productive uses, dissipating their potential benefits. In these cases, improved access to capital can allow firms and sovereigns to accumulate high levels of debt through purchases of unproductive assets. This can ultimately leave firms and countries vulnerable to changes in investor sentiment, possibly contributing to economic crises.

One approach to limiting these risks when legal and financial institutions are poorly developed is to restrict foreign capital flows. Experience, however, suggests that capital controls impose substantial costs. Controls on the movement of capital can distort firms' investment decisions, increase opportunities for corruption, and discourage foreign direct investment. All of these effects can depress growth (Box 13-1).

Box 13-1: Capital Controls in Emerging Markets

Recent economic crises in several emerging economies that opened their markets to capital flows have renewed debate on the desirability of capital controls. Any benefits of restrictions on capital flows, however, must be weighed against the costs and distortions they impose.

Capital controls can take various forms and can target either capital inflows or capital outflows. Countries may adopt *controls on capital inflows* in an attempt to prevent an appreciation of their currency or to direct foreign investments to longer-term ventures. Experience shows that these controls, regardless of whether they achieve their objective, can create problems, including economic distortions and large administrative fees. For example, in the 1990s, the Chilean government required that a portion of capital inflows be temporarily deposited in a non-interest-bearing central bank account. These restrictions lowered the risk of rapid capital flight, and some analyses show that they lengthened the average period of time that capital inflows remained in Chile. These restrictions, however, also increased administrative costs, especially because the government had to

---

Box 13-1 — *continued*

modify them frequently to close numerous loopholes. Research also shows that these controls on capital inflows caused smaller, public firms to face greater financing constraints than they did before the restrictions. These higher financing costs may have stifled an important source of growth and innovation in Chile.

Countries' experiences with *controls on capital outflows* reinforce the view that controls are difficult to implement and often carry unexpected costs. Controls on capital outflows also take a variety of forms, such as limitations on the amount of domestic holdings of foreign currency and restrictions on the ability of foreign investors to repatriate their earnings. The potential to avert financial crises triggered by capital outflows can make controls appealing in theory. In practice, however, any such benefits tend to be eroded over time as firms and individuals find ways to circumvent the restrictions. Such evasive activity can create additional problems, such as reduced financial transparency and tax compliance, distortions from the unequal impact of the controls (as not all sectors have equal access to the evasive measures), and a general reduction in respect for the law. For example, studies indicate that controls on capital outflows in Russia in the mid-1990s were evaded by exporters, particularly in the energy sector, through the underreporting of earnings.

Finally, capital controls can also distort the behavior of foreign investors. For example, research indicates that American multinational firms invest less in their local affiliates in countries with capital controls. In addition, multinationals tend to alter their investment and payment structure in order to minimize the effect of the restrictions. This distortion is yet another way capital controls can reduce the productivity of the world's stock of capital.

Another approach for developing countries to minimize the risks from opening up to capital movements involves the careful timing, or sequencing, of policies designed to "liberalize" financial markets. One variant of this approach suggests that countries should first achieve macroeconomic stability, in part by implementing sound fiscal and monetary policies. Countries should next strengthen financial market institutions, and only then allow for free capital flows. While this approach may work for some countries under specific economic conditions, the pace and timing of reforms appear to be less important than the consistency of the reforms and the government's commitment to them.

Policy makers increasingly realize that there is no simple rule to best achieve free capital flows, and that country characteristics should be considered. There is some consensus, however, that the benefits of international capital mobility can be substantial and that to best achieve these benefits, countries should implement reforms of domestic financial and legal institutions.

Constraints Imposed by Free Capital Flows

One consequence of allowing capital to flow freely in and out of a country is that this constrains a nation's choice of monetary policy and exchange-rate regime. For important but subtle reasons related to the tendency for capital to flow to where returns are the highest, countries can maintain only two of the following three policies—free capital flows, a fixed exchange rate, and an independent monetary policy. Economists refer to this restriction as *the impossible trinity*. As illustrated by Chart 13-3, countries must choose to be on one side of the triangle, adopting the policies at each end, but forgoing the policy on the opposite corner.

Chart 13-3 **"The Impossible Trinity"**
Countries can adopt only two of the following three policies -- free capital flows, a fixed exchange rate, and independent monetary policy.

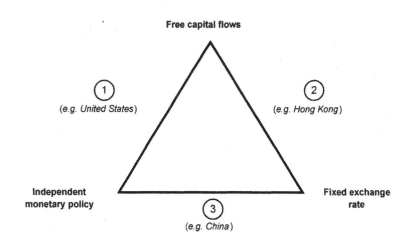

Source: Council of Economic Advisers.

The easiest way to understand this restriction is through specific examples. The United States allows free capital flows and has an independent monetary policy, but it has a flexible exchange rate. (The U.S. government does not attempt to fix, or "peg," the exchange value of the dollar at any particular level against other currencies.) As a simplified example, if the Federal Reserve Board raised its target interest rate relative to foreign interest rates, capital would flow into the United States. By increasing the demand for U.S. dollars relative to other currencies, these capital inflows would increase the price of the dollar against other currencies. This would cause the exchange rate to adjust and the U.S. dollar to appreciate. In the opposite case, if the Federal Reserve Board lowered its target interest rate, net capital outflows would reduce the demand for dollars, thereby causing the dollar to depreciate against foreign currencies.

In contrast, Hong Kong essentially pegs the value of its currency to the U.S. dollar and allows free capital flows. (Hong Kong is a Special Administrative Region of China, but maintains its own currency.) The trade-off is that Hong Kong loses the ability to use monetary policy to influence domestic interest rates. Unlike the United States, Hong Kong cannot cut interest rates to stimulate a weak economy. If Hong Kong's interest rates were to deviate from world rates, capital would flow in or out of the Hong Kong economy, just as in the U.S. case above. Under a flexible exchange rate, these flows would cause the price of the Hong Kong dollar to change relative to that of other currencies. Under a fixed exchange rate, however, the monetary authority must offset these flows by purchasing domestic or foreign currency in order to keep the supply and demand for its currency fixed, and therefore the exchange rate unchanged. The capacity of the government to sustain large purchases and sales of its currency is ultimately limited by several factors, including the amount of foreign exchange reserves held by the government and its willingness to accumulate stocks of relatively low-return foreign currency assets.

Just as in the case of Hong Kong, China pegs its exchange rate to the U.S. dollar. China can operate an independent monetary policy, however, as it maintains restrictions on capital flows. In China's case, world and domestic interest rates can differ, because controls on the transfer of funds in and out of the country limit the resulting changes in the money supply and the corresponding pressures on the exchange rate.

As these three examples show, if a country chooses to allow capital to flow freely, it must also decide between having an independent monetary policy or a fixed exchange rate. Many factors affect how a country makes this crucial decision (Box 13-2).

Box 13-2: Choosing Among a Fixed Exchange Rate, Independent Monetary Policy, and Free Capital Movements

How does a country choose whether to give up a fixed exchange rate, independent monetary policy, or free capital movements? While country-specific factors play a role, experience has shown that these decisions also reflect global trends.

In the late 1920s, many countries, including the United States, adopted an exchange-rate system in which they pegged their currencies to a fixed quantity of gold. This system, which was used previously but was abandoned during World War I, was known as the *gold standard*. It effectively fixed the exchange rates of the currencies for all participating countries. Countries generally coupled this fixed exchange rate with the free movement of capital, relinquishing the ability to influence economic activity at home through the use of independent monetary policy.

This system proved sustainable until the Great Depression of the 1930s, when many governments abandoned exchange-rate stability in order to expand domestic demand by increasing the money supply and lowering interest rates. Following the economic recoveries under this regime, the choice of free capital flows and independent monetary policy remained popular through the end of World War II.

The postwar era, however, saw substantial international integration of markets and increasing cross-border trade. Countries such as the United States wanted to facilitate this increase in trade by eliminating the risks of exchange-rate fluctuations. At a summit held in Bretton Woods, New Hampshire, in 1944, representatives from the major industrial economies designed and implemented a plan that encouraged exchange-rate stability while maintaining autonomous monetary policies. The Bretton Woods system, as it became known, offered countries greater monetary independence while fixing the value of the dollar, yen, deutsche mark, and other currencies. Just as with the previous systems, however, something had to be sacrificed—the Bretton Woods arrangement required capital controls. Capital controls included caps on the interest rates that banks could offer to depositors and limitations on the types of assets in which banks could invest. Further, governments frequently intervened in financial markets to direct capital toward strategic domestic sectors. Though none of these controls alone prevented international capital flows, in combination they allowed governments to restrain the amount of cross-border capital transactions.

Box 13-2 — continued

In the early 1970s, the Bretton Woods system gave way to a more-diverse set of regimes. Ultimately, as growth in other countries outstripped growth in the United States, demand shifted from the U.S. dollar to foreign currencies, putting downward pressure on the dollar's value. After several negotiated devaluations of the dollar, governments agreed to abandon the system rather than continue to be forced to change domestic interest and inflation rates to keep the dollar's value constant. Furthermore, greater financial sophistication and increasing capital mobility made it more difficult and costly to sustain capital controls in the advanced economies.

Since the end of the Bretton Woods system, countries have chosen a variety of exchange-rate regimes. Countries in the euro zone, for instance, have adopted the euro as a common currency. This is equivalent to fixing the exchange rates among the participating countries. The euro, however, is allowed to move freely against other currencies such as the dollar. Each of the countries within the euro zone has had to give up its own independent monetary policy. The value of the U.S. dollar, on the other hand, floats freely against other currencies. The free movement of capital has been uniformly embraced by the advanced industrial economies and is increasingly being adopted by developing economies.

Encouraging Free Capital Flows

The Administration supports the free flow of capital between the United States and other countries and encourages countries to take steps to open their markets to international investment. Such efforts include the negotiation of Bilateral Investment Treaties, as well as Trade and Investment Framework Agreements. Under these agreements, foreign countries commit to treating U.S. investors fairly and to allowing U.S. corporations to operate in foreign countries in closer accordance with standard U.S. practices and procedures. This protection reduces the risks associated with investing abroad and encourages U.S. multinational companies to expand through foreign direct investment.

Investment measures and protections have also played a central role in free trade agreements negotiated by the United States (these are discussed in Chapter 12, *International Trade and Cooperation*). Recent trade agreements, such as that with Chile, have included investment provisions that protect American investors and ensure their access to foreign investment opportunities.

The United States also encourages countries to undertake the reforms that will help them best reap the benefits of greater investment and capital flows. These reforms include improvements in corporate governance and the distribution of accurate, timely, and complete information on economic conditions, government regulations, and corporate performance. The Administration has focused on reducing the risks of destabilizing capital flows in a number of ways.

One important development in this regard has been the increased inclusion of "collective action clauses" in international bonds issued by emerging market countries—a practice that has been supported and encouraged by the United States. These clauses allow a majority of creditors to bind a minority to key financial terms in the event of a debt restructuring. They also help facilitate ongoing discussions and negotiations between a sovereign and its creditors. By making it easier for issuers and bondholders to agree to changes in bond terms in the event of a default or restructuring, collective action clauses provide a contractual method for improving the resolution of situations where sovereign debt levels are unsustainable. Such improvements to the debt-resolution process should reduce the unnecessary loss of value to creditors and thereby lessen the risk of lending to emerging market countries.

The United States has also endorsed the efforts of the International Monetary Fund and the World Bank to increase the availability, frequency, scope, and quality of the reported data of their member countries. Better and more timely information can assist policy makers and investors to make appropriate decisions. Some of these efforts include:

- The Financial Sector Assessment Program, which involves a rigorous and in-depth analysis of a country's financial system.
- The Special Data Dissemination Standard, which sets certain standards of timeliness and quality for economic and financial statistics to guide countries that have (or desire) access to foreign capital markets.
- The implementation of agreed-upon norms, such as the Code of Good Practices and Fiscal Transparency, which emphasize adherence to certain standards of good practice and promote quality accounting procedures and fiscal transparency.

These programs help investors, public-sector lenders, and governments identify weaknesses and vulnerabilities in firms, sectors, and the economy in general. They also target areas for reform in a country's macroeconomic policy, financial sector, and supervisory systems. This combination of policies should help developed and developing countries take advantage of greater capital market integration, while minimizing the risks.

Finally, the Millennium Challenge Account, a Presidential initiative enacted in January 2004, provides incentives for developing countries to adopt policies that spur economic growth and reduce poverty. First-year funding for the

Millennium Challenge Account is $1 billion. The Administration has requested that this amount rise to $5 billion per year by fiscal year 2006. The Millennium Challenge Corporation, which administers the Millennium Challenge Account, will direct development grants to poor countries that have appropriate economic, political, and structural conditions to benefit from foreign assistance. The Millennium Challenge Corporation will partner with countries that demonstrate a strong commitment to ruling justly, investing in their people, and encouraging economic freedom in order to develop their own strategies for catalyzing economic growth and reducing poverty. The Millennium Challenge Account is designed to provide funding for programs that have clear objectives, a sound financial plan, and measured benchmarks for demonstrating progress in overcoming major obstacles to sustained economic growth. The Millennium Challenge Account will not only improve the ability of recipient countries to fight poverty and to grow more quickly, but will also encourage the international investment that helps to strengthen growth.

Conclusion

Underlying each of the policies promoted by the Administration is the goal of helping countries reap the substantial benefits of the free flow of international capital. Foreign direct investment can facilitate the transfer of technology, allow for the development of markets and products, and improve a country's infrastructure. Portfolio flows can reduce the cost of capital, improve competitiveness, and increase investment opportunities. Bank flows can strengthen domestic financial institutions, improve financial intermediation, and reduce vulnerability to crises. These flows are not without their risks, but such risks can be reduced if countries adopt prudent fiscal and monetary policies, strengthen financial and corporate institutions, and develop the regulations and agencies that supervise such institutions. Such steps allow countries to fully gain from free capital flows.

CHAPTER 14

The Link Between Trade
and Capital Flows

M ovements of goods and services across borders are often thought of as
distinct from international capital flows. For example, an individual
who allocates part of his or her retirement savings to a mutual fund that invests
in an international portfolio might not think that this cross-border transaction
has an impact on the price of imports, such as foreign cars or food at the super-
market. Yet, for important but subtle reasons, trade flows and capital flows are
closely intertwined—indeed, they are two sides of the same coin.

This chapter explores the linkages between trade and capital flows. The key
points in this chapter are:

- Changes in a country's net international trade in goods and services,
captured by the current account, must be reflected in equal and opposite
changes in its net capital flows with the rest of the world.
- The United States has experienced a large net inflow of foreign capital in
recent years. Any such inflow must be accompanied by an equally large
current account deficit.
- The size and movement of current and capital accounts reflect fundamental
economic forces, including saving and investment rates, and relative
rates of growth across countries.

The Basic Accounting Identity

The *balance of payments* is the accounting system by which countries report
data on their international borrowing and lending, as well as on the flow of
goods and services in and out of the country. The balance of payments
includes a number of different accounts (Box 14-1). The central relationship
of the balance of payments is that the *net* flow of capital into a country, as
measured by the financial and capital accounts, must balance the *net* flow of
goods, services, transfer payments, and income receipts out of the country, as
measured by the current account.

When the current account balance is negative, this means that purchases of
foreign goods and services (and other outflows) exceed sales of goods and
services to foreigners (and other inflows). This situation is referred to as a
current account deficit. The *trade balance* is generally the largest component of
the current account and captures the net inflows of goods and services. A

positive net flow of capital into the United States means that foreigners are purchasing more U.S. assets than U.S. citizens are purchasing foreign assets. According to the balance of payments, a positive net flow of capital into the United States must be balanced by a current account deficit.

Box 14-1: A New Look for the Balance of Payments

Just as a country's national accounts keep track of macroeconomic variables such as GDP, saving, and investment, a country's balance of payments accounts serve as the bookkeeping for its international transactions, such as exports, imports, and international investment flows. In 1999, the Bureau of Economic Analysis announced that it would adopt new terminology to be consistent with international best practices for balance of payments accounting, as outlined by the International Monetary Fund.

The *old* balance of payments system used two accounts: the *capital account* and the *current account.* The *new* system uses three accounts (Chart 14-1). The new current account includes the trade balance in goods and services, net income receipts, and the balance of most unilateral transfers (one-way transfers of assets, such as pension payments to foreign residents). Some unilateral transfers, including debt forgiveness and the transfer of bank accounts by foreign citizens when immigrating to the United States, have been removed from the *old* current account and are now in a separate account, the *new* capital account. The new capital account represents a very small portion of overall capital flows. Private capital flows and changes in foreign and domestic reserves (formerly in the old capital account) are now in the *financial account.* This new treatment preserves the balance of payments identity that the sum of all the accounts is zero.

To simplify terminology, this *Economic Report of the President* refers to the new capital and financial accounts as *net capital flows—* that is, inflows of capital from foreign countries minus outflows from the United States. Positive net capital flows indicate that more capital is flowing into the United States than out.

Chart 14-1 **Changes to the Balance of Payments Terminology in 1999**

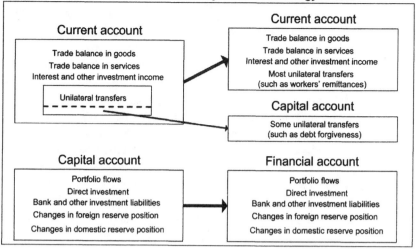

To understand how the balance of payments works in practice, consider a consumer in the United States who purchases a scarf from a foreign seller for one dollar. This transaction is recorded as an import and reduces the U.S. current account balance by one dollar. The foreign seller could spend the dollar on U.S. goods or on U.S assets, such as stocks or bonds. If the foreigner purchases U.S. goods, this would be recorded in the balance of payments as a U.S. export in the current account. The U.S. purchase of the foreign scarf and the foreign purchase of U.S. goods would cancel each other out, so there would be no change in the current account and no change in net capital flows. Alternatively, if the foreigner decided to purchase U.S. assets, this would be recorded as a capital inflow into the United States. The increase in net capital flows would balance the decrease in the U.S. current account. In both examples, the resulting change in the current account, if any, exactly balances any change in net capital flows.

Trade in goods can lead to changes in financial balances (such as with the payment for the scarf in the example above), or financial transactions can lead to changes in trade balances. The latter case would occur if a foreigner purchased a U.S. asset, such as a bond, and the American seller of the bond used the proceeds to purchase foreign goods. In both cases, the balance between the current account and net capital flows still holds.

To understand how financial flows can affect trade balances, suppose that at the prevailing rate of return, investors in the United States seek to undertake $200 billion worth of projects. If U.S. savers were willing to provide only $150 billion in capital through saving, then the other $50 billion could come from the rest of the world as $50 billion in capital inflows. If the U.S. investors choose to spend this capital inflow on foreign goods (perhaps imports of new computers), then net purchases of foreign goods would increase by $50 billion. The resulting $50 billion current account deficit would balance the $50 billion capital inflow. If investors in the United States were not able to obtain the initial $50 billion from abroad, both net capital flows and the current account would equal zero. There would be no current account deficit. Would this be good or bad? One immediate effect would be that the $50 billion gap between desired investment and saving would need to be closed by scaling back investment projects or raising national saving. These changes should be evaluated on their own merits; there is nothing particularly beneficial about having a trade balance or net capital flows exactly equal to zero.

A country's saving and investment decisions are critical to evaluating the implication of any given level of its current account balance. In a world without capital flows, the only funds available for investment come from domestic saving. Capital flows allow a country to finance higher levels of investment by drawing on funds from abroad. This net inflow of funds corresponds to greater net purchases from the world and a decline in the current account balance.

The desirability of positive net capital flows and a current account deficit depend on what the capital inflows are used for. Household borrowing—an excess of household spending or investment over saving—provides a useful analogy. Household debt could reflect borrowing to finance an extravagant vacation, a mortgage to buy a home, or a loan to finance education. Without knowing its purpose, the appropriateness of the borrowing cannot be judged. Similarly for countries, borrowing from abroad can be productive or unproductive. Borrowing from abroad can be justified if it raises the potential output of the economy and this, in turn, generates the resources needed to repay the foreign lenders.

This entire discussion has focused on trade balances and net capital flows with the world as a whole, and not with any individual country. There is no economic basis for concern about trade deficits and the corresponding net capital flows with an individual trading partner when there are many countries in the world (Box 14-2).

Box 14-2: Bilateral Versus Multilateral Balances

A country's aggregate trade deficit matters only to the extent that it reveals information about underlying economic forces, such as relative international growth rates or national saving and investment patterns. In contrast, *bilateral deficits*, such as the U.S. trade deficit with China, reveal *nothing* about underlying economic forces in either country. While trade barriers are a cause for concern, there is no economic sense in which a bilateral deficit is either good or bad. It would be an extraordinary coincidence if all countries had balanced trade with each of their partners. One of the benefits of the international financial system is that it frees countries from these bilateral constraints.

For example, imagine a simplified world that consisted of only the United States, Australia, and China. Suppose the United States ships $100 billion of machine tools to Australia and imports no goods in return. Australia ships $100 billion of wheat to China with no reciprocal goods imports, and China ships $100 billion of toys to the United States. Each country would have $100 billion of exports and $100 billion of imports, so that each would have balanced trade overall. Yet some Americans might complain about their bilateral deficit with China. Some Chinese might complain about their deficit with Australia, and some Australians about their deficit with the United States. All of these complaints would be unfounded; bilateral deficits and surpluses are a natural consequence of a trading world composed of many countries.

Domestic transactions provide a useful analogy. A plumber who spends no more than he earns can still run a bilateral deficit with the local grocer. The plumber can earn money from other sources to pay the grocer and is not constrained to buying only from grocers who have plumbing problems. The bilateral imbalance that exists between the plumber and the grocer is an entirely natural feature of a well-functioning economy with a strong payments system and specialization.

Trends in the U.S. Balance of Payments

The decrease in the U.S. current account balance, from nearly zero in the early 1990s to a deficit of about 5 percent of GDP in the first three quarters of 2003, has been mirrored by a similar increase in net capital flows (Chart 14-2). (The two series in Chart 14-2 are not exact mirror images due to imprecision in the measurement of trade and capital flows.)

Examining the components of the current and financial accounts provides information on the causes of these recent trends in the U.S. balance of payments (Table 14-1). Over the 1990s, a major contributor to the rise in the current account deficit was the increase in imports of foreign goods. The trade balance in goods moved from a deficit of 1.9 percent of GDP in 1990 to a deficit of 4.6 percent of GDP in 2000. Exports of goods increased from 6.7 percent of GDP in 1990 to 7.9 percent of GDP in 2000, but goods imports increased by much more, from 8.6 percent of GDP to 12.5 percent of GDP over the same period. The increase in the current account deficit since 2000 has resulted mainly from lower exports of goods (which fell from 7.9 percent to 6.4 percent of GDP between 2000 and the first three quarters of 2003), rather than increased imports. Imports as a share of GDP actually fell 1 percentage point over the same period (Chart 14-3 and Table 14-1). Most recently, the current account deficit has narrowed from 5.2 percent of GDP in the first quarter of 2003 to 4.9 percent of GDP in the third, reflecting stronger export growth.

Chart 14-2 **Balance of Payments**
The 1990s saw a surge in capital inflows and a corresponding deficit in the current account balance.
Percent of GDP

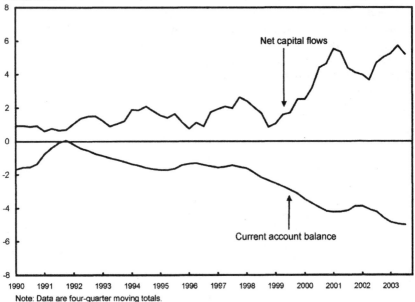

Note: Data are four-quarter moving totals.
Source: Department of Commerce (Bureau of Economic Analysis).

TABLE 14-1.— *Current and Financial Account*
[Percent of GDP]

Accounts	1990	2000	2002	2003: Q1-Q3
Current account balance	-1.4	-4.2	-4.6	-5.1
Trade balance in goods	-1.9	-4.6	-4.6	-5.0
Exports	6.7	7.9	6.5	6.4
Imports	-8.6	-12.5	-11.1	-11.5
Services (net)	.5	.8	.6	.5
Other (net)	.0	-.4	-.6	-.6
Net capital flows	.9	4.6	5.0	5.0
Financial account balance	1.0	4.6	5.0	5.1
Direct investment (net)	.2	1.7	-.9	-.5
Portfolio (net)	-.1	3.0	4.2	3.7
Equity securities (net)	-.4	.9	.3	-.8
Debt securities (net)	.3	2.2	3.8	4.5
Other	1.0	.0	1.8	1.8
Capital account balance	-.1	.0	.0	.0
Memo:				
Foreign purchases of U.S. Government securities	.5	-.5	1.6	2.6

Note: Detail may not add to totals because of rounding and seasonal adjustment.

Source: Department of Commerce (Bureau of Economic Analysis).

Chart 14-3 **Exports and Imports of Goods**
Both exports and imports of goods decreased substantially starting in the first quarter of 2001 and have yet to fully recover.

Percent of GDP

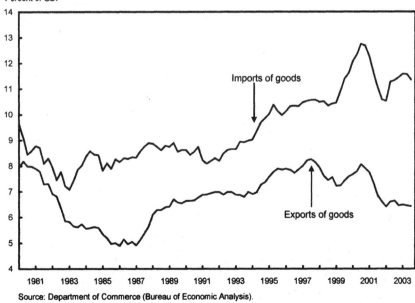

Source: Department of Commerce (Bureau of Economic Analysis).

U.S. net capital flows grew from about 1 percent of GDP in 1990 to over 4½ percent of GDP in 2000. This resulted from roughly equal increases in foreign purchases of debt securities, equity securities, and direct investment. This increase in net capital flows into the United States largely reflected the desire of foreigners to participate in higher-return investment opportunities in the United States. The global economic downturn and the collapse of high-tech stock prices and broader equity indices that began in 2000 contributed to a shift in the composition of capital flows in the United States. Foreign investors moved away from foreign direct investment and private equity assets and toward government and corporate bonds. In addition, foreign governments increased their share of these capital flows, although the foreign private sector still accounts for a far greater proportion.

Over the latter half of the 1990s and the early 2000s, the counterpart to the rising U.S. current account deficit has been a growing wedge between U.S. investment rates and U.S. national saving rates (Chart 14-4). The national saving rate in the United States began to decline in 1999, but increased capital inflows allowed U.S. investment rates to remain at a high level through 2000. As discussed in Chapter 1, *Lessons from the Recent Business Cycle*, investment fell substantially after the collapse of the stock market bubble of the late 1990s. In 2001, the decline in investment outpaced a contemporaneous decline in U.S. saving, so that the current account deficit narrowed. U.S. investment has since leveled off while saving remains low, causing a wider U.S. current account deficit. Over the entire period, the availability of foreign investment permitted the United States to maintain higher investment rates than it could have funded relying solely on domestic financing. These capital inflows have helped finance U.S. investments, expand U.S. productive capacity, and strengthen U.S. economic performance.

Factors that Influence the Balance of Payments

A number of underlying economic factors influence the level of and changes in the balance of payments. One of the most important factors is the differential rate of GDP growth across countries. During the late 1990s, the United States grew faster than many of its major trading partners, such as Japan and a number of major European countries. As a result, capital flowed into the United States, leading to a corresponding trade deficit. Even during the recent business-cycle downturn and recovery, U.S. growth rates have exceeded those of many of our major trading partners. This has contributed to the slow recovery in U.S. exports and has helped to maintain continued capital inflows into the United States.

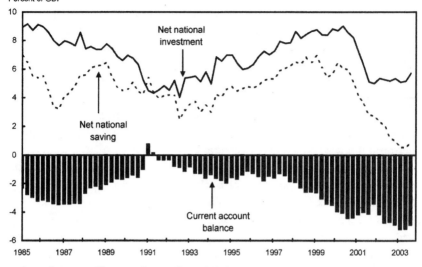

Chart 14-4 Saving, Investment, and the Current Account Balance
In the late 1980s, a decline in the investment rate led to a reduction in the current account deficit, while a sharp decline in the national saving rate accounted for the most recent expansion of the deficit.

Source: Department of Commerce (Bureau of Economic Analysis).

A second determinant of trade and capital flows is the price of domestic goods relative to foreign goods. Relative prices are influenced by a number of factors, including labor and production costs, labor productivity, and exchange rates. For many manufactured products, for example, labor and production costs in developing countries are often below such costs in the United States. As a result, the prices of these goods produced in developing countries may be substantially lower than the price of similar goods produced in the United States. For other products and projects, such as airplanes and the development of new drugs, the availability of factors of production such as skilled engineers may be more important than the availability of low-skilled workers. Exchange rates can also influence relative prices. A depreciation of a country's currency can make its products cheaper and thus more competitive abroad, even if domestic prices do not change. When a country's currency appreciates, domestically produced goods become relatively more expensive in foreign markets.

A third determinant of the direction and size of capital flows is the relative return that investors expect to make in one country compared with another. This return differential can reflect factors discussed earlier, such as relative output growth, labor costs, or exchange rates. This differential can also depend on a country's legal framework, accounting and tax systems, infrastructure, culture, and institutions. The flow of capital into the United States likely reflects a view that the expected risk-adjusted, after-tax return on U.S. assets is higher than the return on similar foreign investments.

These factors—growth rates, relative prices, and rates of return—all drive national saving and investment decisions. Those decisions most directly determine the balance of payments. *National saving* is the sum of *private saving* (saving of households and corporations) and *public saving* (the total saving of Federal, State, and local governments, as reflected in their budget balances). When national saving is less than domestic investment, a country must be borrowing from abroad. This borrowing will be reflected in positive net capital flows and a current account deficit.

Although this suggests that the recent increase in the U.S. budget deficit may be related to the recent increase in the U.S. current account deficit, the historical evidence for a relationship between government deficits and trade deficits is mixed. A number of academic studies suggest that other domestic and international factors are more important influences on current account balances than government deficits. The recent U.S. experience supports this. In the 1990s, the large increase in the U.S. current account deficit occurred while the Federal budget surplus was growing (Chart 14-5). From 1997 to 2000, the U.S. current account deficit increased by almost 3 percentage points. Over the same period, the U.S. budget balance went from a slight deficit to a surplus of 2½ percent of GDP. Since 2000, the U.S. budget has moved into deficit by several percentage points of GDP, but the current account deficit has widened by only about 1 percentage point of GDP. These figures show that the current account and Federal budget do not move in lockstep, and that the government deficit is only one of several factors behind the widening of the current account deficit since the mid-1990s.

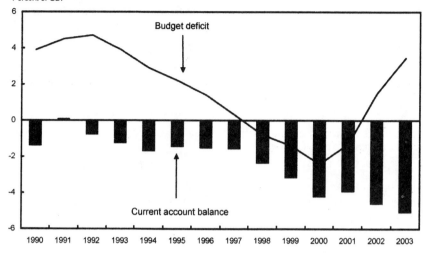

Chart 14-5 **Budget Deficit and the Current Account Balance**
The relatively steady decline in the current account balance contrasts with the initial reduction and subsequent expansion of the budget deficit.

Percent of GDP

Note: Budget deficit data are for fiscal years ending September 30; current account data are for calendar years. Current account balance for 2003 includes data through the third quarter.
Source: Department of Commerce (Bureau of Economic Analysis).

Possible Paths of Balance of Payments Adjustment

The U.S. current account deficit reached about 5 percent of GDP in the first three quarters of 2003. Historically, many countries with sizable current account deficits have experienced reductions in capital flows and corresponding reductions in their current account deficits. Because the U.S. current account deficit and U.S. capital inflows are balanced by trade and capital flows in other countries, any change in the U.S. balance of payments would involve corresponding changes in other countries' flows of trade and capital. The economic implications of any adjustments depend on how it occurs.

An adjustment in the U.S. trade balance could involve a number of domestic and global factors. For example, faster growth in other countries would be expected to increase demand for U.S. exports and narrow the U.S. current account deficit. Slower growth in the United States relative to its major trading partners would dampen U.S. demand for imports and reduce the U.S. trade deficit. Trade flows could also adjust through changes in the relative prices of U.S. goods and services compared to the prices of foreign goods and services. This relative-price adjustment could occur through changes in nominal exchange rates or through different inflation rates in different countries.

An adjustment in the U.S. balance of payments would also require a change in international capital flows. To reduce net capital flows, foreign investors could buy fewer U.S. assets and/or U.S. investors could buy more foreign assets. This might occur if U.S. national saving were to increase, thereby reducing the need for foreign funds to finance U.S. domestic investment. The U.S. investment rate could also fall, so that the United States required less capital inflow. Lower investment is the least desirable form of adjustment for the balance of payments, however, as it would reduce U.S. productive capacity and lead to slower growth.

It is impossible to predict the exact timing or magnitude of any adjustment in the U.S. current account balance. After a large increase in the U.S. current account deficit in the 1980s, the ensuing adjustments were gradual and benign. Public policies can facilitate changes in the U.S. current account and net capital flows by creating a stable macroeconomic and financial environment, encouraging foreign growth, and spurring increased saving in the United States.

Conclusion

Flows of goods and services across borders are linked to international capital flows through the balance of payments. Changes in the current account (which includes international trade in goods and services) must be balanced by equal and opposite changes in net capital flows with the rest of the world. Similarly, movements in net capital flows require offsetting movements in the current account.

In recent years, the United States has received large net inflows of foreign capital, which have been balanced by large U.S. current account deficits. The U.S. balance of payments is mirrored by trade and capital flows in other countries. Thus, over the same period, the rest of the world as a whole has experienced a current account surplus and capital outflows.

The United States' sizable positive net capital flows and the corresponding trade deficits are neither good nor bad in and of themselves. Instead, they represent underlying economic forces, such as relative GDP growth rates, relative prices of domestic and foreign goods, relative returns on investment, and national saving and investment decisions. Changes in these underlying factors would lead to changes in the U.S. balance of payments and corresponding changes in the international flows of trade and capital.

Appendix A
REPORT TO THE PRESIDENT ON THE ACTIVITIES OF THE COUNCIL OF ECONOMIC ADVISERS DURING 2003

LETTER OF TRANSMITTAL

COUNCIL OF ECONOMIC ADVISERS,
Washington, D.C., December 31, 2003.

MR. PRESIDENT:

The Council of Economic Advisers submits this report on its activities during the calendar year 2003 in accordance with the requirements of the Congress, as set forth in section 10(d) of the Employment Act of 1946 as amended by the Full Employment and Balanced Growth Act of 1978.

Sincerely,

N. Gregory Mankiw, *Chairman*
Kristin J. Forbes, *Member*
Harvey S. Rosen, *Member*

Council Members and Their Dates of Service

Name	Position	Oath of office date	Separation date
Edwin G. Nourse	Chairman	August 9, 1946	November 1, 1949.
Leon H. Keyserling	Vice Chairman	August 9, 1946	
	Acting Chairman	November 2, 1949	
	Chairman	May 10, 1950	January 20, 1953.
John D. Clark	Member	August 9, 1946	
	Vice Chairman	May 10, 1950	February 11, 1953.
Roy Blough	Member	June 29, 1950	August 20, 1952.
Robert C. Turner	Member	September 8, 1952	January 20, 1953.
Arthur F. Burns	Chairman	March 19, 1953	December 1, 1956.
Neil H. Jacoby	Member	September 15, 1953	February 9, 1955.
Walter W. Stewart	Member	December 2, 1953	April 29, 1955.
Raymond J. Saulnier	Member	April 4, 1955	
	Chairman	December 3, 1956	January 20, 1961.
Joseph S. Davis	Member	May 2, 1955	October 31, 1958.
Paul W. McCracken	Member	December 3, 1956	January 31, 1959.
Karl Brandt	Member	November 1, 1958	January 20, 1961.
Henry C. Wallich	Member	May 7, 1959	January 20, 1961.
Walter W. Heller	Chairman	January 29, 1961	November 15, 1964.
James Tobin	Member	January 29, 1961	July 31, 1962.
Kermit Gordon	Member	January 29, 1961	December 27, 1962.
Gardner Ackley	Member	August 3, 1962	
	Chairman	November 16, 1964	February 15, 1968.
John P. Lewis	Member	May 17, 1963	August 31, 1964.
Otto Eckstein	Member	September 2, 1964	February 1, 1966.
Arthur M. Okun	Member	November 16, 1964	
	Chairman	February 15, 1968	January 20, 1969.
James S. Duesenberry	Member	February 2, 1966	June 30, 1968.
Merton J. Peck	Member	February 15, 1968	January 20, 1969.
Warren L. Smith	Member	July 1, 1968	January 20, 1969.
Paul W. McCracken	Chairman	February 4, 1969	December 31, 1971.
Hendrik S. Houthakker	Member	February 4, 1969	July 15, 1971.
Herbert Stein	Member	February 4, 1969	
	Chairman	January 1, 1972	August 31, 1974.
Ezra Solomon	Member	September 9, 1971	March 26, 1973.
Marina v.N. Whitman	Member	March 13, 1972	August 15, 1973.
Gary L. Seevers	Member	July 23, 1973	April 15, 1975.
William J. Fellner	Member	October 31, 1973	February 25, 1975.
Alan Greenspan	Chairman	September 4, 1974	January 20, 1977.
Paul W. MacAvoy	Member	June 13, 1975	November 15, 1976.
Burton G. Malkiel	Member	July 22, 1975	January 20, 1977.
Charles L. Schultze	Chairman	January 22, 1977	January 20, 1981.
William D. Nordhaus	Member	March 18, 1977	February 4, 1979.
Lyle E. Gramley	Member	March 18, 1977	May 27, 1980.
George C. Eads	Member	June 6, 1979	January 20, 1981.
Stephen M. Goldfeld	Member	August 20, 1980	January 20, 1981.
Murray L. Weidenbaum	Chairman	February 27, 1981	August 25, 1982.
William A. Niskanen	Member	June 12, 1981	March 30, 1985.
Jerry L. Jordan	Member	July 14, 1981	July 31, 1982.
Martin Feldstein	Chairman	October 14, 1982	July 10, 1984.
William Poole	Member	December 10, 1982	January 20, 1985.
Beryl W. Sprinkel	Chairman	April 18, 1985	January 20, 1989.
Thomas Gale Moore	Member	July 1, 1985	May 1, 1989.
Michael L. Mussa	Member	August 18, 1986	September 19, 1988.
Michael J. Boskin	Chairman	February 2, 1989	January 12, 1993.
John B. Taylor	Member	June 9, 1989	August 2, 1991.
Richard L. Schmalensee	Member	October 3, 1989	June 21, 1991.
David F. Bradford	Member	November 13, 1991	January 20, 1993.
Paul Wonnacott	Member	November 13, 1991	January 20, 1993.
Laura D'Andrea Tyson	Chair	February 5, 1993	April 22, 1995.
Alan S. Blinder	Member	July 27, 1993	June 26, 1994.
Joseph E. Stiglitz	Member	July 27, 1993	
	Chairman	June 28, 1995	February 10, 1997.
Martin N. Baily	Member	June 30, 1995	August 30, 1996.
Alicia H. Munnell	Member	January 29, 1996	August 1, 1997.
Janet L. Yellen	Chair	February 18, 1997	August 3, 1999.
Jeffrey A. Frankel	Member	April 23, 1997	March 2, 1999.
Rebecca M. Blank	Member	October 22, 1998	July 9, 1999.
Martin N. Baily	Chairman	August 12, 1999	January 19, 2001.
Robert Z. Lawrence	Member	August 12, 1999	January 12, 2001.
Kathryn L. Shaw	Member	May 31, 2000	January 19, 2001.
R. Glenn Hubbard	Chairman	May 11, 2001	February 28, 2003.
Mark B. McClellan	Member	July 25, 2001	November 13, 2002.
Randall S. Kroszner	Member	November 30, 2001	July 1, 2003.
N. Gregory Mankiw	Chairman	May 29, 2003	
Kristin J. Forbes	Member	November 21, 2003	
Harvey S. Rosen	Member	November 21, 2003	

Report to the President on the Activities of the Council of Economic Advisers During 2003

The Council of Economic Advisers was established by the Employment Act of 1946 to provide the President with objective economic analysis and advice on the development and implementation of a wide range of domestic and international economic policy issues.

The Chairman of the Council

N. Gregory Mankiw was appointed by the President as Chairman on May 29, 2003. Dr. Mankiw replaced R. Glenn Hubbard, who returned to Columbia University where he is the Russell L. Carson Professor of Economics and Finance and Co-Director of the Entrepreneurship Program in the Graduate School of Business and Professor of Economics in the Faculty of Arts and Sciences. Dr. Mankiw is on leave from Harvard University, where he is the Allie S. Freed Professor of Economics.

Dr. Mankiw is responsible for communicating the Council's views on economic matters directly to the President through personal discussions and written reports. He represents the Council at Cabinet meetings, meetings of the National Economic Council, daily White House senior staff meetings, budget team meetings with the President, and other formal and informal meetings with the President. He also travels within the United States and overseas to present the Administration's views on the economy. Dr. Mankiw is the Council's chief public spokesperson. He directs the work of the Council and exercises ultimate responsibility for the work of the professional staff.

The Members of the Council

Kristin J. Forbes is a Member of the Council of Economic Advisers. Dr. Forbes is on leave from the Massachusetts Institute of Technology Sloan School of Management where she is the Mitsubishi Career Development Chair of International Management and Associate Professor of International Management in the Applied Economics Group. She previously served as Deputy Assistant Secretary for Quantitative Policy Analysis and Latin American and Caribbean Nations at the U.S. Department of the Treasury.

Harvey S. Rosen is also a Member of the Council of Economic Advisers. Dr. Rosen is on leave from Princeton University, where he is the John L. Weinberg Professor of Economics and Business Policy. Dr. Rosen previously served as Deputy Assistant Secretary for Tax Analysis at the U.S. Department of the Treasury.

The Chairman and the Members work as a team on most economic policy issues. Dr. Mankiw is primarily responsible for the Council's macroeconomic analysis including the Administration's economic forecast. Dr. Forbes' responsibilities include international finance and trade issues, with a particular focus on emerging markets and developing economies. Dr. Rosen's responsibilities include policy analysis relating to taxation and microeconomic issues including labor markets, health care, and regulation.

Macroeconomic Policies

As is its tradition, the Council devoted much time during 2003 to assisting the President in formulating economic policy objectives and designing programs to implement them. In this regard the Chairman kept the President informed, on a continuing basis, of important macroeconomic developments and other major policy issues through regular macroeconomic briefings. The Council prepares for the President, the Vice President, and the White House senior staff almost daily memoranda that report key economic data and analyze current economic events. In addition, they prepare weekly discussion and data memos for the President, Vice President and senior White House staff.

The Council, the Department of the Treasury, and the Office of Management and Budget (OMB)—the Administration's economic "troika"—are responsible for producing the economic forecasts that underlie the Administration's budget proposals. The Council, under the leadership of the Chairman and the Chief Economist, initiates the forecasting process twice each year. In preparing these forecasts, the Council consults with a variety of outside sources, including leading private sector forecasters.

In 2003, the Council took part in discussions on a range of macroeconomic issues. An important concern in the first half of the year was in providing analysis related to the President's Jobs and Growth proposal, which took effect in midyear. An important subsequent interest was then in assessing the response of the economy, and the labor market in particular, to fiscal and monetary policies. The Council works closely with the Treasury, the Federal Reserve, and other government agencies in providing analyses to the Administration on these topics of concern. In 2003, the Council worked closely with the National Economic Council, the Office of Management and Budget, and other offices within the Executive Office of the President in assessing the economy and economic policy proposals.

The Council continued its efforts to improve the public's understanding of economic issues and of the Administration's economic agenda through regular briefings with the economic and financial press, frequent discussions with outside economists, and presentations to outside organizations. The Chairman also regularly exchanged views on the economy with the Chairman and Governors of the Federal Reserve System.

International Economic Policies

The Council was involved in a range of international trade issues, including discussions on trade liberalization at the global, regional, and bilateral levels. The Council contributed to the development of U.S. positions in talks on free trade agreements with Australia, Central America, Morocco, the Southern African Customs Union, and to the development of positions for the ongoing negotiations on the Doha Development Agenda at the World Trade Organization and for the Free Trade Agreement of the Americas. The Council participated in deliberations concerning trade policy in a number of industries, including steel and softwood lumber. The Council also provided analysis related to U.S. economic interaction with China and the impact of trade on the manufacturing sector.

The Council participated in discussions concerning international financial policy involving many countries, including Argentina, Bolivia, Brazil, China, the Dominican Republic, Iraq, Japan, the Philippines, and Turkey. The Council participated in the development of U.S. proposals for a number of heads of state summits, including the leaders of the G8 nations and the Special Summit of the Americas in early 2004. The Council also provided analysis in support of efforts to promote economic stability and growth in Iraq.

The Council is a leading participant in the Organization for Economic Cooperation and Development (OECD), the principal forum for economic cooperation among the high-income industrial countries. The Chairman heads the U.S. delegation to the semiannual meetings of the OECD's Economic Policy Committee (EPC) and serves as the EPC Chairman. Dr. Kroszner and Dr. Forbes participated in meetings of the OECD's Working Party 3 on macroeconomic policy and coordination. Council staff participated in the OECD's Working Party 1 on microeconomic policy, in the annual OECD review of U.S. economic policy, and in the OECD Ad Hoc Group on Sustainable Development.

Council members regularly met with representatives of the Council's counterpart agencies in foreign countries, as well as with foreign trade ministers, other government officials, and members of the private sector. During the year the Council represented the United States at other international forums as well, including meetings of the Asian-Pacific Economic Cooperation forum (APEC).

Microeconomic Policies

A wide variety of microeconomic issues received Council attention during 2003. The Council actively participated in the Cabinet-level National Economic Council, dealing with issues including energy policy, the environment, international tax policy, reform of Medicare, pensions, transportation, homeland security, technology, and financial markets. Dr. Rosen was involved in formulating policy concerning the supervisory regime for government-sponsored enterprises in the home mortgage system.

The Council worked on a variety of environmental issues in 2003. The Council played a role in the development of proposed mercury standards, as well as in the proposed Inter-State Air Quality Rule, which seeks to regulate sulfur dioxide and nitrogen oxides emissions from power plants. The Council participated in discussions on the final rule to clarify the routine maintenance, repair and replacement exclusion under EPA's New Source Review program. The Council also helped in the revision of the OMB *Guidelines for the Conduct of Regulatory Analysis and the Format of Accounting Statements*. The Council analyzed proposed revisions to the voluntary registry for greenhouse gases, and aided in the review and updating of models concerning the Administration's Clear Skies legislative proposal.

Energy policy was an important focus of the Council's efforts in 2003, with analysis on topics including the impact of high natural gas prices and problems with the electricity transmission grid. The Council also played a role in the deregulation of computer reservation systems, as well as a number of other technology issues including the exploration of space, telecommunications and broadband, spectrum allocation, and spam. The Council also participated in discussions concerning reforms to corporate governance, government-sponsored enterprises, financial privacy rules, pensions, the Postal Service, and tort reform.

During 2003, the Council participated in discussions on a number of issues related to labor markets and social policies. These issues included Medicare reform and the provision of prescription drug benefits within Medicare, health information technology, medical malpractice liability, unemployment insurance, workers' compensation, immigration, college financial aid, and the President's proposal for re-employment accounts. The Council was also involved in discussions on agriculture, transportation, and homeland security.

The Staff of the Council of Economic Advisers

The professional staff of the Council consists of the Chief of Staff, the Senior Statistician, the Chief Economist, the Director of Macroeconomic Forecasting, eight senior economists, five staff economists, and five research assistants. The professional staff and their areas of concentration at the end of 2003 were:

Chief of Staff
Phillip L. Swagel

Chief Economist
Andrew A. Samwick

Senior Statistician
Catherine H. Furlong

Director
of
Macroeconomic Forecasting
Steven N. Braun

Senior Economists

Karen E. Dynan	Macroeconomics
Ted Gayer	Environment and Regulation
Eric A. Helland	Finance, Regulation, and Technology
Philip I. Levy	International Trade
David W. Meyer	Energy, Regulation, and Transportation
Mark H. Showalter	Labor, Health Care, and Education
Alan D. Viard	Public Finance and Macroeconomics
Beth Anne Wilson	International Finance

Staff Economists

Anne L. Berry	Finance, Regulation, and Technology
Carol L. Cohen	International Trade
William J. Congdon	Education and Labor
Brent I. Neiman	International Finance
Matthew C. Weinzierl	Macroeconomics

Research Assistants

Christine L. Dobridge..................	Environment and Regulation
Namita K. Kalyan.......................	Macroeconomics and Public Finance
Amanda E. Kowalski....................	Health Care and Labor
Therese C. Scharlemann	Macroeconomics and Public Finance
Julia A. Stahl.............................	Public Finance

Statistical Office

Mrs. Furlong directs the Statistical Office. The Statistical Office maintains and updates the Council's statistical information, oversees the publication of the monthly *Economic Indicators* and the statistical appendix to the *Economic Report of the President*, and verifies statistics in Presidential and Council memoranda, testimony, and speeches.

Linda A. Reilly............................	Statistician
Brian A. Amorosi........................	Program Analyst (Statistical)
Dagmara A. Mocala	Research Assistant

Administrative Office

The Administrative Office provides general support for the Council's activities. This includes financial management, human resource management, and travel, facility, security, information, and telecommunications management support.

Rosemary M. Rogers.....................	Acting Administrative Assistant
Brandon L. Schwartz.....................	Information Management Assistant

Office of the Chairman

Alice H. Williams	Executive Assistant to the Chairman
Sandra F. Daigle............................	Executive Assistant to the Chairman and Assistant to the Chief of Staff and Chief Economist
Lisa D. Branch.............................	Executive Assistant to Dr. Forbes
Mary E. Jones	Executive Assistant to Dr. Rosen

Staff Support

Sharon K. Thomas........................	Administrative Support Assistant

Jane Tufts and Barbara Pendergast provided editorial assistance in the preparation of the 2004 *Economic Report of the President*.

John P. Cogbill, Jamie Hall, Joseph J. Prusacki, and John L. Staub served at the Council in 2003 on detail from other government agencies.

John A. List, Michael Moore, and Peter H. Woodward provided consulting services to the Council during 2003.

Student Interns during the year were Jose G. Asturias, Jeffrey P. Clemens, James B. Hargrave, Angela B. Howard, James R. Larson, Yoon-Ho Lee, Evan M. Newman, Christina A. Norair, Michael K. Price, Nirupama S. Rao, Mark T. Silvestri, Richard R. Townsend, Diane T. Tran and Clint W. Wood. Elaine L. Hill joined the staff of the Council in January as a student intern.

Departures

The Council's senior economists, in most cases, are on leave of absence from faculty positions at academic institutions or from other government agencies or research institutions. Their tenure with the Council is usually limited to 1 or 2 years. Some of the senior economists who resigned during the year returned to their previous affiliations. They are Robert N. Collender, (U.S. Department of Agriculture), John L. List (University of Maryland), Michael O. Moore (George Washington University), Robert J. Carroll returned to the Department of the Treasury as Deputy Assistant Secretary for Tax Analysis after joining the Congressional Budget Office as a Visiting Scholar.

Others went on to new positions. Cindy R. Alexander accepted a position at the Securities and Exchange Commission, S. Brock Blomberg accepted a position at Claremont McKenna College, Thomas C. DeLeire went on to a position at Harvard University, and Christopher L. Foote accepted a position with the Federal Reserve Bank of Boston.

Several staff economists went on to new positions. D. Clay Ackerly accepted a position with the Food and Drug Administration. Catherine L. Downard accepted a position with the Department of the Treasury. Brian H. Jenn accepted a position with the Joint Economic Committee. Those who served as research assistants at the Council and resigned during 2003 are Adam R. Saunders (MIT Sloan School of Management), Leandra T. de Silva (University of Pennsylvania), Shelley D. de Alth (Public Policy Institute of California), Paul Landefeld (Federal Reserve Board), and Jeff Lee.

John W. Arnold, Information Management Assistant, resigned to pursue graduate studies. Stephen M. Lineberry, Confidential Assistant to Dr. McClellan accepted a position with the White House Office of Public Liaison. Administrative Officer, Mary C. Fibich, retired after 37 years of Federal service, most of which were with the Council.

Public Information

The Council's annual *Economic Report of the President* is an important vehicle for presenting the Administration's domestic and international economic policies. It is now available for distribution as a bound volume and on the Internet, where it is accessible at www.gpoaccess.gov/eop. The Council also has primary responsibility for compiling the monthly *Economic Indicators*, which is issued by the Joint Economic Committee of the Congress. The Internet address for the *Economic Indicators* is www.gpoaccess.gov/indicators. The Council's home page is located at www.whitehouse.gov/cea.

Appendix B
STATISTICAL TABLES RELATING TO INCOME, EMPLOYMENT, AND PRODUCTION

CONTENTS

NATIONAL INCOME OR EXPENDITURE:

General Notes

Detail in these tables may not add to totals because of rounding.

Because of the formula used for calculating real gross domestic product (GDP), the chained (2000) dollar estimates for the detailed components do not add to the chained-dollar value of GDP or to any intermediate aggregate. The Department of Commerce (Bureau of Economic Analysis) no longer publishes chained-dollar estimates prior to 1990, except for selected series.

Unless otherwise noted, all dollar figures are in current dollars.

Symbols used:

  p Preliminary.

  ... Not available (also, not applicable).

Data in these tables reflect revisions made by the source agencies through January 28, 2004. In particular, tables containing national income and product accounts (NIPA) estimates reflect the comprehensive (benchmark) revision released by the Department of Commerce in December 2003.

NATIONAL INCOME OR EXPENDITURE

TABLE B-1.—*Gross domestic product, 1959-2003*

[Billions of dollars, except as noted; quarterly data at seasonally adjusted annual rates]

Year or quarter	Gross domestic product	Personal consumption expenditures				Gross private domestic investment						
							Fixed investment					Change in private inventories
								Nonresidential			Residential	
		Total	Durable goods	Non-durable goods	Services	Total	Total	Total	Structures	Equipment and software		
1959	506.6	317.6	42.7	148.5	126.5	78.5	74.6	46.5	18.1	28.4	28.1	3.9
1960	526.4	331.7	43.3	152.8	135.6	78.9	75.7	49.4	19.6	29.8	26.3	3.2
1961	544.7	342.1	41.8	156.6	143.8	78.2	75.2	48.8	19.7	29.1	26.4	3.0
1962	585.6	363.3	46.9	162.8	153.6	88.1	82.0	53.1	20.8	32.3	29.0	6.1
1963	617.7	382.7	51.6	168.2	162.9	93.8	88.1	56.0	21.2	34.8	32.1	5.6
1964	663.6	411.4	56.7	178.6	176.1	102.1	97.2	63.0	23.7	39.2	34.3	4.8
1965	719.1	443.8	63.3	191.5	189.0	118.2	109.0	74.8	28.3	46.5	34.2	9.2
1966	787.8	480.9	68.3	208.7	203.8	131.3	117.7	85.4	31.3	54.0	32.3	13.6
1967	832.6	507.8	70.4	217.1	220.3	128.6	118.7	86.4	31.5	54.9	32.4	9.9
1968	910.0	558.0	80.8	235.7	241.6	141.2	132.1	93.4	33.6	59.9	38.7	9.1
1969	984.6	605.2	85.9	253.1	266.1	156.4	147.3	104.7	37.7	67.0	42.6	9.2
1970	1,038.5	648.5	85.0	272.0	291.5	152.4	150.4	109.0	40.3	68.7	41.4	2.0
1971	1,127.1	701.9	96.9	285.5	319.5	178.2	169.9	114.1	42.7	71.5	55.8	8.3
1972	1,238.3	770.6	110.4	308.0	352.2	207.6	198.5	128.8	47.2	81.7	69.7	9.1
1973	1,382.7	852.4	123.5	343.1	385.8	244.5	228.6	153.3	55.0	98.3	75.3	15.9
1974	1,500.0	933.4	122.3	384.5	426.6	249.4	235.4	169.5	61.2	108.2	66.0	14.0
1975	1,638.3	1,034.4	133.5	420.7	480.2	230.2	236.5	173.7	61.4	112.4	62.7	-6.3
1976	1,825.3	1,151.9	158.9	458.3	534.7	292.0	274.8	192.4	65.9	126.4	82.5	17.1
1977	2,030.9	1,278.6	181.2	497.1	600.2	361.3	339.0	228.7	74.6	154.1	110.3	22.3
1978	2,294.7	1,428.5	201.7	550.2	676.6	438.0	412.2	280.6	93.6	187.0	131.6	25.8
1979	2,563.3	1,592.2	214.4	624.5	753.3	492.9	474.9	333.9	117.7	216.2	141.0	18.0
1980	2,789.5	1,757.1	214.2	696.1	846.9	479.3	485.6	362.4	136.2	226.2	123.2	-6.3
1981	3,128.4	1,941.1	231.3	758.9	950.8	572.4	542.6	420.0	167.3	252.7	122.6	29.8
1982	3,255.0	2,077.3	240.2	787.6	1,049.4	517.2	532.1	426.5	177.6	248.9	105.7	-14.9
1983	3,536.7	2,290.6	280.8	831.2	1,178.6	564.3	570.1	417.2	154.3	262.9	152.9	-5.8
1984	3,933.2	2,503.3	326.5	884.6	1,292.2	735.6	670.2	489.6	177.4	312.2	180.6	65.4
1985	4,220.3	2,720.3	363.5	928.7	1,428.1	736.2	714.4	526.2	194.5	331.7	188.2	21.8
1986	4,462.8	2,899.7	403.0	958.4	1,538.3	746.5	739.9	519.8	176.5	343.3	220.1	6.6
1987	4,739.5	3,100.2	421.7	1,015.3	1,663.3	785.0	757.8	524.1	174.2	349.9	233.7	27.7
1988	5,103.8	3,353.6	453.6	1,083.5	1,816.5	821.6	803.1	563.8	182.8	381.0	239.3	18.5
1989	5,484.4	3,598.5	471.8	1,166.7	1,960.0	874.9	847.3	607.7	193.7	414.0	239.5	27.7
1990	5,803.1	3,839.9	474.2	1,249.9	2,115.9	861.0	846.4	622.4	202.9	419.5	224.0	14.5
1991	5,995.9	3,986.1	453.9	1,284.8	2,247.4	802.9	803.3	598.2	183.6	414.6	205.1	-.4
1992	6,337.7	4,235.3	483.6	1,330.5	2,421.2	864.8	848.5	612.1	172.6	439.6	236.3	16.2
1993	6,657.4	4,477.9	526.7	1,379.4	2,571.8	953.4	932.5	666.6	177.2	489.4	266.0	20.9
1994	7,072.2	4,743.3	582.2	1,437.2	2,723.9	1,097.1	1,033.3	731.4	186.8	544.6	301.9	63.7
1995	7,397.7	4,975.8	611.6	1,485.1	2,879.1	1,144.0	1,112.9	810.0	207.3	602.8	302.8	31.0
1996	7,816.9	5,256.8	652.6	1,555.5	3,048.7	1,240.3	1,209.5	875.4	224.6	650.8	334.1	30.8
1997	8,304.3	5,547.4	692.7	1,619.0	3,235.8	1,389.8	1,317.8	968.7	250.3	718.3	349.1	72.0
1998	8,747.0	5,879.5	750.2	1,683.6	3,445.7	1,509.1	1,438.4	1,052.6	275.2	777.3	385.8	70.7
1999	9,268.4	6,282.5	817.6	1,804.8	3,660.0	1,625.7	1,558.8	1,133.9	282.2	851.7	424.9	66.9
2000	9,817.0	6,739.4	863.3	1,947.2	3,928.8	1,735.5	1,679.0	1,232.1	313.2	918.9	446.9	56.5
2001	10,100.8	7,045.4	881.9	2,013.6	4,149.8	1,607.2	1,643.4	1,174.1	322.1	852.0	469.2	-36.3
2002	10,480.8	7,385.3	911.3	2,086.0	4,388.0	1,589.2	1,583.9	1,080.2	266.3	813.9	503.7	5.4
1999:I	9,066.6	6,101.7	785.2	1,748.5	3,568.0	1,596.7	1,514.6	1,101.0	278.3	822.7	413.5	82.1
II	9,174.1	6,237.2	818.5	1,789.2	3,629.6	1,589.9	1,551.7	1,130.1	282.0	848.1	421.7	38.2
III	9,313.5	6,337.2	832.8	1,812.5	3,691.9	1,628.3	1,579.2	1,151.5	281.6	869.8	427.8	49.1
IV	9,519.5	6,453.7	834.1	1,869.0	3,750.7	1,687.7	1,589.5	1,153.0	286.9	866.1	436.5	98.2
2000:I	9,629.4	6,613.9	876.9	1,894.2	3,842.8	1,672.3	1,642.4	1,193.9	295.2	898.7	448.5	29.9
II	9,822.8	6,688.1	854.2	1,938.3	3,895.6	1,781.7	1,685.4	1,236.5	310.4	926.1	448.8	96.3
III	9,862.1	6,783.9	861.3	1,965.8	3,956.7	1,749.0	1,690.6	1,247.5	321.1	926.5	443.1	58.4
IV	9,953.6	6,871.6	860.9	1,990.5	4,020.3	1,738.9	1,697.5	1,250.3	326.0	924.2	447.2	41.4
2001:I	10,024.8	6,934.3	862.0	1,998.6	4,073.8	1,688.3	1,686.2	1,230.3	326.4	903.9	455.9	2.2
II	10,088.2	7,017.4	875.3	2,011.5	4,130.5	1,620.3	1,652.7	1,186.9	327.2	859.6	465.8	-32.5
III	10,096.2	7,058.1	870.6	2,021.8	4,165.7	1,594.3	1,640.3	1,162.9	334.1	828.8	477.4	-46.0
IV	10,193.9	7,171.6	919.6	2,022.6	4,229.4	1,526.1	1,594.2	1,116.4	300.6	815.8	477.8	-68.2
2002:I	10,329.3	7,256.5	914.9	2,051.8	4,289.7	1,553.1	1,580.8	1,092.7	280.0	812.7	488.2	-27.7
II	10,428.3	7,355.5	909.3	2,082.5	4,363.6	1,580.9	1,580.4	1,080.4	269.6	810.8	500.0	.4
III	10,542.0	7,428.2	913.6	2,090.5	4,424.1	1,608.2	1,579.7	1,073.4	259.4	814.0	506.3	28.4
IV	10,623.7	7,501.2	907.3	2,119.2	4,474.7	1,614.7	1,594.6	1,074.3	256.3	817.9	520.3	20.1
2003:I	10,735.8	7,600.7	898.2	2,175.7	4,526.8	1,605.3	1,606.2	1,071.8	256.1	815.8	534.4	-.9
II	10,846.7	7,673.6	926.2	2,170.8	4,576.6	1,624.3	1,630.1	1,086.9	259.2	827.7	543.2	-5.8
III	11,107.0	7,836.3	975.1	2,230.0	4,631.2	1,689.1	1,699.5	1,124.4	259.8	864.6	575.1	-10.4

See next page for continuation of table.

[Billions of dollars, except as noted; quarterly data at seasonally adjusted annual rates]

Year or quarter	Net exports of goods and services			Government consumption expenditures and gross investment					Final sales of domestic product	Gross domestic purchases [1]	Addendum: Gross national product [2]	Percent change from preceding period	
					Federal								
	Net exports	Exports	Imports	Total	Total	National defense	Non-defense	State and local				Gross domestic product	Gross domestic purchases [1]
1959	0.4	22.7	22.3	110.0	65.4	53.8	11.5	44.7	502.7	506.2	509.3	8.4	8.5
1960	4.2	27.0	22.8	111.6	64.1	53.4	10.7	47.5	523.2	522.2	529.5	3.9	3.2
1961	4.9	27.6	22.7	119.5	67.9	56.5	11.4	51.6	541.7	539.8	548.2	3.5	3.4
1962	4.1	29.1	25.0	130.1	75.3	61.1	14.2	54.9	579.5	581.5	589.7	7.5	7.7
1963	4.9	31.1	26.1	136.4	76.9	61.0	15.9	59.5	612.1	612.8	622.2	5.5	5.4
1964	6.9	35.0	28.1	143.2	78.5	60.3	18.2	64.8	658.8	656.7	668.5	7.4	7.2
1965	5.6	37.1	31.5	151.5	80.4	60.6	19.8	71.0	709.9	713.5	724.4	8.4	8.6
1966	3.9	40.9	37.1	171.8	92.5	71.7	20.8	79.2	774.2	783.9	792.9	9.5	9.9
1967	3.6	43.5	39.9	192.7	104.8	83.5	21.3	87.9	822.7	829.0	838.0	5.7	5.8
1968	1.4	47.9	46.6	209.4	111.4	89.3	22.1	98.0	900.9	908.6	916.1	9.3	9.6
1969	1.4	51.9	50.5	221.5	113.4	89.5	23.8	108.2	975.4	983.2	990.7	8.2	8.2
1970	4.0	59.7	55.8	233.8	113.5	87.6	25.8	120.3	1,036.5	1,034.6	1,044.9	5.5	5.2
1971	.6	63.0	62.3	246.5	113.7	84.6	29.1	132.8	1,118.9	1,126.5	1,134.7	8.5	8.9
1972	-3.4	70.8	74.2	263.5	119.7	87.0	32.7	143.8	1,229.2	1,241.7	1,246.8	9.9	10.2
1973	4.1	95.3	91.2	281.7	122.5	88.2	34.3	159.2	1,366.8	1,378.6	1,395.3	11.7	11.0
1974	-.8	126.7	127.5	317.9	134.6	95.6	39.0	183.4	1,486.0	1,500.8	1,515.5	8.5	8.9
1975	16.0	138.7	122.7	357.7	149.1	103.9	45.1	208.7	1,644.6	1,622.4	1,651.3	9.2	8.1
1976	-1.6	149.5	151.1	383.0	159.7	111.1	48.6	223.3	1,808.2	1,826.9	1,842.1	11.4	12.6
1977	-23.1	159.4	182.4	414.1	175.4	120.9	54.5	238.7	2,008.6	2,054.0	2,051.2	11.3	12.4
1978	-25.4	186.9	212.3	453.6	190.9	130.5	60.4	262.6	2,268.9	2,320.1	2,316.3	13.0	13.0
1979	-22.5	230.1	252.7	500.8	210.6	145.2	65.4	290.2	2,545.3	2,585.9	2,595.3	11.7	11.5
1980	-13.1	280.8	293.8	566.2	243.8	168.0	75.8	322.4	2,795.8	2,802.6	2,823.7	8.8	8.4
1981	-12.5	305.2	317.8	627.5	280.2	196.3	84.0	347.3	3,098.6	3,141.0	3,161.4	12.2	12.1
1982	-20.0	283.2	303.2	680.5	310.8	225.9	84.9	369.7	3,269.9	3,275.0	3,291.5	4.0	4.3
1983	-51.7	277.0	328.6	733.5	342.9	250.7	92.3	390.5	3,542.4	3,588.3	3,573.8	8.7	9.6
1984	-102.7	302.4	405.1	797.0	374.4	281.6	92.8	422.6	3,867.8	4,035.9	3,969.5	11.2	12.5
1985	-115.2	302.0	417.2	879.0	412.8	311.2	101.6	466.2	4,198.4	4,335.5	4,246.8	7.3	7.4
1986	-132.7	320.5	453.3	949.3	438.6	330.9	107.8	510.7	4,456.3	4,595.6	4,480.6	5.7	6.0
1987	-145.2	363.9	509.1	999.5	460.1	350.0	110.0	539.4	4,712.3	4,884.7	4,757.4	6.2	6.3
1988	-110.4	444.1	554.5	1,039.0	462.3	354.9	107.4	576.7	5,085.3	5,214.2	5,127.4	7.7	6.7
1989	-88.2	503.3	591.5	1,099.1	482.2	362.2	120.0	616.9	5,456.7	5,572.5	5,510.6	7.5	6.9
1990	-78.0	552.4	630.3	1,180.2	508.3	374.0	134.3	671.9	5,788.5	5,881.1	5,837.9	5.8	5.5
1991	-27.5	596.8	624.3	1,234.4	527.7	383.2	144.5	706.7	5,996.3	6,023.4	6,026.3	3.3	2.4
1992	-33.2	635.3	668.6	1,271.0	533.9	376.9	157.0	737.0	6,321.4	6,371.0	6,367.4	5.7	5.8
1993	-65.0	655.8	720.9	1,291.2	525.2	362.9	162.4	766.0	6,636.6	6,722.4	6,689.3	5.0	5.5
1994	-93.6	720.9	814.5	1,325.5	519.1	353.7	165.5	806.3	7,008.4	7,165.8	7,098.4	6.2	6.6
1995	-91.4	812.2	903.6	1,369.2	519.2	348.7	170.5	850.0	7,366.5	7,489.0	7,433.4	4.6	4.5
1996	-96.2	868.6	964.8	1,416.0	527.4	354.6	172.8	888.6	7,786.1	7,913.1	7,851.9	5.7	5.7
1997	-101.6	955.3	1,056.9	1,468.7	530.9	349.6	181.3	937.8	8,232.3	8,405.9	8,337.3	6.2	6.2
1998	-159.9	955.9	1,115.9	1,518.3	530.4	345.7	184.7	987.9	8,676.2	8,906.9	8,768.3	5.3	6.0
1999	-260.5	991.2	1,251.7	1,620.8	555.8	360.6	195.2	1,065.0	9,201.5	9,528.9	9,302.2	6.0	7.0
2000	-379.5	1,096.3	1,475.8	1,721.6	578.8	370.3	208.5	1,142.8	9,760.5	10,196.4	9,855.9	5.9	7.0
2001	-366.5	1,035.1	1,401.7	1,814.7	612.9	393.0	219.9	1,201.8	10,136.9	10,467.3	10,135.9	2.9	2.7
2002	-426.3	1,006.8	1,433.1	1,932.5	679.5	438.3	241.2	1,253.1	10,475.5	10,907.1	10,502.3	3.8	4.2
1999:I	-207.5	960.1	1,167.6	1,575.6	540.6	350.2	190.4	1,035.0	8,984.4	9,274.1	9,097.2	5.1	6.6
II	-252.1	972.8	1,224.9	1,599.1	545.9	351.7	194.2	1,053.2	9,136.0	9,426.2	9,209.9	4.8	6.7
III	-285.2	1,000.5	1,285.7	1,633.2	560.0	364.9	195.1	1,073.2	9,264.4	9,598.7	9,343.4	6.2	7.5
IV	-297.2	1,031.6	1,328.8	1,675.3	576.8	375.7	201.0	1,098.5	9,421.3	9,816.7	9,558.3	9.1	9.4
2000:I	-346.4	1,055.1	1,401.5	1,689.6	565.3	360.9	204.4	1,124.3	9,599.6	9,975.8	9,661.9	4.7	6.6
II	-366.9	1,091.8	1,458.7	1,720.0	586.6	375.2	211.4	1,133.4	9,726.5	10,189.7	9,859.6	8.3	8.9
III	-400.7	1,122.4	1,523.1	1,729.9	581.2	371.3	209.9	1,148.6	9,803.7	10,262.8	9,893.6	1.6	2.9
IV	-403.9	1,115.8	1,519.7	1,746.9	582.0	373.8	208.2	1,164.9	9,912.2	10,357.5	10,008.4	3.8	3.7
2001:I	-381.3	1,103.1	1,484.4	1,783.5	597.5	384.1	213.4	1,185.9	10,022.8	10,406.1	10,052.1	2.9	1.9
II	-368.2	1,061.1	1,429.3	1,818.8	609.8	388.2	221.6	1,209.0	10,120.6	10,456.4	10,115.5	2.6	1.9
III	-364.9	1,005.4	1,370.4	1,808.8	613.3	392.8	220.5	1,195.4	10,142.2	10,461.2	10,107.8	.3	.2
IV	-351.7	970.8	1,322.5	1,847.8	630.8	406.9	223.9	1,217.1	10,260.0	10,545.5	10,268.3	3.9	3.3
2002:I	-365.6	978.5	1,344.1	1,885.4	652.9	420.3	232.6	1,232.5	10,357.1	10,694.9	10,351.3	5.4	5.8
II	-427.3	1,006.3	1,433.6	1,919.3	673.2	432.5	240.7	1,246.1	10,427.8	10,855.6	10,435.9	3.9	6.1
III	-435.9	1,025.3	1,461.3	1,941.5	681.8	439.3	242.5	1,259.7	10,513.4	10,977.9	10,560.5	4.4	4.6
IV	-476.1	1,017.2	1,493.3	1,983.9	710.0	461.1	248.9	1,273.9	10,603.6	11,099.9	10,661.6	3.1	4.5
2003:I	-487.6	1,021.0	1,508.5	2,017.4	723.0	463.3	259.7	1,294.5	10,736.7	11,223.4	10,763.7	4.3	4.5
II	-505.5	1,020.2	1,525.7	2,054.2	764.7	507.3	257.4	1,289.6	10,852.4	11,352.2	10,880.0	4.2	4.7
III	-490.6	1,048.5	1,539.0	2,072.1	769.6	507.2	262.4	1,302.5	11,117.4	11,597.5	11,144.8	10.0	8.9

[1] Gross domestic product (GDP) less exports of goods and services plus imports of goods and services.
[2] GDP plus net income receipts from rest of the world.

Source: Department of Commerce, Bureau of Economic Analysis.

TABLE B–2.—*Real gross domestic product, 1959–2003*

[Billions of chained (2000) dollars, except as noted; quarterly data at seasonally adjusted annual rates]

Year or quarter	Gross domestic product	Personal consumption expenditures				Gross private domestic investment						
		Total	Durable goods	Non-durable goods	Services	Total	Fixed investment					Change in private inventories
							Total	Nonresidential			Residential	
								Total	Structures	Equipment and software		
1959	2,441.3	1,554.6	....	....	....	266.7	....	....	....	....	....	....
1960	2,501.8	1,597.4	....	....	....	266.6	....	....	....	....	....	....
1961	2,560.0	1,630.3	....	....	....	264.9	....	....	....	....	....	....
1962	2,715.2	1,711.1	....	....	....	298.4	....	....	....	....	....	....
1963	2,834.0	1,781.6	....	....	....	318.5	....	....	....	....	....	....
1964	2,998.6	1,888.4	....	....	....	344.7	....	....	....	....	....	....
1965	3,191.1	2,007.7	....	....	....	393.1	....	....	....	....	....	....
1966	3,399.1	2,121.8	....	....	....	427.7	....	....	....	....	....	....
1967	3,484.6	2,185.0	....	....	....	408.1	....	....	....	....	....	....
1968	3,652.7	2,310.5	....	....	....	431.9	....	....	....	....	....	....
1969	3,765.4	2,396.4	....	....	....	457.1	....	....	....	....	....	....
1970	3,771.9	2,451.9	....	....	....	427.1	....	....	....	....	....	....
1971	3,898.6	2,545.5	....	....	....	475.7	....	....	....	....	....	....
1972	4,105.0	2,701.3	....	....	....	532.1	....	....	....	....	....	....
1973	4,341.5	2,833.8	....	....	....	594.4	....	....	....	....	....	....
1974	4,319.6	2,812.3	....	....	....	550.6	....	....	....	....	....	....
1975	4,311.2	2,876.9	....	....	....	453.1	....	....	....	....	....	....
1976	4,540.9	3,035.5	....	....	....	544.7	....	....	....	....	....	....
1977	4,750.5	3,164.1	....	....	....	627.0	....	....	....	....	....	....
1978	5,015.0	3,303.1	....	....	....	702.6	....	....	....	....	....	....
1979	5,173.4	3,383.4	....	....	....	725.0	....	....	....	....	....	....
1980	5,161.7	3,374.1	....	....	....	645.3	....	....	....	....	....	....
1981	5,291.7	3,422.2	....	....	....	704.9	....	....	....	....	....	....
1982	5,189.3	3,470.3	....	....	....	606.0	....	....	....	....	....	....
1983	5,423.8	3,668.6	....	....	....	662.5	....	....	....	....	....	....
1984	5,813.6	3,863.3	....	....	....	857.7	....	....	....	....	....	....
1985	6,053.7	4,064.0	....	....	....	849.7	....	....	....	....	....	....
1986	6,263.6	4,228.9	....	....	....	843.9	....	....	....	....	....	....
1987	6,475.1	4,369.8	....	....	....	870.0	....	....	....	....	....	....
1988	6,742.7	4,546.9	....	....	....	890.5	....	....	....	....	....	....
1989	6,981.4	4,675.0	....	....	....	926.2	....	....	....	....	....	....
1990	7,112.5	4,770.3	453.5	1,484.0	2,851.7	895.1	886.6	595.1	275.2	355.0	298.9	15
1991	7,100.5	4,778.4	427.9	1,480.5	2,900.0	822.2	829.1	563.2	244.6	345.9	270.2	–
1992	7,336.6	4,934.8	453.0	1,510.1	3,000.8	889.0	878.3	581.3	229.9	371.1	307.6	16
1993	7,532.7	5,099.8	488.4	1,550.4	3,085.7	968.3	953.5	631.9	228.3	417.4	332.7	20
1994	7,835.5	5,290.7	529.4	1,603.9	3,176.6	1,099.6	1,042.3	689.9	232.3	467.2	364.8	63
1995	8,031.7	5,433.5	552.6	1,638.6	3,259.9	1,134.0	1,109.6	762.5	247.1	523.1	353.1	29
1996	8,328.9	5,619.4	595.9	1,680.4	3,356.0	1,234.3	1,209.2	833.6	261.1	578.7	381.3	28
1997	8,703.5	5,831.8	646.9	1,725.3	3,468.0	1,387.7	1,320.6	934.2	280.1	658.3	388.6	71
1998	9,066.9	6,125.8	720.3	1,794.4	3,615.0	1,524.1	1,455.0	1,037.8	294.5	745.6	418.3	72
1999	9,470.3	6,438.6	804.6	1,876.6	3,758.0	1,642.6	1,576.3	1,133.3	293.2	840.2	443.6	68
2000	9,817.0	6,739.4	863.3	1,947.2	3,928.8	1,735.5	1,679.0	1,232.1	313.2	918.9	446.9	56
2001	9,866.6	6,904.6	899.1	1,983.3	4,022.4	1,590.6	1,625.7	1,176.8	305.2	871.3	448.5	-36
2002	10,083.0	7,140.4	957.2	2,043.6	4,141.8	1,572.0	1,565.8	1,092.6	249.0	846.7	470.3	5
1999:I	9,315.5	6,311.3	767.4	1,849.2	3,696.4	1,606.6	1,531.0	1,094.0	292.0	802.7	438.1	75
II	9,392.6	6,409.7	803.6	1,867.9	3,738.5	1,607.8	1,568.6	1,127.3	294.1	833.5	441.8	41
III	9,502.2	6,476.7	820.7	1,873.7	3,782.3	1,647.4	1,598.6	1,154.4	291.8	862.4	444.5	50
IV	9,671.1	6,556.8	826.4	1,915.7	3,815.0	1,708.4	1,606.9	1,157.3	294.8	862.3	449.9	103
2000:I	9,695.6	6,661.3	872.8	1,917.2	3,871.1	1,678.0	1,651.1	1,196.7	299.9	896.7	454.5	28
II	9,847.9	6,703.3	851.3	1,944.0	3,908.2	1,788.6	1,689.1	1,238.6	312.5	926.0	450.4	99
III	9,836.6	6,768.0	863.8	1,955.0	3,949.3	1,742.6	1,686.4	1,245.2	319.7	925.5	441.2	56
IV	9,887.7	6,825.0	865.4	1,972.7	3,986.8	1,732.7	1,689.4	1,247.9	320.6	927.3	441.6	43
2001:I	9,882.2	6,833.7	869.1	1,974.5	3,989.6	1,682.2	1,677.8	1,233.6	315.8	917.8	444.4	4
II	9,866.3	6,872.2	889.6	1,969.1	4,013.3	1,608.5	1,638.0	1,189.4	311.3	877.6	448.5	-28
III	9,834.6	6,904.2	891.1	1,983.4	4,029.3	1,573.1	1,616.1	1,163.7	313.1	849.4	451.9	-44
IV	9,883.6	7,008.2	946.6	2,006.2	4,057.4	1,498.4	1,570.7	1,120.6	280.8	840.5	449.0	-71
2002:I	9,997.9	7,079.2	950.3	2,035.9	4,095.3	1,538.2	1,560.9	1,100.4	262.2	840.0	458.5	-23
II	10,045.1	7,124.5	951.4	2,037.8	4,137.0	1,555.8	1,563.2	1,092.1	252.2	842.6	468.4	-6
III	10,128.4	7,159.2	963.1	2,038.8	4,159.4	1,598.2	1,565.4	1,089.1	242.4	850.3	473.2	32
IV	10,160.8	7,198.9	963.8	2,061.8	4,175.4	1,595.8	1,573.5	1,088.9	239.0	853.9	481.0	21
2003:I	10,210.4	7,244.1	965.0	2,090.5	4,190.7	1,581.6	1,577.7	1,087.3	236.5	855.0	486.4	1
II	10,288.3	7,304.0	1,005.1	2,096.9	4,208.4	1,599.9	1,601.4	1,105.8	238.8	871.6	491.7	–
III	10,493.1	7,426.6	1,069.1	2,134.3	4,237.2	1,656.1	1,661.0	1,139.5	237.7	907.7	516.7	–

See next page for continuation of table.

TABLE B–2.—*Real gross domestic product, 1959–2003*—Continued

[Billions of chained (2000) dollars, except as noted; quarterly data at seasonally adjusted annual rates]

Year or quarter	Net exports of goods and services — Net exports	Exports	Imports	Govt. consumption — Total	Federal — Total	National defense	Non-defense	State and local	Final sales of domestic product	Gross domestic purchases[1]	Addendum: Gross national product[2]	Percent change — Gross domestic product	Gross domestic purchases[1]
1959		77.2	101.9	714.3					2,442.7	2,485.9	2,457.4	7.1	7.1
1960		90.6	103.3	715.4					2,506.8	2,529.6	2,519.4	2.5	1.8
1961		91.1	102.6	751.3					2,566.8	2,587.6	2,579.3	2.3	2.3
1962		95.7	114.3	797.6					2,708.5	2,751.4	2,736.9	6.1	6.3
1963		102.5	117.3	818.1					2,830.3	2,866.0	2,857.2	4.4	4.2
1964		114.6	123.6	836.1					2,999.9	3,023.2	3,023.6	5.8	5.5
1965		117.8	136.7	861.3					3,173.8	3,228.6	3,217.3	6.4	6.8
1966		126.0	157.1	937.1					3,364.8	3,450.3	3,423.7	6.5	6.9
1967		128.9	168.5	1,008.9					3,467.6	3,545.1	3,510.1	2.5	2.7
1968		139.0	193.6	1,040.5					3,640.3	3,727.5	3,680.0	4.8	5.1
1969		145.7	204.6	1,038.0					3,753.7	3,844.1	3,792.0	3.1	3.1
1970		161.4	213.4	1,012.9					3,787.7	3,837.4	3,798.2	.2	–.2
1971		164.1	224.7	990.8					3,893.4	3,974.2	3,927.8	3.4	3.6
1972		176.5	250.0	983.5					4,098.6	4,192.8	4,136.2	5.3	5.5
1973		209.7	261.6	980.0					4,315.9	4,399.1	4,383.6	5.8	4.9
1974		226.3	255.7	1,004.7					4,305.5	4,343.8	4,367.5	–.5	–1.3
1975		224.9	227.3	1,027.4					4,352.5	4,297.0	4,348.4	–.2	–1.1
1976		234.7	271.7	1,031.9					4,522.3	4,575.0	4,585.3	5.3	6.5
1977		240.3	301.4	1,043.3					4,721.6	4,818.5	4,800.3	4.6	5.3
1978		265.7	327.6	1,074.0					4,981.6	5,081.5	5,064.4	5.6	5.5
1979		292.0	333.0	1,094.1					5,161.2	5,206.8	5,240.1	3.2	2.5
1980		323.5	310.9	1,115.4					5,196.7	5,108.9	5,227.6	–.2	–1.9
1981		327.4	319.1	1,125.6					5,265.1	5,244.7	5,349.7	2.5	2.7
1982		302.4	315.0	1,145.4					5,233.4	5,175.1	5,249.7	–1.9	–1.3
1983		294.6	354.8	1,187.3					5,454.0	5,477.6	5,482.5	4.5	5.8
1984		318.7	441.1	1,227.0					5,739.2	5,951.6	5,869.3	7.2	8.7
1985		328.3	469.8	1,312.5					6,042.1	6,215.8	6,093.4	4.1	4.4
1986		353.7	510.0	1,392.5					6,271.8	6,443.6	6,290.6	3.5	3.7
1987		391.8	540.2	1,426.7					6,457.2	6,644.1	6,500.9	3.4	3.1
1988		454.6	561.4	1,445.1					6,734.5	6,857.9	6,775.2	4.1	3.2
1989		506.8	586.0	1,482.5					6,962.2	7,060.8	7,015.4	3.5	3.0
1990	–54.7	552.5	607.1	1,530.0	659.1	479.4	178.6	868.4	7,108.5	7,161.6	7,155.2	1.9	1.4
1991	–14.6	589.1	603.7	1,547.2	658.0	474.2	182.8	886.8	7,115.0	7,101.2	7,136.8	–.2	–.8
1992	–15.9	629.7	645.6	1,555.3	646.6	450.7	195.4	906.5	7,331.1	7,338.9	7,371.8	3.3	3.3
1993	–52.1	650.0	702.1	1,541.1	619.6	425.3	194.1	919.5	7,522.3	7,577.2	7,568.6	2.7	3.2
1994	–79.4	706.5	785.9	1,541.3	596.4	404.6	191.7	943.3	7,777.8	7,911.3	7,864.2	4.0	4.4
1995	–71.0	778.2	849.1	1,549.7	580.3	389.2	191.0	968.3	8,010.2	8,098.4	8,069.8	2.5	2.4
1996	–79.6	843.4	923.0	1,564.9	573.5	383.8	189.6	990.5	8,306.5	8,405.7	8,365.3	3.7	3.8
1997	–104.6	943.7	1,048.3	1,594.0	567.6	373.0	194.5	1,025.9	8,636.6	8,807.6	8,737.5	4.5	4.8
1998	–203.7	966.5	1,170.3	1,624.4	561.2	365.3	195.9	1,063.0	8,997.6	9,272.5	9,088.7	4.2	5.3
1999	–296.2	1,008.2	1,304.4	1,686.9	573.7	372.2	201.5	1,113.2	9,404.0	9,767.7	9,504.7	4.5	5.3
2000	–379.5	1,096.3	1,475.8	1,721.6	578.8	370.3	208.5	1,142.8	9,760.5	10,196.4	9,855.9	3.7	4.4
2001	–398.1	1,039.0	1,437.1	1,768.9	600.5	384.7	215.8	1,168.5	9,901.1	10,265.0	9,901.4	.5	.7
2002	–470.6	1,014.2	1,484.7	1,836.9	648.0	418.8	229.2	1,189.1	10,076.9	10,551.5	10,105.0	2.2	2.8
99: I	–262.1	980.1	1,242.2	1,662.2	562.9	364.1	198.8	1,099.3	9,239.7	9,579.6	9,346.7	3.4	5.1
II	–295.2	991.2	1,286.4	1,672.3	565.3	363.9	201.4	1,107.0	9,353.7	9,689.1	9,429.1	3.4	4.7
III	–313.9	1,017.4	1,331.3	1,693.1	576.7	375.9	200.8	1,116.3	9,453.5	9,816.7	9,532.7	4.8	5.4
IV	–313.7	1,044.1	1,357.9	1,720.2	589.9	385.0	204.9	1,130.2	9,569.3	9,985.4	9,710.4	7.3	7.1
00: I	–350.6	1,060.9	1,411.5	1,707.3	568.2	362.6	205.6	1,139.2	9,668.8	10,046.5	9,729.0	1.0	2.5
II	–374.5	1,092.0	1,466.5	1,730.5	591.2	377.1	214.0	1,139.3	9,748.4	10,222.4	9,885.3	6.4	7.2
III	–395.6	1,120.0	1,515.6	1,721.5	578.6	369.9	208.7	1,142.9	9,780.4	10,232.1	9,867.8	–.5	.4
IV	–397.2	1,112.3	1,509.5	1,727.1	577.2	371.5	205.6	1,149.9	9,844.3	10,284.7	9,941.6	2.1	2.1
01: I	–385.9	1,099.6	1,485.5	1,751.6	589.7	378.5	211.2	1,161.9	9,877.5	10,267.7	9,908.7	–.2	–.7
II	–391.7	1,060.9	1,452.7	1,776.4	599.3	380.9	218.4	1,177.1	9,895.3	10,258.0	9,893.5	–.6	–.4
III	–401.3	1,010.6	1,411.9	1,758.1	599.3	383.2	216.0	1,158.9	9,876.9	10,236.3	9,846.5	–1.3	–.8
IV	–413.4	984.8	1,398.2	1,789.7	613.6	396.2	217.4	1,176.1	9,954.9	10,298.0	9,956.8	2.0	2.4
02: I	–431.2	995.4	1,426.7	1,810.1	626.1	404.1	222.0	1,184.1	10,020.1	10,429.5	10,020.3	4.7	5.2
II	–467.6	1,016.5	1,484.1	1,827.8	641.9	413.4	228.5	1,186.0	10,052.3	10,510.4	10,053.4	1.9	3.1
III	–471.9	1,027.3	1,499.2	1,838.9	648.2	418.1	230.1	1,190.9	10,096.4	10,598.0	10,147.5	3.4	3.4
IV	–511.5	1,017.5	1,529.0	1,870.8	675.8	439.5	236.4	1,195.3	10,138.9	10,668.0	10,198.5	1.3	2.7
03: I	–490.0	1,012.4	1,502.5	1,869.0	675.5	433.2	242.4	1,193.8	10,206.4	10,697.6	10,237.6	2.0	1.1
II	–526.0	1,009.6	1,535.7	1,902.8	712.0	472.8	239.3	1,191.4	10,289.5	10,809.9	10,320.2	3.1	4.3
III	–505.2	1,033.7	1,538.9	1,911.1	714.3	471.2	243.1	1,197.4	10,497.7	10,995.4	10,528.6	8.2	7.0

[1] Gross domestic product (GDP) less exports of goods and services plus imports of goods and services.
[2] GDP plus net income receipts from rest of the world.

Source: Department of Commerce, Bureau of Economic Analysis.

TABLE B–3.—*Quantity and price indexes for gross domestic product, and percent changes, 1959–2003*

[Quarterly data are seasonally adjusted]

Year or quarter	Gross domestic product (GDP)						
	Index numbers, 2000=100			Percent change from preceding period [1]			
	Real GDP (chain-type quantity index)	GDP chain-type price index	GDP implicit price deflator	GDP (current dollars)	Real GDP (chain-type quantity index)	GDP chain-type price index	GDP implicit price deflator
1959	24.868	20.754	20.751	8.4	7.1	1.2	1.2
1960	25.484	21.044	21.041	3.9	2.5	1.4	1.4
1961	26.077	21.281	21.278	3.5	2.3	1.1	1.1
1962	27.658	21.572	21.569	7.5	6.1	1.4	1.4
1963	28.868	21.801	21.798	5.5	4.4	1.1	1.1
1964	30.545	22.134	22.131	7.4	5.8	1.5	1.5
1965	32.506	22.538	22.535	8.4	6.4	1.8	1.8
1966	34.625	23.180	23.176	9.5	6.5	2.8	2.8
1967	35.496	23.897	23.893	5.7	2.5	3.1	3.1
1968	37.208	24.916	24.913	9.3	4.8	4.3	4.3
1969	38.356	26.153	26.149	8.2	3.1	5.0	5.0
1970	38.422	27.538	27.534	5.5	.2	5.3	5.3
1971	39.713	28.916	28.911	8.5	3.4	5.0	5.0
1972	41.815	30.171	30.166	9.9	5.3	4.3	4.3
1973	44.224	31.854	31.849	11.7	5.8	5.6	5.6
1974	44.001	34.721	34.725	8.5	−.5	9.0	9.0
1975	43.916	38.007	38.002	9.2	−.2	9.5	9.4
1976	46.256	40.202	40.196	11.4	5.3	5.8	5.8
1977	48.391	42.758	42.752	11.3	4.6	6.4	6.4
1978	51.085	45.762	45.757	13.0	5.6	7.0	7.0
1979	52.699	49.553	49.548	11.7	3.2	8.3	8.3
1980	52.579	54.062	54.043	8.8	−.2	9.1	9.1
1981	53.904	59.128	59.119	12.2	2.5	9.4	9.4
1982	52.860	62.738	62.726	4.0	−1.9	6.1	6.1
1983	55.249	65.214	65.207	8.7	4.5	3.9	4.0
1984	59.220	67.664	67.655	11.2	7.2	3.8	3.8
1985	61.666	69.724	69.713	7.3	4.1	3.0	3.0
1986	63.804	71.269	71.250	5.7	3.5	2.2	2.2
1987	65.958	73.204	73.196	6.2	3.4	2.7	2.7
1988	68.684	75.706	75.694	7.7	4.1	3.4	3.4
1989	71.116	78.569	78.556	7.5	3.5	3.8	3.8
1990	72.451	81.614	81.590	5.8	1.9	3.9	3.9
1991	72.329	84.457	84.444	3.3	−.2	3.5	3.5
1992	74.734	86.402	86.385	5.7	3.3	2.3	2.3
1993	76.731	88.390	88.381	5.0	2.7	2.3	2.3
1994	79.816	90.265	90.259	6.2	4.0	2.1	2.1
1995	81.814	92.115	92.106	4.6	2.5	2.0	2.0
1996	84.842	93.859	93.852	5.7	3.7	1.9	1.9
1997	88.658	95.415	95.414	6.2	4.5	1.7	1.7
1998	92.359	96.475	96.472	5.3	4.2	1.1	1.1
1999	96.469	97.868	97.868	6.0	4.5	1.4	1.4
2000	100.000	100.000	100.000	5.9	3.7	2.2	2.2
2001	100.506	102.376	102.373	2.9	.5	2.4	2.4
2002	102.710	103.949	103.945	3.8	2.2	1.5	1.5
1999: I	94.892	97.274	97.328	5.1	3.4	1.5	1.6
II	95.677	97.701	97.674	4.8	3.4	1.8	1.4
III	96.794	98.022	98.013	6.2	4.8	1.3	1.4
IV	98.514	98.475	98.432	9.1	7.3	1.9	1.7
2000: I	98.764	99.292	99.317	4.7	1.0	3.4	3.6
II	100.315	99.780	99.745	8.3	6.4	2.0	1.7
III	100.200	100.241	100.259	1.6	−.5	1.9	2.1
IV	100.721	100.687	100.666	3.8	2.1	1.8	1.6
2001: I	100.664	101.478	101.443	2.9	−.2	3.2	3.1
II	100.503	102.273	102.248	2.6	−.6	3.2	3.2
III	100.180	102.676	102.660	.3	−1.3	1.6	1.6
IV	100.679	103.078	103.139	3.9	2.0	1.6	1.9
2002: I	101.843	103.364	103.315	5.4	4.7	1.1	.7
II	102.324	103.738	103.814	3.9	1.9	1.5	1.9
III	103.172	104.123	104.084	4.4	3.4	1.5	1.0
IV	103.502	104.571	104.556	3.1	1.3	1.7	1.8
2003: I	104.008	105.163	105.146	4.3	2.0	2.3	2.3
II	104.801	105.440	105.427	4.2	3.1	1.1	1.1
III	106.887	105.870	105.851	10.0	8.2	1.6	1.6

[1] Quarterly percent changes are at annual rates.

Source: Department of Commerce, Bureau of Economic Analysis.

288

[Percent change from preceding period; quarterly data at seasonally adjusted annual rates]

Year or quarter	Gross domestic product	Personal consumption expenditures				Gross private domestic investment				Exports and imports of goods and services		Government consumption expenditures and gross investment		
						Nonresidential fixed								
		Total	Durable goods	Nondurable goods	Services	Total	Structures	Equipment and software	Residential fixed	Exports	Imports	Total	Federal	State and local
1959	7.1	5.6	12.1	4.1	5.3	8.0	2.4	11.9	25.4	10.3	10.5	3.4	3.1	3.8
1960	2.5	2.8	2.0	1.5	4.5	5.7	7.9	4.2	-7.1	17.4	1.3	.2	-2.7	4.4
1961	2.3	2.1	-3.8	1.8	4.2	-.6	1.4	-1.9	.3	.5	-.7	5.0	4.2	6.2
1962	6.1	5.0	11.7	3.1	5.0	8.7	4.5	11.6	9.6	5.1	11.3	6.2	8.5	3.1
1963	4.4	4.1	9.7	2.1	4.6	5.6	1.1	8.4	11.8	7.1	2.7	2.6	.1	6.0
1964	5.8	6.0	9.3	4.9	6.1	11.9	10.4	12.8	5.8	11.8	5.3	2.2	-1.3	6.8
1965	6.4	6.3	12.7	5.3	5.3	17.4	15.9	18.3	-2.9	2.8	10.6	3.0	.0	6.7
1966	6.5	5.7	8.4	5.5	5.0	12.5	6.8	16.0	-8.9	6.9	14.9	8.8	11.0	6.3
1967	2.5	3.0	1.6	1.6	4.9	-1.4	-2.5	-.7	-3.1	2.3	7.3	7.7	9.9	5.0
1968	4.8	5.7	11.0	4.6	5.2	4.5	1.5	6.2	13.6	7.9	14.9	3.1	.8	5.9
1969	3.1	3.7	3.5	2.7	4.8	7.6	5.4	8.8	3.0	4.8	5.7	-.2	-3.4	3.4
1970	.2	2.3	-3.2	2.4	4.0	-.5	.3	-1.0	-6.0	10.7	4.3	-2.4	-7.4	2.8
1971	3.4	3.8	10.0	1.8	3.9	.0	-1.6	1.0	27.4	1.7	5.3	-2.2	-7.7	3.1
1972	5.3	6.1	12.7	4.4	5.7	9.2	3.1	12.9	17.8	7.5	11.3	-.7	-4.1	2.2
1973	5.8	4.9	10.3	3.3	4.7	14.6	8.2	18.3	-.6	18.9	4.6	-.4	-4.2	2.8
1974	-.5	-.8	-6.9	-2.0	2.3	.8	-2.1	2.6	-20.6	7.9	-2.3	2.5	.9	3.8
1975	-.2	2.3	.0	1.5	3.7	-9.9	-10.5	-9.5	-13.0	-.6	-11.1	2.3	.3	3.7
1976	5.3	5.5	12.8	4.9	4.1	4.9	2.4	6.2	23.6	4.4	19.5	.4	.0	.7
1977	4.6	4.2	9.3	2.4	4.3	11.3	4.1	15.1	21.5	2.4	10.9	1.1	2.1	.4
1978	5.6	4.4	5.3	3.7	4.7	15.0	14.4	15.2	6.3	10.5	8.7	2.9	2.5	3.3
1979	3.2	2.4	-.3	2.7	3.1	10.1	12.7	8.7	-3.7	9.9	1.7	1.9	2.4	1.5
1980	-.2	-.3	-7.8	-.2	1.8	-.3	5.8	-3.6	-21.2	10.8	-6.6	2.0	4.7	-.1
1981	2.5	1.4	1.2	1.2	1.7	5.7	8.0	4.3	-8.0	1.2	2.6	.9	4.8	-2.1
1982	-1.9	1.4	-.1	1.0	2.1	-3.8	-1.7	-5.2	-18.2	-7.6	-1.3	1.8	3.9	.1
1983	4.5	5.7	14.6	3.3	5.5	-1.3	-10.8	5.4	41.4	-2.6	12.6	3.7	6.6	1.2
1984	7.2	5.3	14.6	4.0	4.1	17.7	14.0	19.8	14.8	8.2	24.3	3.3	3.1	3.6
1985	4.1	5.2	10.1	2.7	5.6	6.6	7.1	6.4	1.6	3.0	6.5	7.0	7.8	6.2
1986	3.5	4.1	9.7	3.6	2.9	-2.9	-11.0	1.9	12.3	7.7	8.6	6.1	5.7	6.4
1987	3.4	3.3	1.7	2.4	4.3	-.1	-2.9	1.4	2.0	10.8	5.9	2.5	3.6	1.5
1988	4.1	4.1	6.0	3.3	4.0	5.2	.6	7.5	-1.0	16.0	3.9	1.3	-1.6	3.7
1989	3.5	2.8	2.2	2.8	3.0	5.6	2.0	7.3	-3.0	11.5	4.4	2.6	1.5	3.4
1990	1.9	2.0	-.3	1.6	2.9	.5	1.5	.0	-8.6	9.0	3.6	3.2	2.0	4.1
1991	-.2	.2	-5.6	-.2	1.7	-5.4	-11.1	-2.6	-9.6	6.6	-.6	1.1	-.2	2.2
1992	3.3	3.3	5.9	2.0	3.5	3.2	-6.0	7.3	13.8	6.9	7.0	.5	-1.7	2.2
1993	2.7	3.3	7.8	2.7	2.8	8.7	-.7	12.5	8.2	3.2	8.8	-.9	-4.2	1.4
1994	4.0	3.7	8.4	3.5	2.9	9.2	1.8	11.9	9.6	8.7	11.9	.0	-3.7	2.6
1995	2.5	2.7	4.4	2.2	2.6	10.5	6.4	12.0	-3.2	10.1	8.0	.5	-2.7	2.6
1996	3.7	3.4	7.8	2.6	2.9	9.3	5.6	10.6	8.0	8.4	8.7	1.0	-1.2	2.3
1997	4.5	3.8	8.6	2.7	3.3	12.1	7.3	13.8	1.9	11.9	13.6	1.9	-1.0	3.6
1998	4.2	5.0	11.3	4.0	4.2	11.1	5.1	13.3	7.6	2.4	11.6	1.9	-1.1	3.6
1999	4.5	5.1	11.7	4.6	4.0	9.2	-.4	12.7	6.0	4.3	11.5	3.9	2.2	4.7
2000	3.7	4.7	7.3	3.8	4.5	8.7	6.8	9.4	.8	8.7	13.1	2.1	.9	2.7
2001	.5	2.5	4.1	1.9	2.4	-4.5	-2.5	-5.2	.4	-5.2	-2.6	2.8	3.7	2.2
2002	2.2	3.4	6.5	3.0	3.0	-7.2	-18.4	-2.8	4.9	-2.4	3.3	3.8	7.9	1.8
1999:I	3.4	4.1	-1.5	5.3	4.7	7.4	-7.4	12.9	3.5	-3.4	10.7	2.7	-2.3	5.4
II	3.4	6.4	20.3	4.1	4.6	12.8	2.9	16.2	3.5	4.6	15.0	2.4	1.7	2.8
III	4.8	4.3	8.8	1.2	4.8	10.0	-3.1	14.6	2.4	11.0	14.7	5.1	8.3	3.4
IV	7.3	5.0	2.8	9.3	3.5	1.0	4.2	.0	5.0	10.9	8.2	6.6	9.5	5.1
2000:I	1.0	6.5	24.4	.3	6.0	14.3	7.0	16.9	4.1	6.6	16.7	-3.0	-13.9	3.2
II	6.4	2.5	-9.5	5.7	3.9	14.8	18.0	13.7	-3.5	12.3	16.5	5.5	17.2	.1
III	-.5	3.9	6.0	2.3	4.3	2.2	9.6	-.2	-8.0	10.7	14.1	-2.1	-8.2	1.3
IV	2.1	3.4	.7	3.7	3.9	.9	1.2	.8	.4	-2.7	-1.6	1.3	-1.0	2.5
2001:I	-.2	.5	1.7	.4	.3	-4.5	-5.9	-4.0	2.6	-4.5	-6.2	5.8	8.9	4.3
II	-.6	2.3	9.8	-1.1	2.4	-13.6	-5.6	-16.4	3.7	-13.4	-8.6	5.8	6.7	5.3
III	-1.3	-1.9	.7	2.9	1.6	-8.4	2.2	-12.2	3.1	-17.7	-10.8	-4.1	.0	-6.1
IV	2.0	6.2	27.3	4.7	2.8	-14.0	-35.3	-4.1	-2.5	-9.8	-3.8	7.4	9.9	6.1
2002:I	4.7	4.1	1.6	6.1	3.8	-7.0	-23.9	-.2	8.7	4.4	8.4	4.6	8.4	2.7
II	1.9	2.6	.5	.4	4.1	-3.0	-14.5	1.2	8.9	8.7	17.1	4.0	10.5	.7
III	3.4	2.0	5.0	.2	2.2	-1.1	-14.6	3.7	4.2	4.3	4.1	2.5	3.9	1.7
IV	1.3	2.2	.3	4.6	1.5	-.1	-5.6	1.7	6.8	-3.7	8.2	7.1	18.2	1.5
2003:I	2.0	2.5	.5	5.7	1.5	-.6	-4.0	.5	4.5	-2.0	-6.8	-.4	-.2	-.5
II	3.1	3.3	17.7	1.2	1.7	7.0	3.9	8.0	4.5	-1.1	9.1	7.4	23.5	-.8
III	8.2	6.9	28.0	7.3	2.8	12.8	-1.8	17.6	21.9	9.9	.8	1.8	1.2	2.1

Note.—Percent changes based on unrounded data.

Source: Department of Commerce, Bureau of Economic Analysis.

TABLE B–5.—*Contributions to percent change in real gross domestic product, 1959–2003*

[Percentage points, except as noted; quarterly data at seasonally adjusted annual rates]

Year or quarter	Gross domestic product (percent change)	Personal consumption expenditures				Gross private domestic investment							Change in private inventories
							Fixed investment						
								Nonresidential					
		Total	Durable goods	Non-durable goods	Services	Total	Total	Total	Structures	Equipment and software	Residential		
1959	7.1	3.55	0.97	1.25	1.33	2.80	1.94	0.73	0.09	0.64	1.21		0.86
1960	2.5	1.73	.17	.44	1.12	.00	.13	.52	.28	.24	-.39		-.13
1961	2.3	1.30	-.31	.53	1.08	-.10	-.04	-.06	.05	-.11	.01		-.05
1962	6.1	3.11	.89	.90	1.31	1.81	1.24	.78	.16	.61	.46		.57
1963	4.4	2.56	.77	.59	1.20	1.00	1.08	.50	.04	.46	.58		-.08
1964	5.8	3.71	.77	1.33	1.61	1.25	1.37	1.07	.36	.71	.30		-.13
1965	6.4	3.91	1.07	1.43	1.42	2.16	1.50	1.65	.57	1.07	-.15		.66
1966	6.5	3.50	.73	1.46	1.31	1.44	.87	1.29	.27	1.02	-.43		.58
1967	2.5	1.81	.13	.42	1.26	-.76	-.28	-.15	-.10	-.05	-.13		-.49
1968	4.8	3.50	.93	1.19	1.38	.90	1.00	.46	.06	.41	.53		-.10
1969	3.1	2.27	.31	.69	1.28	.90	.90	.78	.20	.58	.13		.00
1970	.2	1.42	-.28	.61	1.08	-1.04	-.31	-.06	.01	-.07	-.26		-.73
1971	3.4	2.38	.81	.47	1.09	1.67	1.10	.00	-.06	.07	1.10		.58
1972	5.3	3.80	1.07	1.11	1.61	1.87	1.81	.92	.12	.81	.89		.06
1973	5.8	3.05	.90	.82	1.33	1.96	1.46	1.50	.31	1.19	-.04		.50
1974	-.5	-.47	-.61	-.51	.65	-1.30	-1.04	.09	-.09	.18	-1.13		-.27
1975	-.2	1.42	.00	.37	1.05	-2.98	-1.71	-1.14	-.43	-.70	-.57		-1.27
1976	5.3	3.48	1.04	1.24	1.19	2.84	1.42	.52	.09	.43	.90		1.41
1977	4.6	2.68	.80	.60	1.27	2.43	2.18	1.19	.15	1.04	.99		.25
1978	5.6	2.76	.47	.91	1.38	2.16	2.04	1.69	.54	1.15	.35		.12
1979	3.2	1.52	-.03	.65	.90	.61	1.02	1.23	.52	.71	-.21		-.41
1980	-.2	-.17	-.65	-.04	.52	-2.12	-1.21	-.04	.27	-.30	-1.17		-.91
1981	2.5	.90	.09	.29	.51	1.59	.39	.74	.40	.34	-.35		1.20
1982	-1.9	.87	.00	.23	.65	-2.55	-1.22	-.51	-.09	-.42	-.71		-1.34
1983	4.5	3.65	1.07	.80	1.79	1.45	1.17	-.16	-.57	.41	1.33		.29
1984	7.2	3.44	1.15	.93	1.36	4.63	2.68	2.05	.60	1.44	.64		1.95
1985	4.1	3.31	.83	.61	1.87	-.17	.89	.82	.32	.50	.07		-1.06
1986	3.5	2.62	.83	.78	1.01	-.12	.20	-.36	-.50	.15	.55		-.32
1987	3.4	2.17	.16	.52	1.50	.51	.09	-.01	-.11	.10	.10		.42
1988	4.1	2.66	.53	.70	1.43	.39	.52	.57	.02	.55	-.05		-.14
1989	3.5	1.86	.19	.59	1.07	.64	.47	.61	.07	.54	-.14		.17
1990	1.9	1.34	-.02	.33	1.03	-.53	-.32	.05	.05	.00	-.37		-.21
1991	-.2	.11	-.46	-.05	.62	-1.20	-.94	-.57	-.39	-.18	-.37		-.26
1992	3.3	2.18	.44	.43	1.31	1.07	.79	.32	-.18	.50	.47		.29
1993	2.7	2.23	.59	.56	1.09	1.21	1.14	.83	-.02	.85	.31		.07
1994	4.0	2.52	.66	.71	1.14	1.93	1.30	.91	.05	.87	.39		.63
1995	2.5	1.81	.36	.44	1.01	.48	.94	1.08	.17	.91	-.14		-.46
1996	3.7	2.31	.64	.51	1.15	1.35	1.34	1.01	.16	.85	.33		.02
1997	4.5	2.54	.70	.53	1.31	1.95	1.42	1.33	.21	1.12	.08		.54
1998	4.2	3.36	.93	.78	1.66	1.63	1.60	1.28	.16	1.12	.32		.03
1999	4.5	3.44	.99	.89	1.56	1.33	1.36	1.09	-.01	1.11	.27		-.03
2000	3.7	3.17	.63	.74	1.80	.99	1.09	1.06	.21	.85	.03		-.10
2001	.5	1.68	.36	.37	.96	-1.47	-.54	-.56	-.08	-.47	.02		-.93
2002	2.2	2.38	.55	.60	1.23	-.18	-.60	-.82	-.59	-.23	.23		.41
1999: I	3.4	2.68	-.14	1.00	1.82	1.96	1.02	.87	-.24	1.11	.16		.93
II	3.4	4.23	1.64	.79	1.81	.05	1.63	1.47	.09	1.38	.16		-1.57
III	4.8	2.90	.76	.24	1.89	1.72	1.30	1.19	-.10	1.28	.11		.42
IV	7.3	3.47	.25	1.80	1.43	2.65	.36	.12	.13	.00	.23		2.30
2000: I	1.0	4.38	1.96	.06	2.36	-1.30	1.83	1.64	.21	1.44	.19		-3.13
II	6.4	1.78	-.89	1.11	1.55	4.65	1.60	1.76	.53	1.23	-.16		3.05
III	-.5	2.62	.50	.44	1.67	-1.84	-.10	.28	.29	-.02	-.38		-1.74
IV	2.1	2.29	.06	.72	1.51	-.36	.13	.11	.04	.07	.02		-.49
2001: I	-.2	.28	.15	.06	.07	-1.96	-.45	-.56	-.20	-.37	.12		-1.51
II	-.6	1.52	.80	-.22	.94	-2.92	-1.60	-1.76	-.19	-1.57	.16		-1.32
III	-1.3	1.27	.06	.57	.64	-1.39	-.88	-1.02	.07	-1.09	.14		-.51
IV	2.0	4.20	2.14	.91	1.15	-2.98	-1.83	-1.71	-1.36	-.35	-.12		-1.15
2002: I	4.7	2.92	.14	1.19	1.58	1.60	-.41	-.81	-.77	-.03	.40		2.01
II	1.9	1.81	.04	.07	1.70	.69	.08	-.33	-.41	.09	.41		.61
III	3.4	1.39	.43	.04	.92	1.66	.08	-.12	-.40	.28	.20		1.58
IV	1.3	1.57	.02	.90	.65	-.09	.31	-.01	-.14	.13	.32		-.40
2003: I	2.0	1.80	.04	1.13	.63	-.57	.16	-.06	-.10	.04	.22		-.74
II	3.1	2.34	1.38	.25	.71	.73	.90	.68	.09	.59	.22		-.17
III	8.2	4.89	2.23	1.48	1.19	2.17	2.30	1.25	-.04	1.30	1.05		-.13

See next page for continuation of table.

[Percentage points, except as noted; quarterly data at seasonally adjusted annual rates]

Year or quarter	Net exports of goods and services							Government consumption expenditures and gross investment				
	Net exports	Exports			Imports			Total	Federal			State and local
		Total	Goods	Services	Total	Goods	Services		Total	National defense	Nondefense	
1959	0.00	0.45	−0.02	0.48	−0.45	−0.48	0.03	0.76	0.42	−0.23	0.65	0.34
1960	.72	.78	.76	.02	−.06	.05	−.11	.03	−.35	−.17	−.18	.39
1961	.06	.03	.02	.01	.03	.00	.02	1.07	.51	.45	.06	.56
1962	−.21	.25	.17	.08	−.47	−.40	−.07	1.36	1.07	.63	.44	.29
1963	.24	.35	.29	.06	−.12	−.12	.00	.58	.01	−.25	.26	.57
1964	.36	.59	.52	.07	−.23	−.19	−.04	.49	−.17	−.40	.23	.65
1965	−.30	.15	.02	.13	−.45	−.41	−.04	.65	.00	−.19	.19	.66
1966	−.29	.36	.27	.09	−.65	−.49	−.16	1.87	1.24	1.21	.03	.63
1967	−.22	.12	.02	.10	−.34	−.17	−.16	1.68	1.17	1.19	−.02	.51
1968	−.30	.41	.30	.10	−.70	−.68	−.03	.73	.10	.16	−.06	.63
1969	−.04	.25	.20	.05	−.29	−.20	−.09	−.06	−.42	−.49	.06	.37
1970	.34	.56	.44	.12	−.22	−.15	−.07	−.55	−.86	−.83	−.03	.31
1971	−.19	.10	−.02	.11	−.29	−.33	.04	−.50	−.85	−.97	.12	.36
1972	−.21	.42	.43	−.01	−.63	−.57	−.06	−.16	−.42	−.61	.18	.26
1973	.82	1.12	1.01	.11	−.29	−.34	.05	−.08	−.41	−.39	−.02	.33
1974	.75	.58	.46	.12	.18	.17	.00	.52	.08	−.05	.13	.44
1975	.89	−.05	−.16	.10	.94	.87	.07	.48	.03	−.06	.09	.45
1976	−1.08	.37	.31	.05	−1.45	−1.35	−.10	.10	.00	−.02	.03	.09
1977	−.72	.20	.08	.11	−.92	−.84	−.07	.23	.19	.07	.12	.04
1978	.05	.82	.68	.15	−.78	−.67	−.11	.60	.22	.05	.16	.38
1979	.66	.82	.77	.06	−.16	−.14	−.02	.37	.20	.17	.03	.17
1980	1.68	.97	.86	.11	.71	.67	.04	.38	.39	.25	.14	−.01
1981	−.15	.12	−.09	.21	−.27	−.18	−.09	.19	.42	.38	.04	−.23
1982	−.60	−.73	−.67	−.06	.12	.20	−.08	.35	.35	.48	−.13	.01
1983	−1.35	−.22	−.19	−.03	−1.13	−1.00	−.13	.77	.63	.50	.13	.13
1984	−1.58	.63	.46	.17	−2.21	−1.83	−.39	.70	.30	.35	−.05	.40
1985	−.42	.23	.20	.02	−.65	−.52	−.13	1.41	.74	.60	.14	.67
1986	−.30	.54	.26	.28	−.84	−.82	−.02	1.27	.55	.47	.08	.71
1987	.17	.78	.56	.21	−.61	−.39	−.22	.52	.36	.35	.01	.17
1988	.82	1.24	1.04	.20	−.42	−.36	−.07	.27	−.15	−.03	−.12	.42
1989	.52	.99	.75	.24	−.47	−.38	−.10	.52	.14	−.03	.17	.39
1990	.43	.81	.56	.26	−.39	−.26	−.13	.64	.18	.00	.18	.46
1991	.69	.63	.46	.16	.06	.01	.05	.23	−.02	−.07	.06	.24
1992	−.04	.68	.52	.16	−.72	−.77	.05	.11	−.15	−.32	.17	.26
1993	−.59	.32	.23	.09	−.91	−.85	−.06	−.18	−.35	−.33	−.02	.17
1994	−.43	.85	.67	.18	−1.29	−1.18	−.11	.00	−.30	−.27	−.03	.30
1995	.11	1.04	.85	.19	−.93	−.87	−.06	.10	−.20	−.19	−.01	.30
1996	−.14	.91	.68	.22	−1.05	−.94	−.11	.18	−.08	−.07	−.02	.26
1997	−.34	1.30	1.11	.19	−1.64	−1.45	−.19	.34	−.07	−.13	.06	.41
1998	−1.16	.27	.18	.09	−1.43	−1.20	−.23	.34	−.07	−.09	.02	.41
1999	−.99	.47	.29	.18	−1.46	−1.31	−.15	.67	.14	.08	.06	.54
2000	−.86	.93	.84	.09	−1.79	−1.55	−.25	.36	.05	−.02	.07	.31
2001	−.19	−.58	−.48	−.10	.39	.39	−.01	.48	.22	.15	.07	.26
2002	−.70	−.24	−.29	.04	−.45	−.42	−.03	.69	.48	.35	.14	.21
1999: I	−1.67	−.39	−.63	.24	−1.28	−1.16	−.13	.46	−.14	−.22	.08	.60
II	−1.35	.48	.33	.14	−1.83	−1.69	−.14	.41	.09	−.01	.09	.32
III	−.75	1.12	.98	.14	−1.87	−1.67	−.19	.88	.49	.51	−.02	.39
IV	.01	1.13	1.01	.12	−1.11	−1.01	−.11	1.17	.58	.39	.18	.59
2000: I	−1.53	.70	.65	.05	−2.23	−1.79	−.44	−.56	−.93	−.92	−.01	.36
II	−.98	1.30	1.03	.26	−2.27	−2.03	−.24	.96	.96	.61	.35	.01
III	−.87	1.14	1.36	−.22	−2.01	−1.70	−.32	−.37	−.51	−.29	−.22	.15
IV	−.07	−.31	−.45	.14	.24	.19	.04	.22	−.07	.06	−.13	.29
2001: I	.46	−.50	−.44	−.06	.96	.88	.08	.99	.50	.27	.23	.49
II	−.25	−1.54	−1.52	−.02	1.29	1.57	−.28	1.00	.38	.10	.28	.62
III	−.42	−1.99	−1.50	−.48	1.57	1.10	.47	−.74	.00	.09	−.09	−.74
IV	−.50	−1.02	−.54	−.47	.52	.35	.16	1.28	.57	.53	.04	.71
2002: I	−.65	.40	−.19	.59	−1.05	−.66	−.39	.85	.52	.33	.20	.33
II	−1.32	.80	.75	.05	−2.12	−2.20	.09	.72	.64	.38	.27	.08
III	−.15	.41	.28	.13	−.56	−.55	−.02	.46	.26	.19	.07	.20
IV	−1.47	−.37	−.64	.27	−1.10	−.83	−.27	1.29	1.11	.85	.26	.18
2003: I	.81	−.19	.13	−.31	1.00	.81	.19	−.07	−.01	−.25	.24	−.06
II	−1.34	−.11	−.11	.01	−1.24	−1.51	.27	1.36	1.46	1.58	−.12	−.10
III	.80	.92	.56	.36	−.12	.18	−.30	.34	.09	−.06	.15	.25

Source: Department of Commerce, Bureau of Economic Analysis.

[Index numbers, 2000=100; quarterly data seasonally adjusted]

Year or quarter	Gross domestic product	Personal consumption expenditures				Gross private domestic investment					
							Fixed investment				
								Nonresidential			
		Total	Durable goods	Non-durable goods	Services	Total	Total	Total	Structures	Equipment and software	Residential
1959	24.868	23.067	10.822	33.491	20.794	15.367	15.736	10.760	36.530	6.065	37.820
1960	25.484	23.702	11.041	33.994	21.720	15.362	15.870	11.371	39.433	6.322	35.129
1961	26.077	24.191	10.622	34.621	22.626	15.261	15.820	11.299	39.966	6.200	35.227
1962	27.658	25.389	11.865	35.710	23.747	17.197	17.248	12.284	41.775	6.917	38.604
1963	28.868	26.436	13.017	36.463	24.830	18.351	18.584	12.966	42.239	7.500	43.154
1964	30.545	28.020	14.222	38.248	26.345	19.863	20.378	14.504	46.626	8.457	45.662
1965	32.506	29.791	16.025	40.277	27.749	22.650	22.459	17.031	54.058	10.007	44.329
1966	34.625	31.484	17.377	42.487	29.129	24.644	23.745	19.160	57.751	11.609	40.362
1967	35.496	32.422	17.648	43.157	30.552	23.517	23.306	18.900	56.284	11.532	39.092
1968	37.208	34.284	19.594	45.126	32.148	24.887	24.935	19.746	57.102	12.250	44.421
1969	38.356	35.558	20.289	46.326	33.691	26.338	26.486	21.246	60.189	13.334	45.733
1970	38.422	36.381	19.631	47.436	35.038	24.608	25.931	21.134	60.364	13.201	42.998
1971	39.713	37.770	21.593	48.294	36.400	27.413	27.894	21.135	59.370	13.332	54.789
1972	41.815	40.082	24.336	50.422	38.469	30.658	31.246	23.072	61.201	15.052	64.526
1973	44.224	42.048	26.849	52.068	40.274	34.249	34.101	26.429	66.200	17.812	64.112
1974	44.001	41.729	25.001	51.020	41.216	31.729	31.971	26.653	64.785	18.268	50.877
1975	43.916	42.688	24.996	51.771	42.743	26.111	28.541	24.022	57.984	16.529	44.271
1976	46.256	45.041	28.187	54.301	44.475	31.387	31.356	25.200	59.390	17.562	54.698
1977	48.391	46.950	30.809	55.609	46.392	36.130	35.863	28.045	61.841	20.208	66.440
1978	51.085	49.012	32.435	57.687	48.558	40.486	40.205	32.243	70.769	23.284	70.623
1979	52.699	50.204	32.325	59.226	50.044	41.776	42.473	35.489	79.731	25.318	68.032
1980	52.579	50.065	29.788	59.137	50.921	37.182	39.708	35.388	84.350	24.407	53.636
1981	53.904	50.779	30.149	59.839	51.773	40.615	40.591	37.398	91.074	25.445	49.336
1982	52.860	51.493	30.128	60.409	52.865	34.918	37.737	35.981	89.528	24.122	40.378
1983	55.249	54.436	34.535	62.417	55.760	38.172	40.491	35.518	79.865	25.420	57.093
1984	59.220	57.325	39.577	64.898	58.026	49.420	47.331	41.787	91.016	30.462	65.566
1985	61.666	60.303	43.577	66.665	61.303	48.963	49.823	44.561	97.502	32.397	66.604
1986	63.804	62.749	47.785	69.060	63.111	48.629	50.403	43.287	86.817	33.011	74.776
1987	65.958	64.840	48.616	70.715	65.843	50.130	50.682	43.259	84.340	33.463	76.269
1988	68.684	67.468	51.549	73.016	68.506	51.309	52.352	45.520	84.885	35.987	75.496
1989	71.116	69.369	52.686	75.044	70.555	53.369	53.928	48.063	86.583	38.624	73.204
1990	72.451	70.782	52.532	76.209	72.583	51.574	52.803	48.302	87.867	38.636	66.887
1991	72.329	70.903	49.564	76.033	73.812	47.378	49.379	45.712	78.091	37.643	60.460
1992	74.734	73.224	52.470	77.553	76.379	51.223	52.312	47.179	73.423	40.387	68.825
1993	76.731	75.672	56.577	79.619	78.540	55.795	56.788	51.287	72.891	45.428	74.446
1994	79.816	78.504	61.321	82.369	80.854	63.358	62.079	55.999	74.180	50.846	81.621
1995	81.814	80.623	64.011	84.152	82.973	65.340	66.090	61.885	78.903	56.930	79.005
1996	84.842	83.382	69.025	86.300	85.420	71.123	72.018	67.661	83.354	62.981	85.331
1997	88.658	86.533	74.935	88.605	88.270	79.961	78.657	75.820	89.432	71.641	86.942
1998	92.359	90.896	83.432	92.154	92.011	87.821	86.657	84.232	94.019	81.137	93.591
1999	96.469	95.537	93.192	96.374	95.652	94.647	93.884	91.980	93.619	91.437	99.254
2000	100.000	100.000	100.000	100.000	100.000	100.000	100.000	100.000	100.000	100.000	100.000
2001	100.506	102.452	104.144	101.852	102.382	91.650	96.826	95.517	97.465	94.825	100.35
2002	102.710	105.951	110.868	104.949	105.420	90.580	93.258	88.063	79.492	92.144	105.224
1999: I	94.892	93.648	88.891	94.967	94.083	92.577	91.189	88.792	93.238	87.352	98.029
II	95.677	95.108	93.085	95.925	95.155	92.646	93.426	91.499	93.915	90.702	98.860
III	96.794	96.103	95.066	96.223	96.269	94.923	95.212	93.697	93.179	93.848	99.453
IV	98.514	97.291	95.725	98.383	97.103	98.442	95.707	93.931	94.144	93.846	100.67
2000: I	98.764	98.841	101.097	98.458	98.530	96.691	98.339	97.126	95.744	97.587	101.688
II	100.315	99.465	98.609	99.835	99.474	103.060	100.600	100.526	99.785	100.778	100.783
III	100.200	100.424	100.056	100.398	100.521	100.411	100.443	101.066	102.088	100.723	98.714
IV	100.721	101.270	100.238	101.309	101.475	99.838	100.619	101.282	102.383	100.912	98.80
2001: I	100.664	101.400	100.669	101.400	101.547	96.933	99.932	100.125	100.843	99.885	99.45
II	100.503	101.971	103.039	101.124	102.150	92.686	97.560	96.535	99.406	95.506	100.35
III	100.180	102.446	103.219	101.857	102.558	90.646	96.258	94.453	99.958	92.437	101.12
IV	100.679	103.989	109.648	103.029	103.273	86.337	93.554	90.955	89.654	91.470	100.48
2002: I	101.843	105.043	110.076	104.556	104.236	88.634	92.969	89.314	83.728	91.420	102.59
II	102.324	105.715	110.202	104.652	105.298	89.645	93.106	88.641	80.523	91.693	104.80
III	103.172	106.229	111.557	104.703	105.869	92.090	93.238	88.399	77.412	92.536	105.88
IV	103.502	106.819	111.638	105.885	106.276	91.953	93.718	88.378	76.304	92.927	107.62
2003: I	104.008	107.489	111.779	107.358	106.664	91.135	93.968	88.248	75.523	93.047	108.82
II	104.801	108.378	116.420	107.685	107.115	92.186	95.378	89.751	76.244	94.851	110.02
III	106.887	110.197	123.834	109.607	107.849	95.424	98.932	92.485	75.906	98.779	115.61

See next page for continuation of table.

[Index numbers, 2000=100; quarterly data seasonally adjusted]

Year or quarter	Exports of goods and services			Imports of goods and services			Government consumption expenditures and gross investment				
								Federal			State and local
	Total	Goods	Services	Total	Goods	Services	Total	Total	National defense	Non-defense	
1959	7.043	6.198	9.641	6.908	5.403	15.462	41.489	68.666	89.447	33.305	26.999
1960	8.266	7.651	9.797	7.000	5.314	16.669	41.553	66.779	87.977	30.672	28.182
1961	8.309	7.689	9.857	6.953	5.307	16.385	43.639	69.564	91.851	31.599	29.918
1962	8.729	8.031	10.535	7.742	6.092	17.150	46.329	75.492	97.412	38.144	30.839
1963	9.353	8.662	11.070	7.951	6.339	17.137	47.522	75.540	95.085	42.217	32.696
1964	10.454	9.849	11.733	8.374	6.757	17.579	48.563	74.530	91.304	45.880	34.913
1965	10.747	9.901	12.926	9.265	7.714	18.096	50.028	74.508	89.403	48.995	37.252
1966	11.492	10.589	13.814	10.642	8.930	20.395	54.430	82.737	102.205	49.501	39.590
1967	11.757	10.638	14.905	11.417	9.400	22.887	58.604	90.960	115.571	49.059	41.589
1968	12.681	11.481	16.049	13.118	11.342	23.298	60.436	91.681	117.416	47.912	44.048
1969	13.294	12.082	16.646	13.866	11.963	24.767	60.290	88.525	111.604	49.186	45.534
1970	14.723	13.460	18.128	14.457	12.432	26.059	58.833	81.997	101.477	48.674	46.797
1971	14.973	13.408	19.527	15.229	13.474	25.317	57.553	75.686	89.980	50.961	48.232
1972	16.096	14.849	19.404	16.943	15.307	26.390	57.128	72.574	82.921	54.551	49.291
1973	19.131	18.259	20.775	17.729	16.388	25.500	56.926	69.519	78.322	54.213	50.694
1974	20.643	19.709	22.396	17.327	15.932	25.472	58.360	70.134	77.714	57.023	52.603
1975	20.512	19.252	23.773	15.402	13.924	24.367	59.675	70.360	76.977	58.965	54.536
1976	21.408	20.165	24.476	18.413	17.073	26.049	59.940	70.388	76.706	59.523	54.937
1977	21.923	20.429	26.055	20.426	19.153	27.347	60.598	71.880	77.597	62.089	55.137
1978	24.234	22.712	28.234	22.196	20.871	29.297	62.383	73.681	78.259	65.947	56.938
1979	26.637	25.396	29.103	22.565	21.229	29.700	63.549	75.465	80.648	66.640	57.775
1980	29.506	28.422	30.919	21.066	19.653	29.037	64.790	79.043	84.160	70.373	57.736
1981	29.868	28.114	34.211	21.620	20.058	30.711	65.381	82.818	89.486	71.310	56.577
1982	27.586	25.573	33.263	21.348	19.544	32.346	66.530	86.018	96.244	67.888	56.607
1983	26.875	24.838	32.710	24.041	22.210	34.958	68.964	91.726	103.158	71.398	57.268
1984	29.068	26.801	35.627	29.893	27.584	43.724	71.273	94.550	108.186	70.035	59.322
1985	29.951	27.790	36.051	31.833	29.310	47.050	76.240	101.957	117.355	74.169	63.003
1986	32.259	29.217	41.325	34.561	32.314	47.638	80.885	107.754	124.871	76.764	67.064
1987	35.742	32.456	45.502	36.602	33.812	53.205	82.873	111.674	130.779	76.984	68.041
1988	41.469	38.572	49.616	38.039	35.181	55.010	83.940	109.898	130.161	73.037	70.582
1989	46.233	43.172	54.723	39.706	36.686	57.678	86.110	111.594	129.518	79.075	72.994
1990	50.394	46.810	60.480	41.139	37.770	61.430	88.869	113.873	129.472	85.651	75.991
1991	53.736	50.042	64.082	40.905	37.741	59.849	89.872	113.679	128.050	87.700	77.600
1992	57.439	53.785	67.590	43.748	41.263	58.321	90.342	111.713	121.708	93.749	79.318
1993	59.291	55.534	69.726	47.576	45.423	60.026	89.513	107.056	114.860	93.087	80.459
1994	64.447	60.937	74.097	53.256	51.466	63.421	89.525	103.050	109.259	91.957	82.543
1995	70.982	68.070	78.793	57.539	56.104	65.492	90.015	100.254	105.093	91.613	84.728
1996	76.930	74.086	84.483	62.544	61.337	69.094	90.896	99.091	103.648	90.955	86.668
1997	86.082	84.717	89.509	71.037	70.172	75.600	92.588	98.066	100.733	93.320	89.770
1998	88.164	86.614	92.077	79.299	78.364	84.222	94.354	96.970	98.650	93.985	93.014
1999	91.969	89.907	97.207	88.391	88.078	90.038	97.987	99.122	100.515	96.646	97.409
2000	100.000	100.000	100.000	100.000	100.000	100.000	100.000	100.000	100.000	100.000	100.000
2001	94.773	93.903	96.950	97.377	96.802	100.404	102.750	103.746	103.890	103.490	102.248
2002	92.512	90.163	98.348	100.609	100.400	101.787	106.697	111.958	113.086	109.956	104.047
1999: I	89.406	86.963	95.629	84.174	83.489	87.759	96.550	97.248	98.313	95.355	96.195
II	90.419	87.946	96.712	87.170	86.793	89.157	97.136	97.670	98.276	96.595	96.865
III	92.807	90.846	97.786	90.210	90.044	91.091	98.343	99.642	101.501	96.338	97.679
IV	95.243	93.874	98.703	92.011	91.987	92.144	99.920	101.926	103.969	98.297	98.896
2000: I	96.770	95.861	99.055	95.643	95.465	96.598	99.169	98.169	97.925	98.601	99.679
II	99.608	99.017	101.092	99.371	99.427	99.076	100.517	102.139	101.841	102.669	99.696
III	102.163	103.270	99.384	102.700	102.756	102.402	99.995	99.970	99.901	100.091	100.007
IV	101.458	101.852	100.469	102.286	102.352	101.924	100.318	99.722	100.334	98.639	100.618
2001: I	100.304	100.443	99.956	100.659	100.570	101.118	101.742	101.878	102.202	101.300	101.672
II	96.774	95.558	99.810	98.434	97.346	104.151	103.185	103.549	102.871	104.752	103.000
III	92.188	90.691	95.924	95.673	95.032	99.054	102.119	103.539	103.491	103.622	101.404
IV	89.829	88.918	92.111	94.741	94.260	97.293	103.955	106.019	106.995	104.282	102.916
2002: I	90.802	88.323	96.959	96.674	95.704	101.670	105.138	108.175	109.132	106.477	103.610
II	92.721	90.863	97.347	100.567	100.561	100.730	106.168	110.907	111.647	109.592	103.779
III	93.709	91.814	98.426	101.587	101.748	100.906	106.814	111.986	112.894	110.374	104.207
IV	92.818	89.651	100.660	103.610	103.586	103.842	108.666	116.764	118.672	113.381	104.593
2003: I	92.353	90.076	98.010	101.810	101.829	101.828	108.563	116.713	116.972	116.252	104.463
II	92.097	89.693	98.068	104.059	105.144	98.938	110.527	123.025	127.675	114.781	104.248
III	94.290	91.572	101.033	104.277	104.739	102.100	111.008	123.406	127.247	116.596	104.779

Source: Department of Commerce, Bureau of Economic Analysis.

[Index numbers, 2000=100, except as noted; quarterly data seasonally adjusted]

Year or quarter	Gross domestic product	Personal consumption expenditures					Gross private domestic investment				
								Fixed investment			
									Nonresidential		
		Total	Durable goods	Non-durable goods	Services	Total	Total	Total	Structures	Equipment and software	Residential
1959	20.754	20.432	45.662	22.765	15.485	29.474	28.262	35.114	15.923	50.882	16.630
1960	21.044	20.767	45.444	23.089	15.887	29.619	28.414	35.275	15.904	51.305	16.743
1961	21.281	20.985	45.551	23.227	16.173	29.538	28.325	35.076	15.810	51.025	16.769
1962	21.572	21.232	45.755	23.412	16.466	29.558	28.346	35.087	15.941	50.774	16.795
1963	21.801	21.479	45.915	23.683	16.701	29.467	28.267	35.088	16.085	50.495	16.663
1964	22.134	21.786	46.142	23.986	17.016	29.634	28.440	35.268	16.316	50.474	16.796
1965	22.538	22.103	45.721	24.423	17.334	30.107	28.926	35.672	16.791	50.520	17.272
1966	23.180	22.662	45.517	25.232	17.810	30.726	29.536	36.206	17.398	50.654	17.899
1967	23.897	23.237	46.228	25.830	18.349	31.538	30.364	37.129	17.943	51.776	18.521
1968	24.916	24.151	47.749	26.820	19.128	32.714	31.582	38.431	18.835	53.167	19.504
1969	26.153	25.255	49.067	28.062	20.106	34.264	33.140	40.018	20.074	54.645	20.853
1970	27.538	26.448	50.148	29.446	21.175	35.713	34.565	41.908	21.390	56.657	21.526
1971	28.916	27.574	51.975	30.359	22.340	37.493	36.306	43.880	23.040	58.340	22.775
1972	30.171	28.528	52.531	31.373	23.304	39.062	37.865	45.367	24.704	59.044	24.158
1973	31.854	30.081	53.301	33.838	24.381	41.172	39.958	47.115	26.619	60.047	26.297
1974	34.721	33.191	56.676	38.702	26.345	45.263	43.890	51.658	30.295	64.474	29.011
1975	38.007	35.955	61.844	41.735	28.595	50.847	49.384	58.763	33.911	74.001	31.706
1976	40.202	37.948	65.278	43.346	30.603	53.654	52.244	62.018	35.571	78.355	33.743
1977	42.758	40.410	68.129	45.911	32.933	57.677	56.342	66.258	38.651	83.011	37.147
1978	45.762	43.248	72.038	48.985	35.464	62.381	61.101	70.695	42.382	87.391	41.696
1979	49.553	47.059	76.830	54.148	38.316	68.027	66.642	76.440	47.313	92.932	46.374
1980	54.062	52.078	83.277	60.449	42.332	74.424	72.887	83.198	51.740	100.868	51.394
1981	59.128	56.720	88.879	65.130	46.746	81.278	79.670	91.245	58.880	108.077	55.587
1982	62.738	59.859	92.358	66.955	50.528	85.455	84.047	96.295	63.566	112.293	58.564
1983	65.214	62.436	94.181	68.386	53.799	85.237	83.912	95.432	61.939	112.530	59.908
1984	67.664	64.795	95.550	70.004	56.680	85.845	84.399	95.195	62.468	111.547	61.630
1985	69.724	66.936	96.620	71.543	59.295	86.720	85.457	95.936	63.940	111.413	63.219
1986	71.269	68.569	97.685	71.273	62.040	88.599	87.501	97.566	65.168	113.178	65.868
1987	73.204	70.947	100.465	73.731	64.299	90.289	89.118	98.435	66.199	113.796	68.561
1988	75.706	73.755	101.921	76.206	67.493	92.354	91.431	100.625	69.016	115.216	70.928
1989	78.569	76.972	103.717	79.842	70.708	94.559	93.641	102.731	71.707	116.657	73.211
1990	81.614	80.498	104.561	84.226	74.197	96.379	95.542	104.695	74.015	118.168	74.930
1991	84.457	83.419	106.080	86.779	77.497	97.749	96.960	106.314	75.355	119.854	75.912
1992	86.402	85.824	106.756	88.105	80.684	97.395	96.670	105.411	75.330	118.444	76.836
1993	88.390	87.804	107.840	88.973	83.345	98.521	97.805	105.487	77.602	117.243	79.941
1994	90.265	89.654	109.978	89.605	85.748	99.813	99.133	106.008	80.388	116.572	82.754
1995	92.115	91.577	110.672	90.629	88.320	100.941	100.292	106.239	83.879	115.224	85.769
1996	93.859	93.547	109.507	92.567	90.844	100.520	100.028	105.011	86.045	112.451	87.610
1997	95.415	95.124	107.068	93.835	93.305	100.157	99.785	103.696	89.381	109.120	89.843
1998	96.475	95.978	104.152	93.821	95.319	99.035	98.861	101.421	93.474	104.259	92.239
1999	97.868	97.575	101.626	96.173	97.393	98.972	98.888	100.057	96.257	101.366	95.786
2000	100.000	100.000	100.000	100.000	100.000	100.000	100.000	100.000	100.000	100.000	100.000
2001	102.376	102.039	98.086	101.530	103.168	101.070	101.087	99.770	105.518	97.786	104.628
2002	103.949	103.429	95.208	102.075	105.946	101.119	101.155	98.859	106.974	96.121	107.105
1999:I	97.274	96.687	102.292	94.566	96.535	99.036	98.922	100.632	95.302	102.476	94.411
II	97.701	97.319	101.833	95.801	97.094	99.003	98.925	100.235	95.880	101.732	95.441
III	98.022	97.855	101.455	96.751	97.620	98.855	98.790	99.737	96.513	100.844	96.251
IV	98.475	98.438	100.923	97.575	98.322	98.993	98.916	99.625	97.331	100.413	97.010
2000:I	99.292	99.296	100.471	98.816	99.276	99.496	99.481	99.772	98.482	100.212	98.680
II	99.780	99.777	100.337	99.717	99.685	99.788	99.788	99.841	99.366	100.005	99.631
III	100.241	100.239	99.715	100.562	100.194	100.253	100.252	100.191	100.455	100.102	100.412
IV	100.687	100.687	99.477	100.905	100.845	100.463	100.479	100.195	101.697	99.681	101.260
2001:I	101.478	101.475	99.163	101.220	102.114	100.542	100.492	99.731	103.322	98.499	102.584
II	102.273	102.115	98.379	102.152	102.925	100.865	100.855	99.790	105.068	97.973	103.860
III	102.676	102.231	97.678	101.933	103.388	101.433	101.486	99.933	106.686	97.591	105.650
IV	103.078	102.334	97.124	100.815	104.243	101.441	101.484	99.626	106.997	97.079	106.400
2002:I	103.364	102.507	96.268	100.780	104.754	101.266	101.274	99.300	106.759	96.746	106.747
II	103.738	103.245	95.574	102.194	105.485	101.097	101.096	98.925	106.888	96.228	106.767
III	104.123	103.761	94.855	102.538	106.371	100.852	100.908	98.554	106.975	95.730	106.998
IV	104.571	104.203	94.136	102.789	107.174	101.259	101.341	98.658	107.274	95.781	108.188
2003:I	105.163	104.927	93.074	104.079	108.028	101.586	101.808	98.579	108.268	95.404	109.887
II	105.440	105.065	92.147	103.529	108.758	101.589	101.796	98.293	108.559	94.961	110.484
III	105.870	105.522	91.207	104.488	109.306	102.093	102.319	98.678	109.288	95.251	111.321

See next page for continuation of table,

294

[Index numbers, 2000=100, except as noted; quarterly data seasonally adjusted]

Year or quarter	Exports and imports of goods and services — Exports	Imports	Government consumption expenditures and gross investment — Total	Federal — Total	National defense	Non-defense	State and local	Final sales of domestic product	Gross domestic purchases[1] — Total	Less food and energy	Percent change[2] — Gross domestic product	Gross domestic purchases[1] — Total	Less food and energy
1959	29.433	21.901	15.404	16.450	16.257	16.591	14.475	20.581	20.365		1.2	1.2	
1960	29.846	22.110	15.597	16.590	16.383	16.798	14.738	20.872	20.646		1.4	1.4	
1961	30.300	22.110	15.909	16.871	16.619	17.296	15.093	21.108	20.865		1.1	1.1	
1962	30.375	21.849	16.314	17.228	16.940	17.808	15.564	21.398	21.139		1.4	1.3	
1963	30.307	22.273	16.669	17.597	17.320	18.116	15.911	21.629	21.385		1.1	1.2	
1964	30.556	22.743	17.132	18.191	17.822	19.036	16.234	21.963	21.725		1.5	1.6	
1965	31.529	23.059	17.588	18.658	18.314	19.408	16.685	22.368	22.102		1.8	1.7	
1966	32.481	23.596	18.330	19.330	18.950	20.190	17.507	23.010	22.724		2.8	2.8	
1967	33.725	23.688	19.099	19.913	19.518	20.815	18.488	23.729	23.389		3.1	2.9	
1968	34.461	24.048	20.128	20.995	20.539	22.116	19.475	24.752	24.380		4.3	4.2	
1969	35.627	24.675	21.341	22.130	21.664	23.251	20.780	25.988	25.580		5.0	4.9	
1970	36.993	26.135	23.079	23.915	23.321	25.478	22.488	27.369	26.964		5.3	5.4	
1971	38.358	27.739	24.875	25.957	25.387	27.400	24.087	28.741	28.351		5.0	5.1	
1972	40.146	29.682	26.788	28.495	28.319	28.780	25.524	29.994	29.619		4.3	4.5	
1973	45.425	34.841	28.743	30.449	30.396	30.394	27.477	31.673	31.343		5.6	5.8	
1974	55.965	49.847	31.646	33.162	33.217	32.819	30.500	34.517	34.546		9.0	10.2	
1975	61.682	53.997	34.824	36.615	36.460	36.746	33.481	37.789	37.761		9.5	9.3	
1976	63.707	55.622	37.118	39.217	39.117	39.209	35.563	39.987	39.938		5.8	5.8	
1977	66.302	60.523	39.694	42.180	42.079	42.152	37.872	42.546	42.634		6.4	6.8	
1978	70.342	64.798	42.235	44.785	45.035	43.983	40.359	45.551	45.663		7.0	7.1	
1979	78.808	75.879	45.775	48.231	48.628	47.099	43.944	49.322	49.669		8.3	8.8	
1980	86.801	94.513	50.761	53.299	53.908	51.683	48.858	53.806	54.876		9.1	10.5	
1981	93.217	99.594	55.752	58.476	59.229	56.516	53.709	58.859	59.896		9.4	9.1	
1982	93.645	96.235	59.414	62.446	63.392	60.020	57.140	62.489	63.296	62.221	6.1	5.7	
1983	94.015	92.629	61.778	64.612	65.617	62.038	59.666	64.958	65.515	64.685	3.9	3.5	4.0
1984	94.887	91.829	64.955	68.426	70.290	63.577	62.336	67.399	67.822	67.106	3.8	3.5	3.7
1985	91.983	88.813	66.970	69.974	71.621	65.740	64.739	69.494	69.760	69.232	3.0	2.9	3.2
1986	90.639	88.871	68.175	70.352	71.554	67.395	66.624	71.060	71.338	71.474	2.2	2.3	3.2
1987	92.874	94.251	70.056	71.200	72.281	68.616	69.361	72.985	73.527	73.716	2.7	3.1	3.1
1988	97.687	98.774	71.899	72.704	73.631	70.609	71.485	75.519	76.043	76.429	3.4	3.4	3.7
1989	99.310	100.944	74.139	74.677	75.528	72.826	73.940	78.383	78.934	79.151	3.8	3.8	3.6
1990	99.982	103.826	77.139	77.142	78.010	75.260	77.357	81.440	82.144	82.109	3.9	4.1	3.7
1991	101.313	103.420	79.787	80.232	80.821	79.100	79.681	84.286	84.836	84.942	3.5	3.3	3.5
1992	100.892	103.552	81.719	82.602	83.628	80.411	81.300	86.237	86.828	87.169	2.3	2.3	2.6
1993	100.898	102.671	83.789	84.788	85.313	83.728	83.294	88.226	88.730	89.211	2.3	2.2	2.3
1994	102.033	103.634	86.002	87.061	87.412	86.375	85.472	90.108	90.583	91.213	2.1	2.1	2.2
1995	104.376	106.412	88.358	89.503	89.598	89.351	87.778	91.965	92.483	93.176	2.0	2.1	2.2
1996	102.988	104.529	90.491	91.982	92.379	91.216	89.709	93.736	94.145	94.616	1.9	1.8	1.5
1997	101.232	100.816	92.139	93.533	93.716	93.192	91.414	95.320	95.440	95.865	1.7	1.4	1.3
1998	98.905	95.353	93.469	94.511	94.643	94.268	92.934	96.428	96.060	96.797	1.1	.6	1.0
1999	98.313	95.960	96.079	96.884	96.886	96.880	95.667	97.847	97.556	98.165	1.4	1.6	1.4
2000	100.000	100.000	100.000	100.000	100.000	100.000	100.000	100.000	100.000	100.000	2.2	2.5	1.9
2001	99.628	97.537	102.587	102.065	102.158	101.900	102.853	102.381	101.974	101.864	2.4	2.0	1.9
2002	99.273	96.519	105.207	104.858	104.666	105.208	105.382	103.955	103.374	103.557	1.5	1.4	1.7
1999: I	97.956	94.023	94.803	96.055	96.199	95.791	94.162	97.244	96.761	97.618	1.5	1.5	1.5
II	98.145	95.268	95.639	96.583	96.658	96.443	95.157	97.679	97.317	97.989	1.8	2.3	1.5
III	98.345	96.634	96.475	97.120	97.091	97.172	96.146	98.005	97.790	98.296	1.3	2.0	1.3
IV	98.807	97.914	97.397	97.777	97.595	98.114	97.205	98.459	98.356	98.756	1.9	2.3	1.9
2000: I	99.461	99.321	98.970	99.429	99.527	99.421	98.707	99.288	99.275	99.466	3.4	3.8	2.9
II	99.989	99.487	99.395	99.223	99.482	98.765	99.483	99.779	99.714	99.793	2.0	1.8	1.3
III	100.223	100.506	100.486	100.449	100.377	100.576	100.504	100.241	100.283	100.191	1.9	2.3	1.6
IV	100.327	100.686	101.149	100.900	100.614	101.238	101.306	100.691	100.727	100.549	1.8	1.8	1.4
2001: I	100.344	99.967	101.822	101.343	101.504	101.053	102.068	101.473	101.381	101.110	3.2	2.6	2.3
II	100.043	98.439	102.385	101.756	101.903	101.494	102.707	102.279	101.958	101.602	3.2	2.3	2.0
III	99.513	97.106	102.887	102.355	102.126	102.079	103.156	102.687	102.211	102.078	1.6	1.0	1.9
IV	98.610	94.637	103.253	102.803	102.710	102.974	103.481	103.086	102.346	102.663	1.6	.5	2.3
2002: I	98.309	94.249	104.169	104.292	104.014	104.796	104.091	103.365	102.592	102.976	1.1	1.0	1.2
II	99.007	96.631	105.013	104.876	104.618	105.345	105.071	103.737	103.213	103.364	1.5	2.4	1.5
III	99.812	97.503	105.590	105.199	105.090	105.397	105.785	104.132	103.625	103.755	1.5	1.6	1.5
IV	99.964	97.694	106.055	105.066	104.941	105.293	106.580	104.585	104.065	104.132	1.7	1.7	1.5
2003: I	100.842	100.435	107.951	107.032	106.968	107.148	108.435	105.198	104.934	104.585	2.3	3.4	1.8
II	101.044	99.381	107.966	107.399	107.300	107.581	108.246	105.474	105.031	104.811	1.1	.4	.9
III	101.434	100.042	108.433	107.755	107.654	107.942	108.778	105.906	105.496	105.151	1.6	1.8	1.3

[1] Gross domestic product (GDP) less exports of goods and services plus imports of goods and services.
[2] Quarterly percent changes are at annual rates.

Source: Department of Commerce. Bureau of Economic Analysis.

TABLE B–8.—*Gross domestic product by major type of product, 1959–2003*

[Billions of dollars; quarterly data at seasonally adjusted annual rates]

Year or quarter	Gross domestic product	Final sales of domestic product	Change in private inventories	Goods Total Total	Goods Total Final sales	Goods Total Change in private inventories	Goods Durable goods Final sales	Goods Durable goods Change in private inventories [1]	Goods Nondurable goods Final sales	Goods Nondurable goods Change in private inventories [1]	Services [2]	Structures
1959	506.6	502.7	3.9	237.6	233.6	3.9	86.3	2.9	147.3	1.1	206.5	62.5
1960	526.4	523.2	3.2	246.6	243.4	3.2	90.2	1.7	153.2	1.6	217.9	61.9
1961	544.7	541.7	3.0	250.1	247.2	3.0	90.2	-.1	157.0	3.0	231.0	63.6
1962	585.6	579.5	6.1	268.1	262.0	6.1	99.4	3.4	162.6	2.7	249.7	67.8
1963	617.7	612.1	5.6	280.1	274.5	5.6	106.0	2.6	168.5	3.0	265.0	72.7
1964	663.6	658.8	4.8	300.9	296.0	4.8	116.4	3.8	179.7	1.0	284.3	78.4
1965	719.1	709.9	9.2	329.4	320.2	9.2	128.4	6.2	191.8	3.0	305.0	84.7
1966	787.8	774.2	13.6	364.5	350.9	13.6	142.0	10.0	208.9	3.6	335.3	88.0
1967	832.6	822.7	9.9	373.9	364.0	9.9	146.4	4.8	217.6	5.0	369.1	89.6
1968	910.0	900.9	9.1	402.6	393.6	9.1	158.7	4.5	234.8	4.5	407.4	100.0
1969	984.6	975.4	9.2	432.0	422.8	9.2	171.1	6.0	251.7	3.2	444.4	108.3
1970	1,038.5	1,036.5	2.0	446.9	444.9	2.0	173.6	-.2	271.3	2.2	481.9	109.7
1971	1,127.1	1,118.9	8.3	472.9	464.7	8.3	181.1	2.9	283.6	5.3	525.8	128.4
1972	1,238.3	1,229.2	9.1	516.6	507.5	9.1	202.4	6.4	305.1	2.7	574.8	146.9
1973	1,382.7	1,366.8	15.9	597.1	581.2	15.9	236.6	13.0	344.6	2.9	622.7	162.9
1974	1,500.0	1,486.0	14.0	643.3	629.3	14.0	254.5	10.9	374.8	3.1	691.0	165.6
1975	1,638.3	1,644.6	-6.3	691.4	697.7	-6.3	284.5	-7.5	413.2	1.2	780.2	166.7
1976	1,825.3	1,808.2	17.1	777.5	760.4	17.1	321.2	10.8	439.2	6.3	856.6	191.2
1977	2,030.9	2,008.6	22.3	851.5	829.1	22.3	363.8	9.5	465.3	12.8	952.7	226.8
1978	2,294.7	2,268.9	25.8	961.0	935.2	25.8	413.2	18.2	522.0	7.6	1,059.7	273.9
1979	2,563.3	2,545.3	18.0	1,078.1	1,060.1	18.0	472.0	12.8	588.1	5.2	1,171.9	313.3
1980	2,789.5	2,795.8	-6.3	1,145.7	1,152.0	-6.3	500.1	-2.3	651.9	-4.0	1,322.5	321.3
1981	3,128.4	3,098.6	29.8	1,288.2	1,258.3	29.8	542.2	7.3	716.1	22.5	1,487.7	352.6
1982	3,255.0	3,269.9	-14.9	1,277.3	1,292.2	-14.9	539.7	-16.0	752.5	1.1	1,633.2	344.5
1983	3,536.7	3,542.4	-5.8	1,365.0	1,370.8	-5.8	578.1	2.5	792.7	-8.2	1,802.9	368.7
1984	3,933.2	3,867.8	65.4	1,549.6	1,484.2	65.4	650.2	41.4	834.0	24.0	1,957.8	425.8
1985	4,220.3	4,198.4	21.8	1,607.4	1,585.6	21.8	711.0	4.4	874.6	17.4	2,154.1	458.7
1986	4,462.8	4,456.3	6.6	1,657.0	1,650.5	6.6	739.9	-1.9	910.6	8.4	2,325.7	480.1
1987	4,739.5	4,712.3	27.1	1,751.3	1,724.2	27.1	764.9	22.9	959.3	4.2	2,490.5	497.6
1988	5,103.8	5,085.3	18.5	1,903.4	1,884.9	18.5	841.8	22.7	1,043.1	-4.3	2,685.3	515.0
1989	5,484.4	5,456.7	27.7	2,066.6	2,038.9	27.7	917.1	20.0	1,121.9	7.7	2,888.7	529.0
1990	5,803.1	5,788.5	14.5	2,155.8	2,141.3	14.5	950.2	7.7	1,191.1	6.8	3,113.7	533.5
1991	5,995.9	5,996.3	-.4	2,184.7	2,185.1	-.4	944.1	-13.6	1,241.0	13.2	3,311.3	499.9
1992	6,337.7	6,321.4	16.3	2,282.3	2,266.0	16.3	986.1	-3.0	1,279.8	19.3	3,532.7	522.7
1993	6,657.4	6,636.6	20.8	2,387.8	2,367.0	20.8	1,047.9	17.1	1,319.1	3.7	3,711.7	557.8
1994	7,072.2	7,008.4	63.8	2,563.8	2,500.0	63.8	1,125.0	35.7	1,375.0	28.1	3,901.2	607.3
1995	7,397.7	7,366.5	31.1	2,661.1	2,630.0	31.1	1,202.2	33.6	1,427.8	-2.4	4,098.4	638.1
1996	7,816.9	7,786.1	30.8	2,807.0	2,776.3	30.8	1,298.0	19.1	1,478.3	11.7	4,312.7	697.1
1997	8,304.3	8,232.3	72.0	3,007.7	2,935.7	72.0	1,409.1	39.9	1,526.6	32.1	4,548.4	748.2
1998	8,747.0	8,676.2	70.8	3,143.4	3,072.6	70.8	1,487.8	42.8	1,584.8	28.0	4,789.8	813.8
1999	9,268.4	9,201.5	66.9	3,311.3	3,244.4	66.9	1,576.5	40.0	1,667.9	26.9	5,081.8	875.3
2000	9,817.0	9,760.5	56.5	3,449.3	3,392.8	56.5	1,653.3	36.1	1,739.5	20.4	5,425.6	942.1
2001	10,100.8	10,136.9	-36.1	3,400.5	3,436.6	-36.1	1,626.0	-44.2	1,810.6	8.1	5,717.6	982.7
2002	10,480.8	10,475.5	5.4	3,456.2	3,450.9	5.4	1,576.8	6.1	1,874.1	-.7	6,049.8	974.8
1999:I	9,066.6	8,984.4	82.2	3,251.3	3,169.1	82.2	1,529.0	48.0	1,640.2	34.1	4,958.6	856.7
II	9,174.1	9,136.0	38.1	3,272.6	3,234.5	38.1	1,574.5	14.1	1,660.0	24.0	5,033.0	868.5
III	9,313.5	9,264.4	49.1	3,314.1	3,265.0	49.1	1,603.2	32.0	1,661.8	17.1	5,123.0	876.4
IV	9,519.5	9,421.3	98.2	3,407.1	3,308.9	98.2	1,599.4	65.8	1,709.5	32.4	5,212.7	899.7
2000:I	9,629.4	9,599.6	29.9	3,392.9	3,363.1	29.9	1,651.8	18.0	1,711.3	11.9	5,310.5	926.0
II	9,822.8	9,726.5	96.3	3,486.1	3,389.8	96.3	1,654.9	67.1	1,734.9	29.2	5,397.4	939.4
III	9,862.1	9,803.7	58.4	3,461.0	3,402.6	58.4	1,656.2	29.3	1,746.4	29.1	5,454.8	946.3
IV	9,953.6	9,912.2	41.4	3,457.4	3,416.0	41.4	1,650.5	29.9	1,765.5	11.6	5,539.6	956.6
2001:I	10,024.8	10,022.8	2.0	3,430.3	3,428.3	2.0	1,654.3	-12.3	1,774.0	14.3	5,622.4	972.1
II	10,088.2	10,120.6	-32.4	3,401.8	3,434.2	-32.4	1,637.8	-45.9	1,796.4	13.4	5,692.4	994.9
III	10,096.2	10,142.2	-46.0	3,367.2	3,413.2	-46.0	1,591.4	-52.2	1,821.8	6.2	5,737.4	991.6
IV	10,193.9	10,262.0	-68.1	3,402.7	3,470.8	-68.1	1,620.5	-66.6	1,850.3	-1.5	5,818.0	973.
2002:I	10,329.3	10,357.1	-27.8	3,448.4	3,476.1	-27.8	1,595.4	-23.6	1,880.7	-4.1	5,909.0	972.
II	10,428.3	10,427.8	.5	3,443.3	3,442.8	.5	1,573.6	-4.3	1,869.2	4.8	6,012.5	972.
III	10,542.0	10,513.4	28.6	3,478.7	3,450.1	28.6	1,583.7	19.8	1,866.4	8.8	6,091.7	971.
IV	10,623.7	10,603.6	20.2	3,454.5	3,434.4	20.2	1,554.4	32.3	1,880.0	-12.1	6,185.9	983.
2003:I	10,735.8	10,736.7	-.9	3,472.6	3,473.5	-.9	1,558.0	10.9	1,915.5	-11.8	6,267.5	995.
II	10,846.7	10,852.4	-5.8	3,492.8	3,498.5	-5.8	1,588.7	-1.1	1,909.8	-4.7	6,345.6	1,008.
III	11,107.0	11,117.4	-10.5	3,646.0	3,656.5	-10.5	1,688.3	-15.8	1,968.2	5.4	6,412.8	1,048.

[1] Estimates for durable and nondurable goods for 1996 and earlier periods are based on the Standard Industrial Classification (SIC); late estimates are based on the North American Industry Classification System (NAICS).

[2] Includes government consumption expenditures, which are for services (such as education and national defense) produced by government In current dollars, these services are valued at their cost of production.

Source: Department of Commerce, Bureau of Economic Analysis.

TABLE B–9.—*Real gross domestic product by major type of product, 1959–2003*

[Billions of chained (2000) dollars; quarterly data at seasonally adjusted annual rates]

Year or quarter	Gross domestic product	Final sales of domestic product	Change in private inventories	Goods Total — Total	Goods Total — Final sales	Goods Total — Change in private inventories	Durable goods — Final sales	Durable goods — Change in private inventories[1]	Nondurable goods — Final sales	Nondurable goods — Change in private inventories[1]	Services[2]	Structures
1959	2,441.3	2,442.7	12.3	700.7	....	....	....	....	....	....	1,391.1	392.8
1960	2,501.8	2,506.8	10.4	721.1	....	....	....	....	....	....	1,433.0	389.1
1961	2,560.0	2,566.8	9.4	726.7	....	....	....	....	....	....	1,489.4	399.9
1962	2,715.2	2,708.5	19.5	773.8	....	....	....	....	....	....	1,574.3	422.8
1963	2,834.0	2,830.3	18.0	803.4	....	....	....	....	....	....	1,642.4	451.3
1964	2,998.6	2,999.9	15.4	856.4	....	....	....	....	....	....	1,720.1	481.7
1965	3,191.1	3,173.8	29.3	927.3	....	....	....	....	....	....	1,803.6	505.8
1966	3,399.1	3,364.8	42.1	1,005.2	....	....	....	....	....	....	1,916.7	506.4
1967	3,484.6	3,467.6	30.3	1,006.4	....	....	....	....	....	....	2,034.8	499.0
1968	3,652.7	3,640.3	27.4	1,047.9	....	....	....	....	....	....	2,140.4	529.7
1969	3,765.4	3,753.7	27.0	1,082.2	....	....	....	....	....	....	2,212.2	536.5
1970	3,771.9	3,787.7	5.0	1,076.3	....	....	....	....	....	....	2,255.4	513.4
1971	3,898.6	3,893.4	22.3	1,105.7	....	....	....	....	....	....	2,313.6	561.0
1972	4,105.0	4,098.6	23.1	1,180.5	....	....	....	....	....	....	2,393.7	602.7
1973	4,341.5	4,315.9	35.0	1,299.5	....	....	....	....	....	....	2,461.3	615.6
1974	4,319.6	4,305.5	25.9	1,288.1	....	....	....	....	....	....	2,522.8	551.8
1975	4,311.2	4,352.5	–11.3	1,263.7	....	....	....	....	....	....	2,612.1	501.7
1976	4,540.9	4,522.3	30.7	1,359.8	....	....	....	....	....	....	2,676.9	548.7
1977	4,750.5	4,721.6	38.5	1,423.2	....	....	....	....	....	....	2,770.5	600.6
1978	5,015.0	4,981.6	41.1	1,515.6	....	....	....	....	....	....	2,874.9	658.3
1979	5,173.4	5,161.2	25.1	1,577.9	....	....	....	....	....	....	2,943.3	677.0
1980	5,161.7	5,196.7	–8.0	1,567.1	....	....	....	....	....	....	3,004.2	627.8
1981	5,291.7	5,265.1	34.9	1,634.5	....	....	....	....	....	....	3,062.5	619.2
1982	5,189.3	5,233.4	–17.5	1,559.7	....	....	....	....	....	....	3,120.0	566.1
1983	5,423.8	5,454.0	–6.4	1,625.4	....	....	....	....	....	....	3,251.0	607.1
1984	5,813.6	5,739.2	71.3	1,810.9	....	....	....	....	....	....	3,341.1	689.2
1985	6,053.7	6,042.1	23.7	1,851.3	....	....	....	....	....	....	3,520.8	725.1
1986	6,263.6	6,271.8	8.3	1,906.0	....	....	....	....	....	....	3,671.0	735.9
1987	6,475.1	6,457.2	30.3	1,984.9	....	....	....	....	....	....	3,797.3	739.2
1988	6,742.7	6,734.5	20.3	2,108.9	....	....	....	....	....	....	3,930.9	737.9
1989	6,981.4	6,962.2	28.3	2,223.3	....	....	....	....	....	....	4,049.5	732.8
1990	7,112.5	7,108.5	15.4	2,252.7	2,244.3	15.4	872.8	7.2	1,402.1	3.5	4,170.0	718.3
1991	7,100.5	7,115.0	–.5	2,221.5	2,228.9	–.5	852.7	–13.6	1,410.3	6.1	4,251.2	662.8
1992	7,336.6	7,331.1	16.5	2,307.8	2,297.7	16.5	894.7	–3.0	1,434.3	8.7	4,373.7	688.3
1993	7,532.7	7,522.3	20.6	2,394.8	2,380.3	20.6	949.8	16.4	1,457.7	1.5	4,457.5	709.3
1994	7,835.5	7,777.8	63.6	2,550.6	2,493.9	63.6	1,016.4	33.4	1,501.4	12.6	4,558.3	746.0
1995	8,031.7	8,010.2	29.9	2,639.0	2,614.9	29.9	1,096.9	31.0	1,536.9	–1.2	4,654.7	753.5
1996	8,328.9	8,306.5	28.7	2,772.4	2,747.4	28.7	1,193.8	17.8	1,566.5	4.5	4,765.6	803.1
1997	8,703.5	8,636.6	71.2	2,971.3	2,904.6	71.2	1,317.4	38.5	1,593.4	32.4	4,901.1	835.7
1998	9,066.9	8,997.6	72.6	3,132.7	3,063.7	72.6	1,431.8	42.4	1,634.2	29.8	5,057.5	879.1
1999	9,470.3	9,404.0	68.9	3,312.6	3,246.4	68.9	1,554.3	40.4	1,692.6	28.1	5,245.1	913.0
2000	9,817.0	9,760.5	56.5	3,449.3	3,392.8	56.5	1,653.3	36.1	1,739.5	20.4	5,425.6	942.1
2001	9,866.6	9,901.1	–36.0	3,378.7	3,414.0	–36.0	1,650.4	–44.8	1,763.3	8.4	5,548.5	938.5
2002	10,083.0	10,076.9	5.7	3,450.5	3,444.1	5.7	1,631.6	6.2	1,810.5	–.4	5,721.3	910.8
1999: I	9,315.5	9,239.7	79.5	3,241.2	3,165.8	79.5	1,496.3	48.7	1,670.6	30.2	5,169.7	905.7
II	9,392.6	9,353.7	41.7	3,270.7	3,231.3	41.7	1,547.3	14.5	1,684.4	27.4	5,213.3	909.4
III	9,502.2	9,453.5	50.8	3,318.5	3,269.6	50.8	1,585.5	32.4	1,684.0	18.1	5,273.5	910.6
IV	9,671.1	9,569.3	103.5	3,420.2	3,319.0	103.5	1,588.0	66.1	1,731.3	36.9	5,323.8	926.5
2000: I	9,695.6	9,668.8	26.9	3,399.3	3,372.3	26.9	1,648.8	18.0	1,723.4	8.9	5,356.6	939.9
II	9,847.9	9,748.4	99.3	3,484.9	3,385.6	99.3	1,654.4	67.2	1,731.2	32.0	5,419.3	943.6
III	9,836.6	9,780.4	56.2	3,455.7	3,399.5	56.2	1,656.9	29.2	1,742.6	27.0	5,439.1	941.9
IV	9,887.7	9,844.3	43.5	3,457.5	3,414.1	43.5	1,653.2	29.8	1,761.0	13.8	5,487.3	942.8
2001: I	9,882.2	9,877.5	4.3	3,427.3	3,422.9	4.3	1,670.0	–12.4	1,753.2	16.5	5,509.2	945.2
II	9,866.3	9,895.3	–28.8	3,374.8	3,404.3	–28.8	1,659.8	–46.3	1,744.9	16.6	5,535.7	954.6
III	9,834.6	9,876.9	–44.0	3,339.3	3,382.5	–44.0	1,618.2	–52.8	1,763.2	8.3	5,554.9	938.8
IV	9,883.6	9,954.9	–75.5	3,373.3	3,446.1	–75.5	1,653.5	–67.7	1,791.8	–7.7	5,594.3	915.4
2002: I	9,997.9	10,020.1	–23.5	3,436.8	3,459.5	–23.5	1,635.0	–24.0	1,822.2	.4	5,648.3	913.1
II	10,045.1	10,052.3	–8.0	3,426.9	3,434.3	–8.0	1,624.9	–4.3	1,807.2	–3.8	5,706.7	910.6
III	10,128.4	10,096.4	32.8	3,481.4	3,448.2	32.8	1,646.5	20.2	1,800.6	12.5	5,740.2	907.4
IV	10,160.8	10,138.9	21.5	3,457.0	3,434.4	21.5	1,619.9	32.8	1,811.9	–10.6	5,790.1	912.0
2003: I	10,210.4	10,206.4	1.6	3,493.7	3,489.8	1.6	1,636.9	11.1	1,849.5	–8.9	5,805.1	911.4
II	10,288.3	10,289.5	–4.5	3,512.9	3,514.7	–4.5	1,682.7	–1.0	1,831.5	–3.4	5,856.8	917.8
III	10,493.1	10,497.7	–9.1	3,663.3	3,668.6	–9.1	1,799.3	–16.0	1,873.1	6.1	5,887.3	948.2

[1] Estimates for durable and nondurable goods for 1996 and earlier periods are based on the Standard Industrial Classification (SIC); later stimates are based on the North American Industry Classification System (NAICS).
[2] Includes government consumption expenditures, which are for services (such as education and national defense) produced by government. ﬁ current dollars, these services are valued at their cost of production.

Source: Department of Commerce, Bureau of Economic Analysis.

TABLE B–10.—*Gross value added by sector, 1959–2003*

[Billions of dollars; quarterly data at seasonally adjusted annual rates]

Year or quarter	Gross domestic product	Business [1] Total	Business [1] Non-farm [1]	Business [1] Farm	Households and institutions Total	Households and institutions House-holds	Households and institutions Nonprofit institutions serving households [2]	General government [3] Total	General government [3] Federal	General government [3] State and local	Adden-dum: Gross housing value added
1959	506.6	408.2	390.9	17.3	40.1	29.8	10.3	58.3	31.9	26.5	36.9
1960	526.4	420.4	402.3	18.2	43.9	32.3	11.7	62.0	33.1	28.9	39.9
1961	544.7	432.0	413.7	18.3	46.7	34.3	12.4	66.0	34.4	31.6	42.8
1962	585.6	464.5	446.1	18.4	50.4	36.7	13.6	70.7	36.5	34.2	46.0
1963	617.7	488.7	470.2	18.5	53.6	38.8	14.8	75.5	38.4	37.1	48.9
1964	663.6	525.6	508.2	17.3	56.9	40.8	16.1	81.1	40.7	40.4	51.6
1965	719.1	571.4	551.5	19.9	61.0	43.3	17.7	86.7	42.4	44.2	54.9
1966	787.8	625.1	604.3	20.8	65.8	45.9	19.9	96.9	47.3	49.6	58.2
1967	832.6	654.5	634.4	20.1	70.9	48.8	22.1	107.2	51.7	55.5	62.1
1968	910.0	714.5	694.0	20.5	76.5	51.6	25.0	119.0	56.4	62.5	65.9
1969	984.6	770.3	747.5	22.8	84.3	55.6	28.7	130.0	60.0	70.0	71.3
1970	1,038.5	803.6	779.9	23.7	91.4	59.4	32.0	143.6	64.1	79.5	76.7
1971	1,127.1	869.9	844.5	25.4	100.9	65.1	35.7	156.4	67.8	88.6	83.9
1972	1,238.3	959.0	929.4	29.7	109.9	70.3	39.5	169.4	71.6	97.9	91.1
1973	1,382.7	1,079.4	1,032.7	46.8	120.0	76.0	44.0	183.3	74.0	109.3	98.3
1974	1,500.0	1,166.9	1,122.6	44.2	131.7	82.5	49.2	201.4	79.6	121.8	106.8
1975	1,638.3	1,268.5	1,222.8	45.6	145.4	90.3	55.1	224.5	87.3	137.1	117.2
1976	1,825.3	1,423.7	1,380.7	43.0	158.1	98.1	60.0	243.5	93.8	149.7	126.6
1977	2,030.9	1,593.5	1,549.9	43.5	172.8	107.3	65.6	264.6	102.1	162.6	140.3
1978	2,294.7	1,813.4	1,762.7	50.7	193.8	120.4	73.4	287.5	109.7	177.8	155.2
1979	2,563.3	2,032.9	1,972.8	60.1	217.4	135.0	82.5	313.0	117.6	195.4	172.5
1980	2,789.5	2,191.1	2,139.7	51.4	249.9	155.5	94.4	348.6	131.3	217.3	199.4
1981	3,128.4	2,459.4	2,394.5	65.0	283.7	176.8	106.9	385.3	147.4	237.9	228.4
1982	3,255.0	2,520.7	2,460.3	60.4	315.3	195.7	119.6	419.0	161.3	257.7	255.4
1983	3,536.7	2,747.2	2,702.3	44.9	344.0	211.7	132.4	445.4	171.3	274.1	277.4
1984	3,933.2	3,071.8	3,007.7	64.2	376.2	230.2	146.0	485.2	192.1	293.1	301.1
1985	4,220.3	3,290.8	3,227.4	63.4	406.0	249.6	156.4	523.5	205.1	318.4	332.9
1986	4,462.8	3,468.8	3,409.4	59.4	438.0	267.4	170.6	556.1	212.6	343.5	359.5
1987	4,739.5	3,669.9	3,608.4	61.6	478.4	287.6	190.8	591.2	223.4	367.8	385.5
1988	5,103.8	3,948.6	3,887.2	61.3	525.1	312.8	212.4	630.1	234.9	395.2	415.5
1989	5,484.4	4,243.2	4,169.7	73.6	569.6	337.0	232.6	671.5	246.6	424.9	443.8
1990	5,803.1	4,462.6	4,386.0	76.6	618.9	362.9	256.0	721.6	258.9	462.6	478.1
1991	5,995.9	4,569.3	4,499.5	69.9	660.7	383.4	277.3	765.9	275.0	490.9	508.5
1992	6,337.7	4,840.4	4,761.7	78.7	697.9	397.2	300.7	799.4	282.1	517.3	531.0
1993	6,657.4	5,096.2	5,025.6	70.6	732.0	413.7	318.3	829.3	286.3	543.0	549.1
1994	7,072.2	5,444.0	5,362.4	81.6	771.3	439.5	331.7	857.0	286.2	570.7	582.0
1995	7,397.7	5,700.6	5,632.0	68.5	815.5	463.3	352.1	881.6	284.7	596.9	613.3
1996	7,816.9	6,056.7	5,966.0	90.7	852.2	484.7	367.5	908.0	288.6	619.3	638.0
1997	8,304.3	6,471.9	6,383.8	88.1	895.8	509.6	386.2	936.7	290.9	645.8	667.7
1998	8,747.0	6,827.1	6,748.2	78.9	949.7	538.0	411.7	970.3	293.1	677.2	700.2
1999	9,268.4	7,243.4	7,174.7	68.8	1,012.3	576.4	435.9	1,012.7	300.9	711.8	747.8
2000	9,817.0	7,666.7	7,595.1	71.5	1,080.7	615.6	465.1	1,069.6	315.4	754.2	794.3
2001	10,100.8	7,822.5	7,747.0	75.5	1,153.1	661.5	491.6	1,125.1	325.2	799.9	850.3
2002	10,480.8	8,065.6	7,994.9	70.7	1,226.4	704.3	522.2	1,188.8	345.3	843.5	904.0
1999: I	9,066.6	7,081.9	7,001.3	80.6	987.0	561.3	425.7	997.7	300.2	697.5	728.8
II	9,174.1	7,162.6	7,093.1	69.4	1,005.7	570.6	435.1	1,005.9	299.8	706.0	740.7
III	9,313.5	7,280.3	7,216.2	64.1	1,016.5	580.6	435.9	1,016.7	300.9	715.9	753.0
IV	9,519.5	7,449.0	7,388.1	60.9	1,040.0	593.2	446.8	1,030.5	302.7	727.8	768.6
2000: I	9,629.4	7,517.6	7,446.1	71.6	1,059.1	604.3	454.8	1,052.7	312.8	739.9	780.4
II	9,822.8	7,688.0	7,615.2	72.9	1,069.4	609.0	460.4	1,065.4	316.8	748.6	786.1
III	9,862.1	7,698.3	7,626.2	72.2	1,087.9	618.7	469.2	1,075.9	316.4	759.5	798.1
IV	9,953.6	7,762.7	7,693.2	69.5	1,106.5	630.6	475.8	1,084.4	315.5	768.9	812.6
2001: I	10,024.8	7,797.4	7,725.6	71.8	1,125.9	640.4	485.4	1,101.6	321.1	780.4	823.3
II	10,088.2	7,834.3	7,761.5	72.8	1,138.1	649.5	488.6	1,115.8	323.0	792.8	835.6
III	10,096.2	7,797.4	7,723.4	73.9	1,166.1	673.1	493.0	1,132.8	326.4	806.4	865.4
IV	10,193.9	7,861.1	7,777.5	83.6	1,182.3	682.8	499.5	1,150.5	330.3	820.2	876.7
2002: I	10,329.1	7,955.2	7,890.1	65.1	1,205.5	693.6	511.9	1,168.6	341.2	827.4	891.0
II	10,428.3	8,015.1	7,942.5	72.6	1,230.9	711.1	519.8	1,182.2	344.3	838.0	912.3
III	10,542.0	8,110.7	8,040.0	70.7	1,236.4	710.0	526.4	1,194.9	346.7	848.1	910.5
IV	10,623.7	8,181.3	8,106.7	74.6	1,233.0	702.4	530.6	1,209.5	349.1	860.4	902.2
2003: I	10,735.8	8,254.3	8,185.4	69.0	1,248.9	711.8	537.1	1,232.6	363.1	869.4	914.6
II	10,846.7	8,357.5	8,275.8	81.7	1,245.5	701.7	543.8	1,243.7	369.2	874.5	902.7
III	11,107.0	8,592.4	8,506.5	85.9	1,263.4	710.8	552.6	1,251.1	369.8	881.3	912.8

[1] Gross domestic business product equals gross domestic product excluding gross value added of households and institutions and of general government. Nonfarm product equals gross domestic business value added excluding gross farm value added.
[2] Equals compensation of employees of nonprofit institutions, the rental value of nonresidential fixed assets owned and used by nonprofit institutions serving households, and rental income of persons for tenant-occupied housing owned by nonprofit institutions.
[3] Equals compensation of general government employees plus general government consumption of fixed capital.

Source: Department of Commerce, Bureau of Economic Analysis.

298

TABLE B–11.—*Real gross value added by sector, 1959–2003*

[Billions of chained (2000) dollars; quarterly data at seasonally adjusted annual rates]

Year or quarter	Gross domestic product	Business [1]			Households and institutions			General government [3]			Addendum: Gross housing value added
		Total	Non-farm [1]	Farm	Total	House-holds	Non-profit institutions serving households [2]	Total	Federal	State and local	
1959	2,441.3	1,716.0	1,684.1	21.2	261.7	161.6	97.8	514.5	279.4	236.7	195.0
1960	2,501.8	1,748.8	1,713.5	22.4	279.6	171.4	106.6	532.2	284.6	249.3	207.3
1961	2,560.0	1,782.8	1,747.8	22.6	291.5	179.6	109.6	550.9	290.5	262.1	219.2
1962	2,715.2	1,897.7	1,867.0	22.1	307.7	189.8	115.4	572.5	302.5	271.8	232.8
1963	2,834.0	1,985.4	1,954.3	22.8	320.4	197.7	120.0	589.5	305.2	285.9	244.3
1964	2,998.6	2,111.7	2,086.0	22.1	333.7	205.7	125.4	609.7	308.2	303.1	255.4
1965	3,191.1	2,260.6	2,233.5	23.5	350.2	215.2	132.6	630.3	310.4	321.5	268.9
1966	3,399.1	2,413.6	2,393.2	22.7	366.3	224.0	140.2	669.7	330.7	340.6	281.0
1967	3,484.6	2,459.5	2,434.1	24.5	381.6	233.1	146.5	705.2	352.2	354.9	294.0
1968	3,652.7	2,581.7	2,561.5	23.6	400.4	239.3	161.0	732.7	358.1	376.2	304.6
1969	3,765.4	2,660.3	2,639.1	24.5	417.8	249.1	168.8	751.3	359.0	393.4	318.7
1970	3,771.9	2,659.3	2,636.0	25.1	425.0	254.7	170.0	754.1	343.6	410.8	328.9
1971	3,898.6	2,761.5	2,736.2	26.4	443.0	266.5	176.1	755.3	327.8	427.5	343.8
1972	4,105.0	2,939.8	2,918.4	26.4	460.7	277.7	182.4	753.8	311.8	442.3	360.1
1973	4,341.5	3,145.0	3,131.5	26.2	476.3	287.5	188.2	757.2	300.1	457.8	373.0
1974	4,319.6	3,101.3	3,089.1	25.6	493.9	299.9	193.1	772.6	299.2	474.4	390.7
1975	4,311.2	3,071.2	3,037.5	30.5	513.7	308.0	205.2	785.1	297.5	488.9	402.7
1976	4,540.9	3,272.9	3,249.1	29.1	521.5	313.3	207.5	791.8	297.9	495.3	408.3
1977	4,750.5	3,456.2	3,431.1	30.7	528.3	316.2	211.6	800.1	298.8	502.9	418.3
1978	5,015.0	3,673.3	3,656.8	29.6	552.4	335.1	216.3	815.5	302.5	514.6	436.8
1979	5,173.4	3,796.7	3,774.2	32.2	576.7	350.4	225.3	824.2	302.3	523.7	453.9
1980	5,161.7	3,756.1	3,736.1	31.1	606.9	372.9	232.8	836.0	307.0	530.8	481.9
1981	5,291.7	3,859.5	3,814.7	41.0	626.5	384.7	240.5	840.6	311.7	530.6	501.0
1982	5,189.3	3,743.1	3,691.9	43.1	647.2	391.8	254.4	849.2	316.8	534.0	514.7
1983	5,423.8	3,944.3	3,932.8	26.9	665.9	399.4	265.7	854.6	324.2	531.8	526.2
1984	5,813.6	4,286.3	4,254.3	37.2	687.8	413.3	273.6	865.2	331.5	535.0	543.0
1985	6,053.7	4,484.5	4,434.2	46.7	700.1	423.2	275.9	890.0	341.0	550.3	564.4
1986	6,263.6	4,652.0	4,606.2	44.9	718.5	428.7	289.1	911.9	347.0	566.3	574.9
1987	6,475.1	4,815.5	4,769.8	45.5	745.7	440.3	304.8	931.8	356.1	577.2	588.8
1988	6,742.7	5,023.0	4,987.7	40.9	780.6	457.1	323.1	956.0	360.5	596.9	606.2
1989	6,981.4	5,206.6	5,162.3	46.4	812.3	471.5	340.6	978.8	364.9	615.3	620.3
1990	7,112.5	5,287.0	5,237.9	49.3	841.2	483.2	357.9	1,003.9	371.6	633.6	635.7
1991	7,100.5	5,245.4	5,194.7	50.0	865.3	497.8	367.5	1,014.3	373.8	641.7	657.2
1992	7,336.6	5,456.5	5,395.2	57.5	882.6	502.6	379.9	1,017.7	366.0	652.6	666.2
1993	7,532.7	5,625.9	5,576.0	50.6	904.8	507.9	396.9	1,019.8	358.9	661.6	669.9
1994	7,835.5	5,905.3	5,841.4	60.9	923.1	524.7	398.4	1,019.9	347.2	673.1	690.8
1995	8,031.7	6,076.8	6,030.2	49.6	945.1	534.3	410.8	1,020.6	334.1	686.5	705.7
1996	8,328.9	6,356.0	6,300.4	56.1	957.8	540.8	417.0	1,022.1	325.0	697.2	712.1
1997	8,703.5	6,693.8	6,627.2	64.4	983.5	554.0	429.5	1,030.0	318.8	711.2	726.5
1998	9,066.9	7,017.1	6,955.3	61.6	1,010.4	563.8	446.9	1,041.0	315.2	725.8	735.5
1999	9,470.3	7,376.8	7,314.2	62.9	1,042.3	590.7	451.6	1,051.4	312.7	738.7	767.2
2000	9,817.0	7,666.7	7,595.1	71.5	1,080.7	615.6	465.1	1,069.6	315.4	754.2	794.3
2001	9,866.6	7,673.6	7,605.2	68.5	1,104.8	634.5	470.3	1,088.0	316.1	771.9	815.5
2002	10,083.0	7,848.7	7,779.0	69.8	1,128.8	649.9	478.9	1,105.4	321.4	783.9	835.3
1999: I	9,315.5	7,239.5	7,177.5	62.3	1,028.2	579.1	449.1	1,048.4	315.0	733.4	753.0
II	9,392.6	7,307.9	7,243.3	64.7	1,036.2	586.1	450.2	1,048.8	312.4	736.4	761.8
III	9,502.2	7,404.4	7,343.2	61.6	1,046.2	594.2	452.0	1,051.7	311.7	740.1	771.5
IV	9,671.1	7,555.4	7,492.8	62.9	1,058.8	603.5	455.3	1,056.8	311.7	745.1	782.4
2000: I	9,695.6	7,561.7	7,490.6	71.3	1,070.9	608.9	462.0	1,063.0	313.9	749.1	787.1
II	9,847.9	7,699.1	7,626.9	72.2	1,075.7	610.9	464.8	1,073.0	320.3	752.7	789.1
III	9,836.6	7,683.8	7,610.6	73.1	1,083.2	617.8	465.4	1,069.7	314.5	755.2	796.6
IV	9,887.7	7,722.1	7,652.5	69.5	1,093.0	625.0	468.0	1,072.7	312.8	759.8	804.4
2001: I	9,882.2	7,705.7	7,636.7	69.1	1,095.4	627.4	467.9	1,081.1	315.8	765.3	805.8
II	9,866.3	7,682.8	7,616.9	66.2	1,097.2	627.6	469.6	1,086.3	316.0	770.3	807.0
III	9,834.6	7,631.8	7,569.0	63.3	1,112.3	641.7	470.6	1,089.9	316.2	773.7	825.1
IV	9,883.6	7,674.0	7,598.2	75.3	1,114.4	641.3	473.1	1,094.6	316.3	778.2	824.1
2002: I	9,997.9	7,779.6	7,721.7	58.2	1,119.8	644.6	475.3	1,098.2	318.4	779.8	829.1
II	10,045.1	7,806.3	7,737.4	68.8	1,135.2	657.1	478.1	1,102.8	320.0	782.8	844.1
III	10,128.4	7,889.2	7,813.2	76.2	1,132.3	652.2	480.1	1,107.0	321.8	785.2	837.8
IV	10,160.8	7,919.7	7,844.0	75.9	1,127.9	645.9	482.0	1,113.5	325.6	787.9	830.1
2003: I	10,210.4	7,957.9	7,891.0	67.0	1,134.8	651.5	483.3	1,118.1	329.1	789.0	837.3
II	10,288.3	8,039.3	7,964.0	75.2	1,129.4	644.8	484.4	1,121.1	333.1	788.0	828.2
III	10,493.1	8,238.4	8,163.8	74.6	1,137.4	651.4	486.0	1,121.3	333.2	788.2	835.0

[1] Gross domestic business product equals gross domestic product excluding gross value added of households and institutions and of general government. Nonfarm product equals gross domestic business value added excluding gross farm value added.

[2] Equals compensation of employees of nonprofit institutions, the rental value of nonresidential fixed assets owned and used by nonprofit institutions serving households, and rental income of persons for tenant-occupied housing owned by nonprofit institutions.

[3] Equals compensation of general government employees plus general government consumption of fixed capital.

Source: Department of Commerce, Bureau of Economic Analysis.

[Billions of dollars]

Year	Gross domestic product	Private industries											Government
		Total private industries	Agriculture, forestry, and fishing	Mining	Construction	Manufacturing	Transportation and public utilities	Wholesale trade	Retail trade	Finance, insurance, and real estate	Services	Statistical discrepancy[1]	
Based on 1972 SIC:													
1959	507.4	442.1	20.3	12.6	23.6	140.3	45.3	35.7	49.5	65.5	48.4	0.8	65.3
1960	527.4	457.9	21.4	13.0	24.1	142.5	47.5	37.4	50.7	70.3	51.6	-.6	69.5
1961	545.7	472.0	21.7	13.1	25.1	143.0	49.1	38.4	52.0	74.7	55.0	-.2	73.7
1962	586.5	507.6	22.1	13.3	26.9	156.8	52.2	41.0	55.7	79.5	59.4	.7	79.0
1963	618.7	533.9	22.3	13.6	28.8	166.2	55.1	42.8	58.2	83.8	63.5	-.4	84.8
1964	664.4	573.4	21.4	14.0	31.4	178.1	58.6	46.0	63.9	89.5	69.2	1.2	90.9
1965	720.1	623.0	24.2	14.2	34.5	196.6	62.7	49.7	68.4	96.0	74.8	1.9	97.1
1966	789.3	681.6	25.4	14.8	37.6	215.8	67.6	54.1	73.1	103.9	82.8	6.4	107.7
1967	834.1	715.5	24.9	15.3	39.4	221.3	70.9	57.5	78.7	111.6	91.0	4.8	118.6
1968	911.5	779.4	25.7	16.4	43.1	241.8	76.8	63.1	87.1	121.5	99.7	4.3	132.0
1969	985.3	841.1	28.5	17.3	48.3	254.6	83.1	68.3	94.6	132.3	111.1	2.9	144.3
1970	1,039.7	880.7	29.8	18.9	50.9	249.8	88.7	72.0	100.7	142.1	120.9	6.9	158.9
1971	1,128.6	955.4	32.1	19.1	55.9	263.2	97.8	77.7	109.7	157.6	130.8	11.3	173.2
1972	1,240.4	1,051.1	37.3	20.0	62.1	290.5	109.0	86.9	119.2	172.0	145.4	8.7	189.3
1973	1,385.5	1,180.9	55.0	24.0	70.2	321.9	119.7	97.8	131.1	189.5	163.7	8.0	204.6
1974	1,501.0	1,276.4	53.2	37.1	75.0	337.1	130.1	111.1	137.0	206.1	179.6	10.0	224.7
1975	1,635.2	1,386.5	54.9	42.8	75.5	354.8	142.4	121.1	153.2	224.6	199.5	17.7	248.7
1976	1,823.9	1,553.1	53.7	47.5	85.8	405.8	161.4	129.1	172.7	248.0	224.4	24.5	270.8
1977	2,031.4	1,738.3	54.3	54.0	94.8	462.8	179.4	142.2	190.9	282.2	256.2	21.6	293.1
1978	2,295.9	1,976.8	63.3	61.7	112.0	517.5	202.3	162.1	214.8	327.0	295.1	21.0	319.1
1979	2,566.4	2,219.5	74.5	71.5	126.5	571.0	219.0	183.8	233.5	369.7	334.3	35.7	346.8
1980	2,795.6	2,410.8	66.7	113.1	128.9	587.5	242.4	196.9	245.4	416.2	378.9	33.9	384.8
1981	3,131.3	2,704.3	81.1	152.6	131.5	652.2	274.6	218.5	270.6	467.5	428.1	27.5	427.0
1982	3,259.2	2,794.8	77.1	150.4	130.8	650.7	295.4	224.2	288.1	500.7	474.9	2.5	464.5
1983	3,534.9	3,039.7	62.6	129.1	139.8	693.3	324.0	236.9	322.4	559.0	525.5	47.0	495.3
1984	3,932.7	3,392.3	83.8	135.9	166.1	782.5	357.5	271.1	361.9	619.6	595.3	18.6	540.5
1985	4,213.0	3,627.9	84.7	135.3	186.3	804.4	379.0	289.1	394.4	686.5	656.5	11.7	585.1
1986	4,452.9	3,830.8	82.4	88.2	207.9	829.5	395.5	301.2	415.2	750.9	716.3	43.9	622.0
Based on 1987 SIC:													
1987	4,742.5	4,081.4	88.9	92.2	219.3	888.6	426.2	308.9	434.5	829.7	789.9	3.3	661.0
1988	5,108.3	4,401.8	89.1	99.2	237.2	979.9	449.0	346.6	461.5	893.7	887.9	-42.2	706.5
1989	5,489.1	4,735.5	102.0	97.1	245.8	1,017.7	468.7	364.7	492.7	954.5	976.0	16.3	753.6
1990	5,803.2	4,996.7	108.3	111.9	248.7	1,040.6	490.9	376.1	507.8	1,010.3	1,071.5	30.6	806.6
1991	5,986.2	5,129.1	102.9	96.7	232.7	1,043.5	518.3	395.6	523.7	1,072.2	1,123.8	19.6	857.1
1992	6,318.9	5,424.5	111.7	87.6	234.4	1,082.0	538.5	414.6	551.7	1,140.9	1,219.4	43.7	894.4
1993	6,642.3	5,717.5	108.3	88.4	248.9	1,131.4	573.3	432.5	578.0	1,205.3	1,287.7	63.8	924.8
1994	7,054.3	6,096.7	118.5	90.2	275.3	1,223.2	611.4	479.2	620.6	1,254.8	1,365.0	58.5	957.6
1995	7,400.5	6,411.1	109.8	95.7	290.3	1,289.1	642.6	500.6	646.8	1,347.2	1,462.4	26.5	989.5
1996	7,813.2	6,792.8	130.4	113.0	316.4	1,316.0	666.3	529.6	687.1	1,436.8	1,564.2	32.8	1,020.4
1997	8,318.4	7,253.6	130.0	118.9	338.2	1,379.6	688.4	566.8	740.5	1,569.9	1,691.5	29.7	1,064.8
1998	8,781.5	7,678.2	128.0	100.2	380.8	1,431.5	732.0	607.9	790.4	1,708.5	1,829.9	-31.0	1,103.3
1999	9,274.3	8,123.0	127.7	104.1	425.4	1,481.3	770.1	645.3	831.7	1,798.8	1,977.2	-38.8	1,151.3
2000	9,824.6	8,606.9	134.3	133.1	461.3	1,520.3	809.3	696.8	887.3	1,976.7	2,116.4	-128.5	1,217.7
2001	10,082.2	8,800.8	140.7	139.0	480.0	1,423.0	819.5	680.7	931.8	2,076.9	2,226.6	-117.3	1,281.5
2002	10,446.2	9,101.1	142.1	123.2	490.3	1,448.4	839.3	707.7	970.8	2,183.8	2,312.2	-116.7	1,345.1

[1] Equals gross domestic product (GDP) measured as the sum of expenditures less gross domestic income.

Note.—Data shown in Tables B–12 and B–13 do not reflect the benchmark revision of the National Income and Product Accounts release in early December 2003. Data shown here are for information only. For details regarding these data, see *Survey of Current Business,* June 2000 and May 2003.

Source: Department of Commerce, Bureau of Economic Analysis.

TABLE B–13.—Real gross domestic product by industry, 1987–2002

[Billions of chained (1996) dollars]

Year	Gross domestic product	Private industries											Government
		Total private industries	Agriculture, forestry, and fishing	Mining	Construction	Manufacturing	Transportation and public utilities	Wholesale trade	Retail trade	Finance, insurance, and real estate	Services	Statistical discrepancy [1]	
Based on 1987 SIC:													
1987	6,113.3	5,212.0	110.3	98.5	278.4	1,046.3	460.4	353.5	512.1	1,169.1	1,181.0	4.2	938.0
1988	6,368.4	5,445.6	101.2	114.5	294.1	1,120.2	479.0	379.4	544.6	1,209.1	1,255.1	−51.8	961.0
1989	6,591.8	5,648.2	111.4	102.8	296.3	1,111.6	500.4	399.3	562.5	1,234.3	1,313.8	19.3	984.3
1990	6,707.9	5,736.8	118.5	105.8	290.7	1,102.3	525.0	395.1	559.5	1,250.6	1,361.9	34.9	1,008.2
1991	6,676.4	5,707.8	121.3	101.1	268.8	1,066.3	543.1	416.6	554.6	1,270.6	1,352.4	21.7	1,012.1
1992	6,880.0	5,880.3	130.7	95.7	271.7	1,085.0	555.7	444.9	569.7	1,297.4	1,391.4	47.3	1,015.3
1993	7,062.6	6,043.2	122.6	101.1	279.2	1,122.9	576.3	452.4	581.8	1,328.9	1,418.0	67.5	1,013.1
1994	7,347.7	6,314.4	135.8	108.1	297.2	1,206.0	606.1	481.6	617.2	1,347.6	1,458.1	60.7	1,016.0
1995	7,543.8	6,508.7	123.1	113.0	299.6	1,284.7	634.5	483.0	641.4	1,393.0	1,510.4	27.0	1,017.1
1996	7,813.2	6,792.8	130.4	113.0	316.4	1,316.0	666.3	529.6	687.1	1,436.8	1,564.2	32.8	1,020.4
1997	8,159.5	7,151.2	143.7	117.0	324.6	1,387.2	668.7	584.1	745.3	1,520.8	1,632.2	29.2	1,035.5
1998	8,508.9	7,490.6	145.5	119.7	348.9	1,444.3	683.1	663.3	800.0	1,622.1	1,699.0	−30.1	1,047.3
1999	8,859.0	7,851.0	154.6	114.7	367.8	1,513.9	732.2	708.6	846.2	1,688.3	1,768.4	−37.3	1,061.1
2000	9,191.4	8,157.8	166.7	101.9	378.0	1,585.4	781.9	750.2	909.2	1,793.5	1,826.0	−121.3	1,088.8
2001	9,214.5	8,189.4	163.9	106.8	371.9	1,490.3	780.5	748.7	951.2	1,843.5	1,843.3	−108.3	1,107.5
2002	9,439.9	8,390.8	164.0	108.3	372.4	1,516.9	810.8	786.1	1,007.1	1,872.5	1,871.9	−107.0	1,128.2

[1] Equals the current-dollar statistical discrepancy deflated by the implicit price deflator for gross domestic business product.

Note.—Data shown in Tables B–12 and B–13 do not reflect the benchmark revision of the National Income and Product Accounts released in early December 2003. Data shown here are for information only. For details regarding these data, see *Survey of Current Business,* June 2000 and May 2003.

Source: Department of Commerce, Bureau of Economic Analysis.

TABLE B–14.—*Gross value added of nonfinancial corporate business, 1959–2003*

[Billions of dollars; quarterly data at seasonally adjusted annual rates]

Year or quarter	Gross value added of nonfinancial corporate business [1]	Consumption of fixed capital	Net value added										Addenda:	
			Total	Compensation of employees	Taxes on production and imports less subsidies	Net operating surplus						Profits before tax	Inventory valuation adjustment	Capital consumption adjustment
						Total	Net interest and miscellaneous payments	Business current transfer payments	Corporate profits with inventory valuation and capital consumption adjustments					
									Total	Taxes on corporate income	Profits after tax [2]			
1959	266.0	21.1	244.9	170.8	24.4	49.7	2.9	1.3	45.5	20.7	24.8	43.4	−0.3	2.3
1960	276.4	22.6	253.8	180.4	26.6	46.8	3.2	1.4	42.2	19.1	23.1	40.1	−.2	2.3
1961	283.7	23.2	260.5	184.5	27.6	48.4	3.7	1.5	43.2	19.4	23.8	39.9	.3	3.0
1962	309.8	23.9	285.9	199.3	29.9	56.8	4.3	1.7	50.8	20.6	30.2	44.6	.0	6.1
1963	329.9	25.2	304.7	210.1	31.7	62.9	4.7	1.7	56.5	22.8	33.8	49.7	.1	6.8
1964	356.1	26.4	329.7	225.7	33.9	70.2	5.2	2.0	63.0	23.9	39.2	55.9	−.5	7.7
1965	391.2	28.4	362.8	245.4	36.0	81.4	5.8	2.2	73.3	27.1	46.2	66.1	−1.2	8.4
1966	429.0	31.5	397.4	272.9	37.0	87.6	7.0	2.7	77.9	29.5	48.4	71.4	−2.1	8.5
1967	451.2	34.3	416.8	291.1	39.3	86.4	8.4	2.8	75.2	27.8	47.3	67.6	−1.6	9.1
1968	497.8	37.6	460.2	321.9	45.5	92.8	9.7	3.1	80.0	33.5	46.5	74.0	−3.7	9.7
1969	540.5	42.4	498.1	357.1	50.2	90.8	12.7	3.2	74.9	33.3	41.6	71.2	−5.9	9.6
1970	558.3	46.8	511.5	376.5	54.2	80.7	16.6	3.3	60.9	27.3	33.6	58.5	−6.6	8.9
1971	603.0	50.7	552.4	339.4	59.5	93.4	17.6	3.7	72.1	30.0	42.1	67.4	−4.6	9.3
1972	669.5	56.4	613.2	443.9	63.7	105.6	18.6	4.0	83.0	33.8	49.2	79.2	−6.6	10.5
1973	750.8	62.7	688.1	502.2	70.1	115.8	21.8	4.7	89.4	40.4	49.0	99.4	−19.6	9.5
1974	809.8	74.1	735.7	552.2	74.4	109.1	27.5	4.1	77.5	42.8	34.7	110.1	−38.2	5.6
1975	876.7	87.9	788.7	575.5	80.2	133.1	28.4	5.0	99.6	41.9	57.7	110.7	−10.5	−.5
1976	989.7	97.0	892.7	651.4	86.7	154.7	26.0	7.0	121.7	53.5	68.2	138.2	−14.1	−2.4
1977	1,119.4	110.5	1,008.8	735.3	94.6	178.9	28.5	9.0	141.4	60.6	80.9	159.4	−15.7	−2.2
1978	1,272.9	127.8	1,145.1	845.3	102.7	197.0	33.4	9.5	154.1	67.6	86.6	183.7	−23.7	−5.9
1979	1,415.9	147.3	1,268.6	959.9	108.8	200.0	41.8	9.5	148.8	70.6	78.1	197.0	−40.1	−8.1
1980	1,537.1	168.2	1,368.9	1,049.8	121.5	197.6	54.2	10.2	133.2	68.2	65.0	184.0	−42.1	−8.7
1981	1,746.0	191.5	1,554.5	1,161.5	146.7	246.4	67.2	11.4	167.7	66.0	101.7	185.0	−24.6	7.4
1982	1,806.2	211.2	1,594.9	1,203.9	152.9	238.1	77.4	8.8	151.9	48.8	103.1	139.9	−7.5	19.5
1983	1,933.0	217.6	1,715.4	1,266.9	168.0	280.5	77.0	10.5	192.9	61.7	131.2	163.3	−7.4	37.1
1984	2,167.5	230.7	1,936.8	1,406.1	185.0	345.7	86.0	11.7	248.0	75.9	172.0	197.6	−4.0	54.3
1985	2,302.0	247.4	2,054.6	1,504.2	196.6	353.8	91.5	16.1	246.3	71.1	175.2	173.4	.0	72.8
1986	2,387.5	255.3	2,132.2	1,583.1	204.6	344.5	95.1	27.3	222.1	76.2	145.9	149.7	7.1	65.3
1987	2,557.1	266.5	2,290.6	1,687.8	216.8	386.0	96.4	29.9	259.7	94.2	165.5	209.8	−16.2	66.2
1988	2,771.6	281.6	2,490.0	1,812.8	233.8	443.4	109.8	27.4	306.2	104.0	202.3	260.4	−22.2	68.0
1989	2,912.3	301.6	2,610.7	1,914.7	248.2	447.9	142.0	23.0	282.9	101.2	181.7	238.7	−16.3	60.6
1990	3,041.5	319.2	2,722.3	2,012.9	263.5	445.8	146.2	25.4	274.3	98.5	175.8	239.0	−12.9	48.2
1991	3,099.7	341.4	2,758.3	2,048.4	285.7	424.2	135.9	26.7	261.5	88.6	172.9	222.4	4.9	34.2
1992	3,236.0	353.6	2,882.3	2,154.1	302.5	425.7	111.3	25.2	289.2	94.4	194.8	258.2	−2.8	33.8
1993	3,397.8	363.4	3,034.4	2,244.8	318.8	470.8	102.0	29.6	339.2	108.0	231.2	303.3	−4.0	39.9
1994	3,669.5	391.5	3,278.0	2,381.5	349.6	546.9	101.0	30.0	415.9	132.9	283.1	380.1	−12.4	48.3
1995	3,879.5	415.0	3,464.5	2,509.8	356.9	597.8	115.2	30.2	452.5	141.0	311.4	419.3	−18.3	51.5
1996	4,109.5	436.5	3,673.0	2,630.8	369.1	673.1	111.9	38.0	523.2	153.1	370.1	458.5	3.1	61.6
1997	4,401.8	467.1	3,934.7	2,812.9	385.5	736.3	124.0	39.0	573.4	161.9	411.5	494.2	14.1	65.0
1998	4,655.0	493.3	4,161.7	3,045.6	398.7	717.4	143.8	35.2	538.3	158.6	379.7	449.4	20.2	68.7
1999	4,950.8	523.8	4,427.0	3,267.7	416.6	742.7	160.2	45.0	537.6	171.2	366.3	457.9	1.0	78.7
2000	5,272.2	567.8	4,704.3	3,544.4	443.4	716.5	191.7	48.4	476.4	170.2	306.2	423.9	−14.1	66.6
2001	5,299.3	610.5	4,688.9	3,597.0	440.3	651.5	205.8	50.0	395.6	108.7	286.9	309.6	9.1	76.8
2002	5,410.6	618.2	4,792.4	3,570.1	464.5	757.7	206.9	59.1	491.7	101.6	390.2	336.5	−2.2	157.5
1999: I	4,868.1	510.2	4,357.9	3,209.4	408.6	739.9	150.3	43.6	546.0	167.6	378.4	448.6	20.9	76.5
II	4,921.5	517.2	4,404.3	3,236.2	413.2	754.9	155.7	46.0	553.3	174.5	378.8	466.6	6.6	80.1
III	4,961.8	531.4	4,430.3	3,279.5	418.9	731.9	163.1	42.1	526.8	171.0	355.8	455.3	−8.5	79.9
IV	5,052.0	536.6	4,515.4	3,345.5	425.6	744.2	171.9	48.2	524.1	171.9	352.2	461.3	−15.3	78.1
2000: I	5,196.5	549.6	4,647.0	3,485.0	432.0	730.0	183.5	48.5	498.0	183.6	314.4	454.8	−28.6	71.8
II	5,252.7	562.2	4,690.5	3,506.0	440.3	744.2	189.7	47.9	506.6	181.4	325.2	451.3	−11.3	66.6
III	5,316.9	574.3	4,742.6	3,577.5	447.6	717.5	196.0	48.1	473.5	165.9	307.6	415.8	−6.3	64.0
IV	5,322.4	585.3	4,737.1	3,608.9	453.9	674.4	197.6	49.3	427.5	150.0	277.5	373.7	−10.1	63.9
2001: I	5,300.3	592.1	4,708.2	3,611.9	444.0	652.3	204.9	51.2	396.2	124.2	272.1	357.9	−4.9	43.3
II	5,301.0	602.3	4,698.7	3,604.0	438.5	656.2	205.8	55.8	394.6	126.2	268.4	360.4	−1.6	35.8
III	5,284.8	640.8	4,644.0	3,596.3	427.9	619.8	207.0	37.3	375.5	111.1	264.4	316.3	14.3	44.9
IV	5,311.1	606.6	4,704.5	3,576.0	450.8	677.7	205.7	55.8	416.1	73.4	342.8	204.1	28.7	183.4
2002: I	5,322.9	609.2	4,713.7	3,534.2	458.3	721.1	207.1	56.9	457.2	83.5	373.7	271.7	12.1	173.3
II	5,408.0	617.8	4,790.2	3,568.9	462.9	758.4	205.9	58.2	494.3	101.1	393.2	333.3	.9	160.1
III	5,432.0	622.4	4,809.6	3,580.5	465.4	763.6	207.8	59.7	496.1	107.3	388.9	356.2	−11.1	151.1
IV	5,479.3	623.4	4,856.0	3,596.8	471.5	787.6	207.0	61.4	519.3	114.5	404.8	384.7	−10.8	145.4
2003: I	5,479.2	622.9	4,856.3	3,612.6	474.1	769.6	204.5	55.1	510.0	119.8	390.2	398.4	−28.1	139.7
II	5,581.7	619.4	4,962.3	3,640.5	469.0	852.8	201.4	56.7	594.7	117.7	477.0	383.4	1.2	210.1
III	5,708.8	621.3	5,087.4	3,671.7	486.0	929.7	202.9	59.6	667.3	133.6	533.7	433.6	−1.8	235.5

[1] Estimates for nonfinancial corporate business for 2000 and earlier periods are based on the Standard Industrial Classification (SIC); later estimates are based on the North American Industry Classification System (NAICS).
[2] With inventory valuation and capital consumption adjustments.

Source: Department of Commerce, Bureau of Economic Analysis.

TABLE B-15.—*Gross value added and price, costs, and profits of nonfinancial corporate business, 1959–2003*

[Quarterly data at seasonally adjusted annual rates]

Year or quarter	Gross value added of nonfinancial corporate business (billions of dollars)[1]		Price per unit of real gross value added of nonfinancial corporate business (dollars)[1][2]									
				Compensation of employees (unit labor cost)	Unit nonlabor cost				Corporate profits with inventory valuation and capital consumption adjustments[4]		
	Current dollars	Chained (2000) dollars	Total[2]		Total	Consumption of fixed capital	Taxes on production and imports[3]	Net interest and miscellaneous payments	Total	Taxes on corporate income	Profits after tax[5]
1959	266.0	1,000.7	0.266	0.171	0.050	0.021	0.026	0.003	0.045	0.021	0.025
1960	276.4	1,032.4	.268	.175	.052	.022	.027	.003	.041	.019	.022
1961	283.7	1,054.8	.269	.175	.053	.022	.028	.003	.041	.018	.023
1962	309.8	1,143.4	.271	.174	.053	.021	.028	.004	.044	.018	.026
1963	329.9	1,211.1	.272	.173	.053	.021	.028	.004	.047	.019	.028
1964	356.1	1,296.2	.275	.174	.052	.020	.028	.004	.049	.018	.030
1965	391.2	1,403.3	.279	.175	.051	.020	.027	.004	.052	.019	.033
1966	429.0	1,502.6	.285	.182	.052	.021	.026	.005	.052	.020	.032
1967	451.2	1,539.8	.293	.189	.054	.022	.027	.005	.049	.018	.031
1968	497.8	1,637.5	.304	.197	.059	.023	.030	.006	.049	.020	.028
1969	540.5	1,701.2	.318	.210	.063	.025	.031	.007	.044	.020	.024
1970	558.3	1,683.7	.332	.224	.072	.028	.034	.010	.036	.016	.020
1971	603.0	1,751.5	.344	.228	.075	.029	.036	.010	.041	.017	.024
1972	669.5	1,883.8	.355	.236	.076	.030	.036	.010	.044	.018	.026
1973	750.8	1,997.8	.376	.251	.079	.031	.037	.011	.045	.020	.025
1974	809.8	1,964.7	.412	.281	.092	.038	.040	.014	.039	.022	.018
1975	876.7	1,937.8	.452	.297	.104	.045	.044	.015	.051	.022	.030
1976	989.7	2,091.6	.473	.311	.103	.046	.045	.012	.058	.026	.033
1977	1,119.4	2,245.0	.499	.328	.108	.049	.046	.013	.063	.027	.036
1978	1,272.9	2,390.4	.533	.354	.114	.053	.047	.014	.064	.028	.036
1979	1,415.9	2,462.1	.575	.390	.125	.060	.048	.017	.060	.029	.032
1980	1,537.1	2,423.3	.634	.433	.145	.069	.054	.022	.055	.028	.027
1981	1,746.0	2,500.0	.698	.465	.167	.077	.063	.027	.067	.026	.041
1982	1,806.2	2,447.0	.738	.492	.184	.086	.066	.032	.062	.020	.042
1983	1,933.0	2,572.8	.751	.492	.184	.085	.069	.030	.075	.024	.051
1984	2,167.5	2,810.2	.771	.500	.183	.082	.070	.031	.088	.027	.061
1985	2,302.0	2,940.0	.783	.512	.187	.084	.072	.031	.084	.024	.060
1986	2,387.5	3,012.6	.792	.525	.194	.085	.077	.032	.074	.025	.048
1987	2,557.1	3,172.2	.806	.532	.192	.084	.078	.030	.082	.030	.052
1988	2,771.6	3,348.6	.828	.541	.195	.084	.078	.033	.091	.031	.060
1989	2,912.3	3,401.5	.856	.563	.211	.089	.080	.042	.083	.030	.053
1990	3,041.5	3,431.3	.886	.587	.220	.093	.084	.043	.080	.029	.051
1991	3,099.7	3,408.1	.910	.601	.232	.100	.092	.040	.077	.026	.051
1992	3,236.0	3,499.5	.925	.616	.227	.101	.094	.032	.083	.027	.056
1993	3,397.8	3,604.4	.943	.623	.226	.101	.097	.028	.094	.030	.064
1994	3,669.5	3,832.0	.958	.621	.227	.102	.099	.026	.109	.035	.074
1995	3,879.5	3,999.1	.970	.628	.230	.104	.097	.029	.113	.035	.078
1996	4,109.5	4,222.3	.973	.623	.225	.103	.096	.026	.124	.036	.088
1997	4,401.8	4,493.0	.980	.626	.226	.104	.094	.028	.128	.036	.092
1998	4,655.0	4,735.5	.983	.643	.226	.104	.092	.030	.114	.033	.080
1999	4,950.8	5,009.9	.988	.652	.229	.105	.092	.032	.107	.034	.073
2000	5,272.2	5,272.2	1.000	.672	.237	.108	.093	.036	.090	.032	.058
2001	5,299.3	5,235.4	1.012	.687	.250	.117	.094	.039	.076	.021	.055
2002	5,410.6	5,339.0	1.013	.669	.253	.116	.098	.039	.092	.019	.073
1999: I	4,868.1	4,927.8	.988	.651	.226	.104	.092	.030	.111	.034	.077
II	4,921.5	4,982.3	.988	.650	.227	.104	.092	.031	.111	.035	.076
III	4,961.8	5,020.7	.988	.653	.230	.106	.092	.032	.105	.034	.071
IV	5,052.0	5,108.9	.989	.655	.232	.105	.093	.034	.103	.034	.069
2000: I	5,196.5	5,227.0	.994	.667	.232	.105	.092	.035	.095	.035	.060
II	5,252.7	5,257.7	.999	.667	.236	.107	.093	.036	.096	.035	.062
III	5,316.9	5,302.7	1.003	.675	.238	.108	.093	.037	.089	.031	.058
IV	5,322.4	5,301.2	1.004	.681	.242	.110	.095	.037	.081	.028	.052
2001: I	5,300.3	5,272.5	1.005	.685	.245	.112	.094	.039	.075	.024	.052
II	5,301.0	5,237.1	1.012	.688	.248	.115	.094	.039	.075	.024	.051
III	5,284.8	5,207.1	1.015	.691	.252	.123	.089	.040	.072	.021	.051
IV	5,311.1	5,225.1	1.016	.684	.252	.116	.097	.039	.080	.014	.066
2002: I	5,322.9	5,255.0	1.013	.673	.253	.116	.098	.039	.087	.016	.071
II	5,408.0	5,326.6	1.015	.670	.253	.116	.098	.039	.093	.019	.074
III	5,432.0	5,368.7	1.012	.667	.253	.116	.098	.039	.092	.020	.072
IV	5,479.3	5,405.7	1.014	.665	.252	.115	.099	.038	.096	.021	.075
2003: I	5,479.2	5,412.1	1.012	.668	.251	.115	.098	.038	.094	.022	.072
II	5,581.7	5,505.2	1.014	.661	.245	.113	.095	.037	.108	.021	.087
III	5,708.8	5,618.3	1.016	.654	.244	.111	.097	.036	.119	.024	.095

[1] Estimates for nonfinancial corporate business for 2000 and earlier periods are based on the Standard Industrial Classification (SIC); later estimates are based on the North American Industry Classification System (NAICS).
[2] The implicit price deflator for gross value added of nonfinancial corporate business divided by 100.
[3] Less subsidies plus business current transfer payments.
[4] Unit profits from current production.
[5] With inventory valuation and capital consumption adjustments.

Source: Department of Commerce, Bureau of Economic Analysis.

TABLE B–16.—*Personal consumption expenditures, 1959–2003*

[Billions of dollars; quarterly data at seasonally adjusted annual rates]

Year or quarter	Personal con-sumption expendi-tures	Durable goods			Nondurable goods					Services					
		Total¹	Motor vehi-cles and parts	Furni-ture and house-hold equip-ment	Total¹	Food	Cloth-ing and shoes	Gaso-line and oil	Fuel oil and coal	Total¹	Hous-ing²	Household operation		Trans-por-ta-tion	Medi-cal care
												Total¹	Elec-tricity and gas		
1959	317.6	42.7	18.9	18.1	148.5	80.6	26.4	11.3	4.0	126.5	45.0	18.7	7.6	10.6	16.4
1960	331.7	43.3	19.7	18.0	152.8	82.3	27.0	12.0	3.8	135.6	48.2	20.3	8.3	11.2	17.7
1961	342.1	41.8	17.8	18.3	156.6	84.0	27.6	12.0	3.8	143.8	51.2	21.2	8.8	11.6	19.0
1962	363.3	46.9	21.5	19.3	162.8	86.1	29.0	12.6	3.8	153.6	54.7	22.4	9.4	12.3	21.2
1963	382.7	51.6	24.4	20.7	168.2	88.2	29.8	13.0	4.0	162.9	58.0	23.6	9.9	12.9	23.0
1964	411.4	56.7	26.0	23.2	178.6	93.5	32.4	13.6	4.1	176.1	61.4	25.0	10.4	13.8	26.4
1965	443.8	63.3	29.9	25.1	191.5	100.7	34.1	14.8	4.4	189.0	65.4	26.5	10.9	14.7	28.6
1966	480.9	68.3	30.3	28.2	208.7	109.3	37.4	16.0	4.7	203.8	69.5	28.1	11.5	15.9	31.5
1967	507.8	70.4	30.0	30.0	217.1	112.4	39.2	17.1	4.8	220.3	74.1	30.0	12.2	17.4	34.7
1968	558.0	80.8	36.1	32.9	235.7	122.2	43.2	18.6	4.7	241.6	79.8	32.3	13.0	19.3	40.1
1969	605.2	85.9	38.4	34.7	253.1	131.5	46.5	20.5	4.6	266.1	86.9	35.0	14.1	21.6	45.8
1970	648.5	85.0	35.5	35.7	272.0	143.8	47.8	21.9	4.4	291.5	94.1	37.8	15.3	24.0	51.7
1971	701.9	96.9	44.5	37.8	285.5	149.7	51.7	23.2	4.6	319.5	102.8	41.1	16.9	26.8	58.4
1972	770.6	110.4	51.1	42.4	308.0	161.4	56.4	24.4	5.1	352.2	112.6	45.4	18.8	29.6	65.6
1973	852.4	123.5	56.1	47.9	343.1	179.6	62.5	28.1	6.3	385.8	123.3	49.9	20.4	31.6	73.3
1974	933.4	122.3	49.5	51.5	384.5	201.8	66.0	36.1	7.8	426.6	134.8	55.8	24.0	34.1	82.3
1975	1,034.4	133.5	54.8	54.5	420.7	223.2	70.8	39.7	8.4	480.2	147.7	64.0	29.2	37.9	95.6
1976	1,151.9	158.9	71.3	60.2	458.3	242.5	76.6	43.0	10.1	534.7	162.2	72.5	33.2	42.5	109.1
1977	1,278.6	181.2	83.5	67.2	497.1	262.6	84.1	46.9	11.1	600.2	180.2	81.8	38.5	48.7	125.3
1978	1,428.5	201.7	93.1	74.3	550.2	289.6	94.3	50.1	11.5	676.6	202.4	91.2	43.0	53.4	143.1
1979	1,592.2	214.4	93.5	82.7	624.5	324.7	101.2	66.2	14.4	753.3	227.3	100.3	47.8	59.9	161.0
1980	1,757.1	214.2	87.0	86.7	696.1	356.0	107.3	86.7	15.4	846.9	256.2	113.7	57.5	65.2	184.4
1981	1,941.1	231.3	95.8	92.1	758.9	383.5	117.2	97.9	15.8	950.8	289.7	126.8	64.8	70.3	216.7
1982	2,077.3	240.2	102.9	93.4	787.6	403.4	120.5	94.1	14.5	1,049.4	315.2	142.5	74.2	72.9	243.3
1983	2,290.6	280.8	126.5	106.6	831.2	423.8	130.9	93.1	13.6	1,178.6	341.0	157.0	82.4	81.1	274.3
1984	2,503.3	326.5	152.1	119.0	884.6	447.4	142.5	94.6	13.9	1,292.2	374.5	169.4	86.5	93.2	303.2
1985	2,720.3	363.5	175.9	128.5	928.7	467.6	152.1	97.2	13.6	1,428.1	412.7	181.8	90.8	104.5	331.5
1986	2,899.7	403.0	194.1	143.0	958.4	492.0	163.1	80.1	11.3	1,538.3	448.4	187.7	89.2	111.1	357.5
1987	3,100.2	421.7	195.0	153.4	1,015.3	515.2	174.4	85.4	11.2	1,663.3	483.7	195.4	90.9	120.9	392.2
1988	3,353.6	453.6	209.4	163.7	1,083.5	553.5	185.5	88.3	11.7	1,816.5	521.5	207.3	96.3	133.4	442.8
1989	3,598.5	471.8	215.3	171.6	1,166.7	591.6	198.9	98.6	11.9	1,960.0	557.4	221.1	101.0	142.0	492.5
1990	3,839.9	474.2	212.8	171.6	1,249.9	636.8	204.1	111.2	12.9	2,115.9	597.9	227.3	101.0	147.7	556.0
1991	3,986.1	453.9	193.5	171.7	1,284.8	657.5	208.7	108.5	12.4	2,247.4	631.1	238.6	107.4	145.3	608.9
1992	4,235.3	483.6	213.0	178.7	1,330.5	669.3	221.9	112.4	12.2	2,421.2	658.5	250.7	108.9	157.7	672.2
1993	4,477.9	526.7	234.0	193.4	1,379.4	691.9	229.9	114.1	12.4	2,571.8	683.9	269.9	118.2	172.7	715.1
1994	4,743.3	582.2	260.5	213.4	1,437.2	720.6	238.1	116.2	12.8	2,723.9	726.1	286.2	120.7	190.6	752.9
1995	4,975.8	611.6	266.7	228.6	1,485.1	740.9	247.7	120.2	13.1	2,879.1	764.4	298.7	122.2	207.7	797.9
1996	5,256.8	652.6	284.9	242.9	1,555.5	768.7	250.2	130.4	14.3	3,048.7	800.1	318.5	129.4	226.5	833.5
1997	5,547.4	692.7	305.1	256.2	1,619.0	796.2	258.1	134.4	13.3	3,235.8	842.6	337.0	131.3	245.7	873.0
1998	5,879.5	750.2	336.1	273.1	1,683.6	829.8	270.9	122.4	11.5	3,445.7	894.6	350.5	129.8	259.5	921.4
1999	6,282.5	817.6	370.8	293.9	1,804.8	873.1	286.3	137.9	11.9	3,660.0	948.4	364.8	130.6	276.4	961.1
2000	6,739.4	863.3	386.5	312.9	1,947.2	925.2	297.7	175.7	15.8	3,928.8	1,006.5	390.1	143.3	291.3	1,026.8
2001	7,045.4	881.9	406.9	312.0	2,013.6	964.6	297.5	173.1	15.4	4,149.8	1,073.7	407.4	156.2	294.0	1,109.9
2002	7,385.3	911.3	418.1	323.7	2,086.0	1,005.6	304.4	165.8	14.6	4,388.0	1,144.6	408.2	152.3	292.8	1,202.7
1999:I	6,101.7	785.2	352.1	285.0	1,748.5	852.7	281.7	119.8	10.8	3,568.0	930.2	355.6	127.4	269.7	941.8
II	6,237.2	818.5	377.0	290.5	1,789.2	866.3	286.8	134.6	11.9	3,629.6	942.3	362.9	130.3	274.4	952.5
III	6,337.2	832.8	382.0	297.0	1,812.5	875.4	287.8	142.1	12.4	3,691.9	954.5	372.2	135.6	279.1	967.2
IV	6,453.7	834.1	372.1	303.0	1,869.0	898.1	288.9	154.9	12.6	3,750.7	966.7	368.4	129.2	282.4	983.2
2000:I	6,613.9	876.9	402.3	311.4	1,894.2	906.9	292.8	168.6	14.3	3,842.8	983.8	372.0	128.6	286.8	998.1
II	6,688.1	854.2	376.9	313.4	1,938.3	922.1	296.1	173.7	14.9	3,895.6	998.8	385.4	138.7	290.9	1,017.0
III	6,783.9	861.3	382.6	314.7	1,965.8	932.0	300.3	177.5	16.2	3,956.7	1,013.6	393.7	145.4	292.5	1,036.9
IV	6,871.6	860.9	384.3	312.2	1,990.5	939.7	301.6	182.8	18.0	4,020.3	1,029.6	409.4	160.6	294.7	1,055.2
2001:I	6,934.3	862.0	387.4	311.3	1,998.6	953.1	299.5	181.4	17.5	4,073.8	1,047.4	417.0	170.3	296.6	1,077.7
II	7,017.4	875.3	403.5	309.5	2,011.5	959.5	295.5	185.3	15.0	4,130.5	1,065.6	409.5	157.6	296.3	1,098.5
III	7,058.1	870.6	398.5	310.8	2,021.8	968.3	296.3	172.2	15.1	4,165.7	1,082.1	406.7	153.4	293.0	1,120.7
IV	7,171.6	919.6	438.1	316.4	2,022.6	977.5	298.7	153.2	14.0	4,229.4	1,099.8	396.5	143.5	290.3	1,142.9
2002:I	7,256.5	914.9	425.2	321.7	2,051.8	996.0	305.0	151.6	12.8	4,289.7	1,120.0	400.5	146.5	293.3	1,167.5
II	7,355.5	909.3	415.7	324.6	2,082.5	1,003.6	304.5	166.8	14.1	4,363.6	1,137.7	409.7	153.8	294.8	1,191.2
III	7,428.2	913.6	421.1	323.3	2,090.5	1,006.3	301.9	168.4	14.8	4,424.1	1,152.9	409.9	152.8	291.7	1,212.3
IV	7,501.2	907.3	410.4	325.3	2,119.2	1,016.4	306.4	176.3	16.7	4,474.7	1,167.7	412.9	156.0	291.5	1,239.8
2003:I	7,600.7	898.2	402.1	321.8	2,175.7	1,037.4	304.8	203.6	18.9	4,526.8	1,181.5	422.6	163.1	292.3	1,263.1
II	7,673.6	926.2	414.5	329.9	2,170.8	1,049.7	307.5	180.4	16.5	4,576.6	1,191.4	424.2	163.9	292.8	1,289.2
III	7,836.3	975.1	447.2	339.9	2,230.0	1,074.9	315.1	191.7	17.4	4,631.2	1,204.9	428.5	165.8	295.3	1,315.1

¹ Includes other items not shown separately.
² Includes imputed rental value of owner-occupied housing.

Source: Department of Commerce, Bureau of Economic Analysis.

TABLE B–17.—*Real personal consumption expenditures, 1990–2003*

[Billions of chained (2000) dollars; quarterly data at seasonally adjusted annual rates]

Year or quarter	Personal consumption expenditures	Durable goods			Nondurable goods					Services					
		Total[1]	Motor vehicles and parts	Furniture and household equipment	Total[1]	Food	Clothing and shoes	Gasoline and oil	Fuel oil and coal	Total[1]	Housing[2]	Household operation		Transportation	Medical care
												Total[1]	Electricity and gas		
1990	4,770.3	453.5	256.1	119.9	1,484.0	784.4	188.2	141.8	16.7	2,851.7	802.2	266.4	117.4	195.7	797.6
1991	4,778.4	427.9	226.6	121.1	1,480.5	783.3	188.8	140.3	16.6	2,900.0	820.1	269.9	121.1	186.3	824.5
1992	4,934.8	453.0	244.9	127.8	1,510.1	787.9	199.2	146.0	17.0	3,000.8	832.7	277.4	120.4	194.2	863.6
1993	5,099.8	488.4	259.2	141.1	1,550.4	802.2	207.4	149.7	17.4	3,085.7	841.8	291.1	126.8	202.5	877.2
1994	5,290.7	529.4	276.2	156.8	1603.9	821.8	218.5	151.7	18.2	3,176.6	869.3	303.3	128.8	218.4	887.1
1995	5,433.5	552.6	272.3	173.3	1,638.6	827.1	227.4	154.5	18.7	3,259.9	887.5	312.9	130.2	231.8	906.4
1996	5,619.4	595.9	285.4	193.4	1,680.4	834.7	238.7	157.9	18.4	3,356.0	901.1	327.3	134.7	247.5	922.5
1997	5,831.8	646.9	304.7	216.3	1,725.3	845.2	246.0	162.8	16.9	3,468.0	922.5	340.4	133.7	263.2	942.8
1998	6,125.8	720.3	339.0	244.7	1794.4	865.6	263.1	170.3	16.0	3,615.0	948.8	357.1	136.7	272.0	970.7
1999	6,438.6	804.6	372.4	280.7	1,876.6	893.6	282.7	176.3	16.4	3,758.0	978.6	371.9	138.1	283.4	989.0
2000	6,739.4	863.3	386.5	312.9	1,947.2	925.2	297.7	175.7	15.8	3,928.8	1,006.5	390.1	143.3	291.3	1,026.8
2001	6,904.6	899.1	405.4	331.4	1,983.3	937.0	303.5	179.6	15.2	4,022.4	1,033.9	390.2	141.2	289.6	1,070.9
2002	7,140.4	957.2	423.3	364.7	2,043.6	958.2	319.1	183.3	15.9	4,141.8	1,061.9	394.5	145.2	284.8	1,132.1
1999: I	6,311.3	767.4	355.1	266.1	1,849.2	878.4	278.9	177.0	16.1	3,696.4	969.4	362.8	135.5	279.3	978.0
II	6,409.7	803.6	380.2	275.1	1,867.9	889.0	282.3	176.5	17.1	3,738.5	975.2	371.1	138.5	281.9	983.7
III	6,476.7	820.7	382.5	285.7	1,873.7	894.5	284.7	172.3	16.6	3,782.3	981.8	379.9	143.2	285.5	992.5
IV	6,556.8	826.4	371.9	296.1	1,915.7	912.4	284.9	179.2	15.8	3,815.0	987.9	373.7	135.4	287.0	1,001.8
2000: I	6,661.3	872.8	403.3	306.7	1,917.2	916.1	291.3	176.7	14.8	3,871.1	995.7	376.3	133.9	289.9	1,010.7
II	6,703.3	851.3	376.1	311.3	1,944.0	925.6	296.4	174.4	15.7	3,908.2	1,003.3	388.6	142.0	291.9	1,022.0
III	6,768.0	863.8	383.2	315.9	1,955.0	927.8	301.1	173.0	16.1	3,949.3	1,009.9	392.5	143.8	291.6	1,032.1
IV	6,825.0	865.4	383.5	317.8	1,972.7	931.2	302.1	178.5	16.7	3,986.8	1,016.9	403.0	153.6	291.5	1,042.5
2001: I	6,833.7	869.1	384.5	322.5	1,974.5	936.5	300.2	182.3	15.9	3,989.6	1,025.0	397.1	150.4	292.4	1,051.1
II	6,872.2	889.6	401.3	326.7	1,969.1	935.7	300.5	174.5	14.6	4,013.3	1,031.4	389.9	139.7	292.2	1,062.5
III	6,904.2	891.1	397.9	332.9	1,983.4	936.3	304.2	176.4	15.0	4,029.3	1,036.5	389.0	138.8	288.6	1,077.6
IV	7,008.2	946.6	437.8	343.7	2,006.2	939.6	309.1	185.4	15.1	4,057.4	1,042.7	384.9	135.8	285.1	1,092.5
2002: I	7,079.2	950.3	426.5	356.2	2,035.9	952.9	317.6	188.7	14.8	4,095.3	1,051.1	389.2	140.4	287.7	1,110.4
II	7,124.5	951.4	420.1	362.8	2,037.8	957.7	317.9	181.9	15.7	4,137.0	1,059.0	398.3	147.0	286.6	1,125.3
III	7,159.2	963.1	427.8	366.2	2,038.8	958.4	317.6	179.1	15.9	4,159.4	1,065.7	394.7	145.7	283.6	1,137.8
IV	7,198.9	963.8	419.0	373.5	2,061.8	963.9	323.4	183.6	17.4	4,175.4	1,071.7	395.6	147.9	281.3	1,154.8
2003: I	7,244.1	965.0	414.5	374.7	2,090.5	979.6	325.7	186.8	16.3	4,190.7	1,078.0	396.6	148.0	281.6	1,169.3
II	7,304.0	1,005.1	429.5	391.7	2,096.9	985.4	331.9	177.9	15.1	4,208.4	1,082.8	393.4	143.1	278.8	1,182.4
III	7,426.6	1,069.1	466.9	412.4	2,134.3	1,002.8	339.5	178.5	16.2	4,237.2	1,088.7	396.8	144.5	277.2	1,196.9

[1] Includes other items not shown separately.
[2] Includes imputed rental value of owner-occupied housing.

Note.—See Table B-2 for data for total personal consumption expenditures for 1959-89.

Source: Department of Commerce, Bureau of Economic Analysis.

TABLE B–18.—*Private fixed investment by type, 1959–2003*

[Billions of dollars; quarterly data at seasonally adjusted annual rates]

Year or quarter	Private fixed investment	Total nonresidential	Structures	Equipment and software Total	Information processing equipment and software Total	Computers and peripheral equipment	Software	Other	Industrial equipment	Transportation equipment	Other equipment	Total residential [1]	Structures Total [1]	Single family
1959	74.6	46.5	18.1	28.4	4.0	0.0	0.0	4.0	8.5	8.3	7.6	28.1	27.5	16.7
1960	75.7	49.4	19.6	29.8	4.9	.2	.1	4.6	9.4	8.5	7.1	26.3	25.8	14.9
1961	75.2	48.8	19.7	29.1	5.3	.3	.2	4.8	8.8	8.0	7.0	26.4	25.9	14.1
1962	82.0	53.1	20.8	32.3	5.7	.3	.2	5.1	9.3	9.8	7.5	29.0	28.4	15.1
1963	88.1	56.0	21.2	34.8	6.5	.7	.4	5.4	10.0	9.4	8.8	32.1	31.5	16.0
1964	97.2	63.0	23.7	39.2	7.4	.9	.5	5.9	11.4	10.6	9.9	34.3	33.6	17.6
1965	109.0	74.8	28.3	46.5	8.5	1.2	.7	6.7	13.7	13.2	11.0	34.2	33.5	17.8
1966	117.7	85.4	31.3	54.0	10.7	1.7	1.0	8.0	16.2	14.5	12.7	32.3	31.6	16.6
1967	118.7	86.4	31.5	54.9	11.3	1.9	1.2	8.2	16.9	14.3	12.4	32.4	31.6	16.8
1968	132.1	93.4	33.6	59.9	11.9	1.9	1.3	8.7	17.3	17.6	13.0	38.7	37.9	19.5
1969	147.3	104.7	37.7	67.0	14.6	2.4	1.8	10.4	19.1	18.9	14.4	42.6	41.6	19.7
1970	150.4	109.0	40.3	68.7	16.6	2.7	2.3	11.6	20.3	16.2	15.6	41.4	40.2	17.5
1971	169.9	114.1	42.7	71.5	17.3	2.8	2.4	12.2	19.5	18.4	16.3	55.8	54.5	25.8
1972	198.5	128.8	47.2	81.7	19.5	3.5	2.8	13.2	21.4	21.8	19.0	69.7	68.1	32.8
1973	228.6	153.3	55.0	98.3	23.1	3.5	3.2	16.3	26.0	26.6	22.6	75.3	73.6	35.2
1974	235.4	169.5	61.2	108.2	27.0	3.9	3.9	19.2	30.7	26.3	24.3	66.0	64.1	29.7
1975	236.5	173.7	61.4	112.4	28.5	3.6	4.8	20.2	31.3	25.2	27.4	62.7	60.8	29.6
1976	274.8	192.4	65.9	126.4	32.7	4.4	5.2	23.1	34.1	30.0	29.6	82.5	80.4	43.9
1977	339.0	228.7	74.6	154.1	39.2	5.7	5.5	28.0	39.4	39.3	36.3	110.3	107.9	62.2
1978	412.2	280.6	93.6	187.0	48.7	7.6	6.3	34.8	47.7	47.3	43.2	131.6	128.9	72.8
1979	474.9	333.9	117.7	216.2	58.5	10.2	8.1	40.2	56.2	53.6	47.9	141.0	137.8	72.3
1980	485.6	362.4	136.2	226.2	68.8	12.5	9.8	46.4	60.7	48.4	48.3	123.2	119.8	52.9
1981	542.6	420.0	167.3	252.7	81.5	17.1	11.8	52.5	65.5	50.6	55.2	122.6	118.9	52.0
1982	532.1	426.5	177.6	248.9	88.3	18.9	14.0	55.3	62.7	46.8	51.2	105.7	102.0	41.5
1983	570.1	417.2	154.3	262.9	100.1	23.9	16.4	59.8	58.9	53.5	50.4	152.9	148.6	72.5
1984	670.2	489.6	177.4	312.2	121.5	31.6	20.4	69.6	68.1	64.4	58.1	180.6	175.9	86.4
1985	714.4	526.2	194.5	331.7	130.3	33.7	23.8	72.9	72.5	69.0	59.9	188.2	183.1	87.4
1986	739.9	519.8	176.5	343.3	136.8	33.4	25.6	77.7	75.4	70.5	60.7	220.1	214.6	104.1
1987	757.8	524.1	174.2	349.9	141.2	35.8	29.0	76.4	76.7	68.1	63.9	233.7	227.9	117.2
1988	803.1	563.8	182.8	381.0	154.9	38.0	34.2	82.8	84.2	72.9	69.0	239.3	233.2	120.1
1989	847.3	607.7	193.7	414.0	172.6	43.1	41.9	87.6	93.3	67.9	80.2	239.5	233.4	120.9
1990	846.4	622.4	202.9	419.5	177.2	38.6	47.6	90.9	92.1	70.0	80.2	224.0	218.0	112.9
1991	803.3	598.2	183.6	414.6	182.9	37.7	53.7	91.5	89.3	71.5	70.8	205.1	199.4	99.4
1992	848.5	612.1	172.6	439.6	199.9	44.0	57.9	98.1	93.0	74.7	72.0	236.3	230.4	122.0
1993	932.5	666.6	177.2	489.4	217.6	47.9	64.3	105.4	102.2	89.4	80.2	266.0	259.9	140.1
1994	1,033.3	731.4	186.8	544.6	235.2	52.4	68.3	114.6	113.6	107.7	88.1	301.9	295.6	162.3
1995	1,112.9	810.0	207.3	602.8	263.0	66.1	74.6	122.3	129.0	116.1	94.7	302.8	296.5	153.5
1996	1,209.5	875.4	224.6	650.8	290.1	72.8	85.5	131.9	136.5	123.2	101.0	334.1	327.8	170.8
1997	1,317.8	968.7	250.3	718.3	330.3	81.4	107.5	141.4	140.4	135.5	112.1	349.1	342.8	175.2
1998	1,438.4	1,052.6	275.2	777.3	363.4	87.2	124.0	152.2	146.4	144.0	123.5	385.8	379.3	199.4
1999	1,558.8	1,133.9	282.2	851.7	411.0	96.0	152.6	162.4	147.0	167.6	126.0	424.9	417.8	223.8
2000	1,679.0	1,232.1	313.2	918.9	467.6	101.4	176.2	190.0	159.2	160.8	131.2	446.9	439.5	236.8
2001	1,643.4	1,174.1	322.1	852.0	436.4	85.2	173.4	177.7	146.2	141.3	128.2	469.2	461.8	249.1
2002	1,583.9	1,080.2	266.3	813.9	421.3	83.3	167.9	170.1	137.5	128.0	127.1	503.7	496.1	265.9
1999:I	1,514.6	1,101.0	278.3	822.7	389.2	93.4	139.5	156.2	144.6	162.3	126.7	413.5	406.7	218.6
II	1,551.7	1,130.1	282.0	848.1	410.5	98.7	149.6	162.3	146.3	166.7	124.5	421.7	414.7	220.7
III	1,579.2	1,151.5	281.6	869.8	422.7	98.2	157.9	166.6	148.3	173.4	125.5	427.8	420.6	223.8
IV	1,589.5	1,153.0	286.9	866.1	421.6	93.6	163.3	164.7	148.8	168.1	127.5	436.5	429.3	232.3
2000:I	1,642.4	1,193.9	295.2	898.7	446.4	96.2	168.7	181.5	156.0	165.6	130.7	448.5	441.2	240.6
II	1,685.4	1,236.5	310.4	926.1	466.5	103.5	174.8	188.1	159.5	166.7	133.4	448.8	441.5	238.9
III	1,690.6	1,247.5	321.1	926.5	473.6	103.8	177.9	191.9	162.1	160.3	130.6	443.1	435.7	233.3
IV	1,697.5	1,250.3	326.0	924.2	484.0	102.2	183.2	198.5	159.3	150.8	130.1	447.2	439.8	234.3
2001:I	1,686.2	1,230.3	326.4	903.9	468.3	97.1	181.3	189.8	160.9	142.3	132.4	455.9	448.5	241.7
II	1,652.7	1,186.9	327.2	859.6	442.3	88.1	175.9	178.3	148.1	141.7	127.5	465.8	458.5	247.6
III	1,640.3	1,162.9	334.1	828.8	421.6	77.4	170.9	173.3	140.5	137.8	128.8	477.4	470.0	254.4
IV	1,594.2	1,116.4	300.6	815.8	413.3	78.3	165.6	169.4	135.1	143.2	124.2	477.8	470.3	252.7
2002:I	1,580.8	1,092.7	280.0	812.7	413.0	81.5	164.5	167.0	141.5	134.9	123.3	488.2	480.6	256.7
II	1,580.4	1,080.4	269.6	810.8	418.8	81.2	165.9	171.6	136.1	128.3	127.6	500.0	492.4	263.6
III	1,579.7	1,073.4	259.4	814.0	429.4	85.4	171.6	172.4	136.6	119.9	128.1	506.3	498.8	267.1
IV	1,594.6	1,074.3	256.3	817.9	424.1	84.9	169.8	169.3	135.6	128.8	129.4	520.3	512.7	276.1
2003:I	1,606.2	1,071.8	256.1	815.8	436.2	86.8	173.4	175.9	133.4	119.8	126.3	534.4	526.7	287.2
II	1,630.1	1,086.9	259.2	827.7	451.2	93.5	177.6	180.1	133.2	115.3	128.1	543.2	535.3	288.4
III	1,699.5	1,124.4	259.8	864.6	477.0	101.8	185.1	190.2	134.1	117.8	135.7	575.1	566.9	304.7

[1] Includes other items, not shown separately.

Source: Department of Commerce, Bureau of Economic Analysis.

TABLE B–19.—Real private fixed investment by type, 1990–2003

[Billions of chained (2000) dollars; quarterly data at seasonally adjusted annual rates]

Year or quarter	Private fixed invest-ment	Nonresidential — Total non-resi-den-tial	Struc-tures	Equipment and software — Total	Info. proc. equip. and software — Total	Com-puters and periph-eral equip-ment [1]	Soft-ware	Other	Indus-trial equip-ment	Trans-porta-tion equip-ment	Other equip-ment	Residential — Total resi-den-tial [2]	Total [2]	Single family
1990	886.6	595.1	275.2	355.0	100.7	....	39.9	80.1	109.2	81.0	96.0	298.9	292.6	154.2
1991	829.1	563.2	244.6	345.9	105.9	....	45.1	79.6	102.2	78.8	82.0	270.2	264.0	135.1
1992	878.3	581.3	229.9	371.1	122.2	....	53.0	84.4	104.0	80.2	81.6	307.6	301.4	164.1
1993	953.5	631.9	228.3	417.4	138.2	....	59.3	90.9	112.9	95.1	89.3	332.7	326.4	179.7
1994	1,042.3	689.9	232.3	467.2	155.7	....	65.1	99.4	122.9	111.4	96.5	364.8	358.6	198.9
1995	1,109.6	762.5	247.1	523.1	182.7	....	71.6	107.0	134.9	120.6	101.7	353.1	346.8	180.6
1996	1,209.2	833.6	261.1	578.7	218.9	....	84.1	117.2	139.9	125.4	105.6	381.3	375.1	197.3
1997	1,320.6	934.2	280.1	658.3	269.9	....	108.8	127.3	143.0	135.9	115.8	388.6	382.4	196.6
1998	1,455.0	1,037.8	294.5	745.6	328.9	....	129.4	143.2	148.1	145.4	125.7	418.3	411.9	218.1
1999	1,576.3	1,133.3	293.2	840.2	398.5	....	157.2	158.0	147.9	167.7	126.7	443.6	436.6	234.2
2000	1,679.0	1,232.1	313.2	918.9	467.6	....	176.2	190.0	159.2	160.8	131.2	446.9	439.5	236.8
2001	1,625.7	1,176.8	305.2	871.3	457.6	....	171.8	182.3	145.0	142.6	126.4	448.5	441.1	237.2
2002	1,565.8	1,092.6	249.0	846.7	459.3	....	167.5	177.1	136.1	128.2	124.3	470.3	462.7	246.9
1999: I	1,531.0	1,094.0	292.0	802.7	369.5	....	144.9	149.8	145.6	161.4	127.5	438.1	431.3	232.5
II	1,568.6	1,127.3	294.1	833.5	395.8	....	154.5	157.0	147.4	165.7	125.1	441.8	434.9	231.8
III	1,598.6	1,154.4	291.8	862.4	412.8	....	162.2	162.8	149.2	174.6	126.1	444.5	437.3	232.8
IV	1,606.9	1,157.3	294.8	862.3	415.8	....	167.2	162.4	149.3	169.1	128.2	449.9	442.7	239.6
2000: I	1,651.1	1,196.7	299.9	896.7	442.9	....	171.4	179.9	156.3	166.1	131.3	454.5	447.1	243.5
II	1,689.1	1,238.6	312.5	926.0	465.7	....	175.8	187.7	159.7	167.0	133.6	450.4	443.1	239.7
III	1,686.4	1,245.2	319.7	925.5	473.8	....	176.2	192.3	161.9	159.5	130.4	441.2	433.8	232.4
IV	1,689.4	1,247.9	320.6	927.3	488.1	....	181.2	200.2	159.0	150.7	129.6	441.6	434.2	231.5
2001: I	1,677.8	1,233.6	315.8	917.8	482.8	....	179.5	192.9	160.0	144.2	131.1	444.4	437.1	235.4
II	1,638.0	1,189.4	311.3	877.6	460.8	....	173.7	182.8	146.9	144.3	125.9	448.5	441.2	238.3
III	1,616.1	1,163.7	313.1	849.4	445.4	....	169.7	178.5	139.4	137.9	126.9	451.9	444.5	239.6
IV	1,570.7	1,120.6	280.8	840.5	441.4	....	164.4	175.0	133.8	143.9	121.7	449.0	441.6	235.3
2002: I	1,560.9	1,100.4	262.2	840.0	444.2	....	163.3	172.9	140.3	135.0	120.8	458.5	451.0	239.4
II	1,563.2	1,092.1	252.2	842.6	454.7	....	165.7	178.5	135.0	128.7	125.1	468.4	460.8	245.6
III	1,565.4	1,089.1	242.4	850.3	470.0	....	171.2	179.8	135.0	122.0	125.1	473.2	465.6	248.7
IV	1,573.5	1,088.9	239.0	853.9	468.2	....	169.7	177.1	133.9	127.2	126.1	481.0	473.3	253.7
2003: I	1,577.7	1,087.3	236.5	855.0	487.2	....	174.4	184.3	131.4	117.4	122.6	486.4	478.5	259.0
II	1,601.4	1,105.8	238.8	871.6	506.4	....	178.6	188.6	131.0	115.1	123.9	491.7	483.5	259.0
III	1,661.0	1,139.5	237.7	907.7	537.7	....	185.0	200.2	131.4	113.7	131.1	516.7	508.2	271.9

[1] For details on this component see Survey of Current Business, Table 5.3.6, Table 5.3.1 for growth rates, Table 5.3.2 for contributions, and Table 5.3.3 for quantity indexes.

[2] Includes other items, not shown separately.

Source: Department of Commerce, Bureau of Economic Analysis.

TABLE B–20.—*Government consumption expenditures and gross investment by type, 1959–2003*

[Billions of dollars; quarterly data at seasonally adjusted annual rates]

Year or quarter	Total	Government consumption expenditures and gross investment — Federal Total	National defense Total	Consumption expenditures	Gross investment Structures	Gross investment Equipment and software	Nondefense Total	Consumption expenditures	Gross investment Structures	Gross investment Equipment and software	State and local Total	Consumption expenditures	Gross investment Structures	Gross investment Equipment and software
1959	110.0	65.4	53.8	40.1	2.5	11.2	11.5	9.8	1.5	0.2	44.7	30.7	12.8	1.1
1960	111.6	64.1	53.4	41.0	2.2	10.1	10.7	8.7	1.7	.3	47.5	33.5	12.7	1.2
1961	119.5	67.9	56.5	42.7	2.4	11.5	11.4	9.0	1.9	.6	51.6	36.6	13.8	1.3
1962	130.1	75.3	61.1	46.6	2.0	12.5	14.2	11.3	2.1	.8	54.9	39.0	14.5	1.3
1963	136.4	76.9	61.0	48.3	1.6	11.0	15.9	12.4	2.3	1.2	59.5	41.9	16.0	1.5
1964	143.2	78.5	60.3	48.8	1.3	10.2	18.2	14.0	2.5	1.6	64.8	45.8	17.2	1.8
1965	151.5	80.4	60.6	50.6	1.1	8.9	19.8	15.1	2.8	1.9	71.0	50.2	19.0	1.9
1966	171.8	92.5	71.7	60.0	1.3	10.5	20.8	15.9	2.8	2.1	79.2	56.1	21.0	2.1
1967	192.7	104.8	83.5	70.0	1.2	12.3	21.3	17.1	2.2	1.9	87.9	62.6	23.0	2.3
1968	209.4	111.4	89.3	77.2	1.2	10.9	22.1	18.3	2.1	1.7	98.0	70.4	25.2	2.4
1969	221.5	113.4	89.5	78.2	1.5	9.9	23.8	20.2	1.9	1.7	108.2	79.9	25.6	2.7
1970	233.8	113.5	87.6	76.6	1.3	9.8	25.8	22.1	2.1	1.7	120.3	91.5	25.8	3.0
1971	246.5	113.7	84.6	77.1	1.8	5.7	29.1	24.9	2.5	1.7	132.8	102.7	27.0	3.1
1972	263.5	119.7	87.0	79.5	1.8	5.7	32.7	28.2	2.7	1.8	143.8	113.2	27.1	3.5
1973	281.7	122.5	88.2	79.4	2.1	6.6	34.3	29.4	3.1	1.8	159.2	126.0	29.1	4.1
1974	317.9	134.6	95.6	84.5	2.2	8.9	39.0	33.4	3.4	2.2	183.4	143.7	34.7	4.9
1975	357.7	149.1	103.9	90.9	2.3	10.7	45.1	38.7	4.1	2.4	208.7	165.1	38.1	5.5
1976	383.0	159.7	111.1	95.8	2.1	13.2	48.6	41.4	4.6	2.7	223.3	179.5	38.1	5.7
1977	414.1	175.4	120.9	104.2	2.4	14.4	54.5	46.5	5.0	3.0	238.7	195.9	36.9	5.9
1978	453.6	190.9	130.5	112.7	2.5	15.3	60.4	50.6	6.1	3.7	262.6	213.2	42.8	6.6
1979	500.8	210.6	145.2	123.8	2.5	18.9	65.4	55.1	6.3	4.0	290.2	233.3	49.0	7.8
1980	566.2	243.8	168.0	143.7	3.2	21.1	75.8	63.8	7.1	4.9	322.4	258.4	55.1	8.9
1981	627.5	280.2	196.3	167.3	3.2	25.7	84.0	71.0	7.7	5.3	347.3	282.3	55.4	9.5
1982	680.5	310.8	225.9	191.2	4.0	30.8	84.9	72.1	6.8	6.0	369.7	304.9	54.2	10.6
1983	733.5	342.9	250.7	208.8	4.8	37.1	92.3	77.7	6.7	7.8	390.5	324.1	54.2	12.2
1984	797.0	374.4	281.6	232.9	4.9	43.8	92.8	77.1	7.0	8.7	422.6	347.7	60.5	14.4
1985	879.0	412.8	311.2	253.7	6.2	51.3	101.6	84.7	7.3	9.6	466.2	381.8	67.6	16.8
1986	949.3	438.6	330.9	268.0	6.8	56.1	107.8	90.3	8.0	9.5	510.7	417.9	74.2	18.6
1987	999.5	460.1	350.0	283.6	7.7	58.8	110.0	90.6	9.0	10.4	539.4	440.9	78.8	19.6
1988	1,039.0	462.3	354.9	293.6	7.4	53.9	107.4	88.9	6.8	11.7	576.7	470.4	84.8	21.5
1989	1,099.1	482.2	362.2	299.5	6.4	56.3	120.0	99.7	6.9	13.4	616.9	502.1	88.7	26.0
1990	1,180.2	508.3	374.0	308.1	6.1	59.8	134.3	111.7	8.0	14.6	671.9	544.6	98.5	28.7
1991	1,234.4	527.7	383.2	319.8	4.6	58.8	144.5	119.7	9.2	15.7	706.7	574.6	103.2	28.9
1992	1,271.0	533.9	376.9	315.3	5.2	56.3	157.0	129.8	10.3	16.9	737.0	602.7	104.2	30.1
1993	1,291.2	525.2	362.9	307.6	5.1	50.1	162.4	134.2	11.2	16.9	766.0	630.3	104.5	31.2
1994	1,325.5	519.1	353.7	300.7	5.7	47.2	165.5	140.1	10.5	14.9	806.3	663.3	108.7	34.3
1995	1,369.2	519.2	348.7	297.3	6.3	45.1	170.5	143.2	10.8	16.5	850.0	696.1	117.3	36.7
1996	1,416.0	527.4	354.6	302.5	6.7	45.4	172.8	143.8	11.2	17.9	888.6	724.8	126.8	36.9
1997	1,468.7	530.9	349.6	304.7	5.7	39.2	181.3	153.0	9.8	18.5	937.8	758.9	139.5	39.4
1998	1,518.3	530.4	345.7	300.7	5.1	39.9	184.7	153.9	10.6	20.2	987.9	801.4	143.6	43.0
1999	1,620.8	555.8	360.6	312.9	5.0	42.8	195.2	162.2	10.6	22.4	1,065.0	858.9	159.7	46.4
2000	1,721.6	578.8	370.3	321.5	5.0	43.8	208.5	177.8	8.3	22.3	1,142.8	917.8	176.0	49.0
2001	1,814.7	612.9	393.0	342.8	4.6	45.6	219.9	188.8	8.4	22.6	1,201.8	966.1	185.8	50.0
2002	1,932.5	679.5	438.3	382.7	4.4	51.2	241.2	208.1	9.9	23.2	1,253.1	1,004.6	198.1	50.3
1999: I	1,575.6	540.6	350.2	307.1	5.1	37.9	190.4	159.9	10.9	19.7	1,035.0	834.3	155.6	45.1
II	1,599.1	545.9	351.7	304.3	5.2	42.3	194.2	159.7	10.5	24.0	1,053.2	850.8	156.1	46.3
III	1,633.2	560.0	364.9	314.5	4.8	45.6	195.1	163.0	10.4	21.7	1,073.2	867.3	159.0	46.9
IV	1,675.3	576.8	375.7	325.8	4.7	45.2	201.0	166.1	10.8	24.2	1,098.5	883.3	168.0	47.2
2000: I	1,689.6	565.3	360.9	311.9	4.5	44.5	204.4	173.8	9.2	21.5	1,124.3	900.6	176.0	47.8
II	1,720.0	586.6	375.2	326.2	5.2	43.8	211.4	178.9	8.6	24.0	1,133.4	910.8	173.8	48.8
III	1,729.9	581.2	371.3	322.1	5.4	43.8	209.9	179.4	8.1	22.4	1,148.6	923.4	175.9	49.4
IV	1,746.9	582.0	373.8	325.7	4.8	43.3	208.2	179.2	7.5	21.5	1,164.9	936.3	178.5	50.1
2001: I	1,783.5	597.5	384.1	336.6	4.8	42.8	213.4	183.4	7.9	22.0	1,185.9	951.1	184.4	50.4
II	1,818.8	609.8	388.2	338.1	4.7	45.5	221.6	189.0	8.1	24.6	1,209.0	963.3	195.5	50.1
III	1,808.8	613.3	392.8	341.3	4.3	47.3	220.5	189.8	8.7	22.0	1,195.4	971.1	174.5	49.8
IV	1,847.8	630.8	406.9	355.5	4.6	46.8	223.9	193.1	9.1	21.7	1,217.1	978.8	188.6	49.7
2002: I	1,885.4	652.9	420.3	368.5	4.4	47.4	232.6	200.8	9.6	22.2	1,232.5	984.8	197.4	50.3
II	1,919.3	673.2	432.5	376.6	4.4	51.5	240.7	206.0	9.8	24.9	1,246.1	999.5	196.3	50.3
III	1,941.5	681.8	439.3	380.9	4.5	53.9	242.5	209.5	9.9	23.1	1,259.7	1,010.1	199.0	50.6
IV	1,983.9	710.0	461.1	404.6	4.5	52.1	248.9	216.1	10.2	22.6	1,273.9	1,024.2	199.6	50.1
2003: I	2,017.4	723.0	463.3	408.6	4.6	50.2	259.7	227.3	9.8	22.5	1,294.5	1,045.8	198.6	50.1
II	2,054.2	764.7	507.3	447.5	4.5	55.3	257.4	221.4	10.6	25.4	1,289.6	1,040.9	198.7	50.0
III	2,072.1	769.6	507.2	443.7	5.1	58.4	262.4	228.5	10.6	23.3	1,302.5	1,046.3	205.8	50.4

Source: Department of Commerce, Bureau of Economic Analysis.

TABLE B–21.—*Real government consumption expenditures and gross investment by type, 1990–2003*

[Billions of chained (2000) dollars; quarterly data at seasonally adjusted annual rates]

Year or quarter	Total	Federal Total	National defense Total	National defense Consumption expenditures	National defense Gross investment Structures	National defense Gross investment Equipment and software	Nondefense Total	Nondefense Consumption expenditures	Nondefense Gross investment Structures	Nondefense Gross investment Equipment and software	State and local Total	State and local Consumption expenditures	State and local Gross investment Structures	State and local Gross investment Equipment and software
1990	1,530.0	659.1	479.4	404.9	8.6	64.2	178.6	156.5	10.6	12.9	868.4	714.2	132.1	25.0
1991	1,547.2	658.0	474.2	404.4	6.4	61.8	182.8	158.4	11.8	13.7	886.8	729.0	136.5	24.8
1992	1,555.3	646.6	450.7	383.5	7.0	58.7	195.4	168.2	13.2	15.0	906.5	746.5	137.0	25.9
1993	1,541.1	619.6	425.3	367.2	6.4	51.1	194.1	166.0	14.1	15.0	919.5	761.4	133.9	26.8
1994	1,541.3	596.4	404.6	350.6	7.1	46.8	191.7	167.3	12.7	13.3	943.3	780.6	134.9	29.5
1995	1,549.7	580.3	389.2	338.1	7.4	43.7	191.0	164.7	12.6	14.7	968.3	798.4	139.5	31.7
1996	1,564.9	573.5	383.8	332.2	7.7	43.8	189.6	161.1	12.7	16.4	990.5	812.8	146.3	32.7
1997	1,594.0	567.6	373.0	328.1	6.4	38.9	194.5	166.6	10.9	17.5	1,025.9	834.9	155.8	36.1
1998	1,624.4	561.2	365.3	319.8	5.5	40.1	195.9	164.8	11.5	19.8	1,063.0	866.4	155.6	41.2
1999	1,686.9	573.7	372.2	324.6	5.2	42.5	201.5	168.1	11.1	22.3	1,113.2	900.3	167.0	45.9
2000	1,721.6	578.8	370.3	321.5	5.0	43.8	208.5	177.8	8.3	22.3	1,142.8	917.8	176.0	49.0
2001	1,768.9	600.5	384.7	334.0	4.4	46.3	215.8	185.0	8.1	22.6	1,168.5	937.7	179.7	51.1
2002	1,836.9	648.0	418.8	362.2	4.2	52.5	229.2	196.3	9.3	23.6	1,189.1	950.5	186.0	52.6
1999: I	1,662.2	562.9	364.1	321.3	5.4	37.6	198.8	167.9	11.5	19.5	1,099.3	889.8	165.4	44.3
II	1,672.3	565.3	363.9	316.5	5.4	42.0	201.4	166.4	11.0	23.9	1,107.0	897.3	164.0	45.7
III	1,693.1	576.7	375.9	325.5	5.0	45.4	200.8	168.3	10.9	21.7	1,116.3	904.0	165.7	46.6
IV	1,720.2	589.9	385.0	335.2	4.8	44.9	204.9	169.6	11.1	24.2	1,130.2	910.2	173.0	47.1
2000: I	1,707.3	568.2	362.6	313.8	4.5	44.3	205.6	174.8	9.3	21.5	1,139.2	912.4	179.1	47.7
II	1,730.5	591.2	377.1	328.1	5.2	43.8	214.0	181.5	8.6	24.0	1,139.3	916.3	174.2	48.8
III	1,721.5	578.6	369.9	320.7	5.4	43.9	208.7	178.2	8.1	22.4	1,142.9	918.7	174.9	49.3
IV	1,727.1	577.2	371.5	323.4	4.7	43.4	205.6	176.8	7.3	21.5	1,149.9	923.7	175.9	50.2
2001: I	1,751.6	589.7	378.5	330.6	4.6	43.2	211.2	181.3	7.8	22.1	1,161.9	930.9	179.9	51.2
II	1,776.4	599.3	380.9	330.6	4.5	45.9	218.4	186.0	7.8	24.6	1,177.1	936.2	189.9	51.0
III	1,758.1	599.3	383.2	331.3	4.1	47.9	216.0	185.6	8.3	22.1	1,158.9	939.4	168.6	50.9
IV	1,789.7	613.6	396.2	343.6	4.3	48.2	217.4	186.9	8.7	21.8	1,176.1	940.7	180.3	51.4
2002: I	1,810.1	626.1	404.1	351.2	4.1	48.8	222.0	190.4	9.1	22.5	1,184.1	944.9	187.0	52.2
II	1,827.8	641.9	413.4	356.7	4.1	52.8	228.5	194.1	9.3	25.2	1,186.0	949.0	184.5	52.5
III	1,838.9	648.2	418.1	358.9	4.2	55.3	230.1	197.2	9.3	23.5	1,190.9	951.8	165.1	53.1
IV	1,870.8	675.8	439.5	382.0	4.2	53.3	236.4	203.6	9.5	23.1	1,195.3	956.4	186.3	52.7
2003: I	1,869.0	675.5	433.2	377.3	4.2	51.6	242.4	209.9	9.1	23.2	1,193.8	957.8	183.2	52.9
II	1,902.8	712.0	472.8	411.8	4.1	56.9	239.3	203.4	9.8	26.2	1,191.4	956.6	181.7	53.2
III	1,911.1	714.3	471.2	406.9	4.7	59.9	243.1	209.3	9.7	24.0	1,197.4	956.0	187.9	53.7

Note.—See Table B-2 for data for total government consumption expenditures and gross investment for 1959-89.

Source: Department of Commerce, Bureau of Economic Analysis.

[Billions of dollars, except as noted; seasonally adjusted]

Quarter	Private inventories[1]								Final sales of domestic business[3]	Ratio of private inventories to final sales of domestic business	
	Total[2]	Farm	Mining, utilities, and construction[2]	Manufacturing	Wholesale trade	Retail trade	Other industries[2]	Nonfarm[2]		Total	Nonfarm
Fourth quarter:											
1959	132.9	42.1		47.7	16.5	20.5	6.1	90.8	34.0	3.90	2.67
1960	136.2	42.7		48.7	16.9	21.9	6.1	93.5	35.1	3.89	2.67
1961	139.6	44.3		50.1	17.3	21.3	6.6	95.2	36.7	3.80	2.59
1962	147.2	46.7		53.2	18.0	22.7	6.6	100.5	38.8	3.79	2.59
1963	149.7	44.2		55.1	19.5	23.9	7.1	105.5	41.3	3.62	2.55
1964	154.3	42.1		58.6	20.8	25.2	7.7	112.2	44.1	3.50	2.54
1965	169.3	47.1		63.4	22.5	28.0	8.3	122.2	48.9	3.46	2.50
1966	185.7	47.4		73.0	25.8	30.6	8.9	138.3	51.8	3.59	2.67
1967	194.9	45.8		79.9	28.1	30.9	10.1	149.1	55.0	3.54	2.71
1968	208.2	48.9		85.1	29.3	34.2	10.6	159.3	60.7	3.43	2.62
1969	227.7	53.1		92.6	32.5	37.5	12.0	174.6	64.7	3.52	2.70
1970	236.0	52.7		95.5	36.4	38.5	12.9	183.3	68.0	3.47	2.70
1971	253.9	59.5		96.6	39.4	44.7	13.7	194.4	73.9	3.43	2.63
1972	283.9	74.0		102.1	43.1	49.8	14.8	209.9	82.6	3.44	2.54
1973	352.2	102.8		121.5	51.7	58.4	17.7	249.4	91.1	3.86	2.74
1974	406.3	88.2		162.6	66.9	63.9	24.7	318.1	98.8	4.11	3.22
1975	409.3	90.3		162.2	66.5	64.4	25.9	319.0	110.9	3.69	2.88
1976	440.1	85.8		178.7	74.1	73.0	28.5	354.2	121.7	3.62	2.91
1977	482.4	91.0		193.2	84.0	80.9	33.3	391.4	136.1	3.55	2.88
1978	571.4	119.7		219.8	99.0	94.1	38.8	451.7	157.4	3.63	2.87
1979	668.2	135.6		261.8	119.5	104.7	46.6	532.6	174.8	3.82	3.05
1980	739.8	141.1		293.4	139.4	111.7	54.1	598.7	191.5	3.86	3.13
1981	779.2	127.5		313.1	148.8	123.2	66.6	651.7	206.2	3.78	3.16
1982	774.1	131.5		304.6	147.9	123.2	66.8	642.6	216.4	3.58	2.97
1983	797.6	132.5		308.9	153.4	137.6	65.2	665.1	238.1	3.35	2.79
1984	869.3	131.8		344.5	169.1	157.0	66.9	737.6	258.4	3.36	2.85
1985	876.1	125.9		333.3	175.9	171.4	69.5	750.2	277.9	3.15	2.70
1986	858.0	112.9		320.6	182.0	176.2	66.3	745.1	295.2	2.91	2.52
1987	924.2	119.8		339.6	195.8	199.1	69.9	804.4	309.9	2.98	2.60
1988	999.2	130.2		372.4	213.9	213.2	69.5	869.1	337.3	2.96	2.58
1989	1,044.4	129.6		390.5	222.8	231.4	70.1	914.7	358.0	2.92	2.55
1990	1,082.3	133.4		404.5	236.8	236.6	71.0	948.9	373.8	2.90	2.54
1991	1,057.2	123.2		384.1	239.2	240.2	70.5	934.0	384.5	2.75	2.43
1992	1,082.4	132.9		377.6	248.3	249.4	74.3	949.5	412.2	2.63	2.30
1993	1,115.8	132.1		380.1	258.6	268.6	76.5	983.7	433.9	2.57	2.27
1994	1,194.3	134.3		404.3	281.5	293.6	80.6	1,060.0	458.6	2.60	2.31
1995	1,257.0	130.9		424.5	303.7	312.2	85.6	1,126.1	482.4	2.61	2.33
NAICS:											
1996	1,284.4	136.3	31.1	421.0	285.1	328.7	82.1	1,148.1	515.0	2.49	2.23
1997	1,329.5	136.7	33.7	431.7	303.1	337.5	86.9	1,192.9	544.3	2.44	2.19
1998	1,346.8	120.3	37.3	431.5	313.3	353.6	90.9	1,226.5	578.0	2.33	2.12
1999: I	1,362.3	123.5	37.4	431.5	317.2	360.4	92.3	1,238.8	583.3	2.34	2.12
II	1,377.6	123.0	38.9	435.4	320.3	364.9	95.1	1,254.6	593.7	2.32	2.11
III	1,402.9	121.3	39.9	444.6	328.4	371.3	97.5	1,281.6	602.6	2.33	2.13
IV	1,442.2	124.2	39.6	457.7	337.4	383.8	99.5	1,318.0	612.6	2.35	2.15
2000: I	1,467.5	126.8	40.4	463.9	346.1	386.4	104.0	1,340.7	624.0	2.35	2.15
II	1,494.1	125.6	41.6	470.1	352.1	396.8	107.8	1,368.5	632.6	2.36	2.16
III	1,509.6	121.9	43.6	473.8	354.8	403.0	112.6	1,387.7	636.7	2.37	2.18
IV	1,535.9	132.1	44.5	477.0	359.0	409.0	114.4	1,403.8	643.4	2.39	2.18
2001: I	1,542.4	137.3	49.8	475.1	357.2	407.9	115.1	1,405.1	649.6	2.37	2.16
II	1,526.9	135.9	49.5	467.5	355.1	404.2	114.8	1,391.0	655.6	2.33	2.12
III	1,498.0	130.9	47.6	454.8	347.5	403.5	113.6	1,367.1	653.6	2.29	2.09
IV	1,457.3	126.3	48.1	439.0	336.8	395.4	111.9	1,331.1	660.8	2.21	2.01
2002: I	1,456.1	129.9	48.3	436.4	335.2	395.4	110.9	1,326.2	665.2	2.19	1.99
II	1,460.3	126.0	50.6	436.2	335.5	400.1	111.9	1,334.3	667.9	2.19	2.00
III	1,479.6	127.7	49.8	440.3	342.0	407.6	112.1	1,351.8	673.5	2.20	2.01
IV	1,500.2	134.9	51.7	443.0	344.2	413.8	112.6	1,365.3	680.1	2.21	2.01
2003: I	1,525.8	136.8	55.6	448.7	348.1	423.2	113.4	1,389.0	687.9	2.22	2.02
II	1,516.9	138.2	54.3	441.1	343.7	425.7	113.9	1,378.7	696.9	2.18	1.98
III	1,530.8	151.4	53.3	437.7	345.8	428.6	114.1	1,379.4	716.9	2.14	1.92

[1] Inventories at end of quarter. Quarter-to-quarter change calculated from this table is not the current-dollar change in private inventories component of GDP. The former is the difference between two inventory stocks, each valued at its respective end-of-quarter prices. The latter is the change in the physical volume of inventories valued at average prices of the quarter. In addition, changes calculated from this table are at quarterly rates, whereas change in private inventories is stated at annual rates.

[2] Inventories of construction, mining, and utilities establishments are included in other industries through 1995.

[3] Quarterly totals at monthly rates. Final sales of domestic business equals final sales of domestic product less gross value added of households and institutions and of general government and includes a small amount of final sales by farm and by government enterprises.

Note.—The industry classification of inventories is on an establishment basis. Estimates through 1995 are based on the Standard Industrial Classification (SIC). Beginning with 1996, estimates are based on the North American Industry Classification System (NAICS).

Source: Department of Commerce, Bureau of Economic Analysis.

TABLE B–23.—*Real private inventories and domestic final sales by industry, 1990–2003*

[Billions of chained (2000) dollars, except as noted; seasonally adjusted]

Quarter	Total[2]	Farm	Private inventories[1] Mining, utilities, and, construction[2]	Manu-facturing	Whole-sale trade	Retail trade	Other indus-tries[2]	Non-farm[2]	Final sales of domes-tic busi-ness[3]	Ratio of private inventories to final sales of domestic business Total	Nonfarm
Fourth quarter:											
1990	1,092.8	120.9		390.0	242.0	258.9	78.3	971.2	394.0	2.77	2.46
1991	1,092.3	119.4		383.5	246.4	259.5	81.4	972.2	394.6	2.77	2.46
1992	1,108.7	125.1		378.9	254.8	264.1	83.9	982.5	415.7	2.67	2.36
1993	1,129.4	119.1		382.4	261.0	279.4	86.9	1,010.2	429.8	2.63	2.35
1994	1,193.0	130.3		394.1	276.7	299.9	91.1	1,062.2	447.2	2.67	2.38
1995	1,222.8	119.6		407.8	289.9	312.0	93.3	1,103.5	464.2	2.63	2.38
NAICS:											
1996	1,251.6	126.4	33.6	409.9	273.3	325.9	82.7	1,125.2	488.3	2.56	2.30
1997	1,322.7	129.3	36.1	430.7	298.3	340.6	88.1	1,193.7	509.2	2.60	2.34
1998	1,395.3	130.7	43.3	449.3	320.9	357.9	94.0	1,264.9	538.0	2.59	2.35
1999: I	1,415.2	130.9	44.0	452.7	325.9	366.3	96.0	1,284.6	541.5	2.61	2.37
II	1,425.6	131.2	44.2	454.8	328.1	369.5	98.3	1,294.7	549.9	2.59	2.35
III	1,438.3	128.3	43.6	458.8	334.1	373.7	100.1	1,310.1	556.0	2.59	2.36
IV	1,464.2	127.8	42.7	466.3	340.6	385.5	101.3	1,336.4	563.4	2.60	2.37
2000: I	1,470.9	124.2	43.7	465.6	345.4	387.6	104.6	1,346.8	571.2	2.58	2.36
II	1,495.7	125.7	43.0	470.6	351.6	396.7	108.1	1,370.1	575.0	2.60	2.38
III	1,509.8	125.0	43.1	471.5	355.3	402.4	112.5	1,384.8	575.0	2.61	2.40
IV	1,520.7	126.4	41.1	474.2	358.2	407.1	113.7	1,394.3	581.0	2.62	2.40
2001: I	1,521.7	128.0	43.3	471.9	358.2	406.0	114.1	1,393.7	581.5	2.62	2.40
II	1,514.5	127.5	47.3	465.1	357.9	402.3	113.9	1,387.0	581.2	2.61	2.39
III	1,503.5	127.9	50.0	457.2	352.6	401.8	113.6	1,375.5	578.5	2.60	2.38
IV	1,484.7	126.6	52.2	450.7	345.5	396.0	113.2	1,358.0	582.4	2.55	2.33
2002: I	1,478.8	127.9	52.1	446.4	342.3	396.9	112.8	1,350.8	586.3	2.52	2.30
II	1,476.8	124.9	51.5	443.5	341.2	401.7	113.6	1,351.9	587.2	2.52	2.30
III	1,485.0	124.2	50.9	444.1	343.2	408.6	113.7	1,360.9	589.1	2.52	2.31
IV	1,490.4	123.3	50.1	443.2	344.8	415.2	113.5	1,367.2	589.2	2.53	2.32
2003: I	1,490.8	123.6	48.3	440.2	343.6	422.0	113.0	1,367.3	594.0	2.51	2.30
II	1,489.6	123.1	47.8	436.4	342.5	425.8	114.1	1,366.7	597.8	2.49	2.29
III	1,487.4	122.4	47.7	432.4	342.1	428.6	114.3	1,365.2	614.8	2.42	2.22

[1] Inventories at end of quarter. Quarter-to-quarter changes calculated from this table are at quarterly rates, whereas the change in private inventories component of GDP is stated at annual rates.

[2] Inventories of construction, mining, and utilities establishments are included in other industries through 1995.

[3] Quarterly totals at monthly rates. Final sales of domestic business equals final sales of domestic product less gross value added of households and institutions and of general government and includes a small amount of final sales by farm and by government enterprises.

Note.—The industry classification of inventories is on an establishment basis. Estimates for 1990 through 1995 are based on the 1987 Standard Industrial Classification (SIC). Beginning with 1996, estimates are based on the North American Industry Classification System (NAICS).

See *Survey of Current Business*, Table 5.7.6A and 5.7.6B, for detailed information on calculation of the chained (2000) dollar inventory se-es.

Source: Department of Commerce, Bureau of Economic Analysis.

TABLE B–24.—*Foreign transactions in the national income and product accounts, 1959–2003*

[Billions of dollars; quarterly data at seasonally adjusted annual rates]

Year or quarter	Current receipts from rest of the world					Current payments to rest of the world									Balance on current account, NIPA
	Total	Exports of goods and services			In-come re-ceipts	Total	Imports of goods and services			In-come pay-ments	Current taxes and transfer payments to rest of the world (net)				
		Total	Goods[1]	Serv-ices[1]			Total	Goods[1]	Serv-ices[1]		Total	From persons (net)	From govern-ment (net)	From busi-ness (net)	
1959	27.0	22.7	16.5	6.3	4.3	28.2	22.3	15.3	7.0	1.5	4.3	0.5	3.8	0.1	−1.2
1960	31.9	27.0	20.5	6.6	4.9	28.7	22.8	15.2	7.6	1.8	4.1	.5	3.5	.1	3.2
1961	32.9	27.6	20.9	6.7	5.3	28.6	22.7	15.1	7.6	1.8	4.2	.5	3.6	.1	4.3
1962	35.0	29.1	21.7	7.4	5.9	31.1	25.0	16.9	8.1	1.8	4.3	.5	3.6	.1	3.9
1963	37.6	31.1	23.3	7.7	6.5	32.6	26.1	17.7	8.4	2.1	4.4	.7	3.6	.1	5.0
1964	42.3	35.0	26.7	8.3	7.2	34.7	28.1	19.4	8.7	2.3	4.3	.7	3.4	.2	7.5
1965	45.0	37.1	27.8	9.4	7.9	38.8	31.5	22.2	9.3	2.6	4.7	.8	3.7	.2	6.2
1966	49.0	40.9	30.7	10.2	8.1	45.1	37.1	26.3	10.7	3.0	5.0	.8	4.0	.2	3.9
1967	52.1	43.5	32.2	11.3	8.7	48.6	39.9	27.8	12.2	3.3	5.4	1.0	4.1	.2	3.6
1968	58.0	47.9	35.3	12.6	10.1	56.3	46.6	33.9	12.6	4.0	5.7	1.0	4.4	.3	1.7
1969	63.7	51.9	38.3	13.7	11.8	61.9	50.5	36.8	13.7	5.7	5.8	1.1	4.4	.3	1.8
1970	72.5	59.7	44.5	15.2	12.8	68.5	55.8	40.9	14.9	6.4	6.3	1.3	4.7	.4	4.0
1971	77.0	63.0	45.6	17.4	14.0	76.4	62.3	46.6	15.8	6.4	7.6	1.3	5.9	.4	.6
1972	87.1	70.8	51.8	19.0	16.3	90.7	74.2	56.9	17.3	7.7	8.8	1.4	7.0	.5	−3.6
1973	118.8	95.3	73.9	21.3	23.5	109.5	91.2	71.8	19.3	10.9	7.4	1.5	5.2	.7	9.3
1974	156.5	126.7	101.0	25.7	29.8	149.8	127.5	104.5	22.9	14.3	8.1	1.3	5.8	1.0	6.6
1975	166.7	138.7	109.6	29.1	28.0	145.4	122.7	99.0	23.7	15.0	7.6	1.3	5.6	.7	21.4
1976	181.9	149.5	117.8	31.7	32.4	173.0	151.1	124.6	26.5	15.5	6.3	1.3	3.9	1.1	8.9
1977	196.6	159.4	123.7	35.7	37.2	205.6	182.4	152.6	29.8	16.9	6.2	1.3	3.5	1.4	−9.0
1978	233.1	186.9	145.4	41.5	46.3	243.6	212.3	177.4	34.8	24.7	6.7	1.5	3.8	1.4	−10.4
1979	298.5	230.1	184.0	46.1	68.3	297.0	252.7	212.8	39.9	36.4	8.0	1.6	4.3	2.0	1.4
1980	359.9	280.8	225.8	55.0	79.1	348.5	293.8	248.6	45.3	44.9	9.8	1.8	5.5	2.4	11.4
1981	397.3	305.2	239.1	66.1	92.0	390.9	317.8	267.8	49.9	59.1	14.1	5.5	5.4	3.2	6.3
1982	384.2	283.2	215.0	68.2	101.0	384.4	303.2	250.5	52.6	64.5	16.7	6.6	6.7	3.4	−.2
1983	378.9	277.0	207.3	69.7	101.9	410.9	328.6	272.7	56.0	64.8	17.5	6.9	7.2	3.4	−32.1
1984	424.2	302.4	225.6	76.7	121.9	511.2	405.1	336.3	68.8	85.6	20.5	7.8	9.2	3.5	−86.9
1985	414.5	302.0	222.2	79.8	112.4	525.3	417.2	343.3	73.9	85.9	22.2	8.2	11.1	2.9	−110.8
1986	431.9	320.5	226.0	94.5	111.4	571.2	453.3	370.0	83.3	93.6	24.3	9.0	12.2	3.2	−139.2
1987	487.1	363.9	257.5	106.4	123.2	637.9	509.1	414.8	94.3	105.3	23.5	9.9	10.3	3.4	−150.8
1988	596.2	444.1	325.8	118.3	152.1	708.4	554.5	452.1	102.4	128.5	25.5	10.6	10.4	4.5	−112.2
1989	681.0	503.3	369.4	134.0	177.7	769.3	591.5	484.8	106.7	151.5	26.4	11.4	10.4	4.6	−88.3
1990	741.5	552.4	396.6	155.7	189.1	811.5	630.3	508.1	122.3	154.3	26.9	12.0	10.0	4.8	−70.1
1991	765.7	596.8	423.5	173.3	168.9	752.3	624.3	500.7	123.6	138.5	−10.6	13.0	−28.6	5.0	13.5
1992	788.0	635.3	448.0	187.4	152.7	824.9	668.6	544.9	123.6	123.0	33.4	12.3	17.1	3.9	−36.9
1993	812.1	655.8	459.9	195.9	156.2	882.5	720.9	592.8	128.1	124.3	37.3	14.2	17.8	5.4	−70.4
1994	907.3	720.9	510.1	210.8	186.4	1,012.5	814.5	676.8	137.7	160.2	37.8	15.4	15.8	6.6	−105.2
1995	1,046.1	812.2	583.3	228.9	233.9	1,137.1	903.6	757.4	146.1	198.1	35.4	16.2	10.1	9.1	−91.0
1996	1,117.3	868.6	618.3	250.2	248.7	1,217.6	964.8	807.4	157.4	213.7	39.1	18.0	14.1	7.1	−100.3
1997	1,242.0	955.3	687.7	267.6	286.7	1,352.2	1,056.9	885.3	171.5	253.7	41.6	21.0	10.9	9.7	−110.2
1998	1,243.1	955.9	680.9	275.1	287.1	1,430.5	1,115.9	929.0	186.9	265.8	48.8	24.6	11.2	12.9	−187.4
1999	1,312.1	991.2	697.2	294.0	320.8	1,585.9	1,251.7	1,045.5	206.3	287.0	47.2	28.3	11.6	7.3	−273.9
2000	1,478.9	1,096.3	784.3	311.9	382.7	1,875.6	1,475.8	1,243.5	232.3	343.7	56.1	31.5	13.5	11.2	−396.6
2001	1,354.1	1,035.1	731.5	303.6	319.0	1,732.5	1,401.7	1,168.0	233.6	283.8	47.0	33.1	9.5	4.5	−378.4
2002	1,306.0	1,006.8	697.8	309.1	299.1	1,770.1	1,433.1	1,190.3	242.7	277.6	59.3	35.4	14.3	9.6	−464.1
1999: I	1,254.7	960.1	673.2	286.8	294.6	1,475.5	1,167.6	970.1	197.5	264.0	44.0	27.2	8.6	8.2	−220.8
II	1,283.2	972.8	680.3	292.5	310.4	1,545.2	1,224.9	1,021.1	203.8	274.6	45.7	28.8	10.1	6.8	−262.0
III	1,330.4	1,000.5	703.9	296.6	329.9	1,630.5	1,285.7	1,075.3	210.4	300.0	44.8	28.7	8.8	7.3	−300.1
IV	1,379.9	1,031.6	731.3	300.3	348.4	1,692.6	1,328.8	1,115.3	213.4	309.6	54.2	28.4	19.1	6.7	−312.6
2000: I	1,418.0	1,055.1	749.2	305.9	362.9	1,780.8	1,401.5	1,177.0	224.5	330.4	48.9	31.9	8.7	8.3	−362.8
II	1,477.8	1,091.8	776.9	315.0	386.0	1,858.9	1,458.7	1,229.6	229.1	349.2	51.0	31.6	9.1	10.3	−381.1
III	1,502.1	1,122.4	810.9	311.5	379.7	1,925.6	1,523.1	1,284.9	238.3	348.1	54.3	31.3	11.4	11.6	−423.5
IV	1,517.8	1,115.8	800.4	315.4	402.1	1,937.0	1,519.7	1,282.3	237.3	347.2	70.1	31.2	24.6	14.4	−419.2
2001: I	1,458.9	1,103.1	788.9	314.2	355.8	1,859.3	1,484.4	1,247.8	236.6	328.5	46.4	22.4	7.0	16.9	−400.4
II	1,392.9	1,061.1	747.6	313.5	331.8	1,779.5	1,429.3	1,187.4	241.9	304.5	45.7	18.9	8.0	18.9	−386.6
III	1,310.3	1,005.4	704.9	300.5	304.9	1,709.2	1,370.4	1,139.5	230.9	293.3	45.5	71.6	8.7	−34.8	−398.9
IV	1,254.2	970.8	684.5	286.4	283.3	1,582.0	1,322.5	1,097.4	225.1	208.9	50.6	19.7	14.1	16.9	−327.7
2002: I	1,262.9	978.5	677.7	300.8	284.4	1,670.7	1,344.1	1,108.5	235.6	262.4	64.2	28.5	22.7	13.0	−407.8
II	1,305.3	1,006.3	700.9	305.4	299.0	1,779.5	1,433.6	1,194.9	238.7	291.4	54.4	34.5	9.8	10.1	−474.2
III	1,333.7	1,025.3	714.1	311.2	308.3	1,807.6	1,461.3	1,217.1	244.1	289.9	56.5	38.6	9.7	8.2	−473.8
IV	1,322.0	1,017.2	698.3	318.8	304.8	1,822.5	1,493.3	1,240.8	252.5	266.9	62.2	40.2	15.1	6.9	−500.6
2003: I	1,317.8	1,021.0	707.6	313.3	296.8	1,847.1	1,508.5	1,254.2	254.3	269.0	69.6	40.1	21.1	8.5	−529.3
II	1,319.7	1,020.2	707.7	312.5	299.5	1,859.9	1,525.7	1,272.4	253.3	266.2	68.1	37.5	20.2	10.4	−540.2
III	1,360.6	1,048.5	722.1	326.4	312.1	1,879.0	1,539.0	1,275.6	263.5	274.3	65.7	33.9	19.1	12.7	−518.4

[1] Certain goods, primarily military equipment purchased and sold by the Federal Government, are included in services. Beginning with 1986, repairs and alterations of equipment were reclassified from goods to services.

Source: Department of Commerce, Bureau of Economic Analysis.

[Billions of chained (2000) dollars; quarterly data at seasonally adjusted annual rates]

| Year or quarter | Exports of goods and services | | | | | Imports of goods and services | | | | |
| | | Goods [1] | | | Serv-ices [1] | | Goods [1] | | | Serv-ices [1] |
	Total	Total	Dura-ble goods	Non-dura-ble goods		Total	Total	Dura-ble goods	Non-dura-ble goods	
1990	552.5	367.2	226.3	145.1	188.7	607.1	469.7	264.7	218.4	142.7
1991	589.1	392.5	243.1	153.7	199.9	603.7	469.3	266.1	215.9	139.0
1992	629.7	421.9	262.5	163.6	210.8	645.6	513.1	294.0	231.9	135.5
1993	650.0	435.6	276.1	162.4	217.5	702.1	564.8	328.8	248.0	139.4
1994	706.5	478.0	309.6	170.1	231.1	785.9	640.0	383.1	266.0	147.3
1995	778.2	533.9	353.6	181.1	245.8	849.1	697.6	427.1	277.0	152.1
1996	843.4	581.1	394.9	186.7	263.5	923.0	762.7	472.8	295.2	160.5
1997	943.7	664.5	466.2	198.7	279.2	1,048.3	872.6	550.3	326.4	175.6
1998	966.5	679.4	481.2	198.5	287.2	1,170.3	974.4	621.8	355.7	195.6
1999	1,008.2	705.2	503.6	201.7	303.2	1,304.4	1,095.2	711.7	384.3	209.1
2000	1,096.3	784.3	569.2	215.1	311.9	1,475.8	1,243.5	820.7	422.8	232.3
2001	1,039.0	736.5	522.2	214.4	302.4	1,437.1	1,203.7	769.4	434.6	233.2
2002	1,014.2	707.2	493.7	213.7	306.8	1,484.7	1,248.4	801.4	447.4	236.4
1999: I	980.1	682.1	486.3	195.9	298.3	1,242.2	1,038.2	668.0	372.1	203.9
II	991.2	689.8	490.6	199.5	301.7	1,286.4	1,079.2	698.9	381.3	207.1
III	1,017.4	712.5	509.5	203.1	305.0	1,331.3	1,119.7	727.9	392.4	211.6
IV	1,044.1	736.3	528.1	208.3	307.9	1,357.9	1,143.8	752.1	391.6	214.0
2000: I	1,060.9	751.9	543.7	208.2	309.0	1,411.5	1,187.1	785.3	401.5	224.4
II	1,092.0	776.6	566.9	209.8	315.3	1,466.5	1,236.3	813.7	422.5	230.1
III	1,120.0	810.0	586.7	223.3	310.0	1,515.6	1,277.7	842.0	435.8	237.9
IV	1,112.3	798.9	579.7	219.1	313.4	1,509.5	1,272.7	841.8	431.3	236.8
2001: I	1,099.6	787.8	569.8	218.0	311.8	1,485.5	1,250.6	810.7	439.9	234.9
II	1,060.9	749.5	533.7	215.8	311.3	1,452.7	1,210.5	769.9	440.9	241.9
III	1,010.6	711.3	500.9	210.5	299.2	1,411.9	1,181.7	751.2	431.0	230.1
IV	984.8	697.4	484.6	213.1	287.3	1,398.2	1,172.1	746.0	426.8	226.0
2002: I	995.4	692.8	481.4	211.7	302.5	1,426.7	1,190.1	766.5	423.6	236.2
II	1,016.5	712.7	497.9	215.0	303.7	1,484.1	1,250.4	804.4	446.3	234.0
III	1,027.3	720.1	506.5	213.8	307.0	1,499.2	1,265.2	812.2	453.4	234.4
IV	1,017.5	703.2	489.1	214.3	314.0	1,529.0	1,288.1	822.3	466.2	241.2
2003: I	1,012.4	706.5	487.9	218.7	305.7	1,502.5	1,266.2	805.1	461.4	236.5
II	1,009.6	703.5	488.6	215.1	305.9	1,535.7	1,307.4	824.8	482.5	229.8
III	1,033.7	718.2	500.5	218.0	315.2	1,538.9	1,302.4	821.4	480.8	237.2

[1] Certain goods, primarily military equipment purchased and sold by the Federal Government, are included in services. Beginning with 1986, repairs and alterations of equipment were reclassified from goods to services.

Note.—See Table B-2 for data for total exports of goods and services and total imports of goods and services for 1959-89.

Source: Department of Commerce, Bureau of Economic Analysis.

TABLE B–26.—*Relation of gross domestic product, gross national product, net national product, and national income, 1959–2003*

[Billions of dollars; quarterly data at seasonally adjusted annual rates]

Year or quarter	Gross domestic product	Plus: Income receipts from rest of the world	Less: Income payments to rest of the world	Equals: Gross national product	Less: Consumption of fixed capital			Equals: Net national product	Less: Statistical discrepancy	Equals: National income
					Total	Private	Government			
1959	506.6	4.3	1.5	509.3	53.0	38.6	14.5	456.3	0.5	455.8
1960	526.4	4.9	1.8	529.5	55.6	40.5	15.0	473.9	−.9	474.9
1961	544.7	5.3	1.8	548.2	57.2	41.6	15.6	491.0	−.6	491.6
1962	585.6	5.9	1.8	589.7	59.3	42.8	16.5	530.5	.4	530.1
1963	617.7	6.5	2.1	622.2	62.4	44.9	17.5	559.8	−.8	560.6
1964	663.6	7.2	2.3	668.5	65.0	46.9	18.1	603.5	.8	602.7
1965	719.1	7.9	2.6	724.4	69.4	50.5	18.9	655.0	1.6	653.4
1966	787.8	8.1	3.0	792.9	75.6	55.5	20.1	717.3	6.3	711.0
1967	832.6	8.7	3.3	838.0	81.5	59.9	21.6	756.5	4.6	751.9
1968	910.0	10.1	4.0	916.1	88.4	65.2	23.1	827.7	4.6	823.2
1969	984.6	11.8	5.7	990.7	97.9	73.1	24.8	892.8	3.2	889.7
1970	1,038.5	12.8	6.4	1,044.9	106.7	80.0	26.7	938.2	7.3	930.9
1971	1,127.1	14.0	6.4	1,134.7	115.0	86.7	28.3	1,019.7	11.6	1,008.1
1972	1,238.3	16.3	7.7	1,246.8	126.5	97.1	29.5	1,120.3	9.1	1,111.2
1973	1,382.7	23.5	10.9	1,395.3	139.3	107.9	31.4	1,256.0	8.6	1,247.4
1974	1,500.0	29.8	14.3	1,515.5	162.5	126.6	35.9	1,353.0	10.9	1,342.1
1975	1,638.3	28.0	15.0	1,651.3	187.7	147.8	40.0	1,463.6	17.7	1,445.9
1976	1,825.3	32.4	15.5	1,842.1	205.2	162.5	42.6	1,637.0	25.1	1,611.8
1977	2,030.9	37.2	16.9	2,051.2	230.0	184.3	45.7	1,821.2	22.3	1,798.9
1978	2,294.7	46.3	24.7	2,316.3	262.3	212.8	49.5	2,054.0	26.6	2,027.4
1979	2,563.3	68.3	36.4	2,595.3	300.1	245.7	54.5	2,295.1	46.0	2,249.1
1980	2,789.5	79.1	44.9	2,823.7	343.0	281.1	61.8	2,480.7	41.4	2,439.3
1981	3,128.4	92.0	59.1	3,161.4	388.1	317.9	70.1	2,773.3	30.9	2,742.4
1982	3,255.0	101.0	64.5	3,291.5	426.9	349.8	77.1	2,864.6	.3	2,864.3
1983	3,536.7	101.9	64.8	3,573.8	443.8	362.1	81.7	3,130.0	45.7	3,084.2
1984	3,933.2	121.9	85.6	3,969.5	472.6	385.6	87.0	3,496.9	14.6	3,482.3
1985	4,220.3	112.4	85.9	4,246.8	506.7	414.0	92.7	3,740.1	16.7	3,723.4
1986	4,462.8	111.4	93.6	4,480.6	531.3	431.8	99.5	3,949.3	47.0	3,902.3
1987	4,739.5	123.2	105.3	4,757.4	561.9	455.3	106.7	4,195.4	21.7	4,173.7
1988	5,103.8	152.1	128.5	5,127.4	597.6	483.5	114.1	4,529.8	−19.5	4,549.4
1989	5,484.4	177.7	151.5	5,510.6	644.3	522.1	122.2	4,866.3	39.7	4,826.6
1990	5,803.1	189.1	154.3	5,837.9	682.5	551.6	130.9	5,155.4	66.2	5,089.1
1991	5,995.9	168.9	138.5	6,026.3	725.9	586.9	139.1	5,300.4	72.5	5,227.9
1992	6,337.7	152.7	123.0	6,367.4	751.9	607.3	144.6	5,615.5	102.7	5,512.8
1993	6,657.4	156.2	124.3	6,689.3	776.4	624.7	151.8	5,912.9	139.5	5,773.4
1994	7,072.2	186.4	160.2	7,098.4	833.7	675.1	158.6	6,264.7	142.5	6,122.3
1995	7,397.7	233.9	198.1	7,433.4	878.4	713.4	165.0	6,555.1	101.2	6,453.9
1996	7,816.9	248.7	213.7	7,851.9	918.1	748.8	169.3	6,933.8	93.7	6,840.1
1997	8,304.3	286.7	253.7	8,337.3	974.4	800.3	174.1	7,362.8	70.7	7,292.2
1998	8,747.0	287.1	265.8	8,768.3	1,030.2	851.2	179.0	7,738.2	−14.6	7,752.8
1999	9,268.4	320.8	287.0	9,302.2	1,101.3	914.3	187.0	8,200.9	−35.7	8,236.7
2000	9,817.0	382.7	343.7	9,855.9	1,187.8	990.8	197.0	8,668.1	−127.2	8,795.2
2001	10,100.8	319.0	283.8	10,135.9	1,266.9	1,061.0	205.9	8,869.0	−112.2	8,981.2
2002	10,480.8	299.1	277.6	10,502.3	1,288.6	1,077.8	210.8	9,213.7	−77.2	9,290.8
1999: I	9,066.6	294.6	264.0	9,097.2	1,069.5	886.1	183.4	8,027.7	−46.5	8,074.2
II	9,174.1	310.4	274.6	9,209.9	1,087.0	901.2	185.8	8,122.9	−38.4	8,161.3
III	9,313.5	329.9	300.0	9,343.4	1,120.3	932.3	188.0	8,223.1	−31.6	8,254.7
IV	9,519.5	348.4	309.6	9,558.3	1,128.3	937.6	190.6	8,430.0	−26.4	8,456.4
2000: I	9,629.4	362.9	330.4	9,661.9	1,153.1	959.6	193.4	8,508.8	−171.7	8,680.5
II	9,822.8	386.0	349.2	9,859.6	1,177.0	981.0	196.0	8,682.6	−67.8	8,750.4
III	9,862.1	379.7	348.1	9,893.6	1,199.9	1,001.6	198.3	8,693.7	−164.6	8,858.3
IV	9,953.6	402.1	347.2	10,008.4	1,221.3	1,021.1	200.2	8,787.2	−104.6	8,891.7
2001: I	10,024.8	355.8	328.5	10,052.1	1,230.4	1,028.4	202.0	8,821.7	−120.6	8,942.2
II	10,088.2	331.8	304.5	10,115.5	1,257.0	1,053.2	203.8	8,858.5	−87.7	8,946.2
III	10,096.2	304.9	293.3	10,107.8	1,317.3	1,106.0	211.3	8,790.6	−104.1	8,894.7
IV	10,193.9	283.3	208.9	10,268.3	1,263.1	1,056.6	206.5	9,005.2	−136.5	9,141.8
2002: I	10,329.3	284.4	262.4	10,351.3	1,271.6	1,063.2	208.4	9,079.8	−110.7	9,190.5
II	10,428.3	299.0	291.4	10,435.9	1,286.8	1,076.7	210.1	9,149.1	−132.0	9,281.1
III	10,542.0	308.3	289.9	10,560.5	1,295.8	1,084.2	211.6	9,264.7	−50.3	9,314.9
IV	10,623.7	304.8	266.9	10,661.6	1,300.4	1,087.1	213.3	9,361.2	−15.7	9,376.9
2003: I	10,735.8	296.8	269.0	10,763.7	1,305.7	1,090.4	215.3	9,457.9	23.2	9,434.8
II	10,846.7	299.5	266.2	10,880.0	1,303.4	1,086.0	217.4	9,576.6	−8.3	9,584.9
III	11,107.0	312.1	274.3	11,144.8	1,309.1	1,089.9	219.2	9,835.7	54.0	9,781.7

Source: Department of Commerce, Bureau of Economic Analysis.

TABLE B-27.—*Relation of national income and personal income, 1959–2003*

[Billions of dollars; quarterly data at seasonally adjusted annual rates]

Year or quarter	National income	Corporate profits with inventory valuation and capital consumption adjustments	Taxes on production and imports less subsidies	Contributions for government social insurance	Net interest and miscellaneous payments on assets	Business current transfer payments	Current surplus of government enterprises (net)	Wage accruals less disbursements	Personal income receipts on assets	Personal current transfer receipts	Personal income
					Less:				*Plus:*		*Equals:*
1959	455.8	55.7	40.0	13.8	9.6	1.8	1.0	0.0	34.6	24.2	392.8
1960	474.9	53.8	43.4	16.4	10.6	1.9	.9	.0	37.9	25.7	411.5
1961	491.6	54.9	45.0	17.0	12.5	2.0	.8	.0	40.1	29.5	429.0
1962	530.1	63.3	48.2	19.1	14.2	2.2	.9	.0	44.1	30.4	456.7
1963	560.6	69.0	51.2	21.7	15.2	2.7	1.4	.0	47.9	32.2	479.6
1964	602.7	76.5	54.6	22.4	17.4	3.1	1.3	.0	53.8	33.5	514.6
1965	653.4	87.5	57.8	23.4	19.6	3.6	1.3	.0	59.4	36.2	555.7
1966	711.0	93.2	59.3	31.3	22.4	3.5	1.0	.0	64.1	39.6	603.9
1967	751.9	91.3	64.2	34.9	25.5	3.8	.9	.0	69.0	48.0	648.3
1968	823.2	98.8	72.3	38.7	27.1	4.3	1.2	.0	75.2	56.1	712.0
1969	889.7	95.4	79.4	44.1	32.7	4.9	1.0	.0	84.1	62.3	778.5
1970	930.9	83.6	86.7	46.4	39.1	4.5	.0	.0	93.5	74.7	838.8
1971	1,008.1	98.0	95.9	51.2	43.9	4.3	−.2	.6	101.0	88.1	903.5
1972	1,111.2	112.1	101.4	59.2	47.9	4.9	.5	.0	109.6	97.9	992.7
1973	1,247.4	125.5	112.1	75.5	55.2	6.0	−.4	−.1	124.7	112.6	1,110.7
1974	1,342.1	115.8	121.7	85.2	70.8	7.1	−.9	−.5	146.4	133.3	1,222.6
1975	1,445.9	134.8	131.0	89.3	81.6	9.4	−3.2	.1	162.2	170.0	1,335.0
1976	1,611.8	163.3	141.5	101.3	85.5	9.5	−1.8	.1	178.4	184.0	1,474.8
1977	1,798.9	192.4	152.8	113.1	101.1	8.4	−2.6	.1	205.3	194.2	1,633.2
1978	2,027.4	216.6	162.2	131.3	115.0	10.6	−1.9	.3	234.8	209.6	1,837.7
1979	2,249.1	223.2	171.9	152.7	138.9	13.0	−2.6	−.2	274.7	235.3	2,062.2
1980	2,439.3	201.1	190.9	166.2	181.8	14.4	−4.8	.0	338.7	279.5	2,307.9
1981	2,742.4	226.1	224.5	195.7	232.3	17.6	−4.9	.1	421.9	318.4	2,591.3
1982	2,864.3	209.7	226.4	208.9	271.1	20.1	−4.0	.0	488.4	354.8	2,775.3
1983	3,084.2	264.2	242.5	226.0	285.3	22.5	−3.1	−.4	529.6	383.7	2,960.7
1984	3,482.3	318.6	269.3	257.5	327.1	30.1	−1.9	.2	607.9	400.1	3,289.5
1985	3,723.4	330.3	287.3	281.4	341.3	34.8	.8	−.2	654.0	424.9	3,526.7
1986	3,902.3	319.5	298.9	303.4	366.8	36.6	1.3	.0	695.5	451.0	3,722.4
1987	4,173.7	368.8	317.7	323.1	366.4	33.8	1.2	.0	717.0	467.6	3,947.4
1988	4,549.4	432.6	345.5	361.5	385.3	34.0	2.5	.0	769.3	496.6	4,253.7
1989	4,826.6	426.6	372.1	385.2	432.1	39.2	4.9	.0	878.0	543.4	4,587.8
1990	5,089.1	437.8	398.7	410.1	442.2	39.4	1.6	.1	924.0	595.2	4,878.6
1991	5,227.9	451.2	430.2	430.2	418.2	39.9	5.7	−.1	932.0	666.4	5,051.0
1992	5,512.8	479.3	453.9	455.0	388.5	42.4	7.6	−15.8	910.9	749.4	5,362.0
1993	5,773.4	541.9	467.0	477.7	365.7	40.7	7.2	6.4	901.8	790.1	5,558.5
1994	6,122.3	600.3	513.5	508.2	366.4	43.3	8.6	17.6	950.8	827.3	5,842.5
1995	6,453.9	696.7	524.2	532.8	367.1	46.9	11.4	16.4	1,016.4	877.4	6,152.3
1996	6,840.1	786.2	546.8	555.2	376.2	53.1	12.7	3.6	1,089.2	925.0	6,520.6
1997	7,292.2	868.5	579.1	587.2	415.6	49.9	12.6	−2.9	1,181.7	951.2	6,915.1
1998	7,752.8	801.6	604.4	624.2	487.1	64.7	10.3	−.7	1,283.2	978.6	7,423.0
1999	8,236.7	851.3	629.8	661.4	495.4	67.4	10.1	5.2	1,264.2	1,022.1	7,802.4
2000	8,795.2	817.9	664.6	702.7	559.0	87.1	5.3	.0	1,387.0	1,084.0	8,429.7
2001	8,981.2	770.4	674.5	728.5	568.4	92.5	1.2	.0	1,374.9	1,192.6	8,713.1
2002	9,290.8	904.2	721.8	750.3	582.4	89.8	2.8	.0	1,378.5	1,292.2	8,910.3
1999: I	8,074.2	844.2	616.6	652.8	480.6	64.2	11.2	5.2	1,249.4	1,009.5	7,658.4
II	8,161.3	849.3	623.5	656.8	490.6	65.4	10.5	5.2	1,255.4	1,013.3	7,728.8
III	8,254.7	842.3	634.0	662.4	498.8	68.1	10.0	5.2	1,262.3	1,027.4	7,823.7
IV	8,456.4	869.3	645.3	673.8	511.5	71.8	8.6	5.2	1,289.7	1,038.1	7,998.8
2000: I	8,680.5	832.6	653.2	695.5	548.3	81.3	7.9	.0	1,349.9	1,054.6	8,266.2
II	8,750.4	833.0	662.6	696.3	560.6	85.0	7.1	.0	1,385.6	1,080.8	8,372.3
III	8,858.3	811.8	667.9	707.7	564.3	88.9	4.2	.0	1,406.2	1,094.8	8,514.4
IV	8,891.7	794.3	674.6	711.2	563.0	93.1	2.2	.0	1,406.5	1,106.0	8,565.8
2001: I	8,942.2	755.8	672.6	726.3	563.9	97.0	3.0	.0	1,391.8	1,148.0	8,663.5
II	8,946.2	748.6	668.9	727.6	566.7	102.4	1.6	.0	1,378.1	1,181.9	8,690.2
III	8,894.7	713.6	660.3	729.2	568.0	71.1	.6	.0	1,367.4	1,208.0	8,727.4
IV	9,141.8	863.6	696.2	731.1	575.2	99.5	−.3	.0	1,362.3	1,232.3	8,771.2
2002: I	9,190.5	880.1	705.7	743.7	581.2	94.7	1.2	.0	1,359.3	1,260.5	8,803.6
II	9,281.1	901.9	719.7	749.6	572.8	90.6	.6	.0	1,375.4	1,291.1	8,912.2
III	9,314.9	899.8	729.1	752.1	585.7	87.8	5.4	.0	1,387.5	1,301.6	8,944.0
IV	9,376.9	934.9	732.8	755.5	589.7	86.2	4.1	.0	1,392.0	1,315.6	8,981.3
2003: I	9,434.8	927.1	729.4	768.7	589.3	90.1	6.3	1.4	1,388.6	1,337.6	9,048.7
II	9,584.9	1,022.8	725.2	772.3	581.7	92.5	5.8	−1.4	1,390.2	1,369.7	9,145.9
III	9,781.7	1,124.2	745.2	776.9	579.9	97.1	3.7	.0	1,389.2	1,398.7	9,242.5

Source: Department of Commerce, Bureau of Economic Analysis.

TABLE B–28.—*National income by type of income, 1959–2003*

[Billions of dollars; quarterly data at seasonally adjusted annual rates]

Year or quarter	National income	Compensation of employees							Proprietors' income with inventory valuation and capital consumption adjustments			Rental income of persons with capital consumption adjustment
		Total	Wage and salary accruals			Supplements to wages and salaries			Total	Farm	Non-farm	
			Total	Government	Other	Total	Employer contributions for employee pension and insurance funds	Employer contributions for government social insurance				
1959	455.8	281.0	259.8	46.1	213.8	21.1	13.3	7.9	50.7	10.0	40.6	16.2
1960	474.9	296.4	272.9	49.2	223.7	23.6	14.3	9.3	50.8	10.5	40.3	17.1
1961	491.6	305.3	280.5	52.5	228.0	24.8	15.2	9.6	53.2	11.0	42.2	17.9
1962	530.1	327.1	299.4	56.3	243.0	27.8	16.6	11.2	55.4	11.0	44.4	18.8
1963	560.6	345.2	314.9	60.0	254.8	30.4	18.0	12.4	56.5	10.8	45.7	19.5
1964	602.7	370.7	337.8	64.9	272.9	32.9	20.3	12.6	59.4	9.6	49.8	19.6
1965	653.4	399.5	363.8	69.9	293.8	35.7	22.7	13.1	63.9	11.8	52.1	20.2
1966	711.0	442.7	400.3	78.4	321.9	42.3	25.5	16.8	68.2	12.8	55.4	20.8
1967	751.9	475.1	429.0	86.5	342.5	46.1	28.1	18.0	69.8	11.5	58.4	21.2
1968	823.2	524.3	472.0	96.7	375.3	52.3	32.4	20.0	74.3	11.5	62.8	20.9
1969	889.7	577.6	518.3	105.6	412.7	59.3	36.5	22.8	77.4	12.6	64.7	21.2
1970	930.9	617.2	551.6	117.2	434.3	65.7	41.8	23.8	78.4	12.7	65.7	21.4
1971	1,008.1	658.9	584.5	126.8	457.8	74.4	47.9	26.4	84.8	13.2	71.6	22.4
1972	1,111.2	725.1	638.8	137.9	500.9	86.4	55.2	31.2	95.9	16.8	79.1	23.4
1973	1,247.4	811.2	708.8	148.8	560.0	102.5	62.7	39.8	113.5	28.9	84.6	24.3
1974	1,342.1	890.2	772.3	160.5	611.8	118.0	73.3	44.7	113.1	23.2	89.9	24.3
1975	1,445.9	949.1	814.8	176.2	638.6	134.3	87.6	46.7	119.5	21.7	97.8	23.7
1976	1,611.8	1,059.3	899.7	188.9	710.8	159.6	105.2	54.4	132.2	17.0	115.2	22.3
1977	1,798.9	1,180.5	994.2	202.6	791.6	186.4	125.3	61.1	145.7	15.7	130.0	20.7
1978	2,027.4	1,336.1	1,121.2	220.0	901.2	214.9	143.4	71.5	166.6	19.6	147.1	22.1
1979	2,249.1	1,500.8	1,255.8	237.1	1,018.7	245.0	162.4	82.6	180.1	21.8	158.3	23.8
1980	2,439.3	1,651.8	1,377.6	261.5	1,116.2	274.2	185.2	88.9	174.1	11.3	162.8	30.0
1981	2,742.4	1,825.8	1,517.5	285.8	1,231.7	308.3	204.7	103.6	183.0	18.7	164.3	38.0
1982	2,864.3	1,925.8	1,593.7	307.5	1,286.2	332.1	222.4	109.8	176.3	13.1	163.3	38.8
1983	3,084.2	2,042.6	1,684.6	324.8	1,359.8	358.0	238.1	119.9	192.5	6.0	186.5	37.8
1984	3,482.3	2,255.6	1,855.1	348.1	1,507.0	400.5	261.5	139.0	243.3	20.6	222.7	40.2
1985	3,723.4	2,424.7	1,995.5	373.9	1,621.6	429.2	281.5	147.7	262.3	20.8	241.5	41.9
1986	3,902.3	2,570.1	2,114.8	397.0	1,717.9	455.3	297.5	157.9	275.7	22.6	253.1	33.5
1987	4,173.7	2,750.2	2,270.7	422.6	1,848.1	479.5	313.2	166.3	302.2	28.7	273.5	33.5
1988	4,549.4	2,967.2	2,452.9	451.3	2,001.6	514.2	329.6	184.6	341.6	26.8	314.7	40.6
1989	4,826.6	3,145.2	2,596.3	480.2	2,116.2	548.9	355.2	193.7	363.3	33.0	330.3	43.1
1990	5,089.1	3,338.2	2,754.0	517.7	2,236.3	584.2	377.8	206.5	380.6	31.9	348.7	50.7
1991	5,227.9	3,445.2	2,823.0	546.8	2,276.2	622.3	407.1	215.1	377.1	26.7	350.4	60.3
1992	5,512.8	3,635.4	2,964.5	569.2	2,395.3	670.9	442.5	228.4	427.6	34.5	393.0	78.0
1993	5,773.4	3,801.4	3,089.2	586.8	2,502.4	712.2	472.4	239.8	453.8	31.2	422.6	95.6
1994	6,122.3	3,997.2	3,249.8	606.2	2,643.5	747.5	493.3	254.1	473.3	33.9	439.4	119.7
1995	6,453.9	4,193.3	3,435.7	625.5	2,810.2	757.7	493.6	264.0	492.1	22.7	469.5	122.1
1996	6,840.1	4,390.5	3,623.2	644.4	2,978.8	767.3	492.5	274.9	543.2	37.3	505.9	131.5
1997	7,292.2	4,661.7	4,187.7	668.1	3,206.6	787.0	497.5	289.5	576.0	34.2	541.8	128.8
1998	7,752.8	5,019.4	4,182.7	697.3	3,485.5	836.7	529.7	307.0	627.8	29.4	598.4	137.5
1999	8,236.7	5,357.1	4,471.4	729.3	3,742.1	885.7	562.4	323.3	678.3	28.6	649.7	147.3
2000	8,795.2	5,782.7	4,829.2	774.7	4,054.5	953.4	609.9	343.5	728.4	22.7	705.7	150.3
2001	8,981.2	5,940.4	4,942.9	815.8	4,127.1	997.6	642.6	354.9	770.6	25.0	745.6	163.1
2002	9,290.8	6,019.1	4,974.6	859.9	4,114.7	1,044.5	680.4	364.1	797.7	14.3	783.4	173.0
1999: I	8,074.2	5,248.0	4,380.9	718.2	3,662.7	867.0	547.7	319.3	664.3	34.9	629.4	145.2
II	8,161.3	5,302.5	4,425.4	724.3	3,701.1	877.1	556.0	321.1	672.0	29.3	642.7	147.8
III ...	8,254.7	5,376.3	4,486.1	732.3	3,753.8	890.2	566.5	323.7	680.6	25.6	655.1	144.5
IV ...	8,456.4	5,501.7	4,593.2	742.5	3,850.7	908.5	579.3	329.3	696.1	24.6	671.5	152.1
2000: I	8,680.5	5,694.1	4,760.0	762.0	3,998.0	934.1	593.9	340.2	709.3	23.2	686.1	153.8
II	8,750.4	5,727.2	4,783.2	772.8	4,010.5	944.0	603.7	340.3	726.5	23.8	702.7	148.?
III ..	8,858.3	5,837.4	4,874.9	779.2	4,095.8	962.5	616.5	346.0	735.6	23.0	712.6	148.2
IV ..	8,891.7	5,871.9	4,898.8	784.9	4,113.9	973.1	625.6	347.6	742.1	20.7	721.4	150.5
2001: I	8,942.2	5,935.6	4,951.9	798.8	4,153.2	983.7	629.6	354.1	761.3	24.9	736.5	153.?
II	8,946.2	5,936.0	4,945.0	809.1	4,135.9	991.0	636.5	354.5	766.4	24.8	741.5	155.
III ..	8,894.7	5,940.8	4,938.8	821.4	4,117.4	1,002.1	647.0	355.1	769.2	23.5	745.7	171.
IV ..	9,141.8	5,949.3	4,935.8	833.8	4,102.1	1,013.5	657.5	356.0	785.7	26.8	758.9	172.
2002: I	9,190.5	5,972.4	4,945.1	846.6	4,098.5	1,027.3	666.6	360.7	779.3	12.1	767.2	175.
II	9,281.1	6,014.8	4,973.1	856.0	4,117.1	1,041.7	677.9	363.9	796.2	15.2	780.9	184.
III ..	9,314.9	6,031.1	4,980.9	863.2	4,117.7	1,050.2	685.2	365.1	803.2	13.5	789.7	172.
IV ..	9,376.9	6,058.0	4,999.1	873.8	4,125.4	1,058.8	692.1	366.7	812.2	16.3	795.9	159.
2003: I	9,434.8	6,115.8	5,034.6	891.4	4,143.3	1,081.2	706.3	374.9	813.5	13.0	800.5	163.
II	9,584.9	6,164.8	5,070.8	898.1	4,172.7	1,093.9	717.3	376.6	838.8	20.0	818.8	153.
III ..	9,781.7	6,213.6	5,104.1	900.0	4,204.1	1,109.6	730.7	378.8	860.9	21.5	839.4	157

See next page for continuation of table.

[Billions of dollars; quarterly data at seasonally adjusted annual rates]

Year or quarter	Total	Profits with inventory valuation adjustment and without capital consumption adjustment							Capital consumption adjustment	Net interest and miscellaneous payments	Taxes on production and imports	Less: Subsidies	Business current transfer payments	Current surplus of government enterprises
		Total	Profits before tax	Taxes on corporate income	Profits after tax			Inventory valuation adjustment						
					Total	Net dividends	Undistributed profits							
1959	55.7	53.5	53.8	23.7	30.0	12.6	17.5	-0.3	2.2	9.6	41.1	1.1	1.8	1.0
1960	53.8	51.5	51.6	22.8	28.8	13.4	15.5	-.2	2.3	10.6	44.6	1.1	1.9	.9
1961	54.9	51.8	51.6	22.9	28.7	13.9	14.8	.3	3.0	12.5	47.0	2.0	2.0	.8
1962	63.3	57.0	57.0	24.1	32.9	15.0	17.9	.0	6.2	14.2	50.4	2.3	2.2	.9
1963	69.0	62.1	62.1	26.4	35.7	16.2	19.5	.1	6.8	15.2	53.4	2.2	2.7	1.4
1964	76.5	68.6	69.1	28.2	40.9	18.2	22.7	-.5	7.9	17.4	57.3	2.7	3.1	1.3
1965	87.5	78.9	80.2	31.1	49.1	20.2	28.9	-1.2	8.6	19.6	60.8	3.0	3.6	1.3
1966	93.2	84.6	86.7	33.9	52.8	20.7	32.1	-2.1	8.6	22.4	63.3	3.9	3.5	1.0
1967	91.3	82.0	83.5	32.9	50.6	21.5	29.1	-1.6	9.3	25.5	68.0	3.8	3.8	.9
1968	98.8	88.8	92.4	39.6	52.8	23.5	29.3	-3.7	10.0	27.1	76.5	4.2	4.3	1.2
1969	95.4	85.5	91.4	40.0	51.4	24.2	27.2	-5.9	9.9	32.7	84.0	4.5	4.9	1.0
1970	83.6	74.4	81.0	34.8	46.2	24.3	21.9	-6.6	9.2	39.1	91.5	4.8	4.5	.0
1971	98.0	88.3	92.9	38.2	54.7	25.0	29.7	-4.6	9.7	43.9	100.6	4.7	4.3	-.2
1972	112.1	101.2	107.8	42.3	65.5	26.8	38.6	-6.6	10.9	47.9	108.1	6.6	4.9	.5
1973	125.5	115.3	134.8	50.0	84.9	29.9	55.0	-19.6	10.2	55.2	117.3	5.2	6.0	-.4
1974	115.8	109.5	147.8	52.8	95.0	33.2	61.8	-38.2	6.2	70.8	125.0	3.3	7.1	-.9
1975	134.8	135.0	145.5	51.6	93.9	33.0	60.9	-10.5	-.2	81.6	135.5	4.5	9.4	-3.2
1976	163.3	165.6	179.7	65.3	114.4	39.0	75.4	-14.1	-2.3	85.5	146.6	5.1	9.5	-1.8
1977	192.4	194.7	210.4	74.4	136.0	44.8	91.2	-15.7	-2.3	101.1	159.9	7.1	8.4	-2.6
1978	216.6	222.4	246.1	84.9	161.3	50.8	110.5	-23.7	-5.8	115.0	171.2	8.9	10.6	-1.9
1979	223.2	231.8	271.9	90.0	181.9	57.5	124.4	-40.1	-8.5	138.9	180.4	8.5	13.0	-2.6
1980	201.1	211.4	253.5	87.2	166.3	64.1	102.2	-42.1	-10.2	181.8	200.7	9.8	14.4	-4.8
1981	226.1	219.1	243.7	84.3	159.4	73.8	85.6	-24.6	7.0	232.3	236.0	11.5	17.6	-4.9
1982	209.7	191.0	198.5	66.5	132.0	77.7	54.3	-7.5	18.6	271.1	241.3	15.0	20.1	-4.0
1983	264.2	226.5	233.9	80.6	153.3	83.5	69.8	-7.4	37.8	285.3	263.7	21.2	22.5	-3.1
1984	318.6	264.6	268.6	97.5	171.1	90.8	80.3	-4.0	54.0	327.1	290.2	21.0	30.1	-1.9
1985	330.3	257.5	257.4	99.4	158.0	97.6	60.5	.0	72.9	341.3	308.5	21.3	34.8	.8
1986	319.5	253.0	246.0	109.7	136.3	106.2	30.1	7.1	66.5	366.8	323.7	24.8	36.6	1.3
1987	368.8	301.4	317.6	130.4	187.2	112.3	74.9	-16.2	67.5	366.4	347.9	30.2	33.8	1.2
1988	432.6	363.9	386.1	141.6	244.4	129.9	114.5	-22.2	68.7	385.3	374.9	29.4	34.0	2.5
1989	426.6	367.4	383.7	146.1	237.7	158.0	79.7	-16.3	59.2	432.1	399.3	27.2	39.2	4.9
1990	437.8	396.6	409.5	145.4	264.1	169.1	95.0	-12.9	41.2	442.2	425.5	26.8	39.4	1.6
1991	451.2	427.9	423.0	138.6	284.4	180.7	103.7	4.9	23.3	418.2	457.5	27.3	39.9	5.7
1992	479.3	458.3	461.1	148.7	312.4	187.9	124.5	-2.8	21.1	388.5	483.8	29.9	42.4	7.6
1993	541.9	513.1	517.1	171.0	346.1	202.8	143.3	-4.0	28.8	365.7	503.4	36.4	40.7	7.2
1994	600.3	564.6	577.1	193.7	383.3	234.7	148.6	-12.4	35.7	366.4	545.6	32.2	43.3	8.6
1995	696.7	656.0	674.3	218.7	455.6	254.2	201.4	-18.3	40.7	367.1	558.2	34.0	46.9	11.4
1996	786.2	736.1	733.0	231.7	501.4	297.6	203.8	3.1	50.1	376.2	581.1	34.3	53.1	12.7
1997	868.5	812.3	798.2	246.1	552.1	334.5	217.6	14.1	56.2	415.6	612.0	32.9	49.9	12.6
1998	801.6	738.5	718.3	248.3	470.0	351.6	118.3	20.2	63.1	487.1	639.8	35.4	64.7	10.3
1999	851.3	776.8	775.9	258.6	517.2	337.4	179.9	1.0	74.5	495.4	674.0	44.2	67.4	10.1
2000	817.9	759.3	773.4	265.2	508.2	377.9	130.3	-14.1	58.6	559.0	708.9	44.3	87.1	5.3
2001	770.4	705.9	696.8	201.1	495.6	373.2	122.4	9.1	64.5	568.4	729.8	55.3	92.5	1.2
2002	904.2	742.7	745.0	195.0	549.9	398.3	151.6	-2.2	161.5	582.4	760.1	38.2	89.8	2.8
1999: I	844.2	771.3	750.3	251.0	499.3	339.9	159.4	20.9	72.9	480.6	657.9	41.3	64.2	11.2
II	849.3	773.2	766.5	256.5	510.0	333.4	176.6	6.6	76.2	490.6	667.5	44.0	65.4	10.5
III	842.3	766.8	775.3	260.2	515.1	334.2	180.9	-8.5	75.5	498.8	679.6	45.6	68.1	10.0
IV	869.3	796.1	811.4	266.8	544.5	342.0	202.6	-15.3	73.2	511.5	691.2	45.8	71.8	8.6
2000: I	832.6	766.8	795.4	280.8	514.6	360.3	154.4	-28.6	65.8	548.3	697.6	44.4	81.3	7.9
II	833.0	773.5	784.8	272.5	512.2	377.3	135.0	-11.3	59.6	560.6	706.9	44.4	85.0	7.1
III	811.8	756.3	762.6	260.3	502.3	386.6	115.7	-6.3	55.5	564.3	712.2	44.3	88.9	4.2
IV	794.3	740.7	750.8	247.1	503.7	387.6	116.1	-10.1	53.6	563.0	718.7	44.1	93.1	2.2
2001: I	755.8	730.7	735.5	219.1	516.4	380.0	136.4	-4.9	25.1	563.9	752.2	52.5	97.0	3.0
II	748.6	731.4	733.0	217.2	515.8	371.5	144.3	-1.6	17.2	566.7	727.2	58.3	102.4	1.6
III	713.6	685.8	671.5	198.2	473.3	368.7	104.6	14.3	27.8	568.0	727.5	67.2	71.1	.6
IV	863.6	675.7	647.0	170.1	477.0	372.6	104.4	28.7	187.9	575.2	739.4	43.2	99.5	-.3
2002: I	880.1	702.7	690.6	181.6	509.0	382.3	126.7	12.1	177.4	581.2	745.8	40.1	94.7	1.2
II	901.9	738.9	738.0	197.1	540.9	393.5	147.4	.9	163.0	572.8	757.6	37.9	90.6	.6
III	899.8	745.1	756.3	198.6	557.7	404.3	153.4	-11.1	154.7	585.7	767.4	38.2	87.8	5.4
IV	934.9	784.2	795.0	202.9	592.1	413.1	179.1	-10.8	150.7	589.7	769.5	36.7	86.2	4.1
2003: I	927.1	780.9	809.0	213.9	595.0	420.3	174.7	-28.1	146.3	589.3	774.2	44.7	90.1	6.3
II	1,022.8	793.6	792.5	211.4	581.0	427.5	153.5	1.2	229.2	581.7	782.1	56.9	92.5	5.8
III	1,124.2	864.2	865.9	230.6	635.4	434.3	201.1	-1.8	260.1	579.9	791.5	46.3	97.1	3.7

Source: Department of Commerce, Bureau of Economic Analysis.

[Billions of dollars; quarterly data at seasonally adjusted annual rates]

Year or quarter	Personal income	Compensation of employees, received							Proprietors' income with inventory valuation and capital consumption adjustments			Rental income of persons with capital consumption adjustment
		Total	Wage and salary disbursements			Supplements to wages and salaries			Total	Farm	Non-farm	
			Total	Private industries	Government	Total	Employer contributions for employee pension and insurance funds	Employer contributions for government social insurance				
1959	392.8	281.0	259.8	213.8	46.1	21.1	13.3	7.9	50.7	10.0	40.6	16.2
1960	411.5	296.4	272.9	223.7	49.2	23.6	14.3	9.3	50.8	10.5	40.3	17.1
1961	429.0	305.3	280.5	228.0	52.5	24.8	15.2	9.6	53.2	11.0	42.2	17.9
1962	456.7	327.1	299.4	243.0	56.3	27.8	16.6	11.2	55.4	11.0	44.4	18.8
1963	479.6	345.2	314.9	254.8	60.0	30.4	18.0	12.4	56.5	10.8	45.7	19.5
1964	514.6	370.7	337.8	272.9	64.9	32.9	20.3	12.6	59.4	9.6	49.8	19.6
1965	555.7	399.5	363.8	293.8	69.9	35.7	22.7	13.1	63.9	11.8	52.1	20.2
1966	603.9	442.7	400.3	321.9	78.4	42.3	25.5	16.8	68.2	12.8	55.4	20.8
1967	648.3	475.1	429.0	342.5	86.5	46.1	28.1	18.0	69.8	11.5	58.4	21.2
1968	712.0	524.3	472.0	375.3	96.7	52.3	32.4	20.0	74.3	11.5	62.8	20.9
1969	778.5	577.6	518.3	412.7	105.6	59.3	36.5	22.8	77.4	12.6	64.7	21.2
1970	838.8	617.2	551.6	434.3	117.2	65.7	41.8	23.8	78.4	12.7	65.7	21.4
1971	903.5	658.3	584.0	457.4	126.6	74.4	47.9	26.4	84.8	13.2	71.6	22.4
1972	992.7	725.1	638.8	501.2	137.6	86.4	55.2	31.2	95.9	16.8	79.1	23.4
1973	1,110.7	811.3	708.8	560.0	148.8	102.5	62.7	39.8	113.5	28.9	84.6	24.3
1974	1,222.6	890.7	772.8	611.8	161.0	118.0	73.3	44.7	113.1	23.2	89.9	24.3
1975	1,335.0	949.0	814.7	638.6	176.1	134.3	87.6	46.7	119.5	21.7	97.8	23.7
1976	1,474.8	1,059.2	899.6	710.8	188.8	159.6	105.2	54.4	132.2	17.0	115.2	22.7
1977	1,633.2	1,180.4	994.1	791.6	202.5	186.4	125.3	61.1	145.7	15.7	130.0	20.7
1978	1,837.7	1,335.8	1,120.9	901.2	219.7	214.9	143.4	71.5	166.6	19.6	147.1	22.1
1979	2,062.2	1,501.0	1,256.0	1,018.7	237.3	245.0	162.4	82.6	180.1	21.8	158.3	23.8
1980	2,307.9	1,651.8	1,377.7	1,116.2	261.5	274.2	185.2	88.9	174.1	11.3	162.8	30.0
1981	2,591.3	1,825.7	1,517.5	1,231.7	285.8	308.3	204.7	103.6	183.0	18.7	164.3	38.0
1982	2,775.3	1,925.9	1,593.7	1,286.2	307.5	332.1	222.4	109.8	176.3	13.1	163.3	38.8
1983	2,960.7	2,043.0	1,685.0	1,359.8	325.2	358.0	238.1	119.9	192.5	6.0	186.5	37.8
1984	3,289.5	2,255.4	1,854.9	1,507.0	347.9	400.5	261.5	139.0	243.3	20.6	222.7	40.2
1985	3,526.7	2,424.9	1,995.7	1,621.6	374.1	429.2	281.5	147.7	262.3	20.8	241.5	41.9
1986	3,722.4	2,570.1	2,114.8	1,717.9	397.0	455.3	297.5	157.9	275.7	22.6	253.1	33.5
1987	3,947.4	2,750.2	2,270.7	1,848.1	422.6	479.5	313.2	166.3	302.2	28.7	273.5	33.5
1988	4,253.7	2,967.2	2,452.9	2,001.6	451.3	514.2	329.6	184.6	341.6	26.8	314.7	40.6
1989	4,587.8	3,145.2	2,596.3	2,116.2	480.2	548.9	355.2	193.7	363.3	33.0	330.3	43.1
1990	4,878.6	3,338.2	2,754.0	2,236.3	517.7	584.2	377.8	206.5	380.6	31.9	348.7	50.7
1991	5,051.0	3,445.3	2,823.0	2,276.2	546.8	622.3	407.1	215.1	377.1	26.7	350.4	60.3
1992	5,362.0	3,651.2	2,980.3	2,411.1	569.2	670.9	442.5	228.4	427.6	34.5	393.0	78.0
1993	5,558.5	3,794.9	3,082.7	2,496.0	586.8	712.2	472.4	239.8	453.8	31.2	422.6	95.6
1994	5,842.5	3,979.6	3,232.1	2,625.9	606.2	747.5	493.3	254.1	473.3	33.9	439.4	119.7
1995	6,152.3	4,177.0	3,419.3	2,793.8	625.5	757.7	493.6	264.0	492.1	22.7	469.5	122.1
1996	6,520.6	4,386.9	3,619.6	2,975.2	644.4	767.3	492.5	274.9	543.2	37.3	505.9	131.5
1997	6,915.1	4,664.6	3,877.6	3,209.5	668.1	787.0	497.5	289.5	576.0	34.2	541.8	128.8
1998	7,423.0	5,020.1	4,183.4	3,486.2	697.3	836.7	529.7	307.0	627.8	29.4	598.4	137.5
1999	7,802.4	5,352.0	4,466.3	3,736.9	729.3	885.7	562.4	323.3	678.3	28.6	649.7	147.3
2000	8,429.7	5,782.7	4,829.2	4,054.5	774.7	953.4	609.9	343.5	728.4	22.7	705.7	150.3
2001	8,713.1	5,940.4	4,942.9	4,127.1	815.8	997.6	642.6	354.9	770.6	25.0	745.6	163.1
2002	8,910.3	6,019.1	4,974.6	4,114.7	859.9	1,044.5	680.4	364.1	797.7	14.3	783.4	173.0
1999: I	7,658.4	5,242.8	4,375.8	3,657.6	718.2	867.0	547.7	319.3	664.3	34.9	629.4	145.2
II	7,728.8	5,297.3	4,420.2	3,696.0	724.3	877.1	556.0	321.1	672.0	29.3	642.7	147.6
III	7,823.7	5,371.2	4,481.0	3,748.7	732.3	890.2	566.5	323.7	680.6	25.6	655.1	144.5
IV	7,998.8	5,496.5	4,588.0	3,845.5	742.5	908.5	579.3	329.3	696.1	24.6	671.5	152.1
2000: I	8,266.2	5,694.1	4,760.0	3,998.0	762.0	934.1	593.9	340.2	709.3	23.2	686.1	153.8
II	8,372.3	5,727.2	4,783.2	4,010.5	772.8	944.0	603.7	340.3	726.5	23.8	702.7	148.5
III	8,514.4	5,837.4	4,874.9	4,095.8	779.2	962.5	616.5	346.0	735.6	23.0	712.6	148.2
IV	8,565.8	5,871.9	4,898.8	4,113.9	784.9	973.1	625.6	347.6	742.1	20.7	721.4	150.5
2001: I	8,663.5	5,935.6	4,951.9	4,153.2	798.8	983.7	629.6	354.1	761.3	24.9	736.5	153.0
II	8,690.2	5,936.0	4,945.0	4,135.9	809.1	991.0	636.5	354.5	766.4	24.8	741.5	155.6
III	8,727.4	5,940.8	4,938.8	4,117.4	821.4	1,002.1	647.0	355.1	769.2	23.5	745.7	171.1
IV	8,771.2	5,949.3	4,935.8	4,102.1	833.8	1,013.5	657.5	356.0	785.7	26.8	758.9	172.6
2002: I	8,803.6	5,972.4	4,945.1	4,098.5	846.6	1,027.3	666.6	360.7	779.3	12.1	767.2	175.9
II	8,912.2	6,014.8	4,973.1	4,117.1	856.0	1,041.7	677.9	363.9	796.2	15.2	780.9	184.4
III	8,944.0	6,031.1	4,980.9	4,117.7	863.2	1,050.2	685.2	365.1	803.2	13.5	789.7	172.2
IV	8,981.3	6,058.0	4,999.1	4,125.4	873.8	1,058.8	692.1	366.7	812.2	16.3	795.9	159.0
2003: I	9,048.7	6,114.4	5,033.2	4,143.3	890.0	1,081.2	706.3	374.9	813.5	13.0	800.5	163.2
II	9,145.9	6,166.2	5,072.2	4,172.7	899.5	1,093.9	717.3	376.6	838.8	20.0	818.8	153.6
III	9,242.5	6,213.6	5,104.1	4,204.1	900.0	1,109.6	730.7	378.8	860.9	21.5	839.4	157.0

[1] Consists of aid to families with dependent children and, beginning with 1996, assistance programs operating under the Personal Responsibility and Work Opportunity Reconciliation Act of 1996.

See next page for continuation of table.

TABLE B–29.—*Sources of personal income, 1959–2003*—Continued

[Billions of dollars; quarterly data at seasonally adjusted annual rates]

Year or quarter	Personal income receipts on assets			Personal current transfer receipts								Less: Contributions for government social insurance
					Government social benefits to persons						Other current transfer receipts, from business (net)	
	Total	Personal interest income	Personal dividend income	Total	Total	Old-age, survivors, disability, and health insurance benefits	Government unemployment insurance benefits	Veterans benefits	Family assistance[1]	Other		
1959	34.6	22.0	12.6	24.2	22.9	10.2	2.8	4.6	0.9	4.5	1.3	13.8
1960	37.9	24.5	13.4	25.7	24.4	11.1	3.0	4.6	1.0	4.7	1.3	16.4
1961	40.1	26.2	13.9	29.5	28.1	12.6	4.3	5.0	1.1	5.1	1.4	17.0
1962	44.1	29.1	15.0	30.4	28.8	14.3	3.1	4.7	1.3	5.5	1.5	19.1
1963	47.9	31.7	16.2	32.2	30.3	15.2	3.0	4.8	1.4	5.9	1.9	21.7
1964	53.8	35.6	18.2	33.5	31.3	16.0	2.7	4.7	1.5	6.4	2.2	22.4
1965	59.4	39.2	20.2	36.2	33.9	18.1	2.3	4.9	1.7	7.0	2.3	23.4
1966	64.1	43.4	20.7	39.6	37.5	20.8	1.9	4.9	1.9	8.1	2.1	31.3
1967	69.0	47.5	21.5	48.0	45.8	25.8	2.2	5.6	2.3	9.9	2.3	34.9
1968	75.2	51.6	23.5	56.1	53.3	30.5	2.1	5.9	2.8	11.9	2.8	38.7
1969	84.1	59.9	24.2	62.3	59.0	33.1	2.2	6.7	3.5	13.4	3.3	44.1
1970	93.5	69.2	24.3	74.7	71.7	38.6	4.0	7.7	4.8	16.6	2.9	46.4
1971	101.0	75.9	25.0	88.1	85.4	44.7	5.8	8.8	6.2	20.0	2.7	51.2
1972	109.6	82.8	26.8	97.9	94.8	49.8	5.7	9.7	6.9	22.7	3.1	59.2
1973	124.7	94.8	29.9	112.6	108.6	60.9	4.4	10.4	7.2	25.7	3.9	75.5
1974	146.4	113.2	33.2	133.3	128.6	70.3	6.8	11.8	8.0	31.7	4.7	85.2
1975	162.2	129.3	32.9	170.0	163.1	81.5	17.6	14.5	9.3	40.2	6.8	89.3
1976	178.4	139.5	39.0	184.0	177.3	93.3	15.8	14.4	10.1	43.7	6.7	101.3
1977	205.3	160.6	44.7	194.2	189.1	105.3	12.7	13.8	10.6	46.7	5.1	113.1
1978	234.8	184.0	50.7	209.6	203.2	116.9	9.1	13.9	10.8	52.5	6.5	131.3
1979	274.7	217.3	57.4	235.3	227.1	132.5	9.4	14.4	11.1	59.6	8.2	152.7
1980	338.7	274.7	64.0	279.5	270.8	154.8	15.7	15.0	12.5	72.8	8.6	166.2
1981	421.9	348.3	73.6	318.4	307.2	182.1	15.6	16.1	13.1	80.2	11.2	195.7
1982	488.4	410.8	77.6	354.8	342.4	204.6	25.1	16.4	12.9	83.4	12.4	208.9
1983	529.6	446.3	83.3	383.7	369.9	222.2	26.2	16.6	13.8	91.0	13.8	226.0
1984	607.9	517.2	90.6	400.1	380.4	237.8	15.9	16.4	14.5	95.9	19.7	257.5
1985	654.0	556.6	97.4	424.9	402.6	253.0	15.7	16.7	15.2	102.0	22.3	281.4
1986	695.5	589.5	106.0	451.0	428.0	268.9	16.3	16.7	16.1	109.9	22.9	303.4
1987	717.0	604.9	112.2	467.6	447.4	282.6	14.5	16.6	16.4	117.3	20.2	323.1
1988	769.3	639.5	129.7	496.6	476.0	300.2	13.2	16.9	16.9	128.8	20.6	361.5
1989	878.0	720.2	157.8	543.4	519.9	325.6	14.3	17.3	17.5	145.3	23.5	385.2
1990	924.0	755.2	168.8	595.2	573.1	351.8	18.0	17.8	19.2	166.2	22.2	410.1
1991	932.0	751.7	180.3	666.4	648.5	381.7	26.6	18.3	21.1	200.8	17.9	430.2
1992	910.9	723.4	187.4	749.4	729.8	414.4	38.9	19.3	22.2	234.9	19.6	455.0
1993	901.8	699.6	202.2	790.1	775.7	443.4	34.1	20.1	22.8	255.3	14.4	477.7
1994	950.8	716.8	234.0	827.3	812.2	475.4	23.5	20.1	23.2	270.0	15.1	508.2
1995	1,016.4	763.2	253.2	877.4	858.4	506.8	21.4	20.9	22.6	286.7	19.0	532.8
1996	1,089.2	793.0	296.2	925.0	902.1	537.7	22.0	21.7	20.3	300.4	22.9	555.2
1997	1,181.7	848.7	333.0	951.2	931.8	563.2	19.9	22.5	17.9	308.3	19.4	587.2
1998	1,283.2	933.2	349.9	978.6	952.6	575.1	19.5	23.4	17.4	317.3	26.0	624.2
1999	1,264.2	928.6	335.6	1,022.1	988.0	588.9	20.3	24.3	17.9	336.7	34.1	661.4
2000	1,387.0	1,011.0	376.1	1,084.0	1,041.6	620.8	20.3	25.1	18.4	357.0	42.4	702.7
2001	1,374.9	1,003.7	371.2	1,192.6	1,142.6	668.4	31.7	26.7	18.6	397.2	49.9	728.5
2002	1,378.5	982.4	396.2	1,292.2	1,249.5	710.3	53.4	29.9	19.7	436.2	42.6	750.3
1999: I	1,249.4	911.2	338.2	1,009.5	978.7	583.9	20.6	24.1	17.7	332.5	30.8	652.8
II	1,255.4	923.7	331.6	1,013.3	980.5	587.0	20.7	24.2	17.8	330.8	32.8	656.8
III	1,262.3	930.0	332.4	1,027.4	992.0	590.4	20.2	24.3	18.0	339.2	35.4	662.4
IV	1,289.7	949.6	340.1	1,038.1	1,000.8	594.2	19.8	24.4	18.2	344.2	37.2	673.8
2000: I	1,349.9	991.5	358.4	1,054.6	1,014.0	605.7	20.1	25.0	18.3	345.0	40.6	695.5
II	1,385.6	1,010.2	375.4	1,080.8	1,038.9	621.5	19.5	25.0	18.4	354.6	41.8	696.3
III	1,406.2	1,021.4	384.7	1,094.8	1,051.6	625.2	20.1	25.1	18.5	362.8	43.1	707.7
IV	1,406.5	1,020.8	385.7	1,106.0	1,061.8	631.0	21.3	25.4	18.5	365.6	44.1	711.2
2001: I	1,391.8	1,013.7	378.1	1,148.0	1,104.7	655.1	25.3	26.0	18.4	380.0	43.3	726.3
II	1,378.1	1,008.5	369.6	1,181.9	1,135.6	663.3	28.2	26.4	18.5	399.2	46.2	727.6
III	1,367.4	1,000.7	366.7	1,208.0	1,142.7	674.7	33.0	26.7	18.7	389.6	65.3	729.2
IV	1,362.3	991.7	370.6	1,232.3	1,187.5	680.4	40.4	27.8	18.9	420.0	44.9	731.1
2002: I	1,359.3	979.1	380.2	1,260.5	1,216.2	699.4	42.3	28.7	19.4	426.5	44.3	743.7
II	1,375.4	984.0	391.4	1,291.1	1,247.9	707.0	60.2	29.6	19.6	431.4	43.2	749.6
III	1,387.5	985.3	402.2	1,301.6	1,259.4	713.8	57.3	30.4	19.9	438.1	42.1	752.1
IV	1,392.0	981.2	410.8	1,315.6	1,274.6	721.1	53.8	30.9	20.1	448.8	41.0	755.5
2003: I	1,388.6	970.6	418.0	1,337.6	1,292.4	732.3	51.9	31.8	20.2	456.3	45.3	768.7
II	1,390.2	964.9	425.3	1,369.7	1,325.3	741.8	56.3	32.4	20.3	474.5	44.5	772.3
III	1,389.2	957.0	432.2	1,398.7	1,352.6	745.6	58.6	33.0	20.3	495.1	46.1	776.9

Source: Department of Commerce, Bureau of Economic Analysis.

TABLE B–30.—*Disposition of personal income, 1959–2003*

[Billions of dollars, except as noted; quarterly data at seasonally adjusted annual rates]

Year or quarter	Personal income	Less: Personal current taxes	Equals: Disposable personal income	Less: Personal outlays				Equals: Personal saving	Percent of disposable personal income[2]		
				Total	Personal consumption expenditures	Personal interest payments[1]	Personal current transfer payments		Personal outlays		Personal saving
									Total	Personal consumption expenditures	
1959	392.8	42.3	350.5	323.9	317.6	5.5	0.8	26.7	92.4	90.6	7.6
1960	411.5	46.1	365.4	338.8	331.7	6.2	.8	26.7	92.7	90.8	7.3
1961	429.0	47.3	381.8	349.6	342.1	6.5	1.0	32.2	91.6	89.6	8.4
1962	456.7	51.6	405.1	371.3	363.3	7.0	1.1	33.8	91.7	89.7	8.3
1963	479.6	54.6	425.1	391.8	382.7	7.9	1.2	33.3	92.2	90.0	7.8
1964	514.6	52.1	462.5	421.7	411.4	8.9	1.3	40.8	91.2	89.0	8.8
1965	555.7	57.7	498.1	455.1	443.8	9.9	1.4	43.0	91.4	89.1	8.6
1966	603.9	66.4	537.5	493.1	480.9	10.7	1.6	44.4	91.7	89.5	8.3
1967	648.3	73.0	575.3	520.9	507.8	11.1	2.0	54.4	90.5	88.3	9.5
1968	712.0	87.0	625.0	572.2	558.0	12.2	2.0	52.8	91.6	89.3	8.4
1969	778.5	104.5	674.0	621.4	605.2	14.0	2.2	52.5	92.2	89.8	7.8
1970	838.8	103.1	735.7	666.2	648.5	15.2	2.6	69.5	90.6	88.1	9.4
1971	903.5	101.7	801.8	721.2	701.9	16.6	2.8	80.6	89.9	87.5	10.1
1972	992.7	123.6	869.1	791.9	770.6	18.1	3.1	77.2	91.1	88.7	8.9
1973	1,110.7	132.4	978.3	875.6	852.4	19.8	3.4	102.7	89.5	87.1	10.5
1974	1,222.6	151.0	1,071.6	958.0	933.4	21.2	3.4	113.6	89.4	87.1	10.6
1975	1,335.0	147.6	1,187.4	1,061.9	1,034.4	23.7	3.8	125.6	89.4	87.1	10.6
1976	1,474.8	172.3	1,302.5	1,180.2	1,151.9	23.9	4.4	122.3	90.6	88.4	9.4
1977	1,633.2	197.5	1,435.7	1,310.4	1,278.6	27.0	4.8	125.3	91.3	89.1	8.7
1978	1,837.7	229.4	1,608.3	1,465.8	1,428.5	31.9	5.4	142.5	91.1	88.8	8.9
1979	2,062.2	268.7	1,793.5	1,634.4	1,592.2	36.2	5.9	159.1	91.1	88.8	8.9
1980	2,307.9	298.9	2,009.0	1,807.5	1,757.1	43.6	6.8	201.4	90.0	87.5	10.0
1981	2,591.3	345.2	2,246.1	2,001.8	1,941.1	49.3	11.4	244.3	89.1	86.4	10.9
1982	2,775.3	354.1	2,421.2	2,150.4	2,077.3	59.5	13.6	270.8	88.8	85.8	11.2
1983	2,960.7	352.3	2,608.4	2,374.8	2,290.6	69.2	15.0	233.6	91.0	87.8	9.0
1984	3,289.5	377.4	2,912.0	2,597.3	2,503.3	77.0	16.9	314.8	89.2	86.0	10.8
1985	3,526.7	417.4	3,109.3	2,829.3	2,720.3	90.4	18.6	280.0	91.0	87.5	9.0
1986	3,722.4	437.3	3,285.1	3,016.7	2,899.7	96.1	20.9	268.4	91.8	88.3	8.2
1987	3,947.4	489.1	3,458.3	3,216.9	3,100.2	93.6	23.1	241.4	93.0	89.6	7.0
1988	4,253.7	505.0	3,748.7	3,475.8	3,353.6	96.8	25.4	272.9	92.7	89.5	7.3
1989	4,587.8	566.1	4,021.7	3,734.5	3,598.5	108.2	27.8	287.1	92.9	89.5	7.1
1990	4,878.6	592.8	4,285.8	3,986.4	3,839.9	116.1	30.4	299.4	93.0	89.6	7.0
1991	5,051.0	586.7	4,464.3	4,140.1	3,986.1	118.5	35.6	324.2	92.7	89.3	7.3
1992	5,362.0	610.6	4,751.4	4,385.4	4,235.3	111.8	38.3	366.0	92.3	89.1	7.7
1993	5,558.5	646.6	4,911.9	4,627.9	4,477.9	107.3	42.7	284.0	94.2	91.2	5.8
1994	5,842.5	690.7	5,151.8	4,902.4	4,743.3	112.8	46.3	249.5	95.2	92.1	4.8
1995	6,152.3	744.1	5,408.2	5,157.3	4,975.8	132.7	48.9	250.9	95.4	92.0	4.6
1996	6,520.6	832.1	5,688.5	5,460.0	5,256.8	150.3	52.9	228.4	96.0	92.4	4.0
1997	6,915.1	926.3	5,988.8	5,770.5	5,547.4	163.9	59.2	218.3	96.4	92.6	3.6
1998	7,423.0	1,027.0	6,395.9	6,119.1	5,879.5	174.5	65.2	276.8	95.7	91.9	4.3
1999	7,802.4	1,107.5	6,695.0	6,536.4	6,282.5	181.0	73.0	158.6	97.6	93.8	2.4
2000	8,429.7	1,235.7	7,194.0	7,025.6	6,739.4	204.7	81.5	168.5	97.7	93.7	2.3
2001	8,713.1	1,243.7	7,469.4	7,342.2	7,045.4	209.1	87.7	127.2	98.3	94.3	1.7
2002	8,910.3	1,053.1	7,857.2	7,674.0	7,385.3	194.7	94.0	183.2	97.7	94.0	2.3
1999: I	7,658.4	1,071.7	6,586.7	6,346.3	6,101.7	174.6	70.0	240.4	96.4	92.6	3.6
II	7,728.8	1,090.2	6,638.6	6,489.5	6,237.2	179.4	72.8	149.1	97.8	94.0	2.2
III	7,823.7	1,115.5	6,708.2	6,593.2	6,337.2	182.0	74.0	115.0	98.3	94.5	1.7
IV	7,998.8	1,152.5	6,846.2	6,716.6	6,453.7	187.8	75.0	129.7	98.1	94.3	1.9
2000: I	8,266.2	1,207.0	7,059.2	6,888.0	6,613.9	194.1	79.9	171.2	97.6	93.7	2.4
II	8,372.3	1,231.1	7,141.2	6,970.0	6,688.1	201.0	81.0	171.3	97.6	93.7	2.4
III	8,514.4	1,248.0	7,266.4	7,076.3	6,783.9	210.4	82.0	190.1	97.4	93.4	2.6
IV	8,565.8	1,256.6	7,309.3	7,168.1	6,871.6	213.3	83.1	141.2	98.1	94.0	1.9
2001: I	8,663.5	1,302.1	7,361.3	7,219.7	6,934.3	209.9	75.4	141.7	98.1	94.2	1.9
II	8,690.2	1,308.7	7,381.6	7,302.3	7,017.4	211.9	73.0	79.3	98.9	95.1	1.1
III	8,727.4	1,120.9	7,606.4	7,395.7	7,058.1	211.0	126.7	210.7	97.2	92.8	2.8
IV	8,771.2	1,243.0	7,528.1	7,451.0	7,171.6	203.6	75.8	77.1	99.0	95.3	1.0
2002: I	8,803.6	1,069.9	7,733.7	7,538.1	7,256.5	196.1	85.5	195.6	97.5	93.8	2.5
II	8,912.2	1,043.7	7,868.6	7,646.8	7,355.5	198.9	92.5	221.7	97.2	93.5	2.8
III	8,944.0	1,053.0	7,891.0	7,722.0	7,428.2	196.2	97.6	169.0	97.9	94.1	2.1
IV	8,981.3	1,045.6	7,935.6	7,789.2	7,501.2	187.7	100.3	146.4	98.2	94.5	1.8
2003: I	9,048.7	1,009.4	8,039.2	7,888.3	7,600.7	186.2	101.3	151.0	98.1	94.5	1.9
II	9,145.9	1,000.2	8,145.8	7,956.7	7,673.6	183.2	100.0	189.0	97.7	94.2	2.3
III	9,242.5	936.0	8,306.6	8,118.5	7,836.3	184.6	97.6	188.1	97.7	94.3	2.0

[1] Consists of nonmortgage interest paid by households.
[2] Percents based on data in millions of dollars.

Source: Department of Commerce, Bureau of Economic Analysis.

TABLE B–31.—*Total and per capita disposable personal income and personal consumption expenditures, and per capita gross domestic product, in current and real dollars, 1959–2003*

[Quarterly data at seasonally adjusted annual rates, except as noted]

Year or quarter	Disposable personal income				Personal consumption expenditures				Gross domestic product per capita (dollars)		Population (thousands)[1]
	Total (billions of dollars)		Per capita (dollars)		Total (billions of dollars)		Per capita (dollars)				
	Current dollars	Chained (2000) dollars	Current dollars	Chained (2000) dollars	Current dollars	Chained (2000) dollars	Current dollars	Chained (2000) dollars	Current dollars	Chained (2000) dollars	
1959	350.5	1,715.5	1,979	9,685	317.6	1,554.6	1,793	8,776	2,860	13,782	177,130
1960	365.4	1,759.7	2,022	9,735	331.7	1,597.4	1,835	8,837	2,912	13,840	180,760
1961	381.8	1,819.2	2,078	9,901	342.1	1,630.3	1,862	8,873	2,965	13,932	183,742
1962	405.1	1,908.2	2,171	10,227	363.3	1,711.1	1,947	9,170	3,139	14,552	186,590
1963	425.1	1,979.1	2,246	10,455	382.7	1,781.6	2,022	9,412	3,263	14,971	189,300
1964	462.5	2,122.8	2,410	11,061	411.4	1,888.4	2,144	9,839	3,458	15,624	191,927
1965	498.1	2,253.3	2,563	11,594	443.8	2,007.7	2,283	10,331	3,700	16,420	194,347
1966	537.5	2,371.9	2,734	12,065	480.9	2,121.8	2,446	10,793	4,007	17,290	196,599
1967	575.3	2,475.9	2,895	12,457	507.8	2,185.0	2,555	10,994	4,189	17,533	198,752
1968	625.0	2,588.0	3,114	12,892	558.0	2,310.5	2,780	11,510	4,533	18,196	200,745
1969	674.0	2,668.7	3,324	13,163	605.2	2,396.4	2,985	11,820	4,857	18,573	202,736
1970	735.7	2,781.7	3,587	13,563	648.5	2,451.9	3,162	11,955	5,064	18,391	205,089
1971	801.8	2,907.9	3,860	14,001	701.9	2,545.5	3,379	12,256	5,427	18,771	207,692
1972	869.1	3,046.5	4,140	14,512	770.6	2,701.3	3,671	12,868	5,899	19,555	209,924
1973	978.3	3,252.3	4,616	15,345	852.4	2,833.8	4,022	13,371	6,524	20,484	211,939
1974	1,071.6	3,228.5	5,010	15,094	933.4	2,812.3	4,364	13,148	7,013	20,195	213,898
1975	1,187.4	3,302.6	5,498	15,291	1,034.4	2,876.9	4,789	13,320	7,586	19,961	215,981
1976	1,302.5	3,432.2	5,972	15,738	1,151.9	3,035.5	5,282	13,919	8,369	20,822	218,086
1977	1,435.7	3,552.9	6,517	16,128	1,278.6	3,164.1	5,804	14,364	9,219	21,565	220,289
1978	1,608.3	3,718.8	7,224	16,704	1,428.5	3,303.1	6,417	14,837	10,307	22,526	222,629
1979	1,793.5	3,811.2	7,967	16,931	1,592.2	3,383.4	7,073	15,030	11,387	22,982	225,106
1980	2,009.0	3,857.7	8,822	16,940	1,757.1	3,374.1	7,716	14,816	12,249	22,666	227,726
1981	2,246.1	3,960.0	9,765	17,217	1,941.1	3,422.2	8,439	14,879	13,601	23,007	230,008
1982	2,421.2	4,044.9	10,426	17,418	2,077.3	3,470.3	8,945	14,944	14,017	22,346	232,218
1983	2,608.4	4,177.7	11,131	17,828	2,290.6	3,668.6	9,775	15,656	15,092	23,146	234,333
1984	2,912.0	4,494.1	12,319	19,011	2,503.3	3,863.3	10,589	16,343	16,638	24,593	236,394
1985	3,109.3	4,645.2	13,037	19,476	2,720.3	4,064.0	11,406	17,040	17,695	25,382	238,506
1986	3,285.1	4,791.0	13,649	19,906	2,899.7	4,228.9	12,048	17,570	18,542	26,024	240,683
1987	3,458.3	4,874.5	14,241	20,072	3,100.2	4,369.8	12,766	17,994	19,517	26,664	242,843
1988	3,748.7	5,082.6	15,297	20,740	3,353.6	4,546.9	13,685	18,554	20,827	27,514	245,061
1989	4,021.7	5,224.8	16,257	21,120	3,598.5	4,675.0	14,546	18,898	22,169	28,221	247,387
1990	4,285.8	5,324.2	17,131	21,281	3,839.9	4,770.3	15,349	19,067	23,195	28,429	250,181
1991	4,464.3	5,351.7	17,609	21,109	3,986.1	4,778.4	15,722	18,848	23,650	28,007	253,530
1992	4,751.4	5,536.3	18,494	21,548	4,235.3	4,934.8	16,485	19,208	24,668	28,556	256,922
1993	4,911.9	5,594.2	18,872	21,493	4,477.9	5,099.8	17,204	19,593	25,578	28,940	260,282
1994	5,151.8	5,746.4	19,555	21,812	4,743.3	5,290.7	18,004	20,082	26,844	29,741	263,455
1995	5,408.2	5,905.7	20,287	22,153	4,975.8	5,433.5	18,665	20,382	27,749	30,128	266,588
1996	5,688.5	6,080.9	21,091	22,546	5,256.8	5,619.4	19,490	20,835	28,982	30,881	269,714
1997	5,988.8	6,295.8	22,046	23,065	5,547.4	5,831.8	20,323	21,365	30,424	31,886	272,958
1998	6,395.9	6,663.9	23,161	24,131	5,879.5	6,125.8	21,291	22,183	31,674	32,833	276,154
1999	6,695.0	6,861.3	23,968	24,564	6,282.5	6,438.6	22,491	23,050	33,181	33,904	279,328
2000	7,194.0	7,194.0	25,467	25,467	6,739.4	6,739.4	23,858	23,858	34,753	34,753	282,479
2001	7,469.4	7,320.2	26,156	25,633	7,045.4	6,904.6	24,671	24,178	35,370	34,550	285,574
2002	7,857.2	7,596.7	27,223	26,320	7,385.3	7,140.4	25,588	24,739	36,313	34,934	288,627
1999: I	6,586.7	6,812.9	23,684	24,498	6,101.7	6,311.3	21,941	22,694	32,602	33,497	278,103
II	6,638.6	6,822.1	23,806	24,464	6,237.2	6,409.7	22,367	22,985	32,898	33,682	278,864
III	6,708.2	6,856.0	23,979	24,507	6,337.2	6,476.7	22,653	23,152	33,292	33,967	279,751
IV	6,846.2	6,955.6	24,399	24,789	6,453.7	6,556.8	23,000	23,368	33,926	34,467	280,592
2000: I	7,059.2	7,109.7	25,094	25,274	6,613.9	6,661.3	23,511	23,680	34,231	34,466	281,308
II	7,141.2	7,157.5	25,320	25,378	6,688.1	6,703.3	23,713	23,768	34,828	34,917	282,037
III	7,266.4	7,249.3	25,683	25,627	6,783.9	6,768.0	23,982	23,926	34,864	34,774	282,873
IV	7,309.3	7,259.6	25,764	25,589	6,871.6	6,825.0	24,222	24,057	35,085	34,853	283,699
2001: I	7,361.3	7,254.6	25,884	25,508	6,934.3	6,833.7	24,382	24,028	35,249	34,747	284,402
II	7,381.6	7,228.8	25,887	25,352	7,017.4	6,872.2	24,610	24,101	35,380	34,602	285,142
III	7,606.4	7,440.6	26,599	26,019	7,058.1	6,904.2	24,681	24,143	35,305	34,390	285,970
IV	7,528.1	7,356.6	26,250	25,652	7,171.6	7,008.2	25,007	24,438	35,546	34,464	286,781
2002: I	7,733.7	7,544.8	26,903	26,246	7,256.5	7,079.2	25,243	24,626	35,932	34,779	287,468
II	7,868.6	7,621.5	27,302	26,445	7,355.5	7,124.5	25,522	24,721	36,184	34,854	288,202
III	7,891.0	7,605.2	27,303	26,314	7,428.2	7,159.2	25,701	24,771	36,475	35,044	289,019
IV	7,935.6	7,615.8	27,386	26,278	7,501.2	7,198.9	25,882	24,840	36,657	35,059	289,818
2003: I	8,039.2	7,662.0	27,675	26,376	7,600.7	7,244.1	26,165	24,937	36,957	35,149	290,492
II	8,145.8	7,753.5	27,971	26,624	7,673.6	7,304.0	26,350	25,081	37,245	35,328	291,221
III	8,306.6	7,872.3	28,443	26,956	7,836.3	7,426.6	26,833	25,430	38,032	35,930	292,043

[1] Population of the United States including Armed Forces overseas; includes Alaska and Hawaii beginning 1960. Annual data are averages of quarterly data. Quarterly data are averages for the period.

Source: Department of Commerce (Bureau of Economic Analysis and Bureau of the Census).

TABLE B–32.—*Gross saving and investment, 1959–2003*

[Billions of dollars, except as noted; quarterly data at seasonally adjusted annual rates]

Year or quarter	Total gross saving	Gross saving									Consumption of fixed capital		
			Net saving										
		Total net saving	Net private saving				Net government saving			Total	Private	Government
			Total	Personal saving	Undistributed corporate profits [1]	Wage accruals less disbursements	Total	Federal	State and local			
1959	106.2	53.2	46.0	26.7	19.4	0.0	7.1	3.3	3.8	53.0	38.6	14.5
1960	111.3	55.8	44.3	26.7	17.6	.0	11.5	7.2	4.3	55.6	40.5	15.0
1961	114.3	57.1	50.2	32.2	18.1	.0	6.9	2.6	4.3	57.2	41.6	15.6
1962	124.9	65.7	57.9	33.8	24.1	.0	7.8	2.5	5.2	59.3	42.8	16.5
1963	133.2	70.8	59.7	33.3	26.4	.0	11.1	5.4	5.7	62.4	44.9	17.5
1964	143.4	78.4	71.0	40.8	30.1	.0	7.4	1.0	6.4	65.0	46.9	18.1
1965	158.5	89.1	79.2	43.0	36.2	.0	9.9	3.3	6.5	69.4	50.5	18.9
1966	168.7	93.1	83.1	44.4	38.7	.0	10.0	2.3	7.8	75.6	55.5	20.1
1967	170.5	89.0	91.4	54.4	36.9	.0	-2.4	-9.4	7.0	81.5	59.9	21.6
1968	182.0	93.6	88.4	52.8	35.6	.0	5.2	-2.3	7.5	88.4	65.2	23.1
1969	198.3	100.4	83.7	52.5	31.2	.0	16.7	8.7	8.0	97.9	73.1	24.8
1970	192.7	86.0	94.0	69.5	24.6	.0	-8.1	-15.2	7.1	106.7	80.0	26.7
1971	208.9	93.9	115.8	80.6	34.8	.4	-21.9	-28.4	6.5	115.0	86.7	28.3
1972	237.5	111.0	119.8	77.2	42.9	-.3	-8.8	-24.4	15.6	126.5	97.1	29.5
1973	292.0	152.7	148.3	102.7	45.6	.0	4.4	-11.3	15.7	139.3	107.9	31.4
1974	301.5	139.0	143.4	113.6	29.8	.0	-4.4	-13.8	9.3	162.5	126.6	35.9
1975	297.0	109.2	175.8	125.6	50.2	.0	-66.6	-69.0	2.5	187.7	147.8	40.0
1976	342.1	137.0	181.3	122.3	59.0	.0	-44.4	-51.7	7.4	205.2	162.5	42.6
1977	397.5	167.5	198.5	125.3	73.2	.0	-31.0	-44.1	13.1	230.0	184.3	45.7
1978	478.0	215.7	223.5	142.5	81.0	.0	-7.8	-26.5	18.7	262.3	212.8	49.5
1979	536.7	236.6	234.9	159.1	75.7	.0	1.7	-11.3	13.0	300.1	245.7	54.5
1980	549.4	206.5	251.3	201.4	49.9	.0	-44.8	-53.6	8.8	343.0	281.1	61.8
1981	654.7	266.6	312.3	244.3	68.0	.0	-45.7	-53.3	7.6	388.1	317.9	70.1
1982	629.1	202.2	336.2	270.8	65.4	.0	-134.1	-131.9	-2.2	426.9	349.8	77.1
1983	609.4	165.6	333.7	233.6	100.1	.0	-168.1	-173.0	4.9	443.8	362.1	81.7
1984	773.4	300.9	445.0	314.8	130.3	.0	-144.1	-168.1	23.9	472.6	385.6	87.0
1985	767.5	260.7	413.4	280.0	133.4	.0	-152.6	-175.0	22.3	506.7	414.0	92.7
1986	733.5	202.2	372.0	268.4	103.7	.0	-169.9	-190.8	21.0	531.3	431.8	99.5
1987	796.8	234.9	367.4	241.4	126.1	.0	-132.6	-145.0	12.4	561.9	455.3	106.7
1988	915.0	317.4	434.0	272.9	161.1	.0	-116.6	-134.5	17.9	597.6	483.5	114.1
1989	944.7	300.4	409.7	287.1	122.6	.0	-109.3	-130.1	20.8	644.3	522.1	122.2
1990	940.4	258.0	422.7	299.4	123.3	.0	-164.8	-172.0	7.2	682.5	551.6	130.9
1991	964.1	238.2	456.1	324.2	131.9	.0	-217.9	-213.7	-4.2	725.9	586.9	139.1
1992	948.2	196.3	493.0	366.0	142.7	-15.8	-296.7	-297.4	.7	751.9	607.3	144.6
1993	962.4	186.0	458.6	284.0	168.1	6.4	-272.6	-273.5	.9	776.4	624.7	151.8
1994	1,070.7	237.1	438.9	249.5	171.8	17.6	-201.9	-212.3	10.5	833.7	675.1	158.6
1995	1,184.5	306.2	491.1	250.9	223.8	16.4	-184.9	-197.0	12.0	878.4	713.4	165.0
1996	1,291.1	373.0	489.0	228.4	256.9	3.6	-116.0	-141.8	25.8	918.1	748.8	169.3
1997	1,461.1	486.6	503.3	218.3	287.9	-2.9	-16.7	-55.8	39.1	974.4	800.3	174.1
1998	1,598.7	568.6	477.8	276.8	201.7	-.7	90.8	38.8	52.0	1,030.2	851.2	179.0
1999	1,674.3	573.0	419.0	158.6	255.3	5.2	154.0	103.6	50.4	1,101.3	914.3	187.0
2000	1,770.5	582.7	343.3	168.5	174.8	.0	239.4	189.5	50.0	1,187.8	990.8	197.0
2001	1,658.0	391.1	323.2	127.2	196.0	.0	67.8	50.5	17.3	1,266.9	1,061.0	205.9
2002	1,539.4	250.8	494.0	183.2	310.8	.0	-243.3	-240.0	-3.2	1,288.6	1,077.8	210.8
1999: I	1,696.7	627.2	498.8	240.4	253.2	5.2	128.4	79.4	49.0	1,069.5	886.1	183.4
II	1,650.6	563.6	413.7	149.1	259.4	5.2	149.9	104.6	45.3	1,087.0	901.2	185.8
III	1,648.1	527.9	368.1	115.0	247.9	5.2	159.8	107.8	52.0	1,120.3	932.3	188.0
IV	1,701.6	573.3	395.3	129.7	260.5	5.2	178.0	122.7	55.3	1,128.3	937.6	190.6
2000: I	1,784.5	631.4	362.8	171.2	191.6	.0	268.7	212.7	55.9	1,153.1	959.6	193.4
II	1,772.4	595.4	354.5	171.3	183.2	.0	240.9	181.4	59.5	1,177.0	981.0	196.0
III	1,795.1	595.2	355.0	190.1	164.9	.0	240.2	191.2	49.0	1,199.9	1,001.6	198.3
IV	1,730.0	508.7	300.8	141.2	159.6	.0	207.9	172.5	35.4	1,221.3	1,021.1	200.2
2001: I	1,720.8	490.4	298.3	141.7	156.6	.0	192.2	156.1	36.1	1,230.4	1,028.4	202.0
II	1,649.7	392.7	239.2	79.3	159.9	.0	153.6	128.9	24.6	1,257.0	1,053.2	203.8
III	1,606.3	289.0	357.5	210.7	146.8	.0	-68.5	-80.1	11.6	1,317.3	1,106.0	211.3
IV	1,655.2	392.1	398.0	77.1	320.9	.0	-5.9	-2.8	-3.0	1,263.1	1,056.6	206.5
2002: I	1,587.2	315.7	511.8	195.6	316.3	.0	-196.2	-188.8	-7.4	1,271.6	1,063.2	208.4
II	1,575.8	289.1	533.0	221.7	311.3	.0	-244.0	-232.0	-11.9	1,286.8	1,076.7	210.1
III	1,525.6	229.7	465.9	169.0	296.9	.0	-236.1	-242.9	6.8	1,295.8	1,084.2	211.6
IV	1,469.0	168.5	465.3	146.4	318.9	.0	-296.8	-296.3	-.4	1,300.4	1,087.1	213.3
2003: I	1,388.5	82.8	443.9	151.0	292.9	.0	-361.0	-320.4	-40.6	1,305.7	1,090.4	215.3
II	1,436.9	133.5	572.9	189.0	383.8	.0	-439.3	-424.7	-14.7	1,303.4	1,086.0	217.4
III	1,470.2	161.1	647.4	188.1	459.3	.0	-486.3	-499.4	13.1	1,309.1	1,089.9	219.2

[1] With inventory valuation and capital consumption adjustments.

See next page for continuation of table.

TABLE B–32.—*Gross saving and investment, 1959–2003*—Continued

[Billions of dollars, except as noted; quarterly data at seasonally adjusted annual rates]

Year or quarter	Gross domestic investment, capital account transactions, and net lending, NIPA							Addenda:						
	Gross domestic investment				Capital account transactions (net)	Net lending or net borrowing (−), NIPA³	Statistical discrepancy	Gross private saving	Gross government saving			Net domestic investment	Gross saving as a percent of gross national income	Net saving as a percent of gross national income
	Total	Total	Gross private domestic investment	Gross government investment²					Total	Federal	State and local			
1959	106.7	107.8	78.5	29.3		−1.2	0.5	84.6	21.6	13.6	8.0	54.8	20.9	10.4
1960	110.4	107.2	78.9	28.3		3.2	−.9	84.8	26.5	17.8	8.7	51.6	21.0	10.5
1961	113.8	109.5	78.2	31.3		4.3	−.6	91.8	22.5	13.5	9.0	52.3	20.8	10.4
1962	125.3	121.4	88.1	33.3		3.9	.4	100.7	24.3	14.0	10.3	62.2	21.2	11.1
1963	132.4	127.4	93.8	33.6		5.0	−.8	104.6	28.6	17.5	11.1	65.0	21.4	11.4
1964	144.2	136.7	102.1	34.6		7.5	.8	117.9	25.5	13.4	12.1	71.7	21.5	11.7
1965	160.0	153.8	118.2	35.6		6.2	1.6	129.7	28.8	16.0	12.8	84.4	21.9	12.3
1966	175.0	171.1	131.3	39.8		3.9	6.3	138.6	30.1	15.5	14.6	95.5	21.4	11.8
1967	175.1	171.6	128.6	43.0		3.6	4.6	151.3	19.2	4.7	14.5	90.1	20.5	10.7
1968	186.6	184.8	141.2	43.6		1.7	4.6	153.7	28.3	12.5	15.8	96.5	20.0	10.3
1969	201.5	199.7	156.4	43.3		1.8	3.2	156.8	41.5	24.2	17.3	101.8	20.1	10.2
1970	200.0	196.0	152.4	43.6		4.0	7.3	174.1	18.6	.9	17.7	89.3	18.6	8.3
1971	220.5	219.9	178.2	41.8		.6	11.6	202.5	6.4	−11.9	18.3	104.9	18.6	8.4
1972	246.6	250.2	207.6	42.6		−3.6	9.1	216.8	20.7	−7.7	28.5	123.7	19.2	9.0
1973	300.7	291.3	244.5	46.8		9.3	8.6	256.3	35.8	5.8	30.0	152.1	21.1	11.0
1974	312.3	305.7	249.4	56.3		6.6	10.9	270.0	31.5	4.5	27.0	143.2	20.0	9.2
1975	314.7	293.3	230.2	63.1		21.4	17.7	323.6	−26.6	−49.3	22.7	105.6	18.2	6.7
1976	367.2	358.4	292.0	66.4		8.9	25.1	343.8	−1.7	−30.3	28.6	153.2	18.8	7.5
1977	419.8	428.8	361.3	67.5		−9.0	22.3	382.8	14.7	−21.0	35.7	198.8	19.6	8.3
1978	504.6	515.0	438.0	77.1		−10.4	26.6	436.3	41.7	−1.5	43.2	252.7	20.9	9.4
1979	582.8	581.4	492.9	88.5		1.4	46.0	480.5	56.2	15.7	40.5	281.2	21.1	9.3
1980	590.9	579.5	479.3	100.3		11.4	41.4	532.4	17.0	−23.6	40.6	236.6	19.7	7.4
1981	685.6	679.3	572.4	106.9		6.3	30.9	630.3	24.4	−19.4	43.9	291.2	20.9	8.5
1982	629.4	629.5	517.2	112.3	−0.2	.0	.3	686.0	−56.9	−94.2	37.3	202.6	19.1	6.1
1983	655.1	687.2	564.3	122.9	−.2	−31.8	45.7	695.8	−86.5	−132.3	45.8	243.4	17.3	4.7
1984	788.0	875.0	735.6	139.4	−.2	−86.7	14.6	830.6	−57.2	−123.5	66.3	402.4	19.6	7.6
1985	784.1	895.0	736.2	158.8	−.3	−110.5	16.7	827.3	−59.9	−126.9	67.0	388.3	18.1	6.2
1986	780.5	919.7	746.5	173.2	−.3	−138.9	47.0	803.9	−70.4	−139.2	68.8	388.4	16.5	4.6
1987	818.5	969.2	785.0	184.3	−.4	−150.4	21.7	822.7	−25.9	−89.8	63.9	407.3	16.8	5.0
1988	895.5	1,007.7	821.6	186.1	−.5	−111.7	−19.5	917.5	−2.5	−75.2	72.7	410.1	17.8	6.2
1989	984.3	1,072.6	874.9	197.7	−.3	−88.0	39.7	931.8	12.9	−66.7	79.6	428.4	17.3	5.5
1990	1,006.7	1,076.7	861.0	215.7	6.6	−76.6	66.2	974.3	−33.8	−104.1	70.3	394.2	16.3	4.5
1991	1,036.6	1,023.2	802.9	220.3	4.5	9.0	72.5	1,042.9	−78.8	−141.5	62.7	297.3	16.2	4.0
1992	1,051.0	1,087.9	864.8	223.1	.6	−37.5	102.7	1,100.4	−152.1	−222.7	70.6	336.0	15.1	3.1
1993	1,102.0	1,172.4	953.4	219.0	1.3	−71.7	139.5	1,083.3	−120.8	−195.5	74.7	395.9	14.7	2.8
1994	1,213.2	1,318.4	1,097.1	221.4	1.7	−106.9	142.5	1,114.0	−43.2	−132.2	88.9	484.7	15.4	3.4
1995	1,285.7	1,376.7	1,144.0	232.7	.9	−91.9	101.2	1,204.5	−19.9	−115.1	95.2	498.4	16.2	4.2
1996	1,384.8	1,485.2	1,240.3	244.9	.7	−101.0	93.7	1,237.8	53.3	−59.7	113.0	567.1	16.6	4.8
1997	1,531.7	1,641.9	1,389.8	252.2	1.0	−111.3	70.7	1,303.6	157.5	26.7	130.7	667.5	17.7	5.9
1998	1,584.1	1,771.5	1,509.1	262.4	.7	−188.1	−14.6	1,328.9	269.8	121.6	148.2	741.3	18.2	6.5
1999	1,638.5	1,912.4	1,625.7	286.8	4.8	−278.7	−35.7	1,333.3	341.0	188.5	152.5	811.2	17.9	6.1
2000	1,643.3	2,040.0	1,735.5	304.5	.8	−397.4	−127.2	1,334.1	436.4	276.6	159.8	852.1	17.7	5.8
2001	1,545.8	1,924.2	1,607.2	317.0	1.1	−379.5	−112.2	1,384.3	273.7	138.8	135.0	657.3	16.2	3.8
2002	1,462.2	1,926.3	1,589.2	337.1	1.3	−465.4	−77.2	1,571.8	−32.4	−150.9	118.5	637.7	14.6	2.4
1999: I	1,650.3	1,871.1	1,596.7	274.4	.8	−221.6	−46.5	1,384.9	311.9	163.3	148.6	801.6	18.6	6.9
II	1,612.2	1,874.2	1,589.9	284.4	.7	−262.7	−38.4	1,314.9	335.7	189.1	146.6	787.2	17.8	6.1
III	1,616.5	1,916.6	1,628.3	288.3	.7	−300.8	−31.6	1,300.4	347.7	192.9	154.8	796.4	17.6	5.6
IV	1,675.2	1,987.8	1,687.7	300.1	17.2	−329.9	−26.4	1,333.0	368.6	208.5	160.1	859.5	17.8	6.0
2000: I	1,612.8	1,975.6	1,672.3	303.3	.8	−363.6	−171.7	1,322.4	462.1	299.4	162.7	822.6	18.1	6.4
II	1,704.6	2,085.7	1,781.7	304.0	.8	−381.9	−67.8	1,335.5	437.0	268.4	168.6	908.7	17.9	6.0
III	1,630.6	2,054.0	1,749.0	305.0	.9	−424.3	−164.6	1,356.6	438.5	278.7	159.8	854.1	17.8	5.9
IV	1,625.4	2,044.5	1,738.9	305.6	.8	−419.9	−104.6	1,321.9	408.1	260.1	147.9	823.3	17.1	5.0
2001: I	1,600.3	2,000.7	1,688.3	312.4	1.1	−401.5	−120.6	1,326.7	394.2	244.0	150.2	770.3	16.9	4.8
II	1,562.0	1,948.7	1,620.3	328.4	1.0	−387.7	−87.7	1,292.4	357.3	217.2	140.1	691.7	16.2	3.8
III	1,502.1	1,901.0	1,594.3	306.6	1.1	−400.0	−104.1	1,463.5	142.8	8.3	134.5	583.7	15.7	2.8
IV	1,518.7	1,846.6	1,526.1	320.5	1.0	−328.8	−136.5	1,454.6	200.7	85.5	115.2	583.5	15.9	3.8
2002: I	1,476.5	1,884.3	1,553.1	331.3	1.1	−408.9	−110.7	1,575.0	12.2	−100.2	112.4	612.8	15.2	3.0
II	1,443.9	1,918.0	1,580.9	337.1	1.1	−475.3	−132.0	1,609.7	−33.9	−143.2	109.3	631.2	14.9	2.7
III	1,475.3	1,949.2	1,608.2	341.0	1.5	−475.4	−50.3	1,550.1	−24.6	−153.8	129.2	653.4	14.4	2.2
IV	1,453.3	1,953.8	1,614.7	339.0	1.4	−501.9	−15.7	1,552.4	−83.4	−206.5	123.1	653.3	13.8	1.6
2003: I	1,411.7	1,941.0	1,605.3	335.8	1.6	−530.9	23.2	1,534.3	−145.7	−230.4	84.7	635.3	12.9	.8
II	1,428.6	1,968.8	1,624.3	344.5	1.3	−541.5	−8.3	1,658.9	−222.0	−334.1	112.2	665.4	13.2	1.2
III	1,524.1	2,042.6	1,689.1	353.5	3.2	−521.6	54.0	1,737.3	−267.1	−408.2	141.0	733.5	13.3	1.5

² For details on government investment, see Table B–20.

³ Prior to 1982, equals the balance on current account, NIPA (see Table B–24).

Source: Department of Commerce, Bureau of Economic Analysis.

TABLE B–33.—*Median money income (in 2002 dollars) and poverty status of families and persons, by race, selected years, 1988–2002*

Year	Families[1] Number (millions)	Median money income (in 2002 dollars)[2]	Below poverty level Total Number (millions)	Total Percent	Female householder Number (millions)	Female householder Percent	Persons below poverty level Number (millions)	Persons Percent	Median money income (2002 dollars) of persons 15 years old and over with income[2] Males All persons	Males Year-round full-time workers	Females All persons	Females Year-round full-time workers
ALL RACES												
1988	65.8	$47,021	6.9	10.4	3.6	33.4	31.7	13.0	$27,619	$39,938	$12,977	$27,088
1989	66.1	47,916	6.8	10.3	3.5	32.2	31.5	12.8	27,861	39,802	13,479	27,504
1990	66.3	47,167	7.1	10.7	3.8	33.4	33.6	13.5	27,075	38,663	13,435	27,472
1991	67.2	46,275	7.7	11.5	4.2	35.6	35.7	14.2	26,356	39,055	13,489	27,355
1992[3]	68.2	45,940	8.1	11.9	4.3	35.4	38.0	14.8	25,694	38,729	13,458	27,751
1993	68.5	45,295	8.4	12.3	4.4	35.6	39.3	15.1	25,862	38,086	13,537	27,537
1994	69.3	46,549	8.1	11.6	4.2	34.6	38.1	14.5	26,070	37,943	13,762	27,924
1995	69.6	47,588	7.5	10.8	4.1	32.4	36.4	13.8	26,438	37,731	14,214	27,862
1996	70.2	48,272	7.7	11.0	4.2	32.6	36.5	13.7	27,199	38,273	14,624	28,455
1997	70.9	49,797	7.3	10.3	4.0	31.6	35.6	13.3	28,170	39,383	15,311	29,083
1998	71.6	51,495	7.2	10.0	3.8	29.9	34.5	12.7	29,189	39,943	15,899	29,589
1999[4]	73.2	52,694	6.8	9.3	3.6	27.8	32.8	11.9	29,452	40,413	16,515	29,531
2000[5]	73.8	52,977	6.4	8.7	3.3	25.4	31.6	11.3	29,597	40,612	16,774	30,412
2001	74.3	52,225	6.8	9.2	3.5	26.4	32.9	11.7	29,564	40,774	16,878	30,904
2002	75.6	51,680	7.2	9.6	3.6	26.5	34.6	12.1	29,238	40,507	16,812	30,970
WHITE												
1988	56.5	49,539	4.5	7.9	1.9	26.5	20.7	10.1	29,154	41,282	13,297	27,494
1989	56.6	50,384	4.4	7.8	1.9	25.4	20.8	10.0	29,219	41,557	13,742	27,830
1990	56.8	49,251	4.6	8.1	2.0	26.8	22.3	10.7	28,245	40,134	13,765	27,803
1991	57.2	48,650	5.0	8.8	2.2	28.4	23.7	11.3	27,548	39,855	13,804	27,754
1992[3]	57.7	48,574	5.3	9.1	2.2	28.5	25.3	11.9	26,888	39,649	13,771	28,073
1993	57.9	48,164	5.5	9.4	2.4	29.2	26.2	12.2	26,939	39,012	13,807	28,162
1994	58.4	49,072	5.3	9.1	2.3	29.0	25.4	11.7	27,209	38,937	13,959	28,679
1995	58.9	49,973	5.0	8.5	2.2	26.6	24.4	11.2	28,000	39,273	14,432	28,433
1996	58.9	51,074	5.1	8.6	2.3	27.3	24.7	11.2	28,471	39,646	14,791	28,938
1997	59.5	52,239	5.0	8.4	2.3	27.7	24.4	11.0	29,179	40,355	15,410	29,575
1998	60.1	54,014	4.8	8.0	2.1	24.9	23.5	10.5	30,461	40,983	16,105	30,084
1999[4]	61.1	55,120	4.4	7.3	1.9	22.5	22.2	9.8	30,932	42,314	16,566	30,215
2000[5]	61.3	55,376	4.3	7.1	1.8	21.2	21.6	9.5	31,116	42,035	16,791	31,277
2001	61.6	54,927	4.6	7.4	1.9	22.4	22.7	9.9	30,721	41,439	16,917	31,340
2002 Alone[6]	62.3	54,633	4.9	7.8	2.0	22.6	23.5	10.2	30,383	41,375	16,838	31,400
2002 Alone or in combination[6]	63.0	54,449	5.0	7.9	2.1	22.6	24.1	10.3	30,316	41,316	16,805	31,388
BLACK												
1988	7.4	28,233	2.1	28.2	1.6	49.0	9.4	31.3	17,592	30,259	10,735	24,637
1989	7.5	28,303	2.1	27.8	1.5	46.5	9.3	30.7	17,659	28,997	11,029	25,029
1990	7.5	28,582	2.2	29.3	1.6	48.1	9.8	31.9	17,168	28,660	11,111	24,741
1991	7.7	27,745	2.3	30.4	1.8	51.2	10.2	32.7	16,690	29,136	11,352	24,637
1992[3]	8.0	26,508	2.5	31.1	1.9	50.2	10.8	33.4	16,410	28,879	11,163	25,446
1993	8.0	26,401	2.5	31.3	1.9	49.9	10.9	33.1	17,899	28,881	11,653	24,897
1994	8.1	29,644	2.2	27.3	1.7	46.2	10.2	30.6	17,983	29,293	12,656	24,759
1995	8.1	30,432	2.1	26.4	1.7	45.1	9.9	29.3	18,756	29,059	12,844	24,701
1996	8.5	30,266	2.2	26.1	1.7	43.7	9.7	28.4	18,819	30,967	13,434	25,094
1997	8.4	31,958	2.0	23.6	1.6	39.8	9.1	26.5	20,219	30,053	14,579	25,435
1998	8.5	32,398	2.0	23.4	1.6	40.8	9.1	26.1	21,288	30,269	14,474	26,294
1999[4]	8.7	34,370	1.9	21.8	1.5	39.2	8.4	23.6	22,058	32,539	15,945	27,130
2000[5]	8.7	35,166	1.7	19.3	1.3	34.3	8.0	22.5	22,288	31,838	16,584	26,890
2001	8.8	34,132	1.8	20.7	1.4	35.2	8.1	22.7	21,807	32,429	16,541	27,737
2002 Alone[6]	8.9	33,525	1.9	21.5	1.4	35.8	8.6	24.1	21,561	31,932	16,729	27,625
2002 Alone or in combination[6]	9.1	33,634	2.0	21.4	1.5	35.7	8.9	23.9	21,509	31,966	16,671	27,703

[1] The term "family" refers to a group of two or more persons related by birth, marriage, or adoption and residing together. Every family must include a reference person.

[2] Current dollar median money income adjusted by CPI–U–RS.

[3] Based on 1990 census adjusted population controls; comparable with succeeding years.

[4] Reflects implementation of Census 2000-based population controls comparable with succeeding years.

[5] Reflects household sample expansion.

[6] Data are for white alone; for white alone or in combination; for black alone; and, for black alone or in combination. Beginning with data for 2002 the Current Population Survey allowed respondents to choose more than one race; for earlier years respondents could report only one race group.

Note.—Poverty rates (percent of persons below poverty level) for all races for years not shown above are: 1959, 22.4; 1960, 22.2; 1961, 21.9; 1962, 21.0; 1963, 19.5; 1964, 19.0; 1965, 17.3; 1966, 14.7; 1967, 14.2; 1968, 12.8; 1969, 12.1; 1970, 12.6; 1971, 12.5; 1972, 11.9; 1973, 11.1; 1974, 11.2; 1975, 12.3; 1976, 11.8; 1977, 11.6; 1978, 11.4; 1979, 11.7; 1980, 13.0; 1981, 14.0; 1982, 15.0; 1983, 15.2; 1984, 14.4; 1985, 14.0; 1986, 13.6; and 1987, 13.4.

Poverty thresholds are updated each year to reflect changes in the consumer price index (CPI–U).

For details see "Current Population Reports," Series P–60.

Source: Department of Commerce, Bureau of the Census.

TABLE B-34.—*Population by age group, 1929-2003*

[Thousands of persons]

July 1	Total	Age (years)						
		Under 5	5-15	16-19	20-24	25-44	45-64	65 and over
1929	121,767	11,734	26,800	9,127	10,694	35,862	21,076	6,474
1933	125,579	10,612	26,897	9,302	11,152	37,319	22,933	7,363
1939	130,880	10,418	25,179	9,822	11,519	39,354	25,823	8,764
1940	132,122	10,579	24,811	9,895	11,690	39,868	26,249	9,031
1941	133,402	10,850	24,516	9,840	11,807	40,383	26,718	9,288
1942	134,860	11,301	24,231	9,730	11,955	40,861	27,196	9,584
1943	136,739	12,016	24,093	9,607	12,064	41,420	27,671	9,867
1944	138,397	12,524	23,949	9,561	12,062	42,016	28,138	10,147
1945	139,928	12,979	23,907	9,361	12,036	42,521	28,630	10,494
1946	141,389	13,244	24,103	9,119	12,004	43,027	29,064	10,828
1947	144,126	14,406	24,468	9,097	11,814	43,657	29,498	11,185
1948	146,631	14,919	25,209	8,952	11,794	44,288	29,931	11,538
1949	149,188	15,607	25,852	8,788	11,700	44,916	30,405	11,921
1950	152,271	16,410	26,721	8,542	11,680	45,672	30,849	12,397
1951	154,878	17,333	27,279	8,446	11,552	46,103	31,362	12,803
1952	157,553	17,312	28,894	8,414	11,350	46,495	31,884	13,203
1953	160,184	17,638	30,227	8,460	11,062	46,786	32,394	13,617
1954	163,026	18,057	31,480	8,637	10,832	47,001	32,942	14,076
1955	165,931	18,566	32,682	8,744	10,714	47,194	33,506	14,525
1956	168,903	19,003	33,994	8,916	10,616	47,379	34,057	14,938
1957	171,984	19,494	35,272	9,195	10,603	47,440	34,591	15,388
1958	174,882	19,887	36,445	9,543	10,756	47,337	35,109	15,806
1959	177,830	20,175	37,368	10,215	10,969	47,192	35,663	16,248
1960	180,671	20,341	38,494	10,683	11,134	47,140	36,203	16,675
1961	183,691	20,522	39,765	11,025	11,483	47,084	36,722	17,089
1962	186,538	20,469	41,205	11,180	11,959	47,013	37,255	17,457
1963	189,242	20,342	41,626	12,007	12,714	46,994	37,782	17,778
1964	191,889	20,165	42,297	12,736	13,269	46,958	38,338	18,127
1965	194,303	19,824	42,938	13,516	13,746	46,912	38,916	18,451
1966	196,560	19,208	43,702	14,311	14,050	47,001	39,534	18,755
1967	198,712	18,563	44,244	14,200	15,248	47,194	40,193	19,071
1968	200,706	17,913	44,622	14,452	15,786	47,721	40,846	19,365
1969	202,677	17,376	44,840	14,800	16,480	48,064	41,437	19,680
1970	205,052	17,166	44,816	15,289	17,202	48,473	41,999	20,107
1971	207,661	17,244	44,591	15,688	18,159	48,936	42,482	20,561
1972	209,896	17,101	44,203	16,039	18,153	50,482	42,898	21,020
1973	211,909	16,851	43,582	16,446	18,521	51,749	43,235	21,525
1974	213,854	16,487	42,989	16,769	18,975	53,051	43,522	22,061
1975	215,973	16,121	42,508	17,017	19,527	54,302	43,801	22,696
1976	218,035	15,617	42,099	17,194	19,986	55,852	44,008	23,278
1977	220,239	15,564	41,298	17,276	20,499	57,561	44,150	23,892
1978	222,585	15,735	40,428	17,288	20,946	59,400	44,286	24,502
1979	225,055	16,063	39,552	17,242	21,297	61,379	44,390	25,134
1980	227,726	16,451	38,838	17,167	21,590	63,470	44,504	25,707
1981	229,966	16,893	38,144	16,812	21,869	65,528	44,500	26,221
1982	232,188	17,228	37,784	16,332	21,902	67,692	44,462	26,787
1983	234,307	17,547	37,526	15,823	21,844	69,733	44,474	27,361
1984	236,348	17,695	37,461	15,295	21,737	71,735	44,547	27,878
1985	238,466	17,842	37,450	15,005	21,478	73,673	44,602	28,416
1986	240,651	17,963	37,404	15,024	20,942	75,651	44,660	29,008
1987	242,804	18,052	37,333	15,215	20,385	77,338	44,854	29,626
1988	245,021	18,195	37,593	15,198	19,846	78,595	45,471	30,124
1989	247,342	18,508	37,972	14,913	19,442	79,943	45,882	30,682
1990	250,132	18,856	38,632	14,466	19,323	81,291	46,316	31,247
1991	253,493	19,208	39,349	13,992	19,414	82,844	46,874	31,812
1992	256,894	19,528	40,161	13,781	19,314	83,201	48,553	32,356
1993	260,255	19,729	40,904	13,953	19,101	83,766	49,899	32,902
1994	263,436	19,777	41,689	14,228	18,758	84,334	51,318	33,331
1995	266,557	19,627	42,510	14,522	18,391	84,933	52,806	33,769
1996	269,667	19,408	43,172	15,057	17,965	85,527	54,396	34,143
1997	272,912	19,233	43,833	15,433	17,992	85,737	56,283	34,402
1998	276,115	19,145	44,332	15,856	18,250	85,663	58,249	34,619
1999	279,295	19,136	44,755	16,164	18,672	85,408	60,362	34,798
2000 [1]	282,434	19,212	45,108	16,198	19,204	85,138	62,494	35,080
2001	285,545	19,364	45,179	16,226	19,787	85,086	64,550	35,353
2002	288,600	19,609	45,128	16,299	20,292	84,978	66,692	35,602
2003	291,049	....	....	....	....	....	....	....

[1] Revised total population data for 2000, 2001 and 2002 are available as follows: 2000, 282,388; 2001, 285,321; and 2002, 288,205.

Note.—Includes Armed Forces overseas beginning 1940. Includes Alaska and Hawaii beginning 1950.
All estimates are consistent with decennial census enumerations.
Source: Department of Commerce, Bureau of the Census.

TABLE B–35.—*Civilian population and labor force, 1929–2003*

[Monthly data seasonally adjusted, except as noted]

Year or month	Civilian noninstitutional population [1]	Civilian labor force					Not in labor force	Civilian labor force participation rate [2]	Civilian employment/population ratio [3]	Unemployment rate, civilian workers [4]
		Total	Employment			Unemployment				
			Total	Agricultural	Nonagricultural					
	Thousands of persons 14 years of age and over							Percent		
1929	....	49,180	47,630	10,450	37,180	1,550	....	....	....	3.2
1933	....	51,590	38,760	10,090	28,670	12,830	....	....	....	24.9
1939	....	55,230	45,750	9,610	36,140	9,480	....	....	....	17.2
1940	99,840	55,640	47,520	9,540	37,980	8,120	44,200	55.7	47.6	14.6
1941	99,900	55,910	50,350	9,100	41,250	5,560	43,990	56.0	50.4	9.9
1942	98,640	56,410	53,750	9,250	44,500	2,660	42,230	57.2	54.5	4.7
1943	94,640	55,540	54,470	9,080	45,390	1,070	39,100	58.7	57.6	1.9
1944	93,220	54,630	53,960	8,950	45,010	670	38,590	58.6	57.9	1.2
1945	94,090	53,860	52,820	8,580	44,240	1,040	40,230	57.2	56.1	1.9
1946	103,070	57,520	55,250	8,320	46,930	2,270	45,550	55.8	53.6	3.9
1947	106,018	60,168	57,812	8,256	49,557	2,356	45,850	56.8	54.5	3.9
	Thousands of persons 16 years of age and over									
1947	101,827	59,350	57,038	7,890	49,148	2,311	42,477	58.3	56.0	3.9
1948	103,068	60,621	58,343	7,629	50,714	2,276	42,447	58.8	56.6	3.8
1949	103,994	61,286	57,651	7,658	49,993	3,637	42,708	58.9	55.4	5.9
1950	104,995	62,208	58,918	7,160	51,758	3,288	42,787	59.2	56.1	5.3
1951	104,621	62,017	59,961	6,726	53,235	2,055	42,604	59.2	57.3	3.3
1952	105,231	62,138	60,250	6,500	53,749	1,883	43,093	59.0	57.3	3.0
1953 [5]	107,056	63,015	61,179	6,260	54,919	1,834	44,041	58.9	57.1	2.9
1954	108,321	63,643	60,109	6,205	53,904	3,532	44,678	58.8	55.5	5.5
1955	109,683	65,023	62,170	6,450	55,722	2,852	44,660	59.3	56.7	4.4
1956	110,954	66,552	63,799	6,283	57,514	2,750	44,402	60.0	57.5	4.1
1957	112,265	66,929	64,071	5,947	58,123	2,859	45,336	59.6	57.1	4.3
1958	113,727	67,639	63,036	5,586	57,450	4,602	46,088	59.5	55.4	6.8
1959	115,329	68,369	64,630	5,565	59,065	3,740	46,960	59.3	56.0	5.5
1960 [5]	117,245	69,628	65,778	5,458	60,318	3,852	47,617	59.4	56.1	5.5
1961	118,771	70,459	65,746	5,200	60,546	4,714	48,312	59.3	55.4	6.7
1962 [5]	120,153	70,614	66,702	4,944	61,759	3,911	49,539	58.8	55.5	5.5
1963	122,416	71,833	67,762	4,687	63,076	4,070	50,583	58.7	55.4	5.7
1964	124,485	73,091	69,305	4,523	64,782	3,786	51,394	58.7	55.7	5.2
1965	126,513	74,455	71,088	4,361	66,726	3,366	52,058	58.9	56.2	4.5
1966	128,058	75,770	72,895	3,979	68,915	2,875	52,288	59.2	56.9	3.8
1967	129,874	77,347	74,372	3,844	70,527	2,975	52,527	59.6	57.3	3.8
1968	132,028	78,737	75,920	3,817	72,103	2,817	53,291	59.6	57.5	3.6
1969	134,335	80,734	77,902	3,606	74,296	2,832	53,602	60.1	58.0	3.5
1970	137,085	82,771	78,678	3,463	75,215	4,093	54,315	60.4	57.4	4.9
1971	140,216	84,382	79,367	3,394	75,972	5,016	55,834	60.2	56.6	5.9
1972 [5]	144,126	87,034	82,153	3,484	78,669	4,882	57,091	60.4	57.0	5.6
1973 [5]	147,096	89,429	85,064	3,470	81,594	4,365	57,667	60.8	57.8	4.9
1974	150,120	91,949	86,794	3,515	83,279	5,156	58,171	61.3	57.8	5.6
1975	153,153	93,775	85,846	3,408	82,438	7,929	59,377	61.2	56.1	8.5
1976	156,150	96,158	88,752	3,331	85,421	7,406	59,991	61.6	56.8	7.7
1977	159,033	99,009	92,017	3,283	88,734	6,991	60,025	62.3	57.9	7.1
1978 [5]	161,910	102,251	96,048	3,387	92,661	6,202	59,659	63.2	59.3	6.1
1979	164,863	104,962	98,824	3,347	95,477	6,137	59,900	63.7	59.9	5.8
1980	167,745	106,940	99,303	3,364	95,938	7,637	60,806	63.8	59.2	7.1
1981	170,130	108,670	100,397	3,368	97,030	8,273	61,460	63.9	59.0	7.6
1982	172,271	110,204	99,526	3,401	96,125	10,678	62,067	64.0	57.8	9.7
1983	174,215	111,550	100,834	3,383	97,450	10,717	62,665	64.0	57.9	9.6
1984	176,383	113,544	105,005	3,321	101,685	8,539	62,839	64.4	59.5	7.5
1985	178,206	115,461	107,150	3,179	103,971	8,312	62,744	64.8	60.1	7.2
1986 [5]	180,587	117,834	109,597	3,163	106,434	8,237	62,752	65.3	60.7	7.0
1987	182,753	119,865	112,440	3,208	109,232	7,425	62,888	65.6	61.5	6.2
1988	184,613	121,669	114,968	3,169	111,800	6,701	62,944	65.9	62.3	5.5
1989	186,393	123,869	117,342	3,199	114,142	6,528	62,523	66.5	63.0	5.3
1990 [5]	189,164	125,840	118,793	3,223	115,570	7,047	63,324	66.5	62.8	5.6
1991	190,925	126,346	117,718	3,269	114,449	8,628	64,578	66.2	61.7	6.8
1992	192,805	128,105	118,492	3,247	115,245	9,613	64,700	66.4	61.5	7.5
1993	194,838	129,200	120,259	3,115	117,144	8,940	65,638	66.3	61.7	6.9
1994 [5]	196,814	131,056	123,060	3,409	119,651	7,996	65,758	66.6	62.5	6.1
1995	198,584	132,304	124,900	3,440	121,460	7,404	66,280	66.6	62.9	5.6
1996	200,591	133,943	126,708	3,443	123,264	7,236	66,647	66.8	63.2	5.4
1997 [5]	203,133	136,297	129,558	3,399	126,159	6,739	66,837	67.1	63.8	4.9
1998 [5]	205,220	137,673	131,463	3,378	128,085	6,210	67,547	67.1	64.1	4.5
1999 [5]	207,753	139,368	133,488	3,281	130,207	5,880	68,385	67.1	64.3	4.2

[1] Not seasonally adjusted.
[2] Civilian labor force as percent of civilian noninstitutional population.
[3] Civilian employment as percent of civilian noninstitutional population.
[4] Unemployed as percent of civilian labor force.

See next page for continuation of table.

[Monthly data seasonally adjusted, except as noted]

Year or month	Civilian noninsti-tutional popula-tion[1]	Civilian labor force					Not in labor force	Civil-ian labor force par-tici-pation rate[2]	Civil-ian em-ploy-ment/ pop-ula-tion ratio[3]	Unem-ploy-ment rate, civil-ian work-ers[4]
		Total	Employment			Un-employ-ment				
			Total	Agri-cul-tural	Non-agri-cultural					
	Thousands of persons 16 years of age and over							Percent		
2000[5][6]	212,577	142,583	136,891	2,464	134,427	5,692	69,994	67.1	64.4	4.0
2001	215,092	143,734	136,933	2,299	134,635	6,801	71,359	66.8	63.7	4.7
2002	217,570	144,863	136,485	2,311	134,174	8,378	72,707	66.6	62.7	5.8
2003	221,168	146,510	137,736	2,275	135,461	8,774	74,658	66.2	62.3	6.0
2000: Jan[5][6]	211,410	142,258	136,561	2,611	133,912	5,698	69,151	67.3	64.6	4.0
Feb	211,576	142,452	136,599	2,728	133,901	5,853	69,125	67.3	64.6	4.1
Mar	211,772	142,398	136,668	2,578	134,004	5,730	69,374	67.2	64.5	4.0
Apr	212,018	142,747	137,264	2,505	134,778	5,483	69,271	67.3	64.7	3.8
May	212,242	142,369	136,611	2,481	134,118	5,758	69,873	67.1	64.4	4.0
June	212,466	142,571	136,923	2,446	134,515	5,648	69,895	67.1	64.4	4.0
July	212,677	142,265	136,516	2,401	134,217	5,749	70,412	66.9	64.2	4.0
Aug	212,916	142,562	136,701	2,437	134,309	5,861	70,354	67.0	64.2	4.1
Sept	213,163	142,539	136,908	2,388	134,483	5,631	70,624	66.9	64.2	4.0
Oct	213,405	142,663	137,124	2,316	134,820	5,540	70,741	66.9	64.3	3.9
Nov	213,540	142,959	137,316	2,342	134,942	5,643	70,582	66.9	64.3	3.9
Dec	213,736	143,273	137,632	2,389	135,205	5,641	70,463	67.0	64.4	3.9
2001: Jan	213,888	143,787	137,790	2,349	135,407	5,997	70,101	67.2	64.4	4.2
Feb	214,110	143,652	137,581	2,359	135,249	6,072	70,458	67.1	64.3	4.2
Mar	214,305	143,873	137,738	2,340	135,320	6,136	70,432	67.1	64.3	4.3
Apr	214,525	143,549	137,275	2,335	134,989	6,274	70,976	66.9	64.0	4.4
May	214,732	143,290	137,063	2,357	134,699	6,227	71,442	66.7	63.8	4.3
June	214,950	143,323	136,842	2,092	134,725	6,481	71,627	66.7	63.7	4.5
July	215,180	143,674	137,091	2,297	134,859	6,583	71,505	66.8	63.7	4.6
Aug	215,420	143,372	136,314	2,314	133,967	7,057	72,048	66.6	63.3	4.9
Sept	215,665	144,020	136,869	2,327	134,565	7,151	71,646	66.8	63.5	5.0
Oct	215,903	144,171	136,447	2,315	134,141	7,723	71,732	66.8	63.2	5.4
Nov	216,117	144,254	136,234	2,228	134,011	8,020	71,863	66.7	63.0	5.6
Dec	216,315	144,369	136,078	2,289	133,770	8,291	71,946	66.7	62.9	5.7
2002: Jan	216,506	143,842	135,715	2,360	133,359	8,126	72,664	66.4	62.7	5.6
Feb	216,663	144,546	136,362	2,373	134,046	8,184	72,117	66.7	62.9	5.7
Mar	216,823	144,384	136,106	2,348	133,710	8,278	72,440	66.6	62.8	5.7
Apr	217,006	144,675	136,096	2,375	133,782	8,578	72,331	66.7	62.7	5.9
May	217,198	144,902	136,505	2,270	134,236	8,397	72,296	66.7	62.8	5.8
June	217,407	144,738	136,353	2,191	134,087	8,384	72,670	66.6	62.7	5.8
July	217,630	144,879	136,478	2,341	134,094	8,400	72,751	66.6	62.7	5.8
Aug	217,866	145,146	136,811	2,146	134,639	8,335	72,720	66.6	62.8	5.7
Sept	218,107	145,606	137,337	2,288	135,127	8,269	72,500	66.8	63.0	5.7
Oct	218,340	145,442	137,079	2,421	134,666	8,363	72,898	66.6	62.8	5.7
Nov	218,548	145,109	136,545	2,296	134,269	8,565	73,439	66.4	62.5	5.9
Dec	218,741	145,157	136,459	2,345	134,098	8,698	73,584	66.4	62.4	6.0
2003: Jan[5]	219,897	145,875	137,447	2,301	135,176	8,428	74,022	66.3	62.5	5.8
Feb[5]	220,114	145,898	137,318	2,205	135,166	8,581	74,216	66.3	62.4	5.9
Mar	220,317	145,818	137,300	2,235	135,054	8,519	74,499	66.2	62.3	5.8
Apr	220,540	146,377	137,578	2,162	135,486	8,799	74,163	66.4	62.4	6.0
May	220,768	146,462	137,505	2,194	135,311	8,957	74,306	66.3	62.3	6.1
June	221,014	146,917	137,673	2,229	135,348	9,245	74,097	66.5	62.3	6.3
July	221,252	146,652	137,604	2,217	135,240	9,048	74,600	66.3	62.2	6.2
Aug	221,507	146,622	137,693	2,327	135,282	8,929	74,884	66.2	62.2	6.1
Sept	221,779	146,610	137,644	2,341	135,401	8,966	75,168	66.1	62.1	6.1
Oct	222,039	146,892	138,095	2,410	135,722	8,797	75,147	66.2	62.2	6.0
Nov	222,279	147,187	138,533	2,418	136,172	8,653	75,093	66.2	62.3	5.9
Dec	222,509	146,878	138,479	2,245	136,180	8,398	75,631	66.0	62.2	5.7

[5] Not strictly comparable with earlier data due to population adjustments or other changes. See *Employment and Earnings* for details on breaks in series.

[6] Beginning in 2000, data for agricultural employment are for agricultural and related industries; data for this series and for non-agricultural employment are not strictly comparable with data for earlier years. Because of independent seasonal adjustment for these two series, monthly data will not add to total civilian employment.

Note.—Labor force data in Tables B–35 through B–44 are based on household interviews and relate to the calendar week including the 12th of the month. For definitions of terms, area samples used, historical comparability of the data, comparability with other series, etc., see *Employment and Earnings*.

Source: Department of Labor, Bureau of Labor Statistics.

TABLE B–36.—*Civilian employment and unemployment by sex and age, 1959–2003*

[Thousands of persons 16 years of age and over; monthly data seasonally adjusted]

Year or month	Total	Civilian employment						Total	Unemployment					
		Males			Females				Males			Females		
		Total	16-19 years	20 years and over	Total	16-19 years	20 years and over		Total	16-19 years	20 years and over	Total	16-19 years	20 years and over
1959	64,630	43,466	2,198	41,267	21,164	1,640	19,524	3,740	2,420	398	2,022	1,320	256	1,063
1960	65,778	43,904	2,361	41,543	21,874	1,768	20,105	3,852	2,486	426	2,060	1,366	286	1,080
1961	65,746	43,656	2,315	41,342	22,090	1,793	20,296	4,714	2,997	479	2,518	1,717	349	1,368
1962	66,702	44,177	2,362	41,815	22,525	1,833	20,693	3,911	2,423	408	2,016	1,488	313	1,175
1963	67,762	44,657	2,406	42,251	23,105	1,849	21,257	4,070	2,472	501	1,971	1,598	383	1,216
1964	69,305	45,474	2,587	42,886	23,831	1,929	21,903	3,786	2,205	487	1,718	1,581	385	1,195
1965	71,088	46,340	2,918	43,422	24,748	2,118	22,630	3,366	1,914	479	1,435	1,452	395	1,056
1966	72,895	46,919	3,253	43,668	25,976	2,468	23,510	2,875	1,551	432	1,120	1,324	405	921
1967	74,372	47,479	3,186	44,294	26,893	2,496	24,397	2,975	1,508	448	1,060	1,468	391	1,078
1968	75,920	48,114	3,255	44,859	27,807	2,526	25,281	2,817	1,419	426	993	1,397	412	985
1969	77,902	48,818	3,430	45,388	29,084	2,687	26,397	2,832	1,403	440	963	1,429	413	1,015
1970	78,678	48,990	3,409	45,581	29,688	2,735	26,952	4,093	2,238	599	1,638	1,855	506	1,349
1971	79,367	49,390	3,478	45,912	29,976	2,730	27,246	5,016	2,789	693	2,097	2,227	568	1,658
1972	82,153	50,896	3,765	47,130	31,257	2,980	28,276	4,882	2,659	711	1,948	2,222	598	1,625
1973	85,064	52,349	4,039	48,310	32,715	3,231	29,484	4,365	2,275	653	1,624	2,089	583	1,507
1974	86,794	53,024	4,103	48,922	33,769	3,345	30,424	5,156	2,714	757	1,957	2,441	665	1,777
1975	85,846	51,857	3,839	48,018	33,989	3,263	30,726	7,929	4,442	966	3,476	3,486	802	2,684
1976	88,752	53,138	3,947	49,190	35,615	3,389	32,226	7,406	4,036	939	3,098	3,369	780	2,588
1977	92,017	54,728	4,174	50,555	37,289	3,514	33,775	6,991	3,667	874	2,794	3,324	789	2,535
1978	96,048	56,479	4,336	52,143	39,569	3,734	35,836	6,202	3,142	813	2,328	3,061	769	2,292
1979	98,824	57,607	4,300	53,308	41,217	3,783	37,434	6,137	3,120	811	2,308	3,018	743	2,276
1980	99,303	57,186	4,085	53,101	42,117	3,625	38,492	7,637	4,267	913	3,353	3,370	755	2,615
1981	100,397	57,397	3,815	53,582	43,000	3,411	39,590	8,273	4,577	962	3,615	3,696	800	2,895
1982	99,526	56,271	3,379	52,891	43,256	3,170	40,086	10,678	6,179	1,090	5,089	4,499	886	3,613
1983	100,834	56,787	3,300	53,487	44,047	3,043	41,004	10,717	6,260	1,003	5,257	4,457	825	3,632
1984	105,005	59,091	3,322	55,769	45,915	3,122	42,793	8,539	4,744	812	3,932	3,794	687	3,107
1985	107,150	59,891	3,328	56,562	47,259	3,105	44,154	8,312	4,521	806	3,715	3,791	661	3,129
1986	109,597	60,892	3,323	57,569	48,706	3,149	45,556	8,237	4,530	779	3,751	3,707	675	3,032
1987	112,440	62,107	3,381	58,726	50,334	3,260	47,074	7,425	4,101	732	3,369	3,324	616	2,709
1988	114,968	63,273	3,492	59,781	51,696	3,313	48,383	6,701	3,655	667	2,987	3,046	558	2,487
1989	117,342	64,315	3,477	60,837	53,027	3,282	49,745	6,528	3,525	658	2,867	3,003	536	2,467
1990	118,793	65,104	3,427	61,678	53,689	3,154	50,535	7,047	3,906	667	3,239	3,140	544	2,596
1991	117,718	64,223	3,044	61,178	53,496	2,862	50,634	8,628	4,946	751	4,195	3,683	608	3,074
1992	118,492	64,440	2,944	61,496	54,052	2,724	51,328	9,613	5,523	806	4,717	4,090	621	3,469
1993	120,259	65,349	2,994	62,355	54,910	2,811	52,099	8,940	5,055	768	4,287	3,885	597	3,288
1994	123,060	66,450	3,156	63,294	56,610	3,005	53,606	7,996	4,367	740	3,627	3,629	580	3,049
1995	124,900	67,377	3,292	64,085	57,523	3,127	54,396	7,404	3,983	744	3,239	3,421	602	2,819
1996	126,708	68,207	3,310	64,897	58,501	3,190	55,311	7,236	3,880	733	3,146	3,356	573	2,783
1997	129,558	69,685	3,401	66,284	59,873	3,260	56,613	6,739	3,577	694	2,882	3,162	577	2,585
1998	131,463	70,693	3,558	67,135	60,771	3,493	57,278	6,210	3,266	686	2,580	2,944	519	2,424
1999	133,488	71,446	3,685	67,761	62,042	3,487	58,555	5,880	3,066	633	2,433	2,814	529	2,285
2000	136,891	73,305	3,671	69,634	63,586	3,519	60,067	5,692	2,975	599	2,376	2,717	483	2,235
2001	136,933	73,196	3,420	69,776	63,737	3,320	60,417	6,801	3,690	650	3,040	3,111	512	2,599
2002	136,485	72,903	3,169	69,734	63,582	3,162	60,420	8,378	4,597	700	3,896	3,781	553	3,228
2003	137,736	73,332	2,917	70,415	64,404	3,002	61,402	8,774	4,906	697	4,209	3,868	554	3,314
2002: Jan	135,715	72,526	3,203	69,323	63,189	3,171	60,019	8,126	4,458	668	3,790	3,668	584	3,084
Feb	136,362	72,724	3,235	69,490	63,638	3,182	60,456	8,184	4,456	671	3,785	3,728	552	3,175
Mar	136,106	72,679	3,227	69,451	63,427	3,275	60,151	8,278	4,549	726	3,824	3,729	558	3,170
Apr	136,096	72,745	3,190	69,555	63,351	3,162	60,189	8,578	4,607	702	3,905	3,971	578	3,393
May	136,505	73,158	3,203	69,955	63,347	3,123	60,224	8,397	4,557	726	3,832	3,840	544	3,295
June	136,353	72,939	3,150	69,789	63,414	3,189	60,225	8,384	4,606	713	3,893	3,778	554	3,224
July	136,478	73,019	3,165	69,854	63,459	3,160	60,299	8,400	4,579	718	3,861	3,832	565	3,267
Aug	136,811	73,080	3,075	70,004	63,731	3,159	60,572	8,335	4,639	772	3,867	3,696	525	3,171
Sept	137,337	73,405	3,199	70,206	63,932	3,215	60,717	8,269	4,578	709	3,869	3,691	531	3,160
Oct	137,079	73,207	3,229	69,978	63,872	3,169	60,704	8,363	4,559	616	3,943	3,804	523	3,281
Nov	136,545	72,740	3,128	69,612	63,804	3,050	60,754	8,565	4,764	698	4,066	3,801	574	3,226
Dec	136,459	72,615	3,046	69,569	63,844	3,094	60,750	8,698	4,832	675	4,157	3,866	560	3,306
2003: Jan	137,447	72,958	3,018	69,940	64,489	3,098	61,391	8,428	4,764	689	4,075	3,665	565	3,100
Feb	137,318	73,132	2,959	70,174	64,186	3,080	61,106	8,581	4,783	715	4,068	3,798	545	3,253
Mar	137,300	73,015	2,801	70,213	64,285	3,066	61,219	8,519	4,716	720	3,995	3,803	532	3,271
Apr	137,578	73,150	2,860	70,290	64,427	3,084	61,343	8,799	4,945	725	4,220	3,854	565	3,289
May	137,505	73,049	2,867	70,182	64,456	3,059	61,397	8,957	5,072	731	4,341	3,885	583	3,302
June	137,673	73,124	2,935	70,190	64,548	2,938	61,610	9,245	5,214	729	4,485	4,031	652	3,379
July	137,604	73,149	2,880	70,269	64,455	2,976	61,479	9,048	5,128	737	4,391	3,920	563	3,356
Aug	137,693	73,263	2,939	70,324	64,431	2,963	61,467	8,929	4,988	630	4,358	3,941	572	3,369
Sept	137,644	73,488	2,893	70,596	64,155	2,964	61,191	8,966	5,016	707	4,309	3,951	533	3,417
Oct	138,095	73,643	2,917	70,726	64,452	2,928	61,524	8,797	4,887	671	4,216	3,910	535	3,375
Nov	138,533	73,915	2,951	70,964	64,618	3,021	61,597	8,653	4,883	660	4,224	3,770	450	3,320
Dec	138,479	74,085	2,986	71,099	64,394	2,873	61,521	8,398	4,576	631	3,945	3,823	497	3,326

Note.—See footnote 5 and Note, Table B–35.

Source: Department of Labor, Bureau of Labor Statistics.

[Thousands of persons 16 years of age and over; monthly data seasonally adjusted]

Year or month	All civilian workers	White [1]				Black and other [1]				Black or African American [1]			
		Total	Males	Females	Both sexes 16-19	Total	Males	Females	Both sexes 16-19	Total	Males	Females	Both sexes 16-19
1959	64,630	58,006	39,494	18,512	3,475	6,623	3,971	2,652	362	....	....	....	....
1960	65,778	58,850	39,755	19,095	3,700	6,928	4,149	2,779	430	....	....	....	....
1961	65,746	58,913	39,588	19,325	3,693	6,833	4,068	2,765	414	....	....	....	....
1962	66,702	59,698	40,016	19,682	3,774	7,003	4,160	2,843	420	....	....	....	....
1963	67,762	60,622	40,428	20,194	3,851	7,140	4,229	2,911	404	....	....	....	....
1964	69,305	61,922	41,115	20,807	4,076	7,383	4,359	3,024	440	....	....	....	....
1965	71,088	63,446	41,844	21,602	4,562	7,643	4,496	3,147	474	....	....	....	....
1966	72,895	65,021	42,331	22,690	5,176	7,877	4,588	3,289	545	....	....	....	....
1967	74,372	66,361	42,833	23,528	5,114	8,011	4,646	3,365	568	....	....	....	....
1968	75,920	67,750	43,411	24,339	5,195	8,169	4,702	3,467	584	....	....	....	....
1969	77,902	69,518	44,048	25,470	5,508	8,384	4,770	3,614	609	....	....	....	....
1970	78,678	70,217	44,178	26,039	5,571	8,464	4,813	3,650	574	....	....	....	....
1971	79,367	70,878	44,595	26,283	5,670	8,488	4,796	3,692	538	....	....	....	....
1972	82,153	73,370	45,944	27,426	6,173	8,783	4,952	3,832	573	7,802	4,368	3,433	509
1973	85,064	75,708	47,085	28,623	6,623	9,356	5,265	4,092	647	8,128	4,527	3,601	570
1974	86,794	77,184	47,674	29,511	6,796	9,610	5,352	4,258	652	8,203	4,527	3,677	554
1975	85,846	76,411	46,697	29,714	6,487	9,435	5,161	4,275	615	7,894	4,275	3,618	507
1976	88,752	78,853	47,775	31,078	6,724	9,899	5,363	4,536	611	8,227	4,404	3,823	508
1977	92,017	81,700	49,150	32,550	7,068	10,317	5,579	4,739	619	8,540	4,565	3,975	508
1978	96,048	84,936	50,544	34,392	7,367	11,112	5,936	5,177	703	9,102	4,796	4,307	571
1979	98,824	87,259	51,452	35,807	7,356	11,565	6,156	5,409	727	9,359	4,923	4,436	579
1980	99,303	87,715	51,127	36,587	7,021	11,588	6,059	5,529	689	9,313	4,798	4,515	547
1981	100,397	88,709	51,315	37,394	6,588	11,688	6,083	5,606	637	9,355	4,794	4,561	505
1982	99,526	87,903	50,287	37,615	5,984	11,624	5,983	5,641	565	9,189	4,637	4,552	428
1983	100,834	88,893	50,621	38,272	5,799	11,941	6,166	5,775	543	9,375	4,753	4,622	416
1984	105,005	92,120	52,462	39,659	5,836	12,885	6,629	6,256	607	10,119	5,124	4,995	474
1985	107,150	93,736	53,046	40,690	5,768	13,414	6,845	6,569	666	10,501	5,270	5,231	532
1986	109,597	95,660	53,785	41,876	5,792	13,937	7,107	6,830	681	10,814	5,428	5,386	536
1987	112,440	97,789	54,647	43,142	5,898	14,652	7,459	7,192	742	11,309	5,661	5,648	587
1988	114,968	99,812	55,550	44,262	6,030	15,156	7,722	7,434	774	11,658	5,824	5,834	601
1989	117,342	101,584	56,352	45,232	5,946	15,757	7,963	7,795	813	11,953	5,928	6,025	625
1990	118,793	102,261	56,703	45,558	5,779	16,533	8,401	8,131	801	12,175	5,995	6,180	598
1991	117,718	101,182	55,797	45,385	5,216	16,536	8,426	8,110	690	12,074	5,961	6,113	494
1992	118,492	101,669	55,959	45,710	4,985	16,823	8,482	8,342	684	12,151	5,930	6,221	492
1993	120,259	103,045	56,656	46,390	5,113	17,214	8,693	8,521	691	12,382	6,047	6,334	494
1994	123,060	105,190	57,452	47,738	5,398	17,870	8,998	8,872	763	12,835	6,241	6,595	552
1995	124,900	106,490	58,146	48,344	5,593	18,409	9,231	9,179	826	13,279	6,422	6,857	586
1996	126,708	107,808	58,888	48,920	5,667	18,900	9,319	9,580	832	13,542	6,456	7,086	613
1997	129,558	109,856	59,998	49,859	5,807	19,701	9,687	10,014	853	13,969	6,607	7,362	631
1998	131,463	110,931	60,604	50,327	6,089	20,532	10,089	10,443	962	14,556	6,871	7,685	736
1999	133,488	112,235	61,139	51,096	6,204	21,253	10,307	10,945	968	15,056	7,027	8,029	691
2000	136,891	114,424	62,289	52,136	6,160	....	....	....	....	15,156	7,082	8,073	711
2001	136,933	114,430	62,212	52,218	5,817	....	....	....	....	15,006	6,938	8,068	637
2002	136,485	114,013	61,849	52,164	5,441	....	....	....	....	14,872	6,959	7,914	611
2003	137,736	114,235	61,866	52,369	5,064	....	....	....	....	14,739	6,820	7,919	516
2002: Jan	135,715	113,433	61,625	51,808	5,499	....	....	....	....	14,876	7,004	7,871	589
Feb	136,362	114,084	61,856	52,228	5,496	....	....	....	....	14,872	6,974	7,898	636
Mar	136,106	113,853	61,700	52,153	5,598	....	....	....	....	14,782	6,981	7,801	606
Apr	136,096	113,772	61,678	52,095	5,477	....	....	....	....	14,855	6,992	7,863	608
May	136,505	114,088	61,986	52,102	5,407	....	....	....	....	14,951	7,093	7,858	623
June	136,353	113,971	61,882	52,089	5,444	....	....	....	....	14,799	6,917	7,882	630
July	136,478	114,051	61,902	52,149	5,432	....	....	....	....	14,784	6,939	7,845	589
Aug	136,811	114,283	61,983	52,300	5,356	....	....	....	....	14,897	6,965	7,933	597
Sept	137,337	114,434	62,094	52,341	5,486	....	....	....	....	15,100	7,041	8,059	635
Oct	137,079	114,264	61,971	52,293	5,419	....	....	....	....	15,032	7,037	7,995	659
Nov	136,545	114,047	61,807	52,241	5,359	....	....	....	....	14,720	6,776	7,944	587
Dec	136,459	113,876	61,700	52,176	5,330	....	....	....	....	14,799	6,791	8,009	572
2003: Jan	137,447	113,985	61,656	52,329	5,243	....	....	....	....	14,717	6,749	7,968	563
Feb	137,318	114,118	61,830	52,288	5,167	....	....	....	....	14,665	6,800	7,865	553
Mar	137,300	114,057	61,713	52,344	5,019	....	....	....	....	14,678	6,743	7,936	523
Apr	137,578	114,220	61,769	52,451	5,079	....	....	....	....	14,739	6,773	7,966	527
May	137,505	113,978	61,621	52,357	5,068	....	....	....	....	14,838	6,758	8,080	514
June	137,673	114,222	61,653	52,569	5,062	....	....	....	....	14,729	6,815	7,914	473
July	137,604	114,086	61,690	52,396	5,028	....	....	....	....	14,727	6,826	7,901	499
Aug	137,693	114,156	61,753	52,403	5,057	....	....	....	....	14,771	6,832	7,939	512
Sept	137,644	114,015	61,900	52,115	5,020	....	....	....	....	14,826	6,869	7,957	543
Oct	138,095	114,535	62,115	52,420	5,020	....	....	....	....	14,696	6,853	7,843	489
Nov	138,533	114,783	62,324	52,459	5,074	....	....	....	....	14,812	6,890	7,921	505
Dec	138,479	114,678	62,355	52,323	4,942	....	....	....	....	14,679	6,924	7,755	514

[1] Beginning in 2003, persons who selected this race group only. Prior to 2003, persons who selected more than one race were included in the group they identified as the main race. Data for black or African American were for black prior to 2003. Data discontinued for black and other series. See *Employment and Earnings,* for details.

Note.—Beginning with data for 2000, since data for all race groups are not shown here, detail will not sum to total. See footnote 5 and Note, Table B–35.

Source: Department of Labor, Bureau of Labor Statistics.

TABLE B–38.—*Unemployment by demographic characteristic, 1959–2003*

[Thousands of persons 16 years of age and over; monthly data seasonally adjusted]

Year or month	All civilian workers	White[1] Total	Males	Females	Both sexes 16-19	Black and other[1] Total	Males	Females	Both sexes 16-19	Black or African American[1] Total	Males	Females	Both sexes 16-19
1959	3,740	2,946	1,903	1,043	525	793	517	276	128				
1960	3,852	3,065	1,988	1,077	575	788	498	290	138				
1961	4,714	3,743	2,398	1,345	669	971	599	372	159				
1962	3,911	3,052	1,915	1,137	580	861	509	352	142				
1963	4,070	3,208	1,976	1,232	708	863	496	367	176				
1964	3,786	2,999	1,779	1,220	708	787	426	361	165				
1965	3,366	2,691	1,556	1,135	705	678	360	318	171				
1966	2,875	2,255	1,241	1,014	651	622	310	312	186				
1967	2,975	2,338	1,208	1,130	635	638	300	338	203				
1968	2,817	2,226	1,142	1,084	644	590	277	313	194				
1969	2,832	2,260	1,137	1,123	660	571	267	304	193				
1970	4,093	3,339	1,857	1,482	871	754	380	374	235				
1971	5,016	4,085	2,309	1,777	1,011	930	481	450	249				
1972	4,882	3,906	2,173	1,733	1,021	977	486	491	288	906	448	458	279
1973	4,365	3,442	1,836	1,606	955	924	440	484	280	846	395	451	262
1974	5,156	4,097	2,169	1,927	1,104	1,058	544	514	318	965	494	470	297
1975	7,929	6,421	3,627	2,794	1,413	1,507	815	692	355	1,369	741	629	330
1976	7,406	5,914	3,258	2,656	1,364	1,492	779	713	355	1,334	698	637	330
1977	6,991	5,441	2,883	2,558	1,284	1,550	784	766	379	1,393	698	695	354
1978	6,202	4,698	2,411	2,287	1,189	1,505	731	774	394	1,330	641	690	360
1979	6,137	4,664	2,405	2,260	1,193	1,473	714	759	362	1,319	636	683	333
1980	7,637	5,884	3,345	2,540	1,291	1,752	922	830	377	1,553	815	738	343
1981	8,273	6,343	3,580	2,762	1,374	1,930	997	933	388	1,731	891	840	357
1982	10,678	8,241	4,846	3,395	1,534	2,437	1,334	1,104	443	2,142	1,167	975	396
1983	10,717	8,128	4,859	3,270	1,387	2,588	1,401	1,187	441	2,272	1,213	1,059	392
1984	8,539	6,372	3,600	2,772	1,116	2,167	1,144	1,022	384	1,914	1,003	911	353
1985	8,312	6,191	3,426	2,765	1,074	2,121	1,095	1,026	394	1,864	951	913	357
1986	8,237	6,140	3,433	2,708	1,070	2,097	1,097	999	383	1,840	946	894	347
1987	7,425	5,501	3,132	2,369	995	1,924	969	955	353	1,684	826	858	312
1988	6,701	4,944	2,766	2,177	910	1,757	888	869	316	1,547	771	776	288
1989	6,528	4,770	2,636	2,135	863	1,757	889	868	331	1,544	773	772	300
1990	7,047	5,186	2,935	2,251	903	1,860	971	889	308	1,565	806	758	268
1991	8,628	6,560	3,859	2,701	1,029	2,068	1,087	981	330	1,723	890	833	280
1992	9,613	7,169	4,209	2,959	1,037	2,444	1,314	1,130	390	2,011	1,067	944	324
1993	8,940	6,655	3,828	2,827	992	2,285	1,227	1,058	373	1,844	971	872	313
1994	7,996	5,892	3,275	2,617	960	2,104	1,092	1,011	360	1,666	848	818	300
1995	7,404	5,459	2,999	2,460	952	1,945	984	961	394	1,538	762	777	325
1996	7,236	5,300	2,896	2,404	939	1,936	984	952	367	1,592	808	784	310
1997	6,739	4,836	2,641	2,195	912	1,903	935	967	359	1,560	747	813	302
1998	6,210	4,484	2,431	2,053	876	1,726	835	891	329	1,426	671	756	281
1999	5,880	4,273	2,274	1,999	844	1,606	792	814	318	1,309	626	684	268
2000	5,692	4,121	2,177	1,944	795					1,241	620	621	230
2001	6,801	4,969	2,754	2,215	845					1,416	709	706	260
2002	8,378	6,137	3,459	2,678	925					1,693	835	858	260
2003	8,774	6,311	3,643	2,668	909					1,787	891	895	255
2002:Jan	8,126	6,045	3,355	2,690	936					1,645	803	842	269
Feb	8,184	6,014	3,320	2,694	907					1,617	785	832	260
Mar	8,278	6,030	3,396	2,634	940					1,730	871	859	280
Apr	8,578	6,232	3,474	2,759	905					1,784	835	948	325
May	8,397	6,166	3,446	2,720	931					1,665	808	857	254
June	8,384	6,135	3,446	2,689	929					1,723	881	843	265
July	8,400	6,225	3,515	2,709	991					1,626	767	859	212
Aug	8,335	6,150	3,506	2,644	942					1,624	806	818	256
Sept	8,269	6,118	3,487	2,631	908					1,621	839	781	248
Oct	8,363	6,195	3,485	2,710	890					1,629	838	792	211
Nov	8,565	6,170	3,554	2,616	933					1,797	902	895	268
Dec	8,698	6,195	3,561	2,634	870					1,902	914	988	301
2003:Jan	8,428	6,132	3,537	2,595	927					1,727	884	843	249
Feb	8,581	6,129	3,500	2,629	939					1,751	907	845	243
Mar	8,519	6,166	3,503	2,663	918					1,681	848	833	261
Apr	8,799	6,294	3,663	2,631	918					1,782	893	889	259
May	8,957	6,491	3,730	2,762	917					1,776	960	815	287
June	9,245	6,594	3,860	2,734	981					1,926	947	979	296
July	9,048	6,559	3,886	2,673	933					1,836	893	943	271
Aug	8,929	6,502	3,808	2,694	903					1,813	871	942	217
Sept	8,966	6,397	3,671	2,726	896					1,851	945	906	264
Oct	8,797	6,200	3,544	2,657	838					1,893	941	952	290
Nov	8,653	6,258	3,652	2,607	843					1,712	853	860	205
Dec	8,398	6,073	3,455	2,617	857					1,686	778	908	193

[1] See footnote 1 and Note, Table B–37.

Note.—See footnote 5 and Note, Table B–35.

Source: Department of Labor, Bureau of Labor Statistics.

Year or month	Labor force participation rate							Employment/population ratio						
	All civilian workers	Males	Females	Both sexes 16–19 years	White[2]	Black and other[2]	Black or African American[2]	All civilian workers	Males	Females	Both sexes 16–19 years	White[2]	Black and other[2]	Black or African American[2]
1959	59.3	83.7	37.1	46.7	58.7	64.3	....	56.0	79.3	35.0	39.9	55.9	57.5	....
1960	59.4	83.3	37.7	47.5	58.8	64.5	....	56.1	78.9	35.5	40.5	55.9	57.9	....
1961	59.3	82.9	38.1	46.9	58.8	64.1	....	55.4	77.6	35.4	39.1	55.3	56.2	....
1962	58.8	82.0	37.9	46.1	58.3	63.2	....	55.5	77.7	35.6	39.4	55.4	56.3	....
1963	58.7	81.4	38.3	45.2	58.2	63.0	....	55.4	77.1	35.8	37.4	55.3	56.2	....
1964	58.7	81.0	38.7	44.5	58.2	63.1	....	55.7	77.3	36.3	37.3	55.5	57.0	....
1965	58.9	80.7	39.3	45.7	58.4	62.9	....	56.2	77.5	37.1	38.9	56.0	57.8	....
1966	59.2	80.4	40.3	48.2	58.7	63.0	....	56.9	77.9	38.3	42.1	56.8	58.4	....
1967	59.6	80.4	41.1	48.4	59.2	62.8	....	57.3	78.0	39.0	42.2	57.2	58.2	....
1968	59.6	80.1	41.6	48.3	59.3	62.2	....	57.5	77.8	39.6	42.2	57.4	58.0	....
1969	60.1	79.8	42.7	49.4	59.9	62.1	....	58.0	77.6	40.7	43.4	58.0	58.1	....
1970	60.4	79.7	43.3	49.9	60.2	61.8	....	57.4	76.2	40.8	42.3	57.5	56.8	....
1971	60.2	79.1	43.4	49.7	60.1	60.9	....	56.6	74.9	40.4	41.3	56.8	54.9	....
1972	60.4	78.9	43.9	51.9	60.4	60.2	59.9	57.0	75.0	41.0	43.5	57.4	54.1	53.7
1973	60.8	78.8	44.7	53.7	60.8	60.5	60.2	57.8	75.5	42.0	45.9	58.2	55.0	54.5
1974	61.3	78.7	45.7	54.8	61.4	60.3	59.8	57.8	74.9	42.6	46.0	58.3	54.3	53.5
1975	61.2	77.9	46.3	54.0	61.5	59.6	58.8	56.1	71.7	42.0	43.3	56.7	51.4	50.1
1976	61.6	77.5	47.3	54.5	61.8	59.8	59.0	56.8	72.0	43.2	44.2	57.5	52.0	50.8
1977	62.3	77.7	48.4	56.0	62.5	60.4	59.8	57.9	72.8	44.5	46.1	58.6	52.5	51.4
1978	63.2	77.9	50.0	57.8	63.3	62.2	61.5	59.3	73.8	46.4	48.3	60.0	54.7	53.6
1979	63.7	77.8	50.9	57.9	63.9	62.2	61.4	59.9	73.8	47.5	48.5	60.6	55.2	53.8
1980	63.8	77.4	51.5	56.7	64.1	61.7	61.0	59.2	72.0	47.7	46.6	60.0	53.6	52.3
1981	63.9	77.0	52.1	55.4	64.3	61.3	60.8	59.0	71.3	48.0	44.6	60.0	52.6	51.3
1982	64.0	76.6	52.6	54.1	64.3	61.6	61.0	57.8	69.0	47.7	41.5	58.8	50.9	49.4
1983	64.0	76.4	52.9	53.5	64.3	62.1	61.5	57.9	68.8	48.0	41.5	58.9	51.0	49.5
1984	64.4	76.4	53.6	53.9	64.6	62.6	62.2	59.5	70.7	49.5	43.7	60.5	53.6	52.3
1985	64.8	76.3	54.5	54.5	65.0	63.3	62.9	60.1	70.9	50.4	44.4	61.0	54.7	53.4
1986	65.3	76.3	55.3	54.7	65.5	63.7	63.3	60.7	71.0	51.4	44.6	61.5	55.4	54.1
1987	65.6	76.2	56.0	54.7	65.8	64.3	63.8	61.5	71.5	52.5	45.5	62.3	56.8	55.6
1988	65.9	76.2	56.6	55.3	66.2	64.0	63.8	62.3	72.0	53.4	46.8	63.1	57.4	56.3
1989	66.5	76.4	57.4	55.9	66.7	64.7	64.2	63.0	72.5	54.3	47.5	63.8	58.2	56.9
1990	66.5	76.4	57.5	53.7	66.9	64.4	64.0	62.8	72.0	54.3	45.3	63.7	57.9	56.7
1991	66.2	75.8	57.4	51.6	66.6	63.8	63.3	61.7	70.4	53.7	42.0	62.6	56.7	55.4
1992	66.4	75.8	57.8	51.3	66.8	64.6	63.9	61.5	69.8	53.8	41.0	62.4	56.4	54.9
1993	66.3	75.4	57.9	51.5	66.8	63.8	63.2	61.7	70.0	54.1	41.7	62.7	56.3	55.0
1994	66.6	75.1	58.8	52.7	67.1	63.9	63.4	62.5	70.4	55.3	43.4	63.5	57.2	56.1
1995	66.6	75.0	58.9	53.5	67.1	64.3	63.7	62.9	70.8	55.6	44.2	63.8	58.1	57.1
1996	66.8	74.9	59.3	52.3	67.2	64.6	64.1	63.2	70.9	56.0	43.5	64.1	58.6	57.4
1997	67.1	75.0	59.8	51.6	67.5	65.2	64.7	63.8	71.3	56.8	43.4	64.6	59.4	58.2
1998	67.1	74.9	59.8	52.8	67.3	66.0	65.6	64.1	71.6	57.1	45.1	64.7	60.9	59.7
1999	67.1	74.7	60.0	52.0	67.3	65.9	65.8	64.3	71.6	57.4	44.7	64.8	61.3	60.6
2000	67.1	74.8	59.9	52.0	67.3	....	65.8	64.4	71.9	57.5	45.2	64.9	....	60.9
2001	66.8	74.4	59.8	49.6	67.0	....	65.3	63.7	70.9	57.0	42.3	64.2	....	59.7
2002	66.6	74.1	59.6	47.4	66.8	....	64.8	62.7	69.7	56.3	39.6	63.4	....	58.1
2003	66.2	73.5	59.5	44.5	66.5	....	64.3	62.3	68.9	56.1	36.8	63.0	....	57.4
2002: Jan	66.4	74.0	59.4	47.4	66.7	....	65.1	62.7	69.7	56.2	39.6	63.3	....	58.6
Feb	66.7	74.1	59.9	47.6	67.0	....	64.9	62.9	69.9	56.5	39.9	63.7	....	58.5
Mar	66.6	74.1	59.6	48.4	66.9	....	64.9	62.8	69.8	56.3	40.5	63.5	....	58.1
Apr	66.7	74.2	59.7	47.7	66.9	....	65.3	62.7	69.8	56.2	39.7	63.4	....	58.3
May	66.7	74.4	59.6	47.4	67.0	....	65.1	62.8	70.1	56.2	39.5	63.6	....	58.6
June	66.6	74.2	59.5	47.7	66.8	....	64.7	62.7	69.8	56.2	·39.8	63.4	....	57.9
July	66.6	74.2	59.5	47.6	66.9	....	64.1	62.7	69.8	56.2	39.6	63.4	....	57.8
Aug	66.6	74.2	59.6	47.1	66.9	....	64.5	62.8	69.8	56.3	39.0	63.5	....	58.1
Sept	66.8	74.4	59.7	48.0	66.9	....	65.1	63.0	70.0	56.5	40.2	63.5	....	58.8
Oct	66.6	74.1	59.7	47.2	66.8	....	64.8	62.8	69.7	56.3	40.1	63.4	....	58.5
Nov	66.4	73.7	59.6	46.8	66.6	....	64.1	62.5	69.2	56.2	38.8	63.2	....	57.2
Dec	66.4	73.6	59.6	46.3	66.5	....	64.8	62.4	69.0	56.2	38.6	63.1	....	57.4
2003: Jan	66.3	73.5	59.7	46.0	66.6	....	64.5	62.5	69.0	56.5	38.2	63.2	....	57.8
Feb	66.3	73.6	59.5	45.5	66.6	....	64.3	62.4	69.1	56.2	37.7	63.2	....	57.5
Mar	66.2	73.3	59.6	44.4	66.5	....	64.0	62.3	68.9	56.2	36.6	63.1	....	57.4
Apr	66.4	73.6	59.7	45.1	66.6	....	64.6	62.4	68.9	56.3	37.0	63.1	....	57.6
May	66.3	73.5	59.7	45.0	66.6	....	64.8	62.3	68.8	56.3	36.9	63.0	....	57.9
June	66.5	73.7	59.8	45.1	66.7	....	64.9	62.3	68.8	56.3	36.5	63.0	....	57.4
July	66.3	73.5	59.6	44.4	66.5	....	64.4	62.2	68.7	56.2	36.4	62.9	....	57.3
Aug	66.2	73.4	59.5	44.1	66.5	....	64.4	62.2	68.7	56.1	36.6	62.9	....	57.4
Sept	66.1	73.5	59.2	44.0	66.3	....	64.7	62.1	68.8	55.8	36.3	62.8	....	57.5
Oct	66.2	73.5	59.4	43.7	66.4	....	64.2	62.2	68.9	56.0	36.2	63.0	....	56.9
Nov	66.2	73.6	59.3	43.8	66.5	....	63.9	62.3	69.1	56.1	37.0	63.1	....	57.3
Dec	66.0	73.4	59.1	43.2	66.3	....	63.2	62.2	69.2	55.8	36.2	62.9	....	56.7

[1] Civilian labor force or civilian employment as percent of civilian noninstitutional population in group specified.
[2] See footnote 1, Table B–37.

Note.—Data relate to persons 16 years of age and over.
See footnote 5 and Note, Table B–35.

Source: Department of Labor, Bureau of Labor Statistics.

TABLE B–40.—*Civilian labor force participation rate by demographic characteristic, 1965–2003*

[Percent;[1] monthly data seasonally adjusted]

Year or month	All civilian workers	White[2] Total	White Males Total	White Males 16-19 years	White Males 20 years and over	White Females Total	White Females 16-19 years	White Females 20 years and over	Black and other or black or African American[2] Total	Black Males Total	Black Males 16-19 years	Black Males 20 years and over	Black Females Total	Black Females 16-19 years	Black Females 20 years and over
									Black and other						
1965	58.9	58.4	80.8	54.1	83.9	38.1	39.2	38.0	62.9	79.6	51.3	83.7	48.6	29.5	51.1
1966	59.2	58.7	80.6	55.9	83.6	39.2	42.6	38.8	63.0	79.0	51.4	83.3	49.4	33.5	51.6
1967	59.6	59.2	80.6	56.3	83.5	40.1	42.5	39.8	62.8	78.5	51.1	82.9	49.5	35.2	51.6
1968	59.6	59.3	80.4	55.9	83.2	40.7	43.0	40.4	62.2	77.7	49.7	82.2	49.3	34.8	51.4
1969	60.1	59.9	80.2	56.8	83.0	41.8	44.6	41.5	62.1	76.9	49.6	81.4	49.8	34.6	52.0
1970	60.4	60.2	80.0	57.5	82.8	42.6	45.6	42.2	61.8	76.5	47.4	81.4	49.5	34.1	51.8
1971	60.2	60.1	79.6	57.9	82.3	42.6	45.4	42.3	60.9	74.9	44.7	80.0	49.2	31.2	51.8
1972	60.4	60.4	79.6	60.1	82.0	43.2	48.1	42.7	60.2	73.9	46.0	78.6	48.8	32.3	51.2
									Black or African American[2]						
1972	60.4	60.4	79.6	60.1	82.0	43.2	48.1	42.7	59.9	73.6	46.3	78.5	48.7	32.2	51.2
1973	60.8	60.8	79.4	62.0	81.6	44.1	50.1	43.5	60.2	73.4	45.7	78.4	49.3	34.2	51.6
1974	61.3	61.4	79.4	62.9	81.4	45.2	51.7	44.4	59.8	72.9	46.7	77.6	49.0	33.4	51.4
1975	61.2	61.5	78.7	61.9	80.7	45.9	51.5	45.3	58.8	70.9	42.6	76.0	48.8	34.2	51.1
1976	61.6	61.8	78.4	62.3	80.3	46.9	52.8	46.2	59.0	70.0	41.3	75.4	49.8	32.9	52.5
1977	62.3	62.5	78.5	64.0	80.2	48.0	54.5	47.3	59.8	70.6	43.2	75.6	50.8	32.9	53.6
1978	63.2	63.3	78.6	65.0	80.1	49.4	56.7	48.7	61.5	71.5	44.9	76.2	53.1	37.3	55.5
1979	63.7	63.9	78.6	64.8	80.1	50.5	57.4	49.8	61.4	71.3	43.6	76.3	53.1	36.8	55.4
1980	63.8	64.1	78.2	63.7	79.8	51.2	56.2	50.6	61.0	70.3	43.2	75.1	53.1	34.9	55.6
1981	63.9	64.3	77.9	62.4	79.5	51.9	55.4	51.5	60.8	70.0	41.6	74.5	53.5	34.0	56.0
1982	64.0	64.3	77.4	60.0	79.2	52.4	55.0	52.2	61.0	70.1	39.8	74.7	53.7	33.5	56.2
1983	64.0	64.3	77.1	59.4	78.9	52.7	54.5	52.5	61.5	70.6	39.9	75.2	54.2	33.0	56.8
1984	64.4	64.6	77.1	59.0	78.7	53.3	55.4	53.1	62.2	70.8	41.7	74.8	55.2	35.0	57.6
1985	64.8	65.0	77.0	59.7	78.5	54.1	55.2	54.0	62.9	70.8	44.6	74.4	56.5	37.9	58.6
1986	65.3	65.5	76.9	59.3	78.5	55.0	56.3	54.9	63.3	71.2	43.7	74.8	56.9	39.1	58.9
1987	65.6	65.8	76.8	59.0	78.4	55.7	56.5	55.6	63.8	71.1	43.6	74.7	58.0	39.6	60.0
1988	65.9	66.2	76.9	60.0	78.3	56.4	57.2	56.3	63.8	71.0	43.8	74.6	58.0	37.9	60.1
1989	66.5	66.7	77.1	61.0	78.5	57.2	57.1	57.2	64.2	71.0	44.6	74.4	58.7	40.4	60.6
1990	66.5	66.9	77.1	59.6	78.5	57.4	55.3	57.6	64.0	71.0	40.7	75.0	58.3	36.8	60.6
1991	66.2	66.6	76.5	57.3	78.0	57.4	54.1	57.6	63.3	70.4	37.3	74.6	57.5	33.5	60.0
1992	66.4	66.8	76.5	56.9	78.0	57.7	52.5	58.1	63.9	70.7	40.6	74.3	58.5	35.2	60.8
1993	66.3	66.8	76.2	56.6	77.7	58.0	53.5	58.3	63.2	69.6	39.5	73.2	57.9	34.6	60.2
1994	66.6	67.1	75.9	57.7	77.3	58.9	55.1	59.2	63.4	69.1	40.8	72.5	58.7	36.3	60.9
1995	66.6	67.1	75.7	58.5	77.1	59.0	55.5	59.2	63.7	69.0	40.1	72.5	59.5	39.8	61.4
1996	66.8	67.2	75.8	57.1	77.3	59.1	54.7	59.4	64.1	68.7	39.5	72.3	60.4	38.9	62.6
1997	67.1	67.5	75.9	56.1	77.5	59.5	54.1	59.9	64.7	68.3	37.4	72.2	61.7	39.9	64.0
1998	67.1	67.3	75.6	56.6	77.2	59.4	55.4	59.7	65.6	69.0	40.7	72.5	62.8	42.5	64.8
1999	67.1	67.3	75.6	56.4	77.2	59.6	54.5	59.9	65.8	68.7	38.6	72.4	63.5	38.8	66.1
2000	67.1	67.3	75.5	56.5	77.1	59.5	54.5	59.9	65.8	69.2	39.2	72.8	63.1	39.6	65.4
2001	66.8	67.0	75.1	53.7	76.9	59.4	52.4	59.9	65.3	68.4	37.9	72.1	62.8	37.3	65.2
2002	66.6	66.8	74.8	50.3	76.7	59.3	50.8	60.0	64.8	68.4	37.3	72.1	61.8	34.7	64.4
2003	66.2	66.5	74.2	47.5	76.3	59.2	47.9	59.9	64.3	67.3	31.1	71.5	61.9	33.7	64.6
2002: Jan	66.4	66.7	74.7	50.1	76.7	59.2	52.1	59.7	65.1	69.1	38.8	72.7	61.8	32.5	64.6
Feb	66.7	67.0	74.9	50.5	76.8	59.6	51.1	60.2	64.9	68.6	39.3	72.0	61.9	35.1	64.4
Mar	66.6	66.9	74.7	51.2	76.6	59.4	52.6	59.9	64.9	69.3	39.0	72.9	61.3	34.7	63.8
Apr	66.7	66.9	74.8	50.5	76.7	59.5	50.8	60.1	65.3	69.0	39.5	72.5	62.3	37.9	64.6
May	66.7	67.0	‹75.0	50.2	77.0	59.4	50.4	60.0	65.1	69.6	41.1	72.9	61.6	31.7	64.4
June	66.6	66.8	74.8	50.3	76.8	59.3	51.0	59.9	64.7	68.5	38.8	72.0	61.6	35.3	64.0
July	66.6	66.9	74.9	51.1	76.8	59.3	50.9	59.9	64.1	67.6	32.8	71.7	61.3	33.4	64.0
Aug	66.6	66.9	74.9	49.7	76.9	59.4	50.4	60.0	64.5	68.1	35.6	71.9	61.6	34.9	64.1
Sept	66.8	66.9	74.9	50.8	76.8	59.4	50.7	60.0	65.1	68.9	36.9	72.6	62.1	36.1	64.5
Oct	66.6	66.8	74.7	50.1	76.6	59.4	50.1	60.0	64.8	68.7	37.8	72.3	61.6	34.1	64.2
Nov	66.4	66.6	74.5	50.3	76.4	59.2	49.6	59.8	64.1	66.9	36.9	70.4	61.9	33.7	64.6
Dec	66.4	66.5	74.3	49.2	76.3	59.1	49.2	59.8	64.8	67.0	33.7	70.9	63.0	38.2	65.3
2003: Jan	66.3	66.6	74.3	48.8	76.2	59.3	50.0	59.9	64.5	67.2	32.6	71.2	62.4	36.0	64.8
Feb	66.3	66.6	74.3	48.4	76.4	59.2	49.4	59.9	64.3	67.8	34.1	71.6	61.6	33.2	64.2
Mar	66.2	66.5	74.1	46.5	76.3	59.3	48.6	60.0	64.0	66.6	31.6	70.7	61.9	34.7	64.4
Apr	66.4	66.6	74.3	46.9	76.5	59.3	49.1	60.1	64.6	67.2	30.9	71.4	62.4	35.4	65.0
May	66.3	66.6	74.2	47.1	76.3	59.3	48.6	60.1	64.8	67.6	31.5	71.7	62.6	35.9	65.1
June	66.5	66.7	74.3	48.1	76.3	59.5	48.4	60.3	64.9	67.8	30.7	72.1	62.5	33.9	65.2
July	66.3	66.5	74.3	47.7	76.4	59.2	47.4	60.0	64.4	67.3	31.0	71.5	62.1	33.5	64.8
Aug	66.2	66.5	74.2	47.2	76.3	59.1	47.9	59.9	64.4	67.1	29.0	71.5	62.3	32.0	65.1
Sept	66.1	66.3	74.1	47.2	76.2	58.8	47.1	59.6	64.7	67.9	32.2	72.0	62.1	35.3	64.5
Oct	66.2	66.4	74.1	46.3	76.3	59.0	47.0	59.9	64.2	67.6	34.6	71.4	61.5	30.5	64.4
Nov	66.2	66.5	74.4	47.8	76.5	59.0	46.3	59.9	63.9	67.1	27.9	71.6	61.3	31.3	64.1
Dec	66.0	66.3	74.2	47.7	76.2	58.8	44.4	59.8	63.2	66.7	27.0	71.2	60.4	31.8	63.1

[1] Civilian labor force as percent of civilian noninstitutional population in group specified.
[2] See footnote 1, Table B–37.
Note.—Data relate to persons 16 years of age and over.
See footnote 5 and Note, Table B–35.

Source: Department of Labor, Bureau of Labor Statistics.

TABLE B-41.—Civilian employment/population ratio by demographic characteristic, 1965–2003

[Percent;[1] monthly data seasonally adjusted]

Year or month	All civilian workers	White[2] Total	White Males Total	White Males 16-19 years	White Males 20 years and over	White Females Total	White Females 16-19 years	White Females 20 years and over	Black and other or black or African American[2] Total	Males Total	Males 16-19 years	Males 20 years and over	Females Total	Females 16-19 years	Females 20 years and over
									Black and other						
1965	56.2	56.0	77.9	47.1	81.5	36.2	33.7	36.5	57.8	73.7	39.4	78.7	44.1	20.2	47.3
1966	56.9	56.8	78.3	50.1	81.7	37.5	37.5	37.5	58.4	74.0	40.5	79.2	45.1	23.1	48.2
1967	57.3	57.2	78.4	50.2	81.7	38.3	37.7	38.3	58.2	73.8	38.8	79.4	45.0	24.8	47.9
1968	57.5	57.4	78.3	50.3	81.6	38.9	37.8	39.1	58.0	73.3	38.7	78.9	45.2	24.7	48.2
1969	58.0	58.0	78.2	51.1	81.4	40.1	39.5	40.1	58.1	72.8	39.0	78.4	45.9	25.1	48.9
1970	57.4	57.5	76.8	49.6	80.1	40.3	39.5	40.4	56.8	70.9	35.5	76.8	44.9	22.4	48.2
1971	56.6	56.8	75.7	49.2	79.0	39.9	38.6	40.1	54.9	68.1	31.8	74.2	43.9	20.2	47.3
1972	57.0	57.4	76.0	51.5	79.0	40.7	41.3	40.6	54.1	67.3	32.4	73.2	43.3	19.9	46.7
									Black or African American[2]						
1972	57.0	57.4	76.0	51.5	79.0	40.7	41.3	40.6	53.7	66.8	31.6	73.0	43.0	19.2	46.5
1973	57.8	58.2	76.5	54.3	79.2	41.8	43.6	41.6	54.5	67.5	32.8	73.7	43.8	22.0	47.2
1974	57.8	58.3	75.9	54.4	78.6	42.4	44.3	42.2	53.5	65.8	31.4	71.9	43.5	20.9	46.9
1975	56.1	56.7	73.0	50.6	75.7	42.0	42.5	41.9	50.1	60.6	26.3	66.5	41.6	20.2	44.9
1976	56.8	57.5	73.4	51.5	76.0	43.2	44.2	43.1	50.8	60.6	25.8	66.8	42.8	19.2	46.4
1977	57.9	58.6	74.1	54.4	76.5	44.5	45.9	44.4	51.4	61.4	26.4	67.5	43.3	18.5	47.0
1978	59.3	60.0	75.0	56.3	77.2	46.3	48.5	46.1	53.6	63.3	28.5	69.1	45.8	22.1	49.3
1979	59.9	60.6	75.1	55.7	77.3	47.5	49.4	47.3	53.8	63.4	28.7	69.1	46.0	22.4	49.3
1980	59.2	60.0	73.4	53.4	75.6	47.8	47.9	47.8	52.3	60.4	27.0	65.8	45.7	21.0	49.1
1981	59.0	60.0	72.8	51.3	75.1	48.3	46.2	48.5	51.3	59.1	24.6	64.5	45.1	19.7	48.5
1982	57.8	58.8	70.6	47.0	73.0	48.1	44.6	48.4	49.4	56.0	20.3	61.4	44.2	17.7	47.5
1983	57.9	58.9	70.4	47.4	72.6	48.5	44.5	48.9	49.5	56.3	20.4	61.6	44.1	17.0	47.4
1984	59.5	60.5	72.1	49.1	74.3	49.8	47.0	50.0	52.3	59.2	23.9	64.1	46.7	20.1	49.8
1985	60.1	61.0	72.3	49.9	74.3	50.7	47.1	51.0	53.4	60.0	26.3	64.6	48.1	23.1	50.9
1986	60.7	61.5	72.3	49.6	74.3	51.7	47.9	52.0	54.1	60.6	26.5	65.1	48.8	23.8	51.6
1987	61.5	62.3	72.7	49.9	74.7	52.8	49.0	53.1	55.6	62.0	28.5	66.4	50.3	25.8	53.0
1988	62.3	63.1	73.2	51.7	75.1	53.8	50.2	54.0	56.3	62.7	29.4	67.1	51.2	25.8	53.9
1989	63.0	63.8	73.7	52.6	75.4	54.6	50.5	54.9	56.9	62.8	30.4	67.0	52.0	27.1	54.6
1990	62.8	63.7	73.3	51.0	75.1	54.7	48.3	55.2	56.7	62.6	27.7	67.1	51.9	25.8	54.7
1991	61.7	62.6	71.6	47.2	73.5	54.2	45.9	54.8	55.4	61.3	25.8	65.9	50.6	21.5	53.6
1992	61.5	62.4	71.1	46.4	73.1	54.2	44.2	54.9	54.9	59.9	23.6	64.3	50.8	22.1	53.6
1993	61.7	62.7	71.4	46.6	73.3	54.6	45.7	55.2	55.0	60.0	23.6	64.3	50.9	21.6	53.8
1994	62.5	63.5	71.8	48.3	73.6	55.8	47.5	56.4	56.1	60.8	25.4	65.0	52.3	24.5	55.0
1995	62.9	63.8	72.0	49.4	73.8	56.1	48.1	56.7	57.1	61.7	25.2	66.1	53.4	26.1	56.1
1996	63.2	64.1	72.3	48.2	74.2	56.3	47.6	57.0	57.4	61.1	24.9	65.5	54.4	27.1	57.1
1997	63.8	64.6	72.7	48.1	74.7	57.0	47.2	57.8	58.2	61.4	23.7	66.1	55.6	28.5	58.4
1998	64.1	64.7	72.7	48.6	74.7	57.1	49.3	57.7	59.7	62.9	28.4	67.1	57.2	31.8	59.7
1999	64.3	64.8	72.8	49.3	74.8	57.3	48.3	58.0	60.6	63.1	26.7	67.5	58.6	29.0	61.5
2000	64.4	64.9	73.0	49.5	74.9	57.4	44.8	58.0	60.9	63.6	28.9	67.7	58.6	30.6	61.3
2001	63.7	64.2	72.0	46.2	74.0	57.0	46.5	57.7	59.7	62.1	26.4	66.3	57.8	27.0	60.7
2002	62.7	63.4	70.8	42.3	73.1	56.4	44.1	57.3	58.1	61.1	25.6	65.2	55.8	24.9	58.7
2003	62.3	63.0	70.1	39.4	72.5	56.3	41.5	57.3	57.4	59.5	19.9	64.1	55.6	23.4	58.6
2002: Jan	62.7	63.3	70.8	42.8	73.1	56.3	44.5	57.1	58.6	62.0	26.1	66.3	55.9	22.9	59.0
Feb	62.9	63.7	71.1	42.7	73.3	56.7	44.6	57.5	58.5	61.7	27.5	65.7	56.0	25.3	58.9
Mar	62.8	63.5	70.8	43.0	73.1	56.6	46.0	57.3	58.1	61.6	25.5	65.9	55.2	24.8	58.1
Apr	62.7	63.4	70.8	42.7	73.0	56.5	44.3	57.3	58.3	61.7	25.8	65.9	54.6	24.6	58.5
May	62.8	63.6	71.1	42.4	73.4	56.4	43.5	57.4	58.6	62.4	26.9	66.6	55.5	24.8	58.4
June	62.7	63.4	70.9	42.0	73.2	56.4	44.5	57.2	57.9	60.8	26.9	64.8	55.6	25.3	58.5
July	62.7	63.4	70.8	42.1	73.1	56.4	44.3	57.3	57.8	60.9	25.5	65.0	55.3	23.3	58.3
Aug	62.8	63.5	70.9	41.0	73.2	56.5	44.2	57.4	58.1	61.0	24.2	65.3	55.8	25.1	58.7
Sept	63.0	63.5	70.9	43.0	73.1	56.5	44.2	57.4	58.8	61.6	24.0	65.9	56.6	28.4	59.3
Oct	62.8	63.4	70.7	42.7	72.9	56.4	43.4	57.4	58.5	61.4	28.1	65.3	56.1	26.3	58.9
Nov	62.5	63.2	70.5	42.3	72.7	56.3	42.8	57.3	57.2	59.0	25.6	62.9	55.7	22.9	58.7
Dec	62.4	63.1	70.3	41.7	72.5	56.2	42.9	57.2	57.4	59.1	21.8	63.4	56.0	25.3	58.9
2003: Jan	62.5	63.2	70.2	40.9	72.5	56.5	43.1	57.4	57.8	59.4	21.5	63.8	56.4	26.1	59.2
Feb	62.4	63.2	70.4	40.1	72.7	56.4	42.7	57.4	57.5	59.8	21.1	64.2	55.6	25.5	58.4
Mar	62.3	63.1	70.2	38.2	72.7	56.4	42.2	57.4	57.4	59.2	18.0	63.9	56.0	26.2	58.8
Apr	62.3	63.1	70.2	38.8	72.6	56.5	42.6	57.5	57.6	59.4	19.4	63.9	56.2	25.0	59.1
May	62.3	63.0	69.9	39.0	72.4	56.4	42.0	57.4	57.6	59.1	18.5	63.8	56.9	24.7	59.9
June	62.3	63.0	69.9	39.6	72.3	56.5	41.7	57.4	57.6	59.6	19.5	64.1	55.7	20.2	58.9
July	62.2	62.9	69.9	39.2	72.3	56.3	41.1	57.4	57.3	59.6	19.5	64.1	55.5	22.3	58.6
Aug	62.2	62.9	69.9	39.4	72.3	56.3	41.3	57.3	57.4	59.5	21.0	63.9	55.7	24.2	58.8
Sept	62.1	62.8	70.0	38.9	72.4	55.9	41.2	57.4	56.9	59.7	21.2	64.1	55.7	24.2	58.6
Oct	62.2	63.0	70.1	38.9	72.6	56.2	41.1	57.2	56.9	59.5	20.4	63.9	54.8	20.4	58.0
Nov	62.3	63.1	70.3	39.8	72.7	56.2	41.0	57.2	57.3	59.7	18.8	64.4	55.3	23.2	58.3
Dec	62.2	62.9	70.3	40.0	72.6	56.0	38.6	57.2	56.7	59.9	19.3	64.6	54.1	23.3	56.9

[1] Civilian employment as percent of civilian noninstitutional population in group specified.
[2] See footnote 1, Table B-37.

Note.—Data relate to persons 16 years of age and over.
See footnote 5 and Note, Table B-35.

Source: Department of Labor, Bureau of Labor Statistics.

TABLE B–42.—*Civilian unemployment rate, 1959–2003*

[Percent;[1] monthly data seasonally adjusted, except as noted by NSA]

Year or month	All civilian workers	Males			Females			Both sexes 16–19 years	By race				Hispanic or Latino ethnicity[3]	Married men, spouse present	Women who maintain families (NSA)
		Total	16–19 years	20 years and over	Total	16–19 years	20 years and over		White[2]	Black and other[2]	Black or African American[2]	Asian (NSA)[2]			
1959	5.5	5.2	15.3	4.7	5.9	13.5	5.2	14.6	4.8	10.7				3.6	
1960	5.5	5.4	15.3	4.7	5.9	13.9	5.1	14.7	5.0	10.2				3.7	
1961	6.7	6.4	17.1	5.7	7.2	16.3	6.3	16.8	6.0	12.4				4.6	
1962	5.5	5.2	14.7	4.6	6.2	14.6	5.4	14.7	4.9	10.9				3.6	
1963	5.7	5.2	17.2	4.5	6.5	17.2	5.4	17.2	5.0	10.8				3.4	
1964	5.2	4.6	15.8	3.9	6.2	16.6	5.2	16.2	4.6	9.6				2.8	
1965	4.5	4.0	14.1	3.2	5.5	15.7	4.5	14.8	4.1	8.1				2.4	
1966	3.8	3.2	11.7	2.5	4.8	14.1	3.8	12.8	3.4	7.3				1.9	
1967	3.8	3.1	12.3	2.3	5.2	13.5	4.2	12.9	3.4	7.4				1.8	4.9
1968	3.6	2.9	11.6	2.2	4.8	14.0	3.8	12.7	3.2	6.7				1.6	4.4
1969	3.5	2.8	11.4	2.1	4.7	13.3	3.7	12.2	3.1	6.4				1.5	4.4
1970	4.9	4.4	15.0	3.5	5.9	15.6	4.8	15.3	4.5	8.2				2.6	5.4
1971	5.9	5.3	16.6	4.4	6.9	17.2	5.7	16.9	5.4	9.9				3.2	7.3
1972	5.6	5.0	15.9	4.0	6.6	16.7	5.4	16.2	5.1	10.0	10.4			2.8	7.2
1973	4.9	4.2	13.9	3.3	6.0	15.3	4.9	14.5	4.3	9.0	9.4		7.5	2.3	7.1
1974	5.6	4.9	15.6	3.8	6.7	16.6	5.5	16.0	5.0	9.9	10.5		8.1	2.7	7.0
1975	8.5	7.9	20.1	6.8	9.3	19.7	8.0	19.9	7.8	13.8	14.8		12.2	5.1	10.0
1976	7.7	7.1	19.2	5.9	8.6	18.7	7.4	19.0	7.0	13.1	14.0		11.5	4.2	10.1
1977	7.1	6.3	17.3	5.2	8.2	18.3	7.0	17.8	6.2	13.1	14.0		10.1	3.6	9.4
1978	6.1	5.3	15.8	4.3	7.2	17.1	6.0	16.4	5.2	11.9	12.8		9.1	2.8	8.5
1979	5.8	5.1	15.9	4.2	6.8	16.4	5.7	16.1	5.1	11.3	12.3		8.3	2.8	8.3
1980	7.1	6.9	18.3	5.9	7.4	17.2	6.4	17.8	6.3	13.1	14.3		10.1	4.2	9.2
1981	7.6	7.4	20.1	6.3	7.9	19.0	6.8	19.6	6.7	14.2	15.6		10.4	4.3	10.4
1982	9.7	9.9	24.4	8.8	9.4	21.9	8.3	23.2	8.6	17.3	18.9		13.8	6.5	11.7
1983	9.6	9.9	23.3	8.9	9.2	21.3	8.1	22.4	8.4	17.8	19.5		13.7	6.5	12.2
1984	7.5	7.4	19.6	6.6	7.6	18.0	6.8	18.9	6.5	14.4	15.9		10.7	4.6	10.3
1985	7.2	7.0	19.5	6.2	7.4	17.6	6.6	18.6	6.2	13.7	15.1		10.5	4.3	10.4
1986	7.0	6.9	19.0	6.1	7.1	17.6	6.2	18.3	6.0	13.1	14.5		10.6	4.4	9.8
1987	6.2	6.2	17.8	5.4	6.2	15.9	5.4	16.9	5.3	11.6	13.0		8.8	3.9	9.2
1988	5.5	5.5	16.0	4.8	5.6	14.4	4.9	15.3	4.7	10.4	11.7		8.2	3.3	8.1
1989	5.3	5.2	15.9	4.5	5.4	14.0	4.7	15.0	4.5	10.0	11.4		8.0	3.0	8.1
1990	5.6	5.7	16.3	5.0	5.5	14.7	4.9	15.5	4.8	10.1	11.4		8.2	3.4	8.3
1991	6.8	7.2	19.8	6.4	6.4	17.5	5.7	18.7	6.1	11.1	12.5		10.0	4.4	9.3
1992	7.5	7.9	21.5	7.1	7.0	18.6	6.3	20.1	6.6	12.7	14.2		11.6	5.1	10.0
1993	6.9	7.2	20.4	6.4	6.6	17.5	5.9	19.0	6.1	11.7	13.0		10.8	4.4	9.7
1994	6.1	6.2	19.0	5.4	6.0	16.2	5.4	17.6	5.3	10.5	11.5		9.9	3.7	8.9
1995	5.6	5.6	18.4	4.8	5.6	16.1	4.9	17.3	4.9	9.6	10.4		9.3	3.3	8.0
1996	5.4	5.4	18.1	4.6	5.4	15.2	4.8	16.7	4.7	9.3	10.5		8.9	3.0	8.2
1997	4.9	4.9	16.9	4.2	5.0	15.0	4.4	16.0	4.2	8.8	10.0		7.7	2.7	8.1
1998	4.5	4.4	16.2	3.7	4.6	12.9	4.1	14.6	3.9	7.8	8.9		7.2	2.4	7.2
1999	4.2	4.1	14.7	3.5	4.3	13.2	3.8	13.9	3.7	7.0	8.0		6.4	2.2	6.4
2000	4.0	3.9	14.0	3.3	4.1	12.1	3.6	13.1	3.5		7.6	3.6	5.7	2.0	5.9
2001	4.7	4.8	16.0	4.2	4.7	13.4	4.1	14.7	4.2		8.6	4.5	6.6	2.7	6.6
2002	5.8	5.9	18.1	5.3	5.6	14.9	5.1	16.5	5.1		10.2	5.9	7.5	3.6	8.0
2003	6.0	6.3	19.3	5.6	5.7	15.6	5.1	17.5	5.2		10.8	6.0	7.7	3.8	8.5
2002: Jan	5.6	5.8	17.3	5.2	5.5	15.6	4.9	16.4	5.1		10.0	5.6	7.8	3.5	8.2
Feb	5.7	5.8	17.2	5.2	5.5	14.8	5.0	16.0	5.0		9.8	5.6	7.0	3.5	8.3
Mar	5.7	5.9	18.4	5.2	5.6	14.6	5.0	16.5	5.0		10.5	5.6	7.4	3.5	7.9
Apr	5.9	6.0	18.0	5.3	5.9	15.5	5.3	16.8	5.2		10.7	5.9	8.0	3.9	8.2
May	5.8	5.9	18.5	5.2	5.7	14.8	5.2	16.7	5.1		10.0	5.9	7.0	3.6	8.1
June	5.8	5.9	18.5	5.3	5.6	14.8	5.1	16.7	5.1		10.4	6.9	7.2	3.9	8.2
July	5.8	5.9	18.5	5.2	5.7	14.9	5.1	16.8	5.2		9.9	6.2	7.4	3.5	8.6
Aug	5.7	6.0	20.1	5.2	5.5	14.3	5.0	17.2	5.1		9.8	6.5	7.5	3.5	7.6
Sept	5.7	5.9	18.1	5.2	5.5	14.2	4.9	16.2	5.1		9.7	5.4	7.5	3.6	7.0
Oct	5.7	5.9	16.0	5.3	5.6	14.2	5.1	15.1	5.1		9.8	5.6	7.8	3.5	7.7
Nov	5.9	6.1	18.2	5.5	5.6	15.8	5.0	17.1	5.1		10.9	5.6	7.8	3.6	8.0
Dec	6.0	6.2	18.1	5.6	5.7	15.3	5.2	16.7	5.2		11.4	5.9	8.0	3.7	7.9
2003: Jan	5.8	6.1	18.6	5.5	5.4	15.4	4.8	17.0	5.1		10.5	5.6	7.9	3.6	8.0
Feb	5.9	6.1	19.5	5.5	5.6	15.0	5.1	17.3	5.1		10.7	6.0	7.7	3.7	9.0
Mar	5.8	6.1	20.5	5.4	5.6	14.8	5.1	17.6	5.1		10.3	6.5	7.7	3.8	8.4
Apr	6.0	6.3	20.2	5.7	5.6	15.5	5.1	17.8	5.2		10.8	5.8	7.6	3.8	8.5
May	6.1	6.5	20.3	5.8	5.7	16.0	5.1	18.1	5.4		10.7	5.1	8.1	3.9	8.3
June	6.3	6.7	19.9	6.0	5.9	18.2	5.2	19.0	5.5		11.6	7.8	8.2	4.3	8.7
July	6.2	6.6	20.4	5.9	5.7	15.9	5.2	18.2	5.4		11.1	6.2	8.1	3.9	9.0
Aug	6.1	6.4	17.6	5.8	5.8	16.2	5.2	16.9	5.4		10.9	5.9	7.8	3.9	8.4
Sept	6.1	6.4	19.6	5.8	5.8	15.2	5.3	17.5	5.3		11.1	6.2	7.5	3.8	8.5
Oct	6.0	6.2	18.7	5.6	5.7	15.4	5.2	17.1	5.1		11.4	6.1	7.3	3.8	8.4
Nov	5.9	6.2	18.3	5.6	5.5	13.0	5.1	15.7	5.2		10.4	5.2	7.4	3.7	8.3
Dec	5.7	5.8	17.4	5.3	5.6	14.7	5.1	16.1	5.0		10.3	5.3	6.6	3.3	8.4

[1] Unemployed as percent of civilian labor force in group specified.
[2] See footnote 1, Table B–37.
[3] Persons whose ethnicity is identified as Hispanic or Latino may be of any race.

Note.—Data relate to persons 16 years of age and over.
See footnote 5 and Note, Table B–35.
NSA indicates data are not seasonally adjusted.

Source: Department of Labor, Bureau of Labor Statistics.

TABLE B-43.—*Civilian unemployment rate by demographic characteristic, 1965–2003*

[Percent; [1] monthly data seasonally adjusted]

Year or month	All civilian workers	White [2] Total	White Males Total	White Males 16-19 years	White Males 20 years and over	White Females Total	White Females 16-19 years	White Females 20 years and over	Black [2] Total	Black Males Total	Black Males 16-19 years	Black Males 20 years and over	Black Females Total	Black Females 16-19 years	Black Females 20 years and over
									Black and other						
1965	4.5	4.1	3.6	12.9	2.9	5.0	14.0	4.0	8.1	7.4	23.3	6.0	9.2	31.7	7.5
1966	3.8	3.4	2.8	10.5	2.2	4.3	12.1	3.3	7.3	6.3	21.3	4.9	8.7	31.3	6.6
1967	3.8	3.4	2.7	10.7	2.1	4.6	11.5	3.8	7.4	6.0	23.9	4.3	9.1	29.6	7.1
1968	3.6	3.2	2.6	10.1	2.0	4.3	12.1	3.4	6.7	5.6	22.1	3.9	8.3	28.7	6.3
1969	3.5	3.1	2.5	10.0	1.9	4.2	11.5	3.4	6.4	5.3	21.4	3.7	7.8	27.6	5.8
1970	4.9	4.5	4.0	13.7	3.2	5.4	13.4	4.4	8.2	7.3	25.0	5.6	9.3	34.5	6.9
1971	5.9	5.4	4.9	15.1	4.0	6.3	15.1	5.3	9.9	9.1	28.8	7.3	10.9	35.4	8.7
1972	5.6	5.1	4.5	14.2	3.6	5.9	14.2	4.9	10.0	8.9	29.7	6.9	11.4	38.4	8.8
									Black or African American [2]						
1972	5.6	5.1	4.5	14.2	3.6	5.9	14.2	4.9	10.4	9.3	31.7	7.0	11.8	40.5	9.0
1973	4.9	4.3	3.8	12.3	3.0	5.3	13.0	4.3	9.4	8.0	27.8	6.0	11.1	36.1	8.6
1974	5.6	5.0	4.4	13.5	3.5	6.1	14.5	5.1	10.5	9.8	33.1	7.4	11.3	37.4	8.8
1975	8.5	7.8	7.2	18.3	6.2	8.6	17.4	7.5	14.8	14.8	38.1	12.5	14.8	41.0	12.2
1976	7.7	7.0	6.4	17.3	5.4	7.9	16.4	6.8	14.0	13.7	37.5	11.4	14.3	41.6	11.7
1977	7.1	6.2	5.5	15.0	4.7	7.3	15.9	6.2	14.0	13.3	39.2	10.7	14.9	43.4	12.3
1978	6.1	5.2	4.6	13.5	3.7	6.2	14.4	5.2	12.8	11.8	36.7	9.3	13.8	40.8	11.2
1979	5.8	5.1	4.5	13.9	3.6	5.9	14.0	5.0	12.3	11.4	34.2	9.3	13.3	39.1	10.9
1980	7.1	6.3	6.1	16.2	5.3	6.5	14.8	5.6	14.3	14.5	37.5	12.4	14.0	39.8	11.9
1981	7.6	6.7	6.5	17.9	5.6	6.9	16.6	5.9	15.6	15.7	40.7	13.5	15.6	42.2	13.4
1982	9.7	8.6	8.8	21.7	7.8	8.3	19.0	7.3	18.9	20.1	48.9	17.8	17.6	47.1	15.4
1983	9.6	8.4	8.8	20.2	7.9	7.9	18.3	6.9	19.5	20.3	48.8	18.1	18.6	48.2	16.5
1984	7.5	6.5	6.4	16.8	5.7	6.5	15.2	5.8	15.9	16.4	42.7	14.3	15.4	42.6	13.5
1985	7.2	6.2	6.1	16.5	5.4	6.4	14.8	5.7	15.1	15.3	41.0	13.2	14.9	39.2	13.1
1986	7.0	6.0	6.0	16.3	5.3	6.1	14.9	5.4	14.5	14.8	39.3	12.9	14.2	39.2	12.4
1987	6.2	5.3	5.4	15.5	4.8	5.2	13.4	4.6	13.0	12.7	34.4	11.1	13.2	34.9	11.6
1988	5.5	4.7	4.7	13.9	4.1	4.7	12.3	4.1	11.7	11.7	32.7	10.1	11.7	32.0	10.4
1989	5.3	4.5	4.5	13.7	3.9	4.5	11.5	4.0	11.4	11.5	31.9	10.0	11.4	33.0	9.8
1990	5.6	4.8	4.9	14.3	4.3	4.7	12.6	4.1	11.4	11.9	31.9	10.4	10.9	29.9	9.7
1991	6.8	6.1	6.5	17.6	5.8	5.6	15.2	5.0	12.5	13.0	36.3	11.5	12.0	36.0	10.6
1992	7.5	6.6	7.0	18.5	6.4	6.1	15.8	5.5	14.2	15.2	42.0	13.5	13.2	37.2	11.8
1993	6.9	6.1	6.3	17.7	5.7	5.7	14.7	5.2	13.0	13.8	40.1	12.1	12.1	37.4	10.7
1994	6.1	5.3	5.4	16.3	4.8	5.2	13.8	4.6	11.5	12.0	37.6	10.3	11.0	32.6	9.8
1995	5.6	4.9	4.9	15.6	4.3	4.8	13.4	4.3	10.4	10.6	37.1	8.8	10.2	34.3	8.6
1996	5.4	4.7	4.7	15.5	4.1	4.7	12.9	4.1	10.5	11.1	36.9	9.4	10.0	30.3	8.7
1997	4.9	4.2	4.2	14.3	3.6	4.2	12.8	3.7	10.0	10.2	36.5	8.5	9.9	28.7	8.8
1998	4.5	3.9	3.9	14.1	3.2	3.9	10.9	3.4	8.9	8.9	30.1	7.4	9.0	25.3	7.9
1999	4.2	3.7	3.6	12.6	3.0	3.8	11.3	3.3	8.0	8.2	30.9	6.7	7.8	25.1	6.8
2000	4.0	3.5	3.4	12.3	2.8	3.6	10.4	3.1	7.6	8.0	26.2	6.9	7.1	22.8	6.2
2001	4.7	4.2	4.2	13.9	3.7	4.1	11.4	3.6	8.6	9.3	30.4	8.0	8.1	27.5	7.0
2002	5.8	5.1	5.3	15.9	4.7	4.9	13.1	4.4	10.2	10.7	31.3	9.5	9.8	28.3	8.8
2003	6.0	5.2	5.6	17.1	5.0	4.8	13.3	4.4	10.8	11.6	36.0	10.3	10.2	30.3	9.2
2002: Jan	5.6	5.1	5.2	14.6	4.7	4.9	14.5	4.3	10.0	10.3	32.9	8.9	9.7	29.5	8.7
Feb	5.7	5.0	5.1	15.4	4.5	4.9	12.8	4.4	9.8	10.1	29.9	8.8	9.5	28.1	8.6
Mar	5.7	5.0	5.2	16.1	4.6	4.8	12.7	4.3	10.5	11.1	34.4	9.6	9.9	28.5	9.0
Apr	5.9	5.2	5.3	15.5	4.8	5.0	12.8	4.6	10.7	10.7	34.8	9.1	10.8	35.0	9.4
May	5.8	5.1	5.3	15.6	4.7	5.0	13.8	4.4	10.0	10.2	34.5	8.6	9.8	21.8	9.3
June	5.8	5.1	5.3	16.4	4.7	4.9	12.7	4.4	10.4	11.3	30.8	10.1	9.7	28.4	8.7
July	5.8	5.2	5.4	17.7	4.7	4.9	13.0	4.4	9.9	10.0	22.4	9.3	9.9	30.2	8.9
Aug	5.7	5.1	5.4	17.6	4.7	4.8	12.3	4.4	9.8	10.4	31.9	9.1	9.3	28.0	8.4
Sept	5.7	5.1	5.3	15.5	4.8	4.8	12.9	4.3	9.7	10.7	34.8	9.2	8.8	21.4	8.2
Oct	5.7	5.1	5.3	14.9	4.8	4.9	13.3	4.4	9.8	10.6	25.5	9.7	9.0	22.8	8.3
Nov	5.9	5.1	5.4	16.0	4.9	4.8	13.6	4.2	10.9	11.7	30.7	10.6	10.1	32.1	9.1
Dec	6.0	5.2	5.5	15.2	5.0	4.8	12.8	4.3	11.4	11.9	35.3	10.6	11.0	33.7	9.7
2003: Jan	5.8	5.1	5.4	16.3	4.9	4.7	13.8	4.2	10.5	11.6	34.1	10.4	9.6	27.6	8.6
Feb	5.9	5.1	5.4	17.1	4.8	4.8	13.6	4.3	10.7	11.8	38.0	10.3	9.7	23.1	9.4
Mar	5.8	5.1	5.4	17.8	4.8	4.8	13.1	4.4	10.3	11.2	43.1	9.5	9.5	24.5	8.8
Apr	6.0	5.2	5.6	17.4	5.0	4.8	13.2	4.3	10.8	11.6	37.1	10.4	10.0	29.3	9.1
May	6.1	5.4	5.7	17.1	5.2	5.0	13.6	4.5	10.7	12.4	41.1	11.0	9.2	31.3	8.0
June	6.3	5.5	5.9	17.6	5.3	4.9	14.8	4.4	11.6	12.2	36.5	11.0	11.0	40.3	9.6
July	6.2	5.4	5.9	17.9	5.3	4.9	13.3	4.4	11.1	11.6	37.1	10.3	10.7	33.4	9.6
Aug	6.1	5.4	5.8	16.5	5.3	4.9	13.7	4.4	10.9	11.3	27.8	10.5	10.6	31.5	9.7
Sept	6.1	5.3	5.6	17.6	5.0	5.0	12.6	4.5	11.1	12.1	34.2	11.0	10.2	31.4	9.2
Oct	6.0	5.1	5.4	15.9	4.9	4.8	12.6	4.4	11.4	12.1	40.2	10.5	10.8	33.2	9.8
Nov	5.9	5.2	5.5	16.8	5.0	4.7	11.5	4.4	10.4	11.0	32.5	10.1	9.8	25.7	9.1
Dec	5.7	5.0	5.3	16.3	4.7	4.8	13.1	4.3	10.3	10.1	28.4	9.3	10.5	26.5	9.7

[1] Unemployed as percent of civilian labor force in group specified.
[2] See footnote 1, Table B–37.

Note.—Data relate to persons 16 years of age and over.
See footnote 5 and Note, Table B–35.

Source: Department of Labor, Bureau of Labor Statistics.

Year or month	Unemployment	Duration of unemployment						Reason for unemployment					
		Less than 5 weeks	5-14 weeks	15-26 weeks	27 weeks and over	Average (mean) duration (weeks)	Median duration (weeks)	Job losers [3]			Job leavers	Reentrants	New entrants
								Total	On layoff	Other			
1959	3,740	1,585	1,114	469	571	14.4							
1960	3,852	1,719	1,176	503	454	12.8							
1961	4,714	1,806	1,376	728	804	15.6							
1962	3,911	1,663	1,134	534	585	14.7							
1963	4,070	1,751	1,231	535	553	14.0							
1964	3,786	1,697	1,117	491	482	13.3							
1965	3,366	1,628	983	404	351	11.8							
1966	2,875	1,573	779	287	239	10.4							
1967 [2]	2,975	1,634	893	271	177	8.7	2.3	1,229	394	836	438	945	396
1968	2,817	1,594	810	256	156	8.4	4.5	1,070	334	736	431	909	407
1969	2,832	1,629	827	242	133	7.8	4.4	1,017	339	678	436	965	413
1970	4,093	2,139	1,290	428	235	8.6	4.9	1,811	675	1,137	550	1,228	504
1971	5,016	2,245	1,585	668	519	11.3	6.3	2,323	735	1,588	590	1,472	630
1972	4,882	2,242	1,472	601	566	12.0	6.2	2,108	582	1,526	641	1,456	677
1973	4,365	2,224	1,314	483	343	10.0	5.2	1,694	472	1,221	683	1,340	649
1974	5,156	2,604	1,597	574	381	9.8	5.2	2,242	746	1,495	768	1,463	681
1975	7,929	2,940	2,484	1,303	1,203	14.2	8.4	4,386	1,671	2,714	827	1,892	823
1976	7,406	2,844	2,196	1,018	1,348	15.8	8.2	3,679	1,050	2,628	903	1,928	895
1977	6,991	2,919	2,132	913	1,028	14.3	7.0	3,166	865	2,300	909	1,963	953
1978	6,202	2,865	1,923	766	648	11.9	5.9	2,585	712	1,873	874	1,857	885
1979	6,137	2,950	1,946	706	535	10.8	5.4	2,635	851	1,784	880	1,806	817
1980	7,637	3,295	2,470	1,052	820	11.9	6.5	3,947	1,488	2,459	891	1,927	872
1981	8,273	3,449	2,539	1,122	1,162	13.7	6.9	4,267	1,430	2,837	923	2,102	981
1982	10,678	3,883	3,311	1,708	1,776	15.6	8.7	6,268	2,127	4,141	840	2,384	1,185
1983	10,717	3,570	2,937	1,652	2,559	20.0	10.1	6,258	1,780	4,478	830	2,412	1,216
1984	8,539	3,350	2,451	1,104	1,634	18.2	7.9	4,421	1,171	3,250	823	2,184	1,110
1985	8,312	3,498	2,509	1,025	1,280	15.6	6.8	4,139	1,157	2,982	877	2,256	1,039
1986	8,237	3,448	2,557	1,045	1,187	15.0	6.9	4,033	1,090	2,943	1,015	2,160	1,029
1987	7,425	3,246	2,196	943	1,040	14.5	6.5	3,566	943	2,623	965	1,974	920
1988	6,701	3,084	2,007	801	809	13.5	5.9	3,092	851	2,241	983	1,809	816
1989	6,528	3,174	1,978	730	646	11.9	4.8	2,983	850	2,133	1,024	1,843	677
1990	7,047	3,265	2,257	822	703	12.0	5.3	3,387	1,028	2,359	1,041	1,930	688
1991	8,628	3,480	2,791	1,246	1,111	13.7	6.8	4,694	1,292	3,402	1,004	2,139	792
1992	9,613	3,376	2,830	1,453	1,954	17.7	8.7	5,389	1,260	4,129	1,002	2,285	937
1993	8,940	3,262	2,584	1,297	1,798	18.0	8.3	4,848	1,115	3,733	976	2,198	919
1994	7,996	2,728	2,408	1,237	1,623	18.8	9.2	3,815	977	2,838	791	2,786	604
1995	7,404	2,700	2,342	1,085	1,278	16.6	8.3	3,476	1,030	2,446	824	2,525	579
1996	7,236	2,633	2,287	1,053	1,262	16.7	8.3	3,370	1,021	2,349	774	2,512	580
1997	6,739	2,538	2,138	995	1,067	15.8	8.0	3,037	931	2,106	795	2,338	569
1998	6,210	2,622	1,950	763	875	14.5	6.7	2,822	866	1,957	734	2,132	520
1999	5,880	2,568	1,832	755	725	13.4	6.4	2,622	848	1,774	783	2,005	469
2000	5,692	2,558	1,815	669	649	12.6	5.9	2,517	852	1,664	780	1,961	434
2001	6,801	2,853	2,196	951	801	13.1	6.8	3,476	1,067	2,409	835	2,031	459
2002	8,378	2,893	2,580	1,369	1,535	16.6	9.1	4,607	1,124	3,483	866	2,368	536
2003	8,774	2,785	2,612	1,442	1,936	19.2	10.1	4,838	1,121	3,717	818	2,477	641
2002: Jan	8,126	3,011	2,595	1,405	1,182	14.6	8.5	4,446	1,155	3,291	881	2,266	488
Feb	8,184	2,963	2,561	1,408	1,215	15.1	8.3	4,457	1,135	3,322	891	2,314	508
Mar	8,278	3,051	2,535	1,385	1,342	15.5	8.4	4,454	1,099	3,355	881	2,459	533
Apr	8,578	2,940	2,848	1,373	1,459	16.2	8.8	4,665	1,128	3,536	991	2,373	524
May	8,397	2,887	2,573	1,375	1,573	16.9	9.6	4,604	1,091	3,513	900	2,409	502
June	8,384	2,727	2,684	1,389	1,608	16.9	11.1	4,624	1,086	3,539	840	2,350	540
July	8,400	2,905	2,498	1,344	1,579	16.7	8.9	4,594	1,216	3,378	842	2,377	541
Aug	8,335	2,894	2,546	1,306	1,566	16.4	8.9	4,567	1,166	3,402	845	2,314	610
Sept	8,269	2,795	2,511	1,353	1,623	17.7	9.5	4,538	1,042	3,497	798	2,333	534
Oct	8,363	2,779	2,514	1,376	1,695	17.8	9.6	4,733	1,098	3,635	850	2,365	487
Nov	8,565	2,930	2,534	1,339	1,765	17.7	9.4	4,784	1,081	3,703	826	2,399	610
Dec	8,698	2,873	2,591	1,420	1,891	18.5	9.6	4,839	1,122	3,716	866	2,475	534
2003: Jan	8,428	2,795	2,573	1,444	1,731	18.5	9.7	4,631	1,094	3,536	825	2,374	605
Feb	8,581	2,782	2,586	1,292	1,884	18.7	9.5	4,806	1,141	3,665	783	2,418	589
Mar	8,519	2,788	2,531	1,340	1,829	18.1	9.7	4,774	1,151	3,623	802	2,410	620
Apr	8,799	2,815	2,625	1,399	1,919	19.4	10.1	4,851	1,112	3,739	818	2,517	633
May	8,957	3,033	2,617	1,380	1,914	19.2	10.1	5,021	1,197	3,824	778	2,506	635
June	9,245	2,937	2,787	1,500	2,010	19.6	11.7	4,972	1,177	3,795	890	2,646	642
July	9,048	2,739	2,698	1,598	1,961	19.3	10.1	4,947	1,173	3,774	798	2,522	661
Aug	8,929	2,735	2,630	1,561	2,001	19.2	10.0	4,939	1,092	3,847	790	2,530	650
Sept	8,966	2,749	2,736	1,438	2,073	19.6	10.1	4,947	1,110	3,837	836	2,436	684
Oct	8,797	2,733	2,585	1,460	2,018	19.4	10.3	4,877	1,097	3,780	789	2,518	653
Nov	8,653	2,622	2,556	1,448	2,036	20.0	10.4	4,719	1,055	3,664	931	2,440	619
Dec	8,398	2,627	2,450	1,513	1,890	19.6	10.4	4,618	1,060	3,558	783	2,366	694

[1] Because of independent seasonal adjustment of the various series, detail will not add to totals.
[2] Data for 1967 by reason for unemployment are not equal to total unemployment.
[3] Beginning January 1994, job losers and persons who completed temporary jobs.

Note.—Data relate to persons 16 years of age and over.
See footnote 5 and Note, Table B-35.

Source: Department of Labor, Bureau of Labor Statistics.

TABLE B-45.—Unemployment insurance programs, selected data, 1978–2003

Year or month	All programs			State programs					
	Covered employ- ment[1]	Insured unemploy- ment (weekly aver- age)[2][3]	Total benefits paid (millions of dollars)[2][4]	Insured unem- ploy- ment[3]	Initial claims	Exhaus- tions[5]	Insured unemploy- ment as percent of covered employ- ment	Benefits paid Total (millions of dollars)[4]	Benefits paid Average weekly check (dollars)[6]
	Thousands			Weekly average; thousands					
1978	88,804	2,645	9,007	2,359	346	39	3.3	7,717	83.67
1979	92,062	2,592	9,401	2,434	388	39	2.9	8,613	89.67
1980	92,659	3,837	16,175	3,350	488	59	3.9	13,761	98.95
1981	93,300	3,410	15,287	3,047	460	57	3.5	13,262	106.70
1982	91,628	4,592	24,491	4,059	583	80	4.6	20,649	119.34
1983	91,898	3,774	20,968	3,395	438	80	3.9	18,549	123.59
1984	96,474	2,560	13,739	2,475	377	50	2.8	13,237	123.47
1985	99,186	2,699	15,217	2,617	397	49	2.9	14,707	128.11
1986	101,099	2,739	16,563	2,643	378	52	2.8	15,950	135.65
1987	103,936	2,369	14,684	2,300	328	46	2.4	14,211	140.39
1988	107,156	2,135	13,481	2,081	310	38	2.0	13,086	144.74
1989	109,929	2,205	14,569	2,158	330	37	2.1	14,205	151.43
1990	111,500	2,575	18,387	2,522	388	45	2.4	17,932	161.20
1991	109,606	3,406	26,327	3,342	447	67	3.2	25,479	169.56
1992	110,167	3,348	[7]26,035	3,245	408	74	3.1	25,056	173.38
1993	112,146	2,845	[7]22,629	2,751	341	62	2.6	21,661	179.41
1994	115,255	2,746	22,508	2,670	340	57	2.4	21,537	181.91
1995	118,068	2,639	21,991	2,572	357	51	2.3	21,226	187.04
1996	120,567	2,656	22,495	2,595	356	53	2.2	21,820	189.27
1997	121,044	2,370	20,324	2,323	323	48	1.9	19,735	192.84
1998	124,184	2,260	19,941	2,222	321	44	1.8	19,431	200.58
1999	127,042	2,223	21,024	2,188	298	44	1.7	20,563	212.10
2000	129,877	2,146	20,983	2,110	301	41	1.6	20,507	221.01
2001	129,636	3,012	32,228	2,974	404	54	2.3	31,680	238.07
2002	128,234	3,624	[8]42,978	3,585	407	85	2.8	42,130	256.79
2003 [p]		3,575	[8]38,615	3,533	402	85	2.8	37,680	261.61
				**	**		**		
2002: Jan		4,321	4,398.6	3,513	401	81	2.7	4,318.9	251.13
Feb		4,308	3,948.1	3,522	389	77	2.7	3,860.9	254.62
Mar		4,151	3,973.6	3,583	419	89	2.8	3,900.8	256.57
Apr		3,953	3,887.1	3,669	430	101	2.9	3,838.8	256.85
May		3,254	3,442.9	3,705	409	85	2.9	3,401.7	259.10
June		3,542	3,105.7	3,651	392	85	2.8	3,068.8	257.89
July		3,526	3,595.9	3,515	387	94	2.7	3,551.2	255.57
Aug		3,125	3,188.7	3,549	397	82	2.8	3,144.2	254.91
Sept		3,269	3,009.3	3,608	417	82	2.8	2,952.1	259.49
Oct		2,938	3,258.3	3,601	411	79	2.8	3,191.3	260.97
Nov		3,085	2,860.0	3,486	390	75	2.7	2,790.1	258.35
Dec		3,911	3,812.4	3,478	409	85	2.7	3,725.0	259.05
2003: Jan		3,977	4,130.1	3,361	388	84	2.6	4,035.1	261.09
Feb		4,179	3,889.6	3,429	409	83	2.7	3,806.3	263.60
Mar		4,354	4,204.7	3,514	423	88	2.8	4,125.6	264.74
Apr		3,712	3,862.7	3,622	443	92	2.9	3,792.9	263.66
May		3,273	3,305.1	3,716	432	84	2.9	3,244.9	262.72
June		3,676	3,387.0	3,726	427	85	2.9	3,323.9	261.15
July		3,452	3,615.3	3,625	406	89	2.9	3,551.2	258.74
Aug		3,382	3,174.1	3,630	402	84	2.9	3,099.1	257.23
Sept		3,226	3,212.8	3,626	403	83	2.9	3,116.8	261.06
Oct		2,810	2,978.8	3,515	382	78	2.8	2,887.6	262.17
Nov		3,216	2,810.5	3,367	363	81	2.7	2,719.4	260.60
Dec [p]		3,559	3,701.4	3,259	356	86	2.6	3,600.9	261.35

** Monthly data are seasonally adjusted.

[1] Through 1996 includes persons under the State, UCFE (Federal employee, effective January 1955), RRB (Railroad Retirement Board) programs, and UCX (unemployment compensation for ex-servicemembers, effective October 1958) programs. Beginning 1997, covered employment data are State and UCFE programs only. Workers covered by State programs account for about 97 percent of wage and salary earners.
Covered employment data beginning 2001 are based on the North American Industry Classification System (NAICS). Prior data are based on the Standard Industrial Classification (SIC).

[2] Includes State, UCFE, RR, and UCX. Also includes Federal and State extended benefit programs. Does not include FSB (Federal supplemental benefits), SUA (special unemployment assistance), Federal Supplemental Compensation, Emergency Unemployment Compensation, and EUC (Temporary Extended Unemployment Compensation) programs.

[3] Covered workers who have completed at least 1 week of unemployment.

[4] Annual data are net amounts and monthly data are gross amounts.

[5] Individuals receiving final payments in benefit year.

[6] For total unemployment only.

[7] Including Emergency Unemployment Compensation, total benefits paid for 1992 and 1993 would be approximately (in millions of dollars): for 1992, 39,990 and for 1993, 34,876.

[8] Including Temporary Extended Unemployment Compensation, total benefits paid for 2002 and 2003 (not including RRB program) would be approximately (in millions of dollars): for 2002, 53,800 and for 2003, 51,326.

Note.—Insured unemployment and initial claims programs include Puerto Rican sugar cane workers.

Source: Department of Labor, Employment and Training Administration.

—*Employees on nonagricultural payrolls, by major industry, 1959–2003*

[Thousands of persons; monthly data seasonally adjusted]

Year or month	Total	Goods-producing industries						Service-providing industries		
		Total	Natural resources and mining	Construction	Manufacturing			Total	Trade, transportation, and utilities [1]	
					Total	Durable goods	Nondurable goods		Total	Retail trade
1959	53,374	19,163	789	3,050	15,325	8,988	6,337	34,211	10,960	5,453
1960	54,296	19,182	771	2,973	15,438	9,071	6,367	35,114	11,147	5,589
1961	54,105	18,647	728	2,908	15,011	8,711	6,300	35,458	11,040	5,560
1962	55,659	19,203	709	2,997	15,498	9,099	6,399	36,455	11,215	5,672
1963	56,764	19,385	694	3,060	15,631	9,226	6,405	37,379	11,367	5,781
1964	58,391	19,733	697	3,148	15,888	9,414	6,474	38,658	11,677	5,977
1965	60,874	20,595	694	3,284	16,617	9,973	6,644	40,279	12,139	6,262
1966	64,020	21,740	690	3,371	17,680	10,803	6,878	42,280	12,611	6,530
1967	65,931	21,882	679	3,305	17,897	10,952	6,945	44,049	12,950	6,711
1968	68,023	22,292	671	3,410	18,211	11,137	7,074	45,731	13,334	6,977
1969	70,512	22,893	683	3,637	18,573	11,396	7,177	47,619	13,853	7,295
1970	71,006	22,179	677	3,654	17,848	10,762	7,086	48,827	14,144	7,463
1971	71,335	21,602	658	3,770	17,174	10,229	6,944	49,734	14,318	7,657
1972	73,798	22,299	672	3,957	17,669	10,630	7,039	51,499	14,788	8,038
1973	76,912	23,450	693	4,167	18,589	11,414	7,176	53,462	15,349	8,371
1974	78,389	23,364	755	4,095	18,514	11,432	7,082	55,025	15,693	8,536
1975	77,069	21,318	802	3,608	16,909	10,266	6,643	55,751	15,606	8,600
1976	79,502	22,025	832	3,662	17,531	10,640	6,891	57,477	16,128	8,966
1977	82,593	22,972	865	3,940	18,167	11,132	7,035	59,620	16,765	9,359
1978	86,826	24,156	902	4,322	18,932	11,770	7,162	62,670	17,658	9,879
1979	89,932	24,997	1,008	4,562	19,426	12,220	7,206	64,935	18,303	10,180
1980	90,528	24,263	1,077	4,454	18,733	11,679	7,054	66,265	18,413	10,244
1981	91,289	24,118	1,180	4,304	18,634	11,611	7,023	67,172	18,604	10,364
1982	89,677	22,550	1,163	4,024	17,363	10,610	6,753	67,127	18,457	10,372
1983	90,280	22,110	997	4,065	17,048	10,326	6,722	68,171	18,668	10,635
1984	94,530	23,435	1,014	4,501	17,920	11,050	6,870	71,095	19,653	11,223
1985	97,511	23,585	974	4,793	17,819	11,034	6,784	73,926	20,379	11,733
1986	99,474	23,318	829	4,937	17,552	10,795	6,757	76,156	20,795	12,078
1987	102,088	23,470	771	5,090	17,609	10,767	6,842	78,618	21,302	12,419
1988	105,345	23,909	770	5,233	17,906	10,969	6,938	81,436	21,974	12,808
1989	108,014	24,045	750	5,309	17,985	11,004	6,981	83,969	22,510	13,108
1990	109,487	23,723	765	5,263	17,695	10,736	6,959	85,764	22,666	13,182
1991	108,374	22,588	739	4,780	17,068	10,219	6,849	85,787	22,281	12,896
1992	108,726	22,095	689	4,608	16,799	9,945	6,854	86,631	22,125	12,828
1993	110,844	22,219	666	4,779	16,774	9,900	6,873	88,625	22,378	13,021
1994	114,291	22,774	659	5,095	17,021	10,131	6,890	91,517	23,128	13,491
1995	117,298	23,156	641	5,274	17,241	10,372	6,869	94,142	23,834	13,897
1996	119,708	23,410	637	5,536	17,237	10,485	6,752	96,299	24,239	14,143
1997	122,776	23,886	654	5,813	17,419	10,704	6,716	98,890	24,700	14,389
1998	125,930	24,354	645	6,149	17,560	10,910	6,650	101,576	25,186	14,609
1999	128,993	24,465	598	6,545	17,322	10,830	6,492	104,528	25,771	14,970
2000	131,785	24,649	599	6,787	17,263	10,876	6,388	107,136	26,225	15,280
2001	131,826	23,873	606	6,826	16,441	10,335	6,107	107,952	25,983	15,239
2002	130,376	22,619	581	6,732	15,306	9,517	5,789	107,757	25,493	15,047
2003 ᴾ	130,045	22,064	566	6,797	14,701	9,093	5,608	107,981	25,266	14,976
2002: Jan	130,578	22,960	598	6,777	15,585	9,707	5,878	107,618	25,564	15,050
Feb	130,510	22,887	594	6,776	15,517	9,666	5,851	107,623	25,570	15,069
Mar	130,481	22,792	589	6,753	15,450	9,617	5,833	107,689	25,565	15,081
Apr	130,415	22,713	588	6,719	15,406	9,590	5,816	107,702	25,560	15,087
May	130,411	22,667	584	6,716	15,367	9,567	5,800	107,744	25,536	15,069
June	130,383	22,639	580	6,725	15,334	9,541	5,793	107,744	25,530	15,065
July	130,204	22,588	576	6,703	15,309	9,516	5,793	107,616	25,513	15,062
Aug	130,224	22,527	575	6,719	15,233	9,472	5,761	107,697	25,458	15,033
Sept	130,289	22,497	573	6,728	15,196	9,435	5,761	107,792	25,430	15,016
Oct	130,408	22,435	572	6,720	15,143	9,400	5,743	107,973	25,439	15,025
Nov	130,409	33,409	573	6,745	15,091	9,362	5,729	108,000	25,406	15,014
Dec	130,198	22,323	572	6,731	15,020	9,316	5,704	107,875	25,378	15,006
2003: Jan	130,356	22,288	568	6,738	14,982	9,282	5,700	108,068	25,376	15,009
Feb	130,235	22,191	569	6,700	14,922	9,236	5,686	108,044	25,346	14,987
Mar	130,084	22,159	565	6,720	14,874	9,203	5,671	107,925	25,338	14,995
Apr	130,062	22,119	564	6,760	14,795	9,147	5,648	107,943	25,321	15,005
May	129,986	22,098	566	6,786	14,746	9,114	5,632	107,888	25,282	14,979
June	129,903	22,061	569	6,800	14,692	9,081	5,611	107,842	25,238	14,964
July	129,846	22,001	566	6,804	14,631	9,034	5,597	107,845	25,211	14,958
Aug	129,881	21,982	565	6,825	14,592	9,018	5,574	107,899	25,217	14,975
Sept	129,980	21,978	564	6,841	14,573	9,010	5,563	108,002	25,243	14,987
Oct	130,080	21,966	565	6,845	14,556	9,004	5,552	108,114	25,256	14,996
Nov ᴾ	130,123	21,954	565	6,859	14,530	9,001	5,529	108,169	25,236	14,969
Dec ᴾ	130,124	21,942	565	6,873	14,504	8,993	5,511	108,182	25,201	14,931

[1] Includes wholesale trade, transportation and warehousing, and utilities, not shown separately.

Note.—Data in Tables B–46 and B–47 are based on reports from employing establishments and relate to full- and part-time wage and salary workers in nonagricultural establishments who received pay for any part of the pay period that includes the 12th of the month. Not comparable with labor force data (Tables B–35 through B–44), which include proprietors, self-employed persons, unpaid family workers, and

See next page for continuation of table.

[Thousands of persons; monthly data seasonally adjusted]

Year or month	Information	Financial activities	Professional and business services	Education and health services	Leisure and hospitality	Other services	Government			
							Total	Federal	State	Local
1959	1,718	2,454	3,591	2,822	3,365	1,107	8,192	2,342	1,484	4,366
1960	1,728	2,532	3,694	2,937	3,460	1,152	8,464	2,381	1,536	4,547
1961	1,693	2,590	3,744	3,030	3,468	1,188	8,706	2,391	1,607	4,708
1962	1,723	2,656	3,885	3,172	3,557	1,243	9,004	2,455	1,669	4,881
1963	1,735	2,731	3,990	3,288	3,639	1,288	9,341	2,473	1,747	5,121
1964	1,766	2,811	4,137	3,438	3,772	1,346	9,711	2,463	1,856	5,392
1965	1,824	2,878	4,306	3,587	3,951	1,404	10,191	2,495	1,996	5,700
1966	1,908	2,961	4,517	3,770	4,127	1,475	10,910	2,690	2,141	6,080
1967	1,955	3,087	4,720	3,986	4,269	1,558	11,525	2,852	2,302	6,371
1968	1,991	3,234	4,918	4,191	4,453	1,638	11,972	2,871	2,442	6,660
1969	2,048	3,404	5,156	4,428	4,670	1,731	12,330	2,893	2,533	6,904
1970	2,041	3,532	5,267	4,577	4,789	1,789	12,687	2,865	2,664	7,158
1971	2,009	3,651	5,328	4,675	4,914	1,827	13,012	2,828	2,747	7,437
1972	2,056	3,784	5,523	4,863	5,121	1,900	13,465	2,815	2,859	7,790
1973	2,135	3,920	5,774	5,092	5,341	1,990	13,862	2,794	2,923	8,146
1974	2,160	4,023	5,974	5,322	5,471	2,078	14,303	2,858	3,039	8,407
1975	2,061	4,047	6,034	5,497	5,544	2,144	14,820	2,882	3,179	8,758
1976	2,111	4,155	6,287	5,756	5,794	2,244	15,001	2,863	3,273	8,865
1977	2,185	4,348	6,587	6,052	6,065	2,359	15,258	2,859	3,377	9,023
1978	2,287	4,599	6,972	6,427	6,411	2,505	15,812	2,893	3,474	9,446
1979	2,375	4,843	7,312	6,767	6,631	2,637	16,068	2,894	3,541	9,633
1980	2,361	5,025	7,544	7,072	6,721	2,755	16,375	3,000	3,610	9,765
1981	2,382	5,163	7,782	7,357	6,840	2,865	16,180	2,922	3,640	9,619
1982	2,317	5,209	7,848	7,515	6,874	2,924	15,982	2,884	3,640	9,458
1983	2,253	5,334	8,039	7,766	7,078	3,021	16,011	2,915	3,662	9,434
1984	2,398	5,553	8,464	8,193	7,489	3,186	16,159	2,943	3,734	9,482
1985	2,437	5,815	8,871	8,657	7,869	3,366	16,533	3,014	3,832	9,687
1986	2,445	6,128	9,211	9,061	8,156	3,523	16,838	3,044	3,893	9,901
1987	2,507	6,385	9,608	9,515	8,446	3,699	17,156	3,089	3,967	10,100
1988	2,585	6,500	10,090	10,063	8,778	3,907	17,540	3,124	4,076	10,339
1989	2,622	6,562	10,555	10,616	9,062	4,116	17,927	3,136	4,182	10,609
1990	2,688	6,614	10,848	10,984	9,288	4,261	18,415	3,196	4,305	10,914
1991	2,677	6,558	10,714	11,506	9,256	4,249	18,545	3,110	4,355	11,081
1992	2,641	6,540	10,970	11,891	9,437	4,240	18,787	3,111	4,408	11,267
1993	2,668	6,709	11,495	12,303	9,732	4,350	18,989	3,063	4,488	11,438
1994	2,738	6,867	12,174	12,807	10,100	4,428	19,275	3,018	4,576	11,682
1995	2,843	6,827	12,844	13,289	10,501	4,572	19,432	2,949	4,635	11,849
1996	2,940	6,969	13,462	13,683	10,777	4,690	19,539	2,877	4,606	12,056
1997	3,084	7,178	14,335	14,087	11,018	4,825	19,664	2,806	4,582	12,276
1998	3,218	7,462	15,147	14,446	11,232	4,976	19,909	2,772	4,612	12,525
1999	3,419	7,648	15,957	14,798	11,543	5,087	20,307	2,769	4,709	12,829
2000	3,631	7,687	16,666	15,109	11,862	5,168	20,790	2,865	4,786	13,139
2001	3,629	7,807	16,476	15,645	12,036	5,258	21,118	2,764	4,905	13,449
2002	3,420	7,843	16,010	16,184	11,969	5,348	21,489	2,767	5,006	13,716
2003 ᴾ	3,286	7,959	16,063	16,526	12,062	5,319	21,500	2,755	4,949	13,796
2002: Jan	3,492	7,836	16,030	15,968	12,002	5,341	21,385	2,755	5,009	13,621
Feb	3,470	7,826	15,995	16,017	11,969	5,355	21,421	2,758	5,012	13,651
Mar	3,454	7,823	16,013	16,057	11,966	5,364	21,447	2,755	5,019	13,673
Apr	3,443	7,828	16,023	16,100	11,929	5,361	21,458	2,753	5,020	13,685
May	3,434	7,825	16,035	16,130	11,922	5,358	21,504	2,780	5,023	13,701
June	3,424	7,830	16,026	16,183	11,904	5,355	21,492	2,779	5,019	13,694
July	3,410	7,830	15,973	16,194	11,918	5,330	21,448	2,761	5,015	13,672
Aug	3,401	7,830	16,008	16,241	11,940	5,340	21,479	2,765	5,013	13,701
Sept	3,383	7,851	16,008	16,273	11,975	5,346	21,526	2,774	4,993	13,759
Oct	3,392	7,872	16,036	16,315	12,032	5,343	21,544	2,781	4,984	13,779
Nov	3,382	7,880	16,014	16,357	12,069	5,352	21,540	2,782	4,983	13,775
Dec	3,353	7,889	15,972	16,373	12,019	5,335	21,556	2,778	4,984	13,794
2003: Jan	3,328	7,902	16,015	16,405	12,132	5,334	21,576	2,786	4,974	13,816
Feb	3,308	7,916	16,043	16,430	12,084	5,329	21,588	2,791	4,979	13,818
Mar	3,305	7,930	15,980	16,452	12,050	5,323	21,547	2,789	4,958	13,800
Apr	3,303	7,956	15,989	16,483	12,043	5,322	21,526	2,769	4,952	13,805
May	3,294	7,971	16,002	16,509	12,026	5,320	21,484	2,761	4,941	13,782
June	3,285	7,972	16,006	16,503	12,039	5,323	21,476	2,749	4,925	13,802
July	3,278	7,981	16,063	16,487	12,051	5,316	21,458	2,747	4,920	13,791
Aug	3,267	7,980	16,054	16,541	12,051	5,319	21,470	2,745	4,928	13,797
Sept	3,270	7,986	16,107	16,570	12,056	5,314	21,456	2,742	4,948	13,766
Oct	3,266	7,971	16,142	16,625	12,071	5,310	21,473	2,730	4,952	13,791
Nov ᴾ	3,265	7,964	16,179	16,653	12,091	5,309	21,472	2,720	4,954	13,798
Dec ᴾ	3,270	7,952	16,224	16,674	12,087	5,306	21,468	2,710	4,951	13,807

Note (cont'd).—private household workers; which count persons as employed when they are not at work because of industrial disputes, bad weather, etc., even if they are not paid for the time off; which are based on a sample of the working-age population; and which count persons only once—as employed, unemployed, or not in the labor force. In the data shown here, persons who work at more than one job are counted each time they appear on a payroll.

Establishment data for employment, hours, and earnings are classified based on the 2002 North American Industry Classification System (NAICS).

For further description and details see *Employment and Earnings.*

Source: Department of Labor, Bureau of Labor Statistics.

TABLE B–47.—*Hours and earnings in private nonagricultural industries, 1959–2003* [1]

[Monthly data seasonally adjusted]

Year or month	Average weekly hours			Average hourly earnings			Average weekly earnings, total private			
	Total private	Manufacturing		Total private		Manu-facturing (current dollars)	Level		Percent change from year earlier	
		Total	Over-time	Current dollars	1982 dollars²		Current dollars	1982 dollars²	Current dollars	1982 dollars²
1959		40.3	2.7			$2.08				
1960		39.8	2.5			2.15				
1961		39.9	2.4			2.20				
1962		40.5	2.8			2.27				
1963		40.6	2.8			2.34				
1964	38.5	40.8	3.1	$2.53	$7.86	2.41	$97.41	$302.52		
1965	38.6	41.2	3.6	2.63	8.04	2.49	101.52	310.46	4.2	2.6
1966	38.5	41.4	3.9	2.73	8.13	2.60	105.11	312.83	3.5	.8
1967	37.9	40.6	3.3	2.85	8.21	2.71	108.02	311.30	2.8	–.5
1968	37.7	40.7	3.5	3.02	8.37	2.89	113.85	315.37	5.4	1.3
1969	37.5	40.6	3.6	3.22	8.45	3.07	120.75	316.93	6.1	.5
1970	37.0	39.8	2.9	3.40	8.46	3.23	125.80	312.94	4.2	–1.3
1971	36.8	39.9	2.9	3.63	8.64	3.45	133.58	318.05	6.2	1.6
1972	36.9	40.6	3.4	3.90	8.99	3.70	143.91	331.59	7.7	4.3
1973	36.9	40.7	3.8	4.14	8.98	3.97	152.77	331.39	6.2	–.1
1974	36.4	40.0	3.2	4.43	8.65	4.31	161.25	314.94	5.6	–5.0
1975	36.0	39.5	2.6	4.73	8.48	4.71	170.28	305.16	5.6	–3.1
1976	36.1	40.1	3.1	5.06	8.58	5.09	182.67	309.61	7.3	1.5
1977	35.9	40.3	3.4	5.44	8.66	5.55	195.30	310.99	6.9	.4
1978	35.8	40.4	3.6	5.87	8.67	6.05	210.15	310.41	7.6	–.2
1979	35.6	40.2	3.3	6.33	8.40	6.57	225.35	298.87	7.2	–3.7
1980	35.2	39.7	2.8	6.84	7.99	7.15	240.77	281.27	6.8	–5.9
1981	35.2	39.8	2.8	7.43	7.88	7.86	261.54	277.35	8.6	–1.4
1982	34.7	38.9	2.3	7.86	7.86	8.36	272.74	272.74	4.3	–1.7
1983	34.9	40.1	2.9	8.19	7.95	8.70	285.83	277.50	4.8	1.7
1984	35.1	40.7	3.4	8.48	7.95	9.05	297.65	279.22	4.1	.6
1985	34.9	40.5	3.3	8.73	7.91	9.40	304.68	276.23	2.4	–1.1
1986	34.7	40.7	3.4	8.92	7.96	9.59	309.52	276.11	1.6	–.0
1987	34.7	40.9	3.7	9.13	7.86	9.77	316.81	272.88	2.4	–1.2
1988	34.6	41.0	3.8	9.43	7.81	10.05	326.28	270.32	3.0	–.9
1989	34.5	40.9	3.8	9.80	7.75	10.35	338.10	267.27	3.6	–1.1
1990	34.3	40.5	3.8	10.19	7.66	10.78	349.29	262.43	3.3	–1.8
1991	34.1	40.4	3.8	10.50	7.58	11.13	358.06	258.34	2.5	–1.6
1992	34.2	40.7	4.0	10.76	7.55	11.40	367.83	257.95	2.7	–.2
1993	34.3	41.1	4.4	11.03	7.52	11.70	378.40	258.12	2.9	.1
1994	34.5	41.7	5.0	11.32	7.53	12.04	390.73	259.97	3.3	.7
1995	34.3	41.3	4.7	11.64	7.53	12.34	399.53	258.43	2.3	–.6
1996	34.3	41.3	4.8	12.03	7.57	12.75	412.74	259.58	3.3	.4
1997	34.5	41.7	5.1	12.49	7.68	13.14	431.25	265.22	4.5	2.2
1998	34.5	41.4	4.8	13.00	7.89	13.45	448.04	271.87	3.9	2.5
1999	34.3	41.4	4.8	13.47	8.00	13.85	462.49	274.64	3.2	1.0
2000	34.3	41.3	4.7	14.00	8.03	14.32	480.41	275.62	3.9	.4
2001	34.0	40.3	4.0	14.53	8.11	14.76	493.20	275.38	2.7	–.1
2002	33.9	40.5	4.2	14.95	8.24	15.29	506.22	278.91	2.6	1.3
2003 ᴾ	33.8	40.4	4.2	15.38	8.29	15.74	519.56	279.94	2.6	.4
2002: Jan	33.8	40.2	3.9	14.74	8.23	15.05	498.21	278.17	2.0	1.2
Feb	33.9	40.3	4.0	14.77	8.23	15.12	500.70	278.94	2.3	1.5
Mar	33.9	40.6	4.1	14.80	8.22	15.15	501.72	278.58	2.2	1.0
Apr	33.9	40.5	4.1	14.81	8.18	15.17	502.06	277.38	2.3	.9
May	33.9	40.6	4.2	14.86	8.21	15.23	503.75	278.16	2.3	1.5
June	34.0	40.7	4.2	14.93	8.23	15.27	507.62	279.83	2.8	2.0
July	33.8	40.4	4.2	14.97	8.23	15.27	505.99	278.32	2.3	1.0
Aug	33.9	40.5	4.2	15.02	8.24	15.34	509.18	279.46	3.0	1.4
Sept	33.9	40.5	4.2	15.05	8.24	15.38	510.20	279.41	3.2	1.9
Oct	33.8	40.3	4.2	15.10	8.26	15.45	510.38	279.05	3.4	1.5
Nov	33.8	40.4	4.3	15.14	8.27	15.48	511.73	279.63	3.0	.9
Dec	33.8	40.5	4.3	15.20	8.30	15.55	513.76	280.44	2.9	.4
2003: Jan	33.8	40.4	4.4	15.22	8.28	15.59	514.44	279.89	3.3	.6
Feb	33.7	40.4	4.3	15.29	8.26	15.63	515.27	278.52	2.9	–.2
Mar	33.8	40.4	4.1	15.29	8.22	15.64	516.80	277.85	3.0	–.3
Apr	33.7	40.1	4.0	15.30	8.27	15.63	515.61	278.56	2.7	.4
May	33.7	40.2	4.1	15.35	8.31	15.68	517.30	279.92	2.7	.6
June	33.7	40.3	4.0	15.38	8.30	15.72	518.31	279.87	2.1	.0
July	33.6	40.1	4.1	15.43	8.32	15.73	518.45	279.64	2.5	.5
Aug	33.7	40.2	4.1	15.45	8.30	15.79	520.67	279.63	2.3	.1
Sept	33.7	40.5	4.2	15.44	8.27	15.83	520.33	278.70	2.0	–.3
Oct	33.8	40.6	4.3	15.46	8.29	15.83	522.55	280.34	2.4	.5
Nov ᴾ	33.9	40.8	4.5	15.47	8.32	15.85	524.43	282.10	2.5	.9
Dec ᴾ	33.7	40.7	4.6	15.50	8.32	15.90	522.35	280.53	1.7	.0

[1] For production or nonsupervisory workers; total includes private industry groups shown in Table B–46.
² Current dollars divided by the consumer price index for urban wage earners and clerical workers on a 1982=100 base.

Note.—See Note, Table B–46.

Source: Department of Labor, Bureau of Labor Statistics.

TABLE B–48.—*Employment cost index, private industry, 1982–2003*

Year and month	Total private			Goods-producing			Service-producing			Manufacturing			Nonmanufacturing		
	Total compensation	Wages and salaries	Benefits [1]	Total compensation	Wages and salaries	Benefits [1]	Total compensation	Wages and salaries	Benefits [1]	Total compensation	Wages and salaries	Benefits [1]	Total compensation	Wages and salaries	Benefits [1]
Index, June 1989=100; not seasonally adjusted															
December:															
1982	75.8	77.6	71.4	77.8	80.0	73.2	74.1	75.9	69.6	76.9	79.1	72.4	75.1	76.8	70.6
1983	80.1	81.4	76.7	81.6	83.2	78.3	78.9	80.2	75.2	80.8	82.5	77.5	79.6	81.0	76.2
1984	84.0	84.8	81.7	85.4	86.4	83.2	82.9	83.7	80.4	85.0	86.1	82.7	83.4	84.2	81.1
1985	87.3	88.3	84.6	88.2	89.4	85.7	86.6	87.7	83.6	87.8	89.2	85.0	87.0	88.0	84.4
1986	90.1	91.1	87.5	91.0	92.3	88.3	89.3	90.3	86.8	90.7	92.1	87.5	89.7	90.6	87.5
1987	93.1	94.1	90.5	93.8	95.2	90.9	92.6	93.4	90.2	93.4	95.2	89.8	92.9	93.7	91.0
1988	97.6	98.0	96.7	97.9	98.2	97.3	97.3	97.8	96.1	97.6	98.1	96.6	97.5	97.8	96.8
1989	102.3	102.0	102.6	102.1	102.0	102.6	102.3	102.2	102.6	102.0	101.9	102.3	102.3	102.2	102.8
1990	107.0	106.1	109.4	107.0	105.8	109.9	107.0	106.3	109.0	107.2	106.2	109.5	106.9	106.1	109.3
1991	111.7	110.0	116.2	111.9	109.7	116.7	111.6	110.2	115.7	112.2	110.3	116.1	111.5	109.8	116.2
1992	115.6	112.9	122.2	116.1	112.8	123.4	115.2	113.0	121.2	116.5	113.7	122.6	115.1	112.6	122.0
1993	119.8	116.4	128.3	120.6	116.1	130.3	119.3	116.6	126.7	121.3	117.3	130.0	119.0	116.0	127.4
1994	123.5	119.7	133.0	124.3	119.6	134.8	122.8	119.7	131.5	125.1	120.8	134.3	122.6	119.1	132.3
1995	126.7	123.1	135.9	127.3	122.9	137.1	126.2	123.2	134.7	128.3	124.3	136.7	125.9	122.5	135.3
1996	130.6	127.3	138.6	130.9	126.8	139.7	130.2	127.5	137.4	132.1	128.4	139.8	129.8	126.8	137.9
1997	135.1	132.3	141.8	134.1	130.6	141.5	135.3	133.1	141.4	135.3	132.2	141.7	134.7	132.1	141.5
1998	139.8	137.4	145.2	137.8	135.2	143.2	140.5	138.4	145.7	138.9	136.8	142.7	139.7	137.4	145.8
1999	144.6	142.2	150.2	142.5	139.7	148.2	145.3	143.3	150.7	143.6	141.5	147.8	144.5	142.1	150.7
2000	150.9	147.7	158.6	148.8	145.2	156.2	151.7	148.9	159.4	149.3	146.5	154.8	151.1	147.9	159.7
2001	157.2	153.3	166.7	154.4	150.5	162.6	158.2	154.5	168.4	154.6	151.7	160.4	157.6	153.5	168.8
2002	162.3	157.5	174.6	160.1	155.0	171.0	163.1	158.6	175.9	160.5	156.5	168.9	162.5	157.5	176.3
2003:Mar	165.0	159.3	179.6	163.0	156.3	178.0	165.6	160.6	179.9	164.0	158.0	176.9	164.9	159.4	180.3
June	166.4	160.4	182.0	164.5	157.4	180.2	167.0	161.7	182.3	165.4	159.0	179.0	166.4	160.5	182.8
Sept	168.1	161.7	184.3	165.7	158.3	182.3	168.8	163.3	184.7	166.5	159.7	181.1	168.1	162.1	185.1
Index, June 1989=100; seasonally adjusted															
2002:Mar	158.8	154.8	168.6	156.3	151.7	165.2	160.1	156.1	170.5	156.3	153.1	163.2	159.2	155.0	171.0
June	160.5	156.2	170.8	157.8	153.1	167.1	161.8	157.5	173.0	157.8	154.5	165.1	160.9	156.3	173.2
Sept	161.5	156.9	172.6	159.0	153.9	169.1	162.7	158.3	174.7	159.1	155.4	167.2	161.9	157.1	175.0
Dec	162.7	157.7	174.7	160.6	155.0	171.6	163.7	158.9	176.5	160.8	156.5	169.5	162.9	157.8	176.9
2003:Mar	164.9	159.3	178.9	163.1	156.3	177.4	165.7	160.6	179.7	163.7	158.0	176.3	164.8	159.4	180.2
June	166.3	160.3	181.3	164.7	157.4	179.9	167.0	161.5	182.0	165.1	159.0	178.6	166.2	160.3	182.5
Sept	168.0	161.7	183.8	166.2	158.3	182.6	168.8	163.2	184.5	166.5	159.7	181.5	168.0	162.0	184.9
Percent change from 12 months earlier, not seasonally adjusted															
December:															
1982	6.5	6.3	7.2	6.1	5.7	7.3	6.6	6.8	6.9	6.1	5.6	7.3	6.7	6.5	6.8
1983	5.7	4.9	7.4	4.9	4.0	7.0	6.5	5.7	8.0	5.1	4.3	7.0	6.0	5.5	7.9
1984	4.9	4.2	6.5	4.7	3.8	6.3	5.1	4.4	6.9	5.2	4.4	6.7	4.8	4.0	6.4
1985	3.9	4.1	3.5	3.3	3.5	3.0	4.5	4.8	4.0	3.3	3.6	2.8	4.3	4.5	4.1
1986	3.2	3.2	3.4	3.2	3.2	3.0	3.1	3.0	3.8	3.3	3.3	2.9	3.1	3.0	3.7
1987	3.3	3.3	3.4	3.1	3.1	2.9	3.7	3.4	3.9	3.0	3.4	2.6	3.6	3.4	4.0
1988	4.8	4.1	6.9	4.4	3.2	7.0	5.1	4.7	6.5	4.5	3.0	7.6	5.0	4.4	6.4
1989	4.8	4.1	6.1	4.3	3.9	5.4	5.1	4.7	6.7	4.5	3.9	5.9	4.9	4.5	6.2
1990	4.6	4.0	6.6	4.8	3.7	7.1	4.6	4.0	6.2	5.1	4.2	7.0	4.5	3.8	6.3
1991	4.4	3.7	6.2	4.6	3.7	6.2	4.3	3.7	6.1	4.7	3.9	6.0	4.3	3.5	6.3
1992	3.5	2.6	5.2	3.8	2.8	5.7	3.2	2.5	4.8	3.8	3.1	5.6	3.2	2.6	5.0
1993	3.6	3.1	5.0	3.9	2.9	5.6	3.6	3.2	4.5	4.1	3.2	6.0	3.4	3.0	4.4
1994	3.1	2.8	3.7	3.1	3.0	3.5	2.9	2.7	4.1	3.1	3.0	3.3	3.0	2.7	3.8
1995	2.6	2.8	2.2	2.4	2.8	1.7	2.8	2.9	2.4	2.6	2.9	1.8	2.7	2.9	2.3
1996	3.1	3.4	2.0	2.8	3.2	1.9	3.2	3.5	2.0	3.0	3.3	2.3	3.1	3.5	1.9
1997	3.4	3.9	2.3	2.4	3.0	1.3	3.9	4.4	2.9	2.4	3.0	1.4	3.8	4.2	2.6
1998	3.5	3.9	2.4	2.8	3.5	1.2	3.8	4.0	3.0	2.7	3.5	.7	3.7	4.0	3.0
1999	3.4	3.5	3.4	3.4	3.3	3.4	3.4	3.5	3.4	3.4	3.4	4.4	3.4	3.4	3.4
2000	4.4	3.9	5.6	4.4	3.9	5.4	4.4	3.9	5.7	3.5	3.5	3.6	4.7	4.6	6.0
2001	4.2	3.8	5.1	3.8	3.7	4.1	4.3	3.8	5.6	3.5	3.5	3.6	4.3	3.8	5.7
2002	3.2	2.7	4.7	3.7	3.0	5.2	3.1	2.7	4.5	3.8	3.2	5.3	3.1	2.6	4.4
2003:Mar	3.8	3.0	6.1	4.4	3.2	7.4	3.6	2.9	5.4	4.7	3.2	8.1	3.5	2.8	5.4
June	3.5	2.6	6.1	4.4	2.8	7.6	3.2	2.5	5.2	4.6	2.9	8.2	3.3	2.6	5.4
Sept	4.0	3.0	6.5	4.5	2.9	8.0	3.7	3.1	5.6	4.7	2.8	8.6	3.8	3.1	5.7
Percent change from 3 months earlier, seasonally adjusted															
2002:Mar	0.9	0.9	1.1	1.0	0.8	1.2	0.9	0.9	0.9	1.0	0.9	1.1	0.8	0.8	1.0
June	1.1	.9	1.3	1.0	.9	1.2	1.1	.9	1.5	1.0	.9	1.2	1.1	.8	1.3
Sept	.6	.4	1.1	.8	.5	1.2	.6	.5	1.0	.8	.6	1.3	.6	.5	1.0
Dec	.7	.5	1.2	1.0	.7	1.5	.6	.4	1.0	1.1	.7	1.4	.6	.4	1.1
2003:Mar	1.4	1.0	2.4	1.6	.8	3.4	1.2	1.1	1.8	1.8	1.0	4.0	1.2	1.0	1.9
June	.8	.6	1.3	1.0	.7	1.4	.8	.6	1.3	.9	.6	1.3	.8	.6	1.3
Sept	1.0	.9	1.4	.9	.6	1.5	1.1	1.1	1.4	.9	.8	.4	1.6	1.1	1.3

[1] Employer costs for employee benefits.

Note.—The employment cost index is a measure of the change in the cost of labor, free from the influence of employment shifts among occupations and industries.

Data exclude farm and household workers.

Source: Department of Labor, Bureau of Labor Statistics.

TABLE B-49.—*Productivity and related data, business sector, 1959–2003*

[Index numbers, 1992=100; quarterly data seasonally adjusted]

Year or quarter	Output per hour of all persons		Output [1]		Hours of all persons [2]		Compensation per hour [3]		Real compensation per hour [4]		Unit labor costs		Implicit price deflator [5]	
	Business sector	Nonfarm business sector	Business sector	Nonfarm business sector	Business sector	Nonfarm business sector	Business sector	Nonfarm business sector	Business sector	Nonfarm business sector	Business sector	Nonfarm business sector	Business sector	Nonfarm business sector
1959	48.6	51.8	31.9	31.6	65.5	61.0	13.3	13.8	59.2	61.6	27.4	26.7	26.7	26.2
1960	49.5	52.4	32.5	32.1	65.6	61.3	13.9	14.5	60.7	63.2	28.0	27.6	27.0	26.5
1961	51.3	54.2	33.1	32.8	64.5	60.5	14.4	15.0	62.5	64.8	28.1	27.6	27.2	26.7
1962	53.6	56.6	35.2	35.0	65.7	61.9	15.1	15.6	64.6	66.7	28.1	27.5	27.4	26.9
1963	55.7	58.6	36.8	36.6	66.1	62.6	15.6	16.1	66.1	68.1	28.0	27.5	27.6	27.1
1964	57.6	60.4	39.2	39.1	68.0	64.8	16.2	16.6	67.7	69.4	28.1	27.5	27.9	27.5
1965	59.7	62.2	41.9	41.9	70.3	67.3	16.8	17.2	69.1	70.6	28.2	27.6	28.4	27.8
1966	62.1	64.5	44.8	44.9	72.1	69.6	17.9	18.2	71.7	72.6	28.9	28.2	29.1	28.5
1967	63.5	65.6	45.6	45.7	71.9	69.6	19.0	19.3	73.6	74.7	29.9	29.3	29.9	29.4
1968	65.5	67.7	47.9	48.1	73.2	71.1	20.4	20.7	76.0	76.9	31.2	30.5	31.0	30.5
1969	65.8	67.8	49.4	49.5	75.1	73.1	21.9	22.1	77.2	77.9	33.2	32.6	32.4	31.9
1970	67.1	68.8	49.4	49.5	73.6	71.9	23.6	23.7	78.6	79.0	35.1	34.4	33.9	33.3
1971	70.0	71.6	51.3	51.4	73.3	71.7	25.0	25.2	80.1	80.6	35.8	35.2	35.3	34.7
1972	72.2	74.0	54.7	54.9	75.7	74.2	26.6	26.8	82.3	82.9	36.8	36.2	36.5	35.8
1973	74.5	76.3	58.5	58.9	78.6	77.2	28.8	29.0	84.1	84.5	38.7	37.9	38.4	37.0
1974	73.2	75.1	57.6	58.0	78.7	77.2	31.6	31.8	83.1	83.5	43.2	42.3	42.1	40.8
1975	75.8	77.1	57.0	57.0	75.3	73.9	34.8	35.0	83.9	84.3	46.0	45.4	46.1	45.1
1976	78.4	79.9	60.9	61.1	77.7	76.5	37.9	38.0	86.2	86.5	48.3	47.5	48.5	47.6
1977	79.7	81.2	64.3	64.6	80.7	79.5	40.9	41.1	87.4	87.8	51.3	50.6	51.4	50.6
1978	80.6	82.2	68.3	68.8	84.8	83.6	44.5	44.7	88.9	89.4	55.2	54.4	55.1	54.1
1979	80.5	81.9	70.6	70.9	87.7	86.6	48.8	49.0	89.1	89.5	60.6	59.8	59.8	58.7
1980	80.3	81.7	69.8	70.2	86.9	85.9	54.1	54.3	88.9	89.3	67.3	66.4	65.2	64.3
1981	81.9	82.7	71.7	71.6	87.6	86.6	59.2	59.5	89.0	89.6	72.3	72.0	71.2	70.5
1982	81.6	82.3	69.6	69.4	85.2	84.3	63.7	64.0	90.5	91.0	78.1	77.8	75.3	74.8
1983	84.5	85.9	73.3	73.8	86.7	85.9	66.3	66.7	90.4	91.0	78.5	77.7	77.8	77.2
1984	86.8	87.7	79.7	80.0	91.8	91.1	69.2	69.5	90.7	91.2	79.7	79.3	80.0	79.4
1985	88.5	88.9	83.1	83.0	93.8	93.4	72.6	72.8	92.1	92.4	82.0	81.9	82.2	81.9
1986	91.2	91.6	86.1	86.2	94.4	94.1	76.4	76.6	95.2	95.5	83.8	83.6	83.5	83.2
1987	91.6	91.9	89.2	89.3	97.3	97.1	79.3	79.5	95.6	95.8	86.6	86.5	85.6	85.4
1988	93.0	93.4	92.9	93.3	99.9	99.9	83.4	83.4	97.0	97.0	89.7	89.3	88.3	87.9
1989	93.9	94.1	96.2	96.5	102.5	102.5	85.7	85.6	95.5	95.4	91.2	91.0	91.5	91.2
1990	95.3	95.3	97.6	97.8	102.5	102.6	90.7	90.5	96.3	96.1	95.2	94.9	94.8	94.5
1991	96.4	96.5	96.5	96.6	100.1	100.1	95.0	95.0	97.4	97.4	98.6	98.4	98.1	98.0
1992	100.0	100.0	100.0	100.0	100.0	100.0	100.0	100.0	100.0	100.0	100.0	100.0	100.0	100.0
1993	100.5	100.5	103.1	103.3	102.6	102.9	102.4	102.2	99.9	99.7	101.9	101.7	102.2	102.2
1994	101.7	101.8	108.1	108.2	106.3	106.3	104.4	104.3	99.7	99.6	102.6	102.5	104.0	104.1
1995	102.3	102.7	111.5	111.8	108.9	108.9	106.5	106.5	99.4	99.4	104.1	103.7	106.0	106.1
1996	105.1	105.3	116.4	116.7	110.7	110.8	109.9	109.8	99.8	99.7	104.6	104.3	107.7	107.6
1997	107.4	107.4	122.5	122.7	114.0	114.2	113.2	113.0	100.7	100.5	105.4	105.2	109.7	109.8
1998	110.2	110.2	128.5	128.8	116.6	116.9	119.4	119.1	104.8	104.5	108.4	108.1	110.6	110.8
1999	113.0	112.8	134.5	134.8	119.0	119.6	124.8	124.3	107.2	106.8	110.4	110.3	111.6	112.1
2000	116.5	116.1	140.0	140.2	120.1	120.7	133.5	133.0	111.0	110.6	114.6	114.6	113.5	114.1
2001	118.8	118.3	139.8	140.1	117.6	118.4	138.6	137.8	112.1	111.4	116.7	116.5	115.8	116.3
2002	125.1	124.7	143.5	143.9	114.7	115.4	142.5	141.7	113.5	112.8	113.9	113.6	116.3	116.9
2000: I	114.8	114.6	138.4	138.7	120.6	121.0	131.1	130.8	110.3	110.1	114.1	114.2	112.8	113.4
II	116.6	116.1	140.3	140.5	120.3	121.0	131.9	131.4	110.1	109.7	113.1	113.1	113.4	113.9
III	116.8	116.4	140.4	140.6	120.2	120.8	134.6	134.2	111.4	111.4	110.0	115.3	113.7	114.3
IV	117.5	117.0	140.7	141.0	119.7	120.5	135.9	135.3	111.7	111.2	115.6	115.6	114.3	114.8
2001: I	117.4	116.9	140.4	140.7	119.6	120.3	137.4	136.7	111.9	111.3	117.1	117.0	115.2	115.7
II	117.8	117.4	139.4	139.7	118.3	119.0	138.2	137.4	111.6	111.0	117.3	117.1	115.8	116.3
III	118.8	118.3	139.1	139.4	117.1	117.8	139.1	138.2	112.1	111.4	117.1	116.8	116.4	116.8
IV	121.3	120.7	140.3	140.4	115.6	116.3	139.8	138.9	112.8	112.1	115.2	115.1	115.9	116.5
2002: I	123.9	123.4	142.3	142.5	114.9	115.5	141.0	140.2	113.4	112.8	113.8	113.6	116.0	116.4
II	124.1	123.7	142.5	142.9	114.8	115.5	142.4	141.5	113.5	112.9	114.7	114.4	116.2	116.8
III	125.9	125.5	144.4	144.7	114.6	115.3	143.1	142.2	113.5	112.8	113.6	113.3	116.3	116.9
IV	126.4	126.0	145.0	145.3	114.7	115.3	143.7	142.8	113.4	112.7	113.7	113.3	116.8	117.3
2003: I	127.2	126.7	145.5	145.8	114.3	115.1	144.8	143.7	113.3	112.4	113.8	113.4	117.2	117.7
II	129.5	128.9	147.1	147.5	113.6	114.4	146.3	145.0	114.2	113.2	112.9	112.5	117.5	117.9
III	132.2	131.8	150.7	151.1	114.0	114.7	147.1	146.1	114.2	113.4	111.3	110.8	118.0	118.3

[1] Output refers to real gross domestic product in the sector.

[2] Hours at work of all persons engaged in the sector, including hours of proprietors and unpaid family workers. Estimates based primarily on establishment data.

[3] Wages and salaries of employees plus employers' contributions for social insurance and private benefit plans. Also includes an estimate of wages, salaries, and supplemental payments for the self-employed.

[4] Hourly compensation divided by the consumer price index for all urban consumers for recent quarters. The trend from 1978–2002 is based on the consumer price index research series (CPI–U–RS).

[5] Current dollar output divided by the output index.

Note.—Data shown in Tables B–49 and B–50 are based on pre-benchmark GDP data released in late November 2003 and do not reflect either the benchmark revision of the National Income and Product Accounts released in early December or revised GDP data for 2003:III released in late December 2003.

Source: Department of Labor, Bureau of Labor Statistics.

TABLE B–50.—*Changes in productivity and related data, business sector, 1959–2003*

[Percent change from preceding period; quarterly data at seasonally adjusted annual rates]

Year or quarter	Output per hour of all persons		Output [1]		Hours of all persons [2]		Compensation per hour [3]		Real compensation per hour [4]		Unit labor costs		Implicit price deflator [5]	
	Business sector	Nonfarm business sector	Business sector	Nonfarm business sector	Business sector	Nonfarm business sector	Business sector	Nonfarm business sector	Business sector	Nonfarm business sector	Business sector	Nonfarm business sector	Business sector	Nonfarm business sector
1959	4.0	4.0	8.3	8.8	4.2	4.6	4.1	3.9	3.4	3.2	0.1	0.0	0.7	1.2
1960	1.8	1.2	1.9	1.7	.1	.5	4.2	4.4	2.5	2.6	2.4	3.1	1.1	1.2
1961	3.7	3.3	2.0	2.0	-1.6	-1.2	4.0	3.5	3.0	2.5	.4	.2	.8	.8
1962	4.5	4.5	6.4	6.8	1.8	2.2	4.4	4.0	3.4	2.9	-.1	-.5	1.0	1.0
1963	3.9	3.5	4.6	4.6	.7	1.1	3.6	3.4	2.2	2.1	-.3	.0	.6	.7
1964	3.4	3.0	6.4	6.7	2.8	3.6	3.8	3.2	2.5	1.9	.4	.2	1.1	1.2
1965	3.5	3.1	7.0	7.1	3.4	3.8	3.7	3.3	2.1	1.7	.2	.2	1.6	1.4
1966	4.1	3.6	6.8	7.2	2.6	3.5	6.7	5.9	3.7	2.9	2.5	2.2	2.5	2.3
1967	2.2	1.8	1.9	1.7	-.3	-.1	5.8	5.9	2.6	2.8	3.5	4.1	2.7	3.2
1968	3.1	3.1	5.0	5.3	1.9	2.2	7.6	7.4	3.3	3.1	4.4	4.2	3.9	3.8
1969	.5	.2	3.0	3.0	2.5	2.9	7.0	6.8	1.5	1.3	6.5	6.7	4.5	4.4
1970	2.0	1.5	.0	-.1	-2.0	-1.6	7.7	7.2	1.9	1.4	5.6	5.6	4.4	4.5
1971	4.3	4.1	3.9	3.8	-.4	-.3	6.3	6.4	1.9	1.9	1.9	2.2	4.3	4.4
1972	3.2	3.3	6.6	6.9	3.4	3.4	6.1	6.3	2.8	3.0	2.8	2.9	3.3	2.9
1973	3.1	3.1	7.0	7.3	3.7	4.0	8.5	8.2	2.1	1.8	5.2	4.9	5.2	3.6
1974	-1.7	-1.6	-1.5	-1.5	.1	.1	9.7	9.8	-1.2	-1.1	11.6	11.6	9.6	10.2
1975	3.5	2.7	-1.0	-1.7	-4.3	-4.3	10.2	10.1	1.0	.9	6.5	7.2	9.6	10.6
1976	3.5	3.6	6.8	7.2	3.2	3.5	8.7	8.5	2.8	2.6	5.1	4.7	5.2	5.4
1977	1.7	1.6	5.6	5.6	3.8	3.9	7.9	8.1	1.4	1.5	6.1	6.4	6.1	6.4
1978	1.1	1.3	6.2	6.5	5.1	5.2	8.8	8.9	1.8	1.9	7.6	7.6	7.2	6.8
1979	-.1	-.4	3.3	3.2	3.4	3.6	9.7	9.5	.3	.1	9.8	10.0	8.5	8.5
1980	-.3	-.3	-1.1	-1.1	-.9	-.8	10.8	10.8	-.2	-.2	11.1	11.1	9.1	9.7
1981	1.9	1.2	2.7	2.0	.7	.8	9.5	9.7	.1	.3	7.4	8.3	9.2	9.5
1982	-.3	-.5	-2.9	-3.1	-2.6	-2.6	7.6	7.6	1.6	1.6	8.0	8.1	5.7	6.2
1983	3.5	4.4	5.4	6.4	1.7	1.9	4.1	4.2	.0	.0	.5	-.2	3.4	3.2
1984	2.8	2.1	8.8	8.3	5.9	6.1	4.3	4.2	.3	.2	1.5	2.1	2.9	2.8
1985	2.0	1.3	4.2	3.9	2.2	2.5	4.9	4.7	1.6	1.3	2.9	3.3	2.7	3.2
1986	3.0	3.0	3.7	3.8	.7	.8	5.2	5.2	3.3	3.3	2.1	2.1	1.6	1.7
1987	.5	.3	3.5	3.5	3.0	3.2	3.9	3.8	.4	.4	3.4	3.4	2.5	2.5
1988	1.5	1.6	4.3	4.5	2.7	2.9	5.1	4.9	1.4	1.2	3.6	3.2	3.1	3.0
1989	1.0	.7	3.5	3.4	2.6	2.6	2.7	2.6	-1.5	-1.6	1.7	1.9	3.7	3.7
1990	1.5	1.3	1.5	1.4	.0	.1	5.9	5.7	.8	.7	4.3	4.3	3.5	3.6
1991	1.1	1.2	-1.2	-1.3	-2.3	-2.5	4.8	5.0	1.1	1.3	3.6	3.7	3.5	3.7
1992	3.8	3.6	3.7	3.5	-.1	-.1	5.2	5.3	2.7	2.7	1.4	1.6	2.0	2.1
1993	.5	.5	3.1	3.3	2.6	2.9	2.4	2.2	-.1	-.3	1.9	1.7	2.2	2.2
1994	1.2	1.3	4.9	4.7	3.6	3.3	1.9	2.1	-.2	.0	.7	.8	1.8	1.9
1995	.6	.9	3.1	3.4	2.5	2.4	2.1	2.2	-.3	-.3	1.5	1.2	2.0	2.0
1996	2.7	2.5	4.4	4.3	1.6	1.7	3.1	3.1	.4	.4	.4	.5	1.6	1.4
1997	2.2	2.0	5.2	5.1	3.0	3.1	3.0	2.9	.9	.8	.8	1.0	1.8	2.1
1998	2.6	2.6	4.9	5.0	2.2	2.4	5.5	5.4	4.0	3.9	2.8	2.7	.8	.9
1999	2.5	2.3	4.7	4.6	2.1	2.3	4.5	4.3	2.4	2.2	1.9	2.0	1.0	1.2
2000	3.1	3.0	4.1	4.0	.9	1.0	6.9	7.0	3.5	3.6	3.7	3.9	1.7	1.8
2001	2.0	1.9	-.2	-.1	-2.1	-2.0	3.8	3.6	1.0	.8	1.8	1.7	2.0	1.9
2002	5.3	5.4	2.7	2.7	-2.5	-2.5	2.8	2.8	1.2	1.2	-2.3	-2.4	.4	.5
2000: I	.5	.3	2.2	1.9	1.7	1.6	15.2	15.4	11.0	11.3	14.6	15.1	2.4	2.7
II	6.3	5.7	5.4	5.4	-.8	-.2	2.6	1.9	-.8	-1.4	-3.5	-3.6	2.2	1.9
III	.7	.8	.4	.2	-.3	-.6	8.5	8.8	4.7	5.0	7.8	7.9	1.1	1.4
IV	2.6	2.2	.9	1.1	-1.7	-1.0	3.9	3.3	.9	.4	1.2	1.1	1.9	1.6
2001: I	-.5	-.4	-1.0	-.9	-.5	-.5	4.6	4.3	.8	.5	5.1	4.7	3.4	3.3
II	1.5	1.6	-2.8	-2.7	-4.3	-4.3	2.3	2.0	-.9	-1.2	.8	.3	2.2	2.0
III	3.3	3.4	-.9	-.8	-4.1	-4.1	2.5	2.4	1.6	1.5	-.8	-.9	1.8	1.7
IV	8.7	8.3	3.5	2.9	-4.8	-5.0	2.1	2.1	2.7	2.7	-6.1	-5.7	-1.6	-1.0
2002: I	8.7	9.3	5.9	6.2	-2.6	-2.9	3.5	3.7	2.2	2.4	-4.8	-5.2	.3	-.2
II	.8	1.0	.6	.9	-.2	.0	4.0	3.9	.4	.3	3.1	2.9	.7	1.4
III	5.9	5.9	5.3	5.2	-.6	-.6	2.1	2.0	.0	-.2	-3.6	-3.7	.5	.1
IV	1.5	1.7	1.7	1.7	.2	.0	1.6	1.6	-.4	-.4	.1	-.1	1.5	1.4
2003: I	2.7	2.1	1.4	1.4	-1.2	-.7	3.2	2.6	-.6	-1.2	.5	.4	1.6	1.4
II	7.4	7.0	4.5	4.6	-2.7	-2.2	4.1	3.6	3.5	3.0	-3.1	-3.2	1.0	.8
III	8.6	9.4	10.2	10.3	1.4	.8	2.3	3.0	.0	.7	-5.8	-5.8	1.7	1.5

[1] Output refers to real gross domestic product in the sector.

[2] Hours at work of all persons engaged in the sector. See footnote 2, Table B-49.

[3] Wages and salaries of employees plus employers' contributions for social insurance and private benefit plans. Also includes an estimate of wages, salaries, and supplemental payments for the self-employed.

[4] Hourly compensation divided by the consumer price index. See footnote 4, Table B-49.

[5] Current dollar output divided by the output index.

Note.—Percent changes are based on original data and may differ slightly from percent changes based on indexes in Table B-49.

Data shown in Tables B–49 and B–50 are based on pre-benchmark GDP data released in late November 2003 and do not reflect either the benchmark revision of the National Income and Product Accounts released in early December or revised GDP data for 2003:III released in late December 2003.

Source: Department of Labor, Bureau of Labor Statistics.

TABLE B–51.—*Industrial production indexes, major industry divisions, 1959–2003*

[1997=100; monthly data seasonally adjusted]

Year or month	Total industrial production [1]	Manufacturing				Mining	Utilities
		Total [1]	Durable	Nondurable	Other (non-NAICS) [1]		
1959	28.4	26.1					
1960	29.0	26.6					
1961	29.2	26.7					
1962	31.6	29.1					
1963	33.5	30.9					
1964	35.8	33.0					
1965	39.3	36.5					
1966	42.8	39.9					
1967	43.7	40.6					
1968	46.2	42.9					
1969	48.3	44.8					
1970	46.7	42.8					
1971	47.4	43.5					
1972	51.9	48.0	38.8	61.3	66.9	98.7	56.5
1973	56.1	52.3	43.6	64.1	69.1	99.2	59.7
1974	55.9	52.1	43.3	64.4	69.6	97.8	59.4
1975	50.9	46.6	37.5	59.8	66.0	95.4	60.4
1976	54.9	50.8	41.0	65.2	68.1	96.1	63.1
1977	59.1	55.2	45.1	69.7	74.7	98.3	65.5
1978	62.4	58.6	48.6	72.1	77.4	101.4	67.3
1979	64.2	60.4	51.0	72.6	79.0	104.4	68.8
1980	62.5	58.2	48.7	70.3	81.8	106.4	69.3
1981	63.4	58.8	49.2	71.0	83.8	109.2	70.2
1982	60.1	55.6	45.1	69.9	84.7	103.8	68.4
1983	61.7	58.2	47.2	73.2	87.0	98.3	68.
1984	67.3	64.0	54.0	76.6	91.1	104.6	72.
1985	68.1	65.1	55.3	77.0	94.6	102.6	74.
1986	68.8	66.5	56.2	79.2	96.7	95.2	74.
1987	72.3	70.2	59.4	83.5	102.1	96.0	78.
1988	75.9	73.8	63.6	86.3	101.7	98.4	82.
1989	76.6	74.4	64.2	86.8	100.2	97.3	85.
1990	77.2	74.9	64.4	88.2	99.0	98.8	86
1991	76.1	73.4	62.4	87.9	94.9	96.5	88
1992	78.2	76.1	65.6	90.1	92.8	94.4	88
1993	80.8	78.8	69.3	91.4	93.5	94.4	92
1994	85.2	83.6	75.4	94.6	92.8	96.6	93
1995	89.3	88.0	81.9	96.2	92.9	96.4	97
1996	93.1	92.1	89.0	96.5	92.1	98.1	100
1997	100.0	100.0	100.0	100.0	100.0	100.0	100
1998	105.9	106.8	110.7	101.5	106.5	98.2	102
1999	110.6	112.1	119.9	102.2	109.9	94.0	105
2000	115.4	117.4	129.5	102.8	112.2	96.3	108
2001	111.5	112.7	123.5	99.8	105.6	96.8	108
2002	110.9	111.8	122.9	99.2	102.0	93.0	111
2003 P	111.2	112.2	125.4	97.0	105.9	93.2	110
2002:Jan	109.7	111.0	120.8	99.2	103.2	93.5	106
Feb	109.9	111.0	121.1	99.0	102.9	93.7	107
Mar	110.3	111.4	121.4	99.5	103.1	93.0	109
Apr	110.8	111.6	122.0	99.6	101.6	92.8	112
May	110.9	111.9	122.7	99.5	101.6	93.1	111
June	111.7	112.6	123.5	100.2	101.2	93.6	112
July	111.5	112.4	123.3	100.0	101.1	92.8	113
Aug	111.5	112.6	124.1	99.7	101.4	93.0	110
Sept	111.3	112.5	123.8	99.5	102.5	91.3	111
Oct	111.0	111.9	123.5	98.5	102.8	91.8	113
Nov	111.2	111.9	124.5	97.8	101.6	93.8	112
Dec	110.6	111.3	123.6	97.4	100.5	94.2	112
2003:Jan	111.2	112.0	124.8	97.5	103.7	93.4	112
Feb	111.6	112.1	124.5	97.5	106.0	93.3	11
Mar	110.8	111.8	123.6	97.5	107.0	93.1	11
Apr	110.1	111.1	122.8	97.0	106.0	93.4	10
May	110.0	111.0	122.8	96.8	106.1	92.7	11
June	110.0	111.2	123.6	96.3	107.0	93.2	10
July	110.8	111.8	124.8	96.7	105.0	93.4	11
Aug	110.9	111.8	124.9	96.5	105.2	93.1	11
Sept	111.5	112.7	127.1	96.6	104.7	93.5	10
Oct P	111.9	113.0	127.4	96.7	106.2	93.7	11
Nov P	113.1	114.2	128.9	97.5	107.1	94.2	11
Dec P	113.2	114.5	129.7	97.5	106.7	94.2	11

[1] Total industry and total manufacturing series include manufacturing as defined in the North American Industry Classification System (NAICS) plus those industries—logging, and newspaper, periodical, book and directory-publishing—that have traditionally been considered to be manufacturing and included in the industrial sector.

Note.—Data based on the North American Industry Classification System; see footnote 1.

Source: Board of Governors of the Federal Reserve System.

TABLE B-52.—*Industrial production indexes, market groupings, 1959-2003*

[1997=100; monthly data seasonally adjusted]

Year or month	Total industrial production	Final products Total	Consumer goods Total	Automotive products	Other durable goods	Nondurable goods	Equipment Total[1]	Business	Defense and space	Nonindustrial supplies Total	Construction	Business	Materials Total	Nonenergy	Energy
1959	28.4	27.1	33.3	23.6	21.6	38.7	19.0	14.2	48.6	28.7	39.9	23.7	28.9	....	51.4
1960	29.0	28.0	34.6	27.1	21.8	39.9	19.5	14.5	49.9	28.9	39.0	24.5	29.3	....	52.2
1961	29.2	28.2	35.3	24.7	22.4	41.3	19.3	14.1	50.7	29.5	39.4	25.3	29.3	....	52.5
1962	31.6	30.6	37.7	29.9	24.4	43.2	21.4	15.3	58.7	31.3	41.7	26.8	31.9	....	54.4
1963	33.5	32.3	39.7	32.8	26.3	45.1	22.7	16.1	63.3	33.0	43.7	28.6	34.0	....	57.6
1964	35.8	34.2	42.0	34.4	28.7	47.4	24.0	18.0	61.3	35.2	46.3	30.6	36.7	....	59.9
1965	39.3	37.5	45.3	42.3	32.6	49.4	27.2	20.6	67.8	37.5	49.2	32.6	41.0	....	62.6
1966	42.8	41.1	47.6	42.2	35.9	51.8	31.6	23.9	79.7	39.8	51.3	35.1	44.6	....	66.6
1967	43.7	42.8	48.7	37.0	36.4	54.4	33.6	24.4	90.9	41.4	52.6	37.0	44.2	37.6	68.9
1968	46.2	44.8	51.7	44.1	38.9	56.6	34.6	25.4	91.1	43.8	55.3	39.2	47.1	40.3	72.1
1969	48.3	46.2	53.6	44.3	41.5	58.5	35.5	27.1	86.7	46.1	57.7	41.7	49.9	42.8	75.7
1970	46.7	44.6	53.0	37.3	40.2	59.5	33.0	26.1	73.4	45.5	55.7	41.9	48.1	40.3	79.5
1971	47.4	45.0	56.0	47.5	42.6	61.2	30.9	24.8	66.0	46.8	57.5	43.2	48.9	41.0	80.2
1972	51.9	48.8	60.5	51.3	48.8	65.1	33.8	28.3	64.2	52.3	65.2	47.5	53.8	46.0	83.2
1973	56.1	52.6	63.3	55.5	52.1	67.1	38.5	32.7	69.9	55.9	70.7	50.4	58.7	50.9	85.2
1974	55.9	52.4	61.4	48.0	48.9	67.1	40.3	34.5	72.0	55.4	69.0	50.3	58.5	50.8	84.9
1975	50.9	49.3	59.0	46.1	42.8	66.0	36.5	30.5	73.2	49.7	58.5	46.4	52.1	43.7	84.0
1976	54.9	52.7	63.8	52.4	48.1	70.1	38.3	32.3	70.9	53.1	63.1	49.4	56.7	48.6	85.8
1977	59.1	57.0	67.7	59.1	53.8	72.6	42.9	37.4	63.4	57.6	68.7	53.5	60.7	52.7	88.5
1978	62.4	60.5	69.8	58.4	56.3	75.2	47.7	42.3	63.9	60.8	72.6	56.4	63.7	56.1	89.6
1979	64.2	62.5	68.8	52.6	56.6	74.8	53.2	47.6	68.7	62.7	74.4	58.4	65.4	57.7	92.0
1980	62.5	62.1	66.3	41.2	52.5	74.8	55.3	48.2	81.8	60.2	68.8	57.0	63.0	54.3	92.7
1981	63.4	63.6	66.8	42.5	52.8	75.2	57.8	49.5	88.7	60.8	67.6	58.4	63.3	54.5	93.6
1982	60.1	62.2	66.6	41.2	49.0	76.5	55.1	45.4	106.2	58.7	61.4	57.7	58.5	49.1	89.6
1983	61.7	63.3	69.0	47.3	53.1	77.3	54.5	45.3	107.0	61.8	65.7	60.4	60.0	52.4	86.8
1984	67.3	68.6	72.1	52.4	59.3	78.9	62.6	52.5	122.3	67.2	71.6	65.7	65.8	58.6	92.3
1985	68.1	70.4	72.7	52.2	59.4	79.9	65.8	54.6	136.9	69.0	73.4	67.4	65.7	58.6	91.7
1986	68.8	71.4	75.1	55.3	62.8	81.8	65.0	53.9	145.5	71.3	75.9	69.6	65.7	59.8	88.1
1987	72.3	74.6	78.1	58.5	66.1	84.7	68.3	57.3	148.3	75.6	80.5	73.8	69.2	63.8	90.2
1988	75.9	78.3	81.2	62.0	69.6	87.5	73.0	62.4	148.3	78.1	82.3	76.6	73.0	67.8	93.3
1989	76.6	79.1	81.4	64.1	70.3	87.2	74.6	64.4	148.3	78.8	81.9	77.7	73.5	68.2	94.2
1990	77.2	79.8	82.0	61.2	70.2	88.7	75.5	66.1	142.6	80.0	81.1	79.6	74.0	68.3	96.1
1991	76.1	78.8	82.0	57.9	68.2	90.0	72.7	64.6	131.6	78.0	76.6	78.5	72.9	66.9	96.2
1992	78.2	80.6	84.5	67.8	71.3	90.6	73.5	67.1	122.3	80.2	79.8	80.3	75.4	70.2	95.3
1993	80.8	83.2	87.4	75.3	77.7	91.9	75.3	69.7	115.6	83.0	83.4	82.9	77.9	73.4	95.5
1994	85.2	86.8	91.6	85.7	85.2	94.2	78.0	73.5	108.9	87.0	89.5	86.2	83.0	79.4	97.0
1995	89.3	90.4	94.5	89.1	90.2	96.5	82.8	79.4	106.0	90.3	91.4	89.9	87.9	85.1	98.5
1996	93.1	93.9	96.5	92.7	94.3	97.8	88.9	86.9	102.0	93.8	95.5	93.2	92.2	90.1	100.0
1997	100.0	100.0	100.0	100.0	100.0	100.0	100.0	100.0	100.0	100.0	100.0	100.0	100.0	100.0	100.0
1998	105.9	105.7	103.6	106.6	107.3	102.2	110.0	111.2	104.1	105.7	105.2	105.9	106.2	107.8	100.2
1999	110.6	108.3	105.3	116.5	110.8	102.1	114.2	117.1	101.4	109.9	107.9	110.7	113.1	116.7	100.2
2000	115.4	111.6	107.5	119.4	115.8	103.7	119.7	125.5	91.0	114.4	110.3	116.0	119.8	124.9	101.6
2001	111.5	109.1	105.9	113.9	107.4	104.0	115.1	117.6	102.6	109.8	105.2	111.6	114.6	118.2	100.4
2002	110.9	107.6	106.8	124.1	108.3	103.4	108.1	109.5	105.7	108.6	103.1	110.7	115.1	118.9	100.5
2003 [p]	111.2	107.5	106.0	129.4	108.5	101.6	109.7	110.4	112.0	109.0	102.0	111.7	115.8	119.9	100.5
2002: Jan	109.7	107.3	106.3	118.1	108.1	103.6	108.5	110.0	103.7	107.1	101.9	109.2	113.0	116.6	99.3
Feb	109.9	107.3	106.3	119.6	108.6	103.4	108.2	109.8	103.3	107.4	102.7	109.3	113.4	116.8	100.1
Mar	110.3	107.6	106.8	119.9	108.6	104.0	107.9	109.5	103.9	108.1	103.9	109.8	113.9	117.4	100.4
Apr	110.8	107.6	107.0	122.3	107.5	104.1	107.7	109.4	104.3	108.7	103.5	110.7	114.8	118.4	100.7
May	110.9	107.4	106.5	122.7	108.1	103.2	108.0	109.7	104.5	109.2	103.9	111.3	115.3	119.2	100.6
June	111.7	108.3	107.6	125.2	108.2	104.4	108.5	110.1	105.3	109.1	104.0	111.1	116.0	120.0	101.2
July	111.5	108.0	107.5	127.4	107.5	103.9	107.6	109.0	105.0	109.0	102.6	111.6	116.2	120.0	101.6
Aug	111.5	107.9	107.1	128.0	106.9	103.5	108.3	109.7	106.1	109.0	103.4	111.2	116.1	120.3	100.5
Sept	111.3	108.0	107.3	127.1	108.2	103.6	108.2	109.3	107.2	108.9	103.4	111.1	115.7	120.0	99.7
Oct	111.0	107.5	106.7	124.9	108.0	103.2	107.9	108.8	107.9	109.3	103.2	111.7	115.3	119.5	99.8
Nov	111.2	107.5	106.6	129.5	109.5	102.1	108.3	109.6	107.1	108.7	102.8	111.0	115.9	119.8	100.9
Dec	110.6	106.9	105.6	124.9	109.8	101.5	108.4	109.2	109.7	108.4	102.1	110.9	115.3	119.0	100.0
2003: Jan	111.2	107.7	106.6	129.5	110.5	101.9	108.9	109.8	110.3	109.2	102.7	111.8	115.5	119.4	100.6
Feb	111.6	108.2	107.0	127.1	108.6	103.2	109.7	110.6	111.0	109.5	101.9	112.6	115.8	119.3	100.7
Mar	110.8	107.6	106.3	125.7	108.2	102.6	109.1	110.0	111.0	108.8	101.2	111.9	114.7	118.7	99.8
Apr	110.1	106.5	105.3	124.4	107.7	101.4	108.0	108.7	110.3	108.1	100.6	111.1	114.5	118.3	100.2
May	110.0	106.7	105.5	123.5	108.1	101.8	108.3	108.6	111.8	108.1	100.8	111.0	114.1	117.9	99.6
June	110.0	106.5	105.0	125.7	108.0	100.9	108.5	109.0	111.8	108.0	100.8	110.6	114.4	118.3	99.6
July	110.8	107.1	105.8	129.1	108.6	101.3	108.9	109.3	112.1	108.7	101.5	111.5	115.4	119.2	100.9
Aug	110.9	107.2	105.7	127.3	108.8	101.4	109.6	110.0	113.0	108.6	101.9	111.2	115.5	119.2	101.0
Sept	111.5	107.8	106.1	135.0	108.3	100.9	109.4	109.4	113.7	108.7	102.3	111.3	116.4	120.8	100.4
Oct [p]	111.9	107.8	106.2	131.7	109.3	101.3	110.5	111.1	113.8	109.7	103.1	112.4	117.0	121.5	101.0
Nov [p]	113.1	109.0	107.1	131.6	110.9	102.2	112.3	113.2	113.8	110.8	104.2	113.5	118.2	122.9	101.6
Dec [p]	113.2	108.8	106.9	132.2	110.9	101.9	112.2	113.1	113.9	110.6	104.1	113.2	118.7	123.9	101.2

[1] Includes other items, not shown separately.

Note.—See footnote 1 and Note, Table B-51.

Source: Board of Governors of the Federal Reserve System.

TABLE B-53.—*Industrial production indexes, selected manufacturing industries, 1967–2003*

[1997=100; monthly data seasonally adjusted]

Year or month	Durable manufacturing								Nondurable manufacturing					
	Primary metal		Fabricated metal products	Machinery	Computer and electronic products		Transportation equipment		Apparel	Paper	Printing and support	Chemical	Plastics and rubber products	Food
	Total	Iron and steel products			Total	Selected high-technology[1]	Total	Motor vehicles and parts						
1967	....	....	....	....	....	0.8	....	....	....	....	....	....	....	....
1968	....	....	....	....	....	.8	....	....	....	....	....	....	....	....
1969	....	....	....	....	....	.9	....	....	....	....	....	....	....	....
1970	....	....	....	....	....	.9	....	....	....	....	....	....	....	....
1971	....	....	....	....	....	.9	....	....	....	....	....	....	....	....
1972	108.3	115.9	67.4	60.7	3.2	1.0	58.9	51.6	98.9	62.6	46.8	53.1	37.5	64.4
1973	126.0	139.0	74.4	70.2	3.8	1.3	67.2	59.0	101.9	67.7	49.2	58.1	42.2	64.6
1974	129.1	148.4	73.1	73.6	4.1	1.5	62.0	50.7	94.8	70.6	47.7	60.3	41.0	65.2
1975	100.2	110.2	63.2	64.2	3.7	1.3	56.2	44.2	92.8	61.1	44.5	53.1	35.1	64.0
1976	106.3	114.1	67.7	67.0	4.3	1.6	62.9	56.4	98.0	67.5	47.8	59.4	38.8	69.1
1977	107.3	111.5	73.5	73.2	5.5	2.2	68.3	64.2	104.2	70.4	51.8	64.6	45.8	70.4
1978	114.1	119.8	77.1	78.9	6.8	2.7	72.7	66.9	107.2	73.6	54.8	67.9	47.3	72.6
1979	116.7	123.9	80.5	83.2	8.4	3.6	73.4	61.2	101.6	74.7	56.4	69.4	46.5	71.9
1980	102.3	104.9	75.9	79.2	10.1	4.3	65.1	45.0	103.1	74.5	56.8	65.6	41.4	73.2
1981	102.6	109.0	75.4	78.5	11.6	5.1	62.6	43.9	102.5	75.5	58.3	66.7	43.9	74.2
1982	72.7	67.3	67.6	65.7	13.1	5.9	57.6	39.6	103.9	74.2	62.7	62.4	43.1	77.0
1983	74.2	67.5	68.2	59.3	15.0	7.0	63.6	50.5	106.9	79.1	67.4	66.7	46.9	77.9
1984	81.5	74.5	74.3	69.3	18.7	9.3	72.2	60.6	108.5	83.1	73.4	70.6	54.2	79.4
1985	75.2	69.2	75.2	69.5	20.0	9.9	76.0	62.9	104.2	81.4	76.3	70.1	56.3	82.3
1986	73.4	67.4	74.7	68.4	20.8	10.2	77.8	62.8	105.4	84.8	80.2	73.2	58.6	83.5
1987	79.2	77.0	76.1	69.7	23.5	12.3	80.6	65.1	106.1	87.6	86.1	78.9	64.9	85.3
1988	88.6	89.5	80.1	76.8	25.8	14.2	85.2	69.6	104.2	91.1	88.8	83.4	67.9	87.5
1989	86.7	86.4	79.4	79.6	26.5	15.0	86.7	68.8	99.1	92.1	89.2	85.0	70.2	87.7
1990	85.5	85.3	78.3	77.6	28.7	16.8	84.0	64.7	97.1	92.0	92.5	87.0	72.0	90.4
1991	80.3	78.0	74.8	72.9	29.8	18.0	80.5	61.8	97.6	92.2	89.7	86.8	71.3	92.0
1992	82.2	81.6	77.1	72.6	33.6	21.8	83.5	70.4	99.5	94.5	94.6	88.0	76.7	93.8
1993	86.2	86.5	80.0	78.1	37.1	25.6	85.9	77.8	102.0	95.6	94.9	89.0	82.2	96.3
1994	92.6	93.3	87.0	85.5	44.2	33.2	89.9	89.4	104.1	99.7	95.9	91.3	89.0	96.8
1995	93.7	94.8	92.3	91.5	57.5	47.3	90.1	92.0	104.1	101.1	97.3	92.7	91.1	99.3
1996	95.9	97.1	95.8	94.9	73.8	66.7	91.7	92.7	101.3	98.0	98.0	94.6	94.3	97.4
1997	100.0	100.0	100.0	100.0	100.0	100.0	100.0	100.0	100.0	100.0	100.0	100.0	100.0	100.0
1998	102.3	100.3	103.0	102.6	129.1	140.2	108.8	105.2	94.6	101.1	101.0	101.8	103.4	104.3
1999	101.7	99.9	103.8	100.4	169.0	201.3	114.5	116.4	90.7	102.2	101.9	103.8	108.7	105.2
2000	98.5	99.0	107.9	105.8	224.0	286.7	109.5	116.2	87.3	99.9	102.3	105.5	110.5	106.8
2001	89.0	87.7	100.1	93.8	226.1	291.1	105.9	105.6	77.9	94.3	96.9	103.9	104.0	106.9
2002	86.5	89.5	97.4	86.8	234.7	311.4	108.0	114.5	70.8	93.5	93.7	105.3	104.3	107.1
2003 *p*	84.7	89.9	94.6	86.7	267.6	370.7	108.6	117.4	62.4	92.3	89.7	105.6	103.2	106.1
2002: Jan	84.8	84.7	96.5	86.8	224.3	291.3	106.4	108.8	70.7	91.5	95.3	105.7	101.7	108.4
Feb	85.2	85.8	96.8	86.9	225.1	294.1	106.9	110.8	70.0	91.6	94.2	104.6	102.0	107.6
Mar	86.7	87.8	96.8	87.0	226.1	295.8	106.7	110.7	70.3	90.8	93.7	105.4	103.8	107.4
Apr	85.7	86.1	97.4	87.0	226.9	298.9	107.9	113.4	69.4	92.6	94.0	104.9	104.6	107.3
May	86.6	89.8	98.2	87.6	229.2	302.3	107.4	113.5	70.6	94.0	94.4	105.6	105.2	107.3
June	87.3	89.4	98.3	87.8	233.0	308.3	108.6	115.8	72.2	94.0	93.5	106.2	106.1	107.5
July	85.7	88.0	98.1	86.4	233.9	311.2	109.2	117.8	72.2	94.3	94.3	106.8	105.6	107.0
Aug	88.6	93.8	98.0	87.5	238.3	318.9	109.7	117.9	71.6	94.4	93.8	105.9	105.4	106.7
Sept	86.7	91.3	97.4	86.8	241.2	323.2	109.1	117.0	72.2	94.7	92.9	105.9	105.1	107.0
Oct	87.9	93.9	97.7	86.1	242.4	325.8	107.7	115.1	70.2	94.2	92.6	104.7	104.7	106.8
Nov	88.8	96.7	96.5	86.5	246.5	332.5	109.6	118.9	71.1	95.3	92.7	104.3	103.9	105.9
Dec	84.3	86.4	96.6	85.6	248.9	334.7	107.0	114.6	69.2	94.2	93.0	104.0	103.4	106.3
2003: Jan	88.3	97.2	96.2	85.2	251.1	335.7	109.6	118.7	67.6	92.4	92.7	104.5	103.4	106.5
Feb	88.0	93.1	95.7	86.5	253.6	344.0	107.6	116.0	66.2	92.5	92.3	105.3	103.8	106.2
Mar	83.5	84.4	95.0	86.3	254.6	345.9	106.7	114.4	65.2	93.4	90.3	105.0	103.9	106.5
Apr	83.8	91.2	94.0	85.4	254.6	348.3	105.6	113.0	63.4	92.2	90.3	105.6	102.2	106.1
May	82.2	83.8	93.2	86.2	258.0	352.9	105.2	112.0	63.6	92.7	88.8	104.4	103.0	106.1
June	82.7	87.3	93.3	86.3	260.5	359.6	106.3	113.8	61.8	93.1	88.8	103.5	102.5	106.4
July	82.9	87.2	94.2	85.9	266.7	369.1	107.9	116.6	60.9	93.0	89.0	104.5	102.8	106.5
Aug	82.5	84.5	93.2	86.7	273.7	382.6	107.2	114.9	59.1	91.6	88.5	105.5	103.1	105.4
Sept	83.0	88.5	94.4	87.3	277.1	388.1	112.1	122.7	59.1	91.3	88.7	106.1	103.0	105.9
Oct *p*	85.2	91.9	94.9	86.4	284.2	399.6	110.2	119.8	60.7	91.2	88.7	106.5	103.7	105.4
Nov *p*	87.1	93.9	96.0	89.6	289.2	409.1	110.3	119.8	61.2	92.1	89.3	108.2	103.6	106.0
Dec *p*	88.8	97.0	96.1	90.0	290.6	416.8	111.1	120.5	60.0	92.0	88.9	108.9	103.6	106.1

[1] Computers and office equipment, communications equipment, and semiconductors and related electronic components.

Note.—See footnote 1 and Note, Table B-51.

Source: Board of Governors of the Federal Reserve System.

TABLE B–54.—*Capacity utilization rates, 1959–2003*

[Percent [1]; monthly data seasonally adjusted]

Year or month	Total industry [2]	Manufacturing				Mining	Utilities	Stage-of-process		
		Total [2]	Durable goods	Non-durable goods	Other (non-NAICS) [2]			Crude	Primary and semi-finished	Finished
1959	....	81.6	....	....	....	....	....	....	83.0	81.1
1960	....	80.1	....	....	....	....	....	....	79.8	80.5
1961	....	77.3	....	....	....	....	....	....	77.9	77.2
1962	....	81.4	....	....	....	....	....	....	81.5	81.6
1963	....	83.5	....	....	....	....	....	....	83.8	83.4
1964	....	85.6	....	....	....	....	....	....	87.8	84.6
1965	....	89.5	....	....	....	....	....	....	91.0	88.8
1966	....	91.1	....	....	....	....	....	....	91.4	91.1
1967	87.0	87.2	87.5	86.3	....	81.2	94.5	81.1	85.0	88.2
1968	87.3	87.1	87.3	86.4	....	83.6	95.1	83.4	86.8	87.1
1969	87.3	86.5	87.0	86.0	....	86.8	96.8	85.6	88.0	85.5
1970	81.1	79.3	77.6	82.0	....	89.3	96.2	85.1	81.3	78.0
1971	79.4	77.7	75.2	81.6	....	87.9	94.7	84.2	81.4	75.5
1972	84.5	83.2	81.8	85.1	85.2	90.8	95.2	88.5	87.9	79.5
1973	88.3	87.5	88.4	86.5	84.3	91.9	94.4	90.6	92.1	83.0
1974	84.9	84.1	84.3	84.1	82.6	91.1	87.7	91.2	87.1	80.1
1975	75.5	73.4	71.4	76.0	76.8	89.2	84.6	83.9	74.9	73.4
1976	79.5	77.9	76.0	80.9	77.1	90.2	85.3	87.4	79.9	76.2
1977	83.2	82.3	81.0	84.1	83.1	90.4	85.5	89.6	84.5	79.3
1978	85.0	84.5	84.3	84.9	84.8	90.1	84.2	88.8	86.1	82.2
1979	85.1	84.3	84.7	83.7	85.1	91.1	85.5	89.4	86.0	82.1
1980	80.9	78.8	77.9	79.5	87.0	91.7	85.3	89.2	78.9	79.7
1981	79.9	77.3	75.6	78.9	87.6	91.6	84.4	89.6	77.2	78.3
1982	73.9	71.3	66.9	76.8	86.7	83.8	80.5	81.9	70.5	74.1
1983	74.8	73.6	68.7	79.9	87.1	78.4	79.6	78.5	74.2	73.8
1984	80.5	79.5	76.9	82.6	89.3	84.5	83.0	84.7	81.0	78.0
1985	79.5	78.5	75.9	81.1	91.2	83.4	83.2	83.4	80.1	77.3
1986	78.8	78.5	75.4	82.1	89.3	76.7	82.3	79.0	79.9	77.4
1987	81.3	81.2	77.8	85.1	90.1	79.5	84.0	83.0	82.8	79.0
1988	84.3	84.1	82.1	86.5	88.2	83.5	86.1	86.7	85.7	81.8
1989	83.6	83.2	81.3	85.3	86.1	84.3	86.7	87.5	84.5	81.3
1990	82.4	81.6	79.1	84.6	84.3	86.5	86.1	88.8	82.3	80.7
1991	79.6	78.3	74.8	82.6	80.0	84.8	86.8	86.0	79.4	77.9
1992	80.3	79.4	76.8	82.9	78.6	84.4	85.2	85.7	80.9	78.2
1993	81.3	80.3	78.5	82.5	80.8	85.7	87.7	85.5	83.0	78.2
1994	83.4	82.6	81.5	84.1	81.5	87.3	88.9	87.2	86.3	79.1
1995	83.6	82.7	82.0	83.9	80.8	87.1	90.0	87.9	86.4	79.2
1996	82.4	81.1	80.7	82.2	78.1	89.6	90.5	87.6	85.1	78.0
1997	83.6	82.6	82.6	83.0	79.9	90.8	89.1	89.0	85.7	79.8
1998	83.0	82.0	81.9	82.2	81.3	88.1	91.0	86.1	84.4	80.6
1999	82.4	81.4	81.5	80.9	83.1	85.7	92.5	85.9	84.8	78.8
2000	82.6	81.1	81.5	80.1	84.8	89.9	92.9	87.4	85.3	78.2
2001	77.4	75.4	73.2	77.8	80.4	89.0	89.8	85.1	78.6	74.3
2002	75.6	73.9	70.6	77.6	78.6	84.3	87.8	82.9	77.5	71.9
2003 ᴾ	74.9	73.4	70.2	76.4	83.0	85.0	83.7	83.7	76.8	71.0
2002: Jan	75.4	73.7	70.3	77.5	79.0	84.8	86.4	82.6	76.4	72.7
Feb	75.4	73.7	70.3	77.4	78.8	84.9	86.9	82.7	76.7	72.4
Mar	75.6	73.8	70.3	77.8	79.1	84.2	88.2	82.2	77.2	72.4
Apr	75.8	73.9	70.5	77.9	78.0	84.0	89.8	82.8	77.7	72.2
May	75.8	74.1	70.8	77.9	78.1	84.2	88.6	83.5	77.9	71.9
June	76.2	74.4	71.1	78.4	77.9	84.7	89.0	83.6	78.2	72.5
July	76.0	74.3	70.8	78.3	77.9	84.0	89.2	83.6	78.2	72.1
Aug	75.9	74.3	71.1	78.1	78.3	84.2	86.8	83.1	77.9	72.1
Sept	75.7	74.2	70.8	77.9	79.3	82.7	86.9	82.0	77.7	72.1
Oct	75.4	73.7	70.5	77.2	79.7	83.2	87.9	82.1	77.8	71.3
Nov	75.4	73.6	70.9	76.7	78.9	85.1	87.1	83.3	77.7	71.1
Dec	74.9	73.1	70.2	76.4	78.1	85.4	86.7	83.8	77.0	70.8
2003: Jan	75.2	73.6	70.7	76.5	80.7	84.8	85.9	82.9	77.2	71.4
Feb	75.4	73.5	70.4	76.5	82.7	84.7	88.7	83.4	77.8	71.1
Mar	74.8	73.3	69.7	76.6	83.5	84.6	84.1	83.5	76.6	71.0
Apr	74.2	72.7	69.1	76.2	82.8	84.9	82.8	83.5	76.0	70.5
May	74.1	72.6	69.0	76.1	83.0	84.3	83.1	83.0	75.9	70.4
June	74.0	72.7	69.3	75.8	83.8	84.8	81.1	83.6	75.6	70.4
July	74.5	73.0	69.8	76.2	82.3	85.0	83.4	83.9	76.3	70.8
Aug	74.5	73.0	69.8	76.1	82.5	84.8	83.5	83.4	76.4	70.6
Sept	74.9	73.6	70.8	76.2	82.3	85.2	81.8	83.8	76.6	71.2
Oct ᴾ	75.1	73.7	70.9	76.3	83.5	85.3	83.1	83.9	77.2	71.1
Nov ᴾ	75.8	74.4	71.6	77.0	84.4	85.9	84.0	84.5	77.9	71.9
Dec ᴾ	75.8	74.5	71.9	77.0	84.1	85.9	82.6	84.6	77.9	71.8

[1] Output as percent of capacity.
[2] See footnote 1 and Note, Table B–51.

Source: Board of Governors of the Federal Reserve System.

347

TABLE B–55.—*New construction activity, 1964–2003*

[Value put in place, billions of dollars; monthly data at seasonally adjusted annual rates]

Year or month	Total new construc- tion	Private construction										Public construction		
		Total	Residential buildings[1]		Nonresidential buildings and other construction							Total	Federal	State and local
			Total[2]	New housing units[3]	Total	Lodg- ing	Office	Com- mer- cial[4]	Manu- fac- turing	Other[5]				
1964	75.1	54.9	30.5	24.1	24.4							20.2	3.7	16.5
1965	81.9	60.0	30.2	23.8	29.7							21.9	3.9	18.0
1966	85.8	61.9	28.6	21.8	33.3							23.8	3.8	20.0
1967	87.2	61.8	28.7	21.5	33.1							25.4	3.3	22.1
1968	96.8	69.4	34.2	26.7	35.2							27.4	3.2	24.2
1969	104.9	77.2	37.2	29.2	39.9							27.8	3.2	24.6
1970	105.9	78.0	35.9	27.1	42.1							27.9	3.1	24.8
1971	122.4	92.7	48.5	38.7	44.2							29.7	3.8	25.9
1972	139.1	109.1	60.7	50.1	48.4							30.0	4.2	25.8
1973	153.8	121.4	65.1	54.6	56.3							32.3	4.7	27.6
1974	155.2	117.0	56.0	43.4	61.1							38.1	5.1	33.0
1975	152.6	109.3	51.6	36.3	57.8							43.3	6.1	37.2
1976	172.1	128.2	68.3	50.8	59.9							44.0	6.8	37.2
1977	200.5	157.4	92.0	72.2	65.4							43.1	7.1	36.0
1978	239.9	189.7	109.8	85.6	79.9							50.1	8.1	42.0
1979	272.9	216.2	116.4	89.3	99.8							56.6	8.6	48.1
1980	273.9	210.3	100.4	69.6	109.9							63.6	9.6	54.0
1981	289.1	224.4	99.2	69.4	125.1							64.7	10.4	54.3
1982	279.3	216.3	84.7	57.0	131.6							63.1	10.0	53.1
1983	311.9	248.4	125.8	95.0	122.6							63.5	10.6	52.9
1984	370.2	300.0	155.0	114.6	144.9							70.2	11.2	59.0
1985	403.4	325.6	160.5	115.9	165.1							77.8	12.0	65.8
1986	433.5	348.9	190.7	135.2	158.2							84.6	12.4	72.2
1987	446.6	356.0	199.7	142.7	156.3							90.6	14.1	76.6
1988	462.0	367.3	204.5	142.4	162.8							94.7	12.3	82.5
1989	477.5	379.3	204.3	143.2	175.1							98.2	12.2	86.0
1990	476.8	369.3	191.1	132.1	178.2							107.5	12.1	95.4
1991	432.6	322.5	166.3	114.6	156.2							110.1	12.8	97.3
1992	463.7	347.8	199.4	135.1	148.4							115.8	14.4	101.5
1993	491.0	375.1	225.1	150.9	150.0	4.6	20.0	34.4	23.4	67.7		116.0	14.4	101.5
1994	539.2	419.0	258.6	176.4	160.4	4.7	20.4	39.6	28.8	66.9		120.2	14.4	105.8
1995	557.8	427.9	247.4	171.4	180.5	7.1	23.0	44.1	35.4	70.9		129.9	15.8	114.2
1996	615.9	476.6	281.1	191.1	195.5	10.9	26.5	49.4	38.1	70.6		139.3	15.3	123.9
1997	653.4	502.7	289.0	198.1	213.7	12.9	32.8	53.1	37.6	77.3		150.7	14.1	136.6
1998	705.7	551.4	314.6	224.0	236.8	14.8	40.4	55.7	40.5	85.4		154.3	14.3	140.6
1999	766.1	596.3	350.6	251.3	245.8	16.0	45.1	59.4	32.6	92.8		169.7	14.0	155.7
2000	828.8	642.6	374.5	265.0	268.2	16.3	52.4	64.1	31.8	103.6		186.1	14.2	172.4
2001	852.6	652.5	388.3	279.4	264.2	14.5	49.7	63.6	29.5	106.8		200.1	15.1	185.4
2002	860.9	650.5	421.5	298.5	229.0	10.3	35.1	58.2	16.6	108.7		210.4	16.3	194.
2002: Jan	863.7	653.0	399.2	281.2	253.8	11.6	39.7	63.4	21.4	117.7		210.7	15.1	195.
Feb	868.7	654.6	409.5	287.4	245.0	10.8	37.9	60.6	19.8	116.0		214.2	16.7	197.
Mar	858.1	655.1	411.7	292.0	243.4	10.7	36.3	62.3	18.5	115.6		203.0	16.1	186.
Apr	863.6	657.8	415.4	293.5	242.4	11.8	37.5	61.4	17.9	113.8		205.7	16.1	189.
May	861.5	650.1	417.3	294.9	232.8	11.5	35.8	58.8	17.7	108.9		211.5	16.5	195.
June	855.0	646.9	420.1	297.0	226.8	10.5	34.3	57.7	17.0	107.2		208.1	16.1	192.
July	858.7	648.2	423.9	299.5	224.3	10.0	34.7	55.4	16.1	108.1		210.5	16.5	194.
Aug	848.6	638.1	423.6	298.7	214.6	9.5	33.9	56.6	15.1	99.5		210.5	16.4	194.
Sept	854.9	641.5	425.7	302.1	215.8	9.4	33.6	57.8	14.2	100.8		213.3	16.0	197.
Oct	861.9	651.1	429.9	305.7	221.2	9.7	33.5	57.4	14.6	106.1		210.8	17.0	193.
Nov	870.0	656.4	434.4	310.0	222.0	9.0	33.2	56.9	14.6	108.2		213.6	16.6	197.
Dec	872.1	658.2	441.5	315.6	216.8	8.9	32.1	52.3	13.9	109.6		213.8	16.7	197.
2003: Jan	883.2	667.6	450.0	323.6	217.6	9.2	30.8	56.8	14.0	106.7		215.6	16.8	198.
Feb	876.5	665.1	448.5	322.8	216.5	9.3	29.7	54.8	13.6	109.2		211.4	16.7	194.
Mar	875.2	668.8	447.1	321.7	221.6	10.1	29.7	55.6	14.0	112.2		206.5	16.1	190.
Apr	871.9	662.8	443.9	320.3	218.9	10.4	29.3	54.7	13.9	110.6		209.1	17.6	191.
May	871.9	660.9	444.9	324.2	216.1	10.8	28.6	55.3	14.2	107.2		210.9	17.7	193.
June	878.8	661.5	444.4	326.3	217.1	10.3	29.3	56.9	14.5	106.0		217.2	17.8	199.
July	892.6	674.3	457.1	333.4	217.2	9.2	28.5	58.2	13.6	107.6		218.3	17.6	200.
Aug	901.4	681.2	466.8	342.1	214.4	9.5	29.1	58.4	14.1	103.4		220.2	18.5	201.
Sept	913.8	692.5	475.7	350.5	216.7	9.4	29.8	57.0	14.0	106.5		221.4	18.6	202.
Oct	923.8	702.4	486.2	358.9	216.2	9.7	30.3	56.3	14.0	105.9		221.4	18.1	203.
Nov	934.5	710.8	495.7	368.4	215.1	9.6	31.1	56.7	13.8	104.0		223.7	18.0	205.

[1] Includes farm residential buildings.
[2] Includes residential improvements, not shown separately.
[3] New single- and multi-family units.
[4] Including farm.
[5] Health care, educational, religious, public safety, amusement and recreation, transportation, communication, power, highway and stre sewage and waste disposal, water supply, and conservation and development.

Note.—Data beginning 1993 reflect reclassification.

Source: Department of Commerce, Bureau of the Census.

TABLE B–56.—*New private housing units started, authorized, and completed, and houses sold, 1959–2003*

[Thousands; monthly data at seasonally adjusted annual rates]

Year or month	New housing units started Total	1 unit	2 to 4 units[2]	5 units or more	New housing units authorized[1] Total	1 unit	2 to 4 units	5 units or more	New housing units completed	New houses sold
1959	1,517.0	1,234.0	283.0		1,208.3	938.3	77.1	192.9		
1960	1,252.2	994.7	257.5		998.0	746.1	64.6	187.4		
1961	1,313.0	974.3	338.7		1,064.2	722.8	67.6	273.8		
1962	1,462.9	991.4	471.5		1,186.6	716.2	87.1	383.3		
1963	1,603.2	1,012.4	590.8		1,334.7	750.2	118.9	465.6		560
1964	1,528.8	970.5	108.3	450.0	1,285.8	720.1	100.8	464.9		565
1965	1,472.8	963.7	86.7	422.5	1,240.6	709.9	84.8	445.9		575
1966	1,164.9	778.6	61.2	325.1	971.9	563.2	61.0	347.7		461
1967	1,291.6	843.9	71.7	376.1	1,141.0	650.6	73.0	417.5		487
1968	1,507.6	899.4	80.7	527.3	1,353.4	694.7	84.3	574.4	1,319.8	490
1969	1,466.8	810.6	85.1	571.2	1,322.3	624.8	85.2	612.4	1,399.0	448
1970	1,433.6	812.9	84.9	535.9	1,351.5	646.8	88.1	616.7	1,418.4	485
1971	2,052.2	1,151.0	120.5	780.9	1,924.6	906.1	132.9	885.7	1,706.1	656
1972	2,356.6	1,309.2	141.2	906.2	2,218.9	1,033.1	148.6	1,037.2	2,003.9	718
1973	2,045.3	1,132.0	118.2	795.0	1,819.5	882.1	117.0	820.5	2,100.5	634
1974	1,337.7	888.1	68.0	381.6	1,074.4	643.8	64.3	366.2	1,728.5	519
1975	1,160.4	892.2	64.0	204.3	939.2	675.5	63.9	199.8	1,317.2	549
1976	1,537.5	1,162.4	85.8	289.2	1,296.2	893.6	93.1	309.5	1,377.2	646
1977	1,987.1	1,450.9	121.7	414.4	1,690.0	1,126.1	121.3	442.7	1,657.1	819
1978	2,020.3	1,433.3	125.1	462.0	1,800.5	1,182.6	130.6	487.3	1,867.5	817
1979	1,745.1	1,194.1	122.0	429.0	1,551.8	981.5	125.4	444.8	1,870.8	709
1980	1,292.2	852.2	109.5	330.5	1,190.6	710.4	114.5	365.7	1,501.6	545
1981	1,084.2	705.4	91.2	287.7	985.5	564.3	101.8	319.4	1,265.7	436
1982	1,062.2	662.6	80.1	319.6	1,000.5	546.4	88.3	365.8	1,005.5	412
1983	1,703.0	1,067.6	113.5	522.0	1,605.2	901.5	133.6	570.1	1,390.3	623
1984	1,749.5	1,084.2	121.4	543.9	1,681.8	922.4	142.6	616.8	1,652.2	639
1985	1,741.8	1,072.4	93.5	576.0	1,733.3	956.6	120.1	656.6	1,703.3	688
1986	1,805.4	1,179.4	84.0	542.0	1,769.4	1,077.6	108.4	583.5	1,756.4	750
1987	1,620.5	1,146.4	65.1	408.7	1,534.8	1,024.4	89.3	421.1	1,668.8	671
1988	1,488.1	1,081.3	58.7	348.0	1,455.6	993.8	75.7	386.1	1,529.8	676
1989	1,376.1	1,003.3	55.3	317.6	1,338.4	931.7	67.0	339.8	1,422.8	650
1990	1,192.7	894.8	37.6	260.4	1,110.8	793.9	54.3	262.6	1,308.0	534
1991	1,013.9	840.4	35.6	137.9	948.8	753.5	43.1	152.1	1,090.8	509
1992	1,199.7	1,029.9	30.9	139.0	1,094.9	910.7	45.8	138.4	1,157.5	610
1993	1,287.6	1,125.7	29.4	132.6	1,199.1	986.5	52.3	160.2	1,192.7	666
1994	1,457.0	1,198.4	35.2	223.5	1,371.6	1,068.5	62.2	241.0	1,346.9	670
1995	1,354.1	1,076.2	33.8	244.1	1,332.5	997.3	63.7	271.5	1,312.6	667
1996	1,476.8	1,160.9	45.3	270.8	1,425.6	1,069.5	65.8	290.3	1,412.9	757
1997	1,474.0	1,133.7	44.5	295.8	1,441.1	1,062.4	68.5	310.3	1,400.5	804
1998	1,616.9	1,271.4	42.6	302.9	1,612.3	1,187.6	69.2	355.5	1,474.2	886
1999	1,640.9	1,302.4	31.9	306.6	1,663.5	1,246.7	65.8	351.1	1,604.9	880
2000	1,568.7	1,230.9	38.7	299.1	1,592.3	1,198.1	64.9	329.3	1,573.7	877
2001	1,602.7	1,273.3	36.6	292.8	1,636.7	1,235.6	66.0	335.2	1,570.8	908
2002	1,704.9	1,358.6	38.5	307.9	1,747.7	1,332.6	73.7	341.4	1,648.4	973
2003ᵖ	1,848.4	1,498.5	33.3	316.6	1,862.4	1,443.6	82.7	336.0	1,677.7	1,085
2002: Jan	1,681	1,307	68	306	1,679	1,294	72	313	1,631	876
Feb	1,817	1,491	44	282	1,773	1,391	66	316	1,666	949
Mar	1,651	1,284	48	319	1,681	1,281	71	329	1,563	917
Apr	1,587	1,275	27	285	1,662	1,279	70	313	1,643	916
May	1,752	1,389	37	326	1,721	1,286	69	366	1,713	981
June	1,709	1,359	47	303	1,746	1,309	82	355	1,591	959
July	1,666	1,329	31	306	1,742	1,312	70	360	1,612	961
Aug	1,630	1,249	31	350	1,704	1,319	73	312	1,705	1,025
Sept	1,810	1,449	37	324	1,803	1,372	91	340	1,655	1,057
Oct	1,653	1,366	33	254	1,813	1,390	71	352	1,591	1,005
Nov	1,760	1,403	34	323	1,764	1,377	70	317	1,706	1,022
Dec	1,815	1,462	35	318	1,907	1,420	77	410	1,674	1,052
2003: Jan	1,828	1,509	41	278	1,777	1,406	87	284	1,647	1,009
Feb	1,640	1,312	30	298	1,786	1,319	78	389	1,672	935
Mar	1,742	1,393	36	313	1,688	1,311	71	306	1,621	1,008
Apr	1,627	1,357	31	239	1,724	1,332	82	310	1,680	1,004
May	1,745	1,389	27	329	1,803	1,349	84	370	1,742	1,081
June	1,844	1,499	28	317	1,823	1,427	77	319	1,663	1,200
July	1,890	1,533	36	321	1,800	1,434	77	289	1,678	1,145
Aug	1,831	1,490	32	309	1,901	1,484	84	333	1,573	1,190
Sept	1,931	1,547	45	339	1,875	1,487	88	300	1,709	1,129
Oct	1,977	1,640	29	308	1,981	1,539	81	361	1,717	1,149
Novᵖ	2,054	1,674	37	343	1,863	1,473	88	302	1,707	1,117
Decᵖ	2,088	1,664	27	397	1,953	1,530	77	346	1,710	1,060

[1] Authorized by issuance of local building permits in: 19,000 permit-issuing places beginning 1994; 17,000 places for 1984–93; 16,000 places for 1978–83; 14,000 places for 1972–77; 13,000 places for 1967–71; 12,000 places for 1963–66; and 10,000 places prior to 1963.

[2] Monthly data derived.

Note.—Data beginning 1999 for new housing units started and completed and for new houses sold are based on new estimation methods and are not directly comparable with earlier data.

Source: Department of Commerce, Bureau of the Census.

TABLE B–57.—*Manufacturing and trade sales and inventories, 1965–2003*

[Amounts in millions of dollars; monthly data seasonally adjusted]

Year or month	Total manufacturing and trade Sales[1]	Inventories[2]	Ratio[3]	Manufacturing Sales[1]	Inventories[2]	Ratio[3]	Merchant wholesalers Sales[1]	Inventories[2]	Ratio[3]	Retail trade Sales[1,4]	Inventories[2]	Ratio[3]	Retail and food services sales
SIC:[5]													
1965	80,283	120,929	1.51	40,995	68,207	1.66	15,611	18,317	1.17	23,677	34,405	1.45	
1966	87,187	136,824	1.57	44,870	77,986	1.74	16,987	20,765	1.22	25,330	38,073	1.50	
1967	90,820	145,681	1.60	46,486	84,646	1.82	19,576	25,786	1.32	24,757	35,249	1.42	
1968	98,685	156,611	1.59	50,229	90,560	1.80	21,012	27,166	1.29	27,445	38,885	1.42	
1969	105,690	170,400	1.61	53,501	98,145	1.83	22,818	29,800	1.31	29,371	42,455	1.45	
1970	108,221	178,594	1.65	52,805	101,599	1.92	24,167	33,354	1.38	31,249	43,641	1.40	
1971	116,895	188,991	1.62	55,906	102,567	1.83	26,492	36,568	1.38	34,497	49,856	1.45	
1972	131,081	203,227	1.55	63,027	108,121	1.72	29,866	40,297	1.35	38,189	54,809	1.44	
1973	153,677	234,406	1.53	72,931	124,499	1.71	38,115	46,918	1.23	42,631	62,989	1.48	
1974	177,912	287,144	1.61	84,790	157,625	1.86	47,982	58,667	1.22	45,141	70,852	1.57	
1975	182,198	288,992	1.59	86,589	159,708	1.84	46,634	57,774	1.24	48,975	71,510	1.46	
1976	204,150	318,345	1.56	98,797	174,636	1.77	50,698	64,622	1.27	54,655	79,087	1.45	
1977	229,513	350,706	1.53	113,201	188,378	1.66	56,136	73,179	1.30	60,176	89,149	1.48	
1978	260,320	400,931	1.54	126,905	211,691	1.67	66,413	86,934	1.31	67,002	102,306	1.53	
1979	297,701	452,640	1.52	143,936	242,157	1.68	79,051	99,679	1.26	74,713	110,804	1.48	
1980	327,233	508,924	1.56	154,391	265,215	1.72	93,099	122,631	1.32	79,743	121,078	1.52	
1981	355,822	545,786	1.53	168,129	283,413	1.69	101,180	129,654	1.28	86,514	132,719	1.53	
1982	347,625	573,908	1.67	163,351	311,852	1.95	95,211	127,428	1.36	89,062	134,628	1.49	
1983	369,286	590,287	1.56	172,547	312,379	1.78	99,225	130,075	1.28	97,514	147,833	1.44	
1984	410,124	649,780	1.53	190,682	339,516	1.73	112,199	142,452	1.23	107,243	167,812	1.49	
1985	422,583	664,039	1.56	194,538	334,749	1.73	113,459	147,409	1.28	114,586	181,881	1.52	
1986	430,419	662,738	1.55	194,657	322,654	1.68	114,960	153,574	1.32	120,803	186,510	1.56	
1987	457,735	709,848	1.50	206,326	338,109	1.59	122,968	163,903	1.29	128,442	207,836	1.55	
1988	497,157	767,222	1.49	224,619	369,374	1.57	134,521	178,801	1.30	138,017	219,047	1.54	
1989	527,039	815,455	1.52	236,698	391,212	1.63	143,760	187,009	1.28	146,581	237,234	1.58	
1990	545,909	840,594	1.52	242,686	405,073	1.65	149,506	195,833	1.29	153,718	239,688	1.56	
1991	542,815	834,609	1.53	239,847	390,950	1.65	148,306	200,448	1.33	154,661	243,211	1.54	
1992	567,176	842,809	1.48	250,394	382,510	1.54	154,150	208,302	1.32	162,632	251,997	1.52	
NAICS:[5]													
1992	541,227	840,820	1.53	242,002	379,183	1.57	144,302	193,706	1.31	154,923	267,931	1.67	171,875
1993	568,073	868,067	1.50	251,708	380,102	1.51	150,833	201,939	1.31	165,533	286,026	1.68	183,537
1994	610,669	931,353	1.47	269,843	400,335	1.44	161,133	218,856	1.30	179,693	312,162	1.66	198,498
1995	655,227	989,989	1.48	289,973	425,217	1.44	176,227	235,128	1.30	189,028	329,644	1.72	208,496
1996	687,472	1,009,196	1.46	299,766	430,816	1.43	186,649	237,828	1.28	201,058	340,552	1.67	221,299
1997	724,126	1,050,132	1.42	319,558	443,804	1.37	194,541	255,427	1.27	210,027	350,901	1.64	231,530
1998	743,716	1,082,701	1.44	324,984	499,231	1.39	198,319	268,385	1.32	220,413	365,085	1.62	243,133
1999	787,656	1,143,124	1.41	335,991	463,646	1.35	211,797	285,167	1.31	239,869	394,311	1.59	263,696
2000	835,239	1,201,677	1.41	350,715	481,396	1.35	228,549	302,495	1.30	255,974	417,786	1.59	281,497
2001	819,373	1,145,363	1.44	330,875	452,236	1.42	225,722	287,556	1.32	262,776	405,571	1.58	289,300
2002	824,013	1,169,352	1.40	324,313	444,188	1.37	229,250	288,847	1.25	270,451	436,317	1.56	298,334
2002: Jan	810,748	1,144,083	1.41	323,837	448,919	1.39	222,112	286,905	1.29	264,799	408,259	1.54	292,393
Feb	810,406	1,141,534	1.41	320,087	446,363	1.39	224,199	284,463	1.27	266,120	410,708	1.54	293,876
Mar	807,958	1,140,487	1.41	318,481	445,444	1.40	223,530	284,642	1.27	265,947	410,401	1.54	293,575
Apr	823,133	1,139,091	1.38	325,938	444,605	1.36	227,173	282,779	1.24	270,022	411,707	1.52	297,827
May	819,673	1,142,364	1.39	325,999	442,617	1.36	227,446	282,853	1.24	266,228	416,594	1.56	293,876
June	821,495	1,144,988	1.39	322,827	442,415	1.37	228,575	283,920	1.24	270,093	418,653	1.55	298,026
July	831,022	1,152,039	1.39	328,367	442,605	1.35	229,714	286,083	1.25	272,941	423,351	1.55	300,84
Aug	833,117	1,153,106	1.38	326,168	442,827	1.36	232,373	286,685	1.23	274,576	423,594	1.54	302,44
Sept	828,278	1,159,217	1.40	326,165	443,595	1.36	231,752	287,186	1.24	270,361	428,436	1.58	298,23
Oct	833,161	1,160,528	1.39	329,349	443,545	1.35	231,615	285,890	1.23	272,197	431,093	1.58	299,92
Nov	834,536	1,163,281	1.39	326,527	442,499	1.36	234,619	286,317	1.22	273,390	434,465	1.59	301,46
Dec	833,037	1,169,352	1.40	323,862	444,188	1.37	233,732	288,847	1.24	275,943	436,317	1.58	304,65
2003: Jan	844,999	1,172,045	1.39	329,665	444,220	1.35	236,978	288,705	1.22	278,356	439,120	1.58	307,04
Feb	837,850	1,179,647	1.41	325,591	446,088	1.37	238,193	289,680	1.22	274,066	443,879	1.62	302,74
Mar	851,680	1,183,281	1.39	330,764	445,180	1.35	240,547	290,938	1.21	280,369	447,163	1.59	309,56
Apr	836,843	1,183,557	1.41	322,608	445,207	1.38	234,634	290,092	1.24	279,601	448,258	1.60	308,67
May	838,547	1,179,925	1.41	323,920	444,049	1.37	234,049	288,962	1.23	280,578	446,914	1.59	310,21
June	849,696	1,180,343	1.39	328,643	442,666	1.35	237,735	288,919	1.22	283,318	448,758	1.58	313,14
July	863,732	1,178,142	1.36	337,248	440,767	1.31	238,919	289,061	1.21	287,565	448,314	1.56	317,51
Aug	861,312	1,173,573	1.36	331,676	439,632	1.33	239,515	288,717	1.21	290,121	445,224	1.53	320,70
Sept	869,199	1,178,322	1.36	337,598	438,294	1.30	242,007	289,691	1.20	289,594	450,337	1.56	319,62
Oct	875,497	1,183,298	1.35	339,825	438,680	1.29	246,732	291,224	1.18	288,940	453,394	1.57	319,70
Nov[p]	879,768	1,187,426	1.35	339,899	437,904	1.29	247,448	292,743	1.18	292,421	456,779	1.56	323,54

[1] Annual data are averages of monthly not seasonally adjusted figures.
[2] Seasonally adjusted, end of period. Inventories beginning January 1982 for manufacturing and December 1980 for wholesale and retail trade are not comparable with earlier periods.
[3] Inventory/sales ratio. Annual data are: beginning 1982, averages of monthly ratios; for 1965–81, ratio of December inventories to monthly average sales for the year; and for earlier years, weighted averages. Monthly ratios are inventories at end of month to sales for month.
[4] Food services included on SIC basis and excluded on NAICS basis. See last column for retail and food services sales.
[5] Effective in 2001, data classified based on North American Industry Classification System (NAICS). Data on NAICS basis available beginning 1992. Earlier data based on Standard Industrial Classification (SIC).
Data include semiconductors.

Note.—Earlier data are not strictly comparable with data beginning 1967 for wholesale and retail trade.

Source: Department of Commerce, Bureau of the Census.

TABLE B-58.—*Manufacturers' shipments and inventories, 1965–2003*

[Millions of dollars; monthly data seasonally adjusted]

Year or month	Shipments [1]			Inventories [2]								
					Durable goods industries				Nondurable goods industries			
	Total	Durable goods industries	Nondurable goods industries	Total	Total	Materials and supplies	Work in process	Finished goods	Total	Materials and supplies	Work in process	Finished goods
SIC: [3]												
1965	40,995	22,193	18,802	68,207	42,189	13,298	18,055	10,836	26,018	10,487	3,825	11,706
1966	44,870	24,617	20,253	77,986	49,852	15,464	21,908	12,480	28,134	11,197	4,226	12,711
1967	46,486	25,233	21,253	84,646	54,896	16,423	24,933	13,540	29,750	11,760	4,431	13,559
1968	50,229	27,624	22,605	90,560	58,732	17,344	27,213	14,175	31,828	12,328	4,852	14,648
1969	53,501	29,403	24,098	98,145	64,598	18,636	30,282	15,680	33,547	12,753	5,120	15,674
1970	52,805	28,156	24,649	101,599	66,651	19,149	29,745	17,757	34,948	13,168	5,271	16,509
1971	55,906	29,924	25,982	102,567	66,136	19,679	28,550	17,907	36,431	13,686	5,678	17,067
1972	63,027	33,987	29,040	108,121	70,067	20,807	30,713	18,547	38,054	14,677	5,998	17,379
1973	72,931	39,635	33,296	124,499	81,192	25,944	35,490	19,758	43,307	18,147	6,729	18,431
1974	84,790	44,173	40,617	157,625	101,493	35,070	42,530	23,893	56,132	23,744	8,189	24,199
1975	86,589	43,598	42,991	159,708	102,590	33,903	43,227	25,460	57,118	23,565	8,834	24,719
1976	98,797	50,623	48,174	174,636	111,988	37,457	46,074	28,457	62,648	25,847	9,929	26,872
1977	113,201	59,168	54,033	188,378	120,877	40,186	50,226	30,465	67,501	27,387	10,961	29,153
1978	126,905	67,731	59,174	211,691	138,181	45,198	58,848	34,135	73,510	29,619	12,085	31,806
1979	143,936	75,927	68,009	242,157	160,734	52,670	69,325	38,739	81,423	32,814	13,910	34,699
1980	154,391	77,419	76,972	265,215	174,788	55,173	76,945	42,670	90,427	36,606	15,884	37,937
1981	168,129	83,727	84,402	283,413	186,443	57,998	80,998	47,447	96,970	38,165	16,194	42,611
1982	163,351	79,212	84,139	311,852	200,444	59,136	86,707	54,601	111,408	44,039	18,612	48,757
1983	172,547	85,481	87,066	312,379	199,854	60,325	86,899	52,630	112,525	44,816	18,691	49,018
1984	190,682	97,940	92,742	339,516	221,330	66,031	98,251	57,048	118,186	45,692	19,328	53,166
1985	194,538	101,279	93,259	334,749	218,193	63,904	98,162	56,127	116,556	44,106	19,442	53,008
1986	194,657	103,238	91,419	322,654	211,997	61,331	97,000	53,666	110,657	42,335	18,124	50,198
1987	206,326	108,128	98,198	338,109	220,799	63,562	102,393	54,844	117,310	45,319	19,270	52,721
1988	224,619	118,458	106,161	369,374	242,468	69,611	112,958	59,899	126,906	49,396	20,559	56,951
1989	236,698	123,158	113,540	391,212	257,513	72,435	122,251	62,827	133,699	50,674	21,653	61,372
1990	242,686	123,776	118,910	405,073	263,209	73,559	124,130	65,520	141,864	52,645	22,817	66,402
1991	239,847	121,000	118,847	390,950	250,019	70,834	114,960	64,225	140,931	53,011	22,815	65,105
1992	250,394	128,489	121,905	382,510	238,105	69,459	104,424	64,222	144,405	54,007	23,532	66,866
NAICS: [3]												
1992	242,002	126,572	115,430	379,183	238,416	69,823	104,341	64,252	140,767	53,126	23,438	64,203
1993	251,708	133,712	117,996	380,102	239,040	72,752	102,114	64,174	141,062	54,231	23,426	63,405
1994	269,843	147,005	122,838	400,335	253,444	78,680	106,676	68,088	146,891	57,114	24,491	65,286
1995	289,973	158,568	131,405	425,217	267,696	85,612	106,777	75,307	157,521	60,699	25,842	70,980
1996	299,766	164,883	134,883	430,816	272,787	86,365	110,651	75,771	158,029	59,066	26,500	72,463
1997	319,558	178,949	140,610	443,804	281,249	92,364	109,991	78,894	162,555	60,121	28,527	73,907
1998	324,984	185,966	139,019	449,231	290,874	93,614	115,328	81,932	158,357	58,139	27,075	73,143
1999	335,991	193,895	142,096	463,646	296,645	97,835	114,230	84,580	167,001	60,951	28,786	77,264
2000	350,715	197,807	152,908	481,396	306,682	106,018	111,270	89,394	174,714	61,268	30,065	83,381
2001	330,875	181,201	149,674	452,236	283,722	96,251	102,304	85,167	168,514	59,499	28,503	80,512
2002	324,313	177,617	146,696	444,188	271,789	89,408	97,383	84,998	172,399	59,071	30,418	82,910
2002: Jan	323,837	178,520	145,317	448,919	281,384	95,378	101,949	84,057	167,535	58,873	28,831	79,831
Feb	320,087	177,021	143,066	446,363	279,546	94,427	101,379	83,740	166,817	58,996	28,834	78,987
Mar	318,481	174,615	143,866	445,444	276,976	94,673	98,423	83,880	168,468	59,355	29,123	79,990
Apr	325,938	180,692	145,246	446,605	275,800	94,461	97,285	84,054	168,805	59,557	29,170	80,078
May	325,999	179,898	146,101	442,917	274,439	93,277	97,207	83,955	168,478	59,308	29,426	79,744
June	322,827	176,479	146,348	442,415	273,396	92,365	97,240	83,791	169,019	59,234	29,761	80,024
July	328,367	181,527	146,840	442,605	272,636	91,752	96,624	84,260	169,969	59,509	30,216	80,244
Aug	326,168	178,881	147,287	442,827	271,941	91,445	96,186	84,310	170,866	59,390	30,996	80,500
Sept	326,165	178,199	147,966	443,595	271,364	90,965	95,875	84,524	172,231	59,560	31,158	81,513
Oct	329,349	179,936	149,413	443,545	270,836	90,730	95,397	84,709	172,709	59,597	31,037	82,075
Nov	326,527	177,483	149,044	442,499	269,774	89,740	95,051	84,983	172,725	60,036	30,831	81,858
Dec	323,362	172,894	150,468	444,188	271,789	89,408	97,383	84,998	172,399	59,071	30,418	82,910
2003: Jan	329,665	177,331	152,334	444,220	270,964	88,916	97,287	84,761	173,256	60,248	30,606	82,402
Feb	325,591	173,992	151,599	446,088	270,765	88,703	97,432	84,630	175,323	60,758	30,994	83,571
Mar	330,764	175,475	155,289	446,165	269,454	87,948	97,009	84,497	175,726	60,258	31,422	84,046
Apr	322,608	173,512	149,096	445,207	269,285	87,443	97,851	83,991	175,922	60,741	30,859	84,322
May	323,920	173,783	150,137	444,605	268,449	87,129	97,810	83,510	175,600	60,539	30,596	84,465
June	328,643	176,782	151,861	442,666	266,154	86,243	96,243	83,668	176,512	59,786	31,166	85,560
July	337,248	181,761	155,487	440,767	264,638	85,203	96,383	83,052	176,129	58,920	31,502	85,707
Aug	331,676	177,187	154,489	439,632	262,949	84,068	96,258	82,623	176,683	59,117	31,452	86,114
Sept	337,598	182,379	155,219	438,294	261,678	83,637	95,533	82,508	176,616	59,396	31,293	85,927
Oct	339,825	183,740	156,085	438,680	262,351	84,013	96,225	82,113	176,329	59,121	31,655	85,553
Nov ᴾ	339,899	184,158	155,741	437,904	261,721	83,513	95,905	82,303	176,183	59,163	31,972	85,048

[1] Annual data are averages of monthly not seasonally adjusted figures.
[2] Seasonally adjusted, end of period. Data beginning 1982 are not comparable with data for earlier data.
[3] Effective in 2001, data classified based on North American Industry Classification System (NAICS). Data on NAICS basis available beginning 1992. Earlier data based on Standard Industrial Classification (SIC).
Data include semiconductors.

Source: Department of Commerce, Bureau of the Census.

TABLE B–59.—Manufacturers' new and unfilled orders, 1965–2003

[Amounts in millions of dollars; monthly data seasonally adjusted]

Year or month	New orders[1] Total	New orders Durable goods industries — Total	New orders Durable goods industries — Capital goods, nondefense	New orders Nondurable goods industries	Unfilled orders[2] Total	Unfilled orders[2] Durable goods industries	Unfilled orders[2] Nondurable goods industries	Unfilled orders–shipments ratio[2] Total	Unfilled orders–shipments ratio[2] Durable goods industries	Unfilled orders–shipments ratio[2] Nondurable goods industries
SIC:[3]										
1965	42,137	23,286	...	18,851	78,249	74,459	3,790	3.25	3.86	0.79
1966	46,420	26,163	...	20,258	96,846	93,002	3,844	3.74	4.48	.75
1967	47,067	25,803	...	21,265	103,711	99,735	3,976	3.66	4.37	.73
1968	50,657	28,051	6,314	22,606	108,377	104,393	3,984	3.79	4.58	.69
1969	53,990	29,876	7,046	24,114	114,341	110,161	4,180	3.71	4.45	.69
1970	52,022	27,340	6,072	24,682	105,008	100,412	4,596	3.61	4.36	.76
1971	55,921	29,905	6,682	26,016	105,247	100,225	5,022	3.32	4.00	.76
1972	64,182	35,038	7,745	29,144	119,349	113,034	6,315	3.26	3.85	.86
1973	76,003	42,627	9,926	33,376	156,561	149,204	7,357	3.80	4.51	.91
1974	87,327	46,862	11,594	40,465	187,043	181,519	5,524	4.09	4.93	.62
1975	85,139	41,957	9,886	43,181	169,546	161,664	7,882	3.69	4.45	.82
1976	99,513	51,307	11,490	48,206	178,128	169,857	8,271	3.24	3.88	.74
1977	115,109	61,035	13,681	54,073	202,024	193,323	8,701	3.24	3.85	.7
1978	131,629	72,278	17,588	59,351	259,169	248,281	10,888	3.57	4.20	.8
1979	147,604	79,483	21,154	68,121	303,593	291,321	12,272	3.89	4.62	.8
1980	156,359	79,392	21,135	76,967	327,416	315,202	12,214	3.85	4.58	.7
1981	168,025	83,654	21,806	84,371	326,547	314,707	11,840	3.87	4.68	.6
1982	162,140	78,064	19,213	84,077	311,887	300,798	11,089	3.84	4.74	.6
1983	175,451	88,140	19,624	87,311	347,273	333,114	14,159	3.53	4.29	.6
1984	192,879	100,164	23,669	92,715	373,529	359,651	13,878	3.60	4.37	.6
1985	195,706	102,356	24,545	93,351	387,196	372,097	15,099	3.67	4.47	.6
1986	195,204	103,647	23,982	91,557	393,515	376,699	16,816	3.59	4.41	.7
1987	209,389	110,809	26,094	98,579	430,426	408,688	21,738	3.63	4.43	.8
1988	228,270	122,076	31,108	106,194	474,154	452,150	22,004	3.64	4.46	.7
1989	239,572	126,055	32,988	113,516	508,849	487,098	21,751	3.96	4.85	.7
1990	244,507	125,583	33,331	118,924	531,131	509,124	22,007	4.15	5.15	.7
1991	238,805	119,849	30,471	118,957	519,199	495,802	23,397	4.08	5.07	.7
1992	248,212	126,308	31,524	121,905	492,893	469,381	23,512	3.51	4.30	.7
NAICS:[3]										
1992						450,965			4.90	
1993	246,668	128,672	40,681			425,665			4.40	
1994	266,641	143,803	45,175			434,594			4.06	
1995	285,542	154,137	51,011			447,338			3.89	
1996	297,282	162,399	54,066			488,815			4.18	
1997	314,986	174,377	60,697			513,166			4.06	
1998	317,345	178,327	62,133			496,471			3.81	
1999	329,770	187,674	64,392			505,941			3.77	
2000	346,789	193,881	69,278			550,005			4.08	
2001	322,944	173,270	58,336			517,590			4.25	
2002	316,744	170,048	53,991			485,816			4.12	
2002: Jan	311,730	166,413	52,933			510,293			4.15	
Feb	317,675	174,609	56,194			512,426			4.20	
Mar	313,271	169,405	51,840			512,007			4.22	
Apr	317,606	172,360	54,128			508,336			4.09	
May	318,297	172,196	55,528			505,261			4.08	
June	310,680	164,332	50,855			497,705			4.08	
July	324,427	177,587	56,065			498,562			4.01	
Aug	323,955	176,668	58,967			501,299			4.09	
Sept	313,949	165,983	51,702			494,297			4.03	
Oct	320,000	170,587	54,829			490,267			3.98	
Nov	317,869	168,825	54,439			487,009			4.00	
Dec	316,944	166,476	53,807			485,816			4.12	
2003: Jan	322,157	169,823	55,261			483,871			4.01	
Feb	320,664	169,065	53,417			484,649			4.09	
Mar	325,614	170,325	54,838			485,178			4.07	
Apr	317,095	167,999	55,845			485,534			4.11	
May	318,144	168,007	55,367			485,829			4.11	
June	324,098	172,237	57,351			487,360			4.07	
July	330,551	175,064	58,188			485,959			3.94	
Aug	329,401	174,912	57,229			490,036			4.09	
Sept	333,957	178,738	60,225			492,006			4.00	
Oct	341,856	185,771	61,672			500,307			4.05	
Nov[p]	336,909	181,168	58,164			503,633			4.05	

[1] Annual data are averages of monthly not seasonally adjusted figures.

[2] Unfilled orders are seasonally adjusted, end of period. Ratios are unfilled orders at end of period to shipments for period (excludes indutries with no unfilled orders). Annual ratios relate to seasonally adjusted data for December.

[3] Effective in 2001, data classified based on North American Industry Classification System (NAICS). Data on NAICS basis available beginning 1992. Earlier data based on the Standard Industrial Classification (SIC).
Data on SIC basis include semiconductors. Data on NAICS basis do not include semiconductors.

Note.—Since there are no unfilled orders for manufacturers' nondurable goods, manufacturers' nondurable new orders and nondurable shipments are the same (see Table B–58).

Source: Department of Commerce, Bureau of the Census.

PRICES

TABLE B–60.—*Consumer price indexes for major expenditure classes, 1959–2003*

[For all urban consumers; 1982-84=100, except as noted]

Year or month	All items (CPI-U)	Food and beverages — Total¹	Food	Apparel	Housing	Transportation	Medical care	Entertainment	Recreation²	Education and communication²	Other goods and services	Energy³
1959	29.1		29.7	45.0		29.8	21.5					21.9
1960	29.6		30.0	45.7		29.8	22.3					22.4
1961	29.9		30.4	46.1		30.1	22.9					22.5
1962	30.2		30.6	46.3		30.8	23.5					22.6
1963	30.6		31.1	46.9		30.9	24.1					22.6
1964	31.0		31.5	47.3		31.4	24.6					22.5
1965	31.5		32.2	47.8		31.9	25.2					22.9
1966	32.4		33.8	49.0		32.3	26.3					23.3
1967	33.4	35.0	34.1	51.0	30.8	33.3	28.2	40.7			35.1	23.8
1968	34.8	36.2	35.3	53.7	32.0	34.3	29.9	43.0			36.9	24.2
1969	36.7	38.1	37.1	56.8	34.0	35.7	31.9	45.2			38.7	24.8
1970	38.8	40.1	39.2	59.2	36.4	37.5	34.0	47.5			40.9	25.5
1971	40.5	41.4	40.4	61.1	38.0	39.5	36.1	50.0			42.9	26.5
1972	41.8	43.1	42.1	62.3	39.4	39.9	37.3	51.5			44.7	27.2
1973	44.4	48.8	48.2	64.6	41.2	41.2	38.8	52.9			46.4	29.4
1974	49.3	55.5	55.1	69.4	45.8	45.8	42.4	56.9			49.8	38.1
1975	53.8	60.2	59.8	72.5	50.7	50.1	47.5	62.0			53.9	42.1
1976	56.9	62.1	61.6	75.2	53.8	55.1	52.0	65.1			57.0	45.1
1977	60.6	65.8	65.5	78.6	57.4	59.0	57.0	68.3			60.4	49.4
1978	65.2	72.2	72.0	81.4	62.4	61.7	61.8	71.9			64.3	52.5
1979	72.6	79.9	79.9	84.9	70.1	70.5	67.5	76.7			68.9	65.7
1980	82.4	86.7	86.8	90.9	81.1	83.1	74.9	83.6			75.2	86.0
1981	90.9	93.5	93.6	95.3	90.4	93.2	82.9	90.1			82.6	97.7
1982	96.5	97.3	97.4	97.8	96.9	97.0	92.5	96.0			91.1	99.2
1983	99.6	99.5	99.4	100.2	99.5	99.3	100.6	100.1			101.1	99.9
1984	103.9	103.2	103.2	102.1	103.6	103.7	106.8	103.8			107.9	100.9
1985	107.6	105.6	105.6	105.0	107.7	106.4	113.5	107.9			114.5	101.6
1986	109.6	109.1	109.0	105.9	110.9	102.3	122.0	111.6			121.4	88.2
1987	113.6	113.5	113.5	110.6	114.2	105.4	130.1	115.3			128.5	88.6
1988	118.3	118.2	118.2	115.4	118.5	108.7	138.6	120.3			137.0	89.3
1989	124.0	124.9	125.1	118.6	123.0	114.1	149.3	126.5			147.7	94.3
1990	130.7	132.1	132.4	124.1	128.5	120.5	162.8	132.4			159.0	102.1
1991	136.2	136.8	136.3	128.7	133.6	123.8	177.0	138.4			171.6	102.5
1992	140.3	138.7	137.9	131.9	137.5	126.5	190.1	142.3			183.3	103.0
1993	144.5	141.6	140.9	133.7	141.2	130.4	201.4	145.8	90.7	85.5	192.9	104.2
1994	148.2	144.9	144.3	133.4	144.8	134.3	211.0	150.1	92.7	88.8	198.5	104.6
1995	152.4	148.9	148.4	132.0	148.5	139.1	220.5	153.9	94.5	92.2	206.9	105.2
1996	156.9	153.7	153.3	131.7	152.8	143.0	228.2	159.1	97.4	95.3	215.4	110.1
1997	160.5	157.7	157.3	132.9	156.8	144.3	234.6	162.5	99.6	98.4	224.8	111.5
1998	163.0	161.1	160.7	133.0	160.4	141.6	242.1		101.1	100.3	237.7	102.9
1999	166.6	164.6	164.1	131.3	163.9	144.4	250.6		102.0	101.2	258.3	106.6
2000	172.2	168.4	167.8	129.6	169.6	153.3	260.8		103.3	102.5	271.1	124.6
2001	177.1	173.6	173.1	127.3	176.4	154.3	272.8		104.9	105.2	282.6	129.3
2002	179.9	176.8	176.2	124.0	180.3	152.9	285.6		106.2	107.9	293.2	121.7
2003	184.0	180.5	180.0	120.9	184.8	157.6	297.1		107.5	109.8	298.7	136.5
2002: Jan	177.1	176.2	175.8	120.4	177.6	148.6	279.6		105.7	107.2	287.2	111.7
Feb	177.8	176.4	175.9	123.5	178.5	148.4	281.0		105.9	107.3	290.2	111.0
Mar	178.8	176.6	176.1	128.2	179.1	150.5	282.0		106.1	106.6	288.5	115.6
Apr	179.8	176.7	176.2	128.8	179.5	153.7	283.2		106.5	106.2	292.9	122.2
May	179.8	176.4	175.8	127.1	179.7	153.8	284.1		106.4	106.6	291.5	122.9
June	179.9	176.4	175.8	122.7	180.7	153.4	284.7		106.2	106.9	294.4	124.9
July	180.1	176.6	176.0	118.7	181.2	153.7	286.6		106.2	107.6	294.5	125.5
Aug	180.7	176.6	176.0	120.5	181.7	153.9	287.3		106.3	108.9	295.9	125.8
Sept	181.0	176.9	176.4	124.6	181.5	154.0	287.7		106.2	109.5	297.0	126.1
Oct	181.3	177.1	176.5	126.8	181.4	154.9	289.2		106.4	109.4	295.4	125.3
Nov	181.3	177.4	176.8	125.5	181.2	155.2	290.5		106.4	109.3	295.6	125.3
Dec	180.9	177.8	177.3	121.5	181.1	154.2	291.3		106.5	109.2	295.8	123.3
2003: Jan	181.7	178.1	177.5	118.1	182.3	155.5	292.6		106.9	109.7	296.5	127.5
Feb	183.1	178.9	178.3	120.6	183.2	158.9	293.7		107.2	109.7	297.5	135.4
Mar	184.2	179.2	178.6	123.6	184.3	161.0	294.2		107.4	109.4	297.3	142.6
Apr	183.8	179.0	178.4	123.9	184.1	159.3	294.6		107.4	109.0	298.1	138.1
May	183.5	179.4	178.8	122.5	184.5	157.2	295.5		107.6	108.6	298.1	134.0
June	183.7	180.2	179.6	119.5	185.3	156.8	296.3		107.6	108.5	298.1	136.5
July	183.9	180.3	179.7	116.2	185.9	156.8	297.6		107.7	108.9	299.2	136.8
Aug	184.6	180.9	180.4	117.2	186.1	158.3	298.4		107.7	110.1	299.6	140.6
Sept	185.2	181.3	180.7	122.0	185.8	159.4	299.2		107.7	110.9	299.9	144.6
Oct	185.0	182.2	181.7	124.8	185.7	157.1	299.9		107.6	110.9	300.2	136.9
Nov	184.5	182.9	182.4	123.1	185.1	155.7	300.8		107.8	110.8	300.0	133.1
Dec	184.3	184.1	183.6	119.0	185.1	154.7	302.1		107.7	110.9	300.2	131.8

¹ Includes alcoholic beverages, not shown separately.
² December 1997=100.
³ Household fuels—gas (piped), electricity, fuel oil, etc.—and motor fuel. Motor oil, coolant, etc. also included through 1982.

Note.—Data beginning 1983 incorporate a rental equivalence measure for homeowners' costs. Series reflect changes in composition and renaming beginning in 1998, and formula and methodology changes beginning in 1999.

Source: Department of Labor, Bureau of Labor Statistics.

TABLE B-61.—Consumer price indexes for selected expenditure classes, 1959-2003

[For all urban consumers; 1982-84=100, except as noted]

Year or month	Food and beverages	Food			Housing	Shelter			Fuels and utilities	Fuels			Furnishings and operations
	Total [1]	Total	At home	Away from home	Total	Total [2]	Rent of primary residence	Owners' equivalent rent of primary residence [3]	Total [2]	Total	Fuel oil and other fuels	Gas (piped) and electricity	
1959	....	29.7	31.2	24.8	....	24.7	38.2	....	25.4	....	13.9	22.4	....
1960	....	30.0	31.5	25.4	....	25.2	38.7	....	26.0	....	13.8	23.3	....
1961	....	30.4	31.8	26.0	....	25.4	39.2	....	26.3	....	14.1	23.5	....
1962	....	30.6	32.0	26.7	....	25.8	39.7	....	26.3	....	14.2	23.5	....
1963	....	31.1	32.4	27.3	....	26.1	40.1	....	26.6	....	14.4	23.5	....
1964	....	31.5	32.7	27.8	....	26.5	40.5	....	26.6	....	14.4	23.5	....
1965	....	32.2	33.5	28.4	....	27.0	40.9	....	26.6	....	14.6	23.5	....
1966	....	33.8	35.2	29.7	....	27.8	41.5	....	26.7	....	15.0	23.6	....
1967	35.0	34.1	35.1	31.3	30.8	28.8	42.2	....	27.1	21.4	15.5	23.7	42.0
1968	36.2	35.3	36.3	32.9	32.0	30.1	43.3	....	27.4	21.7	16.0	23.9	43.6
1969	38.1	37.1	38.0	34.9	34.0	32.6	44.7	....	28.0	22.1	16.3	24.3	45.2
1970	40.1	39.2	39.9	37.5	36.4	35.5	46.5	....	29.1	23.1	17.0	25.4	46.8
1971	41.4	40.4	40.9	39.4	38.0	37.0	48.7	....	31.1	24.7	18.2	27.1	48.6
1972	43.1	42.1	42.7	41.0	39.4	38.7	50.4	....	32.5	25.7	18.3	28.5	49.7
1973	48.8	48.2	49.7	44.2	41.2	40.5	52.5	....	34.3	27.5	21.1	29.9	51.1
1974	55.5	55.1	57.1	49.8	45.8	44.4	55.2	....	40.7	34.4	33.2	34.5	56.8
1975	60.2	59.8	61.8	54.5	50.7	48.8	58.0	....	45.4	39.4	36.4	40.1	63.4
1976	62.1	61.6	63.1	58.2	53.8	51.5	61.1	....	49.4	43.3	38.8	44.7	67.3
1977	65.8	65.5	66.8	62.6	57.4	54.9	64.8	....	54.7	49.0	43.9	50.5	70.4
1978	72.2	72.0	73.8	68.3	62.4	60.5	69.3	....	58.5	53.0	46.2	55.0	74.7
1979	79.9	79.9	81.8	75.9	70.1	68.9	74.3	....	64.8	61.3	62.4	61.0	79.9
1980	86.7	86.8	88.4	83.4	81.1	81.0	80.9	....	75.4	74.8	86.1	71.4	86.3
1981	93.5	93.6	94.8	90.9	90.4	90.5	87.9	....	86.4	87.2	104.6	81.9	93.0
1982	97.3	97.4	98.1	95.8	96.9	96.9	94.6	....	94.9	95.6	103.4	93.2	98.0
1983	99.5	99.4	99.1	100.0	99.5	99.1	100.1	102.5	100.2	100.5	97.2	101.5	100.2
1984	103.2	103.2	102.8	104.2	103.6	104.0	105.3	107.3	104.8	104.0	99.4	105.4	101.9
1985	105.6	105.6	104.3	108.3	107.7	109.8	111.8	113.2	106.5	104.5	95.9	107.1	103.8
1986	109.1	109.0	107.3	112.5	110.9	115.8	118.3	119.4	104.1	99.2	77.6	105.7	105.2
1987	113.5	113.5	111.9	117.0	114.2	121.3	123.1	124.8	103.0	97.3	77.9	103.8	107.1
1988	118.2	118.2	116.6	121.8	118.5	127.1	127.8	131.1	104.4	98.0	78.1	104.6	109.4
1989	124.9	125.1	124.2	127.4	123.0	132.8	132.8	137.4	107.8	100.9	81.7	107.5	111.2
1990	132.1	132.4	132.3	133.4	128.5	140.0	138.4	144.8	111.6	104.5	99.3	109.3	113.3
1991	136.8	136.3	135.8	137.9	133.6	146.3	143.3	150.4	115.3	106.7	94.6	112.6	116.0
1992	138.7	137.9	136.8	140.7	137.5	151.2	146.9	155.5	117.8	108.1	90.7	114.8	118.0
1993	141.6	140.9	140.1	143.2	141.2	155.7	150.3	160.5	121.3	111.2	90.3	118.5	119.3
1994	144.9	144.3	144.1	145.7	144.8	160.5	154.0	165.8	122.8	111.7	88.8	119.2	121.0
1995	148.9	148.4	148.8	149.0	148.5	165.7	157.8	171.3	123.7	111.5	88.1	119.2	123.0
1996	153.7	153.3	154.3	152.7	152.8	171.0	162.0	176.8	127.5	115.2	99.2	122.1	124.7
1997	157.7	157.3	158.1	157.0	156.8	176.3	166.7	181.9	130.8	117.9	99.8	125.1	125.4
1998	161.1	160.7	161.1	161.1	160.4	182.1	172.1	187.8	128.5	113.7	90.0	121.2	126.6
1999	164.6	164.1	164.2	165.1	163.9	187.3	177.5	192.9	128.8	113.5	91.4	120.9	126.7
2000	168.4	167.8	167.9	169.0	169.6	193.4	183.9	198.7	137.9	122.8	129.7	128.0	128.2
2001	173.6	173.1	173.4	173.9	176.4	200.6	192.1	206.3	150.2	135.4	129.3	142.4	129.1
2002	176.8	176.2	175.6	178.3	180.3	208.1	199.7	214.7	143.6	127.2	115.5	134.4	128.3
2003	180.5	180.0	179.4	182.1	184.8	213.1	205.5	219.9	154.5	138.2	139.5	145.0	126.1
2002: Jan	176.2	175.8	176.2	176.4	177.6	204.5	197.0	211.6	141.5	125.3	112.9	132.4	128.7
Feb	176.4	175.9	176.0	177.0	178.5	206.1	197.7	212.2	140.0	123.7	112.3	130.6	128.6
Mar	176.6	176.1	176.1	177.1	179.1	207.0	198.2	212.8	140.2	123.8	112.8	130.7	128.7
Apr	176.7	176.2	176.4	177.2	179.5	207.5	198.5	213.3	140.3	123.8	115.1	130.6	128.9
May	176.4	175.8	175.5	177.6	179.7	207.5	198.8	213.7	141.5	125.1	114.4	132.1	128.9
June	176.4	175.8	175.0	178.2	180.7	208.1	199.3	214.3	146.2	130.3	112.7	138.0	128.7
July	176.6	176.0	175.2	178.5	181.2	208.8	199.8	214.9	146.8	130.8	111.6	138.6	128.6
Aug	176.6	176.0	174.9	178.8	181.7	209.6	200.2	215.4	146.8	130.7	112.1	138.5	128.1
Sept	176.9	176.4	175.2	179.2	181.5	209.2	200.7	216.2	147.2	131.0	115.2	138.7	128.1
Oct	177.1	176.5	175.1	179.6	181.4	209.7	201.3	216.8	144.4	127.9	119.3	134.9	128.0
Nov	177.4	176.8	175.5	179.8	181.2	209.6	202.0	217.3	143.6	127.0	121.8	133.7	127.8
Dec	177.8	177.3	176.1	180.1	181.1	209.5	202.5	217.9	144.2	127.5	126.4	134.1	127.0
2003: Jan	178.1	177.5	176.7	179.9	182.3	210.9	203.3	218.5	146.1	129.5	136.6	135.6	127.4
Feb	178.9	178.3	177.6	180.7	183.2	211.6	203.7	218.7	148.3	131.9	156.3	136.9	127.7
Mar	179.2	178.6	177.7	181.0	184.3	212.1	204.1	218.9	154.5	138.5	169.0	143.5	127.1
Apr	179.0	178.4	177.3	181.1	184.1	212.1	204.5	218.9	153.1	136.8	147.9	143.0	127.2
May	179.4	178.8	177.8	181.5	184.5	212.8	204.9	219.1	153.7	137.0		144.5	126.3
June	180.2	179.6	178.9	181.9	185.3	213.0	205.1	219.1	159.1	143.4	132.2	151.3	126.2
July	180.9	179.7	178.9	182.3	185.9	213.8	205.6	219.6	159.4	143.6	130.5	151.6	126.1
Aug	180.9	180.4	179.7	182.6	186.1	214.3	206.1	220.1	159.2	143.0	130.7	151.0	125.5
Sept	181.3	180.7	180.1	182.8	185.8	213.8	206.6	220.7	159.6	143.4	130.5	151.5	125.2
Oct	182.2	181.7	181.5	183.3	185.7	214.7	206.9	221.4	155.0	138.2	131.4	145.3	125.1
Nov	182.9	182.4	182.4	183.8	185.1	214.2	207.5	221.9	152.9	135.7	134.8	142.6	124.9
Dec	184.1	183.6	184.1	184.3	185.1	214.1	207.7	222.2	153.6	136.5	137.0	143.3	124.7

[1] Includes alcoholic beverages, not shown separately.
[2] Includes other items, not shown separately.
[3] December 1982=100.

See next page for continuation of table.

[For all urban consumers; 1982-84=100, except as noted]

Year or month	Transportation								Medical care		
	Total	Private transportation							Total	Medical care commodities	Medical care services
		Total²	New vehicles		Used cars and trucks	Motor fuel	Motor vehicle maintenance and repair	Public transportation			
			Total²	New cars							
1959	29.8	30.8	52.3	52.2	26.8	23.7	26.0	21.5	21.5	46.8	18.7
1960	29.8	30.6	51.6	51.5	25.0	24.4	26.5	22.2	22.3	46.9	19.5
1961	30.1	30.8	51.6	51.5	26.0	24.1	27.1	23.2	22.9	46.3	20.2
1962	30.8	31.4	51.4	51.3	28.4	24.3	27.5	24.0	23.5	45.6	20.9
1963	30.9	31.6	51.1	51.0	28.7	24.2	27.8	24.3	24.1	45.2	21.5
1964	31.4	32.0	50.9	50.9	30.0	24.1	28.2	24.7	24.6	45.1	22.0
1965	31.9	32.5	49.8	49.7	29.8	25.1	28.7	25.2	25.2	45.0	22.7
1966	32.3	32.9	48.9	48.8	29.0	25.6	29.2	26.1	26.3	45.1	23.9
1967	33.3	33.8	49.3	49.3	29.9	26.4	30.4	27.4	28.2	44.9	26.0
1968	34.3	34.8	50.7	50.7	....	26.8	32.1	28.7	29.9	45.0	27.9
1969	35.7	36.0	51.5	51.5	30.9	27.6	34.1	30.9	31.9	45.4	30.2
1970	37.5	37.5	53.1	53.0	31.2	27.9	36.6	35.2	34.0	46.5	32.3
1971	39.5	39.4	55.3	55.2	33.0	28.1	39.3	37.8	36.1	47.3	34.7
1972	39.9	39.7	54.8	54.7	33.1	28.4	41.1	39.3	37.3	47.4	35.9
1973	41.2	41.0	54.8	54.8	35.2	31.2	43.2	39.7	38.8	47.5	37.5
1974	45.8	46.2	58.0	57.9	36.7	42.2	47.6	40.6	42.4	49.2	41.4
1975	50.1	50.6	63.0	62.9	43.8	45.1	53.7	43.5	47.5	53.3	46.6
1976	55.1	55.6	67.0	66.9	50.3	47.0	57.6	47.8	52.0	56.5	51.3
1977	59.0	59.7	70.5	70.4	54.7	49.7	61.9	50.0	57.0	60.2	56.4
1978	61.7	62.5	75.9	75.8	55.8	51.8	67.0	51.5	61.8	64.4	61.2
1979	70.5	71.7	81.9	81.8	60.2	70.1	73.7	54.9	67.5	69.0	67.2
1980	83.1	84.2	88.5	88.4	62.3	97.4	81.5	69.0	74.9	75.4	74.8
1981	93.2	93.8	93.9	93.7	76.9	108.5	89.2	85.6	82.9	83.7	82.8
1982	97.0	97.1	97.5	97.4	88.8	102.8	96.0	94.9	92.5	92.3	92.6
1983	99.3	99.3	99.9	99.9	98.7	99.4	100.3	99.5	100.6	100.2	100.7
1984	103.7	103.6	102.6	102.8	112.5	97.9	103.8	105.7	106.8	107.5	106.7
1985	106.4	106.2	106.1	106.1	113.7	98.7	106.8	110.5	113.5	115.2	113.2
1986	102.3	101.2	110.6	110.6	108.8	77.1	110.3	117.0	122.0	122.8	121.9
1987	105.4	104.2	114.4	114.6	113.1	80.2	114.8	121.1	130.1	131.0	130.0
1988	108.7	107.6	116.5	116.9	118.0	80.9	119.7	123.3	138.6	139.9	138.3
1989	114.1	112.9	119.2	119.2	120.4	88.5	124.9	129.5	149.3	150.8	148.9
1990	120.5	118.8	121.4	121.0	117.6	101.2	130.1	142.6	162.8	163.4	162.7
1991	123.8	121.9	126.0	125.3	118.1	99.4	136.0	148.9	177.0	176.8	177.1
1992	126.5	124.6	129.2	128.4	123.2	99.0	141.3	151.4	190.1	188.1	190.5
1993	130.4	127.5	132.7	131.5	133.9	98.0	145.9	167.0	201.4	195.0	202.9
1994	134.3	131.4	137.6	136.0	141.7	98.5	150.2	172.0	211.0	200.7	213.4
1995	139.1	136.3	141.0	139.0	156.5	100.0	154.0	175.9	220.5	204.5	224.2
1996	143.0	140.0	143.7	141.4	157.0	106.3	158.4	181.9	228.2	210.4	232.4
1997	144.3	141.0	144.3	141.7	151.1	106.2	162.7	186.7	234.6	215.3	239.1
1998	141.6	137.9	143.4	140.7	150.6	92.2	167.1	190.3	242.1	221.8	246.8
1999	144.4	140.5	142.9	139.6	152.0	100.7	171.9	197.7	250.6	230.7	255.1
2000	153.3	149.1	142.8	139.6	155.8	129.3	177.3	209.6	260.8	238.1	266.0
2001	154.3	150.0	142.1	138.9	158.7	124.7	183.5	210.6	272.8	247.6	278.8
2002	152.9	148.8	140.0	137.3	152.0	116.6	190.2	207.4	285.6	256.4	292.9
2003	157.6	153.6	137.9	134.7	142.9	135.8	195.6	209.3	297.1	262.8	306.0
2002: Jan	148.6	144.4	142.7	139.7	155.6	97.9	187.1	205.8	279.6	252.6	286.2
Feb	148.4	144.1	141.2	138.6	153.9	98.2	188.0	207.3	281.0	253.7	287.7
Mar	150.5	146.3	140.7	138.2	152.1	107.7	188.5	207.9	282.0	254.1	288.9
Apr	153.7	149.6	140.4	137.8	151.8	121.4	189.0	209.7	283.2	254.8	290.2
May	153.8	149.5	139.8	137.2	151.8	121.4	189.9	211.9	284.1	255.4	291.2
June	153.4	149.1	139.2	136.6	152.2	120.1	190.0	211.3	284.7	256.4	291.7
July	153.7	149.5	138.7	136.1	152.7	120.8	189.8	209.7	286.6	257.5	293.8
Aug	153.9	149.7	138.1	135.4	153.4	121.5	191.0	209.4	287.3	257.7	294.7
Sept	154.0	150.0	138.7	135.8	152.2	121.7	191.4	206.5	287.7	257.9	295.2
Oct	154.9	151.1	139.5	136.7	150.7	124.5	191.8	203.4	289.2	258.3	297.1
Nov	155.2	151.5	140.4	137.6	148.8	124.4	192.8	202.3	290.5	259.1	298.5
Dec	154.2	150.4	140.6	137.7	148.5	119.7	193.3	203.0	291.3	259.5	299.4
2003: Jan	155.5	151.8	139.7	136.7	148.3	126.3	193.7	202.2	292.6	260.3	300.8
Feb	158.9	155.3	139.2	136.0	148.4	140.4	194.5	203.6	293.7	260.4	302.3
Mar	161.0	157.3	139.3	136.1	148.5	148.1	194.3	206.1	294.2	261.4	302.6
Apr	159.3	155.5	138.7	135.5	148.4	140.6	194.6	207.2	294.6	261.6	303.1
May	157.2	153.1	138.1	134.9	147.9	131.3	194.9	211.6	295.5	261.8	304.2
June	156.8	152.6	137.3	134.2	147.4	130.1	195.1	214.4	296.3	262.1	305.2
July	156.8	152.4	136.7	133.5	145.7	130.6	196.0	216.7	297.6	263.6	306.4
Aug	158.3	154.1	136.8	133.6	143.3	139.0	195.7	213.8	298.4	264.1	307.2
Sept	159.4	155.4	136.4	133.1	139.0	147.1	196.2	212.2	299.2	264.9	308.2
Oct	157.1	153.0	136.5	133.5	135.1	136.6	196.9	211.3	299.9	264.7	309.1
Nov	155.7	151.7	137.5	134.3	132.0	131.2	197.2	207.9	300.8	264.0	310.6
Dec	154.7	150.8	138.0	134.8	131.0	127.8	198.0	205.6	302.1	265.0	311.9

Note.—See Note, Table B-60.

Source: Department of Labor, Bureau of Labor Statistics.

TABLE B–62.—*Consumer price indexes for commodities, services, and special groups, 1960–2003*

[For all urban consumers; 1982-84=100, except as noted]

Year or month	All items (CPI-U)	Commodities		Services		Special indexes				All items		
		All commodities	Commodities less food	All services	Services less medical care services	All items less food	All items less energy	All items less food and energy	All items less medical care	CPI-U-X1 (Dec. 1982= 97.6)[1]	CPI-U-RS (Dec. 1977= 100)[2]	C-CPI-U (Dec. 1999= 100)[3]
1960	29.6	33.6	36.0	24.1	25.0	29.7	30.4	30.6	30.2	32.2	....	....
1961	29.9	33.8	36.1	24.5	25.4	30.0	30.7	31.0	30.5	32.5	....	....
1962	30.2	34.1	36.3	25.0	25.9	30.3	31.1	31.4	30.8	32.8	....	....
1963	30.6	34.4	36.6	25.5	26.3	30.7	31.5	31.8	31.1	33.3	....	....
1964	31.0	34.8	36.9	26.0	26.8	31.1	32.0	32.3	31.5	33.7	....	....
1965	31.5	35.2	37.2	26.6	27.4	31.6	32.5	32.7	32.0	34.2	....	....
1966	32.4	36.1	37.7	27.6	28.3	32.3	33.5	33.5	33.0	35.2	....	....
1967	33.4	36.8	38.6	28.8	29.3	33.4	34.4	34.7	33.7	36.3	....	....
1968	34.8	38.1	40.0	30.3	30.8	34.9	35.9	36.3	35.1	37.7	....	....
1969	36.7	39.9	41.7	32.4	32.9	36.8	38.0	38.4	37.0	39.4	....	....
1970	38.8	41.7	43.4	35.0	35.6	39.0	40.3	40.8	39.2	41.3	....	....
1971	40.5	43.2	45.1	37.0	37.5	40.8	42.0	42.7	40.8	43.1	....	....
1972	41.8	44.5	46.1	38.4	38.9	42.0	43.4	44.0	42.1	44.4	....	....
1973	44.4	47.8	47.7	40.1	40.6	43.7	46.1	45.6	44.8	47.2	....	....
1974	49.3	53.5	52.8	43.8	44.3	48.0	50.6	49.4	49.8	51.9	....	....
1975	53.8	58.2	57.6	48.0	48.3	52.5	55.1	53.9	54.3	56.2	....	....
1976	56.9	60.7	60.5	52.0	52.2	56.0	58.2	57.4	57.2	59.4	....	....
1977	60.6	64.2	63.8	56.0	55.9	59.6	61.9	61.0	60.8	63.2	....	....
1978	65.2	68.8	67.5	60.8	60.7	63.9	66.7	65.5	65.4	67.5	104.3	....
1979	72.6	76.6	75.3	67.5	67.5	71.2	73.4	71.9	72.9	74.0	114.1	....
1980	82.4	86.0	85.7	77.9	78.2	81.5	81.9	80.8	82.8	82.3	126.7	....
1981	90.9	93.2	93.1	88.1	88.7	90.4	90.1	89.2	91.4	90.1	138.6	....
1982	96.5	97.0	96.9	96.0	96.4	96.3	96.1	95.8	96.8	95.6	146.8	....
1983	99.6	99.8	100.0	99.4	99.2	99.7	99.6	99.6	99.6	99.6	152.9	....
1984	103.9	103.2	103.1	104.6	104.4	104.0	104.3	104.6	103.7	103.9	159.0	....
1985	107.6	105.4	105.2	109.9	109.6	108.0	108.4	109.1	107.2	107.6	164.3	....
1986	109.6	104.4	101.7	115.4	114.6	109.8	112.6	113.5	108.8	109.6	167.3	....
1987	113.6	107.7	104.3	120.2	119.1	113.6	117.2	118.2	112.6	113.6	173.0	....
1988	118.3	111.5	107.7	125.7	124.3	118.3	122.3	123.4	117.0	118.3	179.3	....
1989	124.0	116.7	112.0	131.9	130.1	123.7	128.1	129.0	122.4	124.0	187.0	....
1990	130.7	122.8	117.4	139.2	136.8	130.3	134.7	135.5	128.8	130.7	196.3	....
1991	136.2	126.6	121.3	146.3	143.3	136.1	140.9	142.1	133.8	136.2	203.4	....
1992	140.3	129.1	124.2	152.0	148.4	140.8	145.4	147.3	137.5	140.3	208.5	....
1993	144.5	131.5	126.3	157.9	153.6	145.1	150.0	152.2	141.2	144.5	213.7	....
1994	148.2	133.8	127.9	163.1	158.4	149.0	154.1	156.5	144.7	148.2	218.2	....
1995	152.4	136.4	129.8	168.7	163.5	153.1	158.7	161.2	148.6	152.4	223.5	....
1996	156.9	139.9	132.6	174.1	168.7	157.5	163.1	165.6	152.8	156.9	229.5	....
1997	160.5	141.8	133.4	179.4	173.9	161.1	167.1	169.5	156.3	160.5	234.4	....
1998	163.0	141.9	132.0	184.2	178.4	163.4	170.9	173.4	158.6	163.0	237.7	....
1999	166.6	144.4	134.0	188.8	182.7	167.0	174.4	177.0	162.0	166.6	242.7	....
2000	172.2	149.2	139.2	195.3	188.9	173.0	178.6	181.3	167.3	172.2	250.8	102.0
2001	177.1	150.7	138.9	203.4	196.6	177.8	183.5	186.1	171.9	177.1	257.8	104.3
2002	179.9	149.7	136.0	209.8	202.5	180.5	187.7	190.5	174.3	179.9	261.9	105.4
2003	184.0	151.2	136.5	216.5	208.7	184.7	190.6	193.2	178.1	184.0	267.9	107.4
2002: Jan	177.1	147.8	133.5	206.3	199.2	177.4	185.7	188.2	171.7	177.1	257.9	104.7
Feb	177.8	148.1	133.9	207.3	200.2	178.2	186.5	189.2	172.4	177.8	258.9	104.8
Mar	178.8	149.4	135.6	208.0	200.8	179.2	187.1	189.8	173.3	178.8	260.3	105.2
Apr	179.8	151.0	137.8	208.4	201.2	180.4	187.5	190.3	174.3	179.8	261.8	105.5
May	179.8	150.5	137.3	208.8	201.6	180.4	187.4	190.2	174.2	179.8	261.7	105.5
June	179.9	149.8	136.3	209.8	202.6	180.6	187.3	190.1	174.4	179.9	262.0	105.3
July	180.1	149.3	135.5	210.7	203.3	180.8	187.5	190.3	174.5	180.1	262.3	105.3
Aug	180.7	149.6	135.9	211.5	204.2	181.5	188.1	191.0	175.0	180.7	263.1	106.0
Sept	181.0	150.2	136.7	211.5	204.1	181.8	188.4	191.3	175.3	181.0	263.5	106.0
Oct	181.3	150.7	137.3	211.7	204.2	182.2	188.8	191.8	175.6	181.3	264.0	106.2
Nov	181.3	150.6	137.0	211.8	204.3	182.1	188.9	191.8	175.6	181.3	264.0	106.2
Dec	180.9	149.7	135.6	211.9	204.3	181.6	188.6	191.4	175.1	180.9	263.4	106.3
2003: Jan	181.7	150.0	135.8	213.1	205.5	182.4	189.0	191.8	175.9	181.7	264.6	106.8
Feb	183.1	152.0	138.3	214.0	206.4	183.9	189.7	192.5	177.3	183.1	266.6	107.3
Mar	184.2	153.1	139.8	215.1	207.4	185.2	190.2	193.0	178.4	184.2	268.3	107.7
Apr	183.8	152.2	138.6	215.1	207.5	184.7	190.2	193.1	178.0	183.8	267.6	107.3
May	183.5	150.9	136.5	215.9	208.2	184.3	190.3	193.2	177.7	183.5	267.2	107.0
June	183.7	150.4	135.5	216.8	209.1	184.5	190.3	193.0	177.9	183.7	267.5	107.0
July	183.9	150.0	134.9	217.6	209.8	184.6	190.5	193.2	178.0	183.9	267.8	107.0
Aug	184.6	150.9	135.9	218.0	210.3	185.3	190.8	193.5	178.7	184.6	268.8	107.5
Sept	185.2	152.0	137.3	218.1	210.3	186.0	191.0	193.6	179.2	185.2	269.7	108.0
Oct	185.0	151.4	136.1	218.4	210.5	185.6	191.7	194.3	179.1	185.0	269.4	108.0
Nov	184.5	150.9	135.0	217.9	209.9	184.9	191.6	193.9	178.5	184.5	268.6	107.9
Dec	184.3	150.4	133.8	217.9	209.9	184.4	191.5	193.6	178.2	184.3	268.4	107.9

[1] CPI-U-X1 is a rental equivalence approach to homeowners' costs for the CPI-U for years prior to 1983, the first year for which the offici[al] index incorporates such a measure. CPI-U-X1 is rebased to the December 1982 value of the CPI-U (1982-84=100) and is identical with CPI-[U] data from December 1982 forward. Data prior to 1967 estimated by moving the series at the same rate as the CPI-U for each year.

[2] CPI research series using current methods (CPI-U-RS) introduced in June 1999. Data for 2003 are preliminary. All data are subject to r[e] vision annually.

[3] Chained consumer price index introduced in August 2002. Data for 2002 and 2003 are subject to revision.

Note.—See Note, Table B-60.

Source: Department of Labor, Bureau of Labor Statistics.

[For all urban consumers; percent change]

Year or month	All items (CPI-U)		All items less food		All items less energy		All items less food and energy		All items less medical care	
	Dec. to Dec.[1]	Year to year	Dec. to Dec.[1]	Year to year	Dec. to Dec.[1]	Year to year	Dec. to Dec.[1]	Year to year	Dec. to Dec.[1]	Year to year
1960	1.4	1.7	1.0	1.7	1.3	1.7	1.0	1.3	1.3	1.3
1961	.7	1.0	1.3	1.0	.7	1.0	1.3	1.3	.3	1.0
1962	1.3	1.0	1.0	1.0	1.3	1.3	1.3	1.3	1.3	1.0
1963	1.6	1.3	1.6	1.3	1.9	1.3	1.6	1.3	1.6	1.0
1964	1.0	1.3	1.0	1.3	1.3	1.6	1.2	1.6	1.0	1.3
1965	1.9	1.6	1.6	1.6	1.9	1.6	1.5	1.2	1.9	1.6
1966	3.5	2.9	3.5	2.2	3.4	3.1	3.3	2.4	3.4	3.1
1967	3.0	3.1	3.3	3.4	3.2	2.7	3.8	3.6	2.7	2.1
1968	4.7	4.2	5.0	4.5	4.9	4.4	5.1	4.6	4.7	4.2
1969	6.2	5.5	5.6	5.4	6.5	5.8	6.2	5.8	6.1	5.4
1970	5.6	5.7	6.6	6.0	5.4	6.1	6.6	6.3	5.2	5.9
1971	3.3	4.4	3.0	4.6	3.4	4.2	3.1	4.7	3.2	4.1
1972	3.4	3.2	2.9	2.9	3.5	3.3	3.0	3.0	3.4	3.2
1973	8.7	6.2	5.6	4.0	8.2	6.2	4.7	3.6	9.1	6.4
1974	12.3	11.0	12.2	9.8	11.7	9.8	11.1	8.3	12.2	11.2
1975	6.9	9.1	7.3	9.4	6.6	8.9	6.7	9.1	6.7	9.0
1976	4.9	5.8	6.1	6.7	4.8	5.6	6.1	6.5	4.5	5.3
1977	6.7	6.5	6.4	6.4	6.7	6.4	6.5	6.3	6.7	6.3
1978	9.0	7.6	8.3	7.2	9.1	7.8	8.5	7.4	9.1	7.6
1979	13.3	11.3	14.0	11.4	11.1	10.0	11.3	9.8	13.4	11.5
1980	12.5	13.5	13.0	14.5	11.7	11.6	12.2	12.4	12.5	13.6
1981	8.9	10.3	9.8	10.9	8.5	10.0	9.5	10.4	8.8	10.4
1982	3.8	6.2	4.1	6.5	4.2	6.7	4.5	7.4	3.6	5.9
1983	3.8	3.2	4.1	3.5	4.5	3.6	4.8	4.0	3.6	2.9
1984	3.9	4.3	3.9	4.3	4.4	4.7	4.7	5.0	3.9	4.1
1985	3.8	3.6	4.1	3.8	4.0	3.9	4.3	4.3	3.5	3.4
1986	1.1	1.9	.5	1.7	3.8	3.9	3.8	4.0	.7	1.5
1987	4.4	3.6	4.6	3.5	4.1	4.1	4.2	4.1	4.3	3.5
1988	4.4	4.1	4.2	4.1	4.7	4.4	4.7	4.4	4.2	3.9
1989	4.6	4.8	4.5	4.6	4.6	4.7	4.4	4.5	4.5	4.6
1990	6.1	5.4	6.3	5.3	5.2	5.2	5.2	5.0	5.9	5.2
1991	3.1	4.2	3.3	4.5	3.9	4.6	4.4	4.9	2.7	3.9
1992	2.9	3.0	3.2	3.5	3.0	3.2	3.3	3.7	2.7	2.8
1993	2.7	3.0	2.7	3.1	3.1	3.2	3.2	3.3	2.6	2.7
1994	2.7	2.6	2.6	2.7	2.6	2.7	2.6	2.8	2.5	2.5
1995	2.5	2.8	2.7	2.8	2.9	3.0	3.0	3.0	2.5	2.7
1996	3.3	3.0	3.1	2.9	2.9	2.8	2.6	2.7	3.3	2.8
1997	1.7	2.3	1.8	2.3	2.1	2.5	2.2	2.4	1.6	2.3
1998	1.6	1.6	1.5	1.4	2.4	2.3	2.4	2.3	1.5	1.5
1999	2.7	2.2	2.8	2.2	2.0	2.0	1.9	2.1	2.6	2.1
2000	3.4	3.4	3.5	3.6	2.6	2.4	2.6	2.4	3.3	3.3
2001	1.6	2.8	1.3	2.8	2.8	2.7	2.7	2.6	1.4	2.7
2002	2.4	1.6	2.6	1.5	1.8	2.3	1.9	2.4	2.2	1.4
2003	1.9	2.3	1.5	2.3	1.5	1.5	1.1	1.4	1.8	2.2

	Percent change from preceding month									
	Unadjusted	Seasonally adjusted	Unadjusted	Seasonally adjusted	Unadjusted	Seasonally adjusted	Unadjusted	Seasonally adjusted	Unadjusted	Seasonally adjusted
2002: Jan	0.2	0.2	0.2	0.2	0.3	0.2	0.2	0.2	0.2	0.2
Feb	.4	.2	.5	.1	.4	.2	.5	.2	.4	.2
Mar	.6	.3	.6	.3	.3	.1	.3	.1	.5	.3
Apr	.6	.4	.7	.6	.2	.2	.3	.3	.6	.5
May	0	.1	0	.2	-.1	.1	-.1	.2	-.1	.1
June	.1	.2	.1	.2	-.1	.1	-.1	.1	.1	.1
July	.1	.2	.1	.2	.1	.2	.1	.2	.1	.2
Aug	.3	.2	.4	.3	.3	.3	.4	.3	.3	.2
Sept	.2	.2	.2	.2	.2	.1	.2	.2	.2	.2
Oct	.2	.2	.2	.3	.2	.2	.3	.1	.2	.2
Nov	0	.1	-.1	.1	.1	.1	0	.1	0	.1
Dec	-.2	.1	-.3	.1	-.2	.2	-.2	.2	-.3	.1
2003: Jan	.4	.3	.4	.4	.2	.1	.2	.1	.5	.3
Feb	.8	.6	.8	.6	.4	.2	.4	.1	.8	.6
Mar	.6	.3	.7	.4	.3	0	.3	0	.6	.4
Apr	-.2	-.3	-.3	-.4	0	0	.1	0	-.2	-.4
May	-.2	0	-.2	-.1	.1	.3	.1	.3	-.2	-.1
June	.1	.2	.1	.1	0	.1	-.1	0	.1	.2
July	.1	.2	.1	.2	.1	.2	.1	.2	.1	.2
Aug	.4	.3	.4	.3	.2	.1	.2	.1	.4	.3
Sept	.3	.3	.4	.3	.1	.1	.1	.1	.3	.3
Oct	-.1	0	-.2	-.2	.4	.3	.4	.2	-.1	-.1
Nov	-.3	-.2	-.4	-.3	-.1	0	-.2	-.1	-.3	-.3
Dec	-.1	.2	-.3	.2	-.1	.2	-.2	.1	-.2	.2

[1] Changes from December to December are based on unadjusted indexes.
Note.—See Note, Table B–60.

Source: Department of Labor, Bureau of Labor Statistics.

TABLE B–64.—*Changes in consumer price indexes for commodities and services, 1929–2003*

[For all urban consumers; percent change]

Year	All items (CPI-U) Dec. to Dec.[1]	All items (CPI-U) Year to year	Commodities Total Dec. to Dec.[1]	Commodities Total Year to year	Commodities Food Dec. to Dec.[1]	Commodities Food Year to year	Services Total Dec. to Dec.[1]	Services Total Year to year	Services Medical care Dec. to Dec.[1]	Services Medical care Year to year	Medical care[2] Dec. to Dec.[1]	Medical care[2] Year to year	Energy[3] Dec. to Dec.[1]	Energy[3] Year to year
1929	0.6	0	....	....	2.5	1.2	....	....	....	....	....	....	....	....
1933	.8	−5.1	....	....	6.9	−2.8	....	....	....	....	....	....	....	....
1939	0	−1.4	−0.7	−2.0	−2.5	−2.5	0	0	1.2	1.2	1.0	0	....	....
1940	.7	.7	1.4	.7	2.5	1.7	.8	.8	0	0	0	1.0	....	....
1941	9.9	5.0	13.3	6.7	15.7	9.2	2.4	.8	1.2	0	1.0	0	....	....
1942	9.0	10.9	12.9	14.5	17.9	17.6	2.3	3.1	3.5	3.5	3.8	2.9	....	....
1943	3.0	6.1	4.2	9.3	3.0	11.0	2.3	2.3	5.6	4.5	4.6	4.7	....	....
1944	2.3	1.7	2.0	1.0	0	−1.2	2.2	2.2	3.2	4.3	2.6	3.6	....	....
1945	2.2	2.3	2.9	3.0	3.5	2.4	.7	1.5	3.1	3.1	2.6	2.6	....	....
1946	18.1	8.3	24.8	10.6	31.3	14.5	3.6	1.4	9.0	5.1	8.3	5.0	....	....
1947	8.8	14.4	10.3	20.5	11.3	21.7	5.6	4.3	6.4	8.7	6.9	8.0	....	....
1948	3.0	8.1	1.7	7.2	−.8	8.3	5.9	6.1	6.9	7.1	5.8	6.7	....	....
1949	−2.1	−1.2	−4.1	−2.7	−3.9	−4.2	3.7	5.1	1.6	3.3	1.4	2.8	....	....
1950	5.9	1.3	7.8	.7	9.8	1.6	3.6	3.0	4.0	2.4	3.4	2.0	....	....
1951	6.0	7.9	5.9	9.0	7.1	11.0	5.2	5.3	5.3	4.7	5.8	5.3	....	....
1952	.8	1.9	−.9	1.3	−1.0	1.8	4.4	4.5	5.8	6.7	4.3	5.0	....	....
1953	.7	.8	−.3	−.3	−1.1	−1.4	4.2	4.3	3.4	3.5	3.5	3.6	....	....
1954	−.7	.7	−1.6	−.9	−1.8	−.4	2.0	3.1	2.6	3.4	2.3	2.9	....	....
1955	.4	−.4	−.3	−.9	−.7	−1.4	2.0	2.0	3.2	2.6	3.3	2.2	....	....
1956	3.0	1.5	2.6	1.0	2.9	.7	3.4	2.5	3.8	3.8	3.2	3.8	....	....
1957	2.9	3.3	2.8	3.2	2.8	3.2	4.2	4.3	4.8	4.3	4.7	4.2	....	....
1958	1.8	2.8	1.2	2.1	2.4	4.5	2.7	3.7	4.6	5.3	4.5	4.6	−0.9	0
1959	1.7	.7	.6	0	−1.0	−1.7	3.9	3.1	4.9	4.5	3.8	4.4	4.7	1.9
1960	1.4	1.7	1.2	.9	3.1	1.0	2.5	3.4	3.7	4.3	3.2	3.7	1.3	2.3
1961	.7	1.0	0	.6	−.7	1.3	2.1	1.7	3.5	3.6	3.1	2.7	−1.3	.4
1962	1.3	1.0	.9	.9	1.3	.7	1.6	2.0	2.9	3.5	2.2	2.6	2.2	.7
1963	1.6	1.3	1.5	.9	2.0	1.6	2.4	2.0	2.8	2.9	2.5	2.6	−.9	0
1964	1.0	1.3	.9	1.2	1.3	1.3	1.6	2.0	2.3	2.3	2.1	2.1	0	−.7
1965	1.9	1.6	1.4	1.1	3.5	2.2	2.7	2.3	3.6	3.2	2.8	2.4	1.8	1.1
1966	3.5	2.9	2.5	2.6	4.0	5.0	4.8	3.8	8.3	5.3	6.7	4.4	1.7	1.3
1967	3.0	3.1	2.5	1.9	1.2	.9	4.3	4.3	8.0	8.8	6.3	7.2	1.7	2.3
1968	4.7	4.2	4.0	3.5	4.4	3.5	5.8	5.2	7.1	7.3	6.2	6.0	1.7	1.3
1969	6.2	5.5	5.4	4.7	7.0	5.1	7.7	6.9	7.3	8.2	6.2	6.7	2.9	2.3
1970	5.6	5.7	3.9	4.5	2.3	5.7	8.1	8.0	8.1	7.0	7.4	6.6	4.8	2.4
1971	3.3	4.4	2.8	3.6	4.3	3.1	4.1	5.7	5.4	7.4	4.6	6.2	3.1	3.3
1972	3.4	3.2	3.4	3.0	4.6	4.2	3.4	3.8	3.7	3.5	3.3	3.3	2.6	2.5
1973	8.7	6.2	10.4	7.4	20.3	14.5	6.2	4.4	6.0	4.5	5.3	4.0	17.0	8.1
1974	12.3	11.0	12.8	11.9	12.0	14.3	11.4	9.2	13.2	10.4	12.6	9.3	21.6	29.3
1975	6.9	9.1	6.2	8.8	6.6	8.5	8.2	9.6	10.3	12.6	9.8	12.0	11.4	10.5
1976	4.9	5.8	3.3	4.3	.5	3.0	7.2	8.3	10.8	10.1	10.0	9.5	7.1	7.1
1977	6.7	6.5	6.1	5.8	8.1	6.3	8.0	7.7	9.0	9.9	8.9	9.6	7.2	9.5
1978	9.0	7.6	8.8	7.2	11.8	9.9	9.3	8.6	9.3	8.5	8.8	8.4	7.9	6.3
1979	13.3	11.3	13.0	11.3	10.2	11.0	13.6	11.0	10.5	9.8	10.1	9.2	37.5	25.1
1980	12.5	13.5	11.0	12.3	10.2	8.6	14.2	15.4	10.1	11.3	9.9	11.0	18.0	30.9
1981	8.9	10.3	6.0	8.4	4.3	7.8	13.0	13.1	12.6	10.7	12.5	10.7	11.9	13.6
1982	3.8	6.2	3.6	4.1	3.1	4.1	4.3	9.0	11.2	11.8	11.0	11.6	1.3	1.5
1983	3.8	3.2	2.9	2.9	2.7	2.1	4.8	3.5	6.2	8.7	6.4	8.8	−.5	.7
1984	3.9	4.3	2.7	3.4	3.8	3.8	5.4	5.2	5.8	6.0	6.1	6.2	.2	1.0
1985	3.8	3.6	2.5	2.1	2.6	2.3	5.1	5.1	6.8	6.1	6.8	6.3	1.8	.7
1986	1.1	1.9	−2.0	−.9	3.8	3.2	4.5	5.0	7.9	7.7	7.7	7.5	−19.7	−13.2
1987	4.4	3.6	4.6	3.2	3.5	4.1	4.3	4.2	5.6	6.6	5.8	6.6	8.2	.5
1988	4.4	4.1	3.8	3.5	5.2	4.1	4.8	4.6	6.9	6.4	6.9	6.5	.5	.8
1989	4.6	4.8	4.1	4.7	5.6	5.8	5.1	4.9	8.6	7.7	8.5	7.7	5.1	5.6
1990	6.1	5.4	6.6	5.2	5.3	5.8	5.7	5.5	9.9	9.3	9.6	9.0	18.1	8.3
1991	3.1	4.2	1.2	3.1	1.9	2.9	4.6	5.1	8.0	8.9	7.9	8.7	−7.4	.4
1992	2.9	3.0	2.0	2.0	1.5	1.2	3.6	3.9	7.0	7.6	6.6	7.4	2.0	.5
1993	2.7	3.0	1.5	1.9	2.9	2.2	3.8	3.9	5.9	6.5	5.4	5.9	−1.4	1.2
1994	2.7	2.6	2.3	1.7	2.9	2.4	2.9	3.3	5.4	5.2	4.9	4.8	2.2	.4
1995	2.5	2.8	1.4	1.9	2.1	2.8	3.5	3.4	4.4	5.1	3.9	4.5	−1.3	.6
1996	3.3	3.0	3.2	2.6	4.3	3.3	3.3	3.2	3.2	3.7	3.0	3.5	8.6	4.6
1997	1.7	2.3	.2	1.4	1.5	2.6	2.8	3.0	2.9	2.9	2.8	2.8	−3.4	1.3
1998	1.6	1.6	.4	.1	2.3	2.2	2.6	2.7	3.2	3.2	3.4	3.2	−8.8	−7.7
1999	2.7	2.2	2.7	1.8	1.9	2.1	2.6	2.5	3.6	3.4	3.7	3.5	13.4	3.6
2000	3.4	3.4	2.7	3.3	2.8	2.3	3.9	3.4	4.6	4.3	4.2	4.1	14.2	16.9
2001	1.6	2.8	−1.4	1.0	2.8	3.2	3.7	4.1	4.8	4.8	4.7	4.6	−13.0	3.6
2002	2.4	1.6	1.2	−.7	1.5	1.8	3.2	3.1	5.6	5.1	5.0	4.7	10.7	−5.9
2003	1.9	2.3	.5	1.0	3.6	2.2	2.8	3.2	4.2	4.5	3.7	4.0	6.9	12.2

[1] Changes from December to December are based on unadjusted indexes.
[2] Commodities and services.
[3] Household fuels—gas (piped), electricity, fuel oil, etc.,—and motor fuel. Motor oil, coolant, etc., also included through 1982.

Note.—See Note, Table B–60.

Source: Department of Labor, Bureau of Labor Statistics.

TABLE B–65.—*Producer price indexes by stage of processing, 1959–2003*

[1982=100]

Year or month	Total finished goods	Consumer foods			Finished goods excluding consumer foods					Total finished consumer goods
						Consumer goods				
		Total	Crude	Processed	Total	Total	Durable	Non-durable	Capital equipment	
1959	33.1	34.8	37.3	34.7	....	33.3	43.9	28.2	32.7	33.3
1960	33.4	35.5	39.8	35.2	....	33.5	43.8	28.4	32.8	33.6
1961	33.4	35.4	38.0	35.3	....	33.4	43.6	28.4	32.9	33.6
1962	33.5	35.7	38.4	35.6	....	33.4	43.4	28.4	33.0	33.7
1963	33.4	35.3	37.8	35.2	....	33.4	43.1	28.5	33.1	33.5
1964	33.5	35.4	38.9	35.2	....	33.3	43.3	28.4	33.4	33.6
1965	34.1	36.8	39.0	36.8	....	33.6	43.2	28.8	33.8	34.2
1966	35.2	39.2	41.5	39.2	....	34.1	43.4	29.3	34.6	35.4
1967	35.6	38.5	39.6	38.8	35.0	34.7	44.1	30.0	35.8	35.6
1968	36.6	40.0	42.5	40.0	35.9	35.5	45.1	30.6	37.0	36.5
1969	38.0	42.4	45.9	42.3	36.9	36.3	45.9	31.5	38.3	37.9
1970	39.3	43.8	46.0	43.9	38.2	37.4	47.2	32.5	40.1	39.1
1971	40.5	44.5	45.8	44.7	39.6	38.7	48.9	33.5	41.7	40.2
1972	41.8	46.9	48.0	47.2	40.4	39.4	50.0	34.1	42.8	41.5
1973	45.6	56.5	63.6	55.8	42.0	41.2	50.9	36.1	44.2	46.0
1974	52.6	64.4	71.6	63.9	48.8	48.2	55.5	44.0	50.5	53.1
1975	58.2	69.8	71.7	70.3	54.7	53.2	61.0	48.9	58.2	58.2
1976	60.8	69.6	76.7	69.0	58.1	56.5	63.7	52.4	62.1	60.4
1977	64.7	73.3	79.5	72.7	62.2	60.6	67.4	56.8	66.1	64.3
1978	69.8	79.9	85.8	79.4	66.7	64.9	73.6	60.0	71.3	69.4
1979	77.6	87.3	92.3	86.8	74.6	73.5	80.8	69.3	77.5	77.5
1980	88.0	92.4	93.9	92.3	86.7	87.1	91.0	85.1	85.8	88.6
1981	96.1	97.8	104.4	97.2	95.6	96.1	96.4	95.8	94.6	96.6
1982	100.0	100.0	100.0	100.0	100.0	100.0	100.0	100.0	100.0	100.0
1983	101.6	101.0	102.4	100.9	101.8	101.2	102.8	100.5	102.8	101.3
1984	103.7	105.4	111.4	104.9	103.2	102.2	104.5	101.1	105.2	103.3
1985	104.7	104.6	102.9	104.8	104.6	103.3	106.5	101.7	107.5	103.8
1986	103.2	107.3	105.6	107.4	101.9	98.5	108.9	93.3	109.7	101.4
1987	105.4	109.5	107.1	109.6	104.0	100.7	111.5	94.9	111.7	103.6
1988	108.0	112.6	109.8	112.7	106.5	103.1	113.8	97.3	114.3	106.2
1989	113.6	118.7	119.6	118.6	111.8	108.9	117.6	103.8	118.8	112.1
1990	119.2	124.4	123.0	124.4	117.4	115.3	120.4	111.5	122.9	118.2
1991	121.7	124.1	119.3	124.4	120.9	118.7	123.9	115.0	126.7	120.5
1992	123.2	123.3	107.6	124.4	123.1	120.8	125.7	117.3	129.1	121.7
1993	124.7	125.7	114.4	126.5	124.4	121.7	128.0	117.6	131.4	123.0
1994	125.5	126.8	111.3	127.9	125.1	121.6	130.9	116.2	134.1	123.3
1995	127.9	129.0	118.8	129.8	127.5	124.0	132.7	118.8	136.7	125.6
1996	131.3	133.6	129.2	133.8	130.5	127.6	134.2	123.3	138.3	129.5
1997	131.8	134.5	126.6	135.1	130.9	128.2	133.7	124.3	138.2	130.2
1998	130.7	134.3	127.2	134.8	129.5	126.4	132.9	122.2	137.6	128.9
1999	133.0	135.1	125.5	135.9	132.3	130.5	133.0	127.9	137.6	132.0
2000	138.0	137.2	123.5	138.3	138.1	138.4	133.9	138.7	138.8	138.2
2001	140.7	141.3	127.7	142.4	140.4	141.4	134.0	142.8	139.7	141.5
2002	138.9	140.1	128.5	141.0	138.3	138.8	133.0	139.8	139.1	139.4
2003	143.3	146.0	130.1	147.3	142.4	144.6	133.1	148.3	139.6	145.2
2002: Jan	137.4	141.1	139.4	141.1	136.3	135.4	133.9	134.4	139.7	137.2
Feb	137.7	142.3	146.4	141.9	136.3	135.4	134.1	134.3	139.8	137.5
Mar	138.7	143.4	160.3	141.9	137.2	136.9	133.6	136.7	139.5	138.9
Apr	138.8	139.2	115.1	141.2	138.5	138.9	133.5	139.8	139.3	139.2
May	138.6	139.4	124.4	140.6	138.2	138.6	133.0	139.5	139.1	139.1
June	139.0	139.8	126.2	140.9	138.6	139.3	132.8	140.6	139.0	139.6
July	138.8	139.8	125.8	140.9	138.3	139.1	131.5	141.0	138.4	139.6
Aug	138.8	139.3	125.4	140.4	138.4	139.3	131.0	141.5	138.2	139.6
Sept	139.1	138.7	119.0	140.3	139.0	140.2	131.1	142.8	138.3	140.0
Oct	140.7	139.2	123.8	140.4	140.8	142.2	134.8	143.8	139.9	141.6
Nov	139.7	139.2	123.2	140.5	139.6	140.5	133.6	142.0	139.5	140.4
Dec	139.0	139.5	112.7	141.8	138.7	139.3	132.2	140.6	139.1	139.6
2003: Jan	140.8	142.0	123.3	143.5	140.3	141.6	133.2	143.8	139.3	141.9
Feb	142.3	142.3	117.5	144.3	142.1	144.4	133.1	147.9	139.2	144.0
Mar	144.2	142.8	123.7	144.4	144.3	147.4	134.4	151.7	139.9	146.3
Apr	142.1	144.0	133.7	144.8	141.5	143.5	132.5	146.9	139.1	143.8
May	142.0	144.6	133.1	145.5	141.1	143.0	132.4	146.3	139.0	143.7
June	143.0	145.2	121.5	147.2	142.2	144.6	131.8	148.9	138.9	145.0
July	143.0	144.9	120.4	146.9	142.2	144.8	131.7	149.2	138.9	145.1
Aug [1]	143.7	146.3	128.2	147.8	142.7	145.4	131.8	150.0	139.2	145.9
Sept	143.9	147.9	136.8	148.8	142.6	145.3	131.1	150.2	139.1	146.3
Oct	145.5	151.0	135.0	152.3	143.8	146.1	135.5	149.2	141.1	147.7
Nov	144.5	150.2	137.0	151.3	142.8	144.7	135.1	147.4	140.7	146.5
Dec	144.5	150.3	150.8	150.2	142.8	144.8	134.4	147.9	140.4	146.6

[1] Data have been revised through August 2003; data are subject to revision 4 months after date of original publication.

See next page for continuation of table.

[1982=100]

Year or month	Intermediate materials, supplies, and components								Crude materials for further processing				
	Total	Foods and feeds[2]	Other	Materials and components		Processed fuels and lubricants	Containers	Supplies	Total	Foodstuffs and feedstuffs	Other		
				For manufacturing	For construction						Total	Fuel	Other
1959	30.8	....	30.5	33.3	32.9	16.2	33.0	33.5	31.1	38.8	....	10.4	28.1
1960	30.8	....	30.7	33.3	32.7	16.6	33.4	33.3	30.4	38.4	....	10.5	26.9
1961	30.6	....	30.3	32.9	32.2	16.8	33.2	33.7	30.2	37.9	....	10.5	27.2
1962	30.6	....	30.2	32.7	32.1	16.7	33.6	34.5	30.5	38.6	....	10.4	27.1
1963	30.7	....	30.1	32.7	32.2	16.6	33.2	35.0	29.9	37.5	....	10.5	26.7
1964	30.8	....	30.3	33.1	32.5	16.2	32.9	34.7	29.6	36.6	....	10.5	27.2
1965	31.2	....	30.7	33.6	32.8	16.5	33.5	35.0	31.1	39.2	....	10.6	27.7
1966	32.0	....	31.3	34.3	33.6	16.8	34.5	36.5	33.1	42.7	....	10.9	28.3
1967	32.2	41.8	31.7	34.5	34.0	16.9	35.0	36.8	31.3	40.3	21.1	11.3	26.5
1968	33.0	41.5	32.5	35.3	35.7	16.5	35.9	37.1	31.8	40.9	21.6	11.5	27.1
1969	34.1	42.9	33.6	36.5	37.7	16.6	37.2	37.8	33.9	44.1	22.5	12.0	28.4
1970	35.4	45.6	34.8	38.0	38.3	17.7	39.0	39.7	35.2	45.2	23.8	13.8	29.1
1971	36.8	46.7	36.2	38.9	40.8	19.5	40.8	40.8	36.0	46.1	24.7	15.7	29.4
1972	38.2	49.5	37.7	40.4	43.0	20.1	42.7	42.5	39.9	51.5	27.0	16.8	32.3
1973	42.4	70.3	40.6	44.1	46.5	22.2	45.2	51.7	54.5	72.6	34.3	18.6	42.9
1974	52.5	83.6	50.5	56.0	55.0	33.6	53.3	56.8	61.4	76.4	44.1	24.8	54.5
1975	58.0	81.6	56.6	61.7	60.1	39.4	60.0	61.8	61.6	77.4	43.7	30.6	50.0
1976	60.9	77.4	60.0	64.0	64.1	42.3	63.1	65.8	63.4	76.8	48.2	34.5	54.9
1977	64.9	79.6	64.1	67.4	69.3	47.7	65.9	69.3	65.5	77.5	51.7	42.0	56.3
1978	69.5	84.8	68.6	72.0	76.5	49.9	71.0	72.9	73.4	87.3	57.5	48.2	61.9
1979	78.4	94.5	77.4	80.9	84.2	61.6	79.4	80.2	85.9	100.0	69.6	57.3	75.5
1980	90.3	105.5	89.4	91.7	91.3	85.0	89.1	89.9	95.3	104.6	84.6	69.4	91.8
1981	98.6	104.6	98.2	98.7	97.9	100.6	96.7	96.9	103.0	103.9	101.8	84.8	109.8
1982	100.0	100.0	100.0	100.0	100.0	100.0	100.0	100.0	100.0	100.0	100.0	100.0	100.0
1983	100.6	103.6	100.5	101.2	102.8	95.4	100.4	101.8	101.3	101.8	100.7	105.1	98.8
1984	103.1	105.7	103.0	104.1	105.6	95.7	105.9	104.1	103.5	104.7	102.2	105.1	101.0
1985	102.7	97.3	103.0	103.3	107.3	92.8	109.0	104.4	95.8	94.8	96.9	102.7	94.3
1986	99.1	96.2	99.3	102.2	108.1	72.7	110.3	105.6	87.7	93.2	81.6	92.2	76.0
1987	101.5	99.2	101.7	105.3	109.8	73.3	114.5	107.7	93.7	96.2	87.9	84.1	88.5
1988	107.1	109.5	106.9	113.2	116.1	71.2	120.1	113.7	96.0	106.1	85.5	82.1	85.9
1989	112.0	113.8	111.9	118.1	121.3	76.4	125.4	118.1	103.1	111.2	93.4	85.3	95.8
1990	114.5	113.3	114.5	118.7	122.9	85.9	127.7	119.4	108.9	113.1	101.5	84.8	107.3
1991	114.4	111.1	114.6	118.1	124.5	85.3	128.1	121.4	101.2	105.5	94.6	82.9	97.5
1992	114.7	110.7	114.9	117.9	126.5	84.5	127.7	122.7	100.4	105.1	93.5	84.0	94.2
1993	116.2	112.7	116.4	118.9	132.0	84.7	126.4	125.0	102.4	108.4	94.7	87.1	94.1
1994	118.5	114.8	118.7	122.1	136.6	83.1	129.7	127.0	101.8	106.5	94.8	82.4	97.0
1995	124.9	114.8	125.5	130.4	142.1	84.2	148.8	132.1	102.7	105.8	96.8	72.1	105.8
1996	125.7	128.1	125.6	128.6	143.6	90.0	141.1	135.9	113.8	121.5	104.5	92.6	105.7
1997	125.6	125.4	125.7	128.3	146.5	89.3	136.0	135.9	111.1	112.2	106.4	101.3	103.5
1998	123.0	116.2	123.4	126.1	146.8	81.1	140.8	134.8	96.8	103.9	88.4	86.7	84.5
1999	123.2	111.1	123.9	124.6	148.9	84.6	142.5	134.2	98.2	98.7	94.3	91.2	91.1
2000	129.2	111.7	130.1	128.1	150.7	102.0	151.6	136.9	120.6	100.2	130.4	136.9	118.0
2001	129.7	115.9	130.5	127.4	150.6	104.5	153.1	138.7	121.0	106.1	126.8	151.4	101.5
2002	127.8	115.5	128.5	126.1	151.3	96.3	152.1	138.9	108.1	99.5	111.4	117.3	101.0
2003	133.7	125.8	134.2	129.7	153.6	112.6	153.7	141.5	135.3	113.5	148.2	186.1	116.8
2002:Jan	125.5	113.6	126.1	124.5	150.2	90.0	152.6	138.2	98.9	99.6	95.0	100.5	86.0
Feb	125.2	113.6	125.9	124.6	150.2	88.8	151.9	138.1	98.0	102.0	91.4	85.0	89.5
Mar	126.1	114.3	126.8	125.1	150.7	91.3	151.7	138.3	103.7	102.8	100.9	98.0	96.4
Apr	127.2	113.6	127.9	125.5	151.1	95.3	151.2	138.5	108.3	96.5	114.0	124.4	100.8
May	127.1	112.9	127.9	125.5	151.4	94.8	151.0	138.4	109.9	98.2	115.6	120.1	105.8
June	127.7	114.2	128.4	125.9	151.5	96.4	151.3	138.7	105.7	96.8	109.2	113.7	99.9
July	128.1	115.8	128.8	126.3	151.7	97.3	151.4	139.1	106.8	98.0	110.2	109.8	103.5
Aug	128.4	116.8	129.0	126.5	152.1	97.6	151.5	139.3	108.7	99.7	112.1	111.1	105.8
Sept	129.3	118.0	130.0	126.9	152.1	100.6	152.5	139.6	110.9	100.7	115.4	115.4	108.3
Oct	129.7	117.4	130.4	127.4	151.7	101.6	153.3	139.5	112.6	99.9	119.0	126.0	107.5
Nov	129.7	117.5	130.3	127.6	151.2	101.2	153.4	139.6	116.1	99.7	125.3	150.6	102.6
Dec	129.4	118.8	130.0	127.2	151.1	100.9	153.2	139.6	118.1	100.5	128.2	153.0	105.7
2003:Jan	131.1	120.4	131.7	127.9	151.4	106.9	153.4	140.1	127.3	105.6	140.4	169.9	114.5
Feb	133.5	121.2	134.2	129.5	152.1	113.6	153.7	140.7	134.0	106.3	151.7	186.6	121.9
Mar	136.2	121.0	137.0	130.1	152.3	124.8	153.8	141.2	152.2	105.7	184.4	271.5	121.8
Apr	133.0	121.2	133.7	129.4	152.9	110.8	154.0	141.3	128.0	107.0	140.6	176.9	110.5
May	132.5	122.8	133.1	129.3	152.9	108.0	153.9	141.5	130.9	111.0	142.4	183.7	109.2
June	133.5	125.1	134.0	129.6	153.0	112.1	154.1	141.5	136.5	110.4	152.8	203.0	113.8
July	133.7	124.4	134.2	129.2	153.0	113.7	153.8	141.5	132.6	107.6	148.2	189.1	115.0
Aug[1]	134.1	125.0	134.6	129.8	153.7	114.5	153.6	141.2	131.3	111.5	142.7	171.2	117.1
Sept	134.1	128.0	134.5	129.8	155.1	113.3	153.6	141.7	135.6	118.7	144.5	180.1	114.6
Oct	134.1	131.7	134.4	130.5	155.2	111.9	153.2	141.8	138.3	127.9	141.9	165.8	119.1
Nov	134.0	134.8	134.1	130.7	155.6	109.7	153.5	142.6	137.4	126.1	141.9	163.8	120.2
Dec	134.5	133.9	134.7	131.0	155.6	111.7	153.4	142.7	139.9	124.6	147.4	172.1	123.8

[2] Intermediate materials for food manufacturing and feeds.

Source: Department of Labor, Bureau of Labor Statistics.

TABLE B–66.—*Producer price indexes by stage of processing, special groups, 1974–2003*

[1982=100]

Year or month	Finished goods						Intermediate materials, supplies, and components				Crude materials for further processing			
	Total	Foods	Energy	Excluding foods and energy			Total	Foods and feeds[1]	Energy	Other	Total	Foodstuffs and feedstuffs	Energy	Other
				Total	Capital equipment	Consumer goods excluding foods and energy								
1974	52.6	64.4	26.2	53.6	50.5	55.5	52.5	83.6	33.1	54.0	61.4	76.4	27.8	83.3
1975	58.2	69.8	30.7	59.7	58.2	60.6	58.0	81.6	38.7	60.2	61.6	77.4	33.3	69.3
1976	60.8	69.6	34.3	63.1	62.1	63.7	60.9	77.4	41.5	63.8	63.4	76.8	35.3	80.2
1977	64.7	73.3	39.7	66.9	66.1	67.3	64.9	79.6	46.8	67.6	65.5	77.5	40.4	79.8
1978	69.8	79.9	42.3	71.9	71.3	72.2	69.5	84.8	49.1	72.5	73.4	87.3	45.2	87.8
1979	77.6	87.3	57.1	78.3	77.5	78.8	78.4	94.5	61.1	80.7	85.9	100.0	54.9	106.2
1980	88.0	92.4	85.2	87.1	85.8	87.8	90.3	105.5	84.9	90.3	95.3	104.6	73.1	113.1
1981	96.1	97.8	101.5	94.6	94.6	94.6	98.6	104.6	100.5	97.7	103.0	103.9	97.7	111.7
1982	100.0	100.0	100.0	100.0	100.0	100.0	100.0	100.0	100.0	100.0	100.0	100.0	100.0	100.0
1983	101.6	101.0	95.2	103.0	102.8	103.1	100.6	103.6	95.3	101.6	101.3	101.8	98.7	105.3
1984	103.7	105.4	91.2	105.5	105.2	105.7	103.1	105.7	95.5	104.7	103.5	104.7	98.0	111.7
1985	104.7	104.6	87.6	108.1	107.5	108.4	102.7	97.3	92.6	105.2	95.8	94.8	93.3	104.9
1986	103.2	107.3	63.0	110.6	109.7	111.1	99.1	96.2	72.6	104.9	87.7	93.2	71.8	103.1
1987	105.4	109.5	61.8	113.3	111.7	114.2	101.5	99.2	73.0	107.8	93.7	96.2	75.0	115.7
1988	108.0	112.6	59.8	117.0	114.3	118.5	107.1	109.5	70.9	115.2	96.0	106.1	67.7	133.0
1989	113.6	118.7	65.7	122.1	118.8	124.0	112.0	113.8	76.1	120.2	103.1	111.2	75.9	137.9
1990	119.2	124.4	75.0	126.6	122.9	128.8	114.5	113.3	85.5	120.9	108.9	113.1	85.9	136.3
1991	121.7	124.1	78.1	131.1	126.7	133.7	114.4	111.1	85.1	121.4	101.2	105.5	80.4	128.2
1992	123.2	123.3	77.8	134.2	129.1	137.3	114.7	110.7	84.3	122.0	100.4	105.1	78.8	128.4
1993	124.7	125.7	78.0	135.8	131.4	138.5	116.2	112.7	84.6	123.8	102.4	108.4	76.7	140.2
1994	125.5	126.8	77.0	137.1	134.1	139.0	118.5	114.8	83.0	127.1	101.8	106.5	72.1	156.2
1995	127.9	129.0	78.1	140.0	136.7	141.9	124.9	114.8	84.1	135.2	102.7	105.8	69.4	173.6
1996	131.3	133.6	83.2	142.0	138.3	144.3	125.7	128.1	89.8	134.0	113.8	121.5	85.0	155.8
1997	131.8	134.5	83.4	142.4	138.2	145.1	125.6	125.4	89.0	134.2	111.1	112.2	87.3	156.5
1998	130.7	134.3	75.1	143.7	137.6	147.7	123.0	116.2	80.8	133.5	96.8	103.9	68.6	142.1
1999	133.0	135.1	78.8	146.1	137.6	151.7	123.2	111.1	84.3	133.1	98.2	98.7	78.5	135.2
2000	138.0	137.2	94.1	148.0	138.8	154.0	129.2	111.7	101.7	136.6	120.6	100.2	122.1	145.2
2001	140.7	141.3	96.7	150.0	139.7	156.9	129.7	115.9	104.1	136.4	121.0	106.1	122.3	130.7
2002	138.9	140.1	88.8	150.2	139.1	157.6	127.8	115.5	95.9	135.8	108.1	99.5	102.0	135.7
2003	143.3	146.0	102.0	150.5	139.6	157.8	133.7	125.8	111.9	138.5	135.3	113.5	147.4	152.2
2002: Jan	137.4	141.1	81.3	150.4	139.7	157.6	125.5	113.6	89.6	134.6	98.9	99.6	82.8	126.1
Feb	137.7	142.3	81.3	150.4	139.8	157.6	125.2	113.6	88.4	134.6	98.0	102.0	76.9	128.1
Mar	138.7	143.4	85.0	150.2	139.5	157.4	126.1	114.3	90.9	135.0	103.7	102.8	89.9	129.0
Apr	138.8	139.2	88.8	150.4	139.3	157.9	127.2	113.6	94.9	135.4	108.3	96.5	107.3	131.8
May	138.6	139.4	88.4	150.2	139.1	157.7	127.1	112.9	94.6	135.4	109.9	98.2	108.3	134.9
June	139.0	139.8	89.8	150.2	139.0	157.8	127.7	114.2	96.2	135.7	105.7	96.8	97.8	138.6
July	138.8	139.8	90.5	149.5	138.4	157.1	128.1	115.8	96.7	136.0	106.8	98.0	98.1	141.0
Aug	138.8	139.3	91.3	149.3	138.2	156.8	128.4	116.8	97.0	136.2	108.7	99.7	101.2	140.3
Sept	139.1	138.7	93.0	149.5	138.3	157.1	129.3	118.0	100.4	136.5	110.9	100.7	105.9	140.0
Oct	140.7	139.2	94.5	151.3	139.9	159.1	129.7	117.4	101.6	136.6	112.6	99.9	111.3	139.8
Nov	139.7	139.2	91.3	150.9	139.5	158.6	129.7	117.5	101.0	136.7	116.1	99.7	120.0	139.8
Dec	139.0	139.5	90.7	149.9	139.1	157.2	129.4	118.8	100.0	136.6	118.1	100.5	124.0	139.9
2003: Jan	140.8	142.0	95.3	150.3	139.3	157.7	131.1	120.4	105.8	137.1	127.3	105.6	140.1	143.0
Feb	142.3	142.3	101.7	150.2	139.2	157.6	133.5	121.2	113.2	138.1	134.0	106.3	153.9	148.3
Mar	144.2	142.8	107.4	151.0	139.9	158.4	136.2	121.0	124.2	138.7	152.2	105.7	200.2	148.1
Apr	142.1	144.0	100.0	150.0	139.1	157.4	133.0	121.2	110.1	138.4	128.0	107.0	138.8	146.7
May	142.0	144.6	98.9	150.0	139.0	157.4	132.5	122.8	107.1	138.5	130.9	111.0	141.4	146.5
June	143.0	145.2	103.1	149.8	138.9	157.1	133.5	125.1	111.3	138.4	136.5	110.4	156.2	146.3
July	143.0	144.9	103.4	149.8	138.9	157.1	133.7	124.4	113.0	138.3	132.6	107.6	148.7	148.8
Aug[2]	143.7	146.3	104.7	149.9	139.2	157.2	134.1	125.0	114.3	138.3	131.3	111.5	139.2	150.9
Sept	143.9	147.9	105.0	149.7	139.1	156.9	134.1	128.0	112.4	138.8	135.6	118.7	140.7	155.5
Oct	145.5	151.0	103.2	152.0	141.1	159.2	134.1	131.7	111.1	139.0	138.3	127.9	135.7	158.8
Nov	144.5	150.2	100.3	151.7	140.7	159.0	134.0	134.8	109.0	139.2	137.4	126.1	133.6	163.7
Dec	144.5	150.3	101.1	151.4	140.4	158.8	134.5	133.9	110.9	139.5	139.9	124.6	139.3	169.0

[1] Intermediate materials for food manufacturing and feeds.
[2] Data have been revised through August 2003; data are subject to revision 4 months after date of original publication.

Source: Department of Labor, Bureau of Labor Statistics.

TABLE B–67.—*Producer price indexes for major commodity groups, 1959–2003*

[1982=100]

Year or month	Farm products and processed foods and feeds			Industrial commodities				
	Total	Farm products	Processed foods and feeds	Total	Textile products and apparel	Hides, skins, leather, and related products	Fuels and related products and power	Chemicals and allied products[1]
1959	37.6	40.2	35.6	30.5	48.1	35.9	13.7	34.8
1960	37.7	40.1	35.6	30.5	48.6	34.6	13.9	34.8
1961	37.7	39.7	36.2	30.4	47.8	34.9	14.0	34.5
1962	38.1	40.4	36.5	30.4	48.2	35.3	14.0	33.9
1963	37.7	39.6	36.8	30.3	48.2	34.3	13.9	33.5
1964	37.5	39.0	36.7	30.5	48.5	34.4	13.5	33.6
1965	39.0	40.7	38.0	30.9	48.8	35.9	13.8	33.9
1966	41.6	43.7	40.2	31.5	48.9	39.4	14.1	34.0
1967	40.2	41.3	39.8	32.0	48.9	38.1	14.4	34.2
1968	41.1	42.3	40.6	32.8	50.7	39.3	14.3	34.1
1969	43.4	45.0	42.7	33.9	51.8	41.5	14.6	34.2
1970	44.9	45.8	44.6	35.2	52.4	42.0	15.3	35.0
1971	45.8	46.6	45.5	36.5	53.3	43.4	16.6	35.6
1972	49.2	51.6	48.0	37.8	55.5	50.0	17.1	35.6
1973	63.9	72.7	58.9	40.3	60.5	54.5	19.4	37.6
1974	71.3	77.4	68.0	49.2	68.0	55.2	30.1	50.2
1975	74.0	77.0	72.6	54.9	67.4	56.5	35.4	62.0
1976	73.6	78.8	70.8	58.4	72.4	63.9	38.3	64.0
1977	75.9	79.4	74.0	62.5	75.3	68.3	43.6	65.9
1978	83.0	87.7	80.6	67.0	78.1	76.1	46.5	68.0
1979	92.3	99.6	88.5	75.7	82.5	96.1	58.9	76.0
1980	98.3	102.9	95.9	88.0	89.7	94.7	82.8	89.0
1981	101.1	105.2	98.9	97.4	97.6	99.3	100.2	98.4
1982	100.0	100.0	100.0	100.0	100.0	100.0	100.0	100.0
1983	102.0	102.4	101.8	101.1	100.3	103.2	95.9	100.3
1984	105.5	105.5	105.4	103.3	102.7	109.0	94.8	102.9
1985	100.7	95.1	103.5	103.7	102.9	108.9	91.4	103.7
1986	101.2	92.9	105.4	100.0	103.2	113.0	69.8	102.6
1987	103.7	95.5	107.9	102.6	105.1	120.4	70.2	106.4
1988	110.0	104.9	112.7	106.3	109.2	131.4	66.7	116.3
1989	115.4	110.9	117.8	111.6	112.3	136.3	72.9	123.0
1990	118.6	112.2	121.9	115.8	115.0	141.7	82.3	123.6
1991	116.4	105.7	121.9	116.5	116.3	138.9	81.2	125.6
1992	115.9	103.6	122.1	117.4	117.8	140.4	80.4	125.9
1993	118.4	107.1	124.0	119.0	118.0	143.7	80.0	128.2
1994	119.1	106.3	125.5	120.7	118.3	148.5	77.8	132.1
1995	120.5	107.4	127.0	125.5	120.8	153.7	78.0	142.5
1996	129.7	122.4	133.3	127.3	122.4	150.5	85.8	142.1
1997	127.0	112.9	134.0	127.7	122.6	154.2	86.1	143.6
1998	122.7	104.6	131.6	124.8	122.9	148.0	75.3	143.9
1999	120.3	98.4	131.1	126.5	121.1	146.0	80.5	144.2
2000	122.0	99.5	133.1	134.8	121.4	151.5	103.5	151.0
2001	126.2	103.8	137.3	135.7	121.3	158.4	105.3	151.8
2002	123.9	99.0	136.2	132.4	119.9	157.6	93.2	151.9
2003	132.9	111.5	143.3	139.1	119.7	162.3	112.9	161.8
2002: Jan	123.9	99.9	135.7	129.4	120.3	152.4	84.0	147.1
Feb	125.1	101.8	136.5	129.1	119.9	152.5	82.5	147.3
Mar	125.9	104.4	136.4	130.5	120.0	154.3	87.4	148.8
Apr	122.0	94.3	135.8	132.4	119.8	154.4	93.7	150.5
May	122.5	96.6	135.3	132.3	119.8	156.5	93.4	150.6
June	122.6	96.2	135.6	132.4	119.9	158.0	92.9	151.3
July	123.5	97.9	136.2	132.6	119.9	158.5	93.5	152.9
Aug	124.0	99.7	136.0	132.8	119.8	160.4	94.5	153.6
Sept	124.2	99.8	136.3	133.7	119.8	161.0	97.5	154.1
Oct	124.1	99.1	136.4	134.8	119.7	160.9	99.7	155.3
Nov	124.1	99.1	136.5	134.7	119.8	160.9	99.5	155.6
Dec	124.8	99.1	137.5	134.4	120.0	161.0	99.4	155.1
2003: Jan	127.5	104.1	139.2	136.7	119.7	160.8	106.5	158.0
Feb	128.2	104.6	139.9	139.3	119.6	162.2	114.9	162.2
Mar	128.1	104.0	140.1	143.6	119.7	162.3	129.6	164.5
Apr	129.0	105.6	140.7	138.2	119.7	162.8	110.0	162.2
May	130.7	109.2	141.4	137.8	119.9	161.0	108.5	162.1
June	131.2	107.3	143.2	139.2	119.7	160.8	114.3	162.2
July	130.3	105.5	142.7	139.1	119.6	160.8	114.0	160.9
Aug[2]	132.1	109.0	143.6	139.1	119.9	161.9	113.7	161.2
Sep	136.1	116.1	145.0	139.2	119.5	162.8	113.1	161.2
Oct	141.1	124.1	148.5	139.3	119.7	163.8	111.1	161.9
Nov	140.3	124.0	148.3	138.7	119.7	163.9	108.5	162.4
Dec	139.8	124.2	147.3	139.4	119.5	164.6	110.6	163.3

[1] Prices for some items in this grouping are lagged and refer to 1 month earlier than the index month.
[2] Data have been revised through August 2003; data are subject to revision 4 months after date of original publication.

See next page for continuation of table.

TABLE B–67.—*Producer price indexes for major commodity groups, 1959–2003*—Continued

[1982=100]

Year or month	Rubber and plastic products	Lumber and wood products	Pulp, paper, and allied products	Metals and metal products	Machinery and equipment	Furniture and household durables	Non-metallic mineral products	Transportation equipment		Miscellaneous products
								Total	Motor vehicles and equipment	
1959	42.6	34.7	33.7	30.6	32.8	48.0	30.3	....	39.9	33.4
1960	42.7	33.5	34.0	30.6	33.0	47.8	30.4	....	39.3	33.6
1961	41.1	32.0	33.0	30.5	33.0	47.5	30.5	....	39.2	33.7
1962	39.9	32.2	33.4	30.2	33.0	47.2	30.5	....	39.2	33.9
1963	40.1	32.8	33.1	30.3	33.1	46.9	30.3	....	38.9	34.2
1964	39.6	33.5	33.0	31.1	33.3	47.1	30.4	....	39.1	34.4
1965	39.7	33.7	33.3	32.0	33.7	46.8	30.4	....	39.2	34.7
1966	40.5	35.2	34.2	32.8	34.7	47.4	30.7	....	39.2	35.3
1967	41.4	35.1	34.6	33.2	35.9	48.3	31.2	....	39.8	36.2
1968	42.8	39.8	35.0	34.0	37.0	49.7	32.4	....	40.9	37.0
1969	43.6	44.0	36.0	36.0	38.2	50.7	33.6	40.4	41.7	38.1
1970	44.9	39.9	37.5	38.7	40.0	51.9	35.3	41.9	43.3	39.8
1971	45.2	44.7	38.1	39.4	41.4	53.1	38.2	44.2	45.7	40.8
1972	45.3	50.7	39.3	40.9	42.3	53.8	39.4	45.5	47.0	41.5
1973	46.6	62.2	42.3	44.0	43.7	55.7	40.7	46.1	47.4	43.3
1974	56.4	64.5	52.5	57.0	50.0	61.8	47.8	50.3	51.4	48.1
1975	62.2	62.1	59.0	61.5	57.9	67.5	54.4	56.7	57.6	53.4
1976	66.0	72.2	62.1	65.0	61.3	70.3	58.2	60.5	61.2	55.6
1977	69.4	83.0	64.6	69.3	65.2	73.2	62.6	64.6	65.2	59.4
1978	72.4	96.9	67.7	75.3	70.3	77.5	69.6	69.5	70.0	66.7
1979	80.5	105.5	75.9	86.0	76.7	82.8	77.6	75.3	75.8	75.5
1980	90.1	101.5	86.3	95.0	86.0	90.7	88.4	82.9	83.1	93.6
1981	96.4	102.8	94.8	99.6	94.4	95.9	96.7	94.3	94.6	96.1
1982	100.0	100.0	100.0	100.0	100.0	100.0	100.0	100.0	100.0	100.0
1983	100.8	107.9	103.3	101.8	102.7	103.4	101.6	102.8	102.2	104.8
1984	102.3	108.0	110.3	104.8	105.1	105.7	105.4	105.2	104.1	107.0
1985	101.9	106.6	113.3	104.4	107.2	107.1	108.6	107.9	106.4	109.4
1986	101.9	107.2	116.1	103.2	108.8	108.2	110.0	110.5	109.1	111.6
1987	103.0	112.8	121.8	107.1	110.4	109.9	110.0	112.5	111.7	114.9
1988	109.3	118.9	130.4	118.7	113.2	113.1	111.2	114.3	113.1	120.2
1989	112.6	126.7	137.8	124.1	117.4	116.9	112.6	117.7	116.2	126.5
1990	113.6	129.7	141.2	122.9	120.7	119.2	114.7	121.5	118.2	134.2
1991	115.1	132.1	142.9	120.2	123.0	121.2	117.2	126.4	122.1	140.8
1992	115.1	146.6	145.2	119.2	123.4	122.2	117.3	130.4	124.9	145.3
1993	116.0	174.0	147.3	119.2	124.0	123.7	120.0	133.7	128.0	145.4
1994	117.6	180.0	152.5	124.8	125.1	126.1	124.2	137.2	131.4	141.9
1995	124.3	178.1	172.2	134.5	126.6	128.2	129.0	139.7	133.0	145.4
1996	123.8	176.1	168.7	131.0	126.5	130.4	131.0	141.7	134.1	147.7
1997	123.2	183.8	167.9	131.8	125.9	130.8	133.2	141.6	132.7	150.9
1998	122.6	179.1	171.7	127.8	124.9	131.3	135.4	141.2	131.4	156.0
1999	122.5	183.6	174.1	124.6	124.3	131.7	138.9	141.8	131.7	166.6
2000	125.5	178.2	183.7	128.1	124.0	132.6	142.5	143.8	132.3	170.8
2001	127.2	174.4	184.8	125.4	123.7	133.2	144.3	145.2	131.5	181.3
2002	126.8	173.3	185.9	125.9	122.9	133.5	146.2	144.6	129.9	182.4
2003	130.1	177.5	190.0	129.2	122.0	133.8	148.1	145.6	129.5	179.7
2002: Jan	126.4	171.7	184.7	123.7	123.3	133.5	145.7	145.4	131.1	182.0
Feb	125.8	173.0	184.4	124.0	123.3	133.4	145.3	145.8	131.7	181.8
Mar	126.0	175.3	184.4	124.5	123.4	133.2	145.1	145.3	131.0	181.4
Apr	126.2	175.6	184.9	125.0	123.2	133.2	145.7	145.1	130.6	183.0
May	126.6	174.4	184.9	125.6	123.0	133.1	146.4	144.5	130.0	182.9
June	127.1	173.3	185.6	126.4	122.9	133.4	146.5	144.4	129.7	183.0
July	126.7	173.3	186.2	126.8	122.7	133.8	146.4	143.0	127.8	183.0
Aug	127.1	173.8	186.6	126.6	122.7	133.7	146.6	142.5	127.0	182.9
Sept	127.8	173.0	186.8	127.1	122.7	133.8	146.7	142.5	127.0	183.2
Oct	127.8	172.3	187.2	127.0	122.5	133.9	146.7	146.4	132.0	183.2
Nov	127.3	171.8	187.5	127.3	122.5	133.9	146.5	145.5	130.7	183.1
Dec	127.3	171.8	187.4	127.2	122.3	133.5	146.3	144.8	129.8	179.1
2003: Jan	127.8	171.7	188.5	127.6	122.3	133.7	146.8	145.3	129.9	179.5
Feb	128.7	173.2	188.8	128.3	122.1	133.6	147.5	145.5	130.0	179.5
Mar	129.9	172.6	189.1	128.5	122.1	133.6	147.8	146.9	131.7	179.9
Apr	130.9	172.9	189.6	128.2	122.1	133.8	148.5	144.9	128.9	179.1
May	131.0	173.1	189.9	128.3	122.1	133.9	148.4	144.8	128.8	179.1
June	130.5	173.8	190.2	128.3	122.0	134.0	148.2	144.3	127.8	179.3
July	130.4	176.9	190.3	128.4	121.9	134.1	148.2	144.3	127.5	179.0
Aug [2]	130.5	177.8	190.4	129.0	121.8	133.9	148.3	144.6	127.7	179.3
Sept	130.5	184.4	190.7	129.6	122.0	133.7	148.4	144.0	126.8	179.7
Oct	130.4	184.3	190.8	130.2	121.9	134.1	148.1	148.3	132.6	180.4
Nov	130.3	185.2	191.1	131.2	121.7	134.0	148.6	147.8	131.9	180.7
Dec	130.8	184.0	190.9	132.8	121.6	133.8	148.8	147.2	131.0	180.7

Source: Department of Labor, Bureau of Labor Statistics.

TABLE B–68.—*Changes in producer price indexes for finished goods, 1965–2003*

[Percent change]

Year or month	Total finished goods		Finished consumer foods		Finished goods excluding consumer foods						Finished energy goods		Finished goods excluding foods and energy	
					Total		Consumer goods		Capital equipment					
	Dec. to Dec.¹	Year to year	Dec. to Dec.¹	Year to year	Dec. to Dec.¹	Year to year	Dec. to Dec.¹	Year to year	Dec. to Dec.¹	Year to year	Dec. to Dec.¹	Year to year	Dec. to Dec.¹	Year to year
1965	3.3	1.8	9.1	4.0			0.9	0.9	1.5	1.2				
1966	2.0	3.2	1.3	6.5			1.8	1.5	3.8	2.4				
1967	1.7	1.1	-.3	-1.8			2.0	1.8	3.1	3.5				
1968	3.1	2.8	4.6	3.9	2.5	2.6	2.0	2.3	3.0	3.4				
1969	4.9	3.8	8.1	6.0	3.3	2.8	2.8	2.3	4.8	3.5				
1970	2.1	3.4	-2.3	3.3	4.3	3.5	3.8	3.0	4.8	4.7				
1971	3.3	3.1	5.8	1.6	2.0	3.7	2.1	3.5	2.4	4.0				
1972	3.9	3.2	7.9	5.4	2.3	2.0	2.1	1.8	2.1	2.6				
1973	11.7	9.1	22.7	20.5	6.6	4.0	7.5	4.6	5.1	3.3				
1974	18.3	15.4	12.8	14.0	21.1	16.2	20.3	17.0	22.7	14.3			17.7	11.4
1975	6.6	10.6	5.6	8.4	7.2	12.1	6.8	10.4	8.1	15.2	16.3	17.2	6.0	11.4
1976	3.8	4.5	-2.5	-.3	6.2	6.2	6.0	6.2	6.5	6.7	11.6	11.7	5.7	5.7
1977	6.7	6.4	6.9	5.3	6.8	7.1	6.7	7.3	7.2	6.4	12.0	15.7	6.2	6.0
1978	9.3	7.9	11.7	9.0	8.3	7.2	8.5	7.1	8.0	7.9	8.5	6.5	8.4	7.5
1979	12.8	11.2	7.4	9.3	14.8	11.8	17.6	13.3	8.8	8.7	58.1	35.0	9.4	8.9
1980	11.8	13.4	7.5	5.8	13.4	16.2	14.1	18.5	11.4	10.7	27.9	49.2	10.8	11.2
1981	7.1	9.2	1.5	5.8	8.7	10.3	8.6	10.3	9.2	10.3	14.1	19.1	7.7	8.6
1982	3.6	4.1	2.0	2.2	4.2	4.6	4.2	4.1	3.9	5.7	-.1	-1.5	4.9	5.7
1983	.6	1.6	2.3	1.0	0	1.8	-.9	1.2	2.0	2.8	-9.2	-4.8	1.9	3.0
1984	1.7	2.1	3.5	4.4	1.1	1.4	.8	1.0	1.8	2.3	-4.2	-4.2	2.0	2.4
1985	1.8	1.0	.6	-.8	2.2	1.4	2.1	1.1	2.7	2.2	-.2	-3.9	2.7	2.5
1986	-2.3	-1.4	2.8	2.6	-4.0	-2.6	-6.6	-4.6	2.1	2.0	-38.1	-28.1	2.7	2.3
1987	2.2	2.1	-.2	2.1	3.2	2.1	4.1	2.2	1.3	1.8	11.2	-1.9	2.1	2.4
1988	4.0	2.5	5.7	2.8	3.2	2.4	3.1	2.4	3.6	2.3	-3.6	-3.2	4.3	3.3
1989	4.9	5.2	5.2	5.4	4.8	5.0	5.3	5.6	3.8	3.9	9.5	9.9	4.2	4.4
1990	5.7	4.9	2.6	4.8	6.9	5.0	8.7	5.9	3.4	3.5	30.7	14.2	3.5	3.7
1991	-.1	2.1	-1.5	-.2	.3	3.0	-.7	2.9	2.5	3.1	-9.6	4.1	3.1	3.6
1992	1.6	1.2	1.6	-.6	1.6	1.8	1.6	1.8	1.7	1.9	-.3	-.4	2.0	2.4
1993	.2	1.2	2.4	1.9	-.4	1.1	-1.4	.7	1.8	1.8	-4.1	.3	.4	1.2
1994	1.7	.6	1.1	.9	1.9	.6	2.0	-.1	2.0	2.1	3.5	-1.3	1.6	1.0
1995	2.3	1.9	1.9	1.7	2.3	1.9	2.3	2.0	2.2	1.9	1.1	1.4	2.6	2.1
1996	2.8	2.7	3.4	3.6	2.6	2.4	3.7	2.9	.4	1.2	11.7	6.5	.6	1.4
1997	-1.2	.4	-.8	.7	-1.2	.3	-1.5	.5	-.6	-.1	-6.4	.2	0	.3
1998	0	-.8	.1	-.1	-.1	-1.1	-.1	-1.4	0	-.4	-11.7	-10.0	2.5	.9
1999	2.9	1.8	.8	.6	3.5	2.2	5.1	3.2	.3	0	18.1	4.9	.9	1.7
2000	3.6	3.8	1.7	1.6	4.1	4.4	5.5	6.1	1.2	.9	16.6	19.4	1.3	1.3
2001	-1.6	2.0	1.8	3.0	-2.6	1.7	-3.9	2.2	0	.6	-17.1	2.8	.9	1.4
2002	1.2	-1.3	-.6	-.8	1.7	-1.5	2.9	-1.8	-.6	-.4	12.3	-8.2	-.5	.1
2003	4.0	3.2	7.7	4.2	3.0	3.0	3.9	4.2	.9	.4	11.5	14.9	1.0	.2

	Percent change from preceding month													
	Unadjusted	Seasonally adjusted	Unadjusted	Seasonally adjusted	Unadjusted	Seasonally adjusted	Unadjusted	Seasonally adjusted	Unadjusted	Seasonally adjusted	Unadjusted	Seasonally adjusted	Unadjusted	Seasonally adjusted
2002: Jan	0	0	0.5	0.5	-0.1	-0.1	0	-0.1	-0.1	-0.1	0.6	-0.2	-0.2	-0.1
Feb	.2	.3	.9	1.1	0	.1	0	.1	.1	0	0	.6	0	0
Mar	.7	.8	.8	.6	.7	.8	1.1	1.3	-.2	0	4.6	4.6	-.1	-.1
Apr	.1	-.1	-2.9	-2.9	.9	.7	1.5	1.1	-.1	-.2	4.5	3.1	.1	.1
May	-.1	-.4	.1	-.3	-.2	-.5	-.2	-.7	-.1	-.1	-.5	-2.3	-.1	0
June	.3	.1	.3	.2	.3	.1	.5	.2	-.1	-.1	1.6	.1	0	.1
July	-.1	0	0	-.1	-.2	-.1	-.1	.1	-.4	-.3	.8	1.1	-.5	-.3
Aug	0	0	-.4	-.4	.1	.2	.1	.3	-.1	-.1	.9	1.4	-.1	.1
Sep	.2	.3	-.4	-.4	.4	.4	.6	.6	.1	.3	1.9	1.2	.1	.3
Oct	1.2	.8	.4	.4	1.3	.9	1.4	1.2	1.2	.2	1.6	3.4	1.2	.3
Nov	-.7	-.3	0	.4	-.9	-.4	-1.2	-.6	-.3	-.1	-3.4	-1.6	-.3	-.1
Dec	-.5	-.3	.2	.4	-.6	-.4	-.9	-.6	-.3	-.2	-.7	.2	-.7	-.6
2003: Jan	1.3	1.4	1.8	1.9	1.2	1.2	1.7	1.6	.1	.3	5.1	4.6	.3	.3
Feb	1.1	1.1	.2	.4	1.3	1.4	2.0	2.2	-.1	-.1	6.7	7.4	-.1	-.1
Mar	1.3	1.4	.4	.2	1.5	1.6	2.1	2.1	.5	.6	5.6	5.4	.5	.7
Apr	-1.5	-1.7	.8	.8	-1.9	-2.3	-2.6	-3.1	-.6	-.6	-6.9	-8.1	-.7	-.7
May	-.1	-.4	.4	.1	-.3	-.5	-.5	-.3	-.8	-.1	-1.1	-2.9	0	-.1
June	.7	.5	.4	.3	.8	.6	1.1	.8	-.1	0	4.2	2.9	-.1	-.1
July	0	.1	-.2	-.3	0	.2	.1	.3	0	.1	.3	.7	0	.1
Aug[2]	.5	.6	1.0	.9	.4	.5	.4	.6	.2	.3	1.3	1.6	-.1	0
Sept	.1	.2	1.1	1.0	-.1	-.1	-.1	-.1	-.1	0	.3	-.3	-.1	0
Oct	1.1	.8	2.1	2.2	.8	.4	.6	.3	1.4	.6	-1.7	-.1	1.5	.1
Nov	-.7	-.3	-.5	-.3	-.7	-.3	-1.0	-.3	-.3	-.1	-2.8	-1.2	-.2	-.1
Dec	0	.3	.1	.2	0	.3	.1	.5	-.2	-.1	.8	1.8	-.2	-.1

¹ Changes from December to December are based on unadjusted indexes.
² Data have been revised through August 2003; data are subject to revision 4 months after date of original publication.

Source: Department of Labor, Bureau of Labor Statistics.

TABLE B–69.—*Money stock and debt measures, 1959–2003*

[Averages of daily figures, except debt end-of-period basis; billions of dollars, seasonally adjusted]

Year and month	M1 — Sum of currency, demand deposits, travelers checks, and other checkable deposits (OCDs)	M2 — M1 plus retail MMMF balances, savings deposits (including MMDAs), and small time deposits	M3 — M2 plus large time deposits, RPs, Euro-dollars, and institution-only MMMF balances	Debt [1] — Debt of domestic nonfinancial sectors	Percent change — From year or 6 months earlier [2] — M1	M2	M3	From previous period [3] — Debt
December:								
1959	140.0	297.8	299.7	689.5	....	....	....	7.8
1960	140.7	312.4	315.2	724.3	0.5	4.9	5.2	5.0
1961	145.2	335.5	340.8	767.8	3.2	7.4	8.1	6.0
1962	147.8	362.7	371.3	820.6	1.8	8.1	8.9	6.9
1963	153.3	393.2	405.9	876.1	3.7	8.4	9.3	6.8
1964	160.3	424.7	442.4	940.0	4.6	8.0	9.0	7.3
1965	167.8	459.2	482.1	1,007.2	4.7	8.1	9.0	7.1
1966	172.0	480.2	505.4	1,074.7	2.5	4.6	4.8	6.7
1967	183.3	524.8	557.9	1,152.7	6.6	9.3	10.4	7.3
1968	197.4	566.8	607.2	1,242.8	7.7	8.0	8.8	7.9
1969	203.9	587.9	615.9	1,332.3	3.3	3.7	1.4	7.2
1970	214.3	626.4	677.0	1,422.5	5.1	6.5	9.9	6.9
1971	228.2	710.1	775.9	1,557.7	6.5	13.4	14.6	9.5
1972	249.1	802.1	885.8	1,713.7	9.2	13.0	14.2	10.0
1973	262.7	855.3	984.9	1,898.2	5.5	6.6	11.2	10.7
1974	274.0	901.9	1,069.7	2,073.1	4.3	5.4	8.6	9.2
1975	286.8	1,016.0	1,169.9	2,264.7	4.7	12.7	9.4	9.3
1976	305.9	1,151.7	1,309.7	2,508.3	6.7	13.4	11.9	10.8
1977	330.5	1,269.9	1,470.1	2,829.6	8.0	10.3	12.2	12.8
1978	356.9	1,365.6	1,644.2	3,214.5	8.0	7.5	11.8	13.8
1979	381.4	1,473.3	1,808.3	3,606.5	6.9	7.9	10.0	12.2
1980	408.1	1,599.4	1,995.1	3,957.9	7.0	8.6	10.3	9.5
1981	436.2	1,754.9	2,254.0	4,366.4	6.9	9.7	13.0	10.4
1982	474.3	1,909.8	2,460.2	4,788.3	8.7	8.8	9.1	10.1
1983	520.8	2,125.9	2,697.0	5,364.8	9.8	11.3	9.6	12.0
1984	551.2	2,309.6	2,990.5	6,151.2	5.8	8.6	10.9	14.7
1985	619.1	2,494.9	3,207.6	7,132.3	12.3	8.0	7.3	15.7
1986	724.0	2,731.6	3,498.7	7,975.1	16.9	9.5	9.1	11.9
1987	749.4	2,830.6	3,685.9	8,677.6	3.5	3.6	5.4	9.0
1988	786.0	2,993.8	3,928.3	9,461.7	4.9	5.8	6.6	9.1
1989	792.1	3,157.4	4,076.0	10,166.2	.8	5.5	3.8	7.3
1990	824.1	3,277.2	4,152.1	10,850.4	4.0	3.8	1.9	6.5
1991	896.3	3,376.7	4,204.8	11,313.1	8.8	3.0	1.3	4.3
1992	1,024.3	3,430.8	4,215.8	11,831.7	14.3	1.6	.3	4.6
1993	1,129.3	3,483.3	4,277.6	12,413.5	10.3	1.5	1.5	4.8
1994	1,149.9	3,496.2	4,360.0	12,993.3	1.8	.4	1.9	4.6
1995	1,126.7	3,640.0	4,625.2	13,682.8	-2.0	4.1	6.1	5.3
1996	1,078.4	3,815.3	4,972.0	14,412.5	-4.3	4.8	7.5	5.3
1997	1,071.4	4,031.5	5,446.5	15,199.1	-.6	5.7	9.5	5.5
1998	1,094.8	4,384.4	6,036.6	16,241.1	2.2	8.8	10.8	6.9
1999	1,121.5	4,650.2	6,535.4	17,302.3	2.4	6.1	8.3	6.3
2000	1,084.7	4,932.1	7,100.5	18,165.7	-3.3	6.1	8.6	4.9
2001	1,172.9	5,445.1	8,006.2	19,302.2	8.1	10.4	12.8	6.3
2002	1,210.4	5,792.9	8,525.9	20,677.1	3.2	6.4	6.5	7.1
2003 *p*	1,287.1	6,044.6	8,806.9	....	6.3	4.3	3.3	....
2002: Jan	1,179.0	5,469.1	8,017.9	....	7.2	9.0	9.1	....
Feb	1,185.2	5,507.4	8,069.6	....	6.3	9.1	10.2	....
Mar	1,187.1	5,508.3	8,082.8	19,571.9	-2.3	4.9	6.3	5.6
Apr	1,172.6	5,494.8	8,085.0	....	1.5	4.9	5.4	....
May	1,183.3	5,557.5	8,152.4	....	3.1	5.7	5.2	....
June	1,188.9	5,587.7	8,180.9	19,939.4	2.7	5.2	4.4	7.5
July	1,195.7	5,635.5	8,227.1	....	2.8	6.1	5.2	....
Aug	1,184.5	5,673.4	8,293.7	....	-.1	6.0	5.6	....
Sept	1,191.3	5,699.1	8,335.3	20,261.4	.7	6.9	6.2	6.5
Oct	1,202.6	5,737.0	8,346.9	....	5.1	8.8	6.5	....
Nov	1,202.2	5,777.3	8,470.0	....	3.2	7.9	7.8	....
Dec	1,210.4	5,792.9	8,525.9	20,677.1	3.6	7.3	8.4	8.2
2003: Jan	1,212.8	5,821.8	8,526.0	....	2.9	6.6	7.3	....
Feb	1,233.4	5,875.0	8,572.9	....	8.3	7.1	6.7	....
Mar	1,236.7	5,887.1	8,599.4	21,011.9	7.6	6.6	6.3	6.5
Apr	1,236.9	5,910.0	8,617.6	....	5.7	6.0	6.5	....
May	1,257.8	5,998.6	8,711.7	....	9.2	7.7	5.7	....
June	1,271.9	6,047.5	8,780.2	21,595.3	10.2	8.8	6.0	11.1
July	1,277.8	6,099.5	8,916.9	....	10.7	9.5	9.2	....
Aug	1,285.8	6,143.6	8,956.5	....	8.5	9.1	8.9	....
Sept	1,288.1	6,122.4	8,953.7	21,997.0	8.3	8.0	8.2	7.4
Oct	1,286.9	6,092.1	8,896.0	....	8.1	6.2	6.5	....
Nov	1,281.8	6,071.5	8,856.1	....	3.8	2.4	3.3	....
Dec *p*	1,287.1	6,044.6	8,806.9	....	2.4	-.1	.6	....

[1] Consists of outstanding credit market debt of the U.S. Government, State and local governments, and private nonfinancial sectors.
[2] Annual changes are from December to December; monthly changes are from 6 months earlier at a simple annual rate.
[3] Annual changes are from fourth quarter to fourth quarter. Quarterly changes are from previous quarter at annual rate.
Note.—See Table B–70, for components.
Source: Board of Governors of the Federal Reserve System.

[Averages of daily figures; billions of dollars, seasonally adjusted]

Year and month	Currency	Nonbank travelers checks	Demand deposits	Other checkable deposits (OCDs)	Small denomination time deposits[1]	Savings deposits, including money market deposit accounts (MMDAs)[2]
December:						
1959	28.8	0.3	110.8	0.0	11.4	146.5
1960	28.7	.3	111.6	.0	12.5	159.1
1961	29.3	.4	115.5	.0	14.8	175.5
1962	30.3	.4	117.1	.0	20.1	194.8
1963	32.2	.4	120.6	.1	25.5	214.4
1964	33.9	.5	125.8	.1	29.2	235.2
1965	36.0	.5	131.3	.1	34.5	256.9
1966	38.0	.6	133.4	.1	55.0	253.1
1967	40.0	.6	142.5	.1	77.8	263.7
1968	43.0	.7	153.6	.1	100.5	268.9
1969	45.7	.8	157.3	.2	120.4	263.7
1970	48.6	.8	164.7	.1	151.2	261.0
1971	52.0	.9	175.1	.2	189.7	292.2
1972	56.2	1.1	191.6	.2	231.6	321.4
1973	60.8	1.2	200.3	.3	265.8	326.8
1974	67.0	1.5	205.1	.4	287.9	338.6
1975	72.8	1.9	211.3	.9	337.9	388.9
1976	79.5	2.3	221.5	2.7	390.7	453.2
1977	87.4	2.6	236.4	4.2	445.5	492.2
1978	96.0	2.9	249.5	8.5	521.0	481.9
1979	104.8	3.1	256.6	16.8	634.3	423.8
1980	115.3	3.5	261.2	28.1	728.5	400.3
1981	122.5	3.6	231.4	78.7	823.1	343.9
1982	132.5	3.6	234.1	104.1	850.9	400.1
1983	146.2	4.0	238.5	132.1	784.1	684.9
1984	156.1	4.3	243.4	147.4	888.8	704.7
1985	167.7	4.8	266.7	179.8	885.7	815.3
1986	180.4	5.2	302.7	235.6	858.4	940.9
1987	196.7	5.7	287.5	259.5	921.0	937.4
1988	212.0	6.1	287.0	280.9	1,037.1	926.4
1989	222.2	6.1	278.6	285.1	1,151.3	893.7
1990	246.5	7.0	276.9	293.7	1,173.4	922.9
1991	267.1	7.1	289.7	332.4	1,065.6	1,043.6
1992	292.2	7.6	340.0	384.6	868.1	1,186.8
1993	321.6	7.5	385.5	414.8	782.0	1,219.4
1994	354.0	8.0	383.6	404.2	816.4	1,149.8
1995	372.1	8.5	389.3	356.8	931.4	1,134.1
1996	394.1	8.3	400.3	275.7	946.8	1,273.9
1997	424.6	8.1	393.1	245.7	968.0	1,400.6
1998	459.9	8.2	377.1	249.5	951.6	1,605.2
1999	517.7	8.3	352.2	243.4	954.1	1,740.7
2000	531.5	8.0	306.9	238.2	1,044.2	1,877.2
2001	581.9	7.8	326.1	257.2	973.2	2,307.0
2002	627.3	7.5	297.0	278.6	893.2	2,762.8
2003 *p*	664.0	7.5	306.5	309.1	805.8	3,144.9
2002: Jan	587.5	7.9	325.4	258.3	961.0	2,348.4
Feb	592.2	7.8	325.7	259.5	950.0	2,398.6
Mar	595.9	7.8	323.9	259.5	940.9	2,421.5
Apr	600.0	7.7	305.8	259.1	933.3	2,450.6
May	605.0	7.8	307.1	263.4	927.5	2,499.2
June	609.5	8.2	306.2	265.0	923.5	2,531.4
July	613.7	8.5	305.1	268.4	919.3	2,568.5
Aug	616.4	8.3	290.0	269.8	914.4	2,625.8
Sept	618.3	7.9	292.7	272.4	907.3	2,664.5
Oct	620.9	7.7	299.7	274.4	902.2	2,699.6
Nov	623.6	7.5	294.5	276.6	898.1	2,743.6
Dec	627.3	7.5	297.0	278.6	893.2	2,762.8
2003: Jan	631.0	7.6	295.6	278.6	888.3	2,807.4
Feb	636.2	7.6	305.9	283.7	882.1	2,851.6
Mar	640.3	7.5	304.1	284.8	877.2	2,871.4
Apr	643.2	7.4	304.0	282.3	871.6	2,914.1
May	645.8	7.5	315.0	289.6	863.6	2,981.8
June	646.5	7.9	322.2	295.3	854.9	3,029.7
July	646.2	8.2	322.5	301.0	843.0	3,096.7
Aug	649.2	8.0	322.3	306.2	832.0	3,148.2
Sept	653.0	7.8	317.3	310.0	823.9	3,142.2
Oct	658.2	7.6	313.9	307.2	817.2	3,147.6
Nov	661.4	7.4	306.9	306.1	810.4	3,155.3
Dec *p*	664.0	7.5	306.5	309.1	805.8	3,144.9

[1] Small denomination deposits are those issued in amounts of less than $100,000.
[2] Data prior to 1982 are savings deposits only; MMDA data begin December 1982.

See next page for continuation of table.

[Averages of daily figures; billions of dollars, seasonally adjusted]

Year and month	Money market mutual fund (MMMF) balances		Large denomination time deposits[3]	Overnight and term repurchase agreements (RPs) (net)	Overnight and term Euro-dollars (net)
	Retail	Institution only			
December:					
1959	0.0	0.0	1.2	0.0	0.7
1960	.0	.0	2.0	.0	.8
1961	.0	.0	3.9	.0	1.5
1962	.0	.0	7.0	.0	1.6
1963	.0	.0	10.8	.0	1.9
1964	.0	.0	15.2	.0	2.4
1965	.0	.0	21.2	.0	1.8
1966	.0	.0	23.1	.0	2.2
1967	.0	.0	30.9	.0	2.2
1968	.0	.0	37.4	.0	2.9
1969	.0	.0	20.4	4.9	2.7
1970	.0	.0	45.2	3.0	2.4
1971	.0	.0	57.7	5.2	2.9
1972	.0	.0	73.3	6.6	3.8
1973	.1	.0	110.9	12.8	5.8
1974	1.4	.2	144.7	14.5	8.5
1975	2.4	.5	129.7	13.8	10.0
1976	1.8	.6	118.1	24.0	15.2
1977	1.8	1.0	145.2	32.2	21.7
1978	5.8	3.5	195.6	44.4	35.1
1979	33.9	10.4	223.1	48.8	52.7
1980	62.5	16.0	260.2	58.1	61.4
1981	151.7	38.2	304.3	67.8	88.8
1982	184.5	48.8	325.6	71.8	104.2
1983	136.1	40.9	316.1	97.5	116.6
1984	164.9	62.3	402.2	107.6	108.9
1985	174.9	65.3	421.7	121.5	104.2
1986	208.4	86.3	419.0	146.2	115.7
1987	222.8	93.7	461.9	178.3	121.5
1988	244.3	93.8	512.4	196.7	131.7
1989	320.3	112.3	527.9	169.0	109.4
1990	356.8	140.5	479.6	151.5	103.3
1991	370.9	189.8	414.8	131.2	92.3
1992	351.6	213.8	350.1	141.6	79.5
1993	352.6	217.0	331.8	172.6	72.8
1994	380.1	211.3	369.8	196.4	86.3
1995	447.7	264.6	428.1	198.5	94.0
1996	516.2	322.9	508.6	210.5	114.7
1997	591.5	395.8	617.7	254.0	147.5
1998	732.7	539.3	669.4	293.4	150.2
1999	833.9	634.8	744.2	335.7	170.5
2000	926.0	789.4	821.2	363.5	194.3
2001	992.0	1,191.7	785.8	375.0	208.6
2002	926.5	1,236.8	793.6	474.6	227.9
2003 ᵖ	806.8	1,102.6	884.7	493.8	281.1
2002: Jan	980.6	1,176.6	790.6	373.0	208.6
Feb	973.6	1,181.8	793.3	372.8	214.3
Mar	958.8	1,186.9	797.0	374.5	216.1
Apr	938.4	1,191.0	808.5	375.3	215.5
May	947.5	1,190.7	821.1	371.3	211.8
June	943.9	1,199.3	813.4	371.7	208.8
July	952.0	1,195.0	815.2	373.3	208.1
Aug	948.8	1,194.3	815.6	400.9	209.6
Sept	936.0	1,186.2	812.9	424.3	212.8
Oct	932.5	1,145.8	818.8	423.4	221.8
Nov	933.4	1,211.4	811.6	443.4	226.4
Dec	926.5	1,236.8	793.6	474.6	227.9
2003: Jan	913.3	1,201.0	802.9	466.3	234.0
Feb	907.8	1,181.2	800.6	480.9	235.2
Mar	901.7	1,168.5	805.2	499.4	239.3
Apr	887.4	1,146.8	804.9	509.3	246.6
May	895.4	1,127.9	808.2	517.5	259.5
June	890.9	1,147.6	805.8	520.2	259.1
July	882.0	1,188.4	865.7	496.2	267.1
Aug	877.7	1,170.4	871.1	494.3	277.2
Sept	868.2	1,179.6	876.5	498.5	276.7
Oct	840.4	1,149.1	865.4	505.9	283.4
Nov	824.0	1,125.1	869.8	507.7	281.9
Dec ᵖ	806.8	1,102.6	884.7	493.8	281.1

[3] Large denomination deposits are those issued in amounts of more than $100,000.

Note.—See also Table B–69.

Source: Board of Governors of the Federal Reserve System.

TABLE B-71.—Aggregate reserves of depository institutions and the monetary base, 1959–2003

[Averages of daily figures [1]; millions of dollars; seasonally adjusted, except as noted]

Year and month	Adjusted for changes in reserve requirements [2] Reserves of depository institutions				Mone-tary base	Borrowings of depository institutions from the Federal Reserve (NSA)				Adjust-ment
	Total	Nonbor-rowed	Required	Execess (NSA)		Total	Primary	Secondary	Seasonal	
December:										
1959	11,109	10,168	10,603	506	40,880	941				941
1960	11,247	11,172	10,503	743	40,977	74				74
1961	11,499	11,366	10,915	584	41,853	133				133
1962	11,604	11,344	11,033	572	42,957	260				260
1963	11,730	11,397	11,239	490	45,003	332				332
1964	12,011	11,747	11,605	406	47,161	264				264
1965	12,316	11,872	11,892	423	49,620	444				444
1966	12,223	11,690	11,884	339	51,565	532				532
1967	13,180	12,952	12,805	375	54,579	228				228
1968	13,767	13,021	13,341	426	58,357	746				746
1969	14,168	13,049	13,882	286	61,569	1,119				1,119
1970	14,558	14,225	14,309	249	65,013	332				332
1971	15,230	15,104	15,049	182	69,108	126				126
1972	16,645	15,595	16,361	284	75,167	1,050				1,050
1973	17,021	15,723	16,717	304	81,073	1,298			41	1,257
1974	17,550	16,823	17,292	258	87,535	727			32	548
1975	17,822	17,692	17,556	266	93,887	130			14	104
1976	18,388	18,335	18,115	274	101,515	53			13	40
1977	18,990	18,420	18,800	190	110,324	569			55	514
1978	19,753	18,885	19,521	232	120,445	868			135	734
1979	20,720	19,248	20,279	442	131,143	1,473			82	1,390
1980	22,015	20,325	21,501	514	142,004	1,690			116	1,571
1981	22,443	21,807	22,124	319	149,021	636			54	433
1982	23,600	22,966	23,100	500	160,127	634			33	415
1983	25,367	24,593	24,806	561	175,467	774			96	676
1984	26,896	23,710	26,061	835	187,241	3,186			113	469
1985	31,541	30,223	30,478	1,063	203,540	1,318			56	763
1986	38,841	38,015	37,668	1,173	223,430	827			38	486
1987	38,918	38,141	37,899	1,019	239,846	777			93	201
1988	40,428	38,712	39,366	1,061	256,866	1,716			130	342
1989	40,430	40,164	39,489	941	267,669	265			84	162
1990	41,699	41,374	40,035	1,664	293,267	326			76	227
1991	45,451	45,258	44,461	989	317,507	192			38	153
1992	54,332	54,208	53,178	1,154	350,754	124			18	105
1993	60,460	60,378	59,390	1,070	386,462	82			31	51
1994	59,369	59,160	58,209	1,159	418,194	209			100	109
1995	56,430	56,173	55,140	1,290	434,400	257			40	217
1996	50,149	49,994	48,733	1,416	451,921	155			68	87
1997	46,848	46,523	45,163	1,685	479,838	324			79	245
1998	45,141	45,024	43,627	1,514	513,708	117			15	101
1999	41,809	41,488	40,512	1,297	593,155	3 320			67	179
2000	38,537	38,327	37,110	1,427	584,765	210			111	99
2001	41,243	41,177	39,595	1,649	635,617	67			33	34
2002	40,217	40,138	38,208	2,009	681,899	80			45	35
2003	43,020	42,974	41,359	1,661	721,040	46	17	0	29	
2002: Jan	41,576	41,526	40,181	1,395	641,597	50			17	33
Feb	41,335	41,305	39,964	1,371	646,583	30			17	12
Mar	40,768	40,689	39,347	1,421	649,991	79			20	59
Apr	40,635	40,565	39,424	1,211	654,077	71			50	21
May	39,406	39,294	38,145	1,261	657,784	112			105	7
June	39,469	39,327	38,231	1,238	662,317	142			136	6
July	39,679	39,487	38,301	1,377	666,838	191			176	16
Aug	39,961	39,628	38,353	1,608	669,833	333			185	148
Sept	39,209	38,980	37,722	1,486	671,399	229			169	60
Oct	39,171	39,028	37,636	1,535	674,250	143			120	23
Nov	39,760	39,489	38,122	1,638	677,611	272			60	211
Dec	40,217	40,138	38,208	2,009	681,899	80			45	35
2003: Jan	40,731	40,704	39,024	1,707	685,725	27	12	0	13	2
Feb	40,820	40,795	38,855	1,965	691,300	25	21	0	5	
Mar	40,973	40,951	39,337	1,636	695,141	22	14	0	8	
Apr	40,806	40,777	39,274	1,532	698,221	29	8	0	21	
May	40,986	40,931	39,367	1,619	701,177	55	3	0	53	
June	42,795	42,634	40,942	1,854	703,172	161	87	0	74	
July	43,927	43,796	42,003	1,924	703,534	130	21	0	110	
Aug	46,282	45,954	42,519	3,763	709,233	329	168	15	146	
Sept	44,963	44,783	43,458	1,505	711,231	181	23	0	158	
Oct	43,992	43,884	42,525	1,467	715,778	107	13	0	94	
Nov	43,430	43,362	41,882	1,548	719,012	68	25	0	43	
Dec	43,020	42,974	41,359	1,661	721,040	46	17	0	29	

[1] Data are prorated averages of biweekly (maintenance period) averages of daily figures.
[2] Aggregate reserves incorporate adjustments for discontinuities associated with regulatory changes to reserve requirements. For details on aggregate reserves series see Federal Reserve Bulletin.
[3] Total includes borrowing under the terms and conditions established for the Century Date Change Special Liquidity Facility in effect from October 1, 1999 through April 7, 2000.

Note.—NSA indicates data are not seasonally adjusted.

Source: Board of Governors of the Federal Reserve System.

TABLE B-72.—Bank credit at all commercial banks, 1959-2003

[Monthly average; billions of dollars, seasonally adjusted [1]]

Year and month	Total bank credit	Securities in bank credit			Loans and leases in bank credit							
		Total securities	U.S. Treasury and agency securities	Other securities	Total loans and leases[2]	Commercial and industrial	Real estate			Consumer	Security	Other
							Total	Revolving home equity	Other			
December:												
1959	189.5	77.4	61.9	15.5	112.1	39.5	28.1	....	....	24.1	5.0	15.4
1960	197.6	79.5	63.9	15.6	118.1	42.4	28.7			26.3	5.2	15.6
1961	213.1	88.2	70.4	17.9	124.8	44.1	30.2			27.6	6.1	16.8
1962	231.0	92.2	70.7	21.5	138.8	47.7	34.0			30.3	6.6	20.2
1963	250.7	92.6	67.4	25.2	158.1	52.5	38.9			34.2	7.9	24.6
1964	270.4	94.7	66.7	28.1	175.6	58.7	43.5			39.5	8.3	25.7
1965	297.1	96.1	64.3	31.9	201.0	69.5	48.9			45.0	8.0	29.7
1966	318.6	97.2	61.0	36.2	221.4	79.3	53.8			47.7	8.3	32.4
1967	350.5	111.4	70.7	40.6	239.2	86.5	58.2			51.2	9.6	33.8
1968	390.5	121.9	73.8	48.1	268.6	96.5	64.8			57.7	10.5	39.2
1969	401.6	112.4	64.2	48.2	289.2	106.9	69.9			62.6	10.0	39.8
1970	434.4	129.7	73.4	56.3	304.6	111.6	72.9			65.3	10.4	44.5
1971	485.2	147.5	79.8	67.7	337.6	118.0	81.7			73.3	10.9	53.9
1972	555.3	160.6	85.4	75.2	394.7	133.6	98.8			85.4	14.4	62.5
1973	638.6	168.4	89.7	78.7	470.1	162.8	119.4		119.4	98.3	11.2	78.4
1974	701.7	173.8	87.9	85.9	527.9	193.0	132.5		132.5	102.1	10.6	89.6
1975	732.9	206.7	117.9	88.9	526.2	184.3	137.2		137.2	104.6	12.7	87.5
1976	790.7	228.6	137.3	91.3	562.1	186.3	151.3		151.3	115.9	17.7	91.0
1977	876.0	236.3	137.4	98.9	639.7	205.8	178.0		178.0	138.1	20.7	97.2
1978	989.4	242.2	138.4	103.8	747.2	239.0	213.5		213.5	164.6	19.1	110.9
1979	1,111.4	260.7	147.2	113.4	850.7	282.2	245.0		245.0	184.5	17.4	121.6
1980	1,207.1	296.8	173.2	123.6	910.3	314.5	265.7		265.7	179.2	17.2	133.6
1981	1,302.7	311.1	181.8	129.3	991.6	353.3	287.5		287.5	182.7	20.2	148.0
1982	1,412.3	338.6	204.7	133.9	1,073.7	396.4	303.8		303.8	188.2	23.6	161.7
1983	1,566.7	403.8	263.4	140.4	1,163.0	419.1	334.8		334.8	213.2	26.5	169.4
1984	1,733.4	406.6	262.9	143.7	1,326.9	479.4	380.8		380.8	253.6	34.1	179.0
1985	1,922.2	455.9	273.8	182.2	1,466.3	506.5	431.0		431.0	294.5	42.9	191.4
1986	2,106.6	510.0	312.8	197.2	1,596.5	544.0	499.9		499.9	314.5	38.6	199.5
1987	2,255.3	535.0	338.9	196.1	1,720.2	575.0	595.7	32.2	563.5	327.7	34.8	187.0
1988	2,434.7	562.2	366.6	195.6	1,872.5	611.6	678.0	42.6	635.5	354.8	40.3	187.7
1989	2,604.2	585.1	400.0	185.1	2,019.1	642.6	771.0	53.5	717.5	375.4	40.9	189.3
1990	2,751.5	635.1	456.3	178.8	2,116.4	645.5	858.2	66.3	791.9	380.9	44.6	187.2
1991	2,857.7	747.0	566.8	180.3	2,110.7	623.3	884.3	74.3	810.0	364.1	53.9	185.0
1992	2,956.7	843.1	666.2	176.9	2,113.6	599.4	907.3	78.4	828.9	356.4	63.4	187.1
1993	3,116.0	917.9	733.1	184.8	2,198.0	590.3	948.3	78.0	870.3	387.6	86.5	185.3
1994	3,322.4	942.6	724.2	218.4	2,379.8	650.3	1,012.1	80.5	931.7	448.3	75.9	193.3
1995	3,605.1	986.7	703.7	283.0	2,618.3	723.8	1,091.0	84.4	1,006.5	491.5	83.3	228.7
1996	3,757.2	981.9	701.8	280.1	2,775.3	784.9	1,142.4	90.8	1,051.6	513.2	75.4	259.5
1997	4,101.3	1,096.6	755.2	341.4	3,004.7	854.5	1,245.5	104.9	1,140.6	503.0	94.6	307.2
1998	4,537.4	1,236.1	797.6	438.5	3,301.3	948.0	1,336.3	103.8	1,232.5	497.3	145.8	313.9
1999	4,769.2	1,281.4	814.6	466.8	3,487.8	999.8	1,475.5	101.5	1,374.0	491.2	150.4	370.8
2000	5,223.8	1,346.8	791.8	555.0	3,877.0	1,088.4	1,656.0	130.0	1,526.1	540.1	177.2	415.3
2001	5,434.1	1,491.8	852.4	639.4	3,942.4	1,029.0	1,784.4	155.5	1,628.8	557.5	145.6	426.0
2002	5,889.4	1,718.4	1,028.1	690.4	4,171.0	964.0	2,028.5	213.4	1,815.1	588.0	188.8	401.7
2003	6,247.6	1,850.6	1,100.5	750.1	4,397.0	897.7	2,217.0	280.9	1,936.1	635.1	196.6	450.6
2002:Jan	5,413.9	1,482.8	835.4	647.4	3,931.0	1,019.2	1,782.4	158.6	1,623.8	560.3	151.8	417.3
Feb	5,420.2	1,480.2	829.8	650.4	3,940.0	1,023.3	1,790.2	161.7	1,628.5	562.3	154.0	410.2
Mar	5,411.2	1,479.8	846.7	633.1	3,931.4	1,016.4	1,792.3	167.0	1,625.2	560.8	161.7	400.3
Apr	5,435.6	1,499.4	868.4	630.9	3,936.2	1,005.6	1,796.8	171.1	1,625.6	565.3	168.3	400.3
May	5,484.3	1,529.1	889.7	639.4	3,955.2	998.4	1,819.6	178.6	1,641.1	568.5	170.0	398.7
June	5,528.9	1,559.6	908.7	650.9	3,969.4	990.0	1,842.6	185.2	1,657.4	567.8	169.6	399.4
July	5,580.9	1,591.7	917.4	674.3	3,989.2	978.6	1,874.7	192.3	1,682.4	564.1	178.1	393.7
Aug	5,662.9	1,629.4	943.6	685.7	4,033.5	978.5	1,906.7	197.3	1,709.4	574.5	177.0	396.9
Sept	5,722.4	1,642.5	962.6	679.9	4,079.9	972.8	1,940.0	200.7	1,739.3	583.0	181.0	403.1
Oct	5,755.0	1,645.2	981.6	663.6	4,109.8	967.4	1,971.5	204.7	1,766.8	584.7	183.1	403.2
Nov	5,835.3	1,687.3	1,012.3	675.0	4,148.0	966.3	2,006.5	208.7	1,797.8	585.5	185.9	403.9
Dec	5,889.4	1,718.4	1,028.1	690.4	4,171.0	964.0	2,028.5	213.4	1,815.1	588.0	188.8	401.7
2003:Jan	5,881.2	1,713.6	1,029.7	683.8	4,167.6	957.4	2,046.8	217.6	1,829.2	591.9	171.5	399.9
Feb	5,957.2	1,756.2	1,058.4	697.8	4,201.0	951.2	2,080.0	222.7	1,857.3	591.9	177.9	400.0
Mar	5,988.8	1,769.0	1,071.1	697.9	4,219.8	945.6	2,095.2	230.5	1,864.7	587.0	190.0	400.0
Apr	6,028.1	1,782.9	1,103.5	679.4	4,245.2	945.4	2,111.1	234.8	1,876.4	584.6	187.1	416.9
May	6,140.7	1,841.4	1,134.5	706.9	4,299.3	937.2	2,134.1	238.4	1,895.7	594.5	207.8	425.9
June	6,196.6	1,868.2	1,152.1	716.2	4,328.3	924.4	2,156.9	244.8	1,912.2	600.5	209.9	436.6
July	6,201.1	1,828.6	1,116.7	711.9	4,372.5	923.7	2,195.6	249.0	1,946.6	602.2	211.3	439.7
Aug	6,190.6	1,785.6	1,079.6	706.0	4,405.0	917.1	2,242.3	253.4	1,988.9	603.4	203.7	438.4
Sept	6,198.2	1,789.7	1,064.5	725.3	4,408.5	907.2	2,259.5	258.8	2,000.8	607.9	199.1	434.7
Oct	6,178.1	1,809.6	1,080.8	728.8	4,368.5	896.8	2,238.3	265.6	1,972.6	603.0	206.7	423.8
Nov	6,217.9	1,839.2	1,101.3	738.0	4,378.7	893.0	2,222.7	273.4	1,949.3	631.7	212.4	438.6
Dec	6,247.6	1,850.6	1,100.5	750.1	4,397.0	897.7	2,217.0	280.9	1,936.1	635.1	196.6	450.6

[1] Data are prorated averages of Wednesday values for domestically chartered commercial banks, branches and agencies of foreign banks, New York State investment companies (through September 1996), and Edge Act and agreement corporations.
[2] Excludes Federal funds sold to, reverse repurchase agreements (RPs) with, and loans to commercial banks in the United States.
Source: Board of Governors of the Federal Reserve System.

TABLE B–73.—Bond yields and interest rates, 1929–2003

[Percent per annum]

Year and month	U.S. Treasury securities — Bills (new issues)[1] 3-month	6-month	Constant maturities[2] 3-year	10-year	30-year	Corporate bonds (Moody's) Aaa[3]	Baa	High-grade municipal bonds (Standard & Poor's)	New-home mortgage yields[4]	Prime rate charged by banks[5]	Discount window (Federal Reserve Bank of New York)[5][6] Primary credit	Discount rate	Federal funds rate[7]
1929						4.73	5.90	4.27		5.50-6.00		5.16	
1933	0.515					4.49	7.76	4.71		1.50-4.00		2.56	
1939	.023					3.01	4.96	2.76		1.50		1.00	
1940	.014					2.84	4.75	2.50		1.50		1.00	
1941	.103					2.77	4.33	2.10		1.50		1.00	
1942	.326					2.83	4.28	2.36		1.50		[8] 1.00	
1943	.373					2.73	3.91	2.06		1.50		[8] 1.00	
1944	.375					2.72	3.61	1.86		1.50		[8] 1.00	
1945	.375					2.62	3.29	1.67		1.50		[8] 1.00	
1946	.375					2.53	3.05	1.64		1.50		[8] 1.00	
1947	.594					2.61	3.24	2.01		1.50-1.75		1.00	
1948	1.040					2.82	3.47	2.40		1.75-2.00		1.34	
1949	1.102					2.66	3.42	2.21		2.00		1.50	
1950	1.218					2.62	3.24	1.98		2.07		1.59	
1951	1.552					2.86	3.41	2.00		2.56		1.75	
1952	1.766					2.96	3.52	2.19		3.00		1.75	
1953	1.931		2.47	2.85		3.20	3.74	2.72		3.17		1.99	
1954	.953		1.63	2.40		2.90	3.51	2.37		3.05		1.60	
1955	1.753		2.47	2.82		3.06	3.53	2.53		3.16		1.89	1.78
1956	2.658		3.19	3.18		3.36	3.88	2.93		3.77		2.77	2.73
1957	3.267		3.98	3.65		3.89	4.71	3.60		4.20		3.12	3.11
1958	1.839		2.84	3.32		3.79	4.73	3.56		3.83		2.15	1.57
1959	3.405	3.832	4.46	4.33		4.38	5.05	3.95		4.48		3.36	3.30
1960	2.928	3.247	3.98	4.12		4.41	5.19	3.73		4.82		3.53	3.22
1961	2.378	2.605	3.54	3.88		4.35	5.08	3.46		4.50		3.00	1.96
1962	2.778	2.908	3.47	3.95		4.33	5.02	3.18		4.50		3.00	2.68
1963	3.157	3.253	3.67	4.00		4.26	4.86	3.23	5.89	4.50		3.23	3.18
1964	3.549	3.686	4.03	4.19		4.40	4.83	3.22	5.83	4.50		3.55	3.50
1965	3.954	4.055	4.22	4.28		4.49	4.87	3.27	5.81	4.54		4.04	4.07
1966	4.881	5.082	5.23	4.92		5.13	5.67	3.82	6.25	5.63		4.50	5.11
1967	4.321	4.630	5.03	5.07		5.51	6.23	3.98	6.46	5.61		4.19	4.22
1968	5.339	5.470	5.68	5.65		6.18	6.94	4.51	6.97	6.30		5.16	5.66
1969	6.677	6.853	7.02	6.67		7.03	7.81	5.81	7.81	7.96		5.87	8.20
1970	6.458	6.562	7.29	7.35		8.04	9.11	6.51	8.45	7.91		5.95	7.18
1971	4.348	4.511	5.65	6.16		7.39	8.56	5.70	7.74	5.72		4.88	4.66
1972	4.071	4.466	5.72	6.21		7.21	8.16	5.27	7.60	5.25		4.50	4.43
1973	7.041	7.178	6.95	6.84		7.44	8.24	5.18	7.96	8.03		6.44	8.73
1974	7.886	7.926	7.82	7.56		8.57	9.50	6.09	8.92	10.81		7.83	10.50
1975	5.838	6.122	7.49	7.99		8.83	10.61	6.89	9.00	7.86		6.25	5.82
1976	4.989	5.266	6.77	7.61		8.43	9.75	6.49	9.00	6.84		5.50	5.04
1977	5.265	5.510	6.69	7.42	7.75	8.02	8.97	5.56	9.02	6.83		5.46	5.54
1978	7.221	7.572	8.29	8.41	8.49	8.73	9.49	5.90	9.56	9.06		7.46	7.93
1979	10.041	10.017	9.71	9.44	9.28	9.63	10.69	6.39	10.78	12.67		10.28	11.19
1980	11.506	11.374	11.55	11.46	11.27	11.94	13.67	8.51	12.66	15.27		11.77	13.36
1981	14.029	13.776	14.44	13.91	13.45	14.17	16.04	11.23	14.70	18.87		13.42	16.38
1982	10.686	11.084	12.92	13.00	12.76	13.79	16.11	11.57	15.14	14.86		11.02	12.26
1983	8.63	8.75	10.45	11.10	11.18	12.04	13.55	9.47	12.57	10.79		8.50	9.09
1984	9.58	9.80	11.89	12.44	12.41	12.71	14.19	10.15	12.38	12.04		8.80	10.23
1985	7.48	7.66	9.64	10.62	10.79	11.37	12.72	9.18	11.55	9.93		7.69	8.10
1986	5.98	6.03	7.06	7.68	7.78	9.02	10.39	7.38	10.17	8.33		6.33	6.81
1987	5.82	6.05	7.68	8.39	8.59	9.38	10.58	7.73	9.31	8.21		5.66	6.66
1988	6.69	6.92	8.26	8.85	8.96	9.71	10.83	7.76	9.19	9.32		6.20	7.57
1989	8.12	8.04	8.55	8.49	8.45	9.26	10.18	7.24	10.13	10.87		6.93	9.21
1990	7.51	7.47	8.26	8.55	8.61	9.32	10.36	7.25	10.05	10.01		6.98	8.10
1991	5.42	5.49	6.82	7.86	8.14	8.77	9.80	6.89	9.32	8.46		5.45	5.69
1992	3.45	3.57	5.30	7.01	7.67	8.14	8.98	6.41	8.24	6.25		3.25	3.52
1993	3.02	3.14	4.44	5.87	6.59	7.22	7.93	5.63	7.20	6.00		3.00	3.02
1994	4.29	4.66	6.27	7.09	7.37	7.96	8.62	6.19	7.49	7.15		3.60	4.21
1995	5.51	5.59	6.25	6.57	6.88	7.59	8.20	5.95	7.87	8.83		5.21	5.83
1996	5.02	5.09	5.99	6.44	6.71	7.37	8.05	5.75	7.80	8.27		5.02	5.30
1997	5.07	5.18	6.10	6.35	6.61	7.26	7.86	5.55	7.71	8.44		5.00	5.46
1998	4.81	4.85	5.14	5.26	5.58	6.53	7.22	5.12	7.07	8.35		4.92	5.35
1999	4.66	4.76	5.49	5.65	5.87	7.04	7.87	5.43	7.04	8.00		4.62	4.97
2000	5.85	5.92	6.22	6.03	5.94	7.62	8.36	5.77	7.52	9.23		5.73	6.24
2001	3.45	3.39	4.09	5.02	5.49	7.08	7.95	5.19	7.00	6.91		3.40	3.88
2002	1.62	1.69	3.10	4.61		6.49	7.80	5.05	6.43	4.67		1.17	1.67
2003	1.02	1.06	2.10	4.01		5.67	6.77	4.73	5.80	4.12	2.12		1.13

[1] Rate on new issues within period; bank-discount basis.

[2] Yields on the more actively traded issues adjusted to constant maturities by the Department of the Treasury. In February 2002, the Department of the Treasury discontinued publication of the 30-year series.

[3] Beginning December 7, 2001, data for corporate Aaa series are industrial bonds only.

[4] Effective rate (in the primary market) on conventional mortgages, reflecting fees and charges as well as contract rate and assuming, on the average, repayment at end of 10 years. Rates beginning January 1973 not strictly comparable with prior rates.

See next page for continuation of table.

TABLE B–73.—*Bond yields and interest rates, 1929–2003*—Continued

[Percent per annum]

Year and month	U.S. Treasury securities					Corporate bonds (Moody's)		High-grade municipal bonds (Standard & Poor's)	New-home mortgage yields[4]	Prime rate charged by banks[5]	Discount window (Federal Reserve Bank of New York)[5][6]		Federal funds rate[7]
	Bills (new issues)[1]		Constant maturities[2]										
	3-month	6-month	3-year	10-year	30-year	Aaa[3]	Baa				Primary credit	Discount rate	
										High-low	High-low	High-low	
1999:													
Jan	4.34	4.36	4.61	4.72	5.16	6.24	7.29	5.04	6.96	7.75-7.75	....	4.50-4.50	4.63
Feb	4.45	4.43	4.90	5.00	5.37	6.40	7.39	5.03	6.92	7.75-7.75	....	4.50-4.50	4.76
Mar	4.48	4.52	5.11	5.23	5.58	6.62	7.53	5.10	6.86	7.75-7.75	....	4.50-4.50	4.81
Apr	4.28	4.36	5.03	5.18	5.55	6.64	7.48	5.07	6.85	7.75-7.75	....	4.50-4.50	4.74
May	4.51	4.55	5.33	5.54	5.81	6.93	7.72	5.17	6.89	7.75-7.75	....	4.50-4.50	4.74
June	4.59	4.81	5.70	5.90	6.04	7.23	8.02	5.34	7.03	7.75-7.75	....	4.50-4.50	4.76
July	4.60	4.62	5.62	5.79	5.98	7.19	7.95	5.36	7.29	8.00-8.00	....	4.50-4.50	4.99
Aug	4.76	4.88	5.77	5.94	6.07	7.40	8.15	5.59	7.09	8.25-8.00	....	4.75-4.50	5.07
Sept	4.73	4.91	5.75	5.92	6.07	7.39	8.20	5.70	7.09	8.25-8.25	....	4.75-4.75	5.22
Oct	4.88	4.98	5.94	6.11	6.26	7.55	8.38	5.92	7.17	8.25-8.25	....	4.75-4.75	5.20
Nov	5.07	5.17	5.92	6.03	6.15	7.36	8.15	5.85	7.24	8.50-8.25	....	5.00-4.75	5.42
Dec	5.23	5.43	6.14	6.28	6.35	7.55	8.19	5.93	7.28	8.50-8.50	....	5.00-5.00	5.30
2000:													
Jan	5.34	5.52	6.49	6.66	6.63	7.78	8.33	6.10	7.45	8.50-8.50	....	5.00-5.00	5.45
Feb	5.57	5.75	6.65	6.52	6.23	7.68	8.29	6.06	7.54	8.75-8.50	....	5.25-5.00	5.73
Mar	5.72	5.85	6.53	6.26	6.05	7.68	8.37	5.89	7.60	9.00-8.75	....	5.50-5.25	5.85
Apr	5.67	5.82	6.36	5.99	5.85	7.64	8.40	5.76	7.63	9.00-9.00	....	5.50-5.50	6.02
May	5.92	6.12	6.77	6.44	6.15	7.99	8.90	6.04	7.55	9.50-9.00	....	6.00-5.50	6.27
June	5.74	6.02	6.43	6.10	5.93	7.67	8.48	5.84	7.50	9.50-9.50	....	6.00-6.00	6.53
July	5.93	5.99	6.28	6.05	5.85	7.65	8.35	5.72	7.51	9.50-9.50	....	6.00-6.00	6.54
Aug	6.11	6.09	6.17	5.83	5.72	7.55	8.26	5.63	7.54	9.50-9.50	....	6.00-6.00	6.50
Sept	6.00	5.98	6.02	5.80	5.83	7.62	8.35	5.64	7.52	9.50-9.50	....	6.00-6.00	6.52
Oct	6.10	6.04	5.85	5.74	5.80	7.55	8.34	5.65	7.53	9.50-9.50	....	6.00-6.00	6.51
Nov	6.19	6.07	5.79	5.72	5.78	7.45	8.28	5.60	7.47	9.50-9.50	....	6.00-6.00	6.51
Dec	5.83	5.70	5.26	5.24	5.49	7.21	8.02	5.30	7.40	9.50-9.50	....	6.00-6.00	6.40
2001:													
Jan	5.27	5.04	4.77	5.16	5.54	7.15	7.93	5.15	7.20	9.50-9.00	....	6.00-5.00	5.98
Feb	4.93	4.78	4.71	5.10	5.45	7.10	7.87	5.21	7.10	8.50-8.50	....	5.00-5.00	5.49
Mar	4.50	4.36	4.43	4.89	5.34	6.98	7.84	5.19	7.04	8.50-8.00	....	5.00-4.50	5.31
Apr	3.92	3.89	4.42	5.14	5.65	7.20	8.07	5.33	7.07	8.00-7.50	....	4.50-4.00	4.80
May	3.67	3.66	4.51	5.39	5.78	7.29	8.07	5.35	7.12	7.50-7.00	....	4.00-3.50	4.21
June	3.48	3.44	4.35	5.28	5.67	7.18	7.97	5.24	7.12	7.00-6.75	....	3.50-3.25	3.97
July	3.54	3.48	4.31	5.24	5.61	7.13	7.97	5.22	7.11	6.75-6.75	....	3.25-3.25	3.77
Aug	3.39	3.31	4.04	4.97	5.48	7.02	7.85	5.06	7.15	6.75-6.50	....	3.25-3.00	3.65
Sept	2.87	2.84	3.45	4.73	5.48	7.17	8.03	5.09	6.89	6.50-6.00	....	3.00-2.50	3.07
Oct	2.22	2.19	3.14	4.57	5.32	7.03	7.91	5.07	6.73	6.00-5.50	....	2.50-2.00	2.49
Nov	1.93	1.94	3.22	4.65	5.12	6.97	7.81	5.06	6.63	5.50-5.00	....	2.00-1.50	2.09
Dec	1.72	1.81	3.62	5.09	5.48	6.76	8.05	5.28	6.79	5.00-4.75	....	1.50-1.25	1.82
2002:													
Jan	1.66	1.74	3.56	5.04	5.45	6.55	7.87	5.19	6.87	4.75-4.75	....	1.25-1.25	1.73
Feb	1.73	1.83	3.55	4.91	....	6.51	7.89	5.14	6.82	4.75-4.75	....	1.25-1.25	1.74
Mar	1.81	2.02	4.14	5.28	....	6.81	8.11	5.27	6.76	4.75-4.75	....	1.25-1.25	1.73
Apr	1.72	1.97	4.01	5.21	....	6.76	8.03	5.27	6.74	4.75-4.75	....	1.25-1.25	1.75
May	1.74	1.88	3.80	5.16	....	6.75	8.09	5.22	6.59	4.75-4.75	....	1.25-1.25	1.75
June	1.71	1.83	3.49	4.93	....	6.63	7.95	5.11	6.47	4.75-4.75	....	1.25-1.25	1.75
July	1.68	1.71	3.01	4.65	....	6.53	7.90	5.01	6.37	4.75-4.75	....	1.25-1.25	1.73
Aug	1.63	1.62	2.52	4.26	....	6.37	7.58	4.92	6.26	4.75-4.75	....	1.25-1.25	1.74
Sept	1.63	1.61	2.32	3.87	....	6.15	7.40	4.73	6.17	4.75-4.75	....	1.25-1.25	1.75
Oct	1.60	1.57	2.25	3.94	....	6.32	7.73	4.85	6.09	4.75-4.75	....	1.25-1.25	1.75
Nov	1.26	1.29	2.32	4.05	....	6.31	7.62	4.98	6.08	4.75-4.25	....	1.25-0.75	1.34
Dec	1.20	1.26	2.23	4.03	....	6.21	7.45	4.91	6.04	4.25-4.25	....	0.75-0.75	1.24
2003:													
Jan	1.17	1.21	2.18	4.05	....	6.17	7.35	4.88	6.12	4.25-4.25	2.25-2.25	0.75-0.75	1.24
Feb	1.16	1.18	2.05	3.90	....	5.95	7.06	4.80	5.82	4.25-4.25	2.25-2.25	....	1.26
Mar	1.13	1.12	1.98	3.81	....	5.89	6.95	4.72	5.75	4.25-4.25	2.25-2.25	....	1.25
Apr	1.14	1.15	2.06	3.96	....	5.74	6.85	4.71	5.92	4.25-4.25	2.25-2.25	....	1.26
May	1.08	1.09	1.75	3.57	....	5.22	6.38	4.35	5.75	4.25-4.25	2.25-2.25	....	1.26
June	0.95	0.94	1.51	3.33	....	4.97	6.19	4.32	5.51	4.25-4.00	2.25-2.00	....	1.22
July	0.90	0.95	1.93	3.98	....	5.49	6.62	4.71	5.53	4.00-4.00	2.00-2.00	....	1.01
Aug	0.96	1.04	2.44	4.45	....	5.88	7.01	5.08	5.77	4.00-4.00	2.00-2.00	....	1.03
Sept	0.95	1.02	2.23	4.27	....	5.72	6.79	4.91	5.97	4.00-4.00	2.00-2.00	....	1.01
Oct	0.93	1.01	2.26	4.29	....	5.70	6.73	4.84	5.92	4.00-4.00	2.00-2.00	....	1.01
Nov	0.94	1.02	2.45	4.30	....	5.65	6.66	4.74	5.92	4.00-4.00	2.00-2.00	....	1.00
Dec	0.90	1.00	2.44	4.27	....	5.62	6.60	4.65	5.59	4.00-4.00	2.00-2.00	....	0.98

[5] For monthly data, high and low for the period. Prime rate for 1929–33 and 1947–48 are ranges of the rate in effect during the period.

[6] Discount window borrowing for primary credit and discount rate (adjustment credit). The rate for primary credit replaced the rate for adjustment credit under an amendment to the Federal Reserve Board's Regulation A, effective January 9, 2003.

[7] Since July 19, 1975, the daily effective rate is an average of the rates on a given day weighted by the volume of transactions at these rates. Prior to that date, the daily effective rate was the rate considered most representative of the day's transactions, usually the one at which most transactions occurred.

[8] From October 30, 1942, to April 24, 1946, a preferential rate of 0.50 percent was in effect for advances secured by Government securities maturing in 1 year or less.

Sources: Department of the Treasury, Board of Governors of the Federal Reserve System, Federal Housing Finance Board, Moody's Investors Service, and Standard & Poor's.

371

TABLE B–74.—*Credit market borrowing, 1994–2003*

[Billions of dollars; quarterly data at seasonally adjusted annual rates]

Item	1994	1995	1996	1997	1998	1999	2000	2001	2002
NONFINANCIAL SECTORS									
DOMESTIC	573.6	690.0	729.7	788.1	1,042.0	1,026.0	852.2	1,135.9	1,374.9
FEDERAL GOVERNMENT	155.9	144.4	144.9	23.1	−52.6	−71.2	−295.9	−5.6	257.5
Treasury securities	155.7	142.9	146.6	23.2	−54.6	−71.0	−294.9	−5.0	257.0
Budget agency securities and mortgages	.2	1.5	−1.6	−.1	2.0	−.2	−1.0	−.5	.5
NONFEDERAL, BY INSTRUMENT	417.7	545.6	584.7	765.0	1,094.6	1,097.8	1,148.1	1,141.5	1,117.4
Commercial paper	21.4	18.1	−.9	13.7	24.4	37.4	48.1	−88.3	−64.2
Municipal securities and loans ..	−35.9	−57.6	−6.5	56.9	84.2	54.4	23.6	122.9	161.0
Corporate bonds	23.3	91.1	116.3	150.5	235.2	221.7	162.6	348.5	132.3
Bank loans n.e.c.	75.2	103.7	70.4	106.4	109.8	82.9	101.8	−82.0	−87.1
Other loans and advances	36.3	52.6	22.2	43.1	68.5	26.1	84.5	5.6	18.6
Mortgages	162.6	190.6	279.7	322.4	485.5	563.3	562.4	697.1	875.5
Home	182.1	176.8	241.7	258.3	384.6	424.4	418.2	533.2	724.0
Multifamily residential	−2.7	4.6	9.9	7.2	23.1	35.2	30.1	44.4	41.1
Commercial	−19.1	7.8	25.4	53.8	71.3	98.0	107.5	112.1	101.9
Farm	2.3	1.4	2.7	3.1	6.5	5.8	6.5	7.5	8.4
Consumer credit	134.8	147.0	103.6	71.9	87.0	112.1	165.2	137.7	81.4
NONFEDERAL, BY SECTOR	417.7	545.6	584.7	765.0	1,094.6	1,097.8	1,148.1	1,141.5	1,117.4
Household sector	325.1	330.5	345.7	330.7	451.1	490.5	565.5	637.8	771.1
Nonfinancial business	138.9	276.0	254.9	392.7	575.8	568.8	567.1	397.9	200.9
Corporate	126.5	227.1	182.8	291.8	408.1	381.0	372.2	233.6	61.0
Nonfarm noncorporate	8.0	46.1	67.3	94.7	159.7	182.4	184.1	156.8	132.0
Farm	4.4	2.7	4.9	6.2	8.0	5.5	10.9	7.5	7.9
State and local governments	−46.3	−60.9	−15.9	41.5	67.7	38.5	15.5	105.8	145.5
FOREIGN BORROWING IN THE UNITED STATES	−13.9	78.5	88.4	71.8	31.2	13.0	57.0	−49.7	6.0
Commercial paper	−26.1	13.5	11.3	3.7	7.8	16.3	31.7	−14.2	36.1
Bonds	12.2	57.1	67.0	61.4	22.8	1.9	15.2	−24.5	−33.5
Bank loans n.e.c.	1.4	8.5	9.1	8.5	6.6	.5	11.4	−7.3	5.3
Other loans and advances	−1.4	−.5	1.0	−1.8	−6.0	−5.7	−1.3	−3.8	−1.9
NONFINANCIAL DOMESTIC AND FOREIGN BORROWING	559.6	768.5	818.1	859.9	1,073.2	1,039.6	909.2	1,086.2	1,381.0
FINANCIAL SECTORS									
BY INSTRUMENT	468.3	454.0	550.1	662.2	1,084.6	1,068.5	815.3	935.4	911.2
Federal Government related	287.4	204.2	231.4	212.9	470.9	592.0	433.5	629.3	554.0
Government-sponsored enterprises securities	176.9	105.9	90.4	98.4	278.3	318.2	234.1	290.8	225.9
Mortgage pool securities	115.3	98.3	141.0	114.6	192.6	273.8	199.4	338.5	328.1
U.S. Government loans	−4.8	0	0	0	0	0	0	0	0
Private financial sectors	180.9	249.8	318.7	449.3	613.7	476.5	381.8	306.1	357.2
Open market paper	40.5	42.7	92.2	166.7	161.0	176.2	131.7	−45.3	−63.5
Corporate bonds	121.8	195.9	178.1	218.9	309.2	202.4	201.8	302.1	397.0
Bank loans n.e.c.	−13.7	2.5	12.6	13.3	28.5	−14.4	−.4	13.1	1.1
Other loans and advances	22.6	3.4	27.9	35.6	90.2	107.1	42.5	34.9	16.6
Mortgages	9.8	5.3	7.9	14.9	24.8	5.1	6.2	1.3	5.9
BY SECTOR	468.3	454.0	550.1	662.2	1,084.6	1,068.5	815.3	935.4	911.2
Commercial banking	20.1	22.5	13.0	46.1	72.9	67.2	60.0	52.9	49.9
Savings institutions	12.8	2.6	25.5	19.7	52.2	48.0	27.3	7.4	−13.7
Government-sponsored enterprises	172.1	105.9	90.4	98.4	278.3	318.2	234.1	290.8	225.9
Federally related mortgage pools	115.3	98.3	141.0	114.6	192.6	273.8	199.4	338.5	328.1
Asset-backed securities issuers	76.5	142.4	150.8	202.2	320.4	207.2	195.3	293.5	256.4
Finance companies	48.7	50.2	50.6	57.8	57.1	70.7	82.0	1.5	43.1
Funding corporations	23.1	34.9	63.8	79.9	40.0	91.5	−.4	−55.2	−.6
Other [1]	−.2	−2.8	15.1	43.5	71.1	−8.0	17.6	6.0	22.0
ALL SECTORS									
BY INSTRUMENT	1,028.0	1,222.6	1,368.1	1,522.1	2,157.8	2,108.0	1,724.5	2,021.6	2,292.2
Open market paper	35.7	74.3	102.6	184.1	193.1	229.9	211.6	−147.8	−91.5
U.S. Government securities	448.0	348.6	376.3	236.0	418.3	520.7	137.6	623.8	811.5
Municipal securities and loans	−35.9	−57.6	−6.5	56.9	84.2	54.4	23.6	122.9	161.0
Corporate and foreign bonds	157.3	344.1	361.3	430.8	567.2	426.1	379.5	626.2	495.8
Bank loans n.e.c.	62.9	114.7	92.1	128.2	145.0	69.0	112.8	−76.2	−80.6
Other loans and advances	52.7	55.6	51.1	76.9	152.7	127.5	125.6	36.7	33.3
Mortgages	172.4	195.9	287.6	337.3	510.3	568.4	568.6	698.4	881.3
Consumer credit	134.8	147.0	103.6	71.9	87.0	112.1	165.2	137.7	81.4

[1] Credit unions, life insurance companies, mortgage companies, real estate investment trusts, and brokers and dealers.

See next page for continuation of table.

[Billions of dollars; quarterly data at seasonally adjusted annual rates]

Item	2002				2003		
	I	II	III	IV	I	II	III
NONFINANCIAL SECTORS							
DOMESTIC	1,078.9	1,470.2	1,287.8	1,662.8	1,339.3	2,333.6	1,606.5
FEDERAL GOVERNMENT	102.8	421.4	261.5	244.4	164.2	749.0	317.5
Treasury securities	104.6	419.6	259.9	244.0	165.8	748.5	317.5
Budget agency securities and mortgages	−1.8	1.8	1.6	.4	−1.6	.5	.1
NONFEDERAL, BY INSTRUMENT	976.1	1,048.8	1,026.3	1,418.4	1,175.1	1,584.6	1,289.0
Commercial paper	−144.4	−81.7	−17.4	−13.2	−15.2	−87.3	−1.1
Municipal securities and loans	87.4	177.2	162.1	217.3	103.1	187.2	156.7
Corporate bonds	264.4	185.1	−20.3	99.8	185.9	292.6	85.5
Bank loans n.e.c.	−38.1	−175.6	−106.2	−28.4	−83.1	−43.3	−104.8
Other loans and advances	−39.6	39.8	38.7	35.4	−24.1	−3.8	−6.3
Mortgages	731.2	799.9	889.5	1,081.3	925.4	1,125.8	1,037.7
Home	631.7	633.9	750.3	880.3	792.3	937.9	826.8
Multifamily residential	27.6	40.4	31.0	65.5	35.2	50.0	67.7
Commercial	65.0	116.5	95.2	130.8	89.2	127.0	137.4
Farm	6.9	9.1	13.0	4.7	8.7	10.9	5.9
Consumer credit	115.2	104.1	79.9	26.2	83.0	113.4	121.3
NONFEDERAL, BY SECTOR	976.1	1,048.8	1,026.3	1,418.4	1,175.1	1,584.6	1,289.0
Household sector	734.6	679.6	753.3	916.7	844.9	1,032.5	906.5
Nonfinancial business	166.7	203.0	125.3	308.4	248.7	378.1	245.2
Corporate	51.0	61.8	−17.1	148.3	128.1	229.9	58.4
Nonfarm noncorporate	110.2	132.0	128.0	158.0	113.2	145.2	180.2
Farm	5.6	9.2	14.4	2.2	7.4	2.9	6.6
State and local governments	74.8	166.2	147.7	193.2	81.5	174.1	137.3
FOREIGN BORROWING IN THE UNITED STATES	65.2	3.1	−45.9	1.8	20.0	−62.9	−68.8
Commercial paper	66.8	36.5	3.9	37.3	52.6	73.5	−55.4
Bonds	−14.5	−54.0	−35.3	−30.1	−28.9	−102.2	−4.9
Bank loans n.e.c.	13.9	22.0	−11.7	−2.9	−4.0	−31.4	−3.1
Other loans and advances	−1.0	−1.3	−2.9	−2.5	.2	−2.7	−5.4
NONFINANCIAL DOMESTIC AND FOREIGN BORROWING	1,144.1	1,473.3	1,241.8	1,664.6	1,359.3	2,270.7	1,537.7
FINANCIAL SECTORS							
BY INSTRUMENT	918.9	862.4	823.2	1,040.4	1,195.1	909.3	1,177.8
Federal Government related	703.1	484.0	425.6	603.3	531.0	502.0	831.1
Government-sponsored enterprise securities	191.3	141.7	249.1	321.5	247.5	255.8	497.4
Mortgage pool securities	511.8	342.3	176.5	281.8	283.5	246.2	333.7
U.S. Government loans	0	0	0	0	0	0	0
Private financial sectors	215.7	378.4	397.6	437.1	664.1	407.3	346.6
Open market paper	−117.7	−85.0	32.7	−83.9	1.3	−67.5	−30.4
Corporate bonds	322.8	400.9	226.5	638.0	593.2	457.7	386.0
Bank loans n.e.c.	5.8	26.2	76.2	−103.7	−35.3	15.4	13.1
Other loans and advances	−1.7	29.3	57.0	−18.1	108.4	−1.7	−28.9
Mortgages	6.6	7.0	5.3	4.7	−3.5	3.3	6.8
BY SECTOR	918.9	862.4	823.2	1,040.4	1,195.1	909.3	1,177.8
Commercial banking	26.5	22.1	68.7	82.3	78.6	30.5	1.5
Savings institutions	−33.0	−8.0	15.8	−29.6	48.8	−25.6	−28.1
Government-sponsored enterprises	191.3	141.7	249.1	321.5	247.5	255.8	497.4
Federally related mortgage pools	511.8	342.3	176.5	281.8	283.5	246.2	333.7
Asset-backed securities issuers	248.4	219.3	204.7	353.3	334.9	302.3	233.2
Finance companies	−24.0	86.7	80.4	29.6	37.7	192.3	108.5
Funding corporations	1.4	12.4	−20.0	4.0	101.0	−92.0	−19.8
Other [1]	−3.5	46.1	48.1	−2.5	63.2	−.3	51.3
ALL SECTORS							
BY INSTRUMENT	2,063.0	2,335.7	2,065.1	2,705.0	2,554.4	3,180.0	2,715.5
Open market paper	−195.3	−130.2	19.2	−59.8	38.7	−81.4	−86.9
U.S. Government securities	805.9	905.3	687.1	847.7	695.2	1,251.0	1,148.7
Municipal securities and loans	87.4	177.2	162.1	217.3	103.1	187.2	156.7
Corporate and foreign bonds	572.7	532.0	170.9	707.7	750.2	648.1	466.6
Bank loans n.e.c.	−18.3	−127.4	−41.7	−134.9	−122.4	−59.3	−94.8
Other loans and advances	−42.4	67.8	92.8	14.8	84.6	−8.2	−40.5
Mortgages	737.8	806.9	894.7	1,085.9	922.0	1,129.2	1,044.5
Consumer credit	115.2	104.1	79.9	26.2	83.0	113.4	121.3

Source: Board of Governors of the Federal Reserve System.

TABLE B–75.—*Mortgage debt outstanding by type of property and of financing, 1949–2003*

[Billions of dollars]

End of year or quarter	All proper- ties	Farm proper- ties	Nonfarm properties				Nonfarm properties by type of mortgage					
							Government underwritten				Conventional [2]	
			Total	1- to 4- family houses	Multi- family proper- ties	Com- mercial proper- ties	Total [1]	1- to 4-family houses			Total	1- to 4- family houses
								Total	FHA insured	VA guar- anteed		
1949	62.3	5.6	56.7	37.3	8.6	10.8	17.1	15.0	6.9	8.1	39.6	22.3
1950	72.7	6.0	66.6	45.1	10.1	11.5	22.1	18.8	8.5	10.3	44.6	26.2
1951	82.1	6.6	75.6	51.6	11.5	12.5	26.6	22.9	9.7	13.2	49.0	28.8
1952	91.4	7.2	84.2	58.6	12.3	13.4	29.3	25.4	10.8	14.6	55.0	33.2
1953	101.2	7.7	93.5	66.1	12.9	14.6	32.1	28.1	12.0	16.1	61.4	38.0
1954	113.7	8.1	105.6	75.8	13.5	16.3	36.2	32.1	12.8	19.3	69.4	43.7
1955	130.1	9.0	121.1	88.4	14.3	18.4	42.9	38.9	14.3	24.6	78.1	49.5
1956	144.7	9.8	134.8	99.2	14.9	20.8	47.8	43.9	15.5	28.4	87.0	55.3
1957	156.7	10.4	146.3	107.8	15.3	23.2	51.6	47.2	16.5	30.7	94.8	60.6
1958	172.0	11.1	160.9	117.9	16.8	26.2	55.2	50.1	19.7	30.4	105.8	67.8
1959	190.9	12.1	178.8	130.9	18.7	29.2	59.3	53.8	23.8	30.0	119.5	77.1
1960	207.5	12.8	194.7	141.9	20.3	32.4	62.3	56.4	26.7	29.7	132.3	85.5
1961	228.1	13.9	214.2	154.7	23.0	36.5	65.6	59.1	29.5	29.6	148.6	95.5
1962	251.6	15.2	236.4	169.4	25.8	41.2	69.4	62.2	32.3	29.9	167.1	107.3
1963	278.7	16.8	261.9	186.6	29.0	46.3	73.4	65.9	35.0	30.9	188.5	120.7
1964	306.2	18.9	287.3	203.6	33.6	50.1	77.2	69.2	38.3	30.9	210.1	134.3
1965	333.7	21.2	312.5	220.8	37.2	54.5	81.2	73.1	42.0	31.1	231.3	147.6
1966	356.9	23.1	333.8	233.3	40.3	60.3	84.1	76.1	44.8	31.3	249.7	157.2
1967	381.6	25.1	356.5	247.7	43.9	64.8	88.2	79.9	47.4	32.5	268.3	167.8
1968	411.5	27.5	383.9	265.2	47.3	71.4	93.4	84.4	50.6	33.8	290.5	180.8
1969	442.3	29.4	412.9	283.6	52.2	77.1	100.2	90.2	54.5	35.7	312.7	193.4
1970	474.4	30.5	443.9	297.8	60.1	86.0	109.2	97.3	59.9	37.3	334.7	200.6
1971	525.1	32.4	492.7	326.2	70.1	96.4	120.7	105.2	65.7	39.5	372.0	221.0
1972	598.1	35.4	562.8	366.7	82.8	113.3	131.1	113.0	68.2	44.7	431.7	253.8
1973	673.4	39.8	633.6	407.9	93.2	132.6	135.0	116.2	66.2	50.0	498.6	291.6
1974	734.0	44.9	689.1	440.7	100.0	148.3	140.2	121.3	65.1	56.2	548.8	319.4
1975	793.5	49.9	743.7	482.0	100.7	161.0	147.0	127.7	66.1	61.6	596.7	354.2
1976	880.3	55.4	824.9	544.8	105.9	174.2	154.0	133.5	66.5	67.0	670.9	411.3
1977	1,012.0	63.8	948.2	640.6	114.3	193.3	161.7	141.6	68.0	73.6	786.4	499.0
1978	1,164.6	72.8	1,091.9	752.2	125.2	214.5	176.4	153.4	71.4	82.0	915.5	598.8
1979	1,330.0	86.8	1,243.3	868.8	135.0	239.4	199.0	172.9	81.0	92.0	1,044.3	695.9
1980	1,464.8	97.5	1,367.3	966.2	141.1	259.9	225.1	195.2	93.6	101.6	1,142.2	771.1
1981	1,590.1	107.2	1,482.9	1,044.1	139.2	299.7	238.9	207.6	101.3	106.2	1,244.0	836.5
1982	1,675.5	111.3	1,564.2	1,089.5	141.1	333.6	248.9	217.9	108.0	109.9	1,315.3	871.6
1983	1,869.1	113.7	1,755.3	1,211.6	154.3	389.4	279.8	248.8	127.4	121.4	1,475.5	962.8
1984	2,113.1	112.4	2,000.7	1,351.4	177.4	471.9	294.8	265.9	136.7	129.1	1,705.8	1,085.5
1985	2,376.8	105.9	2,271.0	1,523.5	205.9	541.6	328.3	288.8	153.0	135.8	1,942.7	1,234.7
1986	2,663.3	95.1	2,568.3	1,726.4	239.3	602.5	370.5	328.6	185.5	143.1	2,197.8	1,397.8
1987	3,001.5	87.7	2,913.7	1,953.6	262.1	698.0	431.4	387.9	235.5	152.4	2,482.3	1,565.7
1988	3,319.6	83.0	3,236.6	2,188.1	279.0	769.6	459.7	414.2	258.8	155.4	2,776.9	1,773.9
1989	3,591.3	80.5	3,510.8	2,421.5	289.9	799.5	486.8	440.1	282.8	157.3	3,024.0	1,981.4
1990	3,807.8	78.9	3,728.9	2,619.9	288.3	820.7	517.9	470.9	310.9	160.0	3,210.9	2,149.0
1991	3,959.8	79.2	3,880.6	2,788.6	284.9	807.1	537.2	493.3	330.6	162.7	3,343.4	2,295.3
1992	4,072.3	79.7	3,992.5	2,957.1	272.0	763.4	533.3	489.8	326.0	163.8	3,459.2	2,467.4
1993	4,208.8	80.7	4,128.1	3,119.1	269.1	739.9	513.4	469.5	303.2	166.2	3,614.7	2,649.7
1994	4,381.2	83.0	4,298.3	3,301.5	269.6	727.2	559.3	514.2	336.8	177.3	3,738.9	2,787.3
1995	4,576.8	84.6	4,492.3	3,478.2	275.5	738.5	584.3	537.1	352.3	184.7	3,908.0	2,941.2
1996	4,864.3	87.1	4,777.2	3,719.9	288.0	769.2	620.3	571.2	379.2	192.0	4,156.8	3,148.8
1997	5,201.8	90.3	5,111.5	3,978.7	301.1	831.7	656.7	605.7	405.7	200.0	4,454.8	3,373.0
1998	5,711.7	96.5	5,615.2	4,362.9	331.3	921.0	674.1	623.8	417.9	205.9	4,941.1	3,739.1
1999	6,315.1	103.0	6,212.2	4,787.2	368.4	1,056.5	731.5	678.8	462.3	216.5	5,480.7	4,108.4
2000	6,883.1	108.9	6,774.2	5,205.4	400.6	1,168.2	773.1	720.0	499.9	220.1	6,001.1	4,485.5
2001	7,581.0	116.3	7,464.7	5,738.1	445.4	1,281.2	772.7	718.5	497.4	221.2	6,692.0	5,019.6
2002	8,463.0	124.8	8,338.2	6,462.7	488.4	1,387.1	759.3	704.0	486.2	217.7	7,578.9	5,758.7
2001: I	7,010.2	110.0	6,900.2	5,301.1	409.6	1,189.5	776.6	723.1	502.8	220.3	6,123.6	4,578.0
II	7,210.0	113.0	7,097.0	5,460.8	420.6	1,215.7	772.3	718.2	497.8	220.4	6,324.7	4,742.5
III	7,400.5	114.6	7,285.9	5,605.0	432.4	1,248.5	773.7	719.7	499.3	220.4	6,512.2	4,885.3
IV	7,581.0	116.3	7,464.7	5,738.1	445.4	1,281.2	772.7	718.5	497.4	221.2	6,692.0	5,019.6
2002: I	7,747.8	118.1	7,629.7	5,877.2	452.8	1,299.6	778.5	723.9	503.5	220.4	6,851.2	5,153.4
II	7,962.6	120.5	7,842.2	6,049.6	463.5	1,329.1	781.0	726.2	508.7	217.5	7,061.2	5,323.4
III	8,196.7	123.6	8,073.1	6,247.7	471.7	1,353.7	778.3	723.7	505.9	217.8	7,294.8	5,524.1
IV	8,463.0	124.8	8,338.2	6,462.7	488.4	1,387.1	759.3	704.0	486.2	217.7	7,578.9	5,758.7
2003: I	8,672.7	126.9	8,545.8	6,640.4	496.9	1,408.5	749.9	694.3	477.8	216.5	7,795.9	5,946.1
II	8,970.6	129.7	8,841.0	6,890.4	509.6	1,440.9	730.1	673.3	457.5	215.9	8,110.8	6,217.1
III ᵖ	9,241.9	131.0	9,110.9	7,107.5	527.1	1,476.2	709.2	653.1	438.3	214.8	8,401.6	6,454.4

[1] Includes FHA insured multifamily properties, not shown separately.
[2] Derived figures. Total includes commercial properties, and multifamily properties, not shown separately.

Source: Board of Governors of the Federal Reserve System, based on data from various Government and private organizations.

TABLE B-76.—*Mortgage debt outstanding by holder, 1949-2003*

[Billions of dollars]

End of year or quarter	Total	Major financial institutions				Other holders	
		Total	Savings institutions[1]	Commercial banks[2]	Life insurance companies	Federal and related agencies[3]	Individuals and others[4]
1949	62.3	42.9	18.3	11.6	12.9	2.0	17.5
1950	72.7	51.7	21.9	13.7	16.1	2.6	18.4
1951	82.1	59.5	25.5	14.7	19.3	3.3	19.3
1952	91.4	67.0	29.8	16.0	21.3	3.9	20.4
1953	101.2	75.1	34.8	17.0	23.3	4.4	21.7
1954	113.7	85.8	41.1	18.7	26.0	4.7	23.2
1955	130.1	99.5	48.9	21.2	29.4	5.3	25.3
1956	144.7	111.4	55.5	22.9	33.0	6.2	27.1
1957	156.7	120.0	61.2	23.6	35.2	7.7	29.1
1958	172.0	131.7	68.9	25.8	37.1	8.0	32.3
1959	190.9	145.6	78.1	28.2	39.2	10.2	35.1
1960	207.5	157.6	86.9	28.9	41.8	11.5	38.4
1961	228.1	172.7	98.0	30.6	44.2	12.2	43.1
1962	251.6	192.6	111.1	34.7	46.9	12.6	46.3
1963	278.7	217.4	127.2	39.6	50.5	11.8	49.5
1964	306.2	241.3	141.9	44.3	55.2	12.2	52.7
1965	333.7	265.0	154.9	50.0	60.0	13.5	55.2
1966	356.9	281.2	161.8	54.8	64.6	17.5	58.2
1967	381.6	299.2	172.3	59.5	67.4	20.9	61.4
1968	411.5	320.3	184.3	66.1	70.0	25.1	66.1
1969	442.3	339.8	196.4	71.4	72.0	31.1	71.4
1970	474.4	356.7	208.3	74.1	74.4	38.3	79.4
1971	525.1	395.2	236.2	83.4	75.5	46.3	83.6
1972	598.1	450.8	273.6	100.2	76.9	54.5	92.8
1973	673.4	506.3	305.0	120.1	81.3	64.7	102.4
1974	734.0	544.1	324.2	133.6	86.2	82.2	107.7
1975	793.5	582.9	355.8	137.9	89.2	101.1	109.6
1976	880.3	649.3	404.6	153.1	91.6	116.7	114.4
1977	1,012.0	747.0	469.4	180.8	96.8	140.5	124.6
1978	1,164.6	849.8	528.0	215.7	106.2	170.6	144.3
1979	1,330.0	939.9	574.6	246.9	118.4	216.0	174.2
1980	1,464.8	998.6	603.1	264.5	131.1	256.8	209.4
1981	1,590.1	1,042.8	618.5	286.5	137.7	289.4	257.9
1982	1,675.5	1,023.4	578.1	303.4	142.0	355.4	296.7
1983	1,869.1	1,109.9	626.6	332.3	151.0	433.3	325.8
1984	2,113.1	1,247.8	709.7	381.4	156.7	490.6	374.7
1985	2,376.8	1,363.5	760.5	431.2	171.8	580.9	432.4
1986	2,663.3	1,476.5	778.0	504.7	193.8	733.7	453.1
1987	3,001.5	1,667.6	860.5	594.8	212.4	857.9	475.9
1988	3,319.6	1,834.3	924.5	676.9	232.9	937.8	547.6
1989	3,591.3	1,935.2	910.3	770.7	254.2	1,067.3	588.8
1990	3,807.8	1,918.8	801.6	849.3	267.9	1,258.9	630.1
1991	3,959.8	1,846.2	705.4	881.3	259.5	1,422.5	691.2
1992	4,072.3	1,770.4	627.9	900.5	242.0	1,558.1	743.7
1993	4,208.8	1,770.1	598.4	947.8	223.9	1,682.8	755.9
1994	4,381.2	1,824.7	596.2	1,012.7	215.8	1,787.6	768.9
1995	4,576.8	1,900.1	596.8	1,090.2	213.1	1,878.2	798.5
1996	4,864.3	1,981.9	628.3	1,145.4	208.2	2,005.6	876.8
1997	5,201.8	2,084.0	631.8	1,245.3	206.8	2,111.0	1,006.8
1998	5,711.7	2,194.6	644.0	1,337.0	213.6	2,310.1	1,207.0
1999	6,315.1	2,394.3	668.1	1,495.4	230.8	2,612.0	1,308.9
2000	6,883.1	2,619.0	723.0	1,660.1	235.9	2,832.7	1,431.4
2001	7,581.0	2,791.1	758.2	1,789.8	243.0	3,202.8	1,587.1
2002	8,463.0	3,089.8	781.4	2,058.4	250.0	3,594.4	1,778.8
2001: I	7,010.2	2,663.2	740.5	1,687.7	235.1	2,878.4	1,468.6
II	7,210.0	2,711.3	751.6	1,722.4	237.2	2,989.1	1,509.7
III	7,400.5	2,734.2	758.3	1,736.6	239.2	3,117.9	1,548.4
IV	7,581.0	2,791.1	758.2	1,789.8	243.0	3,202.8	1,587.1
2002: I	7,747.8	2,790.9	748.3	1,799.1	243.4	3,335.6	1,621.4
II	7,962.6	2,861.2	742.7	1,873.4	245.1	3,432.8	1,668.6
III	8,196.7	2,981.8	773.7	1,962.2	245.9	3,491.5	1,723.4
IV	8,463.0	3,089.8	781.4	2,058.4	250.0	3,594.4	1,778.8
2003: I	8,672.7	3,166.4	815.9	2,099.4	251.1	3,681.9	1,824.4
II	8,970.6	3,281.1	833.6	2,193.0	254.5	3,778.5	1,911.0
III *p*	9,241.9	3,373.2	852.1	2,263.9	257.3	3,900.6	1,968.0

[1] Includes savings banks and savings and loan associations. Data reported by Federal Savings and Loan Insurance Corporation-insured institutions include loans in process for 1987 and exclude loans in process beginning 1988.
[2] Includes loans held by nondeposit trust companies, but not by bank trust departments.
[3] Includes Government National Mortgage Association (GNMA), Federal Housing Administration, Veterans Administration, Farmers Home Administration (FmHA), Federal Deposit Insurance Corporation, Resolution Trust Corporation (through 1995), and in earlier years Reconstruction Finance Corporation, Homeowners Loan Corporation, Federal Farm Mortgage Corporation, and Public Housing Administration. Also includes U.S.-sponsored agencies such as Federal National Mortgage Association (FNMA), Federal Land Banks, Federal Home Loan Mortgage Corporation (FHLMC), Federal Home Loan Banks (beginning 1997), and mortgage pass-through securities issued or guaranteed by GNMA, FHLMC, FNMA or FmHA. Other U.S. agencies (amounts small or current separate data not readily available) included with "individuals and others."
[4] Includes private mortgage pools.

Source: Board of Governors of the Federal Reserve System, based on data from various Government and private organizations.

[Amount outstanding (end of month); millions of dollars, seasonally adjusted]

Year and month	Total consumer credit [1]	Revolving	Nonrevolving [2]
December:			
1955	41,869.0	....	41,869.0
1956	45,448.2	....	45,448.2
1957	48,078.3	....	48,078.3
1958	48,394.3	....	48,394.3
1959	56,010.7	....	56,010.7
1960	60,025.3	....	60,025.3
1961	62,248.5	....	62,248.5
1962	68,126.7	....	68,126.7
1963	76,581.4	....	76,581.4
1964	85,959.6	....	85,959.6
1965	95,954.7	....	95,954.7
1966	101,788.2	....	101,788.2
1967	106,842.6	....	106,842.6
1968	117,399.1	2,041.5	115,357.5
1969	127,156.2	3,604.8	123,551.3
1970	131,551.6	4,961.5	126,590.1
1971	146,930.2	8,245.3	138,684.8
1972	166,189.1	9,379.2	156,809.9
1973	190,086.3	11,342.2	178,744.1
1974	198,917.8	13,241.3	185,676.6
1975	204,002.0	14,495.3	189,506.7
1976	225,721.6	16,489.1	209,232.5
1977	260,562.7	37,414.8	223,147.9
1978	306,100.4	45,691.0	260,409.4
1979	348,589.1	53,596.4	294,992.7
1980	351,920.1	54,970.1	296,950.0
1981	371,301.4	60,928.0	310,373.4
1982	389,848.7	66,348.3	323,500.4
1983	437,068.9	79,027.3	358,041.6
1984	517,279.0	100,385.6	416,893.4
1985	599,711.2	124,465.8	475,245.4
1986	654,750.2	141,068.2	513,682.1
1987	686,318.8	160,853.9	525,464.9
1988 [3]	731,917.8	184,593.1	547,324.6
1989	794,612.2	211,229.8	583,382.3
1990	808,230.6	238,642.6	569,588.0
1991	798,029.0	263,768.6	534,260.4
1992	806,118.7	278,449.7	527,669.0
1993	865,650.6	309,908.0	555,742.6
1994	997,126.9	365,569.6	631,557.3
1995	1,140,629.6	443,126.9	697,502.7
1996	1,242,168.9	498,931.0	743,238.0
1997	1,305,033.3	521,663.0	783,370.3
1998	1,400,260.7	562,807.8	837,452.9
1999	1,512,769.0	590,496.8	922,272.1
2000	1,686,221.8	658,855.3	1,027,366.5
2001	1,822,183.3	703,881.7	1,118,301.6
2002	1,902,731.3	716,702.3	1,186,029.0
2002: Jan	1,828,402.9	705,862.5	1,122,540.4
Feb	1,838,334.2	705,576.2	1,132,758.0
Mar	1,850,775.7	708,504.1	1,142,271.6
Apr	1,858,954.3	710,792.0	1,148,162.3
May	1,867,701.5	712,684.9	1,155,016.6
June	1,876,605.9	716,176.9	1,160,429.0
July	1,886,143.4	718,453.6	1,167,689.8
Aug	1,892,855.7	722,183.8	1,170,671.9
Sept	1,896,378.2	721,410.9	1,174,967.3
Oct	1,901,407.1	721,764.5	1,179,642.6
Nov	1,902,586.2	721,743.9	1,180,842.3
Dec	1,902,731.3	716,702.3	1,186,029.0
2003: Jan	1,915,183.1	719,709.2	1,195,473.9
Feb	1,924,581.9	723,200.3	1,201,381.6
Mar	1,923,487.5	724,801.3	1,198,686.2
Apr	1,933,140.1	726,911.6	1,206,228.5
May	1,951,072.1	731,017.8	1,220,054.3
June	1,951,846.9	729,744.5	1,222,102.4
July	1,959,267.8	730,979.5	1,228,288.3
Aug	1,970,829.3	733,160.9	1,237,668.4
Sept	1,982,178.8	737,330.1	1,244,848.7
Oct	1,990,515.0	739,960.2	1,250,554.8
Nov [p]	1,994,554.9	739,396.6	1,255,158.3

[1] Covers most short- and intermediate-term credit extended to individuals. Credit secured by real estate is excluded.
[2] Includes automobile loans and all other loans not included in revolving credit, such as loans for mobile homes, education, boats, trailers or vacations. These loans may be secured or unsecured. Beginning 1977 includes student loans extended by the Federal Government and SLM Holding Corporation, the parent company of Sallie Mae.
[3] Data newly available in January 1989 result in breaks in these series between December 1988 and subsequent months.

Source: Board of Governors of the Federal Reserve System.

TABLE B–78.—*Federal receipts, outlays, surplus or deficit, and debt, selected fiscal years, 1939–2005*

[Billions of dollars; fiscal years]

Fiscal year or period	Total			On-budget			Off-budget			Federal debt (end of period)		Addendum: Gross domestic product
	Receipts	Outlays	Surplus or deficit (−)	Receipts	Outlays	Surplus or deficit (−)	Receipts	Outlays	Surplus or deficit (−)	Gross Federal	Held by the public	
1939	6.3	9.1	−2.8	5.8	9.2	−3.4	0.5	−0.0	0.5	48.2	41.4	89.1
1940	6.5	9.5	−2.9	6.0	9.5	−3.5	.6	−.0	.6	50.7	42.8	96.8
1941	8.7	13.7	−4.9	8.0	13.6	−5.6	.7	.0	.7	57.5	48.2	114.1
1942	14.6	35.1	−20.5	13.7	35.1	−21.3	.9	.1	.8	79.2	67.8	144.3
1943	24.0	78.6	−54.6	22.9	78.5	−55.6	1.1	.1	1.0	142.6	127.8	180.3
1944	43.7	91.3	−47.6	42.5	91.2	−48.7	1.3	.1	1.2	204.1	184.8	209.2
1945	45.2	92.7	−47.6	43.8	92.6	−48.7	1.3	.1	1.2	260.1	235.2	221.4
1946	39.3	55.2	−15.9	38.1	55.0	−17.0	1.2	.2	1.0	271.0	241.9	222.7
1947	38.5	34.5	4.0	37.1	34.2	2.9	1.5	.3	1.2	257.1	224.3	233.2
1948	41.6	29.8	11.8	39.9	29.4	10.5	1.6	.4	1.2	252.0	216.3	256.7
1949	39.4	38.8	.6	37.7	38.4	−.7	1.7	.4	1.3	252.6	214.3	271.3
1950	39.4	42.6	−3.1	37.3	42.0	−4.7	2.1	.5	1.6	256.9	219.0	273.2
1951	51.6	45.5	6.1	48.5	44.2	4.3	3.1	1.3	1.8	255.3	214.3	320.3
1952	66.2	67.7	−1.5	62.6	66.0	−3.4	3.6	1.7	1.9	259.1	214.8	348.7
1953	69.6	76.1	−6.5	65.5	73.8	−8.3	4.1	2.3	1.8	266.0	218.4	372.6
1954	69.7	70.9	−1.2	65.1	67.9	−2.8	4.6	2.9	1.7	270.8	224.5	377.1
1955	65.5	68.4	−3.0	60.4	64.5	−4.1	5.1	4.0	1.1	274.4	226.6	395.9
1956	74.6	70.6	3.9	68.2	65.7	2.5	6.4	5.0	1.5	272.7	222.2	427.0
1957	80.0	76.6	3.4	73.2	70.6	2.6	6.8	6.0	.8	272.3	219.3	450.9
1958	79.6	82.4	−2.8	71.6	74.9	−3.3	8.0	7.5	.5	279.7	226.3	460.0
1959	79.2	92.1	−12.8	71.0	83.1	−12.1	8.3	9.0	−.7	287.5	234.7	490.2
1960	92.5	92.2	.3	81.9	81.3	.5	10.6	10.9	−.2	290.5	236.8	518.9
1961	94.4	97.7	−3.3	82.3	86.0	−3.8	12.1	11.7	.4	292.6	238.4	529.9
1962	99.7	106.8	−7.1	87.4	93.3	−5.9	12.3	13.5	−1.3	302.9	248.0	567.8
1963	106.6	111.3	−4.8	92.4	96.4	−4.0	14.2	15.0	−.8	310.3	254.0	599.2
1964	112.6	118.5	−5.9	96.2	102.8	−6.5	16.4	15.7	.6	316.1	256.8	641.4
1965	116.8	118.2	−1.4	100.1	101.7	−1.6	16.7	16.5	.2	322.3	260.8	687.5
1966	130.8	134.5	−3.7	111.7	114.8	−3.1	19.1	19.7	−.6	328.5	263.7	755.8
1967	148.8	157.5	−8.6	124.4	137.0	−12.6	24.4	20.4	4.0	340.4	266.6	810.2
1968	153.0	178.1	−25.2	128.1	155.8	−27.7	24.9	22.3	2.6	368.7	289.5	868.5
1969	186.9	183.6	3.2	157.9	158.4	−.5	29.0	25.2	3.7	365.8	278.1	948.3
1970	192.8	195.6	−2.8	159.3	168.0	−8.7	33.5	27.6	5.9	380.9	283.2	1,012.9
1971	187.1	210.2	−23.0	151.3	177.3	−26.1	35.8	32.8	3.0	408.2	303.0	1,080.3
1972	207.3	230.7	−23.4	167.4	193.8	−26.4	39.9	36.9	3.1	435.9	322.4	1,176.9
1973	230.8	245.7	−14.9	184.7	200.1	−15.4	46.1	45.6	.5	466.3	340.9	1,311.0
1974	263.2	269.4	−6.1	209.3	217.3	−8.0	53.9	52.1	1.8	483.9	343.7	1,438.9
1975	279.1	332.3	−53.2	216.6	271.9	−55.3	62.5	60.4	2.0	541.9	394.7	1,560.8
1976	298.1	371.8	−73.7	231.7	302.2	−70.5	66.4	69.6	−3.2	629.0	477.4	1,738.8
Transition quarter ...	81.2	96.0	−14.7	63.2	76.6	−13.3	18.0	19.4	−1.4	643.6	495.5	459.6
1977	355.6	409.2	−53.7	278.7	328.5	−49.8	76.8	80.7	−3.9	706.4	549.1	1,974.4
1978	399.6	458.7	−59.2	314.2	369.1	−54.9	85.4	89.7	−4.3	776.6	607.1	2,218.3
1979	463.3	504.0	−40.7	365.3	404.1	−38.7	98.0	100.0	−2.0	829.5	640.3	2,502.4
1980	517.1	590.9	−73.8	403.9	476.6	−72.7	113.2	114.3	−1.1	909.0	711.9	2,725.4
1981	599.3	678.2	−79.0	469.1	543.0	−73.9	130.2	135.2	−5.0	994.8	789.4	3,058.6
1982	617.8	745.7	−128.0	474.3	594.3	−120.0	143.5	151.4	−7.9	1,137.3	924.6	3,225.5
1983	600.6	808.4	−207.8	453.2	661.3	−208.0	147.3	147.1	.2	1,371.7	1,137.3	3,442.7
1984	666.5	851.9	−185.4	500.4	686.0	−185.6	166.1	165.8	.3	1,564.6	1,307.0	3,846.7
1985	734.1	946.4	−212.3	547.9	769.6	−221.7	186.2	176.8	9.4	1,817.4	1,507.3	4,148.9
1986	769.2	990.4	−221.2	569.0	806.9	−237.9	200.2	183.5	16.7	2,120.5	1,740.6	4,406.7
1987	854.4	1,004.1	−149.7	641.0	810.2	−169.3	213.4	193.8	19.6	2,346.0	1,889.8	4,654.4
1988	909.3	1,064.5	−155.2	667.8	861.8	−194.0	241.5	202.7	38.8	2,601.1	2,051.6	5,011.9
1989	991.2	1,143.6	−152.5	727.5	932.7	−205.2	263.7	210.9	52.8	2,867.8	2,190.7	5,401.7
1990	1,032.0	1,253.2	−221.2	750.3	1,028.1	−277.8	281.7	225.1	56.6	3,206.3	2,411.6	5,737.0
1991	1,055.0	1,324.4	−269.3	761.2	1,082.7	−321.5	293.9	241.7	52.2	3,598.2	2,689.0	5,934.2
1992	1,091.3	1,381.7	−290.4	788.9	1,129.3	−340.5	302.4	252.3	50.1	4,001.8	2,999.7	6,240.6
1993	1,154.4	1,409.5	−255.1	842.5	1,142.9	−300.4	311.9	266.6	45.3	4,351.0	3,248.4	6,578.4
1994	1,258.6	1,461.9	−203.3	923.6	1,182.5	−258.9	335.0	279.4	55.7	4,643.3	3,433.1	6,964.2
1995	1,351.8	1,515.8	−164.0	1,000.8	1,227.1	−226.4	351.1	288.7	62.4	4,920.6	3,604.4	7,325.1
1996	1,453.1	1,560.5	−107.5	1,085.6	1,259.6	−174.1	367.5	300.9	66.6	5,181.5	3,734.1	7,697.4
1997	1,579.3	1,601.3	−22.0	1,187.3	1,290.6	−103.3	392.0	310.6	81.4	5,369.2	3,772.3	8,186.6
1998	1,721.8	1,652.6	69.2	1,306.0	1,336.0	−30.0	415.8	316.6	99.2	5,478.2	3,721.1	8,626.3
1999	1,827.5	1,701.9	125.6	1,383.0	1,381.1	1.9	444.5	320.8	123.7	5,605.5	3,632.4	9,127.0
2000	2,025.2	1,788.8	236.4	1,544.6	1,458.0	86.6	480.6	330.8	149.8	5,628.7	3,409.8	9,708.4
2001	1,991.2	1,863.8	127.4	1,483.7	1,516.9	−33.3	507.5	346.8	160.7	5,769.9	3,319.6	10,040.7
2002	1,853.2	2,011.0	−157.8	1,337.9	1,655.3	−317.5	515.3	355.7	159.7	6,198.4	3,540.4	10,373.4
2003	1,782.3	2,157.6	−375.3	1,258.5	1,794.6	−536.1	523.8	363.0	160.8	6,760.0	3,913.6	10,828.3
2004 [1]	1,798.1	2,318.8	−520.7	1,264.1	1,938.9	−674.8	534.0	380.0	154.0	7,486.4	4,420.8	11,466.0
2005 [1]	2,036.3	2,399.8	−363.6	1,461.2	2,004.1	−542.9	575.1	395.7	179.4	8,132.9	4,791.9	12,042.4

[1] Estimates.

Note.—Through fiscal year 1976, the fiscal year was on a July 1-June 30 basis; beginning October 1976 (fiscal year 1977), the fiscal year is on an October 1-September 30 basis. The transition quarter is the 3-month period from July 1, 1976 through September 30, 1976.
Refunds of receipts are excluded from receipts and outlays.
See *Budget of the United States Government, Fiscal Year 2005,* for additional information.

Sources: Department of Commerce (Bureau of Economic Analysis), Department of the Treasury, and Office of Management and Budget.

TABLE B–79.—*Federal receipts, outlays, surplus or deficit, and debt, as percent of gross domestic product, fiscal years 1934–2005*

[Percent; fiscal years]

Fiscal year or period	Receipts	Outlays		Surplus or deficit (–)	Federal debt (end of period)	
		Total	National defense		Gross Federal	Held by public
1934	4.8	10.7		–5.9		
1935	5.2	9.2		–4.0		
1936	5.0	10.5		–5.5		
1937	6.1	8.6		–2.5		
1938	7.6	7.7		–.1		
1939	7.1	10.3		–3.2	54.2	46.6
1940	6.8	9.8	1.7	–3.0	52.4	44.2
1941	7.6	12.0	5.6	–4.3	50.4	42.3
1942	10.1	24.3	17.8	–14.2	54.9	47.0
1943	13.3	43.6	37.0	–30.3	79.1	70.9
1944	20.9	43.6	37.8	–22.7	97.6	88.3
1945	20.4	41.9	37.5	–21.5	117.5	106.2
1946	17.6	24.8	19.2	–7.2	121.7	108.6
1947	16.5	14.8	5.5	1.7	110.3	96.2
1948	16.2	11.6	3.5	4.6	98.2	84.3
1949	14.5	14.3	4.8	.2	93.1	79.0
1950	14.4	15.6	5.0	–1.1	94.0	80.2
1951	16.1	14.2	7.4	1.9	79.7	66.9
1952	19.0	19.4	13.2	–.4	74.3	61.6
1953	18.7	20.4	14.2	–1.7	71.4	58.6
1954	18.5	18.8	13.1	–.3	71.8	59.5
1955	16.5	17.3	10.8	–.8	69.3	57.2
1956	17.5	16.5	10.0	.9	63.9	52.0
1957	17.7	17.0	10.1	.8	60.4	48.6
1958	17.3	17.9	10.2	–.6	60.8	49.2
1959	16.2	18.8	10.0	–2.6	58.6	47.9
1960	17.8	17.8	9.3	.1	56.0	45.6
1961	17.8	18.4	9.4	–.6	55.2	45.0
1962	17.6	18.8	9.2	–1.3	53.4	43.7
1963	17.8	18.6	8.9	–.8	51.8	42.4
1964	17.6	18.5	8.5	–.9	49.3	40.0
1965	17.0	17.2	7.4	–.2	46.9	37.9
1966	17.3	17.8	7.7	–.5	43.5	34.9
1967	18.4	19.4	8.8	–1.1	42.0	32.9
1968	17.6	20.5	9.4	–2.9	42.5	33.3
1969	19.7	19.4	8.7	.3	38.6	29.3
1970	19.0	19.3	8.1	–.3	37.6	28.0
1971	17.3	19.5	7.3	–2.1	37.8	28.1
1972	17.6	19.6	6.7	–2.0	37.0	27.4
1973	17.6	18.7	5.8	–1.1	35.6	26.0
1974	18.3	18.7	5.5	–.4	33.6	23.9
1975	17.9	21.3	5.5	–3.4	34.7	25.3
1976	17.1	21.4	5.2	–4.2	36.2	27.5
Transition quarter	17.7	20.9	4.8	–3.2	35.0	27.0
1977	18.0	20.7	4.9	–2.7	35.8	27.8
1978	18.0	20.7	4.7	–2.7	35.0	27.4
1979	18.5	20.1	4.6	–1.6	33.1	25.6
1980	19.0	21.7	4.9	–2.7	33.4	26.1
1981	19.6	22.2	5.1	–2.6	32.5	25.8
1982	19.2	23.1	5.7	–4.0	35.3	28.7
1983	17.4	23.5	6.1	–6.0	39.8	33.0
1984	17.3	22.1	5.9	–4.8	40.7	34.0
1985	17.7	22.8	6.1	–5.1	43.8	36.3
1986	17.5	22.5	6.2	–5.0	48.1	39.5
1987	18.4	21.6	6.1	–3.2	50.4	40.6
1988	18.1	21.2	5.8	–3.1	51.9	40.9
1989	18.3	21.2	5.6	–2.8	53.1	40.6
1990	18.0	21.8	5.2	–3.9	55.9	42.0
1991	17.8	22.3	4.6	–4.5	60.6	45.3
1992	17.5	22.1	4.8	–4.7	64.1	48.1
1993	17.5	21.4	4.4	–3.9	66.1	49.4
1994	18.1	21.0	4.0	–2.9	66.7	49.3
1995	18.5	20.7	3.7	–2.2	67.2	49.2
1996	18.9	20.3	3.5	–1.4	67.3	48.5
1997	19.3	19.6	3.3	–.3	65.6	46.1
1998	20.0	19.2	3.1	.8	63.5	43.1
1999	20.0	18.6	3.0	1.4	61.4	39.8
2000	20.9	18.4	3.0	2.4	58.0	35.1
2001	19.8	18.6	3.0	1.3	57.5	33.1
2002	17.9	19.4	3.4	–1.5	59.8	34.1
2003	16.5	19.9	3.7	–3.5	62.4	36.1
2004 [1]	15.7	20.2	4.0	–4.5	65.3	38.6
2005 [1]	16.9	19.9	3.7	–3.0	67.5	39.8

[1] Estimates.

Note.—See Note, Table B–78.

Sources: Department of the Treasury and Office of Management and Budget.

TABLE B–80.—*Federal receipts and outlays, by major category, and surplus or deficit, fiscal years 1940–2005*

[Billions of dollars; fiscal years]

Fiscal year or period	Receipts (on-budget and off-budget)					Outlays (on-budget and off-budget)										Surplus or deficit (–) (on-budget and off-budget)
	Total	Individual income taxes	Corporation income taxes	Social insurance and retirement receipts	Other	Total	National defense		International affairs	Health	Medicare	Income security	Social security	Net interest	Other	
							Total	Department of Defense, military								
1940	6.5	0.9	1.2	1.8	2.7	9.5	1.7		0.1	0.1		1.5	0.0	0.9	5.3	–2.9
1941	8.7	1.3	2.1	1.9	3.3	13.7	6.4		.1	.1		1.9	.1	.9	4.1	–4.9
1942	14.6	3.3	4.7	2.5	4.2	35.1	25.7		1.0	.1		1.8	.1	1.1	5.4	–20.5
1943	24.0	6.5	9.6	3.0	4.9	78.6	66.7		1.3	.1		1.7	.2	1.5	7.0	–54.6
1944	43.7	19.7	14.8	3.5	5.7	91.3	79.1		1.4	.2		1.5	.2	2.2	6.6	–47.6
1945	45.2	18.4	16.0	3.5	7.3	92.7	83.0		1.9	.2		1.1	.3	3.1	3.1	–47.6
1946	39.3	16.1	11.9	3.1	8.2	55.2	42.7		1.9	.2		2.4	.4	4.1	3.6	–15.9
1947	38.5	17.9	8.6	3.4	8.5	34.5	12.8		5.8	.2		2.8	.5	4.2	8.2	4.0
1948	41.6	19.3	9.7	3.8	8.8	29.8	9.1		4.6	.2		2.5	.6	4.3	8.5	11.8
1949	39.4	15.6	11.2	3.8	8.9	38.8	13.2		6.1	.2		3.2	.7	4.5	11.1	.6
1950	39.4	15.8	10.4	4.3	8.9	42.6	13.7		4.7	.3		4.1	.8	4.8	14.2	–3.1
1951	51.6	21.6	14.1	5.7	10.2	45.5	23.6		3.6	.3		3.4	1.6	4.7	8.4	6.1
1952	66.2	27.9	21.2	6.4	10.6	67.7	46.1		2.7	.3		3.7	2.1	4.7	8.1	–1.5
1953	69.6	29.8	21.2	6.8	11.7	76.1	52.8		2.1	.3		3.8	2.7	5.2	9.1	–6.5
1954	69.7	29.5	21.1	7.2	11.9	70.9	49.3		1.6	.3		4.4	3.4	4.8	7.1	–1.2
1955	65.5	28.7	17.9	7.9	11.0	68.4	42.7		2.2	.3		5.1	4.4	4.9	8.9	–3.0
1956	74.6	32.2	20.9	9.3	12.2	70.6	42.5		2.4	.4		4.7	5.5	5.1	10.1	3.9
1957	80.0	35.6	21.2	10.0	13.2	76.6	45.4		3.1	.5		5.4	6.7	5.4	10.1	3.4
1958	79.6	34.7	20.1	11.2	13.6	82.4	46.8		3.4	.5		7.5	8.2	5.6	10.3	–2.8
1959	79.2	36.7	17.3	11.7	13.5	92.1	49.0		3.1	.7		8.2	9.7	5.8	15.5	–12.8
1960	92.5	40.7	21.5	14.7	15.6	92.2	48.1		3.0	.8		7.4	11.6	6.9	14.4	.3
1961	94.4	41.3	21.0	16.4	15.7	97.7	49.6		3.2	.9		9.7	12.5	6.7	15.2	–3.3
1962	99.7	45.6	20.5	17.0	16.5	106.8	52.3	50.1	5.6	1.2		9.2	14.4	6.9	17.2	–7.1
1963	106.6	47.6	21.6	19.8	17.6	111.3	53.4	51.1	5.3	1.5		9.3	15.8	7.7	18.3	–4.8
1964	112.6	48.7	23.5	22.0	18.5	118.5	54.8	52.6	4.9	1.8		9.7	16.6	8.2	22.6	–5.9
1965	116.8	48.8	25.5	22.2	20.3	118.2	50.6	48.8	5.3	1.8		9.5	17.5	8.6	25.0	–1.4
1966	130.8	55.4	30.1	25.5	19.8	134.5	58.1	56.6	5.6	2.5	0.1	9.7	20.7	9.4	28.5	–3.7
1967	148.8	61.5	34.0	32.6	20.7	157.5	71.4	70.1	5.6	3.4	2.7	10.3	21.7	10.3	32.1	–8.6
1968	153.0	68.7	28.7	33.9	21.7	178.1	81.9	80.4	5.3	4.4	4.6	11.8	23.9	11.1	35.1	–25.2
1969	186.9	87.2	36.7	39.0	23.9	183.6	82.5	80.8	4.6	5.2	5.7	13.1	27.3	12.7	32.6	3.2
1970	192.8	90.4	32.8	44.4	25.2	195.6	81.7	80.1	4.3	5.9	6.2	15.7	30.3	14.4	37.2	–2.8
1971	187.1	86.2	26.8	47.3	26.8	210.2	78.9	77.5	4.2	6.8	6.6	22.9	35.9	14.8	40.0	–23.0
1972	207.3	94.7	32.2	52.6	27.8	230.7	79.2	77.6	4.8	8.7	7.5	27.7	40.2	15.5	47.3	–23.4
1973	230.8	103.2	36.2	63.1	28.3	245.7	76.7	75.0	4.1	9.4	8.1	28.3	49.1	17.3	52.8	–14.9
1974	263.2	119.0	38.6	75.1	30.6	269.4	79.3	77.9	5.7	10.7	9.6	33.7	55.9	21.4	52.9	–6.1
1975	279.1	122.4	40.6	84.5	31.5	332.3	86.5	84.9	7.1	12.9	12.9	50.2	64.7	23.2	74.8	–53.2
1976	298.1	131.6	41.4	90.8	34.3	371.8	89.6	87.9	6.4	15.7	15.8	60.8	73.9	26.7	82.7	–73.7
Transition quarter	81.2	38.8	8.5	25.2	8.8	96.0	22.3	21.8	2.5	3.9	4.3	15.0	19.8	6.9	21.4	–14.7
1977	355.6	157.6	54.9	106.5	36.6	409.2	97.2	95.1	6.4	17.3	19.3	61.1	85.1	29.9	93.0	–53.7
1978	399.6	181.0	60.0	121.0	37.7	458.7	104.5	102.3	7.5	18.5	22.8	61.5	93.9	35.5	114.7	–59.2
1979	463.3	217.8	65.7	138.9	40.8	504.0	116.3	113.6	7.5	20.5	26.5	66.4	104.1	42.6	120.2	–40.7
1980	517.1	244.1	64.6	157.8	50.6	590.9	134.0	130.9	12.7	23.2	32.1	86.6	118.5	52.5	131.3	–73.8
1981	599.3	285.9	61.1	182.7	69.5	678.2	157.5	153.9	13.1	26.9	39.1	100.3	139.6	68.8	133.0	–79.0
1982	617.8	297.7	49.2	201.5	69.3	745.7	185.3	180.7	12.3	27.4	46.6	108.2	156.0	85.0	125.0	–128.0
1983	600.6	288.9	37.0	209.0	65.6	808.4	209.9	204.4	11.8	28.6	52.6	123.0	170.7	89.8	121.8	–207.8
1984	666.5	298.4	56.9	239.4	71.8	851.9	227.4	220.9	15.9	30.4	57.5	113.4	178.2	111.1	117.9	–185.4
1985	734.1	334.5	61.3	265.2	73.1	946.4	252.7	245.1	16.2	33.5	65.8	129.0	188.6	129.5	131.0	–212.3
1986	769.2	349.0	63.1	283.9	73.2	990.4	273.4	265.4	14.2	35.9	70.2	120.6	198.8	136.0	141.4	–221.2
1987	854.4	392.6	83.9	303.3	74.6	1,004.1	282.0	273.9	11.6	40.0	75.1	124.1	207.4	138.6	125.3	–149.7
1988	909.3	401.2	94.5	334.3	79.3	1,064.5	290.4	281.9	10.5	44.5	78.9	130.4	219.3	151.8	138.7	–155.2
1989	991.2	445.7	103.3	359.4	82.8	1,143.6	303.6	294.8	9.6	48.4	85.0	137.4	232.5	169.0	158.2	–152.5
1990	1,032.0	466.9	93.5	380.0	91.5	1,253.2	299.3	289.7	13.8	57.7	98.1	148.7	248.6	184.3	202.6	–221.2
1991	1,055.0	467.8	98.1	396.0	93.1	1,324.4	273.3	262.3	15.9	71.2	104.5	172.4	269.0	194.4	223.7	–269.3
1992	1,091.3	476.0	100.3	413.7	101.4	1,381.7	298.4	286.8	16.1	89.5	119.0	199.5	287.6	199.3	172.2	–290.4
1993	1,154.4	509.7	117.5	428.3	98.9	1,409.5	291.1	278.5	17.2	99.4	130.6	209.9	304.6	198.7	158.0	–255.1
1994	1,258.6	543.1	140.4	461.5	113.7	1,461.9	281.6	268.6	17.1	107.1	144.7	217.1	319.6	202.9	171.7	–203.3
1995	1,351.8	590.2	157.0	484.5	120.1	1,515.8	272.1	259.4	16.4	115.4	159.9	223.7	335.8	232.1	160.3	–164.0
1996	1,453.1	656.4	171.8	509.4	115.4	1,560.5	265.8	253.1	13.5	119.4	174.2	229.7	349.7	241.1	167.3	–107.5
1997	1,579.3	737.5	182.3	539.4	120.2	1,601.3	270.5	258.3	15.2	123.8	190.0	235.0	365.3	244.0	157.5	–22.0
1998	1,721.8	828.6	188.7	571.8	132.7	1,652.6	268.5	256.1	13.1	131.4	192.8	237.7	379.2	241.1	188.8	69.2
1999	1,827.5	879.5	184.7	611.8	151.5	1,701.9	274.9	261.3	15.2	141.1	190.4	242.4	390.0	229.8	218.1	125.6
2000	2,025.2	1,004.5	207.3	652.9	160.6	1,788.8	294.5	281.2	17.2	154.5	197.1	253.6	409.4	223.0	239.5	236.4
2001	1,991.2	994.3	151.1	694.0	151.8	1,863.8	305.5	291.0	16.5	172.3	217.4	269.6	433.0	206.2	243.4	127.4
2002	1,853.2	858.3	148.0	700.8	146.0	2,011.0	348.6	332.0	22.4	196.5	230.9	312.5	456.0	171.0	273.2	–157.8
2003	1,782.3	793.7	131.8	713.0	143.9	2,157.6	404.9	387.3	21.2	219.6	249.4	334.4	474.7	153.1	300.3	–375.3
2004 [1]	1,798.1	765.4	168.7	732.4	131.6	2,318.8	453.7	434.8	34.2	243.5	270.5	339.5	496.2	156.3	325.0	–520.7
2005 [1]	2,036.3	873.8	230.2	793.9	138.3	2,399.8	450.6	429.6	37.8	252.6	294.2	348.1	515.0	177.9	323.5	–363.6

[1] Estimates.

Note.—See Note, Table B–78.

Sources: Department of the Treasury and Office of Management and Budget.

[Millions of dollars; fiscal years]

Description	Actual				Estimates	
	2000	2001	2002	2003	2004	2005
RECEIPTS AND OUTLAYS:						
Total receipts	2,025,218	1,991,194	1,853,173	1,782,342	1,798,093	2,036,273
Total outlays	1,788,773	1,863,770	2,010,970	2,157,637	2,318,834	2,399,843
Total surplus or deficit (–)	236,445	127,424	–157,797	–375,295	–520,741	–363,570
On-budget receipts	1,544,634	1,483,675	1,337,852	1,258,500	1,264,089	1,461,172
On-budget outlays	1,458,008	1,516,932	1,655,308	1,794,628	1,938,855	2,004,104
On-budget surplus or deficit (–)	86,626	–33,257	–317,456	–536,128	–674,766	–542,932
Off-budget receipts	480,584	507,519	515,321	523,842	534,004	575,101
Off-budget outlays	330,765	346,838	355,662	363,009	379,979	395,739
Off-budget surplus or deficit (–)	149,819	160,681	159,659	160,833	154,025	179,362
OUTSTANDING DEBT, END OF PERIOD:						
Gross Federal debt	5,628,700	5,769,881	6,198,401	6,760,014	7,486,447	8,132,945
Held by Federal Government accounts	2,218,896	2,450,266	2,658,006	2,846,407	3,065,659	3,341,083
Held by the public	3,409,804	3,319,615	3,540,395	3,913,607	4,420,788	4,791,862
Federal Reserve System	511,413	534,135	604,191	656,116	....	....
Other	2,898,391	2,785,480	2,936,203	3,257,491	....	....
RECEIPTS: ON-BUDGET AND OFF-BUDGET	2,025,218	1,991,194	1,853,173	1,782,342	1,798,093	2,036,273
Individual income taxes	1,004,462	994,339	858,345	793,699	765,399	873,837
Corporation income taxes	207,289	151,075	148,044	131,778	168,741	230,196
Social insurance and retirement receipts	652,852	693,967	700,760	712,978	732,392	793,948
On-budget	172,268	186,448	185,439	189,136	198,388	218,847
Off-budget	480,584	507,519	515,321	523,842	534,004	575,101
Excise taxes	68,865	66,232	66,989	67,524	70,776	73,210
Estate and gift taxes	29,010	28,400	26,507	21,959	23,909	21,442
Customs duties and fees	19,914	19,369	18,602	19,862	22,595	22,095
Miscellaneous receipts	42,826	37,812	33,926	34,542	34,281	36,545
Deposits of earnings by Federal Reserve System	32,293	26,124	23,683	21,878	22,880	25,262
All other [1]	10,533	11,688	10,243	12,664	11,401	11,283
Adjustment for revenue uncertainty	....	....	....	....	–20,000	–15,000
OUTLAYS: ON-BUDGET AND OFF-BUDGET	1,788,773	1,863,770	2,010,970	2,157,637	2,318,834	2,399,843
National defense	294,495	305,500	348,555	404,920	453,684	450,586
International affairs	17,216	16,493	22,351	21,208	34,236	37,838
General science, space and technology	18,633	19,784	20,767	20,873	22,291	24,353
Energy	–1,061	38	482	–775	957	1,774
Natural resources and environment	25,031	25,623	29,454	29,703	31,665	30,899
Agriculture	36,465	26,204	21,957	22,600	20,121	22,322
Commerce and housing credit	3,207	5,878	–391	–1,607	7,723	2,714
On-budget	1,178	3,576	260	3,638	12,679	2,964
Off-budget	2,029	2,302	–651	–5,245	–4,956	–250
Transportation	46,853	54,447	61,833	67,069	68,144	69,899
Community and regional development	10,623	11,773	12,981	18,850	18,757	17,017
Education, training, employment, and social services	53,754	57,143	70,544	82,568	87,211	89,020
Health	154,533	172,270	196,544	219,576	243,501	252,597
Medicare	197,113	217,384	230,855	249,433	270,451	294,249
Income security	253,575	269,615	312,530	334,432	339,495	348,149
Social security	409,423	432,958	455,980	474,680	496,174	514,989
On-budget	13,254	11,701	13,969	13,279	14,299	15,124
Off-budget	396,169	421,257	442,011	461,401	481,875	499,865
Veterans benefits and services	47,083	45,039	50,984	57,018	60,454	67,473
Administration of justice	28,501	30,205	35,171	35,408	41,603	42,782
General government	12,959	14,259	16,814	22,987	25,424	19,148
Net interest	222,951	206,168	170,951	153,076	156,264	177,909
On-budget	282,747	274,979	247,771	236,621	242,550	269,827
Off-budget	–59,796	–68,811	–76,820	–83,545	–86,286	–91,918
Allowances	....	....	....	....	....	–76
Undistributed offsetting receipts	–42,581	–47,011	–47,392	–54,382	–59,321	–63,10
On-budget	–34,944	–39,101	–38,514	–44,780	–48,667	–51,15
Off-budget	–7,637	–7,910	–8,878	–9,602	–10,654	–11,95

[1] Beginning 1984, includes universal service fund receipts.

Note.—See Note, Table B-78.

Sources: Department of the Treasury and Office of Management and Budget.

TABLE B-82.—*Federal and State and local government current receipts and expenditures, national income and product accounts (NIPA), 1959–2003*

[Billions of dollars; quarterly data at seasonally adjusted annual rates]

Year or quarter	Total government			Federal Government			State and local Government			Addendum: Grants-in-aid to State and local governments
	Current receipts	Current expenditures	Net government saving (NIPA)	Current receipts	Current expenditures	Net Federal Government saving (NIPA)	Current receipts	Current expenditures	Net State and local government saving (NIPA)	
1959	123.0	115.8	7.1	87.0	83.6	3.3	40.6	36.9	3.8	3.8
1960	134.4	122.9	11.5	93.9	86.7	7.2	44.5	40.2	4.3	4.0
1961	139.0	132.1	6.9	95.5	92.8	2.6	48.1	43.8	4.3	4.5
1962	150.6	142.8	7.8	103.6	101.1	2.5	52.0	46.8	5.2	5.0
1963	162.2	151.1	11.1	111.8	106.4	5.4	56.0	50.3	5.7	5.6
1964	166.6	159.2	7.4	111.8	110.8	1.0	61.3	54.9	6.4	6.5
1965	180.3	170.4	9.9	120.9	117.6	3.3	66.5	60.0	6.5	7.2
1966	202.8	192.8	10.0	137.9	135.7	2.3	74.9	67.2	7.8	10.1
1967	217.6	220.0	-2.4	146.9	156.2	-9.4	82.5	75.5	7.0	11.7
1968	252.0	246.8	5.2	171.2	173.5	-2.3	93.5	86.0	7.5	12.7
1969	283.4	266.7	16.7	192.5	183.8	8.7	105.5	97.5	8.0	14.6
1970	286.7	294.8	-8.1	186.0	201.1	-15.2	120.1	113.0	7.1	19.3
1971	303.4	325.3	-21.9	191.7	220.0	-28.4	134.9	128.5	6.5	23.2
1972	346.8	355.5	-8.8	220.1	244.4	-24.4	158.4	142.8	15.6	31.7
1973	390.0	385.6	4.4	250.4	261.7	-11.3	174.3	158.6	15.7	34.8
1974	431.3	435.8	-4.4	279.5	293.3	-13.8	188.1	178.7	9.3	36.3
1975	441.6	508.2	-66.6	277.2	346.2	-69.0	209.6	207.1	2.5	45.1
1976	505.5	549.9	-44.4	322.5	374.3	-51.7	233.7	226.3	7.4	50.7
1977	566.8	597.7	-31.0	363.4	407.5	-44.1	259.9	246.8	13.1	56.6
1978	645.6	653.4	-7.8	423.5	450.0	-26.5	287.6	268.9	18.7	65.5
1979	728.2	726.5	1.7	486.2	497.5	-11.3	308.4	295.4	13.0	66.3
1980	798.0	842.8	-44.8	532.1	585.7	-53.6	338.2	329.4	8.8	72.3
1981	917.2	962.9	-45.7	619.4	672.7	-53.3	370.2	362.7	7.6	72.5
1982	938.5	1,072.6	-134.1	616.6	748.5	-131.9	391.4	393.6	-2.2	69.5
1983	999.4	1,167.5	-168.1	642.3	815.4	-173.0	428.6	423.7	4.9	71.6
1984	1,112.5	1,256.6	-144.1	709.0	877.1	-168.1	480.2	456.2	23.9	76.7
1985	1,213.5	1,366.1	-152.6	773.3	948.2	-175.0	521.1	498.7	22.3	80.9
1986	1,289.3	1,459.1	-169.9	815.2	1,006.0	-190.8	561.6	540.7	21.0	87.6
1987	1,403.2	1,535.8	-132.6	896.6	1,041.6	-145.0	590.6	578.1	12.4	83.9
1988	1,502.2	1,618.7	-116.6	958.2	1,092.7	-134.5	635.5	617.6	17.9	91.6
1989	1,626.3	1,735.6	-109.3	1,037.4	1,167.5	-130.1	687.3	666.5	20.8	98.3
1990	1,707.8	1,872.6	-164.8	1,081.5	1,253.5	-172.0	737.8	730.5	7.2	111.4
1991	1,758.8	1,976.7	-217.9	1,101.3	1,315.0	-213.7	789.2	793.3	-4.2	131.6
1992	1,843.7	2,140.4	-296.7	1,147.2	1,444.6	-297.4	845.7	845.0	.7	149.1
1993	1,945.8	2,218.4	-272.6	1,222.5	1,496.0	-273.5	886.9	886.0	.9	163.7
1994	2,089.0	2,290.8	-201.9	1,320.8	1,533.1	-212.3	942.9	932.4	10.5	174.7
1995	2,212.6	2,397.6	-184.9	1,406.5	1,603.5	-197.0	990.2	978.2	12.0	184.1
1996	2,376.1	2,492.1	-116.0	1,524.0	1,665.8	-141.8	1,043.3	1,017.5	25.8	191.2
1997	2,551.9	2,568.6	-16.7	1,653.1	1,708.9	-55.8	1,097.4	1,058.3	39.1	198.6
1998	2,724.2	2,633.4	90.8	1,773.8	1,734.9	38.8	1,163.2	1,111.2	52.0	212.8
1999	2,895.0	2,741.0	154.0	1,891.2	1,787.6	103.6	1,236.7	1,186.3	50.4	232.9
2000	3,125.9	2,886.5	239.4	2,053.8	1,864.4	189.5	1,319.5	1,269.5	50.0	247.3
2001	3,124.2	3,056.4	67.8	2,017.8	1,967.3	50.5	1,382.7	1,365.4	17.3	276.3
2002	2,980.7	3,224.0	-243.3	1,860.7	2,100.7	-240.0	1,424.7	1,427.9	-3.2	304.6
1999: I	2,821.8	2,693.3	128.4	1,843.6	1,764.2	79.4	1,205.1	1,156.1	49.0	227.0
II	2,862.8	2,712.9	149.9	1,869.5	1,764.8	104.6	1,217.1	1,171.8	45.3	223.7
III	2,912.2	2,752.5	159.8	1,900.2	1,792.4	107.8	1,249.6	1,197.6	52.0	237.6
IV	2,983.3	2,805.3	178.0	1,951.6	1,828.9	122.7	1,275.0	1,219.7	55.3	243.2
2000: I	3,091.1	2,822.4	268.7	2,035.7	1,823.0	212.7	1,294.4	1,238.5	55.9	239.0
II	3,121.1	2,880.2	240.9	2,044.9	1,863.5	181.4	1,319.0	1,259.5	59.5	242.8
III	3,142.3	2,902.1	240.2	2,066.8	1,875.5	191.2	1,330.5	1,281.6	49.0	255.0
IV	3,149.3	2,941.4	207.9	2,068.0	1,895.5	172.5	1,333.9	1,298.5	35.4	252.6
2001: I	3,193.3	3,001.2	192.2	2,088.5	1,932.4	156.1	1,370.5	1,334.4	36.1	265.7
II	3,200.8	3,047.2	153.6	2,082.9	1,953.9	128.9	1,396.5	1,371.8	24.6	278.5
III	2,999.4	3,067.9	-68.5	1,901.8	1,981.9	-80.1	1,371.4	1,359.7	11.6	273.7
IV	3,103.5	3,109.4	-5.9	1,998.2	2,001.1	-2.8	1,392.6	1,395.6	-3.0	287.3
2002: I	2,960.1	3,156.3	-196.2	1,857.7	2,046.5	-188.8	1,393.0	1,400.3	-7.4	290.6
II	2,967.0	3,211.0	-244.0	1,865.4	2,097.4	-232.0	1,406.2	1,418.2	-11.9	304.6
III	2,995.9	3,232.1	-236.1	1,859.9	2,102.8	-242.9	1,442.8	1,436.1	6.8	306.8
IV	2,999.9	3,239.7	-296.8	1,859.7	2,156.1	-296.3	1,456.6	1,457.0	-.4	316.4
2003: I	2,993.9	3,354.9	-361.0	1,863.5	2,184.0	-320.4	1,441.2	1,481.8	-40.6	310.8
II	2,996.3	3,435.7	-439.3	1,863.9	2,288.5	-424.7	1,477.9	1,492.6	-14.7	345.5
III	2,966.0	3,452.3	-486.3	1,784.3	2,283.7	-499.4	1,528.0	1,514.9	13.1	346.3

Note.—Federal grants-in-aid to State and local governments are reflected in Federal current expenditures and State and local current re-
pts. Total government current receipts and expenditures have been adjusted to eliminate this duplication.

Source: Department of Commerce, Bureau of Economic Analysis.

TABLE B-83.—*Federal and State and local government current receipts and expenditures, national income and product accounts (NIPA), by major type, 1959-2003*

[Billions of dollars; quarterly data at seasonally adjusted annual rates]

Year or quarter	Current receipts									Current expenditures					Net government saving
	Total	Current tax receipts				Contributions for government social insurance	Income receipts on assets	Current transfer receipts	Current surplus of government enterprises	Total²	Consumption expenditures	Current transfer payments	Interest payments	Subsidies	
		Total¹	Personal current taxes	Taxes on production and imports	Taxes on corporate income										
1959	123.0	107.1	42.3	41.1	23.6	13.8	0.3	0.8	1.0	115.8	80.7	26.8	7.3	1.1	7.1
1960	134.4	113.4	46.1	44.6	22.7	16.4	2.7	.9	.9	122.9	83.3	28.0	10.4	1.1	11.5
1961	139.0	117.1	47.3	47.0	22.8	17.0	2.9	1.1	.8	132.1	88.2	31.8	10.2	2.0	6.9
1962	150.6	126.1	51.6	50.4	24.0	19.1	3.2	1.2	.9	142.8	96.8	32.6	11.1	2.3	7.8
1963	162.2	134.4	54.6	53.4	26.2	21.7	3.4	1.3	1.4	151.1	102.7	34.1	12.0	2.2	11.1
1964	166.6	137.6	52.1	57.3	28.0	22.4	3.7	1.6	1.3	159.2	108.6	34.9	12.9	2.7	7.4
1965	180.3	149.5	57.7	60.8	30.9	23.4	4.1	1.9	1.3	170.4	115.9	37.8	13.7	3.0	9.9
1966	202.8	163.5	66.4	63.3	33.7	31.3	4.7	2.2	1.0	192.8	132.0	41.8	15.1	3.9	10.0
1967	217.6	173.9	73.0	68.0	32.7	34.9	5.5	2.5	.9	220.0	149.7	50.1	16.4	3.8	−2.4
1968	252.0	203.2	87.0	76.5	39.4	38.7	6.4	2.6	1.2	246.8	165.8	58.1	18.8	4.2	5.2
1969	283.4	228.5	104.5	84.0	39.7	44.1	7.0	2.7	1.0	266.7	178.2	63.7	20.2	4.5	16.7
1970	286.7	229.3	103.1	91.5	34.4	46.4	8.2	2.9	.0	294.8	190.2	76.8	23.1	4.8	−8.1
1971	303.4	240.4	101.7	100.6	37.7	51.2	9.0	3.1	−.2	325.3	204.7	91.6	24.5	4.7	−21.9
1972	346.8	274.0	123.6	108.1	41.9	59.2	9.5	3.6	.5	355.5	220.8	102.2	26.3	6.6	−8.8
1973	390.0	299.4	132.4	117.3	49.3	75.5	11.6	3.9	−.4	385.6	234.8	114.2	31.3	5.2	4.4
1974	431.3	328.3	151.0	125.0	51.8	85.2	14.4	4.5	−.9	435.8	261.7	134.7	35.6	3.3	−4.4
1975	441.6	334.4	147.6	135.5	50.9	89.3	16.1	5.1	−3.2	508.2	294.6	169.2	40.0	4.5	−66.6
1976	505.5	383.8	172.3	146.6	64.2	101.3	16.3	5.8	−1.8	549.9	316.6	181.9	46.3	5.1	−44.4
1977	566.8	431.2	197.5	159.9	73.0	113.1	18.4	6.8	−2.6	597.7	346.6	193.3	50.8	7.1	−31.0
1978	645.6	485.0	229.4	171.2	83.5	131.3	23.2	8.0	−1.9	653.4	376.5	207.9	60.2	8.9	−7.8
1979	728.2	538.2	268.7	180.4	88.0	152.7	30.8	9.1	−2.6	726.5	412.3	232.6	72.9	8.5	1.7
1980	798.0	586.0	298.9	200.7	84.8	166.2	39.9	10.7	−4.8	842.8	465.9	278.0	89.1	9.8	−44.8
1981	917.2	663.9	345.2	236.0	81.1	195.7	50.2	12.3	−4.9	962.9	520.6	314.2	116.7	11.5	−45.7
1982	938.5	659.9	354.1	241.3	63.1	208.9	58.9	14.8	−4.0	1,072.6	568.2	350.5	138.9	15.0	−134.1
1983	999.4	694.5	352.3	263.7	77.2	226.0	65.3	16.8	−3.1	1,167.5	610.6	378.4	156.9	21.2	−168.1
1984	1,112.5	763.0	377.4	290.2	94.0	257.5	74.3	19.6	−1.9	1,256.6	657.6	390.9	187.3	21.0	−144.1
1985	1,213.5	824.3	417.4	308.5	96.5	281.4	84.0	23.0	.8	1,366.1	720.2	415.7	208.8	21.3	−152.6
1986	1,289.3	869.2	437.3	323.7	106.5	303.4	89.8	25.6	1.3	1,459.1	776.1	441.9	216.3	24.8	−169.9
1987	1,403.2	966.1	489.1	347.9	127.1	323.1	86.1	26.8	1.2	1,535.8	815.2	459.7	230.8	30.2	−132.6
1988	1,502.2	1,019.4	505.0	374.9	137.2	361.5	90.5	28.2	2.5	1,618.7	852.8	488.8	247.7	29.4	−116.6
1989	1,626.3	1,109.7	566.1	399.3	141.5	385.2	94.3	32.2	4.9	1,735.6	901.4	533.1	274.0	27.2	−109.3
1990	1,707.8	1,161.9	592.8	425.5	140.6	410.1	98.7	35.6	1.6	1,872.6	964.4	586.1	295.3	26.8	−164.8
1991	1,758.8	1,180.3	586.7	457.5	133.6	430.2	98.1	44.6	5.7	1,976.7	1,014.1	622.5	312.7	27.3	−217.9
1992	1,843.7	1,240.2	610.6	483.8	143.1	455.0	90.5	50.5	7.6	2,140.4	1,047.8	749.5	313.2	29.9	−296.7
1993	1,945.8	1,318.2	646.6	503.4	165.4	477.7	87.6	55.1	7.2	2,218.4	1,072.2	796.3	313.6	36.4	−272.6
1994	2,089.0	1,426.1	690.7	545.6	186.7	508.2	86.6	59.5	8.6	2,290.8	1,104.1	831.2	323.4	32.2	−201.9
1995	2,212.6	1,517.2	744.1	558.2	211.0	532.8	92.1	59.1	11.4	2,397.6	1,136.5	872.5	354.6	34.0	−184.9
1996	2,376.1	1,642.0	832.1	581.1	223.6	555.2	100.2	66.0	12.7	2,492.1	1,171.1	921.4	365.3	34.3	−116.0
1997	2,551.9	1,780.5	926.3	612.0	237.1	587.2	103.7	67.9	12.6	2,568.6	1,216.6	947.8	371.4	32.9	−16.7
1998	2,724.2	1,911.7	1,027.0	639.8	239.2	624.2	102.4	75.5	10.3	2,633.4	1,256.0	969.6	372.4	35.4	90.8
1999	2,895.0	2,036.2	1,107.5	674.0	248.8	661.4	106.8	80.6	10.1	2,741.0	1,334.0	1,005.5	357.3	44.2	154.0
2000	3,125.9	2,206.8	1,235.7	708.9	255.0	702.7	117.4	93.7	5.3	2,886.5	1,417.1	1,062.4	362.8	44.3	239.4
2001	3,124.2	2,172.6	1,243.7	729.8	192.0	728.5	120.0	101.9	1.2	3,056.4	1,497.7	1,159.2	344.1	55.3	67.8
2002	2,980.7	2,006.2	1,053.1	760.1	185.9	750.3	116.1	105.3	2.8	3,224.0	1,595.4	1,271.1	319.3	38.2	−243.3
1999: I	2,821.8	1,976.1	1,071.7	657.9	241.2	652.8	103.9	77.8	11.2	2,693.3	1,301.2	992.6	358.2	41.3	128.4
II	2,862.8	2,010.6	1,090.2	667.5	247.0	656.8	105.7	79.3	10.5	2,712.9	1,314.8	996.5	357.6	44.0	149.9
III	2,912.2	2,051.3	1,115.5	679.8	249.8	662.4	107.5	81.0	10.0	2,752.5	1,344.9	1,007.1	354.9	45.6	159.7
IV	2,983.3	2,106.7	1,152.5	691.2	257.0	673.8	110.0	84.3	8.6	2,805.3	1,375.2	1,025.9	358.4	45.8	178.0
2000: I	3,091.1	2,182.2	1,207.0	697.6	270.8	695.5	114.9	90.5	7.9	2,822.4	1,386.3	1,029.6	362.2	44.4	268.7
II	3,121.1	2,207.8	1,231.1	706.9	262.2	696.3	117.4	92.6	7.1	2,880.2	1,416.0	1,055.7	364.2	44.4	240.9
III	3,142.3	2,218.0	1,248.0	712.2	250.5	707.7	117.8	94.6	4.2	2,902.1	1,424.8	1,070.2	362.8	44.3	240.3
IV	3,149.3	2,219.2	1,256.6	718.7	236.4	711.2	119.6	97.1	2.2	2,941.4	1,441.3	1,093.9	362.0	44.1	207.9
2001: I	3,193.3	2,244.2	1,302.1	725.2	209.7	726.3	120.6	99.2	3.0	3,001.2	1,471.1	1,119.0	358.6	52.5	192.1
II	3,200.8	2,250.2	1,308.7	727.2	207.8	727.6	120.6	100.8	1.6	3,047.2	1,490.4	1,150.0	348.6	58.3	153.6
III	2,999.4	2,045.1	1,120.9	727.5	189.5	729.2	120.1	104.4	.6	3,067.9	1,502.1	1,158.7	339.9	67.2	−68.5
IV	3,103.5	2,151.0	1,243.0	739.4	160.9	731.1	118.6	103.0	−.3	3,109.4	1,527.4	1,209.3	329.5	43.2	−5.9
2002: I	2,960.1	1,995.4	1,069.9	745.8	172.4	743.7	116.2	103.6	1.2	3,156.3	1,554.1	1,246.2	315.8	40.1	−196.2
II	2,967.0	1,996.8	1,043.7	757.6	187.8	749.6	115.3	104.7	.6	3,211.0	1,582.1	1,265.5	325.5	37.9	−244.0
III	2,995.9	2,016.6	1,053.0	767.4	189.2	752.1	115.9	106.0	5.4	3,232.1	1,600.5	1,276.2	317.1	38.2	−236.3
IV	2,999.9	2,016.0	1,045.6	769.5	194.2	755.5	117.1	107.2	4.1	3,296.7	1,644.9	1,296.5	318.6	36.7	−296.8
2003: I	2,993.9	1,995.3	1,009.4	774.2	204.9	768.7	116.9	106.7	6.3	3,354.9	1,681.7	1,320.2	309.7	44.7	−361.0
II	2,996.3	1,992.0	1,000.2	782.1	203.9	773.3	117.5	108.7	5.8	3,435.7	1,709.8	1,352.4	315.3	56.9	−439.3
III	2,966.0	1,955.7	936.0	791.5	221.6	776.9	118.7	111.0	3.7	3,452.3	1,718.6	1,378.3	309.1	46.3	−486.3

¹ Includes taxes from the rest of the world, not shown separately.
² Includes an item for the difference between wage accruals and disbursements, not shown separately.

Source: Department of Commerce, Bureau of Economic Analysis.

TABLE B–84.—*Federal Government current receipts and expenditures, national income and product accounts (NIPA), 1959–2003*

[Billions of dollars; quarterly data at seasonally adjusted annual rates]

Year or quarter	Current receipts									Current expenditures					Net Federal Government saving
	Total	Current tax receipts				Contributions for government social insurance	Income receipts on assets	Current transfer receipts	Current surplus of government enterprises	Total [2]	Consumption expenditures	Current transfer payments [3]	Interest payments	Subsidies	
		Total [1]	Personal current taxes	Taxes on production and imports	Taxes on corporate income										
1959	87.0	73.3	38.5	12.2	22.5	13.4	0.0	0.4	−0.1	83.6	50.0	26.2	6.3	1.1	3.3
1960	93.9	76.5	41.8	13.1	21.4	16.0	1.4	.4	−.3	86.7	49.8	27.5	8.4	1.1	7.2
1961	95.5	77.5	42.7	13.2	21.5	16.5	1.5	.5	−.5	92.8	51.6	31.3	7.9	2.0	2.6
1962	103.6	83.3	46.5	14.2	22.5	18.6	1.7	.5	−.5	101.1	57.8	32.3	8.6	2.3	2.5
1963	111.8	88.6	49.1	14.7	24.6	21.0	1.8	.6	−.3	106.4	60.8	34.1	9.3	2.2	5.4
1964	111.8	87.8	46.0	15.5	26.1	21.7	1.8	.7	−.3	110.8	62.8	35.2	10.0	2.7	1.0
1965	120.9	95.7	51.1	15.5	28.9	22.7	1.9	1.1	−.3	117.6	65.7	38.3	10.6	3.0	3.3
1966	137.9	104.8	58.6	14.9	31.4	30.5	2.1	1.2	−.6	135.7	75.9	44.2	11.6	3.9	2.3
1967	146.9	109.9	64.4	15.2	30.0	34.0	2.5	1.1	−.6	156.2	87.1	52.6	12.7	3.8	−9.4
1968	171.2	129.8	76.4	17.0	36.1	37.8	2.9	1.1	−.3	173.5	95.4	59.3	14.6	4.1	−2.3
1969	192.5	146.1	91.7	17.9	36.1	43.1	2.7	1.1	−.5	183.8	98.4	65.1	15.8	4.5	8.7
1970	186.0	138.0	88.9	18.2	30.6	45.3	3.1	1.1	−1.5	201.1	98.6	80.0	17.7	4.8	−15.2
1971	191.7	138.7	85.8	19.1	33.5	50.0	3.5	1.1	−1.6	220.0	102.0	95.5	17.9	4.6	−28.4
1972	220.1	158.4	102.8	18.6	36.6	57.9	3.6	1.3	−1.1	244.4	107.7	111.9	18.8	6.6	−24.4
1973	250.4	173.1	109.6	19.9	43.3	74.0	3.8	1.3	−1.8	261.7	108.9	124.9	22.8	5.1	−11.3
1974	279.5	192.2	126.5	20.2	45.1	83.5	4.2	1.4	−1.8	293.3	118.0	145.7	26.0	3.2	−13.8
1975	277.2	187.0	120.7	22.2	43.6	87.5	4.9	1.5	−3.6	346.2	129.6	183.5	28.9	4.3	−69.0
1976	322.5	218.1	141.2	21.6	54.6	99.1	5.9	1.6	−2.2	374.3	137.2	198.5	33.8	4.9	−51.7
1977	363.4	247.4	162.2	22.9	61.6	110.3	6.7	1.9	−2.9	407.5	150.7	212.9	37.1	6.9	−44.1
1978	423.5	286.9	188.9	25.6	71.4	127.9	8.5	2.4	−2.1	450.0	163.3	237.2	45.3	8.7	−26.5
1979	486.2	326.2	224.6	26.0	74.4	148.9	10.7	2.8	−2.3	497.5	179.0	254.6	55.7	8.2	−11.3
1980	532.1	355.9	250.0	34.0	70.3	162.6	13.7	3.5	−3.6	585.7	207.5	299.1	69.7	9.4	−53.6
1981	619.4	408.1	290.6	50.3	65.7	191.8	18.3	3.8	−2.5	672.7	238.3	329.5	93.9	11.1	−53.3
1982	616.6	386.8	295.0	41.4	49.0	204.9	22.2	5.2	−2.4	748.5	263.3	358.8	111.8	14.5	−131.9
1983	642.3	393.6	286.2	44.8	61.3	221.8	23.8	6.0	−2.9	815.4	286.5	383.0	124.6	20.8	−173.0
1984	709.0	425.7	301.4	47.8	75.2	252.8	26.6	7.3	−3.4	877.1	310.0	396.5	150.3	20.6	−168.1
1985	773.3	460.6	336.0	46.4	76.3	276.5	29.1	9.4	−2.4	948.2	338.4	419.3	169.4	20.9	−175.0
1986	815.2	479.6	350.1	44.0	83.8	297.5	31.4	8.2	−1.5	1,006.0	358.2	445.1	178.2	24.5	−190.8
1987	896.6	544.0	392.5	46.3	103.2	315.9	27.9	10.7	−2.0	1,041.6	374.3	452.9	184.6	29.9	−145.0
1988	958.2	566.7	402.9	50.3	111.1	353.1	30.0	10.8	−2.3	1,092.7	382.5	481.9	199.3	29.0	−134.5
1989	1,037.4	621.7	451.5	50.2	117.2	376.3	28.6	12.4	−1.6	1,167.5	399.2	522.0	219.3	26.8	−130.1
1990	1,081.5	642.8	470.2	51.4	118.1	400.1	30.2	13.5	−5.1	1,253.5	419.8	569.9	237.5	26.4	−172.0
1991	1,101.3	636.1	461.3	62.2	109.9	418.6	30.1	17.9	−1.4	1,315.0	439.5	597.6	250.9	26.9	−213.7
1992	1,147.2	660.4	475.3	63.7	118.8	441.8	25.7	19.4	−.1	1,444.6	445.2	718.7	251.3	29.5	−297.4
1993	1,222.5	713.4	505.5	66.7	138.5	463.6	26.2	21.1	−1.8	1,496.0	441.9	764.7	253.4	36.0	−273.5
1994	1,320.8	781.9	542.7	79.4	156.7	493.7	23.4	22.3	−.4	1,533.1	440.8	799.2	261.3	31.8	−212.3
1995	1,406.5	845.1	586.0	75.9	179.3	519.2	23.7	19.1	−.6	1,603.5	440.5	839.0	290.4	33.7	−197.0
1996	1,524.0	932.4	663.4	73.2	190.6	542.8	26.9	23.1	−1.2	1,665.8	446.3	888.3	297.3	34.0	−141.8
1997	1,653.1	1,030.6	744.3	78.2	203.0	576.4	25.9	19.9	.3	1,708.9	457.7	918.8	300.0	32.4	−55.8
1998	1,773.8	1,116.8	825.8	81.1	204.2	613.8	21.5	21.5	.1	1,734.9	454.6	946.5	298.8	35.0	38.8
1999	1,891.2	1,195.7	893.0	83.9	213.0	651.6	21.5	22.7	−.3	1,787.6	475.1	986.1	282.7	43.8	103.6
2000	2,053.8	1,313.6	999.1	87.8	219.4	691.7	25.2	25.7	−2.3	1,864.4	499.3	1,038.1	283.3	43.8	189.5
2001	2,017.8	1,254.9	1,000.0	86.0	161.8	715.4	24.4	27.4	−4.1	1,967.3	531.7	1,130.5	257.5	47.6	50.5
2002	1,860.7	1,080.7	831.1	87.6	154.8	736.7	20.6	25.4	−3.1	2,100.7	590.8	1,243.4	229.3	37.2	−240.0
1999: I	1,843.6	1,157.5	864.1	81.7	206.3	643.0	20.8	21.9	.4	1,764.2	467.0	971.9	284.4	40.9	79.4
II	1,869.5	1,179.2	879.7	82.1	211.4	647.1	21.2	22.1	−.2	1,764.8	463.9	973.9	283.3	43.6	104.6
III	1,900.2	1,203.9	899.5	84.2	213.9	652.6	21.5	22.5	−.4	1,792.4	477.6	989.5	280.1	45.2	107.8
IV	1,951.6	1,242.4	928.7	87.5	220.2	663.9	22.3	24.2	−1.2	1,828.9	491.8	1,008.9	282.8	45.4	122.7
2000: I	2,035.7	1,301.9	975.4	86.7	233.0	685.3	24.5	24.8	−.8	1,823.0	485.7	1,008.2	285.1	43.9	212.7
II	2,044.9	1,309.4	987.4	88.9	225.5	685.6	25.5	25.3	−.9	1,863.5	505.1	1,028.8	285.7	43.8	181.4
III	2,066.8	1,322.6	1,011.7	88.1	215.6	696.5	25.0	25.8	−3.1	1,875.5	501.5	1,047.8	282.5	43.7	191.2
IV	2,068.0	1,320.4	1,021.7	87.5	203.7	699.4	25.9	26.7	−4.5	1,895.5	505.0	1,067.4	279.6	43.5	172.5
2001: I	2,088.5	1,324.4	1,051.2	87.9	178.1	713.7	26.1	27.4	−3.1	1,932.4	520.0	1,094.2	273.7	44.5	156.1
II	2,082.9	1,319.9	1,050.2	86.8	176.5	714.5	25.0	27.5	−4.1	1,953.9	527.0	1,120.6	262.4	43.9	128.9
III	1,901.8	1,138.9	887.0	84.4	160.2	715.7	24.0	27.5	−4.3	1,981.9	531.1	1,135.8	252.7	62.3	−80.1
IV	1,998.2	1,236.5	1,011.5	84.9	132.4	717.5	22.3	27.1	−5.1	2,001.1	548.6	1,171.3	241.4	39.8	−2.8
2002: I	1,857.7	1,085.2	849.0	85.4	143.4	730.3	20.2	26.1	−4.0	2,046.5	569.4	1,211.9	227.1	38.2	−188.8
II	1,865.4	1,088.8	836.6	88.1	156.4	736.1	19.7	25.8	−5.2	2,097.4	582.6	1,241.6	235.9	37.2	−232.0
III	1,859.9	1,076.1	823.6	87.9	157.5	738.6	20.5	25.7	−1.0	2,102.8	590.4	1,249.2	226.7	36.5	−242.9
IV	1,859.7	1,072.7	815.4	89.0	161.7	741.9	22.0	25.4	−2.3	2,156.1	620.7	1,270.8	227.6	37.0	−296.3
2003: I	1,863.5	1,060.3	794.3	88.3	171.0	755.1	22.5	26.0	−.4	2,184.0	635.9	1,287.3	217.7	44.5	−320.4
II	1,863.9	1,057.1	794.6	87.7	167.9	758.5	23.6	26.3	−1.6	2,288.5	668.9	1,339.5	222.5	56.3	−424.7
III	1,784.3	972.1	696.3	86.3	182.8	763.1	24.9	26.9	−2.5	2,283.7	672.3	1,348.9	215.6	47.0	−499.4

[1] Includes taxes from the rest of the world, not shown separately.
[2] Includes an item for the difference between wage accruals and disbursements, not shown separately.
[3] Includes Federal grants-in-aid.

Source: Department of Commerce, Bureau of Economic Analysis.

TABLE B–85.—*State and local government current receipts and expenditures, national income and product accounts (NIPA), 1959–2003*

[Billions of dollars; quarterly data at seasonally adjusted annual rates]

Year or quarter	Current receipts									Current expenditures					Net State and local government saving
	Total	Current tax receipts				Contributions for government social insurance	Income receipts on assets	Current transfer receipts [1]	Current surplus of government enterprises	Total [2]	Consumption expenditures	Government social benefit payments to persons	Interest payments	Subsidies	
		Total	Personal current taxes	Taxes on production and imports	Taxes on corporate income										
1959	40.6	33.8	3.8	28.8	1.2	0.4	1.1	4.2	1.1	36.9	30.7	4.3	1.8	0.0	3.8
1960	44.5	37.0	4.2	31.5	1.2	.5	1.3	4.5	1.2	40.2	33.5	4.6	2.1	.0	4.3
1961	48.1	39.7	4.6	33.8	1.3	.5	1.4	5.2	1.3	43.8	36.6	5.0	2.2	.0	4.3
1962	52.0	42.8	5.0	36.3	1.5	.5	1.5	5.8	1.4	46.8	39.0	5.3	2.4	.0	5.2
1963	56.0	45.8	5.4	38.7	1.7	.6	1.6	6.4	1.6	50.3	41.9	5.7	2.7	.0	5.7
1964	61.3	49.8	6.1	41.8	1.8	.7	1.9	7.3	1.6	54.9	45.8	6.2	2.9	.0	6.4
1965	66.5	53.9	6.6	45.3	2.0	.8	2.2	8.0	1.7	60.0	50.2	6.7	3.1	.0	6.5
1966	74.9	58.8	7.8	48.8	2.2	.8	2.6	11.1	1.6	67.2	56.1	7.6	3.4	.0	7.8
1967	82.5	64.0	8.6	52.8	2.6	.9	3.0	13.1	1.5	75.5	62.6	9.2	3.7	.0	7.0
1968	93.5	73.4	10.6	59.5	3.3	.9	3.5	14.2	1.5	86.0	70.4	11.4	4.2	.0	7.5
1969	105.5	82.5	12.8	66.0	3.6	1.0	4.3	16.2	1.5	97.5	79.9	13.2	4.4	.0	8.0
1970	120.1	91.3	14.2	73.3	3.7	1.1	5.2	21.1	1.5	113.0	91.5	16.1	5.3	.0	7.1
1971	134.9	101.7	15.9	81.5	4.3	1.2	5.5	25.2	1.4	128.5	102.7	19.3	6.5	.0	6.5
1972	158.4	115.6	20.9	89.4	5.3	1.3	5.9	34.0	1.6	142.8	113.2	22.0	7.5	.1	15.6
1973	174.3	126.3	22.8	97.4	6.0	1.5	7.8	37.3	1.5	158.6	126.0	24.1	8.5	.1	15.7
1974	188.1	136.0	24.5	104.8	6.7	1.7	10.2	39.3	.9	178.7	143.7	25.3	9.6	.1	9.3
1975	209.6	147.4	26.9	113.2	7.3	1.8	11.2	48.7	.4	207.1	165.1	30.8	11.1	.2	2.5
1976	233.7	165.7	31.1	125.0	9.6	2.2	10.4	55.0	.4	226.3	179.5	34.1	12.5	.2	7.4
1977	259.9	183.7	35.4	136.9	11.4	2.8	11.7	61.4	.3	246.8	195.9	37.0	13.7	.2	13.1
1978	287.6	198.2	40.5	145.6	12.1	3.4	14.7	71.1	.3	268.9	213.2	40.8	14.9	.2	18.7
1979	308.4	212.0	44.0	154.4	13.6	3.9	20.1	72.7	-.3	295.4	233.3	44.3	17.2	.3	13.0
1980	338.2	230.0	48.9	166.7	14.5	3.6	26.3	79.5	-1.2	329.4	258.4	51.2	19.4	.4	8.8
1981	370.2	255.8	54.6	185.7	15.4	3.9	32.0	81.0	-2.4	362.7	282.3	57.1	22.8	.4	7.6
1982	391.4	273.2	59.1	200.0	14.0	4.0	36.7	79.1	-1.6	393.6	304.9	61.2	27.1	.5	-2.2
1983	428.6	300.9	66.1	218.9	15.9	4.1	41.4	82.4	-.2	423.7	324.1	66.9	32.3	.4	4.9
1984	480.2	337.3	76.0	242.5	18.8	4.7	47.7	89.0	1.5	456.2	347.7	71.2	37.0	.4	23.9
1985	521.1	363.7	81.4	262.1	20.2	4.9	54.9	94.5	3.2	498.7	381.8	77.3	39.4	.3	22.3
1986	561.6	389.5	87.2	279.7	22.7	6.0	58.4	105.0	2.8	540.7	417.9	84.3	38.2	.3	21.0
1987	590.6	422.1	96.6	301.6	23.9	7.2	58.1	100.0	3.1	578.1	440.9	90.7	46.2	.3	12.4
1988	635.5	452.8	102.1	324.6	26.0	8.4	60.5	109.0	4.8	617.6	470.4	98.5	48.4	.4	17.9
1989	687.3	488.0	114.6	349.1	24.2	9.0	65.7	118.1	6.5	666.5	502.1	109.3	54.6	.4	20.8
1990	737.8	519.1	122.6	374.1	22.5	10.0	68.4	133.5	6.7	730.5	544.6	127.7	57.9	.4	7.2
1991	789.2	543.3	125.3	395.3	23.6	11.6	68.0	158.2	7.1	793.3	574.6	156.5	61.7	.4	-4.2
1992	845.7	579.8	135.3	420.1	24.4	13.1	64.8	180.3	7.7	845.0	602.7	180.0	61.9	.4	.7
1993	886.9	604.7	141.1	436.8	26.9	14.1	61.4	197.7	9.0	886.0	630.3	195.2	60.2	.4	.9
1994	942.9	644.2	148.0	466.3	30.0	14.5	63.2	211.9	9.0	932.4	663.3	206.7	62.0	.3	10.5
1995	990.2	672.1	158.1	482.4	31.7	15.8	68.4	224.1	12.0	978.2	696.1	217.6	64.2	.3	12.0
1996	1,043.3	709.6	168.7	507.9	33.0	12.5	73.3	234.1	13.9	1,017.5	724.8	224.3	68.1	.3	25.8
1997	1,097.4	749.9	182.0	533.8	34.1	10.8	77.8	246.6	12.3	1,058.3	758.9	227.6	71.4	.4	39.1
1998	1,163.2	794.9	201.2	558.8	34.9	10.4	80.9	266.8	10.2	1,111.2	801.4	235.8	73.6	.4	52.0
1999	1,236.7	840.4	214.5	590.2	35.8	9.8	85.3	290.8	10.4	1,186.3	858.9	252.4	74.6	.4	50.4
2000	1,319.5	893.2	236.6	621.1	35.5	11.0	92.2	315.4	7.7	1,269.5	917.8	271.7	79.5	.5	50.0
2001	1,382.7	917.7	243.7	643.8	30.2	13.2	95.6	350.8	5.4	1,365.4	966.1	305.1	86.6	7.7	17.3
2002	1,424.7	925.5	221.9	672.5	31.1	13.5	95.5	384.2	5.9	1,427.9	1,004.6	332.3	89.9	1.0	-3.2
1999: I	1,205.1	818.6	207.6	576.1	34.9	9.8	83.0	282.8	10.8	1,156.1	834.3	247.7	73.8	.4	49.0
II	1,217.1	831.4	210.4	585.4	35.6	9.7	84.4	280.9	10.7	1,171.8	850.8	246.3	74.2	.4	45.3
III	1,249.6	847.3	216.0	595.4	35.9	9.7	86.0	296.1	10.4	1,197.6	867.3	255.1	74.8	.4	52.0
IV	1,275.0	864.3	223.8	603.7	36.8	9.9	87.7	303.3	9.8	1,219.7	883.3	260.3	75.6	.4	55.3
2000: I	1,294.4	880.3	231.6	610.9	37.8	10.3	90.4	304.7	8.8	1,238.5	900.6	260.4	77.0	.5	55.9
II	1,319.0	898.4	243.7	618.0	36.7	10.7	91.9	310.0	8.0	1,259.5	910.8	269.6	78.5	.5	59.5
III	1,330.5	895.4	236.3	624.1	35.0	11.2	92.8	323.8	7.3	1,281.6	923.4	277.4	80.3	.6	49.0
IV	1,333.9	898.8	234.8	631.2	32.8	11.8	93.7	323.0	6.6	1,298.5	936.3	279.2	82.4	.6	35.4
2001: I	1,370.5	919.8	250.9	637.3	31.6	12.6	94.5	337.5	6.0	1,334.4	951.1	290.4	84.9	8.0	36.1
II	1,396.5	930.2	258.4	640.5	31.3	13.1	95.6	351.8	5.7	1,371.8	963.3	307.9	86.2	14.4	24.6
III	1,371.4	906.3	233.9	643.1	29.3	13.6	96.1	350.7	4.9	1,359.7	971.1	296.6	87.2	4.8	11.6
IV	1,392.6	914.5	231.6	654.5	28.5	13.6	96.3	363.3	4.8	1,395.6	978.8	325.4	88.1	3.4	-3.0
2002: I	1,393.0	910.2	220.9	660.3	29.0	13.5	96.1	368.0	5.2	1,400.3	984.8	324.9	88.8	1.9	-7.4
II	1,406.2	908.0	207.1	669.5	31.3	13.5	95.6	383.4	5.7	1,418.2	999.5	328.4	89.6	.7	-11.9
III	1,442.8	940.5	229.4	679.5	31.6	13.5	95.4	387.1	6.3	1,436.1	1,010.1	333.8	90.4	1.8	6.8
IV	1,456.6	943.3	230.3	680.5	32.5	13.6	95.0	398.2	6.5	1,457.0	1,024.2	342.1	91.0	-.3	-.4
2003: I	1,441.2	935.0	215.1	685.9	33.9	13.7	94.4	391.5	6.6	1,481.8	1,045.8	343.7	92.0	.3	-40
II	1,477.9	934.9	205.6	694.4	35.0	13.8	93.9	427.9	7.4	1,492.6	1,040.9	358.4	92.7	.6	-14.
III	1,528.0	983.6	239.7	705.1	38.8	13.9	93.9	430.4	6.2	1,514.9	1,046.3	375.7	93.5	-.7	13.

[1] Includes Federal grants-in-aid.
[2] Includes an item for the difference between wage accruals and disbursements, not shown separately.

Source: Department of Commerce, Bureau of Economic Analysis.

TABLE B–86.—*State and local government revenues and expenditures, selected fiscal years, 1927–2001*

[Millions of dollars]

Fiscal year[1]	General revenues by source[2]							General expenditures by function[2]				
	Total	Property taxes	Sales and gross receipts taxes	Individual income taxes	Corporation net income taxes	Revenue from Federal Government	All other[3]	Total	Education	Highways	Public welfare	All other[4]
1927	7,271	4,730	470	70	92	116	1,793	7,210	2,235	1,809	151	3,015
1932	7,267	4,487	752	74	79	232	1,643	7,765	2,311	1,741	444	3,269
1934	7,678	4,076	1,008	80	49	1,016	1,449	7,181	1,831	1,509	889	2,952
1936	8,395	4,093	1,484	153	113	948	1,604	7,644	2,177	1,425	827	3,215
1938	9,228	4,440	1,794	218	165	800	1,811	8,757	2,491	1,650	1,069	3,547
1940	9,609	4,430	1,982	224	156	945	1,872	9,229	2,638	1,573	1,156	3,862
1942	10,418	4,537	2,351	276	272	858	2,123	9,190	2,586	1,490	1,225	3,889
1944	10,908	4,604	2,289	342	451	954	2,269	8,863	2,793	1,200	1,133	3,737
1946	12,356	4,986	2,986	422	447	855	2,661	11,028	3,356	1,672	1,409	4,591
1948	17,250	6,126	4,442	543	592	1,861	3,685	17,684	5,379	3,036	2,099	7,170
1950	20,911	7,349	5,154	788	593	2,486	4,541	22,787	7,177	3,803	2,940	8,867
1952	25,181	8,652	6,357	998	846	2,566	5,763	26,098	8,318	4,650	2,788	10,342
1953	27,307	9,375	6,927	1,065	817	2,870	6,252	27,910	9,390	4,987	2,914	10,619
1954	29,012	9,967	7,276	1,127	778	2,966	6,897	30,701	10,557	5,527	3,060	11,557
1955	31,073	10,735	7,643	1,237	744	3,131	7,584	33,724	11,907	6,452	3,168	12,197
1956	34,667	11,749	8,691	1,538	890	3,335	8,465	36,711	13,220	6,953	3,139	13,399
1957	38,164	12,864	9,467	1,754	984	3,843	9,252	40,375	14,134	7,816	3,485	14,940
1958	41,219	14,047	9,829	1,759	1,018	4,865	9,699	44,851	15,919	8,567	3,818	16,547
1959	45,306	14,983	10,437	1,994	1,001	6,377	10,516	48,887	17,283	9,592	4,136	17,876
1960	50,505	16,405	11,849	2,463	1,180	6,974	11,634	51,876	18,719	9,428	4,404	19,325
1961	54,037	18,002	12,463	2,613	1,266	7,131	12,563	56,201	20,574	9,844	4,720	21,063
1962	58,252	19,054	13,494	3,037	1,308	7,871	13,489	60,206	22,216	10,357	5,084	22,549
1963	62,890	20,089	14,456	3,269	1,505	8,722	14,850	64,816	23,776	11,136	5,481	24,423
1962-63	62,269	19,833	14,446	3,267	1,505	8,663	14,556	63,977	23,729	11,150	5,420	23,678
1963-64	68,443	21,241	15,762	3,791	1,695	10,002	15,951	69,302	26,286	11,664	5,766	25,586
1964-65	74,000	22,583	17,118	4,090	1,929	11,029	17,250	74,678	28,563	12,221	6,315	27,579
1965-66	83,036	24,670	19,085	4,760	2,038	13,214	19,269	82,843	33,287	12,770	6,757	30,029
1966-67	91,197	26,047	20,530	5,825	2,227	15,370	21,198	93,350	37,919	13,932	8,218	33,281
1967-68	101,264	27,747	22,911	7,308	2,518	17,181	23,599	102,411	41,158	14,481	9,857	36,915
1968-69	114,550	30,673	26,519	8,908	3,180	19,153	26,117	116,728	47,238	15,417	12,110	41,963
1969-70	130,756	34,054	30,322	10,812	3,738	21,857	29,973	131,332	52,718	16,427	14,679	47,508
1970-71	144,927	37,852	33,233	11,900	3,424	26,146	32,372	150,674	59,413	18,095	18,226	54,940
1971-72	167,535	42,877	37,518	15,227	4,416	31,342	36,156	168,549	65,813	19,021	21,117	62,598
1972-73	190,222	45,283	42,047	17,994	5,425	39,264	40,210	181,357	69,713	18,615	23,582	69,447
1973-74	207,670	47,705	46,098	19,491	6,015	41,820	46,542	198,959	75,833	19,946	25,085	78,095
1974-75	228,171	51,491	49,815	21,454	6,642	47,034	51,735	230,722	87,858	22,528	28,156	92,180
1975-76	256,176	57,001	54,547	24,575	7,273	55,589	57,191	256,731	97,216	23,907	32,604	103,004
1976-77	285,157	62,527	60,641	29,246	9,174	62,444	61,125	274,215	102,780	23,058	35,906	112,472
1977-78	315,960	66,422	67,596	33,176	10,738	69,592	68,435	296,984	110,758	24,609	39,140	122,478
1978-79	343,236	64,944	74,247	36,932	12,128	75,164	79,822	327,517	119,448	28,440	41,898	137,731
1979-80	382,322	68,499	79,927	42,080	13,321	83,029	95,467	369,086	133,211	33,311	47,288	155,276
1980-81	423,404	74,969	85,971	46,426	14,143	90,294	111,599	407,449	145,784	34,603	54,105	172,957
1981-82	457,654	82,067	93,613	50,738	15,028	87,282	128,925	436,733	154,282	34,520	57,996	189,935
1982-83	486,753	89,105	100,247	55,129	14,258	90,007	138,008	466,516	163,876	36,655	60,906	205,080
1983-84	542,730	96,457	114,097	64,529	17,141	96,935	153,571	505,008	176,108	39,419	66,414	223,068
1984-85	598,121	103,757	126,376	70,361	19,152	106,158	172,317	553,899	192,686	44,989	71,479	244,745
1985-86	641,486	111,709	135,005	74,365	19,994	113,099	187,314	605,623	210,819	49,368	75,868	269,568
1986-87	686,860	121,203	144,091	83,935	22,425	114,857	200,350	657,134	226,619	52,355	82,650	295,510
1987-88	726,762	132,212	156,452	88,350	23,663	117,602	208,482	704,921	242,683	55,621	89,090	317,527
1988-89	786,129	142,400	166,336	97,806	25,926	125,824	227,838	762,360	263,898	58,105	97,879	342,479
1989-90	849,502	155,613	177,885	105,640	23,566	136,802	249,996	834,818	288,148	61,057	110,518	375,094
1990-91	902,207	167,999	185,570	109,341	22,242	154,099	262,955	908,108	309,302	64,937	130,402	403,467
1991-92	979,137	180,337	197,731	115,638	23,880	179,174	282,376	981,253	324,652	67,351	158,723	430,526
1992-93	1,041,643	189,744	209,649	123,235	26,417	198,663	293,935	1,030,434	342,287	68,370	170,705	449,072
1993-94	1,100,490	197,141	223,628	128,810	28,320	215,492	307,099	1,077,665	353,287	72,067	183,394	468,916
1994-95	1,169,505	203,451	237,268	137,931	31,406	228,771	330,677	1,149,863	378,273	77,109	196,703	497,779
1995-96	1,222,821	209,440	248,993	146,844	32,009	234,891	350,645	1,193,276	398,859	79,092	197,354	517,971
1996-97	1,289,237	218,877	261,418	159,042	33,820	244,847	371,233	1,249,984	418,416	82,062	203,779	545,727
1997-98	1,365,762	230,150	274,883	175,630	34,412	255,048	395,639	1,318,042	450,365	87,214	208,120	572,343
1998-99	1,434,464	240,107	290,993	189,309	33,922	270,628	409,505	1,402,369	483,259	90,018	218,957	607,134
1999-2000	1,541,322	249,178	309,290	211,661	36,059	291,950	443,186	1,506,797	521,612	101,336	237,336	646,512
2000-01	1,647,161	263,689	320,217	226,334	35,296	324,033	477,592	1,626,063	563,572	107,235	257,380	697,876

[1] Fiscal years not the same for all governments. See Note.
[2] Excludes revenues or expenditures of publicly owned utilities and liquor stores, and of insurance-trust activities. Intergovernmental receipts and payments between State and local governments are also excluded.
[3] Includes other taxes and charges and miscellaneous revenues.
[4] Includes expenditures for libraries, hospitals, health, employment security administration, veterans' services, air transportation, water transport and terminals, parking facilities, transit subsidies, police protection, fire protection, correction, protective inspection and regulation, sewerage, natural resources, parks and recreation, housing and community development, solid waste management, financial administration, judicial and legal, general public buildings, other government administration, interest on general debt, and general expenditures, n.e.c.

Note.—Except for States listed, data for fiscal years listed from 1962-63 to 2000-01 are the aggregation of data for government fiscal years that ended in the 12-month period from July 1 to June 30 of those years (Texas used August and Alabama and Michigan used September). Data for 1963 and earlier years include data for governments fiscal years ending during that particular calendar year.

Data are not available for intervening years.

Source: Department of Commerce, Bureau of the Census.

TABLE B–87.—*U.S. Treasury securities outstanding by kind of obligation, 1967–2003*

[Billions of dollars]

End of year or month	Total Treasury securities outstanding [1]	Marketable						Nonmarketable				
		Total [2]	Treasury bills	Treasury notes	Treasury bonds	Treasury inflation-indexed		Total	U.S. savings securities [3]	Foreign series [4]	Government account series	Other [5]
						Notes	Bonds					
Fiscal year:												
1967	322.3	[6] 210.7	58.5	49.1	97.4	....	....	111.6	51.2	1.5	56.2	2.7
1968	344.4	226.6	64.4	71.1	91.1	....	....	117.8	51.7	3.7	59.5	2.8
1969	351.7	226.1	68.4	78.9	78.8	....	....	125.6	51.7	4.1	66.8	3.1
1970	369.0	232.6	76.2	93.5	63.0	....	....	136.4	51.3	4.8	76.3	4.1
1971	396.3	245.5	86.7	104.8	54.0	....	....	150.8	53.0	9.3	82.8	5.8
1972	425.4	257.2	94.6	113.4	49.1	....	....	168.2	55.9	19.0	89.6	3.7
1973	456.4	263.0	100.1	117.8	45.1	....	....	193.4	59.4	28.5	101.7	3.7
1974	473.2	266.6	105.0	128.4	33.1	....	....	206.7	61.9	25.0	115.4	4.3
1975	532.1	315.6	128.6	150.3	36.8	....	....	216.5	65.5	23.2	124.2	3.6
1976	619.3	392.6	161.2	191.8	39.6	....	....	226.7	69.7	21.5	130.6	4.9
1977	697.6	443.5	156.1	241.7	45.7	....	....	254.1	75.4	21.8	140.1	16.8
1978	767.0	485.2	160.9	267.9	56.4	....	....	281.8	79.8	21.7	153.3	27.1
1979	819.0	506.7	161.4	274.2	71.1	....	....	312.3	80.4	28.1	176.4	27.4
1980	906.4	594.5	199.8	310.9	83.8	....	....	311.9	72.7	25.2	189.8	24.2
1981	996.5	683.2	223.4	363.6	96.2	....	....	313.3	68.0	20.5	201.1	23.7
1982	1,140.9	824.4	277.9	442.9	103.6	....	....	316.5	67.3	14.6	210.5	24.1
1983	1,375.8	1,024.0	340.7	557.5	125.7	....	....	351.8	70.0	11.5	234.7	35.6
1984	1,559.6	1,176.6	356.8	661.7	158.1	....	....	383.0	72.8	8.8	259.5	41.8
1985	1,821.0	1,360.2	384.2	776.4	199.5	....	....	460.8	77.0	6.6	313.9	63.3
1986	2,122.7	[2] 1,564.3	410.7	896.9	241.7	....	....	558.4	85.6	4.1	365.9	102.8
1987	2,347.8	[2] 1,676.0	378.3	1,005.1	277.6	....	....	671.8	97.0	4.4	440.7	129.8
1988	2,599.9	[2] 1,802.9	398.5	1,089.6	299.9	....	....	797.0	106.2	6.3	536.5	148.0
1989	2,836.3	[2] 1,892.8	406.6	1,133.2	338.0	....	....	943.5	114.0	6.8	663.7	159.0
1990	3,210.9	[2] 2,092.8	482.5	1,218.1	377.2	....	....	1,118.2	122.2	36.0	779.4	180.6
1991	3,662.8	[2] 2,390.7	564.6	1,387.7	423.4	....	....	1,272.1	133.5	41.6	908.4	188.5
1992	4,061.8	[2] 2,677.5	634.3	1,566.3	461.8	....	....	1,384.3	148.3	37.0	1,011.0	188.0
1993	4,408.6	[2] 2,904.9	658.4	1,734.2	497.4	....	....	1,503.7	167.0	42.5	1,114.3	179.9
1994	4,689.5	[2] 3,091.6	697.3	1,867.5	511.8	....	....	1,597.9	176.4	42.0	1,211.7	167.8
1995	4,950.6	[2] 3,260.4	742.5	1,980.3	522.6	....	....	1,690.2	181.2	41.0	1,324.3	143.8
1996	5,220.8	[2] 3,418.4	761.2	2,098.7	543.5	....	....	1,802.4	184.1	37.5	1,454.7	126.1
1997	5,407.5	[2] 3,439.6	701.9	2,122.2	576.2	24.4	....	1,967.9	182.7	34.9	1,608.5	141.9
1998	5,518.7	[2] 3,331.0	637.6	2,009.1	610.4	41.9	17.0	2,187.7	180.8	35.1	1,777.3	194.4
1999	5,647.2	[2] 3,233.0	653.2	1,828.8	643.7	67.6	24.8	2,414.2	180.0	31.0	2,005.2	198.1
2000	5,622.1	[2] 2,992.8	616.2	1,611.3	635.3	81.6	33.4	2,629.3	177.7	25.4	2,242.9	183.3
2001 [1]	5,807.5	[2] 2,930.7	734.9	1,433.0	613.0	95.1	39.7	2,876.7	186.5	18.3	2,492.1	179.9
2002	6,228.2	[2] 3,136.7	868.3	1,521.6	593.0	93.7	45.1	3,091.5	193.3	12.5	2,707.3	178.4
2003	6,783.2	3,460.7	918.2	1,799.5	576.9	120.0	46.1	3,322.5	201.6	11.0	2,912.2	197.7
2002: Jan	5,937.2	[2] 2,968.2	792.7	1,411.9	602.7	101.1	44.7	2,969.0	190.9	16.4	2,584.8	176.9
Feb	6,003.5	[2] 3,033.6	833.2	1,443.2	596.8	100.7	44.6	2,969.8	191.5	14.8	2,588.1	175.5
Mar	6,006.0	[2] 3,035.0	834.4	1,443.3	596.8	100.9	44.7	2,971.0	192.0	14.6	2,589.7	174.8
Apr	5,984.7	[2] 2,992.7	793.5	1,445.4	593.0	101.3	44.6	2,991.9	192.4	14.8	2,610.5	174.2
May	6,019.3	[2] 3,045.1	816.1	1,474.3	593.0	101.9	44.8	2,974.2	192.6	14.4	2,587.0	180.2
June	6,126.5	[2] 3,052.3	822.5	1,474.3	593.0	102.4	45.1	3,074.2	192.8	13.3	2,691.4	176.7
July	6,159.7	[2] 3,095.9	862.3	1,487.0	593.0	93.6	45.1	3,063.8	193.0	12.9	2,689.2	168.8
Aug	6,210.5	[2] 3,145.6	890.7	1,508.2	593.0	93.6	45.1	3,064.9	193.1	12.7	2,683.5	175.6
Sept	6,228.2	[2] 3,136.7	868.3	1,521.6	593.0	93.7	45.1	3,091.5	193.3	12.5	2,707.3	178.4
Oct	6,282.5	3,148.7	881.9	1,527.4	593.0	101.1	45.3	3,133.9	193.9	12.7	2,743.6	183.7
Nov	6,343.5	3,205.7	901.4	1,568.9	588.8	101.3	45.4	3,137.8	194.4	12.5	2,742.6	188.2
Dec	6,405.7	3,205.3	888.8	1,580.9	588.8	101.4	45.4	3,200.4	194.9	11.2	2,806.9	187.4
2003: Jan	6,401.4	3,197.2	869.3	1,586.2	588.8	107.5	45.4	3,204.2	195.8	11.2	2,814.6	182.5
Feb	6,445.8	3,273.7	918.8	1,616.6	585.8	107.2	45.3	3,172.1	196.4	11.6	2,780.5	183.5
Mar	6,460.8	[2] 3,332.0	955.0	1,622.9	585.8	107.7	45.5	3,128.8	196.9	12.2	2,736.8	182.9
Apr	6,460.4	[2] 3,316.4	929.9	1,631.3	585.7	108.5	45.9	3,144.0	197.7	12.2	2,754.2	179.9
May	6,558.1	[2] 3,353.9	910.8	1,690.3	582.5	109.2	46.2	3,204.2	198.5	11.8	2,819.2	174.8
June	6,670.1	3,379.1	927.8	1,713.8	582.5	109.0	46.1	3,291.0	199.2	11.7	2,905.5	174.7
July	6,751.2	3,413.1	937.0	1,727.8	582.5	119.8	46.0	3,338.1	200.0	11.6	2,900.9	225.6
Aug	6,790.0	3,454.2	961.7	1,749.7	576.9	119.9	46.0	3,335.8	200.8	11.1	2,895.2	228.8
Sept	6,783.2	3,460.7	918.2	1,799.5	576.9	120.0	46.1	3,322.5	201.6	11.0	2,912.2	197.7
Oct	6,872.7	3,519.3	943.9	1,822.7	576.9	129.5	46.3	3,353.4	203.0	11.0	2,935.2	204.1
Nov	6,925.1	3,563.0	954.8	1,867.4	564.4	130.0	46.3	3,362.1	203.6	9.9	2,945.4	203.3
Dec	6,998.0	3,575.2	928.8	1,905.8	564.4	129.8	46.4	3,422.8	203.9	9.7	3,007.0	202.2

[1] Data beginning January 2001 are interest-bearing and noninterest-bearing securities; prior data are interest-bearing securities only.
[2] Includes Federal Financing Bank securities, not shown separately, in the amount of $15 billion.
[3] Through 1996, series is U.S. savings bonds. Beginning 1997, includes U.S. retirement plan bonds, U.S. individual retirement bonds, and U.S. savings notes previously included in "other" nonmarketable securities.
[4] Nonmarketable certificates of indebtedness, notes, bonds, and bills in the Treasury foreign series of dollar-denominated and foreign-currency denominated issues.
[5] Includes depository bonds, retirement plan bonds, Rural Electrification Administration bonds, State and local bonds, special issues held only by U.S. Government agencies and trust funds and the Federal home loan banks and, beginning in July 2003, depositary compensation securities.
[6] Includes $5,610 million in certificates not shown separately.

Note.—Through fiscal year 1976, the fiscal year was on a July 1-June 30 basis; beginning October 1976 (fiscal year 1977), the fiscal year is on an October 1-September 30 basis.

Source: Department of the Treasury.

TABLE B–88.—*Maturity distribution and average length of marketable interest-bearing public debt securities held by private investors, 1967–2003*

End of year or month	Amount out-standing, privately held	Maturity class					Average length [1]	
		Within 1 year	1 to 5 years	5 to 10 years	10 to 20 years	20 years and over	Years	Months
	Millions of dollars						Years	Months
Fiscal year:								
1967	150,321	56,561	53,584	21,057	6,153	12,968	5	1
1968	159,671	66,746	52,295	21,850	6,110	12,670	4	5
1969	156,008	69,311	50,182	18,078	6,097	12,337	4	2
1970	157,910	76,443	57,035	8,286	7,876	8,272	3	8
1971	161,863	74,803	58,557	14,503	6,357	7,645	3	6
1972	165,978	79,509	57,157	16,033	6,358	6,922	3	3
1973	167,869	84,041	54,139	16,385	8,741	4,564	3	1
1974	164,862	87,150	50,103	14,197	9,930	3,481	2	11
1975	210,382	115,677	65,852	15,385	8,857	4,611	2	8
1976	279,782	150,296	90,578	24,169	8,087	6,652	2	7
1977	326,674	161,329	113,319	33,067	8,428	10,531	2	11
1978	356,501	163,819	132,993	33,500	11,383	14,805	3	3
1979	380,530	181,883	127,574	32,279	18,489	20,304	3	7
1980	463,717	220,084	156,244	38,809	25,901	22,679	3	9
1981	549,863	256,187	182,237	48,743	32,569	30,127	4	0
1982	682,043	314,436	221,783	75,749	33,017	37,058	3	11
1983	862,631	379,579	294,955	99,174	40,826	48,097	4	1
1984	1,017,488	437,941	332,808	130,417	49,664	66,658	4	6
1985	1,185,675	472,661	402,766	159,383	62,853	88,012	4	11
1986	1,354,275	506,903	467,348	189,995	70,664	119,365	5	3
1987	1,445,366	483,582	526,746	209,160	72,862	153,016	5	9
1988	1,555,208	524,201	552,993	232,453	74,186	171,375	5	9
1989	1,654,660	546,751	578,333	247,428	80,616	201,532	6	0
1990	1,841,903	626,297	630,144	267,573	82,713	235,176	6	1
1991	2,113,799	713,778	761,243	280,574	84,900	273,304	6	0
1992	2,363,802	808,705	866,329	295,921	84,706	308,141	5	11
1993	2,562,336	858,135	978,714	306,663	94,345	324,479	5	10
1994	2,719,861	877,932	1,128,322	289,998	88,208	335,401	5	8
1995	2,870,781	1,002,875	1,157,492	290,111	87,297	333,006	5	4
1996	3,011,185	1,058,558	1,212,258	306,643	111,360	322,366	5	3
1997	2,998,846	1,017,913	1,206,993	321,622	154,205	298,113	5	5
1998	2,856,637	940,572	1,105,175	319,331	157,347	334,212	5	10
1999	2,728,011	915,145	962,644	378,163	149,703	322,356	6	0
2000	2,469,152	858,903	791,540	355,382	167,082	296,246	6	2
2001	2,328,302	900,178	650,522	329,247	174,653	273,702	6	1
2002	2,492,821	939,986	802,032	311,176	203,816	235,811	5	6
2003	2,804,092	1,057,049	955,239	351,552	243,755	196,497	5	1
2002: Jan	2,371,510	906,466	712,370	307,869	197,484	247,321	5	10
Feb	2,430,599	959,624	719,279	308,109	197,408	246,179	5	9
Mar	2,400,776	953,703	696,282	307,424	197,398	245,968	5	9
Apr	2,375,274	904,061	725,849	306,097	195,227	244,040	5	9
May	2,419,549	912,351	761,718	305,994	195,227	244,258	5	8
June	2,402,091	916,256	740,340	305,792	195,227	244,478	5	8
July	2,457,756	922,600	781,212	314,301	195,227	244,416	5	7
Aug	2,483,538	968,597	764,257	311,100	203,816	235,768	5	7
Sept	2,492,821	939,986	802,032	311,176	203,816	235,811	5	6
Oct	2,519,727	951,452	810,083	318,435	203,816	235,940	5	5
Nov	2,555,144	992,371	794,585	328,363	209,639	230,186	5	5
Dec	2,575,371	981,309	825,882	328,290	209,639	230,251	5	4
2003: Jan	2,567,292	964,715	845,144	317,542	209,639	230,253	5	4
Feb	2,636,316	995,366	878,201	322,940	222,785	217,023	5	4
Mar	2,675,019	1,031,783	880,646	322,672	222,785	217,132	5	2
Apr	2,653,534	1,007,588	882,574	323,174	222,785	217,412	5	2
May	2,666,851	1,020,653	885,966	319,770	222,785	217,678	5	3
June	2,726,476	1,042,539	923,907	319,643	222,785	217,602	5	1
July	2,759,673	1,066,487	922,326	330,539	222,785	217,536	5	1
Aug	2,786,706	1,090,480	916,129	339,736	243,835	196,526	5	1
Sept	2,804,092	1,057,049	955,239	351,552	243,755	196,497	5	1
Oct	2,859,992	1,090,086	968,750	360,755	243,755	196,646	5	0
Nov	2,877,933	1,127,794	953,987	355,619	243,755	196,778	5	0

[1] In 2002, the average length calculation was revised to include Treasury inflation-indexed notes (first offered in 1997) and bonds (first offered in 1998).

Note.—Through fiscal year 1976, the fiscal year was on a July 1-June 30 basis; beginning October 1976 (fiscal year 1977), the fiscal year is on an October 1-September 30 basis.

Source: Department of the Treasury.

TABLE B-89.—Estimated ownership of U.S. Treasury securities, 1992–2003

[Billions of dollars]

End of month	Total public debt [1]	Federal Reserve and Government accounts [2]	Total privately held	Depository institutions [3]	U.S. savings bonds [4]	Pension funds: Private [5]	Pension funds: State and local governments	Insurance companies	Mutual funds [6]	State and local governments	Foreign and international [7]	Other investors [8]
1992: Mar	3,881.3	1,215.5	2,665.8	300.5	142.0	116.9	141.7	188.4	193.8	460.0	536.4	586.0
June	3,984.7	1,272.3	2,712.4	315.1	145.4	116.8	146.7	192.8	193.7	435.6	558.2	608.1
Sept	4,064.6	1,282.4	2,782.2	337.2	150.3	120.1	166.4	194.8	195.9	429.3	562.8	625.4
Dec	4,177.0	1,329.7	2,847.3	348.3	157.3	121.2	172.3	197.5	200.4	418.2	576.7	655.3
1993: Mar	4,230.6	1,328.6	2,902.0	362.6	163.6	112.3	171.2	208.0	202.0	434.0	585.9	662.5
June	4,352.0	1,400.6	2,951.4	360.9	166.5	111.8	176.9	217.8	207.5	441.2	596.8	672.0
Sept	4,411.5	1,422.2	2,989.3	366.2	169.1	125.3	189.2	229.4	217.6	434.0	619.1	639.4
Dec	4,535.7	1,476.1	3,059.6	373.0	171.9	119.6	186.6	234.5	227.1	447.8	650.3	648.9
1994: Mar	4,575.9	1,476.0	3,099.9	397.4	175.0	119.9	195.3	233.4	212.8	443.4	661.1	661.6
June	4,645.8	1,547.5	3,098.3	383.8	177.1	129.2	193.4	238.0	204.6	425.2	659.9	687.1
Sept	4,692.8	1,562.8	3,130.0	364.0	178.6	136.2	191.9	243.7	201.6	398.2	682.0	733.8
Dec	4,800.2	1,622.6	3,177.6	339.6	179.9	139.9	191.9	240.1	209.4	370.0	667.3	839.5
1995: Mar	4,864.1	1,619.3	3,244.8	353.0	181.4	141.6	203.1	244.2	210.6	350.5	707.0	853.5
June	4,951.4	1,690.1	3,261.3	340.0	182.6	142.5	197.2	245.0	202.5	313.7	762.5	875.5
Sept	4,974.0	1,688.0	3,286.0	330.8	183.5	141.9	193.0	245.2	211.6	304.3	820.4	855.4
Dec	4,988.7	1,681.0	3,307.7	315.4	185.0	142.6	191.7	241.5	225.1	289.8	835.2	881.4
1996: Mar	5,117.8	1,731.1	3,386.7	322.1	185.8	144.2	198.9	239.4	240.9	283.6	908.1	863.6
June	5,161.1	1,806.7	3,354.4	318.7	186.5	144.5	208.2	229.5	230.6	283.3	929.7	823.4
Sept	5,224.8	1,831.6	3,393.2	310.9	186.8	141.1	202.4	226.8	226.8	263.7	993.4	841.3
Dec	5,323.2	1,892.0	3,431.2	296.6	187.0	139.9	203.5	214.1	227.4	257.0	1,102.1	803.6
1997: Mar	5,380.9	1,928.7	3,452.2	317.3	186.5	141.4	203.7	181.8	221.9	248.1	1,157.6	793.9
June	5,376.2	1,998.9	3,377.3	300.1	186.3	141.9	209.3	183.1	216.8	243.3	1,182.7	713.7
Sept	5,413.1	2,011.5	3,401.6	292.8	186.2	142.9	219.7	186.8	221.6	235.2	1,230.5	685.8
Dec	5,502.4	2,087.8	3,414.6	300.3	186.5	144.1	216.9	176.6	232.4	239.3	1,241.6	677.0
1998: Mar	5,542.4	2,104.9	3,437.5	308.3	186.2	136.5	211.9	169.4	234.7	238.1	1,250.5	701.8
June	5,547.9	2,198.6	3,349.3	290.9	186.0	129.6	214.8	160.6	230.7	258.5	1,256.0	622.2
Sept	5,526.2	2,213.0	3,313.2	244.4	186.0	121.1	211.2	151.3	231.8	266.4	1,224.2	676.8
Dec	5,614.2	2,280.2	3,334.0	237.4	186.6	113.2	217.7	141.7	253.5	269.3	1,278.7	635.9
1999: Mar	5,651.6	2,324.1	3,327.5	247.4	186.5	109.5	218.4	137.5	254.0	272.5	1,272.3	629.4
June	5,638.8	2,439.6	3,199.2	240.6	186.5	111.0	222.5	133.6	227.9	279.1	1,258.8	539.2
Sept	5,656.3	2,480.9	3,175.4	241.2	186.2	110.8	215.3	128.0	224.4	271.6	1,281.4	516.5
Dec	5,776.1	2,542.2	3,233.9	248.6	186.4	110.5	211.2	123.4	228.7	266.8	1,268.7	589.6
2000: Mar	5,773.4	2,590.6	3,182.8	237.7	185.3	108.5	211.1	120.0	222.0	260.0	1,106.9	731.2
June	5,685.9	2,698.6	2,987.3	222.1	184.6	110.0	210.5	116.5	204.9	262.9	1,082.0	593.9
Sept	5,674.2	2,737.9	2,936.3	220.5	184.3	110.3	200.7	113.7	207.4	251.4	1,057.9	590.0
Dec	5,662.2	2,781.8	2,880.4	201.4	184.8	109.1	195.7	110.2	220.8	247.7	1,034.2	576.5
2001: Mar	5,773.7	2,880.9	2,892.8	188.0	184.8	106.7	195.3	109.1	220.7	259.3	1,029.9	599.0
June	5,726.8	3,004.2	2,722.6	188.1	185.5	106.9	204.4	108.1	217.4	272.0	1,000.5	439.8
Sept	5,807.5	3,027.8	2,779.7	189.1	186.4	104.7	187.7	106.8	231.5	286.8	1,005.5	481.2
Dec	5,943.4	3,123.9	2,819.5	181.5	190.3	105.8	177.4	105.7	257.5	295.4	1,051.2	454.7
2002: Mar	6,006.0	3,156.8	2,849.2	187.6	192.0	107.9	187.0	114.0	264.8	298.9	1,067.1	430.1
June	6,126.5	3,276.7	2,849.8	204.6	192.8	110.5	177.2	122.0	252.1	311.8	1,134.3	344.6
Sept	6,228.2	3,303.5	2,924.8	210.4	193.3	112.9	174.1	130.4	255.7	308.9	1,199.6	339.5
Dec	6,405.7	3,387.2	3,018.5	222.8	194.9	116.4	176.3	139.7	279.0	315.0	1,245.3	329.1
2003: Mar	6,460.8	3,390.9	3,069.8	153.1	196.9	120.3	177.2	151.2	296.3	306.2	1,287.4	381.4
June	6,670.1	3,505.4	3,164.7	144.8	199.1	123.0	185.4	161.7	298.5	318.5	1,384.0	347.9
Sept	6,783.2	3,515.3	3,268.0	....	201.6	....	....	....	....	....	1,458.5	....

[1] Face value.
[2] Federal Reserve holdings exclude Treasury securities held under repurchase agreements.
[3] Includes commercial banks, savings institutions, and credit unions.
[4] Current accrual value.
[5] Includes Treasury securities held by the Federal Employees Retirement System Thrift Savings Plan "G Fund."
[6] Includes money market mutual funds, mutual funds, and closed-end investment companies.
[7] Includes nonmarketable foreign series Treasury securities and Treasury deposit funds. Excludes Treasury securities held under repurchase agreements in custody accounts at the Federal Reserve Bank of New York.
Estimates reflect the 1989 benchmark to December 1994, the 1994 benchmark to March 2000, the March 2000 benchmark to June 2002, and the June 2002 benchmark (released in December 2003) to date.
[8] Includes individuals, Government-sponsored enterprises, brokers and dealers, bank personal trusts and estates, corporate and noncorporate businesses, and other investors.

Note.—Data shown in this table are as of December 2003.

Source: Department of the Treasury.

CORPORATE PROFITS AND FINANCE

TABLE B–90.—*Corporate profits with inventory valuation and capital consumption adjustments, 1959–2003*

[Billions of dollars; quarterly data at seasonally adjusted annual rates]

Year or quarter	Corporate profits with inventory valuation and capital consumption adjustments	Taxes on corporate income	Corporate profits after tax with inventory valuation and capital consumption adjustments		
			Total	Net dividends	Undistributed profits with inventory valuation and capital consumption adjustments
1959	55.7	23.7	32.0	12.6	19.4
1960	53.8	22.8	31.0	13.4	17.6
1961	54.9	22.9	32.0	13.9	18.1
1962	63.3	24.1	39.2	15.0	24.1
1963	69.0	26.4	42.6	16.2	26.4
1964	76.5	28.2	48.3	18.2	30.1
1965	87.5	31.1	56.4	20.2	36.2
1966	93.2	33.9	59.3	20.7	38.7
1967	91.3	32.9	58.4	21.5	36.9
1968	98.8	39.6	59.2	23.5	35.6
1969	95.4	40.0	55.4	24.2	31.2
1970	83.6	34.8	48.9	24.3	24.6
1971	98.0	38.2	59.9	25.0	34.8
1972	112.1	42.3	69.7	26.8	42.9
1973	125.5	50.0	75.5	29.9	45.6
1974	115.8	52.8	63.0	33.2	29.8
1975	134.8	51.6	83.2	33.0	50.2
1976	163.3	65.3	98.1	39.0	59.0
1977	192.4	74.4	118.0	44.8	73.2
1978	216.6	84.9	131.8	50.8	81.0
1979	223.2	90.0	133.2	57.5	75.7
1980	201.1	87.2	113.9	64.1	49.9
1981	226.1	84.3	141.8	73.8	68.0
1982	209.7	66.5	143.2	77.7	65.4
1983	264.2	80.6	183.6	83.5	100.1
1984	318.6	97.5	221.1	90.8	130.3
1985	330.3	99.4	230.9	97.6	133.4
1986	319.5	109.7	209.8	106.2	103.7
1987	368.8	130.4	238.4	112.3	126.1
1988	432.6	141.6	291.0	129.9	161.1
1989	426.6	146.1	280.5	158.0	122.6
1990	437.8	145.4	292.4	169.1	123.3
1991	451.2	138.6	312.6	180.7	131.9
1992	479.3	148.7	330.6	187.9	142.7
1993	541.9	171.0	370.9	202.8	168.1
1994	600.3	193.7	406.5	234.7	171.8
1995	696.7	218.7	478.0	254.2	223.8
1996	786.2	231.7	554.5	297.6	256.9
1997	868.5	246.1	622.4	334.5	287.9
1998	801.6	248.3	553.3	351.6	201.7
1999	851.3	258.6	592.6	337.4	255.3
2000	817.9	265.2	552.7	377.9	174.8
2001	770.4	201.1	569.3	373.2	196.0
2002	904.2	195.0	709.1	398.3	310.8
1999: I	844.2	251.0	593.2	339.9	253.2
II	849.3	256.5	592.9	333.4	259.4
III	842.3	260.2	582.1	334.2	247.9
IV	869.3	266.8	602.5	342.0	260.5
2000: I	832.6	280.8	551.8	360.3	191.6
II	833.0	272.5	560.5	377.3	183.2
III	811.8	260.3	551.5	386.6	164.9
IV	794.3	247.1	547.2	387.6	159.6
2001: I	755.8	219.1	536.7	380.0	156.6
II	748.6	217.2	531.4	371.5	159.9
III	713.6	198.2	515.5	368.7	146.8
IV	863.6	170.1	693.5	372.6	320.9
2002: I	880.1	181.6	698.6	382.3	316.3
II	901.9	197.1	704.8	393.5	311.3
III	899.8	198.6	701.2	404.3	296.9
IV	934.9	202.9	732.0	413.1	318.9
2003: I	927.1	213.9	713.2	420.3	292.9
II	1,022.8	211.4	811.3	427.5	383.8
III	1,124.2	230.6	893.7	434.3	459.3

Source: Department of Commerce, Bureau of Economic Analysis.

389

TABLE B-91.—*Corporate profits by industry, 1959-2003*

[Billions of dollars; quarterly data at seasonally adjusted annual rates]

Year or quarter	Total	Corporate profits with inventory valuation adjustment and without capital consumption adjustment — Domestic industries — Financial — Total	Federal Reserve banks	Other	Nonfinancial — Total¹	Manufacturing²	Transportation and public utilities	Utilities	Wholesale trade	Retail trade	Other	Rest of the world
SIC:³												
1959	53.5	50.8	7.6	0.7	6.9	43.2	26.5	7.1	....	2.9	3.3	3.4	2.7
1960	51.5	48.3	8.4	.9	7.5	39.9	23.8	7.5	....	2.5	2.8	3.3	3.1
1961	51.8	48.5	8.3	.8	7.6	40.2	23.4	7.9	....	2.5	3.0	3.4	3.3
1962	57.0	53.3	8.6	.9	7.7	44.7	26.3	8.5	....	2.8	3.4	3.6	3.8
1963	62.1	58.1	8.3	1.0	7.3	49.8	29.7	9.5	....	2.8	3.6	4.1	4.1
1964	68.6	64.1	8.8	1.1	7.6	55.4	32.6	10.2	....	3.4	4.5	4.7	4.5
1965	78.9	74.2	9.3	1.3	8.0	64.9	39.8	11.0	....	3.8	4.9	5.4	4.7
1966	84.6	80.1	10.7	1.7	9.1	69.3	42.6	12.0	....	4.0	4.9	5.9	4.5
1967	82.0	77.2	11.2	2.0	9.2	66.0	39.2	10.9	....	4.1	5.7	6.1	4.8
1968	88.8	83.2	12.8	2.5	10.3	70.4	41.9	11.0	....	4.6	6.4	6.6	5.6
1969	85.5	78.9	13.6	3.1	10.5	65.3	37.3	10.7	....	4.9	6.4	6.1	6.6
1970	74.4	67.3	15.4	3.5	11.9	52.0	27.5	8.3	....	4.4	6.0	5.8	7.1
1971	88.3	80.4	17.6	3.3	14.3	62.8	35.1	8.9	....	5.2	7.2	6.4	7.9
1972	101.2	91.7	19.1	3.3	15.8	72.6	41.9	9.5	....	6.9	7.4	7.0	9.5
1973	115.3	100.4	20.5	4.5	16.0	79.9	47.2	9.1	....	8.2	6.6	8.7	14.9
1974	109.5	92.1	20.2	5.7	14.5	71.9	41.4	7.6	....	11.5	2.3	9.1	17.5
1975	135.0	120.4	20.2	5.6	14.6	100.2	55.2	11.0	....	13.8	8.2	12.0	14.6
1976	165.6	149.0	25.0	5.9	19.1	124.1	71.3	15.3	....	12.9	10.5	14.0	16.5
1977	194.7	175.6	31.9	6.1	25.8	143.7	79.3	18.6	....	15.6	12.4	17.8	19.1
1978	222.4	199.6	39.5	7.6	31.9	160.0	90.5	21.8	....	15.6	12.3	19.8	22.9
1979	231.8	197.2	40.3	9.4	30.9	156.8	89.6	17.0	....	18.8	9.8	21.6	34.6
1980	211.4	175.9	34.0	11.8	22.2	141.9	78.3	18.4	....	17.2	6.2	21.8	35.5
1981	219.1	189.4	29.1	14.4	14.7	160.3	91.1	20.3	....	22.4	9.9	16.7	29.7
1982	191.0	158.5	26.0	15.2	10.8	132.4	67.1	23.1	....	19.6	13.4	9.2	32.6
1983	226.5	191.4	35.5	14.6	20.9	155.9	76.2	29.5	....	21.0	18.7	10.4	35.1
1984	264.6	228.1	34.4	16.4	18.0	193.7	91.8	40.1	....	29.5	21.1	11.1	36.6
1985	257.5	219.4	45.9	16.3	29.5	173.5	84.3	33.8	....	23.9	22.2	9.2	38.1
1986	253.0	213.5	56.8	15.5	41.2	156.8	57.9	35.8	....	24.1	23.5	15.5	39.5
1987	301.4	253.4	59.8	15.7	44.1	193.5	86.3	41.9	....	18.6	23.4	23.4	48.0
1988	363.9	306.9	68.7	17.6	51.1	238.2	121.2	48.4	....	20.1	20.3	28.3	57.0
1989	367.4	300.3	77.9	20.2	57.8	222.3	110.9	43.3	....	21.8	20.8	25.5	67.1
1990	396.6	320.5	94.4	21.4	73.0	226.1	113.1	44.2	....	19.2	20.7	29.0	76.1
1991	427.9	351.4	124.2	20.3	103.9	227.3	98.0	53.3	....	21.7	26.7	27.5	76.5
1992	458.3	385.2	129.8	17.8	111.9	255.4	99.5	58.4	....	25.1	32.6	39.7	73.1
1993	513.1	436.1	136.8	16.2	120.6	299.3	115.6	69.5	....	26.3	39.1	48.9	76.9
1994	564.6	487.6	119.9	18.1	101.8	367.7	147.0	83.2	....	30.9	46.2	60.4	77.1
1995	656.0	563.2	162.2	22.5	139.7	401.0	173.7	85.8	....	27.3	43.1	71.2	92.8
1996	736.1	634.2	172.6	22.1	150.5	461.6	188.8	91.3	....	39.8	51.9	89.7	101.9
1997	812.3	701.4	193.0	23.8	169.2	508.4	209.0	84.2	....	47.6	64.2	103.4	110.9
1998	738.5	635.5	165.9	25.2	140.7	469.6	173.5	78.9	....	52.3	73.4	91.5	103.0
1999	776.8	655.3	196.4	26.3	170.1	458.9	175.2	56.8	....	52.6	74.6	99.7	121.5
2000	759.3	613.6	203.8	30.8	173.0	409.8	166.3	43.8	....	56.9	70.1	72.8	145.7
NAICS:³												
1998	738.5	635.5	165.4	25.2	140.2	470.1	157.0	....	32.7	53.2	66.4	119.8	103.0
1999	776.8	655.3	194.3	26.3	168.0	461.1	150.6	....	33.1	55.5	65.2	130.1	121.5
2000	759.3	613.6	200.2	30.8	169.4	413.4	144.3	....	24.4	59.7	59.6	128.2	145.7
2001	705.9	544.4	225.6	28.3	197.3	318.8	54.0	....	24.1	51.6	71.1	145.3	161.5
2002	742.7	589.4	255.1	22.9	232.2	334.3	73.3	....	22.0	49.1	76.7	135.5	153.4
2001:I	730.7	581.3	228.3	31.3	197.0	353.0	86.8	....	26.0	46.1	64.2	149.2	149.3
II	731.4	578.6	219.9	29.2	190.6	358.8	79.3	....	27.1	47.7	66.8	156.2	152.8
III	685.8	541.7	211.1	27.4	183.7	330.6	50.1	....	25.0	54.1	74.3	152.4	144.1
IV	675.7	476.0	243.2	25.2	218.0	232.7	-.2	....	18.4	58.5	79.1	123.3	199.7
2002:I	702.7	551.4	267.5	23.8	243.8	283.8	42.0	....	18.5	48.8	75.8	127.5	151.3
II	738.9	594.8	260.6	23.9	236.7	334.2	69.2	....	25.3	53.9	79.7	135.5	144.1
III	745.1	594.0	249.0	22.6	226.4	345.0	87.2	....	21.5	45.7	77.5	136.7	151.1
IV	784.2	617.2	243.4	21.2	222.1	373.9	95.1	....	22.8	47.9	73.9	144.4	166.9
2003:I	780.9	632.1	261.8	21.2	240.7	370.3	87.1	....	28.1	39.8	72.9	148.1	148.7
II	793.6	645.1	260.6	20.5	240.1	384.5	80.3	....	21.1	42.6	85.0	150.7	148.5
III	864.2	706.4	274.6	18.9	255.7	431.8	97.7	....	21.5	51.0	84.3	160.2	157.7

¹ Data on NAICS basis include transportation and warehousing, and information, not shown separately.

² See Table B-92 for industry detail.

³ Industry data based on the Standard Industrial Classification (SIC) are based on the 1987 SIC for data beginning 1987 and on the 1972 SIC for earlier data shown. Data on the North American Industry Classification System (NAICS) are based on the 1997 NAICS. Industry groups shown on SIC and NAICS basis are not necessarily the same and are not strictly comparable.

Source: Department of Commerce, Bureau of Economic Analysis.

TABLE B-92.—Corporate profits of manufacturing industries, 1959–2003

[Billions of dollars; quarterly data at seasonally adjusted annual rates]

Year or quarter	Total manu-fac-turing	Corporate profits with inventory valuation adjustment and without capital consumption adjustment											
		Durable goods [2]							Nondurable goods [2]				
		Total [1]	Fabri-cated metal prod-ucts	Ma-chinery	Compu-ter and elec-tronic prod-ucts	Elec-trical equip-ment, appli-ances, and compo-nents	Motor vehi-cles, bodies and trail-ers, and parts	Other	Total	Food and bev-erage and tobacco prod-ucts	Chem-ical prod-ucts	Petro-leum and coal prod-ucts	Other
SICS: [3]													
1959	26.5	13.7	1.1	2.2	....	1.7	3.0	3.5	12.9	2.5	3.5	2.6	4.3
1960	23.8	11.6	.8	1.8	....	1.3	3.0	2.7	12.2	2.2	3.1	2.6	4.2
1961	23.4	11.3	1.0	1.9	....	1.3	2.5	2.9	12.1	2.4	3.3	2.3	4.2
1962	26.3	14.1	1.2	2.4	....	1.5	4.0	3.4	12.3	2.4	3.2	2.2	4.4
1963	29.7	16.4	1.3	2.6	....	1.6	4.9	4.0	13.3	2.7	3.7	2.2	4.7
1964	32.6	18.1	1.5	3.3	....	1.7	4.6	4.4	14.5	2.7	4.1	2.4	5.3
1965	39.8	23.3	2.1	4.0	....	2.7	6.2	5.2	16.5	2.9	4.6	2.9	6.1
1966	42.6	24.1	2.4	4.6	....	3.0	5.2	5.2	18.6	3.3	4.9	3.4	6.9
1967	39.2	21.3	2.5	4.2	....	3.0	4.0	4.9	18.0	3.3	4.3	4.0	6.4
1968	41.9	22.5	2.3	4.2	....	2.9	5.5	5.6	19.4	3.2	5.3	3.8	7.1
1969	37.3	19.2	2.0	3.8	....	2.3	4.8	4.9	18.1	3.1	4.6	3.4	7.0
1970	27.5	10.5	1.1	3.1	....	1.3	1.3	2.9	17.0	3.2	3.9	3.7	6.1
1971	35.1	16.6	1.5	3.1	....	2.0	5.2	4.1	18.5	3.6	4.5	3.8	6.6
1972	41.9	22.7	2.2	4.5	....	2.9	6.0	5.6	19.2	3.0	5.3	3.3	7.6
1973	47.2	25.1	2.7	4.9	....	3.2	5.9	6.2	22.0	2.5	6.2	5.4	7.9
1974	41.4	15.3	1.8	3.3	....	.6	.7	4.0	26.1	2.6	5.3	10.9	7.3
1975	55.2	20.6	3.3	5.1	....	2.6	2.3	4.7	34.5	8.6	6.4	10.1	9.5
1976	71.3	31.4	3.9	6.9	....	3.8	7.4	7.3	39.9	7.1	8.2	13.5	11.1
1977	79.3	37.9	4.5	8.6	....	5.9	9.4	8.5	41.4	6.9	7.8	13.1	13.6
1978	90.5	45.4	5.0	10.7	....	6.7	9.0	10.5	45.1	6.2	8.3	15.8	14.8
1979	89.6	37.1	5.3	9.5	....	5.6	4.7	8.5	52.5	5.8	7.2	24.8	14.7
1980	78.3	18.9	4.4	8.0	....	5.2	−4.3	2.7	59.5	6.1	5.7	34.7	13.1
1981	91.1	19.5	4.5	9.0	....	5.2	.3	−2.6	71.6	9.2	8.0	40.0	14.5
1982	67.1	5.0	2.7	3.1	....	1.7	.0	2.1	62.1	7.3	5.1	34.7	15.0
1983	76.2	19.5	3.1	4.0	....	3.5	5.3	8.4	56.7	6.3	7.4	23.9	19.1
1984	91.8	39.3	4.7	6.0	....	5.1	9.2	14.6	52.6	6.8	8.2	17.6	20.1
1985	84.3	29.7	4.9	5.7	....	2.6	7.4	10.1	54.6	8.8	6.6	18.7	20.5
1986	57.9	26.3	5.2	.8	....	2.7	4.6	12.1	31.7	7.5	7.5	−4.7	21.3
1987	86.3	40.7	5.5	5.4	....	5.9	3.7	17.6	45.6	11.4	14.4	−1.5	21.3
1988	121.2	54.1	6.3	11.1	....	7.7	6.2	16.5	67.1	12.0	18.6	12.7	23.7
1989	110.9	51.2	6.4	12.2	....	9.3	2.7	14.2	59.7	11.1	18.2	6.5	23.9
1990	113.1	43.8	6.0	11.8	....	8.5	−1.9	15.9	69.2	14.3	16.8	16.4	21.7
1991	98.0	34.4	5.3	5.7	....	10.0	−5.4	17.3	63.6	18.1	16.2	7.3	22.0
1992	99.5	40.6	6.2	7.5	....	10.4	−1.0	17.4	59.0	18.2	16.0	−.9	25.6
1993	115.6	55.8	7.4	7.5	....	15.2	6.0	19.4	59.7	16.4	15.9	2.7	24.7
1994	147.0	74.4	11.1	9.1	....	22.8	7.8	21.3	72.6	19.9	23.2	1.2	28.3
1995	173.7	80.9	11.8	14.8	....	21.5	.0	25.8	92.8	27.1	27.9	7.1	30.6
1996	188.8	90.6	14.5	16.9	....	20.1	4.2	29.2	98.2	22.1	26.4	15.0	34.7
1997	209.0	103.1	17.0	16.7	....	25.3	4.8	33.0	105.9	24.6	32.3	17.3	31.7
1998	173.5	87.3	16.4	19.5	....	8.9	5.9	30.1	86.2	21.9	26.5	6.7	31.1
1999	175.2	78.8	16.2	12.4	....	5.3	7.3	35.3	96.4	28.1	25.2	4.3	38.9
2000	166.3	64.8	15.4	16.3	....	4.7	−1.5	28.2	101.5	25.7	16.0	29.1	30.7
NAICS: [3]													
1998	157.0	83.4	16.7	15.6	3.9	6.1	6.4	34.6	73.6	21.8	25.1	4.9	21.8
1999	150.6	72.3	16.5	12.4	−6.5	6.3	7.3	36.4	78.3	30.7	23.0	1.8	22.7
2000	144.3	60.0	15.5	8.2	4.0	5.6	−1.0	27.7	84.3	25.4	14.2	26.9	17.8
2001	54.0	−24.9	9.7	3.2	−49.4	2.0	−7.2	16.7	78.9	27.5	13.8	29.9	7.7
2002	73.3	8.8	9.7	1.5	−18.4	1.7	−1.0	15.3	64.6	32.8	17.5	6.4	7.9
2001: I	86.8	13.9	11.4	9.6	−19.3	3.0	−5.8	15.0	72.8	23.0	5.8	34.1	9.8
II	79.3	−4.4	10.5	5.8	−38.3	2.7	−8.2	22.9	83.7	27.6	14.6	33.4	8.1
III	50.1	−37.6	9.9	−5.2	−60.9	2.2	−4.0	20.4	87.7	28.5	16.7	32.5	10.0
IV	−.2	−71.7	6.9	2.5	−79.0	.3	−10.9	8.5	71.4	31.0	18.1	19.6	2.7
2002: I	42.0	−16.4	8.8	2.0	−40.1	3.1	−5.7	15.5	58.3	31.4	16.2	4.1	6.6
II	69.2	5.8	9.3	2.6	−23.6	1.5	2.3	13.7	63.3	32.9	16.6	5.1	8.7
III	87.2	20.4	8.4	2.6	−8.7	1.6	1.1	15.3	66.8	34.4	17.7	7.7	7.0
IV	95.1	25.2	12.1	−1.3	−1.2	.7	−1.7	16.6	69.9	32.4	19.4	8.7	9.4
2003: I	87.1	17.1	8.9	−2.8	−5.6	.7	7.3	8.6	70.0	32.4	18.9	20.2	−1.5
II	80.3	13.9	12.1	−2.7	−1.8	−.9	−1.9	9.1	66.4	30.6	15.8	20.6	−.5
III	97.7	19.4	12.6	−2.4	−1.5	−1.5	−3.5	15.7	78.4	31.8	23.7	19.5	3.4

[1] For SIC data, includes primary metal industries, not shown separately.

[2] Industry groups shown in column headings reflect NAICS classification for data beginning 1998. For data on SIC basis, the industry groups would be, machinery—industrial machinery and equipment; electrical equipment, appliances, and components—electronic and other electric equipment; motor vehicles, bodies and trailers, and parts—motor vehicles and equipment; food and beverage and tobacco products—food and kindred products; and chemical products—chemicals and allied products.

[3] Industry data based on the Standard Industrial Classification (SIC) are based on the 1987 SIC for data beginning 1987 and on the 1972 SIC for earlier data shown. Data on the North American Industry Classification System (NAICS) are based on the 1997 NAICS. Industry groups shown on SIC and NAICS basis are not necessarily the same and are not strictly comparable.

Source: Department of Commerce, Bureau of Economic Analysis.

TABLE B-93.—*Sales, profits, and stockholders' equity, all manufacturing corporations, 1965-2003*

[Billions of dollars]

Year or quarter	All manufacturing corporations				Durable goods industries				Nondurable goods industries			
	Sales (net)	Before income taxes[1]	After income taxes	Stockholders' equity[2]	Sales (net)	Before income taxes[1]	After income taxes	Stockholders' equity[2]	Sales (net)	Before income taxes[1]	After income taxes	Stockholders' equity[2]
1965	492.2	46.5	27.5	211.7	257.0	26.2	14.5	105.4	235.2	20.3	13.0	106.3
1966	554.2	51.8	30.9	230.3	291.7	29.2	16.4	115.2	262.4	22.6	14.6	115.1
1967	575.4	47.8	29.0	247.6	300.6	25.7	14.6	125.0	274.8	22.0	14.4	122.6
1968	631.9	55.4	32.1	265.9	335.5	30.6	16.5	135.6	296.4	24.8	15.5	130.3
1969	694.6	58.1	33.2	289.9	366.5	31.5	16.9	147.6	328.1	26.6	16.4	142.3
1970	708.8	48.1	28.6	306.8	363.1	23.0	12.9	155.1	345.7	25.2	15.7	151.7
1971	751.1	52.9	31.0	320.8	381.8	26.5	14.5	160.4	369.3	26.5	16.5	160.5
1972	849.5	63.2	36.5	343.4	435.8	33.6	18.4	171.4	413.7	29.6	18.0	172.0
1973	1,017.2	81.4	48.1	374.1	527.3	43.6	24.8	188.7	489.9	37.8	23.3	185.4
1973: IV	275.1	21.4	13.0	386.4	140.1	10.8	6.3	194.7	135.0	10.6	6.7	191.7
New series:												
1973: IV	236.6	20.6	13.2	368.0	122.7	10.1	6.2	185.8	113.9	10.5	7.0	182.1
1974	1,060.6	92.1	58.7	395.0	529.0	41.1	24.7	196.0	531.6	51.0	34.1	199.0
1975	1,065.2	79.9	49.1	423.4	521.1	35.3	21.4	208.1	544.1	44.6	27.7	215.3
1976	1,203.2	104.9	64.5	462.7	589.6	50.7	30.8	224.3	613.7	54.3	33.7	238.4
1977	1,328.1	115.1	70.4	496.7	657.3	57.9	34.8	239.9	670.8	57.2	35.5	256.8
1978	1,496.4	132.5	81.1	540.5	760.7	69.6	41.8	262.6	735.7	62.9	39.3	277.9
1979	1,741.8	154.2	98.7	600.5	865.7	72.4	45.2	292.5	876.1	81.8	53.5	308.0
1980	1,912.8	145.8	92.6	668.1	889.1	57.4	35.6	317.7	1,023.7	88.4	56.9	350.4
1981	2,144.7	158.6	101.3	743.4	979.5	67.2	41.6	350.4	1,165.2	91.3	59.6	393.0
1982	2,039.4	108.2	70.9	770.2	913.1	34.7	21.7	355.5	1,126.4	73.6	49.3	414.7
1983	2,114.3	133.1	85.8	812.8	973.5	48.7	30.0	372.4	1,140.8	84.4	55.8	440.4
1984	2,335.0	165.6	107.6	864.2	1,107.6	75.5	48.9	395.6	1,227.5	90.0	58.8	468.5
1985	2,331.4	137.0	87.6	866.2	1,142.6	61.5	38.6	420.9	1,188.8	75.6	49.1	445.3
1986	2,220.9	129.3	83.1	874.7	1,125.5	52.1	32.6	436.3	1,095.4	77.2	50.5	438.4
1987	2,378.2	173.0	115.6	900.9	1,178.0	78.0	53.0	444.3	1,200.3	95.1	62.6	456.6
1988 [3]	2,596.2	215.3	153.8	957.6	1,284.7	91.6	66.9	468.7	1,311.5	123.7	86.8	488.9
1989	2,745.1	187.6	135.1	999.0	1,356.6	75.1	55.5	501.3	1,388.5	112.6	79.6	497.7
1990	2,810.7	158.1	110.1	1,043.8	1,357.2	57.3	40.7	515.0	1,453.5	100.8	69.4	528.9
1991	2,761.1	98.7	66.4	1,064.1	1,304.0	13.9	7.2	506.8	1,457.1	84.8	59.3	557.4
1992 [4]	2,890.2	31.4	22.1	1,034.7	1,389.8	-33.7	-24.0	473.9	1,500.4	65.1	46.0	560.8
1993	3,015.1	117.9	83.2	1,039.7	1,490.2	38.9	27.4	482.7	1,524.9	79.0	55.7	557.1
1994	3,255.8	243.5	174.9	1,110.1	1,657.6	121.0	87.1	533.3	1,598.2	122.5	87.8	576.8
1995	3,528.3	274.5	198.2	1,240.6	1,807.7	130.6	94.3	613.7	1,720.6	143.9	103.9	627.0
1996	3,757.6	306.6	224.9	1,348.0	1,941.6	146.6	106.1	673.9	1,816.0	160.0	118.8	674.2
1997	3,920.0	331.4	244.5	1,462.7	2,075.8	167.0	121.4	743.4	1,844.2	164.4	123.1	719.3
1998	3,949.4	314.7	234.4	1,482.9	2,168.8	175.1	127.8	779.9	1,780.7	139.6	106.5	703.0
1999	4,148.9	355.3	257.8	1,569.3	2,314.2	198.8	140.3	869.6	1,834.6	156.5	117.5	699.7
2000	4,548.2	381.1	275.3	1,823.1	2,457.4	190.7	131.8	1,054.3	2,090.8	190.5	143.5	768.7
2000: IV	1,163.6	69.2	46.8	1,892.4	620.4	31.2	19.3	1,101.5	543.2	38.0	27.4	790.9
NAICS:[5]												
2000: IV	1,128.8	62.1	41.7	1,833.8	623.0	26.9	15.4	1,100.0	505.8	35.2	26.3	733.8
2001	4,295.0	83.2	36.2	1,843.0	2,321.2	-69.0	-76.1	1,080.5	1,973.8	152.2	112.3	762.5
2002	4,220.7	196.8	136.0	1,805.2	2,262.4	47.1	22.8	1,025.6	1,958.3	149.7	113.2	779.6
2001: I	1,082.2	12.0	-.2	1,846.3	591.6	-28.0	-31.6	1,101.7	490.6	40.0	31.4	744.6
II	1,116.6	39.6	24.0	1,858.2	600.6	-8.3	-12.2	1,100.5	516.0	47.9	36.3	757.7
III	1,062.4	20.1	9.8	1,840.8	567.4	-18.9	-18.1	1,068.6	495.0	39.0	27.9	772.2
IV	1,033.7	11.5	2.5	1,826.6	561.5	-13.8	-14.2	1,051.2	472.2	25.3	16.6	775.5
2002: I	994.1	36.1	24.7	1,796.5	546.4	.8	-1.8	1,035.9	447.6	35.2	26.6	760.5
II	1,071.6	64.6	46.2	1,819.3	583.4	22.4	15.1	1,046.8	488.1	42.2	31.2	772.5
III	1,068.7	59.3	40.1	1,830.0	564.8	16.4	8.5	1,029.9	503.8	42.9	31.6	800.1
IV	1,086.4	36.9	25.0	1,775.1	567.7	7.5	1.1	989.8	518.7	29.4	23.8	785.3
2003: I	1,069.3	72.7	54.1	1,801.5	548.0	12.1	14.0	1,000.9	521.3	51.6	40.1	800.7
II	1,097.8	77.0	57.3	1,854.9	573.3	29.4	21.4	1,029.1	524.5	47.6	35.9	825.8
III	1,107.3	74.3	54.4	1,878.0	571.3	31.0	23.6	1,041.1	536.0	43.3	30.8	836.9

[1] In the old series, "income taxes" refers to Federal income taxes only, as State and local income taxes had already been deducted. In the new series, no income taxes have been deducted.

[2] Annual data are average equity for the year (using four end-of-quarter figures).

[3] Beginning 1988, profits before and after income taxes reflect inclusion of minority stockholders' interest in net income before and after income taxes.

[4] Data for 1992 (most significantly 1992:I) reflect the early adoption of Financial Accounting Standards Board Statement 106 (Employer's Accounting for Post-Retirement Benefits Other Than Pensions) by a large number of companies during the fourth quarter of 1992. Data for 1993 (1993:I) also reflect adoption of Statement 106. Corporations must show the cumulative effect of a change in accounting principle in the first quarter of the year in which the change is adopted.

[5] Data based on the North American Industry Classification System (NAICS). Other data shown are based on the Standard Industrial Classification (SIC).

Note.—Data are not necessarily comparable from one period to another due to changes in accounting principles, industry classifications, sampling procedures, etc. For explanatory notes concerning compilation of the series, see "Quarterly Financial Report for Manufacturing, Mining, and Trade Corporations," Department of Commerce, Bureau of the Census.

Source: Department of Commerce, Bureau of the Census.

TABLE B–94.—*Relation of profits after taxes to stockholders' equity and to sales, all manufacturing corporations, 1955–2003*

Year or quarter	Ratio of profits after income taxes (annual rate) to stockholders' equity—percent [1]			Profits after income taxes per dollar of sales—cents		
	All manufacturing corporations	Durable goods industries	Nondurable goods industries	All manufacturing corporations	Durable goods industries	Nondurable goods industries
1955	12.6	13.8	11.4	5.4	5.7	5.1
1956	12.3	12.8	11.8	5.3	5.2	5.3
1957	10.9	11.3	10.6	4.8	4.8	4.9
1958	8.6	8.0	9.2	4.2	3.9	4.4
1959	10.4	10.4	10.4	4.8	4.8	4.9
1960	9.2	8.5	9.8	4.4	4.0	4.8
1961	8.9	8.1	9.6	4.3	3.9	4.7
1962	9.8	9.6	9.9	4.5	4.4	4.7
1963	10.3	10.1	10.4	4.7	4.5	4.9
1964	11.6	11.7	11.5	5.2	5.1	5.4
1965	13.0	13.8	12.2	5.6	5.7	5.5
1966	13.4	14.2	12.7	5.6	5.6	5.6
1967	11.7	11.7	11.8	5.0	4.8	5.3
1968	12.1	12.2	11.9	5.1	4.9	5.2
1969	11.5	11.4	11.5	4.8	4.6	5.0
1970	9.3	8.3	10.3	4.0	3.5	4.5
1971	9.7	9.0	10.3	4.1	3.8	4.5
1972	10.6	10.8	10.5	4.3	4.2	4.4
1973	12.8	13.1	12.6	4.7	4.7	4.8
1973: IV	13.4	12.9	14.0	4.7	4.5	5.0
New series:						
1973: IV	14.3	13.3	15.3	5.6	5.0	6.1
1974	14.9	12.6	17.1	5.5	4.7	6.4
1975	11.6	10.3	12.9	4.6	4.1	5.1
1976	13.9	13.7	14.2	5.4	5.2	5.5
1977	14.2	14.5	13.8	5.3	5.3	5.3
1978	15.0	16.0	14.2	5.4	5.5	5.3
1979	16.4	15.4	17.4	5.7	5.2	6.1
1980	13.9	11.2	16.3	4.8	4.0	5.6
1981	13.6	11.9	15.2	4.7	4.2	5.1
1982	9.2	6.1	11.9	3.5	2.4	4.4
1983	10.6	8.1	12.7	4.1	3.1	4.9
1984	12.5	12.4	12.5	4.6	4.4	4.8
1985	10.1	9.2	11.0	3.8	3.4	4.1
1986	9.5	7.5	11.5	3.7	2.9	4.6
1987	12.8	11.9	13.7	4.9	4.5	5.2
1988 [2]	16.1	14.3	17.8	5.9	5.2	6.6
1989	13.5	11.1	16.0	4.9	4.1	5.7
1990	10.6	7.9	13.1	3.9	3.0	4.8
1991	6.2	1.4	10.6	2.4	.5	4.1
1992 [3]	2.1	−5.1	8.2	.8	−1.7	3.1
1993	8.0	5.7	10.0	2.8	1.8	3.7
1994	15.8	16.3	15.2	5.4	5.3	5.5
1995	16.0	15.4	16.6	5.6	5.2	6.0
1996	16.7	15.7	17.6	6.0	5.5	6.5
1997	16.7	16.3	17.1	6.2	5.8	6.7
1998	15.8	16.4	15.2	5.9	5.9	6.0
1999	16.4	16.1	16.8	6.2	6.1	6.4
2000	15.1	12.5	18.7	6.1	5.4	6.9
2000: IV	9.9	7.0	13.9	4.0	3.1	5.1
NAICS: [4]						
2000: IV	9.1	5.6	14.3	3.7	2.5	5.2
2001	2.0	−7.0	14.7	.8	−3.3	5.7
2002	7.5	2.2	14.5	3.2	1.0	5.8
2001: I	.0	−11.5	16.9	.0	−5.3	6.4
II	5.2	−4.5	19.2	2.2	−2.0	7.0
III	2.1	−6.8	14.5	.9	−3.2	5.6
IV	.5	−5.4	8.6	.2	−2.5	3.5
2002: I	5.5	−.7	14.0	2.5	−.3	5.9
II	10.2	5.8	16.1	4.3	2.6	6.4
III	8.8	3.3	15.8	3.7	1.5	6.3
IV	5.6	.5	12.1	2.3	.2	4.6
2003: I	12.0	5.6	20.0	5.1	2.6	7.7
II	12.4	8.3	17.4	5.2	3.7	6.9
III	11.6	9.1	14.7	4.9	4.1	5.7

[1] Annual ratios based on average equity for the year (using four end-of-quarter figures). Quarterly ratios based on equity at end of quarter.
[2] See footnote 3, Table B-93.
[3] See footnote 4, Table B-93.
[4] See footnote 5, Table B-93.

Note.—Based on data in millions of dollars.
See Note, Table B-93.

Source: Department of Commerce, Bureau of the Census.

TABLE B–95.—*Common stock prices and yields, 1969–2003*

Year or month	Common stock prices [1]								Common stock yields (S&P) (percent) [4]	
	New York Stock Exchange indexes [2]					Dow Jones industrial average [2]	Standard & Poor's composite index (1941-43=10) [2]	Nasdaq composite index (Feb. 5, 1971=100) [2]	Dividend-price ratio [5]	Earnings-price ratio [6]
	Composite (Dec. 31, 2002=5,000)	Industrial	December 31, 1965=50							
			Transpor-tation	Utility [3]	Finance					
1969	578.01	57.44	46.96	85.60	70.49	876.72	97.84		3.24	6.08
1970	483.39	48.03	32.14	74.47	60.00	753.19	83.22		3.83	6.45
1971	573.33	57.92	44.35	79.05	70.38	884.76	98.29	107.44	3.14	5.41
1972	637.52	65.73	50.17	76.95	78.35	950.71	109.20	128.52	2.84	5.50
1973	607.11	63.08	37.74	75.38	70.12	923.88	107.43	109.90	3.06	7.12
1974	463.54	48.08	31.89	59.58	49.67	759.37	82.85	76.29	4.47	11.59
1975	483.55	50.52	31.10	63.00	47.14	802.49	86.16	77.20	4.31	9.15
1976	575.85	60.44	39.57	73.94	52.94	974.92	102.01	89.90	3.77	8.90
1977	567.66	57.86	41.09	81.84	55.25	894.63	98.20	98.71	4.62	10.79
1978	567.81	58.23	43.50	78.44	56.65	820.23	96.02	117.53	5.28	12.03
1979	616.68	64.76	47.34	76.41	61.42	844.40	103.01	136.57	5.47	13.46
1980	720.15	78.70	60.61	74.69	64.25	891.41	118.78	168.61	5.26	12.66
1981	782.62	85.44	72.61	77.81	73.52	932.92	128.05	203.18	5.20	11.96
1982	728.84	78.18	60.41	79.49	71.99	884.36	119.71	188.97	5.81	11.60
1983	979.52	107.45	89.36	93.99	95.34	1,190.34	160.41	285.43	4.40	8.03
1984	977.33	108.01	85.63	92.89	89.28	1,178.48	160.46	248.88	4.64	10.02
1985	1,142.97	123.79	104.11	113.49	114.21	1,328.23	186.84	290.19	4.25	8.12
1986	1,438.02	155.85	119.87	142.72	147.20	1,792.76	236.34	366.96	3.49	6.09
1987	1,709.79	195.31	140.39	148.59	146.48	2,275.99	286.83	402.57	3.08	5.48
1988	1,585.14	180.95	134.12	143.53	127.26	2,060.82	265.79	374.43	3.64	8.01
1989	1,903.36	216.23	175.28	174.87	151.88	2,508.91	322.84	437.81	3.45	7.42
1990	1,939.47	225.78	158.62	181.20	133.26	2,678.94	334.59	409.17	3.61	6.47
1991	2,181.72	258.14	173.99	185.32	150.82	2,929.33	376.18	491.69	3.24	4.79
1992	2,421.51	284.62	201.09	198.91	179.26	3,284.29	415.74	599.26	2.99	4.22
1993	2,638.96	299.99	242.84	228.90	216.42	3,522.06	451.41	715.16	2.78	4.46
1994	2,687.02	315.25	247.29	209.06	209.73	3,793.77	460.42	751.65	2.82	5.83
1995	3,078.56	367.34	269.41	220.30	238.45	4,493.76	541.72	925.19	2.56	6.09
1996	3,787.20	453.98	327.33	249.77	303.89	5,742.89	670.50	1,164.96	2.19	5.24
1997	4,827.35	574.52	414.60	283.82	424.48	7,441.15	873.43	1,469.49	1.77	4.57
1998	5,818.26	681.57	468.69	378.12	516.35	8,625.52	1,085.50	1,794.91	1.49	3.46
1999	6,546.81	774.78	491.60	473.73	530.86	10,464.88	1,327.33	2,728.15	1.25	3.17
2000	6,805.89	810.63	413.60	477.65	553.13	10,734.90	1,427.22	3,783.67	1.15	3.63
2001	6,397.85	748.26	443.59	377.30	595.61	10,189.13	1,194.18	2,035.00	1.32	2.95
2002	5,578.89	657.37	431.10	260.85	555.27	9,226.43	993.94	1,539.73	1.61	2.92
2003	5,447.93	633.18	436.51	237.77	565.75	8,993.59	965.23	1,647.17	1.77	
2002: Jan	6,151.15	723.56	446.13	322.49	591.94	9,923.80	1,140.21	1,976.77	1.38	
Feb	6,022.23	715.80	453.51	301.32	570.18	9,891.05	1,100.67	1,799.72	1.43	
Mar	6,352.08	751.79	490.51	316.27	609.72	10,500.95	1,153.79	1,863.05	1.37	2.15
Apr	6,212.88	732.71	470.00	300.66	610.24	10,165.18	1,112.03	1,758.80	1.42	
May	6,087.85	718.12	459.55	287.10	603.15	10,080.48	1,079.27	1,660.31	1.47	
June	5,755.89	677.58	449.42	265.21	577.05	9,492.44	1,014.05	1,505.49	1.58	2.70
July	5,139.94	603.04	416.10	230.19	524.01	8,616.52	903.59	1,346.09	1.76	
Aug	5,200.62	611.34	409.96	225.52	533.60	8,685.48	912.55	1,327.36	1.72	
Sept	4,980.65	589.14	388.19	210.76	506.05	8,160.78	867.81	1,251.07	1.80	3.68
Oct	4,862.70	574.45	383.41	207.83	494.06	8,048.12	854.63	1,241.91	1.86	
Nov	5,104.89	597.75	405.03	229.41	523.50	8,625.72	909.93	1,409.15	1.73	
Dec	5,075.76	593.15	401.39	233.38	519.72	8,526.66	899.18	1,387.15	1.77	3.14
2003: Jan	5,055.78	587.78	394.84	236.43	522.51	8,474.59	895.84	1,389.56	1.80	
Feb	4,738.56	553.90	367.55	214.63	485.33	7,916.18	837.62	1,313.26	1.95	
Mar	4,724.22	558.10	366.90	211.45	486.71	7,977.73	846.62	1,348.50	1.93	3.57
Apr	4,977.45	583.74	395.85	221.06	522.05	8,332.09	890.03	1,409.83	1.83	
May	5,269.96	613.26	425.12	238.33	549.91	8,623.41	935.96	1,524.18	1.75	
June	5,583.42	649.25	441.81	254.16	579.48	9,098.07	988.00	1,631.75	1.66	3.55
July	5,567.94	648.00	445.29	244.67	588.81	9,154.39	992.54	1,716.85	1.71	
Aug	5,580.87	651.19	451.31	238.06	582.20	9,284.78	989.53	1,724.82	1.78	
Sept	5,748.42	670.18	464.61	243.37	593.10	9,492.54	1,019.44	1,856.22	1.73	3.88
Oct	5,894.39	678.51	477.99	245.96	616.46	9,682.46	1,038.73	1,907.89	1.71	
Nov	5,989.42	689.30	497.44	248.01	624.02	9,762.20	1,049.90	1,939.25	1.69	
Dec	6,244.68	714.93	509.35	257.12	638.41	10,124.66	1,080.64	1,956.98	1.67	

[1] Averages of daily closing prices.

[2] Includes stocks as follows: for NYSE, all stocks listed (nearly 3,000); for Dow Jones industrial average, 30 stocks; for S&P composite index, 500 stocks; and for Nasdaq composite index, over 5,000.

[3] Effective April 1993, the NYSE doubled the value of the utility index to facilitate trading of options and futures on the index. Annual indexes prior to 1993 reflect the doubling.

[4] Based on 500 stocks in the S&P composite index.

[5] Aggregate cash dividends (based on latest known annual rate) divided by aggregate market value based on Wednesday closing prices. Monthly data are averages of weekly figures; annual data are averages of monthly figures.

[6] Quarterly data are ratio of earnings (after taxes) for 4 quarters ending with particular quarter to price index for last day of that quarter. Annual data are averages of quarterly ratios.

Note.—Data for NYSE composite index reflect the new composite index, released on January 9, 2003 by the NYSE, incorporating new methodology, definitions and base value.

Sources: New York Stock Exchange (NYSE), Dow Jones & Co., Inc., Standard & Poor's (S&P), and Nasdaq Stock Market.

TABLE B–96.—*Business formation and business failures, 1955–97*

Year or month	Index of net business formation (1967=100)	New business incorpo- rations (number)	Business failure rate [2]	Business failures [1]					
				Number of failures			Amount of current liabilities (millions of dollars)		
				Total	Liability size class		Total	Liability size class	
					Under $100,000	$100,000 and over		Under $100,000	$100,000 and over
1955	96.6	139,915	42	10,969	10,113	856	449.4	206.4	243.0
1956	94.6	141,163	48	12,686	11,615	1,071	562.7	239.8	322.9
1957	90.3	137,112	52	13,739	12,547	1,192	615.3	267.1	348.2
1958	90.2	150,781	56	14,964	13,499	1,465	728.3	297.6	430.7
1959	97.9	193,067	52	14,053	12,707	1,346	692.8	278.9	413.9
1960	94.5	182,713	57	15,445	13,650	1,795	938.6	327.2	611.4
1961	90.8	181,535	64	17,075	15,006	2,069	1,090.1	370.1	720.0
1962	92.6	182,057	61	15,782	13,772	2,010	1,213.6	346.5	867.1
1963	94.4	186,404	56	14,374	12,192	2,182	1,352.6	321.0	1,031.6
1964	98.2	197,724	53	13,501	11,346	2,155	1,329.2	313.6	1,015.6
1965	99.8	203,897	53	13,514	11,340	2,174	1,321.7	321.7	1,000.0
1966	99.3	200,010	52	13,061	10,833	2,228	1,385.7	321.5	1,064.1
1967	100.0	206,569	49	12,364	10,144	2,220	1,265.2	297.9	967.3
1968	108.3	233,635	39	9,636	7,829	1,807	941.0	241.1	699.9
1969	115.8	274,267	37	9,154	7,192	1,962	1,142.1	231.3	910.8
1970	108.8	264,209	44	10,748	8,019	2,729	1,887.8	269.3	1,618.4
1971	111.1	287,577	42	10,326	7,611	2,715	1,916.9	271.3	1,645.6
1972	119.3	316,601	38	9,566	7,040	2,526	2,000.2	258.8	1,741.5
1973	119.1	329,358	36	9,345	6,627	2,718	2,298.6	235.6	2,063.0
1974	113.2	319,149	38	9,915	6,733	3,182	3,053.1	256.9	2,796.3
1975	109.9	326,345	43	11,432	7,504	3,928	4,380.2	298.6	4,081.6
1976	120.4	375,766	35	9,628	6,176	3,452	3,011.3	257.8	2,753.4
1977	130.8	436,170	28	7,919	4,861	3,058	3,095.3	208.3	2,887.0
1978	138.1	478,019	24	6,619	3,712	2,907	2,656.0	164.7	2,491.3
1979	138.3	524,565	28	7,564	3,930	3,634	2,667.4	179.9	2,487.5
1980	129.9	533,520	42	11,742	5,682	6,060	4,635.1	272.5	4,362.6
1981	124.8	581,242	61	16,794	8,233	8,561	6,955.2	405.8	6,549.3
1982	116.4	566,942	88	24,908	11,509	13,399	15,610.8	541.7	15,069.1
1983	117.5	600,420	110	31,334	15,572	15,762	16,072.9	635.1	15,437.8
1984	121.3	634,991	107	52,078	33,527	18,551	29,268.6	409.8	28,858.8
1985	120.9	664,235	115	57,253	36,551	20,702	36,937.4	423.9	36,513.5
1986	120.4	702,738	120	61,616	38,908	22,708	44,724.0	838.3	43,885.7
1987	121.2	685,572	102	61,111	38,949	22,162	34,723.8	746.0	33,977.8
1988	124.1	685,095	98	57,097	38,300	18,797	39,573.0	686.9	38,886.1
1989	124.8	676,565	65	50,361	33,312	17,049	42,328.8	670.5	41,658.2
1990	120.7	647,366	74	60,747	40,833	19,914	56,130.1	735.6	55,394.5
1991	115.2	628,604	107	88,140	60,617	27,523	96,825.3	1,044.9	95,780.4
1992	116.3	666,800	110	97,069	68,264	28,805	94,317.5	1,096.7	93,220.8
1993	121.1	706,537	109	86,133	61,188	24,945	47,755.5	947.6	46,807.9
1994	125.5	741,778	86	71,558	50,814	20,744	28,977.9	845.0	28,132.9
1995	(3)	766,988	82	71,128	49,495	21,633	37,283.6	866.1	36,417.4
1996	(3)	786,482	80	71,931	49,667	22,264	29,568.7	914.9	28,653.8
1997	(3)	798,779	88	83,384	56,050	27,334	37,436.9	1,111.3	36,325.6

[1] Commercial and industrial failures only through 1983, excluding failures of banks, railroads, real estate, insurance, holding, and financial companies, steamship lines, travel agencies, etc.
Data beginning 1984 are based on expanded coverage and new methodology and are therefore not generally comparable with earlier data.
[2] Failure rate per 10,000 listed enterprises.
[3] Series discontinued in 1995.

Note.—Data are no longer published.

Sources: Department of Commerce (Bureau of Economic Analysis) and The Dun & Bradstreet Corporation.

TABLE B–97.—*Farm income, 1945–2003*

[Billions of dollars]

Year	Total[1]	Cash marketing receipts			Value of inventory changes[3]	Direct Government payments[4]	Production expenses	Net farm income
		Total	Livestock and products	Crops[2]				
1945	25.4	21.7	12.0	9.7	-0.4	0.7	13.1	12.3
1946	29.6	24.8	13.8	11.0	.0	.8	14.5	15.1
1947	32.4	29.6	16.5	13.1	-1.8	.3	17.0	15.4
1948	36.5	30.2	17.1	13.1	1.7	.3	18.8	17.7
1949	30.8	27.8	15.4	12.4	-.9	.2	18.0	12.8
1950	33.1	28.4	16.1	12.4	.8	.3	19.5	13.6
1951	38.3	32.8	19.6	13.2	1.2	.3	22.3	15.9
1952	37.7	32.5	18.2	14.3	.9	.3	22.8	14.9
1953	34.4	31.0	16.9	14.1	-.6	.2	21.5	13.0
1954	34.2	29.8	16.3	13.6	.5	.3	21.8	12.4
1955	33.4	29.5	16.0	13.5	.2	.2	22.2	11.3
1956	33.9	30.4	16.4	14.0	-.5	.6	22.7	11.2
1957	34.8	29.7	17.4	12.3	.6	1.0	23.7	11.1
1958	39.0	33.5	19.2	14.2	.8	1.1	25.8	13.2
1959	37.9	33.6	18.9	14.7	.0	.7	27.2	10.7
1960	38.6	34.0	19.0	15.0	.4	.7	27.4	11.2
1961	40.5	35.2	19.5	15.7	.3	1.5	28.6	12.0
1962	42.3	36.5	20.2	16.3	.6	1.7	30.3	12.1
1963	43.4	37.5	20.0	17.4	.6	1.7	31.6	11.8
1964	42.3	37.3	19.9	17.4	-.8	2.2	31.8	10.5
1965	46.5	39.4	21.9	17.5	1.0	2.5	33.6	12.9
1966	50.5	43.4	25.0	18.4	-.1	3.3	36.5	14.0
1967	50.5	42.8	24.4	18.4	.7	3.1	38.2	12.3
1968	51.8	44.2	25.5	18.7	.1	3.5	39.5	12.3
1969	56.4	48.2	28.6	19.6	.1	3.8	42.1	14.3
1970	58.8	50.5	29.5	21.0	.0	3.7	44.5	14.4
1971	62.1	52.7	30.5	22.3	1.4	3.1	47.1	15.0
1972	71.1	61.1	35.6	25.5	.9	4.0	51.7	19.5
1973	98.9	86.9	45.8	41.1	3.4	2.6	64.6	34.4
1974	98.2	92.4	41.3	51.1	-1.6	.5	71.0	27.3
1975	100.6	88.9	43.1	45.8	3.4	.8	75.0	25.5
1976	102.9	95.4	46.3	49.0	-1.5	.7	82.7	20.2
1977	108.8	96.2	47.6	48.6	1.1	1.8	88.9	19.9
1978	128.4	112.4	59.2	53.2	1.9	3.0	103.2	25.2
1979	150.7	131.5	69.2	62.3	5.0	1.4	123.3	27.4
1980	149.3	139.7	68.0	71.7	-6.3	1.3	133.1	16.1
1981	166.3	141.6	69.2	72.5	6.5	1.9	139.4	26.9
1982	164.1	142.6	70.3	72.3	-1.4	3.5	140.3	23.8
1983	153.9	136.8	69.6	67.2	-10.9	9.3	139.6	14.3
1984	168.0	142.8	72.9	69.9	6.0	8.4	142.0	26.0
1985	161.1	144.0	70.1	73.9	-2.3	7.7	132.6	28.5
1986	156.1	135.4	71.6	63.8	-2.2	11.8	125.0	31.1
1987	168.4	141.8	76.0	65.8	-2.3	16.7	130.4	38.0
1988	177.8	151.1	79.5	71.6	-4.1	14.5	138.3	39.5
1989	191.6	160.5	83.6	76.9	3.8	10.9	145.1	46.5
1990	197.9	169.4	89.1	80.3	3.3	9.3	151.5	46.3
1991	192.0	167.9	85.8	82.1	-.2	8.2	151.8	40.2
1992	200.7	171.5	85.8	85.8	4.2	9.2	151.2	49.5
1993	205.1	178.3	90.5	87.7	-4.2	13.4	158.3	46.8
1994	216.2	181.4	88.3	93.1	8.3	7.9	164.8	51.4
1995	210.9	188.2	87.2	101.0	-5.0	7.3	171.2	39.7
1996	235.9	199.5	92.9	106.5	7.9	7.3	178.1	57.8
1997	238.3	207.9	96.5	111.4	.6	7.5	187.1	51.3
1998	232.3	196.2	94.1	102.1	-.6	12.4	186.0	46.2
1999	234.5	187.6	95.6	92.0	-.2	21.5	187.7	46.8
2000	241.4	192.0	99.5	92.4	1.6	22.9	193.6	47.8
2001	248.4	199.8	106.4	93.4	1.2	20.7	197.8	50.6
2002	228.2	192.9	93.5	99.5	-3.1	11.0	192.8	35.3
2003 ᵖ	259.2	209.9	104.3	105.6	1.0	19.7	203.5	55.8

[1] Cash marketing receipts, Government payments, value of changes in inventories, other farm related cash income, and nonmoney income produced by farms including imputed rent of operator residences.
[2] Crop receipts include proceeds received from commodities placed under Commodity Credit Corporation loans.
[3] Physical changes in beginning and ending year inventories of crop and livestock commodities valued at weighted average market prices during the year.
[4] Includes only Government payments made directly to farmers.

Note.—Data for 2003 are forecasts.

Source: Department of Agriculture, Economic Research Service.

TABLE B–98.—*Farm business balance sheet, 1950–2002*

[Billions of dollars]

End of year	Total assets	Assets								Claims			
		Physical assets					Financial assets		Total claims	Real estate debt[5]	Nonreal estate debt[6]	Proprietors' equity
		Real estate	Nonreal estate			Purchased inputs[3]	Investments in cooperatives	Other[4]				
			Livestock and poultry[1]	Machinery and motor vehicles	Crops[2]							
1950	121.6	75.4	17.1	12.3	7.1		2.7	7.0	121.6	5.2	5.7	110.7
1951	136.0	83.8	19.5	14.3	8.2		2.9	7.3	136.0	5.7	6.9	123.4
1952	133.1	85.1	14.8	15.0	7.9		3.2	7.1	133.1	6.2	7.1	119.8
1953	128.7	84.3	11.7	15.6	6.8		3.3	7.0	128.7	6.6	6.3	115.8
1954	132.6	87.8	11.2	15.7	7.5		3.5	6.9	132.6	7.1	6.7	118.8
1955	137.0	93.0	10.6	16.3	6.5		3.7	6.9	137.0	7.8	7.3	121.9
1956	145.7	100.3	11.0	16.9	6.8		4.0	6.7	145.7	8.5	7.4	129.8
1957	154.5	106.4	13.9	17.0	6.4		4.2	6.6	154.5	9.0	8.2	137.3
1958	168.7	114.6	17.7	18.1	6.9		4.5	6.9	168.7	9.7	9.4	149.6
1959	172.9	121.2	15.2	19.3	6.2		4.8	6.2	172.9	10.6	10.7	151.6
1960	174.4	123.3	15.6	19.1	6.4		4.2	5.8	174.4	11.3	11.1	151.9
1961	181.6	129.1	16.4	19.3	6.5		4.5	5.9	181.6	12.3	11.8	157.5
1962	188.9	134.6	17.3	19.9	6.5		4.6	5.9	188.9	13.5	13.2	162.2
1963	196.7	142.4	15.9	20.4	7.4		5.0	5.7	196.7	15.0	14.6	167.1
1964	204.2	150.5	14.5	21.2	7.0		5.2	5.8	204.2	16.9	15.3	172.1
1965	220.8	161.5	17.6	22.4	7.9		5.4	6.0	220.8	18.9	16.9	185.0
1966	234.0	171.2	19.0	24.1	8.1		5.7	6.0	234.0	20.7	18.5	194.8
1967	246.1	180.9	18.8	26.3	8.0		5.8	6.1	246.1	22.6	19.6	203.9
1968	257.2	189.4	20.2	27.7	7.4		6.1	6.3	257.2	24.7	19.2	213.2
1969	267.8	195.3	22.8	28.6	8.3		6.4	6.4	267.8	26.4	20.0	221.4
1970	278.8	202.4	23.7	30.4	8.7		7.2	6.5	278.8	27.2	21.3	230.3
1971	301.8	217.6	27.3	32.4	10.0		7.9	6.7	301.8	28.8	24.0	248.9
1972	339.9	243.0	33.7	34.6	12.9		8.7	6.9	339.9	31.4	26.7	281.8
1973	418.5	298.3	42.4	39.7	21.4		9.7	7.1	418.5	35.2	31.6	351.7
1974[7]	449.2	335.6	24.6	48.5	22.5		11.2	6.9	449.2	39.6	35.1	374.5
1975	510.8	383.6	29.4	57.4	20.5		13.0	6.9	510.8	43.8	39.8	427.3
1976	590.7	456.5	29.0	63.3	20.6		14.3	6.9	590.7	48.5	45.7	496.5
1977	651.5	509.3	31.9	69.3	20.4		13.5	7.0	651.5	55.8	52.6	543.1
1978	777.7	601.8	50.1	78.8	23.8		16.1	7.1	777.7	63.4	60.4	653.9
1979	914.7	706.1	61.4	91.9	29.9		18.1	7.3	914.7	75.8	71.7	767.2
1980	1,000.4	782.8	60.6	97.5	32.8		19.3	7.4	1,000.4	85.3	77.2	838.0
1981	997.9	785.6	53.5	101.1	29.5		20.6	7.6	997.9	93.9	83.8	820.2
1982	962.5	750.0	53.0	103.9	25.9		21.9	7.8	962.5	96.8	87.2	778.5
1983	959.3	753.4	49.5	101.7	23.7		22.8	8.1	959.3	98.1	88.1	773.1
1984	897.8	661.8	49.5	125.8	26.1	2.0	24.3	8.3	897.8	101.4	87.4	709.0
1985	775.9	586.2	46.3	86.1	22.9	1.2	24.3	9.0	775.9	94.1	78.1	603.8
1986	722.0	542.4	47.8	79.0	16.3	2.1	24.4	10.0	722.0	84.1	67.2	570.7
1987	756.5	563.7	58.0	78.7	17.8	3.2	25.3	9.9	756.5	75.8	62.7	618.0
1988	788.5	582.3	62.2	81.0	23.7	3.5	25.6	10.4	788.5	70.8	62.3	655.4
1989	813.7	600.1	66.2	84.1	23.9	2.6	26.3	10.4	813.7	68.8	62.3	682.7
1990	840.6	619.1	70.9	86.3	23.2	2.8	27.5	10.9	840.6	67.6	63.5	709.5
1991	844.2	624.8	68.1	85.9	22.2	2.6	28.7	11.8	844.2	67.4	64.4	712.3
1992	867.8	640.8	71.0	84.8	24.2	3.9	29.4	13.6	867.8	67.9	63.7	736.2
1993	909.2	677.6	72.8	85.4	23.3	3.8	31.0	13.3	909.2	68.4	65.9	774.9
1994	934.7	704.1	67.9	86.8	23.3	5.0	32.1	-15.5	934.7	69.9	69.0	795.8
1995	965.7	740.5	57.8	87.6	27.4	3.4	34.1	15.0	965.7	71.7	71.3	822.8
1996	1,002.9	769.5	60.3	88.0	31.7	4.4	34.9	14.1	1,002.9	74.4	74.2	854.3
1997	1,051.3	808.2	67.1	88.7	32.7	4.9	35.7	13.9	1,051.3	78.5	78.4	894.4
1998	1,083.1	840.4	63.4	89.8	29.7	5.0	40.5	14.2	1,083.1	83.1	81.5	918.5
1999	1,138.8	887.0	73.2	89.8	28.3	4.0	41.9	14.6	1,138.8	87.2	80.5	971.1
2000	1,203.2	946.4	76.8	90.1	27.9	4.9	43.0	14.1	1,203.2	91.1	86.5	1,025.6
2001	1,255.9	996.2	78.5	92.8	25.2	4.2	43.6	15.3	1,255.9	96.0	89.7	1,070.2
2002	1,304.0	1,045.7	75.6	93.6	23.1	5.6	44.7	15.8	1,304.0	103.4	90.0	1,110.7

[1] Excludes commercial broilers; excludes horses and mules beginning 1959; excludes turkeys beginning 1986.
[2] Non-Commodity Credit Corporation (CCC) crops held on farms plus value above loan rate for crops held under CCC.
[3] Includes fertilizer, chemicals, fuels, parts, feed, seed, and other supplies.
[4] Currency and demand deposits.
[5] Includes CCC storage and drying facilities loans.
[6] Does not include CCC crop loans.
[7] Beginning 1974, data are for farms included in the new farm definition, that is, places with sales of $1,000 or more annually.

Note.—Data exclude operator households.
Beginning 1959, data include Alaska and Hawaii.

Source: Department of Agriculture, Economic Research Service.

[1996=100]

Year	Farm output				Productivity indicators	
		Primary output				
	Total	Livestock and products	Crops	Secondary output	Farm output per unit of total factor input	Farm output per unit of labor input
1948	43	49	41	27	43	13
1949	42	50	39	25	40	13
1950	42	52	37	22	39	13
1951	44	54	39	23	41	14
1952	45	55	41	23	42	15
1953	45	55	41	22	43	16
1954	46	58	40	22	44	17
1955	47	59	42	22	44	17
1956	48	62	41	23	44	18
1957	47	61	41	27	44	19
1958	50	62	45	31	46	21
1959	52	64	45	38	46	22
1960	53	65	48	42	48	23
1961	54	68	48	42	50	24
1962	55	69	48	41	50	25
1963	57	71	50	43	51	27
1964	56	72	49	37	51	28
1965	58	70	52	36	53	29
1966	58	72	51	35	52	31
1967	59	74	53	35	54	34
1968	60	74	54	34	56	36
1969	62	74	56	32	56	37
1970	61	76	54	28	55	37
1971	66	79	60	31	60	41
1972	66	81	60	30	59	42
1973	69	81	64	32	61	43
1974	64	78	59	30	58	44
1975	68	75	67	31	63	46
1976	69	79	66	30	61	47
1977	73	80	72	31	66	52
1978	74	80	74	33	63	56
1979	79	81	81	33	66	60
1980	75	82	74	29	63	60
1981	81	83	85	21	70	64
1982	83	83	86	51	73	68
1983	72	84	66	59	64	60
1984	82	83	83	47	75	69
1985	85	85	87	55	80	77
1986	82	86	82	56	80	80
1987	84	87	83	74	82	81
1988	80	88	73	99	79	75
1989	86	88	83	105	86	82
1990	90	90	89	99	89	86
1991	91	92	89	105	89	84
1992	96	95	96	98	96	94
1993	91	96	87	101	91	93
1994	102	101	103	98	101	103
1995	97	102	92	105	93	94
1996	100	100	100	100	100	100
1997	104	103	104	115	102	104
1998	105	104	103	121	101	107
1999	107	108	104	129	101	106

Note.—Farm output includes primary agricultural activities and certain secondary activities that are closely linked to agricultural production for which information on production and input use cannot be separately observed.

See Table B-100 for farm inputs.

Source: Department of Agriculture, Economic Research Service.

TABLE B–100.—*Farm input use, selected inputs, 1948–2003*

Year	Farm population, April [1] — Number (thousands)	As percent of total population [2]	Farm employment (thousands) [3] — Total	Self-employed and unpaid workers [4]	Hired workers	Crops harvested (millions of acres) [5]	Selected indexes of input use (1996=100) — Total	Farm labor	Farm real estate	Durable equipment	Energy	Agricultural chemicals	Feed, seed, and purchased livestock	Other purchased inputs
1948	24,383	16.6	10,363	8,026	2,337	356	101	341	116	70	66	22	55	14
1949	24,194	16.2	9,964	7,712	2,252	360	106	334	116	82	73	24	59	31
1950	23,048	15.2	9,926	7,597	2,329	345	106	321	117	94	75	29	59	32
1951	21,890	14.2	9,546	7,310	2,236	344	108	308	117	105	77	28	62	34
1952	21,748	13.9	9,149	7,005	2,144	349	107	298	118	114	81	29	61	35
1953	19,874	12.5	8,864	6,775	2,089	348	106	282	118	119	83	29	62	38
1954	19,019	11.7	8,651	6,570	2,081	346	104	275	117	125	82	30	59	36
1955	19,078	11.5	8,381	6,345	2,036	340	108	279	117	127	85	31	65	41
1956	18,712	11.1	7,852	5,900	1,952	324	109	264	116	129	85	33	68	46
1957	17,656	10.3	7,600	5,660	1,940	324	108	246	116	127	83	31	72	52
1958	17,128	9.8	7,503	5,521	1,982	324	109	235	115	125	81	32	76	51
1959	16,592	9.3	7,342	5,390	1,952	324	111	234	115	125	82	38	77	59
1960	15,635	8.7	7,057	5,172	1,885	324	111	228	115	127	83	45	77	60
1961	14,803	8.1	6,919	5,029	1,890	302	110	222	115	124	85	48	76	58
1962	14,313	7.7	6,700	4,873	1,827	295	111	220	115	122	87	46	80	57
1963	13,367	7.1	6,518	4,738	1,780	298	112	214	116	122	88	50	82	56
1964	12,954	6.7	6,110	4,506	1,604	298	109	202	116	124	89	56	80	57
1965	12,363	6.4	5,610	4,128	1,482	298	109	196	116	126	91	60	80	58
1966	11,595	5.9	5,214	3,854	1,360	294	110	183	116	129	92	69	86	55
1967	10,875	5.5	4,903	3,650	1,253	306	110	174	115	134	92	70	86	60
1968	10,454	5.2	4,749	3,535	1,213	300	108	168	115	139	92	60	87	62
1969	10,307	5.1	4,596	3,419	1,176	290	109	165	115	142	94	61	91	60
1970	9,712	4.7	4,523	3,348	1,175	293	110	163	114	143	94	72	93	58
1971	9,425	4.5	4,436	3,275	1,161	305	110	160	113	144	92	72	94	60
1972	9,610	4.6	4,373	3,228	1,146	294	112	158	112	145	91	77	99	58
1973	9,472	4.5	4,337	3,169	1,168	321	112	159	111	147	92	80	98	49
1974	9,264	4.3	4,389	3,075	1,314	328	110	147	111	156	88	86	94	48
1975	8,864	4.1	4,331	3,021	1,310	336	109	147	112	162	103	77	91	53
1976	8,253	3.8	4,363	2,992	1,371	337	113	145	112	166	116	91	95	58
1977	6,194 [6]	2.8 [6]	4,143	2,852	1,291	345	111	140	113	171	122	80	94	62
1978	6,501 [6]	2.9 [6]	3,937	2,680	1,256	338	117	133	114	175	127	87	106	77
1979	6,241 [6]	2.8 [6]	3,765	2,495	1,270	348	119	130	113	180	116	95	109	78
1980	6,051 [6]	2.7 [6]	3,699	2,401	1,298	352	120	126	115	186	113	112	109	73
1981	5,850 [6]	2.5 [6]	3,582 [7]	2,324 [7]	1,258 [7]	366	115	128	114	186	108	101	103	71
1982	5,628 [6]	2.4 [6]	3,466 [7]	2,248 [7]	1,218 [7]	362	113	122	110	183	102	82	107	79
1983	5,787 [6]	2.5 [6]	3,349 [7]	2,171 [7]	1,178 [7]	306	113	121	110	174	99	81	107	79
1984	5,754	2.4	3,233 [7]	2,095 [7]	1,138 [7]	348	109	119	111	166	103	88	99	74
1985	5,355	2.2	3,116	2,018	1,098	342	106	111	111	158	92	90	100	81
1986	5,226	2.2	2,912	1,873	1,039	325	104	103	109	147	86	105	101	81
1987	4,986	2.1	2,897	1,846	1,051	302	102	103	107	136	95	96	100	84
1988	4,951	2.1	2,954	1,967	1,037	297	102	106	107	129	95	80	99	83
1989	4,801	2.0	2,863	1,935	928	318	100	105	107	123	94	82	95	86
1990	4,591	1.9	2,891	2,000	892	322	102	105	106	119	94	95	101	87
1991	4,632	1.9	2,877	1,968	910	318	102	108	105	116	94	96	101	90
1992	....	....	2,810	1,944	866	319	100	102	104	113	94	98	101	89
1993	....	....	2,800	1,942	857	308	100	98	103	109	94	94	103	99
1994	....	....	2,767	1,925	842	321	101	99	102	106	97	101	103	104
1995	....	....	2,836	1,967	869	314	104	103	101	103	102	92	109	110
1996	....	....	2,842	2,010	832	326	100	100	100	100	100	100	100	100
1997	....	....	2,867	1,990	877	333	103	101	99	98	102	108	105	108
1998	....	....	2,827	1,947	880	327	103	98	98	98	104	105	111	119
1999	....	....	2,977	2,048	929	327	106	101	97	99	105	104	117	127
2000 ...	....	....	2,952	2,062	890	324								
2001 ...	....	....	2,923	2,050	873	321								
2002 ...	....	....	....	....	886	317								
2003 p	....	....	....	....	836	324								

[1] Farm population as defined by Department of Agriculture and Department of Commerce, i.e., civilian population living on farms in rural areas, regardless of occupation. Series discontinued in 1992.

[2] Total population of United States including Armed Forces overseas, as of July 1.

[3] Includes persons doing farmwork on all farms. These data, published by the Department of Agriculture, differ from those on agricultural employment by the Department of Labor (see Table B-35) because of differences in the method of approach, in concepts of employment, and in time of month for which the data are collected.

[4] Prior to 1982 this category was termed "family workers" and did not include nonfamily unpaid workers. Series discontinued in 2002.

[5] Acreage harvested plus acreages in fruits, tree nuts, and vegetables and minor crops.

[6] Based on new definition of a farm. Under old definition of a farm, farm population (in thousands and as percent of total population) for 1977, 1978, 1979, 1980, 1981, 1982, and 1983 is 7,806 and 3.6; 8,005 and 3.6; 7,553 and 3.4; 7,241 and 3.2; 7,014 and 3.1; 6,880 and 3.0; 7,029 and 3.0, respectively.

[7] Basis for farm employment series was discontinued for 1981 through 1984. Employment is estimated for these years.

Note.—Population includes Alaska and Hawaii beginning 1960.

Sources: Department of Agriculture (Economic Research Service) and Department of Commerce (Bureau of the Census).

TABLE B-101.—*Agricultural price indexes and farm real estate value, 1975–2003*

[1990-92=100, except as noted]

Year or month	Prices received by farmers			Prices paid by farmers											Addendum:
	All farm products	Crops	Livestock and products	All commodities, services, interest, taxes, and wage rates¹	Production items									Wage rates	Average farm real estate value per acre (dollars)³
					Total²	Feed	Livestock and poultry	Fertilizer	Agricultural chemicals	Fuels	Farm machinery	Farm services	Rent		
1975	73	88	62	47	55	83	39	87	72	40	38	48		44	340
1976	75	87	64	50	59	83	47	74	78	43	43	52		48	397
1977	73	83	64	53	61	82	48	72	71	46	47	57		51	474
1978	83	89	78	58	67	80	65	72	66	48	51	60		55	531
1979	94	98	90	66	76	89	88	77	67	61	56	66		60	628
1980	98	107	89	75	85	98	85	96	71	86	63	81		65	737
1981	100	111	89	82	92	110	80	104	77	98	70	89		70	819
1982	94	98	90	86	94	99	78	105	83	97	76	96		74	823
1983	98	108	88	86	92	107	76	100	87	94	81	82		76	788
1984	101	111	91	89	94	112	73	103	90	93	85	86		77	801
1985	91	97	86	86	91	95	74	98	90	93	85	85		78	713
1986	87	87	88	85	86	88	73	90	89	76	83	83		81	640
1987	89	86	91	87	87	83	85	86	87	76	85	84		85	599
1988	99	105	93	91	90	104	91	94	89	77	89	85		87	632
1989	104	109	100	96	95	110	93	99	93	83	94	91		95	668
1990	104	103	105	99	99	103	102	97	95	100	96	96	96	96	683
1991	100	101	99	100	100	98	102	103	101	104	100	98	100	100	703
1992	99	101	97	101	101	99	96	100	103	96	104	103	104	105	713
1993	101	102	100	104	104	102	104	96	109	93	107	110	100	108	736
1994	100	105	95	106	106	106	94	105	112	89	113	110	108	111	798
1995	102	112	92	109	108	103	82	121	116	89	120	115	117	114	844
1996	112	127	99	115	115	129	75	125	119	102	125	116	128	117	887
1997	107	115	98	118	119	125	94	121	121	106	128	116	136	123	926
1998	101	107	97	115	113	111	88	112	122	84	132	115	120	129	974
1999	96	97	95	115	111	100	95	105	121	93	135	116	113	135	1,020
2000	96	96	97	120	116	102	110	110	120	134	139	119	110	140	1,080
2001	102	99	106	123	120	109	111	123	121	119	144	121	117	146	1,150
2002	98	105	90	124	119	112	102	108	119	112	148	120	119	153	1,210
2003	107	111	103	128	124	116	109	124	121	144	149	122	120	157	1,270
2002: Jan	95	94	96	122	117	108	109	108	120	83	146	120	119	155	1,210
Feb	98	101	96	122	117	107	110	108	118	86	146	120	119	155	....
Mar	105	117	94	123	118	109	106	107	119	101	147	120	119	155	....
Apr	94	100	89	123	118	109	102	107	119	114	147	119	119	153	....
May	96	104	89	123	118	108	98	107	119	110	148	120	119	153	....
June	97	105	90	123	118	110	95	108	119	108	147	121	119	153	....
July	98	109	88	123	119	114	96	107	119	112	148	121	119	148	....
Aug	100	113	87	124	120	116	97	107	120	117	148	121	119	148	....
Sept	98	109	85	124	121	118	99	107	120	129	148	121	119	148	....
Oct	95	101	87	125	121	116	101	107	119	139	148	120	119	155	....
Nov	97	104	89	125	120	114	105	109	119	123	149	120	119	155	....
Dec	100	107	91	125	121	114	109	109	121	123	149	120	119	155	....
2003: Jan	100	103	96	126	122	114	105	112	122	140	149	121	120	161	1,270
Feb	99	103	95	127	123	114	101	117	122	171	149	121	120	161	....
Mar	99	106	93	128	124	114	98	126	120	178	149	121	120	161	....
Apr	101	111	94	128	124	114	102	129	121	143	149	122	120	158	....
May	106	116	97	127	123	116	102	127	121	129	149	122	120	158	....
June	107	117	99	128	123	115	103	124	121	134	149	123	120	158	....
July	105	109	101	127	123	113	106	122	121	136	149	123	120	153	....
Aug	109	113	106	127	123	110	107	123	121	141	149	123	120	153	....
Sept	110	111	110	129	125	114	117	124	121	138	149	124	120	153	....
Oct	113	111	116	130	126	115	125	125	122	144	150	123	120	156	....
Nov	117	117	117	130	127	121	122	126	122	137	150	122	120	156	....
Dec	115	117	113	130	128	129	119	127	122	137	150	122	120	156	....

¹ Includes items used for family living, not shown separately.
² Includes other production items not shown separately.
³ Average for 48 States. Annual data are: March 1 for 1975, February 1 for 1976-81, April 1 for 1982-85, February 1 for 1986-89, and January 1 for 1990-2003.

Note.—Data on a 1990-92 base prior to 1975 have not been calculated by Department of Agriculture.

Source: Department of Agriculture, National Agricultural Statistics Service.

TABLE B–102.—U.S. exports and imports of agricultural commodities, 1945–2003

[Billions of dollars]

Year	Exports							Imports					Agri-cultural trade balance
	Total[1]	Feed grains	Food grains[2]	Oil-seeds and products	Cot-ton	To-bacco	Ani-mals and products	Total[1]	Fruits, nuts, and vege-tables[3]	Ani-mals and products	Cof-fee	Cocoa beans and products	
1945	2.3	(4)	0.4	(4)	0.3	0.2	0.9	1.7	0.1	0.4	0.3	(4)	0.5
1946	3.1	0.1	.7	(4)	.5	.4	.9	2.3	.2	.4	.5	0.1	.8
1947	4.0	.4	1.4	0.1	.4	.3	.7	2.8	.1	.4	.6	.2	1.2
1948	3.5	.1	1.5	.2	.5	.2	.5	3.1	.2	.6	.7	.2	.3
1949	3.6	.3	1.1	.3	.9	.3	.4	2.9	.2	.4	.8	.1	.7
1950	2.9	.2	.6	.2	1.0	.3	.3	4.0	.2	.7	1.1	.2	−1.1
1951	4.0	.3	1.1	.3	1.1	.3	.5	5.2	.2	1.1	1.4	.2	−1.1
1952	3.4	.3	1.1	.2	.9	.2	.3	4.5	.2	.7	1.4	.2	−1.1
1953	2.8	.3	.7	.2	.5	.3	.4	4.2	.2	.6	1.5	.2	−1.3
1954	3.1	.2	.5	.3	.8	.3	.5	4.0	.2	.5	1.5	.3	−.9
1955	3.2	.3	.6	.4	.5	.4	.6	4.0	.2	.5	1.4	.2	−.8
1956	4.2	.4	1.0	.5	.7	.3	.7	4.0	.2	.4	1.4	.2	.2
1957	4.5	.3	1.0	.5	1.0	.4	.7	4.0	.2	.5	1.4	.2	.6
1958	3.9	.5	.8	.4	.7	.4	.5	3.9	.2	.7	1.2	.2	(4)
1959	4.0	.6	.9	.6	.4	.3	.6	4.1	.2	.8	1.1	.2	−.1
1960	4.8	.5	1.2	.6	1.0	.4	.6	3.8	.2	.6	1.0	.2	1.0
1961	5.0	.5	1.4	.6	.9	.4	.6	3.7	.2	.7	1.0	.2	1.3
1962	5.0	.8	1.3	.7	.5	.4	.6	3.9	.2	.9	1.0	.2	1.2
1963	5.6	.8	1.5	.8	.6	.4	.7	4.0	.3	.9	1.0	.2	1.6
1964	6.3	.9	1.7	1.0	.7	.4	.8	4.1	.3	.8	1.2	.2	2.3
1965	6.2	1.1	1.4	1.2	.5	.4	.8	4.1	.3	.9	1.1	.1	2.1
1966	6.9	1.3	1.8	1.2	.4	.5	.7	4.5	.4	1.2	1.1	.1	2.4
1967	6.4	1.1	1.5	1.3	.5	.5	.7	4.5	.4	1.1	1.0	.2	1.9
1968	6.3	.9	1.4	1.3	.5	.5	.7	5.0	.5	1.3	1.2	.2	1.3
1969	6.0	.9	1.2	1.3	.3	.6	.8	5.0	.5	1.4	.9	.2	1.1
1970	7.3	1.1	1.4	1.9	.4	.5	.9	5.8	.5	1.6	1.2	.3	1.5
1971	7.7	1.0	1.3	2.2	.6	.5	1.0	5.8	.6	1.5	1.2	.2	1.9
1972	9.4	1.5	1.8	2.4	.5	.7	1.1	6.5	.7	1.8	1.3	.2	2.9
1973	17.7	3.5	4.7	4.3	.9	.7	1.6	8.4	.8	2.6	1.7	.3	9.3
1974	21.9	4.6	5.4	5.7	1.3	.8	1.8	10.2	.8	2.2	1.6	.5	11.7
1975	21.9	5.2	6.2	4.5	1.0	.9	1.7	9.3	.8	1.8	1.7	.5	12.6
1976	23.0	6.0	4.7	5.1	1.0	.9	2.4	11.0	.9	2.3	2.9	.6	12.0
1977	23.6	4.9	3.6	6.6	1.5	1.1	2.7	13.4	1.2	2.3	4.2	1.0	10.2
1978	29.4	5.9	5.5	8.2	1.7	1.4	3.0	14.8	1.5	3.1	4.0	1.4	14.6
1979	34.7	7.7	6.3	8.9	2.2	1.2	3.8	16.7	1.7	3.9	4.2	1.2	18.0
1980	41.2	9.8	7.9	9.4	2.9	1.3	3.8	17.4	1.7	3.8	4.2	.9	23.8
1981	43.3	9.4	9.6	9.6	2.3	1.5	4.2	16.9	2.0	3.5	2.9	.9	26.4
1982	36.6	6.4	7.9	9.1	2.0	1.5	3.9	15.3	2.3	3.7	2.9	.7	21.3
1983	36.1	7.3	7.4	8.7	1.8	1.5	3.8	16.5	2.3	3.8	2.8	.8	19.6
1984	37.8	8.1	7.5	8.4	2.4	1.5	4.2	19.3	3.1	4.1	3.3	1.1	18.5
1985	29.0	6.0	4.5	5.8	1.6	1.5	4.1	20.0	3.5	4.2	3.3	1.4	9.1
1986	26.2	3.1	3.8	6.5	.8	1.2	4.5	21.5	3.6	4.5	4.6	1.1	4.7
1987	28.7	3.8	3.8	6.4	1.6	1.1	5.2	20.4	3.6	4.9	2.9	1.2	8.3
1988	37.1	5.9	5.9	7.7	2.0	1.3	6.4	21.0	3.8	5.2	2.5	1.0	16.1
1989	40.1	7.7	7.1	6.4	2.2	1.3	6.4	21.9	4.2	5.0	2.4	1.0	18.2
1990	39.5	7.0	4.8	5.7	2.8	1.4	6.6	22.9	4.9	5.6	1.9	1.1	16.6
1991	39.3	5.7	4.2	6.4	2.5	1.4	7.1	22.9	4.8	5.5	1.9	1.1	16.5
1992	43.1	5.7	5.4	7.2	2.0	1.7	8.0	24.8	4.9	5.7	1.7	1.1	18.3
1993	42.9	5.0	5.6	7.3	1.5	1.3	8.0	25.1	5.0	5.9	1.5	1.0	17.7
1994	46.2	4.7	5.3	7.2	2.7	1.3	9.2	27.0	5.4	5.7	2.5	1.0	19.2
1995	56.3	8.2	6.7	9.0	3.7	1.4	10.9	30.3	5.9	6.0	3.3	1.1	26.0
1996	60.3	9.4	7.4	10.8	2.7	1.4	11.1	33.5	6.9	6.1	2.8	1.4	26.8
1997	57.2	6.0	5.2	12.1	2.7	1.6	11.3	36.1	7.2	6.5	3.9	1.5	21.0
1998	51.8	5.0	5.0	9.5	2.5	1.5	10.6	36.9	7.9	6.9	3.4	1.7	14.9
1999	48.4	5.5	4.7	8.1	1.0	1.3	10.4	37.7	8.9	7.3	2.9	1.5	10.7
2000	51.2	5.2	4.3	8.6	1.9	1.2	11.6	39.0	9.0	8.3	2.7	1.4	12.3
2001	53.7	5.2	4.2	9.2	2.2	1.3	12.4	39.4	9.3	9.1	1.7	1.5	14.3
2002	53.1	5.5	4.5	9.6	2.0	1.0	11.1	41.9	10.1	9.0	1.7	1.8	11.2
Jan-Nov:													
2002	48.2	5.0	3.9	8.6	1.8	1.0	10.2	38.2	8.5	8.2	1.5	1.6	10.0
2003	53.5	4.8	4.5	10.2	2.7	.9	11.4	42.9	9.6	8.0	1.8	2.2	10.6

[1] Total includes items not shown separately.
[2] Rice, wheat, and wheat flour.
[3] Includes fruit, nut, and vegetable preparations.
[4] Less than $50 million.

Note.—Data derived from official estimates released by the Bureau of the Census, Department of Commerce. Agricultural commodities are defined as (1) nonmarine food products and (2) other products of agriculture which have not passed through complex processes of manufacture. Export value, at U.S. port of exportation, is based on the selling price and includes inland freight, insurance, and other charges to the port. Import value, defined generally as the market value in the foreign country, excludes import duties, ocean freight, and marine insurance.

Source: Department of Agriculture, Economic Research Service.

TABLE B–103.—*U.S. international transactions, 1946–2003*

[Millions of dollars; quarterly data seasonally adjusted. Credits (+), debits (−)]

Year or quarter	Goods[1] Exports	Goods[1] Imports	Goods[1] Balance on goods	Services Net military transactions[2]	Services Net travel and transportation	Services Other services, net	Services Balance on goods and services	Income receipts and payments Receipts	Income receipts and payments Payments	Income receipts and payments Balance on income	Unilateral current transfers, net[2]	Balance on current account
1946	11,764	−5,067	6,697	−424	733	310	7,316	772	−212	560	−2,991	4,885
1947	16,097	−5,973	10,124	−358	946	145	10,857	1,102	−245	857	−2,722	8,992
1948	13,265	−7,557	5,708	−351	374	175	5,906	1,921	−437	1,484	−4,973	2,417
1949	12,213	−6,874	5,339	−410	230	208	5,367	1,831	−476	1,355	−5,849	873
1950	10,203	−9,081	1,122	−56	−120	242	1,188	2,068	−559	1,509	−4,537	−1,840
1951	14,243	−11,176	3,067	169	298	254	3,788	2,633	−583	2,050	−4,954	884
1952	13,449	−10,838	2,611	528	83	309	3,531	2,751	−555	2,196	−5,113	614
1953	12,412	−10,975	1,437	1,753	−238	307	3,259	2,736	−624	2,112	−6,657	−1,286
1954	12,929	−10,353	2,576	902	−269	305	3,514	2,929	−582	2,347	−5,642	219
1955	14,424	−11,527	2,897	−113	−297	299	2,786	3,406	−676	2,730	−5,086	430
1956	17,556	−12,803	4,753	−221	−361	447	4,618	3,837	−735	3,102	−4,990	2,730
1957	19,562	−13,291	6,271	−423	−189	482	6,141	4,180	−796	3,384	−4,763	4,762
1958	16,414	−12,952	3,462	−849	−633	486	2,466	3,790	−825	2,965	−4,647	784
1959	16,458	−15,310	1,148	−831	−821	573	69	4,132	−1,061	3,071	−4,422	−1,282
1960	19,650	−14,758	4,892	−1,057	−964	639	3,508	4,616	−1,238	3,379	−4,062	2,824
1961	20,108	−14,537	5,571	−1,131	−978	732	4,195	4,999	−1,245	3,755	−4,127	3,822
1962	20,781	−16,260	4,521	−912	−1,152	912	3,370	5,618	−1,324	4,294	−4,277	3,387
1963	22,272	−17,048	5,224	−742	−1,309	1,036	4,210	6,157	−1,560	4,596	−4,392	4,414
1964	25,501	−18,700	6,801	−794	−1,146	1,161	6,022	6,824	−1,783	5,041	−4,240	6,823
1965	26,461	−21,510	4,951	−487	−1,280	1,480	4,664	7,437	−2,088	5,350	−4,583	5,431
1966	29,310	−25,493	3,817	−1,043	−1,331	1,497	2,940	7,528	−2,481	5,047	−4,955	3,031
1967	30,666	−26,866	3,800	−1,187	−1,750	1,742	2,604	8,021	−2,747	5,274	−5,294	2,583
1968	33,626	−32,991	635	−596	−1,548	1,759	250	9,367	−3,378	5,990	−5,629	611
1969	36,414	−35,807	607	−718	−1,763	1,964	91	10,913	−4,869	6,044	−5,735	399
1970	42,469	−39,866	2,603	−641	−2,038	2,330	2,254	11,748	−5,515	6,233	−6,156	2,331
1971	43,319	−45,579	−2,260	653	−2,345	2,649	−1,303	12,707	−5,435	7,272	−7,402	−1,433
1972	49,381	−55,797	−6,416	1,072	−3,063	2,965	−5,443	14,765	−6,572	8,192	−8,544	−5,795
1973	71,410	−70,499	911	740	−3,158	3,406	1,900	21,808	−9,655	12,153	−6,913	7,140
1974	98,306	−103,811	−5,505	165	−3,184	4,231	−4,292	27,587	−12,084	15,503	−9,249	1,962
1975	107,088	−98,185	8,903	1,461	−2,812	4,854	12,404	25,351	−12,564	12,787	−7,075	18,116
1976	114,745	−124,228	−9,483	931	−2,558	5,027	−6,082	29,375	−13,311	16,063	−5,686	4,295
1977	120,816	−151,907	−31,091	1,731	−3,565	5,680	−27,246	32,354	−14,217	18,137	−5,226	−14,335
1978	142,075	−176,002	−33,927	857	−3,573	6,879	−29,763	42,088	−21,680	20,408	−5,788	−15,143
1979	184,439	−212,007	−27,568	−1,313	−2,935	7,251	−24,565	63,834	−32,961	30,873	−6,593	−285
1980	224,250	−249,750	−25,500	−1,822	−997	8,912	−19,407	72,606	−42,532	30,073	−8,349	2,317
1981	237,044	−265,067	−28,023	−844	144	12,552	−16,172	86,529	−53,626	32,903	−11,702	5,030
1982	211,157	−247,642	−36,485	112	−992	13,209	−24,156	91,747	−56,583	35,164	−16,544	−5,536
1983	201,799	−268,901	−67,102	−563	−4,227	14,124	−57,767	90,000	−53,614	36,386	−17,310	−38,691
1984	219,926	−332,418	−112,492	−2,547	−8,438	14,404	−109,073	108,819	−73,756	35,063	−20,335	−94,344
1985	215,915	−338,088	−122,173	−4,390	−9,798	14,483	−121,880	98,542	−72,819	25,723	−21,998	−118,155
1986	223,344	−368,425	−145,081	−5,181	−8,779	20,502	−138,538	97,064	−81,571	15,494	−24,132	−147,177
1987	250,208	−409,765	−159,557	−3,844	−8,010	19,728	−151,684	108,184	−93,891	14,293	−23,265	−160,655
1988	320,230	−447,189	−126,959	−6,320	−3,013	21,725	−114,566	136,713	−118,026	18,687	−25,274	−121,153
1989	359,916	−477,665	−117,749	−6,749	3,551	27,805	−93,142	161,287	−141,463	19,824	−26,169	−99,486
1990	387,401	−498,435	−111,034	−7,599	7,501	30,270	−80,861	171,742	−143,192	28,550	−26,654	−78,965
1991	414,083	−491,020	−76,937	−5,274	16,561	34,516	−31,135	149,214	−125,084	24,130	10,752	3,747
1992	439,631	−536,528	−96,897	−1,448	19,969	40,191	−38,385	132,427	−109,101	23,325	−33,154	−48,013
1993	456,943	−589,394	−132,451	1,385	19,714	42,185	−69,166	134,545	−110,255	24,290	−37,113	−81,989
1994	502,859	−668,690	−165,831	2,570	16,305	49,767	−97,189	165,838	−148,744	17,094	−37,583	−117,678
1995	575,204	−749,374	−174,170	4,600	21,772	52,729	−95,069	211,920	−186,880	25,040	−35,188	−105,217
1996	612,113	−803,113	−191,000	5,385	25,015	57,731	−102,869	226,271	−201,743	24,528	−38,862	−117,203
1997	678,366	−876,485	−198,119	4,968	22,152	63,952	−107,047	261,026	−240,371	20,655	−41,292	−127,684
1998	670,416	−917,112	−246,696	5,220	10,210	68,113	−163,153	258,648	−251,751	6,897	−48,435	−204,691
1999	683,965	−1,029,987	−346,022	2,593	7,085	75,143	−261,201	290,198	−273,088	17,110	−46,755	−290,846
2000	771,994	−1,224,417	−452,423	317	2,486	74,236	−375,384	346,861	−327,256	19,605	−55,679	−411,458
2001	718,712	−1,145,927	−427,215	−2,436	−3,254	75,086	−357,819	277,362	−266,673	10,689	−46,615	−393,745
2002	681,874	−1,164,746	−482,872	−7,302	−3,781	75,917	−418,038	255,542	−259,512	−3,970	−58,853	−480,861
2001: I	194,145	−306,871	−112,726	−772	1,182	18,876	−93,440	79,087	−78,157	930	−11,494	−104,004
II	184,457	−291,627	−107,170	101	−1,157	18,770	−89,456	72,607	−71,794	813	−11,321	−99,964
III	172,526	−278,847	−106,321	−376	−719	18,373	−89,043	65,701	−69,038	−3,337	−11,256	−103,636
IV	167,584	−268,582	−100,998	−1,389	−2,563	19,068	−85,882	59,967	−47,683	12,284	−12,542	−86,140
2002: I	165,298	−271,331	−106,033	−1,609	−597	18,182	−90,057	60,632	−61,365	−733	−15,938	−106,728
II	171,421	−292,707	−121,286	−1,917	−1,322	19,637	−104,888	63,920	−68,378	−4,458	−13,481	−122,827
III	174,315	−297,627	−123,312	−1,572	−1,118	19,022	−106,980	66,124	−67,871	−1,747	−13,997	−122,724
IV	170,840	−303,081	−132,241	−2,204	−746	19,075	−116,116	64,864	−61,898	2,966	−15,436	−128,586
2003: I	173,346	−309,364	−136,018	−2,847	−2,339	19,575	−121,629	62,901	−62,710	191	−17,269	−138,707
II	174,247	−312,335	−138,088	−3,107	−3,012	20,023	−124,184	64,310	−62,580	1,730	−16,940	−139,394
III *p*	177,858	−314,090	−136,232	−2,519	−2,664	20,098	−121,317	67,344	−64,749	2,595	−16,319	−135,041

[1] Adjusted from Census data for differences in valuation, coverage, and timing; excludes military.
[2] Includes transfers of goods and services under U.S. military grant programs.

See next page for continuation of table.

TABLE B-103.—*U.S. international transactions, 1946-2003*—Continued

[Millions of dollars; quarterly data seasonally adjusted. Credits (+), debits (−)]

Year or quarter	Capital account trans-actions, net	Financial account							Statistical discrepancy	
		U.S.-owned assets abroad, net [increase/financial outflow (−)]				Foreign-owned assets in the U.S., net [increase/financial inflow (+)]			Total (sum of the items with sign reversed)	Of which: Seasonal adjust-ment discrep-ancy
		Total	U.S. official reserve assets [3]	Other U.S. Govern-ment assets	U.S. private assets	Total	Foreign official assets	Other foreign assets		
1946			−623							
1947			−3,315							
1948			−1,736							
1949			−266							
1950			1,758							
1951			−33							
1952			−415							
1953			1,256							
1954			480							
1955			182							
1956			−869							
1957			−1,165							
1958			2,292							
1959			1,035							
1960		−4,099	2,145	−1,100	−5,144	2,294	1,473	821	−1,019	
1961		−5,538	607	−910	−5,235	2,705	765	1,939	−989	
1962		−4,174	1,535	−1,085	−4,623	1,911	1,270	641	−1,124	
1963		−7,270	378	−1,662	−5,986	3,217	1,986	1,231	−360	
1964		−9,560	171	−1,680	−8,050	3,643	1,660	1,983	−907	
1965		−5,716	1,225	−1,605	−5,336	742	134	607	−457	
1966		−7,321	570	−1,543	−6,347	3,661	−672	4,333	629	
1967		−9,757	53	−2,423	−7,386	7,379	3,451	3,928	−205	
1968		−10,977	−870	−2,274	−7,833	9,928	−774	10,703	438	
1969		−11,585	−1,179	−2,200	−8,206	12,702	−1,301	14,002	−1,516	
1970		−8,470	3,348	−1,589	−10,229	6,359	6,908	−550	−219	
1971		−11,758	3,066	−1,884	−12,940	22,970	26,879	−3,909	−9,779	
1972		−13,787	706	−1,568	−12,925	21,461	10,475	10,986	−1,879	
1973		−22,874	158	−2,644	−20,388	18,388	6,026	12,362	−2,654	
1974		−34,745	−1,467	366	−33,643	35,341	10,546	24,796	−2,558	
1975		−39,703	−849	−3,474	−35,380	17,170	7,027	10,143	4,417	
1976		−51,269	−2,558	−4,214	−44,498	38,018	17,693	20,326	8,955	
1977		−34,785	−375	−3,693	−30,717	53,219	36,816	16,403	−4,099	
1978		−61,130	732	−4,660	−57,202	67,036	33,678	33,358	9,236	
1979		−64,915	6	−3,746	−61,176	40,852	−13,665	54,516	24,349	
1980		−85,815	−7,003	−5,162	−73,651	62,612	15,497	47,115	20,886	
1981		−113,054	−4,082	−5,097	−103,875	86,232	4,960	81,272	21,792	
1982	199	−127,882	−4,965	−6,131	−116,786	96,589	3,593	92,997	36,630	
1983	209	−66,373	−1,196	−5,006	−60,172	88,694	5,845	82,849	16,162	
1984	235	−40,376	−3,131	−5,489	−31,757	117,752	3,140	114,612	16,733	
1985	315	−44,752	−3,858	−2,821	−38,074	146,115	−1,119	147,233	16,478	
1986	301	−111,723	312	−2,022	−110,014	230,009	35,648	194,360	28,590	
1987	365	−79,296	9,149	1,006	−89,450	248,634	45,387	203,247	−9,048	
1988	493	−106,573	−3,912	2,967	−105,628	246,522	39,758	206,764	−19,289	
1989	336	−175,383	−25,293	1,233	−151,323	224,928	8,503	216,425	49,605	
1990	−6,579	−81,234	−2,158	2,317	−81,393	141,571	33,910	107,661	25,208	
1991	−4,479	−64,388	5,763	2,924	−73,075	110,808	17,389	93,420	−45,688	
1992	−557	−74,410	3,901	−1,667	−76,644	170,663	40,477	130,186	−47,683	
1993	−1,299	−200,552	−1,379	−351	−198,822	282,040	71,753	210,287	1,799	
1994	−1,723	−176,056	5,346	−390	−181,012	305,989	39,583	266,406	−10,532	
1995	−927	−352,376	−9,742	−984	−341,650	438,562	109,880	328,682	19,958	
1996	−654	−413,923	6,668	−989	−419,602	551,096	126,724	424,372	−19,316	
1997	−1,044	−487,599	−1,010	68	−486,657	706,809	19,036	687,773	−90,482	
1998	−740	−347,829	−6,783	−422	−340,624	423,569	−19,903	443,472	129,691	
1999	−4,843	−503,640	8,747	2,750	−515,137	740,210	43,543	696,667	59,119	
2000	−799	−569,798	−290	−941	−568,567	1,026,139	37,724	988,415	−44,084	
2001	−1,062	−349,939	−4,911	−486	−344,542	765,531	5,104	760,427	−20,785	
2002	−1,285	−178,985	−3,681	−32	−175,272	706,983	94,860	612,123	−45,852	
2001: I	−267	−192,224	190	77	−192,491	313,923	4,290	309,633	−17,428	6,244
II	−260	−92,213	−1,343	−783	−90,087	213,471	−21,197	234,668	−21,034	799
III	−286	37,353	−3,559	77	40,835	24,084	16,702	7,382	42,485	−8,244
IV	−249	−102,853	−199	143	−102,797	214,051	5,309	208,742	−24,809	1,200
2002: I	−277	−35,227	390	133	−35,750	146,813	6,106	140,707	−4,581	8,579
II	−286	−128,567	−1,843	42	−126,766	221,242	47,552	173,690	30,438	2,091
III	−364	29,712	−1,416	−27	31,155	141,478	8,992	132,486	−48,102	−12,409
IV	−358	−44,902	−812	−180	−43,910	197,448	32,210	165,238	−23,602	1,744
2003: I	−388	−101,331	83	−70	−101,344	242,004	40,978	201,026	−1,578	9,479
II	−1,553	−112,818	−170	427	−113,075	262,819	57,000	205,819	−9,054	1,454
III *p*	−795	−4,891	−611	530	−4,810	128,200	43,895	84,305	12,527	−12,200

[3] Consists of gold, special drawing rights, foreign currencies, and the U.S. reserve position in the International Monetary Fund (IMF).

Source: Department of Commerce, Bureau of Economic Analysis.

TABLE B–104.—U.S. international trade in goods by principal end-use category, 1965–2003

[Billions of dollars; quarterly data seasonally adjusted]

Year or quarter	Exports							Imports						
	Total	Agricultural products	Nonagricultural products					Total	Petroleum and products	Nonpetroleum products				
			Total	Industrial supplies and materials	Capital goods except automotive	Automotive	Other			Total	Industrial supplies and materials	Capital goods except automotive	Automotive	Other
1965	26.5	6.3	20.2	7.6	8.1	1.9	2.6	21.5	2.0	19.5	9.1	1.5	0.9	8.0
1966	29.3	6.9	22.4	8.2	8.9	2.4	2.9	25.5	2.1	23.4	10.2	2.2	1.8	9.2
1967	30.7	6.5	24.2	8.5	9.9	2.8	3.0	26.9	2.1	24.8	10.0	2.5	2.4	9.9
1968	33.6	6.3	27.3	9.6	11.1	3.5	3.2	33.0	2.4	30.6	12.0	2.8	4.0	11.8
1969	36.4	6.1	30.3	10.3	12.4	3.9	3.7	35.8	2.6	33.2	11.8	3.4	4.9	13.0
1970	42.5	7.4	35.1	12.3	14.7	3.9	4.3	39.9	2.9	36.9	12.4	4.0	5.5	15.0
1971	43.3	7.8	35.5	10.9	15.4	4.7	4.5	45.6	3.7	41.9	13.8	4.3	7.4	16.4
1972	49.4	9.5	39.9	11.9	16.9	5.5	5.6	55.8	4.7	51.1	16.3	5.9	8.7	20.2
1973	71.4	18.0	53.4	17.0	22.0	6.9	7.6	70.5	8.4	62.1	19.6	8.3	10.3	23.9
1974	98.3	22.4	75.9	26.3	30.9	8.6	10.0	103.8	26.6	77.2	27.8	9.8	12.0	27.5
1975	107.1	22.2	84.8	26.8	36.6	10.6	10.8	98.2	27.0	71.2	24.0	10.2	11.7	25.3
1976	114.7	23.4	91.4	28.4	39.1	12.1	11.7	124.2	34.6	89.7	29.8	12.3	16.2	31.4
1977	120.8	24.3	96.5	29.8	39.8	13.4	13.5	151.9	45.0	106.9	35.7	14.0	18.6	38.6
1978 [1]	142.1	29.9	112.2	34.2	47.5	15.2	15.3	176.0	42.6	133.4	40.7	19.3	25.0	48.4
1979	184.4	35.5	149.0	52.2	60.2	17.9	18.7	212.0	60.4	151.6	47.5	24.6	26.6	52.8
1980	224.3	42.0	182.2	65.1	76.3	17.4	23.4	249.8	79.5	170.2	53.0	31.6	28.3	57.4
1981	237.0	44.1	193.0	63.6	84.2	19.7	25.5	265.1	78.4	186.7	56.1	37.1	31.0	62.4
1982	211.2	37.3	173.9	57.7	76.5	17.2	22.4	247.6	62.0	185.7	48.6	38.4	34.3	64.3
1983	201.8	37.1	164.7	52.7	71.7	18.5	21.8	268.9	55.1	213.8	53.7	43.7	43.0	73.3
1984	219.9	38.4	181.5	56.8	77.0	22.4	25.3	332.4	58.1	274.4	66.1	60.4	56.5	91.4
1985	215.9	29.6	186.3	54.8	79.3	24.9	27.2	338.1	51.4	286.7	62.6	61.3	64.9	97.9
1986	223.3	27.2	196.2	59.4	82.8	25.1	28.9	368.4	34.3	334.1	69.9	72.0	78.1	114.2
1987	250.2	29.8	220.4	63.7	92.7	27.6	36.4	409.8	42.9	366.8	70.8	85.1	85.2	125.7
1988	320.2	38.8	281.4	82.6	119.1	33.4	46.3	447.2	39.6	407.6	83.1	102.2	87.9	134.4
1989 [1]	359.9	41.1	318.8	90.4	136.9	35.0	56.4	477.7	50.9	426.8	84.6	112.4	87.2	142.5
1990	387.4	40.2	347.2	97.0	153.1	36.1	61.1	498.4	62.3	436.1	83.0	116.3	88.4	148.5
1991	414.1	40.1	374.0	101.6	166.7	39.7	66.0	491.0	51.7	439.3	81.3	121.0	85.7	151.4
1992	439.6	44.1	395.5	101.7	176.5	46.7	70.6	536.5	51.6	484.9	89.1	134.6	91.7	169.5
1993	456.9	43.6	413.3	105.1	182.9	51.3	74.1	589.4	51.5	537.9	100.7	152.9	102.4	181.9
1994	502.9	47.1	455.8	112.6	205.8	57.3	80.0	668.7	51.3	617.4	113.7	185.0	118.1	200.6
1995	575.2	57.3	518.0	135.5	234.5	61.3	86.7	749.4	56.0	693.3	128.8	222.2	123.6	218.7
1996	612.1	61.5	550.6	137.9	254.0	64.2	94.4	803.1	72.7	730.4	136.8	228.5	128.7	236.4
1997	678.4	58.5	619.9	147.7	295.9	73.3	103.0	876.5	71.7	804.7	145.5	253.4	139.5	266.3
1998	670.4	53.2	617.3	138.5	299.9	72.4	106.5	917.1	50.6	866.5	152.1	269.5	148.7	296.2
1999	684.0	49.7	634.3	140.3	311.3	75.3	107.5	1,030.0	67.8	962.2	156.3	295.7	179.0	331.2
2000	772.0	52.8	719.2	163.9	357.0	80.4	117.9	1,224.4	120.2	1,104.2	181.9	347.0	195.9	379.4
2001	718.7	54.9	663.8	150.5	321.7	75.4	116.2	1,145.9	103.6	1,042.3	172.5	298.0	189.8	382.0
2002	681.9	54.5	627.4	147.7	290.5	78.9	110.2	1,164.7	103.5	1,061.3	164.6	283.3	203.7	409.6
2001: I	194.1	13.6	180.5	40.8	91.1	18.5	30.1	306.9	29.2	277.7	49.0	84.5	47.1	97.1
II	184.5	13.6	170.8	39.0	82.5	19.2	30.2	291.6	28.5	263.1	44.3	75.0	47.6	96.1
III	172.5	13.8	158.7	35.8	75.7	19.0	28.2	278.8	25.6	253.2	40.5	70.1	47.8	94.8
IV	167.6	13.9	153.7	34.9	72.4	18.7	27.7	268.6	20.2	248.3	38.7	68.3	47.3	94.0
2002: I	165.3	13.7	151.6	34.6	71.4	18.9	26.7	271.3	19.1	252.2	38.3	69.0	48.1	96.7
II	171.4	13.5	157.9	37.2	73.1	20.1	27.5	292.7	27.1	265.7	41.0	71.5	51.0	102.1
III	174.3	13.6	160.8	37.6	74.7	20.3	28.1	297.6	27.9	269.7	42.0	71.4	52.2	104.1
IV	170.8	13.7	157.1	38.2	71.3	19.6	27.9	303.1	29.4	273.7	43.3	71.4	52.3	106.6
2003: I	173.3	14.2	159.1	40.2	70.8	20.0	28.2	309.4	34.0	275.4	45.4	70.9	51.1	107.9
II	174.2	14.4	159.9	40.4	70.5	19.9	29.0	312.3	32.6	279.7	45.4	73.0	52.9	108.5
III p	177.9	15.2	162.7	40.1	73.4	19.7	29.5	314.1	34.3	279.8	46.6	74.0	50.8	108.5

[1] End-use commodity classifications beginning 1978 and 1989 are not strictly comparable with data for earlier periods. See *Survey of Current Business*, June 1988 and July 2001.

Note.—Data are on a balance of payments basis and exclude military.

In June 1990, end-use categories for goods exports were redefined to include reexports; beginning with data for 1978, reexports (exports of foreign goods) are assigned to detailed end-use categories in the same manner as exports of domestic goods.

Source: Department of Commerce, Bureau of Economic Analysis.

TABLE B–105.—*U.S. international trade in goods by area, 1994–2003*

[Billions of dollars]

Item	1994	1995	1996	1997	1998	1999	2000	2001	2002	2003 first 3 quarters at annual rate[1]
EXPORTS	502.9	575.2	612.1	678.4	670.4	684.0	772.0	718.7	681.9	700.6
Industrial countries	295.7	338.5	354.3	385.4	389.6	401.5	438.3	406.1	381.0	395.0
Canada	114.7	127.4	134.3	151.9	156.7	166.7	178.9	163.3	160.9	168.4
Japan	52.4	63.6	66.5	64.4	56.5	56.1	63.5	55.9	49.7	50.3
Western Europe[2]	115.4	132.5	136.9	152.4	159.3	162.7	178.7	171.4	153.4	159.1
Australia, New Zealand, and South Africa	13.2	15.0	16.6	16.7	17.1	16.0	17.2	15.6	17.1	17.1
Australia	9.6	10.5	11.7	11.7	11.6	11.5	12.2	10.6	12.8	12.8
Other countries, except Eastern Europe	201.7	231.0	250.5	285.1	273.3	276.9	327.8	305.8	294.5	299.1
OPEC[3]	16.3	17.4	19.2	23.7	22.9	18.3	17.6	19.5	17.8	16.3
Other[4]	185.4	213.6	231.3	261.4	250.3	258.6	310.2	286.3	276.7	282.8
Eastern Europe[2]	5.3	5.7	7.3	7.9	7.4	5.6	5.9	6.8	6.4	6.5
International organizations and unallocated	.1	....	....	....	.1	....	....	....	....	....
IMPORTS	668.7	749.4	803.1	876.5	917.1	1,030.0	1,224.4	1,145.9	1,164.7	1,247.7
Industrial countries	389.9	425.2	442.9	476.7	502.0	557.3	636.3	599.4	591.9	618.1
Canada	131.1	146.9	158.5	170.1	175.8	201.3	233.7	218.7	211.8	226.6
Japan	119.1	123.5	115.2	121.7	121.9	130.9	146.5	126.5	121.4	116.6
Western Europe[2]	133.0	147.7	161.6	176.0	194.2	214.9	243.4	241.0	245.9	261.6
Australia, New Zealand, and South Africa	6.7	7.0	7.6	9.0	10.1	10.2	12.7	13.1	12.8	13.3
Australia	3.2	3.4	3.8	4.9	5.4	5.3	6.4	6.5	6.4	6.3
Other countries, except Eastern Europe	273.0	317.2	353.2	391.3	404.3	460.9	572.0	532.2	558.0	610.7
OPEC[3]	31.7	34.3	42.7	44.0	33.7	42.0	67.0	59.8	53.2	67.9
Other[4]	241.3	282.9	310.5	347.3	370.6	419.0	505.0	472.5	504.8	542.8
Eastern Europe[2]	5.8	7.0	7.0	8.5	10.9	11.8	16.1	14.3	14.9	18.9
International organizations and unallocated	....	....	....	....	....	....	....	....	....	....
BALANCE (excess of exports +)	−165.8	−174.2	−191.0	−198.1	−246.7	−346.0	−452.4	−427.2	−482.9	−547.1
Industrial countries	−94.2	−86.7	−88.6	−91.3	−112.3	−155.7	−198.0	−193.2	−210.9	−223.1
Canada	−16.5	−19.5	−24.3	−18.2	−19.1	−34.6	−54.8	−55.5	−50.9	−58.1
Japan	−66.7	−59.9	−48.7	−57.3	−65.4	−74.8	−83.0	−70.6	−71.8	−66.3
Western Europe[2]	−17.5	−15.2	−24.7	−23.6	−34.9	−52.1	−64.7	−69.6	−92.5	−102.4
Australia, New Zealand, and South Africa	6.6	7.9	9.0	7.7	7.0	5.8	4.5	2.5	4.3	3.8
Australia	6.4	7.1	7.9	6.9	6.2	6.3	5.8	4.1	6.3	6.5
Other countries, except Eastern Europe	−71.2	−86.2	−102.6	−106.2	−131.0	−184.0	−244.2	−226.5	−263.5	−311.6
OPEC[3]	−15.4	−16.9	−23.5	−20.3	−10.7	−23.6	−49.4	−40.3	−35.4	−51.6
Other[4]	−55.9	−69.3	−79.2	−85.9	−120.2	−160.4	−194.8	−186.2	−228.1	−260.0
Eastern Europe[2]	−.5	−1.3	.3	−.6	−3.5	−6.3	−10.2	−7.5	−8.5	−12.4
International organizations and unallocated	.1	....	....	....	.1	....	....	....	....	....

[1] Preliminary; seasonally adjusted.
[2] The former German Democratic Republic (East Germany) included in Western Europe beginning fourth quarter 1990 and in Eastern Europe prior to that time.
[3] Organization of Petroleum Exporting Countries, consisting of Algeria, Ecuador (through 1992), Gabon (through 1994), Indonesia, Iran, Iraq, Kuwait, Libya, Nigeria, Qatar, Saudi Arabia, United Arab Emirates, and Venezuela.
[4] Latin America, other Western Hemisphere, and other countries in Asia and Africa, less members of OPEC.

Note.—Data are on a balance of payments basis and exclude military.

Source: Department of Commerce, Bureau of Economic Analysis.

TABLE B–106.—*U.S. international trade in goods on balance of payments (BOP) and Census basis, and trade in services on BOP basis, 1979–2003*

[Billions of dollars; monthly data seasonally adjusted]

Year or month	Goods: Exports (f.a.s. value)[1][2] Census basis (by end-use category)							Goods: Imports (customs value, except as noted)[5] Census basis (by end-use category)							Services (BOP basis)	
	Total, BOP basis[3]	Total, Census basis[3][4]	Foods, feeds, and beverages	Industrial supplies and materials	Capital goods except automotive	Automotive vehicles, parts, and engines	Consumer goods (nonfood) except automotive	Total, BOP basis	Total, Census basis[4]	Foods, feeds, and beverages	Industrial supplies and materials	Capital goods except automotive	Automotive vehicles, parts, and engines	Consumer goods (nonfood) except automotive	Exports	Imports
	F.a.s. value[2]							F.a.s. value[2]								
1979	184.4	186.4						212.0	210.3						39.7	36.7
1980	224.3	225.6						249.8	245.3						47.6	41.5
								Customs value								
1981	237.0	238.7						265.1	261.0						57.4	45.5
1982	211.2	216.4	31.3	61.7	72.7	15.7	14.3	247.6	244.0	17.1	112.0	35.4	33.3	39.7	64.1	51.7
1983	201.8	205.6	30.9	56.7	67.2	16.8	13.4	268.9	258.0	18.2	107.0	40.9	40.8	44.9	64.3	55.0
1984	219.9	224.0	31.5	61.7	72.0	20.6	13.3	332.4	[6]330.7	21.0	123.7	59.8	53.5	60.0	71.2	67.7
1985	215.9	[7]218.8	24.0	58.5	73.9	22.9	12.6	338.1	[6]336.5	21.9	113.9	65.1	66.8	68.3	73.2	72.9
1986	223.3	[7]227.2	22.3	57.3	75.8	21.7	14.2	368.4	365.4	24.4	101.3	71.8	78.2	79.4	86.7	80.1
1987	250.2	254.1	24.3	66.7	86.2	24.6	17.7	409.8	406.2	24.8	111.0	84.5	85.2	88.7	98.7	90.8
1988	320.2	322.4	32.3	85.1	109.2	29.3	23.1	447.2	441.0	24.8	118.3	101.4	87.7	95.9	110.9	98.5
1989	359.9	363.8	37.2	99.3	138.8	34.8	36.4	477.7	473.2	25.1	132.3	113.3	86.1	102.9	127.1	102.5
1990	387.4	393.6	35.1	104.4	152.7	37.4	43.3	498.4	495.3	26.6	143.2	116.4	87.3	105.7	147.8	117.7
1991	414.1	421.7	35.7	109.7	166.7	40.0	45.9	491.0	488.5	26.5	131.6	120.7	85.7	108.0	164.3	118.5
1992	439.6	448.2	40.3	109.1	175.9	47.0	51.4	536.5	532.7	27.6	138.6	134.3	91.8	122.7	176.8	118.1
1993	456.9	465.1	40.6	111.8	181.7	52.4	54.7	589.4	580.7	27.9	145.6	152.4	102.4	134.0	185.4	122.1
1994	502.9	512.6	42.0	121.4	205.0	57.8	60.0	668.7	663.3	31.0	162.1	184.4	118.3	146.3	199.8	131.1
1995	575.2	584.7	50.5	146.2	233.0	61.8	64.4	749.4	743.5	33.2	181.8	221.4	123.8	159.9	218.5	139.4
1996	612.1	625.1	55.5	147.7	253.0	65.0	70.1	803.1	795.3	35.7	204.5	228.1	128.9	172.0	238.8	150.6
1997	678.4	689.2	51.5	158.2	294.5	74.0	77.4	876.5	869.7	39.7	213.8	253.3	139.8	193.8	255.5	164.4
1998	670.4	682.1	46.4	148.3	299.4	72.4	80.3	917.1	911.9	41.2	200.1	269.5	148.7	217.0	262.1	178.6
1999	684.0	695.8	46.0	147.5	310.8	75.3	80.9	1,030.0	1,024.6	43.6	221.4	295.7	179.0	241.9	281.5	196.7
2000	772.0	781.9	47.9	172.6	356.9	80.4	89.4	1,224.4	1,218.0	46.0	299.0	347.0	195.9	281.8	298.1	221.0
2001	718.7	729.1	49.4	160.1	321.7	75.4	88.3	1,145.9	1,141.0	46.6	273.9	298.0	189.8	284.3	288.9	219.5
2002	681.9	693.1	49.6	156.8	290.5	78.9	84.4	1,164.7	1,161.4	49.7	267.7	283.3	203.7	307.9	292.2	227.4
2002: Jan	55.2	56.0	4.2	12.4	23.8	6.2	6.9	88.7	88.5	3.9	18.9	22.8	15.5	23.4	23.4	18.2
Feb	55.0	55.9	4.2	12.3	23.5	6.4	6.9	90.9	90.6	4.0	19.0	23.0	16.4	24.4	23.6	18.8
Mar	55.1	56.1	3.9	12.4	24.0	6.3	6.8	91.7	91.5	4.0	19.6	23.2	16.2	24.2	24.2	18.2
Apr	56.9	57.7	4.0	13.0	24.2	6.7	7.1	96.6	96.3	4.0	22.6	23.7	16.9	25.1	23.8	18.3
May	56.8	58.1	4.0	13.2	24.2	6.7	6.9	97.7	97.4	4.1	22.9	23.8	17.0	25.5	24.2	18.5
June	57.7	58.6	4.3	13.3	24.7	6.7	7.1	98.4	98.1	4.1	22.3	24.0	17.1	26.1	24.3	19.2
July	58.6	59.6	4.3	13.2	25.1	6.9	7.2	97.9	97.7	4.2	22.7	23.8	17.2	25.7	24.3	19.1
Aug	57.9	58.9	4.1	13.4	24.7	6.8	7.0	99.9	99.6	4.2	23.6	23.7	17.4	26.7	24.7	18.9
Sept	57.8	58.7	4.1	13.3	24.8	6.7	7.1	99.7	99.4	4.2	23.5	23.8	17.7	26.2	24.5	19.2
Oct	57.3	58.3	3.9	13.2	24.5	6.7	7.1	97.9	97.6	4.1	24.5	22.3	17.1	25.5	24.9	19.4
Nov	57.8	58.7	4.3	13.5	24.4	6.5	7.2	101.9	101.6	4.4	23.8	24.4	17.6	27.5	25.2	19.6
Dec	55.8	56.7	4.4	13.6	22.5	6.5	7.0	103.2	103.0	4.5	24.3	24.7	17.7	27.7	25.3	20.2
2003: Jan	57.1	57.9	4.4	14.1	23.0	6.6	7.3	102.0	101.8	4.5	25.0	24.5	17.0	26.9	24.9	20.1
Feb	57.9	58.8	4.4	14.0	24.1	6.7	7.0	101.6	101.4	4.4	26.0	23.2	16.8	26.9	24.8	19.7
Mar	58.3	59.3	4.3	14.4	23.7	6.7	7.3	105.8	105.6	4.6	28.4	23.2	17.3	28.0	24.3	19.8
Apr	57.2	58.3	4.3	14.2	23.0	6.6	7.2	103.6	103.3	4.7	26.1	24.1	16.9	27.7	23.9	19.5
May	57.8	58.6	4.2	14.3	23.3	6.8	7.2	104.4	104.1	4.6	25.6	24.5	17.8	27.7	24.5	19.8
June	59.3	60.1	4.4	14.5	24.2	6.6	7.7	104.3	103.9	4.5	25.9	24.4	18.2	26.7	24.9	20.2
July	60.4	61.2	4.6	14.8	24.8	6.8	7.5	105.4	105.2	4.6	26.8	24.5	18.0	27.3	25.2	20.6
Aug	57.7	58.6	4.3	14.0	23.9	6.1	7.5	102.4	101.9	4.5	26.0	24.0	15.6	27.2	25.6	20.5
Sept	59.7	60.5	4.5	14.1	24.7	6.7	7.7	106.3	106.0	4.8	27.0	25.3	17.4	27.6	26.0	20.8
Oct	61.6	62.4	4.7	14.7	25.6	6.9	7.6	108.8	108.5	4.8	26.8	25.5	18.3	29.0	26.4	20.9
Nov	63.8	64.6	5.1	14.7	27.3	6.7	8.1	107.4	107.2	4.9	25.6	25.7	18.2	28.8	26.8	21.2

[1] Department of Defense shipments of grant-aid military supplies and equipment under the Military Assistance Program are excluded from total exports through 1985 and included beginning 1986.

[2] F.a.s. (free alongside ship) value basis at U.S. port of exportation for exports and at foreign port of exportation for imports.

[3] Beginning 1989, exports have been adjusted for undocumented exports to Canada and are included in the appropriate end-use categories. For prior years, total exports include this adjustment.

[4] Total includes "other" exports or imports, not shown separately.

[5] Total arrivals of imported goods other than intransit shipments.

[6] Total includes revisions not reflected in detail.

[7] Total exports are on a revised statistical month basis; end-use categories are on a statistical month basis.

Note.—Goods on a Census basis are adjusted to a BOP basis by the Bureau of Economic Analysis, in line with concepts and definitions used to prepare international and national accounts. The adjustments are necessary to supplement coverage of Census data, to eliminate duplication of transactions recorded elsewhere in international accounts, and to value transactions according to a standard definition. Data include trade of the U.S. Virgin Islands, Puerto Rico, and U.S. Foreign Trade Zones.

Source: Department of Commerce (Bureau of the Census and Bureau of Economic Analysis).

[Billions of dollars]

Type of investment	1994	1995	1996	1997	1998	1999	2000	2001	2002 p
NET INTERNATIONAL INVESTMENT POSITION OF THE UNITED STATES:									
With direct investment at current cost ..	−311.9	−496.0	−521.5	−833.2	−918.7	−797.6	−1,387.7	−1,979.9	−2,387.2
With direct investment at market value	−123.7	−343.3	−386.5	−835.2	−1,094.1	−1,068.8	−1,588.2	−2,314.3	−2,605.2
U.S.-OWNED ASSETS ABROAD:									
With direct investment at current cost ...	2,998.6	3,452.0	4,012.7	4,567.9	5,090.9	5,965.1	6,229.4	6,187.4	6,189.2
With direct investment at market value	3,326.7	3,930.3	4,631.3	5,379.1	6,174.5	7,390.4	7,393.7	6,891.3	6,473.6
U.S. official reserve assets	163.4	176.1	160.7	134.8	146.0	136.4	128.4	130.0	158.6
Gold [1]	100.1	101.3	96.7	75.9	75.3	76.0	71.8	72.3	90.8
Special drawing rights	10.0	11.0	10.3	10.0	10.6	10.3	10.5	10.8	12.2
Reserve position in the International Monetary Fund	12.0	14.6	15.4	18.1	24.1	18.0	14.8	17.9	22.0
Foreign currencies	41.2	49.1	38.3	30.8	36.0	32.2	31.2	29.0	33.7
U.S. Government assets, other than official reserves	83.9	85.1	86.1	86.2	86.8	84.2	85.2	85.7	85.7
U.S. credits and other long-term assets	81.9	82.8	84.0	84.1	84.9	81.7	82.6	83.1	83.1
Repayable in dollars	81.4	82.4	83.6	83.8	84.5	.81.4	82.3	82.9	82.8
Other	.5	.4	.4	.4	.3	.3	.3	.3	.3
U.S. foreign currency holdings and U.S. short-term assets	2.0	2.3	2.1	2.1	1.9	2.6	2.6	2.5	2.6
U.S. private assets:									
With direct investment at current cost ..	2,751.3	3,190.9	3,765.9	4,346.9	4,858.2	5,744.5	6,015.8	5,971.8	5,944.9
With direct investment at market value	3,079.3	3,669.1	4,384.4	5,158.1	5,941.7	7,169.8	7,180.1	6,675.6	6,229.3
Direct investment abroad:									
At current cost	786.6	885.5	989.8	1,068.1	1,196.0	1,414.4	1,529.7	1,598.1	1,751.9
At market value	1,114.6	1,363.8	1,608.3	1,879.3	2,279.6	2,839.6	2,694.0	2,301.9	2,036.2
Foreign securities	948.7	1,169.6	1,468.0	1,751.2	2,053.0	2,525.3	2,385.4	2,114.7	1,847.0
Bonds	321.2	392.8	465.1	543.4	578.0	521.6	532.5	502.1	501.8
Corporate stocks	627.5	776.8	1,002.9	1,207.8	1,475.0	2,003.7	1,852.9	1,612.7	1,345.2
U.S. claims on unaffiliated foreigners reported by U.S. nonbanking concerns ...	323.0	367.6	450.6	545.5	588.3	704.5	836.6	835.8	891.0
U.S. claims reported by U.S. banks, not included elsewhere	693.1	768.1	857.5	982.1	1,020.8	1,100.3	1,264.1	1,423.2	1,455.1
FOREIGN-OWNED ASSETS IN THE UNITED STATES:									
With direct investment at current cost ..	3,310.5	3,947.9	4,534.3	5,401.1	6,009.6	6,762.7	7,617.1	8,167.3	8,576.4
With direct investment at market value	3,450.4	4,273.6	5,017.8	6,214.3	7,268.6	8,459.2	8,981.8	9,205.5	9,078.7
Foreign official assets in the United States ...	535.2	682.9	820.8	873.7	896.2	951.1	1,014.5	1,027.2	1,132.5
U.S. Government securities	407.2	507.5	631.1	648.2	669.8	693.8	749.9	798.8	898.0
U.S. Treasury securities	396.9	490.0	606.4	615.1	622.9	617.7	625.2	650.7	710.6
Other	10.3	17.5	24.7	33.1	46.8	76.1	124.7	148.1	187.4
Other U.S. Government liabilities	23.7	23.6	22.6	21.7	18.4	21.1	19.3	17.0	17.1
U.S. liabilities reported by U.S. banks, not included elsewhere	73.4	107.4	113.1	135.4	125.9	138.8	153.4	123.4	141.0
Other foreign official assets	31.0	44.4	54.0	68.4	82.1	97.3	91.8	87.9	76.4
Other foreign assets in the United States:									
With direct investment at current cost ..	2,775.3	3,265.1	3,713.5	4,527.3	5,113.4	5,811.6	6,602.6	7,140.1	7,443.9
With direct investment at market value	2,915.2	3,590.7	4,197.0	5,340.6	6,372.4	7,508.1	7,967.3	8,178.3	7,946.2
Direct investment in the United States:									
At current cost	618.0	680.1	745.6	824.1	920.0	1,101.7	1,418.5	1,514.4	1,504.4
At market value	757.9	1,005.7	1,229.1	1,637.4	2,179.0	2,798.2	2,783.2	2,552.6	2,006.7
U.S. Treasury securities	235.7	330.2	440.8	550.6	562.0	462.8	401.0	389.0	503.6
U.S. securities other than U.S. Treasury securities	739.7	969.8	1,165.1	1,512.7	1,903.4	2,351.3	2,623.7	2,855.7	2,861.1
Corporate and other bonds	368.1	459.1	539.3	618.8	724.6	825.2	1,076.0	1,391.6	1,690.3
Corporate stocks	371.6	510.8	625.8	893.9	1,178.8	1,526.1	1,547.7	1,464.1	1,170.8
U.S. currency	157.2	169.5	186.8	211.6	228.3	250.7	251.8	275.6	297.1
U.S. liabilities to unaffiliated foreigners reported by U.S. nonbanking concerns ...	239.8	300.4	346.8	459.4	485.7	578.0	738.9	799.1	870.3
U.S. liabilities reported by U.S. banks, not included elsewhere	784.9	815.0	828.2	968.8	1,014.0	1,067.2	1,168.7	1,306.4	1,407.4

[1] Valued at market price.

Note.—For details regarding these data, see *Survey of Current Business*, July 2003.

Source: Department of Commerce, Bureau of Economic Analysis.

TABLE B–108.—*Industrial production and consumer prices, major industrial countries, 1979–2003*

Year or quarter	United States[1]	Canada	Japan	European Union[2]	France	Germany[3]	Italy	United Kingdom
	Industrial production (Index, 1997=100)[4]							
1979	64.2	68.6	63.1	78.2	85.3	82.1	77.6	79.8
1980	62.5	66.5	66.0	78.1	84.4	82.1	81.9	74.6
1981	63.4	66.8	66.7	76.7	83.5	80.6	80.2	72.2
1982	60.1	61.7	66.9	75.4	82.9	78.0	77.6	73.6
1983	61.7	65.1	69.0	76.0	83.0	78.4	75.9	76.4
1984	67.3	73.2	75.4	78.1	84.3	80.8	78.3	76.4
1985	68.1	76.9	78.2	80.1	84.9	84.7	78.4	80.5
1986	68.8	76.3	78.1	82.1	87.1	86.3	81.6	82.5
1987	72.3	79.5	80.8	83.7	88.6	86.6	83.8	85.8
1988	75.9	84.8	88.4	87.5	91.7	89.8	89.6	90.0
1989	76.6	84.6	93.5	91.0	94.9	94.2	93.1	91.9
1990	77.2	82.2	97.5	92.7	96.4	99.0	91.2	91.6
1991	76.1	79.3	99.2	92.8	95.9	102.5	90.4	88.5
1992	78.2	80.3	93.6	91.6	94.2	100.0	89.5	88.7
1993	80.8	84.2	90.4	88.3	90.5	92.1	87.5	90.7
1994	85.2	89.4	91.5	92.6	94.0	95.0	92.6	95.6
1995	89.3	93.5	94.4	95.7	96.2	95.8	98.0	97.3
1996	93.1	94.7	96.6	96.3	95.8	96.5	96.4	98.6
1997	100.0	100.0	100.0	100.0	100.0	100.0	100.0	100.0
1998	105.9	103.5	93.5	103.7	103.4	104.2	101.2	101.0
1999	110.6	109.5	93.8	105.6	105.7	105.7	101.2	102.2
2000	115.4	118.5	99.0	110.5	110.1	112.3	105.3	104.2
2001	111.5	115.0	92.7	110.7	111.3	112.8	104.1	102.5
2002	110.9	117.3	91.7	109.9	109.9	111.6	102.7	99.7
2003 P	111.2	....	....	....	....	....	....	....
2002: I	110.0	115.2	88.8	109.6	110.0	110.9	102.9	100.1
II	111.1	117.2	91.3	110.1	110.4	111.2	103.3	100.0
III	111.5	118.3	93.1	110.3	110.3	112.3	103.5	99.7
IV	110.9	118.3	93.5	109.8	109.1	111.8	103.0	99.1
2003: I	111.2	118.3	93.8	110.3	109.1	112.9	102.6	98.9
II	110.0	116.4	93.1	109.6	108.6	111.5	101.7	99.2
III	111.1	116.4	94.0	110.0	109.8	111.6	103.1	99.1
IV P	112.7	....	....	....	....	....	....	....
	Consumer prices (Index, 1982-84=100)							
1979	72.6	69.2	84.4	65.7	63.6	82.3	52.8	66.6
1980	82.4	76.1	91.0	74.5	72.2	86.7	63.9	78.5
1981	90.9	85.6	95.3	83.6	81.8	92.2	75.5	87.9
1982	96.5	94.9	98.1	92.4	91.7	97.0	87.8	95.4
1983	99.6	100.4	99.8	100.1	100.3	100.3	100.8	99.8
1984	103.9	104.7	102.1	107.4	108.0	102.7	111.4	104.8
1985	107.6	109.0	104.2	114.1	114.3	104.8	121.7	111.1
1986	109.6	113.5	104.9	118.2	117.2	104.6	128.9	114.9
1987	113.6	118.4	104.9	122.1	121.1	104.9	135.1	119.7
1988	118.3	123.2	105.6	126.5	124.3	106.3	141.9	125.6
1989	124.0	129.3	108.0	133.2	128.7	109.2	150.7	135.4
1990	130.7	135.5	111.4	140.7	132.9	112.2	160.4	148.2
1991	136.2	143.1	115.0	148.2	137.2	116.3	170.5	156.9
1992	140.3	145.3	117.0	154.9	140.4	122.2	179.5	162.7
1993	144.5	147.9	118.5	160.5	143.4	127.6	187.7	165.3
1994	148.2	148.2	119.3	165.4	145.8	131.1	195.3	169.3
1995	152.4	151.4	119.2	170.6	148.4	133.3	205.6	175.2
1996	156.9	153.8	119.3	174.8	151.4	135.3	213.8	179.4
1997	160.5	156.3	121.5	178.4	153.2	137.8	218.2	185.1
1998	163.0	157.8	122.2	181.6	154.2	139.1	222.5	191.4
1999	166.6	160.5	121.8	183.9	155.0	140.0	226.2	194.3
2000	172.2	164.9	121.0	188.1	157.6	142.0	231.9	200.1
2001	177.1	169.1	120.1	192.7	160.2	144.8	238.3	203.6
2002	179.9	172.9	119.0	196.8	163.3	146.7	244.3	207.0
2003 P	184.0	177.7	....	....	166.7	148.3	250.8	213.0
2002: I	177.9	169.9	118.7	194.9	162.0	146.4	241.9	204.3
II	179.8	172.4	119.2	196.6	163.2	146.7	243.7	206.8
III	180.6	174.2	119.0	197.2	163.6	147.0	244.9	207.5
IV	181.2	175.2	118.9	198.4	164.3	146.8	246.5	209.4
2003: I	183.0	177.5	118.4	199.7	165.8	148.2	248.5	210.4
II	183.7	177.2	119.0	200.9	166.4	148.0	250.3	213.3
III	184.6	177.9	118.7	201.4	166.8	148.4	251.6	213.3
IV P	184.6	178.2	....	....	167.9	148.5	252.8	214.

[1] See Note, Table B–51 for information on U.S. industrial production series.
[2] Consists of Austria, Belgium, Denmark, Finland, France, Germany, Greece, Ireland, Italy, Luxembourg, Netherlands, Portugal, Spain, Sweden, and United Kingdom.
[3] Prior to 1991 data are for West Germany only.
[4] All data exclude construction. Quarterly data are seasonally adjusted.

Sources: National sources as reported by Department of Commerce (International Trade Administration, Office of Trade and Economic Analysis), Department of Labor (Bureau of Labor Statistics), and Board of Governors of the Federal Reserve System.

[Quarterly data seasonally adjusted]

Year or quarter	United States	Canada	Japan	France	Germany [1]	Italy	United Kingdom
	Civilian unemployment rate (Percent) [2]						
1979	5.8	7.3	2.1	6.1	2.9	4.4	5.4
1980	7.1	7.3	2.0	6.5	2.8	4.4	7.0
1981	7.6	7.3	2.2	7.6	4.0	4.9	10.5
1982	9.7	10.6	2.4	8.3	5.6	5.4	11.3
1983	9.6	11.5	2.7	8.6	[3] 6.9	5.9	11.8
1984	7.5	10.9	2.8	10.0	7.1	5.9	11.7
1985	7.2	10.2	2.6	10.5	7.2	6.0	11.2
1986	7.0	9.2	2.8	10.6	6.6	[3] 7.5	11.2
1987	6.2	8.4	2.9	10.8	6.3	7.9	10.3
1988	5.5	7.3	2.5	10.3	6.3	7.9	8.6
1989	5.3	7.1	2.3	9.6	5.7	7.8	7.2
1990	[3] 5.6	7.7	2.1	9.1	5.0	7.0	6.9
1991	6.8	9.8	2.1	9.5	[3] 5.6	[3] 6.9	8.8
1992	7.5	10.6	2.2	[3] 9.9	6.7	7.3	10.1
1993	6.9	10.8	2.5	11.3	8.0	[3] 10.2	10.4
1994	[3] 6.1	9.5	2.9	11.8	8.5	11.2	9.5
1995	5.6	8.6	3.2	11.3	8.2	11.8	8.7
1996	5.4	8.8	3.4	11.9	9.0	11.7	8.1
1997	4.9	8.4	3.4	11.8	9.9	11.9	7.0
1998	4.5	7.7	4.1	11.3	9.3	12.0	6.3
1999	4.2	7.0	4.7	10.6	8.6	11.5	6.0
2000	4.0	6.1	4.8	9.1	8.1	10.7	5.5
2001	4.7	6.4	5.1	8.4	8.0	9.6	5.1
2002	5.8	7.0	5.4	8.7	8.4	9.1	5.2
2003	6.0	....	....	....	....	....	....
2002: I	5.7	7.1	5.3	8.5	8.2	9.2	5.1
II	5.8	6.9	5.4	8.6	8.3	9.2	5.2
III	5.7	7.0	5.5	8.8	8.5	9.1	5.3
IV	5.9	6.9	5.4	8.8	8.7	9.0	5.1
2003: I	5.8	6.7	5.4	9.0	9.0	9.0	5.1
II	6.1	6.9	5.4	9.2	9.2	8.8	5.0
III	6.1	7.2	5.2	9.3	9.1	8.7	5.0
IV	5.9	....	....	....	....	....	....
	Manufacturing hourly compensation in U.S. dollars (Index, 1992=100) [4]						
1979	49.6	44.0	32.0	44.6	42.0	38.6	31.8
1980	55.6	49.1	32.8	51.7	46.1	43.8	42.2
1981	61.1	54.2	36.0	46.7	39.3	39.1	42.8
1982	67.0	59.7	33.5	45.6	38.8	38.4	40.8
1983	68.8	64.0	36.0	43.5	38.6	39.4	38.1
1984	71.2	64.4	37.1	41.2	36.3	39.1	36.5
1985	75.1	63.6	38.5	43.4	37.2	40.7	38.9
1986	78.5	63.5	57.3	58.5	52.4	54.4	47.9
1987	80.7	68.1	68.2	69.8	66.0	66.0	59.7
1988	84.0	76.2	78.3	72.8	70.4	70.6	69.3
1989	86.6	84.3	77.2	71.4	69.1	72.7	68.4
1990	90.8	91.5	79.2	88.3	86.4	90.1	83.7
1991	95.6	100.1	90.9	90.4	86.1	93.5	93.9
1992	100.0	100.0	100.0	100.0	100.0	100.0	100.0
1993	102.7	95.5	117.2	95.8	100.4	82.8	89.3
1994	105.6	91.7	129.9	101.1	107.6	81.7	93.7
1995	107.9	93.3	146.1	116.8	128.3	84.2	97.8
1996	109.4	94.8	127.2	116.0	128.0	95.0	98.4
1997	111.5	95.3	117.9	101.5	113.2	88.9	107.2
1998	117.4	90.0	111.7	101.0	113.3	86.7	115.0
1999	122.1	91.4	128.0	100.0	111.1	84.2	118.7
2000	131.1	92.6	133.7	90.0	101.1	75.1	118.0
2001	134.3	91.9	119.4	91.7	101.1	75.4	117.2
2002	140.6	94.8	114.1	99.9	109.1	81.6	126.4

[1] Prior to 1991 data are for West Germany only.
[2] Civilian unemployment rates, approximating U.S. concepts. Quarterly data for France and Germany should be viewed as less precise indicators of unemployment under U.S. concepts than the annual data.
[3] There are breaks in the series for Germany (1983 and 1991), France (1992), Italy (1986, 1991, and 1993), and United States (1990 and 1994). Also, for Italy, data reflect new estimation procedures and updated population data introduced in July 1999. For details on break in series in 1990 and 1994 for United States, see footnote 5, Table B-35. For details on break in series for other countries, see U.S. Department of Labor *Comparative Civilian Labor Force Statistics, Ten Countries: 1959–2002,* April 2003.
[4] Hourly compensation in manufacturing, U.S. dollar basis. Data relate to all employed persons (employees and self-employed workers) in the United States, Canada, Japan, France, Germany, and United Kingdom, and to employees (wage and salary earners) in Italy. For Canada, France and United Kingdom, compensation adjusted to include changes in employment taxes that are not compensation to employees, but are labor costs to employers.
Data for U.S. are as of early December 2003; other data are as of September 2003.

Source: Department of Labor, Bureau of Labor Statistics.

TABLE B-110.—*Foreign exchange rates, 1983–2003*

[Foreign currency units per U.S. dollar, except as noted; certified noon buying rates in New York]

Period	Canada (dollar)	EMU Members (euro)[1][2]	Belgium (franc)[1]	France (franc)[1]	Germany (mark)[1]	Italy (lira)[1]	Nether-lands (guild-er)[1]	Japan (yen)	Sweden (krona)	Switzer-land (franc)	United Kingdom (pound)[2]
March 1973	0.9967	....	39.408	4.5156	2.8132	568.17	2.8714	261.90	4.4294	3.2171	2.4724
1983	1.2325	....	51.122	7.6204	2.5539	1519.32	2.8544	237.55	7.6718	2.1007	1.5159
1984	1.2952	....	57.752	8.7356	2.8455	1756.11	3.2085	237.46	8.2708	2.3500	1.3368
1985	1.3659	....	59.337	8.9800	2.9420	1908.88	3.3185	238.47	8.6032	2.4552	1.2974
1986	1.3896	....	44.664	6.9257	2.1705	1491.16	2.4485	168.35	7.1273	1.7979	1.4677
1987	1.3259	....	37.358	6.0122	1.7981	1297.03	2.0264	144.60	6.3469	1.4918	1.6398
1988	1.2306	....	36.785	5.9595	1.7570	1302.39	1.9778	128.17	6.1370	1.4643	1.7813
1989	1.1842	....	39.409	6.3802	1.8808	1372.28	2.1219	138.07	6.4559	1.6369	1.6382
1990	1.1668	....	33.424	5.4467	1.6166	1198.27	1.8215	145.00	5.9231	1.3901	1.7841
1991	1.1460	....	34.195	5.6468	1.6610	1241.28	1.8720	134.59	6.0521	1.4356	1.7674
1992	1.2085	....	32.148	5.2935	1.5618	1232.17	1.7587	126.78	5.8258	1.4064	1.7663
1993	1.2902	....	34.581	5.6669	1.6545	1573.41	1.8585	111.08	7.7956	1.4781	1.5016
1994	1.3664	....	33.426	5.5459	1.6216	1611.49	1.8190	102.18	7.7161	1.3667	1.5319
1995	1.3725	....	29.472	4.9864	1.4321	1629.45	1.6044	93.96	7.1406	1.1812	1.5785
1996	1.3638	....	30.970	5.1158	1.5049	1542.76	1.6863	108.78	6.7082	1.2361	1.5607
1997	1.3849	....	35.807	5.8393	1.7348	1703.81	1.9525	121.06	7.6446	1.4514	1.6376
1998	1.4836	....	36.310	5.8995	1.7597	1736.85	1.9837	130.99	7.9522	1.4506	1.6573
1999	1.4858	1.0653	....	....	....	....	....	113.73	8.2740	1.5045	1.6172
2000	1.4855	.9232	....	....	....	....	....	107.80	9.1735	1.6904	1.5156
2001	1.5487	.8952	....	....	....	....	....	121.57	10.3425	1.6891	1.4396
2002	1.5704	.9454	....	....	....	....	....	125.22	9.7233	1.5567	1.5025
2003	1.4008	1.1321	....	....	....	....	....	115.94	8.0787	1.3450	1.6347
2002: I	1.5946	.8770	....	....	....	....	....	132.42	10.4428	1.6802	1.4261
II	1.5552	.9186	....	....	....	....	....	126.92	9.9831	1.5960	1.4615
III	1.5633	.9842	....	....	....	....	....	119.27	9.3841	1.4872	1.5497
IV	1.5696	1.0003	....	....	....	....	....	122.52	9.0974	1.4664	1.5714
2003: I	1.5098	1.0733	....	....	....	....	....	118.93	8.5572	1.3662	1.6025
II	1.3992	1.1356	....	....	....	....	....	118.55	8.0607	1.3370	1.6183
III	1.3806	1.1264	....	....	....	....	....	117.41	8.1385	1.3720	1.6107
IV	1.3162	1.1920	....	....	....	....	....	108.78	7.5647	1.3044	1.7079

Trade-weighted value of the U.S. dollar

	Nominal				Real[7]		
	G–10 index (March 1973=100)[3]	Broad index (January 1997=100)[4]	Major cur-rencies index (March 1973=100)[5]	OITP index (January 1997=100)[6]	Broad index (March 1997=100)[4]	Major cur-rencies index (March 1973=100)[5]	OITP index (March 1973=100)[6]
1983	125.3	52.8	120.4	7.4	110.5	110.8	109.0
1984	138.2	60.1	128.7	9.8	117.7	118.3	115.5
1985	143.0	67.2	133.5	13.1	122.5	122.1	123.4
1986	112.2	62.4	109.8	16.5	107.0	99.6	127.5
1987	96.9	60.4	97.2	19.9	98.3	89.1	124.9
1988	92.7	60.9	90.4	24.1	91.7	84.0	114.2
1989	98.6	66.9	94.3	29.6	93.4	88.2	108.7
1990	89.1	71.4	89.9	40.1	91.7	84.8	111.7
1991	89.8	74.4	88.6	46.7	90.3	83.1	111.2
1992	86.6	76.9	87.0	53.2	88.4	82.0	107.5
1993	93.2	83.8	89.9	63.4	89.7	85.2	104.9
1994	91.3	90.9	88.4	80.5	89.6	84.9	105.1
1995	84.2	92.7	83.4	92.5	87.2	81.0	105.1
1996	87.3	97.5	87.2	98.2	89.2	85.9	102.0
1997	96.4	104.4	93.9	104.6	94.0	93.2	103.0
1998	98.8	115.9	98.4	125.9	101.9	98.2	116.5
1999	....	116.0	96.9	129.2	101.3	98.0	115.2
2000	....	119.4	101.6	129.8	105.3	104.7	115.4
2001	....	125.9	107.7	135.9	111.3	112.2	120.0
2002	....	126.8	106.0	140.6	111.6	110.6	122.7
2003	....	119.3	93.0	144.0	104.9	97.7	124.5
2002: I	....	129.0	111.4	137.5	113.4	116.1	119.9
II	....	126.9	107.3	139.0	112.0	111.9	121.9
III	....	125.0	102.8	141.5	110.3	107.4	123.9
IV	....	126.0	102.6	144.2	110.6	107.1	125.0
2003: I	....	123.4	97.9	146.0	108.3	102.5	126.1
II	....	119.1	93.4	143.0	104.8	97.9	123.9
III	....	119.0	93.1	143.1	105.1	98.0	124.5
IV	....	115.6	87.8	144.1	101.3	92.2	123.4

[1] European Economic and Monetary Union members include Austria, Belgium, Finland, France, Germany, Ireland, Italy, Luxembourg, Nether-lands, Portugal, Spain, and beginning in 2001, Greece.
[2] U.S. dollars per foreign currency unit.
[3] G-10 comprises the individual countries shown in this table. Discontinued after December 1998.
[4] Weighted average of the foreign exchange value of the dollar against the currencies of a broad group of U.S. trading partners.
[5] Subset of the broad index. Includes currencies of the euro area, Australia, Canada, Japan, Sweden, Switzerland, and the United Kingdom.
[6] Subset of the broad index. Includes other important U.S. trading partners (OITP) whose currencies are not heavily traded outside their home markets.
[7] Adjusted for changes in the consumer price index.

Source: Board of Governors of the Federal Reserve System.

[Millions of SDRs; end of period]

Area and country	1962	1972	1982	1992	2001	2002	2003 Sept	2003 Oct
All countries	62,851	146,658	361,239	752,566	1,737,257	1,881,480	2,096,812	2,137,411
Industrial countries [1]	53,502	113,362	214,025	424,229	710,779	749,487	819,376	834,602
United States	17,220	12,112	29,918	52,995	55,030	59,160	60,483	60,215
Canada	2,561	5,572	3,439	8,662	27,061	27,225	25,612	25,002
Euro area:								
Austria	1,081	2,505	5,544	9,703	10,345	7,480	6,710	6,481
Belgium	1,753	3,564	4,757	10,914	9,255	9,010	7,977	7,884
Finland	237	664	1,420	3,862	6,408	6,885	6,914	6,919
France	4,049	9,224	17,850	22,522	28,667	24,268	24,182	24,844
Germany	6,958	21,908	43,909	69,489	44,717	41,516	40,322	40,241
Greece	287	950	916	3,606	4,239	6,083	3,225	3,331
Ireland	359	1,038	2,390	2,514	4,451	3,989	2,655	2,684
Italy	4,068	5,605	15,108	22,438	22,190	23,798	27,273	26,516
Luxembourg	....	....	....	....	87	114	177	175
Netherlands	1,943	4,407	10,723	17,492	8,184	7,993	9,102	9,046
Portugal	680	2,129	1,179	14,474	8,375	8,889	5,185	4,923
Spain	1,045	4,618	7,450	33,640	24,128	25,992	16,765	16,951
Australia	1,168	5,656	6,053	8,429	14,377	15,307	19,372	21,801
Japan	2,021	16,916	22,001	52,937	315,292	340,088	417,234	431,630
New Zealand	251	767	577	2,239	2,394	2,750	2,694	3,090
Denmark	256	787	2,111	8,090	13,690	19,924	24,767	24,735
Iceland	32	78	133	364	271	326	412	460
Norway	304	1,220	6,273	8,725	12,366	15,254	15,472	15,282
Sweden	802	1,453	3,397	16,667	11,330	12,807	13,522	....
Switzerland	2,919	6,961	16,930	27,100	27,941	31,693	33,208	33,459
United Kingdom	3,308	5,201	11,904	27,300	30,067	29,305	28,957	28,616
Developing countries: Total [2]	9,349	33,295	147,213	328,337	1,026,478	1,131,994	1,277,436	1,302,809
By area:								
Africa	2,110	3,962	7,737	13,044	52,351	54,158	60,370	60,480
Asia [2]	2,772	8,130	44,490	190,363	633,878	720,121	818,817	840,711
Europe	381	2,680	5,359	16,006	113,744	140,118	161,529	164,073
Middle East	1,805	9,436	64,039	44,149	99,498	98,645	102,563	102,156
Western Hemisphere	2,282	9,089	25,563	64,774	127,007	118,953	134,157	135,389
Memo:								
Oil-exporting countries	2,030	9,956	67,108	46,144	111,826	110,077	117,420	117,789
Non-oil developing countries [2]	7,319	23,339	80,105	282,193	914,652	1,021,916	1,160,016	1,185,020

[1] Includes data for Luxembourg 1962–92. Includes data for European Central Bank (ECB) beginning 1999. Detail does not add to totals shown.

[2] Includes data for Taiwan Province of China.

Note.—International reserves is comprised of monetary authorities' holdings of gold (at SDR 35 per ounce), special drawing rights (SDRs), reserve positions in the International Monetary Fund, and foreign exchange.
U.S. dollars per SDR (end of period) are: 1962—1.00000; 1972—1.08571; 1982—1.10311; 1992—1.37500; 2001—1.2567; 2002—1.3595; September 2003—1.4298; and October 2003—1.4318.

Source: International Monetary Fund, *International Financial Statistics*.

TABLE B–112.—*Growth rates in real gross domestic product, 1985–2003*

[Percent change at annual rate]

Area and country	1985–94	1995	1996	1997	1998	1999	2000	2001	2002	2003 [1]
World	3.3	3.7	4.0	4.2	2.8	3.6	4.8	2.4	3.0	3.2
Advanced economies	3.0	2.8	3.0	3.5	2.7	3.4	3.9	1.0	1.8	1.8
Major advanced economies	2.8	2.4	2.7	3.2	2.8	3.0	3.5	.8	1.6	1.8
United States [2]	2.9	2.7	3.6	4.4	4.3	4.1	3.8	.3	2.4	2.6
Japan	3.4	1.8	3.5	1.9	-1.1	.2	2.8	.4	.2	2.0
Germany	2.7	1.7	.8	1.4	2.0	2.0	2.9	.8	.2	(5)
France	2.1	1.8	1.1	1.9	3.6	3.2	4.2	2.1	1.2	.5
Italy	2.1	2.9	1.1	2.0	1.8	1.7	3.1	1.8	.4	.4
United Kingdom	2.6	2.9	2.6	3.4	2.9	2.4	3.1	2.1	1.9	1.7
Canada	2.5	2.8	1.6	4.2	4.1	5.5	5.3	1.9	3.3	1.9
Other advanced economies	3.8	4.3	3.6	4.2	1.9	4.8	5.1	1.6	3.0	1.9
Memorandum:										
European Union	2.4	2.5	1.7	2.6	3.0	2.8	3.6	1.7	1.1	.8
Euro area	....	2.2	1.4	2.3	2.9	2.8	3.5	1.5	.9	.5
Newly industrialized Asian economies	7.8	7.5	6.3	5.8	-2.4	8.0	8.4	.8	4.8	2.3
Developing countries	5.2	6.1	6.6	5.9	3.5	3.9	5.7	4.1	4.6	5.0
Africa	1.9	3.0	5.6	3.0	3.2	2.7	3.0	3.7	3.1	3.7
Developing Asia	7.7	9.0	8.3	6.6	4.0	6.2	6.8	5.8	6.4	6.4
Middle East and Turkey [3]	3.0	4.0	5.3	6.1	3.7	.9	6.0	2.0	4.8	5.1
Western Hemisphere	3.1	1.8	3.6	5.2	2.3	.2	4.0	.7	-.1	1.1
Countries in transition	-2.1	-1.5	-.6	1.9	-.9	4.1	7.1	5.1	4.2	4.9
Central and eastern Europe	....	5.5	4.0	2.5	2.5	2.3	3.9	3.1	3.0	3.4
CIS and Mongolia [4]	....	-5.5	-3.5	1.4	-3.2	5.2	9.1	6.4	4.9	5.8
Russia	....	-4.1	-3.6	1.4	-5.3	6.3	10.0	5.0	4.3	6.0

[1] All figures are forecasts as published by the International Monetary Fund.
[2] U.S. GDP data were revised historically by the Department of Commerce in December 2003; data shown in this table are pre-benchmark estimates. See Table B–2 for revised GDP data.
[3] Includes Malta.
[4] CIS—Commonwealth of Independent States.
[5] Figure is zero or negligible.

Sources: Department of Commerce (Bureau of Economic Analysis) and International Monetary Fund.

○